The Lawrence brothers. 1910
Seated, from left to right, Ned, Frank, Will

THE HOME LETTERS OF
T. E. LAWRENCE AND HIS BROTHERS

THE HOME LETTERS OF T. E. LAWRENCE AND HIS BROTHERS

L

THE MACMILLAN COMPANY
NEW YORK
1954

First published in the United States in 1954
by the Macmillan Company

CONTENTS

The following letters were printed in part or whole in *The Letters of T. E. Lawrence*, edited by David Garnett (Jonathan Cape 1938, and copyright 1938, 1939 by Doubleday & Company Inc., New York): Aug. 4, 16, 24, 26, 1906; April, Aug. 11, 1907; July 23, 1908; Aug. 2, 5, 29, Sept. 7, 1909; Aug. Dec., Dec. 16, 1910; Mar. 31, May 3, 23, June 13, July 29, 1911; May 18, 1916. The letters of Aug. 2, 29, and Sept. 7, 1909; Aug. Dec. and Dec. 16, 1910; Mar. 31 and June 13, 1911; and May 18, 1916 are reprinted, and the letter of Aug. 28, 1908 is first printed in *Selected Letters of T. E. Lawrence*, edited by David Garnett (Jonathan Cape, 1952). Grateful acknowledgement is made to these publishers for permission to print these letters in particular, and to the T. E. Lawrence Trustees for permission to print the letters in general

LIST OF ILLUSTRATIONS

LIST OF ILLUSTRATIONS

PUBLISHER'S NOTE

Mr. Lionel Curtis, C.H., is greatly to thank for the publication of these letters. Having learned from Mr. M. R. Lawrence of his achievement in deciphering and transcribing them, he urged that they should be printed together in one volume. Friend and confidant of great men, *omni illis et virtute et laude par*, he recognised in Will and Frank Lawrence the promise of greatness which he saw fulfilled in their elder brother. Their letters are printed for the first time; part of some of the letters of T. E. Lawrence have appeared before, either in *Crusader Castles* or in David Garnett's selection, but very few have been previously published in their entirety. These have been included to complete the collection. Thanks also are due to another friend of T. E. Lawrence, Mr. F. S. Thornton of Oxford, for the loan of a copy of Sir Winston Churchill's allocution, which appeared with his imprint in 1937

NOTE BY M. R. LAWRENCE

The letters of this book are not literary documents but were all written without the slightest idea of subsequent publication. I have transcribed them with great care both in regard to idiosyncrasies of spelling and punctuation. Throughout, words enclosed within brackets, thus { }, are my additions or explanations added to help the reader. Passages omitted are clearly indicated in the text.

Many of the letters by T.E. were damaged by water and have been exceedingly difficult to read. It was his habit to indicate a pause in the thought, or the end of a sentence, by a series of dots and many instances of this will be noticed; they do not mark omissions. His letters are in the Bodleian Library, Oxford.

It was the Grace of God which made my brothers what they were, and to me these letters are sacred.

M. R. LAWRENCE

Oxford
February 9th 1954

NOTE ON THE LIFE OF T. E. LAWRENCE

Born 1888

Oxford High School, September 1896 to July 1907

   In northern France studying castles, summers of 1906 and 1907

Jesus College, Oxford, October 1907 to June 1910 (First Class Honours History)

   In France studying castles, summer of 1908

   In Syria studying castles, summer of 1909

   Wrote *Crusader Castles*, winter of 1909–1910

In France studying medieval pottery, summer of 1910

At Jebail in Syria studying Arabic, winter of 1910–1911

Excavating at Carchemish (Jerablus) under D. G. Hogarth and R. Campbell
   Thompson, March and April 1911; under Campbell Thompson, April to
   July 1911

   Walk through northern Mesopotamia, summer of 1911

Excavating in Egypt under Flinders Petrie beginning of 1912

Excavating at Carchemish under C. L. Woolley, spring 1912 to spring 1914

   At home in Oxford, summer of 1913

   Survey on Sinai, January to February 1914

At Oxford and London, summer of 1914, completing *Wilderness of Zin* (report
   on Sinai work), eventually at the War Office

In Egypt, December 1914 to October 1916

   Journey to 'Iraq, March to May 1916

With Arab forces, October 1916 to October 1918

In London and Oxford, October to December 1918

In Paris for Peace Conference, January to October 1919

   By air to Egypt, May 1919

At All Souls College, Oxford, and in London, October 1919–1921

Adviser, Colonial Office, 1921–1922

   On missions to Aden, Jedda and Transjordan, August to December 1921

Aircraftsman Ross, Royal Air Force, latter half of 1922 to January 1923

   Discharged on discovery of his identity

Private Shaw, Royal Tank Corps, March 1923 to August 1925

   Acquired cottage at Clouds Hill, Dorset

   Transferred to Royal Air Force

Aircraftsman Shaw, Royal Air Force, August 1925 to March 1935

   Seven Pillars of Wisdom published 1926, at 30 guineas

   In India, January 1927 to 1928; *Revolt in the Desert* published and withdrawn
   in British Empire; *The Mint* completed; Marine Craft (speed boats)
   1930–35

Died after motor-cycling accident near Clouds Hill, May 1935

Mrs. Lawrence has sought my permission to print, as an introduction to the Home Letters of the most famous of her sons, the words which I spoke when I unveiled his Memorial at his old school in Oxford in 1936; and I readily give my consent.

Eighteen years have passed since those words were spoken, but now, pondering them again, I find not one to alter. The vast perils and catastrophes of the years between have not dimmed the splendour of his fame, nor blurred the impress of his personality upon the memory of his friends. It is the measure of his greatness that his multiple achievement has passed beyond opinion into history.

Winston S. Churchill

4 March, 1954.

THE ALLOCUTION

ALTHOUGH more than a year has passed since Lawrence was taken from us, the impression of his personality remains living and vivid upon the minds of his friends, and the sense of his loss is in no way dimmed among his countrymen. All feel the poorer that he has gone from us. In these days danger and difficulties gather upon Britain and her Empire, and we are also conscious of a lack of outstanding figures with which to overcome them. Here was a man in whom there existed not only an immense capacity for service, but that touch of genius which every one recognizes and no one can define. Whether in his great period of adventure and command or in those later years of self-suppression and self-imposed eclipse, he always reigned over those with whom he came in contact. They felt themselves in the presence of an extraordinary being. They felt that his latent reserves of force and willpower were beyond measurement. If he roused himself to action, who should say what crisis he could not surmount or quell? If things were going very badly, how glad one would be to see him come round the corner.

Part of the secret of this stimulating ascendancy lay of course in his disdain for most of the prizes, the pleasures and comforts of life. The world naturally looks with some awe upon a man who appears unconcernedly indifferent to home, money, comfort, rank, or even power and fame. The world feels not without a certain apprehension, that here is some one outside its jurisdiction; some one before whom its allurements may be spread in vain; some one strangely enfranchised, untamed, untrammelled by convention, moving independently of the ordinary currents of human action; a being readily capable of violent revolt or supreme sacrifice, a man, solitary, austere, to whom existence is no more than a duty, yet a duty to be faithfully discharged. He was indeed a dweller upon the mountain tops where the air is cold, crisp, rarefied, and where the view on clear days commands all the kingdoms of the world and the glory of them.

Lawrence was one of those beings whose pace of life was faster and more intense than what is normal. Just as an aeroplane only flies by its speed and pressure against the air, so he flew best and easiest in the hurricane. He was not in complete harmony with the normal. The fury of the Great War raised the pitch of life to the Lawrence standard. The multitudes were swept forward till their pace was the same as his. In this heroic period he found himself in perfect relation both to men and events.

I have often wondered what would have happened to Lawrence if the Great War had continued for several more years. His fame was spreading fast and with the momentum of the fabulous throughout Asia. The earth trembled with the wrath of the warring nations. All the metals were molten. Everything was in motion. No one could say what was impossible. Lawrence might have realized Napoleon's young dream of conquering the East; he might have arrived at Constantinople in 1919 or 1920 with most of the tribes and races of Asia Minor and Arabia at his back. But the storm wind ceased as suddenly as it had arisen. The skies were clear; the bells of Armistice rang out. Mankind returned with indescribable relief to its long interrupted, fondly cherished ordinary life, and Lawrence was left once more moving alone on a different plane and at a different speed.

In this we find an explanation of the last phase of his all too brief life. It is not the only explanation. The sufferings and stresses he had undergone, both physical and psychic, during the war had left their scars and injuries upon him. These were aggravated by the distress which he felt at what he deemed the ill-usage of his Arab friends and allies to whom he had pledged the word of Britain, and the word of Lawrence. He was capable of suffering mental pain in an exceptional degree. I am sure that the ordeal of watching the helplessness of his Arab friends in the grand confusions of the Peace Conference was the main cause which decided his renunciation of all power, and so far as possible of all interest in great public affairs.

In this premature retirement he had to lay hold of detailed tasks wherewith to fill the days and the hours. The writing of his book *The Seven Pillars* was a powerful solace to him. To all of us it is one of the treasures of English literature. *The Seven Pillars* as a narrative of war and adventure, as a portrayal of all that the Arabs mean in the world, is unsurpassed; it ranks with the greatest books ever written in the English language. It is not I think excessive to class it in interest and charm with *Pilgrim's Progress*, *Robinson Crusoe*, and *Gulliver's Travels*. If

Lawrence had never done anything except write this book as a mere work of the imagination, his fame would last in Macaulay's familiar phrase, "as long as the English language is spoken in any quarter of the globe." But this was a book of fact, not fiction; and the author was also the commander. When most of the vast literature of the Great War has been sifted and superseded by the epitomes, commentaries, and histories of future generations, when the complicated and infinitely costly operation of ponderous armies are the concern only of the military student, when our struggles are viewed in a fading perspective and a truer proportion, Lawrence's tale of the revolt in the desert will gleam with immortal fire.

When this literary masterpiece was written, lost, and written again; when every illustration had been profoundly considered and every incident of typography and paragraphing settled with meticulous care; when Lawrence on his bicycle had carried the precious volume to the few—the very few he deemed worthy to read them—happily he found another task to his hands which cheered and comforted his soul. He saw as clearly as any one the vision of air power and all that it would mean in traffic and war. He found in the life of an aircraftsman that balm of peace and equipoise which no great station or command could have bestowed upon him. He felt that in living the life of a private in the Royal Air Force he would dignify that honourable calling and help to attract all that is keenest in our youthful manhood to the sphere where it is most urgently needed. For this service and example, to which he devoted the last twelve years of his life, we owe him a separate debt. It was in itself a princely gift.

If on this occasion I have seemed to dwell upon Lawrence's sorrows and heart-searching rather than upon his achievements and prowess, it is because the latter are so justly famous. He had a full measure of the versatility of genius. He held one of those master keys which unlock the doors of many kinds of treasure-houses. He was a savant as well as a soldier. He was an archæologist as well as a man of action. He was an accomplished scholar as well as an Arab partisan. He was a mechanic as well as a philosopher. His background of sombre experience and reflection only seemed to set forth more brightly the charm and gaiety of his companionship, and the generous majesty of his nature. Those who knew him best miss him most; but our country misses him most of all; and misses him most of all now. For this is a time when the great problems upon which his thought and work had so long centred, problems of aerial defence, problems of our relations with the Arab peoples, fill an even larger space in our affairs. For all his reiterated renunciations I always felt that he was a man who held himself ready for a call. While Lawrence lived one always felt—I certainly felt it strongly—that some overpowering need would draw him from the modest path he chose to tread and set him once again in full action at the centre of memorable events. It was not to be. The summons which reached him, and for which he was equally prepared, was of a different order. It came as he would have wished it, swift and sudden on the wings of Speed. He had reached the last leap in his gallant course through life.

> *All is over! Fleet career,*
> > *Dash of greyhound slipping thongs,*
> *Flight of falcon, bound of deer,*
> *Mad hoof-thunder in our rear,*
> > *Cold air rushing up our lungs,*
> > *Din of many tongues.*

King George the Fifth wrote to Lawrence's brother, "His name will live in history." Can we doubt that that is true? It will live in English letters; it will live in the traditions of the Royal Air Force; it will live in the annals of war and in the legends of Arabia. It will also live here in his old school, for ever proclaimed and honoured by the monument we have to-day unveiled.

WINSTON S. CHURCHILL

T. E. LAWRENCE

T. E. Lawrence

DEAR MOTHER

It seems rather a long time since I wrote to you, and so, as its Sunday, we have decided that it is my turn to write to you. This morning Father and I went to St. Botolph's, the modern church near the old Priory Ruins. We have Picture P. Cards of the present state of the ruins so you will be able to compare the two views. The Ruins are all made of Roman tiles;—thousands of them,—and even the arcading is made of tiles. The actual large Norman Arch in the centre is, however, faced with stone. Behind this entrance there are a number of Norman Piers all made of rubble and bricks; they were once faced

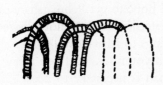

with plaster. The modern church (Built in 1836) is a very good specimen of modern Norman; in fact Father and I had only two holes to pick in it, and it harmonises excellently with the old being made of a greyish brick. Colchester is all over Roman remains; all the churches are full of Roman tiles and brick work, from Saxon Holy Trinity to Italian Renaissance St. Peter's: the Castle is brick from top to bottom; and large portions of the old walls still remain all round the town. The West Gate (Roman) still exists entire. It is rather like a tunnel and is about 11 feet high but only 5 feet wide. Its masonry is rubble and every two feet up are four courses of Roman tile. The stone work is regular at the bottom and has been squared. Up above it degenerates. There are about four rows of tiling altogether; and the wall is about 13 ft. high. The mortar is as soft as cheese. Next the gate was a guard room; nearly perfect; all except its roof, which had been of wood. The stone vaulting of the gate & guard room passage was perfect.

a. Guard Room.
b–b. Town wall.
c–c. Gate.
d–d. Guard Passage.

The dotted part is where the vaulting remains.

If possible I shall get post cards of the gate. It was far in a way the most interesting thing I have seen this trip. We came here from Ipswich over a rather hilly road 18 miles long. Still we took two hours over it; and walked about six hills; a proceeding Father does not like. We are feeding splendidly.

Father is much better and has not coughed since Lynn. I have had to give up Bures {A rubbing of a monumental brass}. We came by the other road because of the wind; still I hope to get Pebmarsh {another brass} tomorrow; and I got one yesterday so I'm not altogether mournful. I have sent off all my rubbings to Miss Powell; hope she'll like them. I expect you have Will with you now. Will you please tell him not to let you do more work than is necessary to keep you in condition? Also tickle Arnie when he gets up and when he goes to bed all from me. Tell him there are dozens of butterflies of all sorts about here, some Red Admirals; and a lot of other very queer ones. Ask Beadle {Will} to come up here as he has never seen a Death's Head or some such insect. Norwich Museum he would have enjoyed. There was the largest collection of raptorial birds in existence 409 out of 470 species: I wonder if he'll shriek with horror when he hears that I did not look at them but went off and examined the Norman W.C.s. In the hall was a thrilling stuffed group a boa constrictor strangling a tiger. We hope to return to Oxford Wednesday. Kindly take heaps of love from me for yourself; and when you've had enough, divide the remainder into three portions, and give them to the three worms you have with you. I wonder how the Doctor is enjoying Jerry {a Dog}. Don't forget the Canon's {Canon Christopher} birthday next Sunday. We have had one post card from Will, 1 from yourself and one letter from you. Loud snores to all. Love to yourself.

(NED)

Le Clos Briant
Dinard
Friday, August 4, 1906

Dear Mother

I have arrived here quite right after an excellent crossing. The Kerrys almost missed the train at Oxford of course, and came to the boat just with a minute to spare. The journey down to Southampton was uneventful, except for scares about the luggage going wrong. I rode straight to Netley, and caused a spirit of eager enquiry to be manifested by the youth of Southampton. Netley is as fine as if not finer than I had imagined. It is certainly the finest ruin I have seen, and much the most picturesque. I do not think that the Chapter House and guest room can be equalled. Coming back from Netley I went to Bakers and got my hat and then got note paper and Post Card Album. In the Hartley Institute they have some excellent Encaustic Tiles, well worth going to see: the collection of local objects is also good. On going to the boat I passed the *Deutschland*, having her bows repaired as a sequel to the Dover collision. On board the boat I found my berth, and deposited all my spare goods, and then put on the extra thick coat (this information is for Mother). The Moon was full and glorious: Mr. Kerry and I stayed up till about 11.30 looking at it; I cannot say whether the cloud effects or the reflection on the water were the best but the "ensemble" was perfect and left nothing to be desired. I never before understood properly Tennyson's "Long glories of the Autumn Moon" but I see his reasons now for mentioning it so often, it was so different from the pale moon of the land. The moon was out from about seven to four, and there were heavy clouds with continuous lightning in the East. We only had about ½ hour's rain. The sunrise was on the whole a failure, there was nothing so good as the sunset before. About 2 we passed between Sark and Jersey. Tell Chimp {Frank} I was not much impressed with the latter. It was all too dark and gloomy, for a residence; the only bright spot was the Corbière Light-house. St. Malo was reached before six, but we had to wait till seven before landing. The sea was very choppy and irregular with a strong swell around the Channel Islands. Everyone in the boat appears to have been sick with the exception of four or five, among whom Mr. Kerry and myself were prominent. I found Mons. Chaignon at the Douanne (?); we recognised each other at the same moment. He

has hardly changed at all, if anything he is a trifle stouter. The Customs
people were chalking all the baggages as fast as it appeared, they do
not seem to have opened any: there was a fearful crush; I should think
there were 120 bicycles. I saw Mr. Fécélier for a moment but had no
time to discuss any economical questions with him. The Chaignons
have some most wonderful carved furniture, and most valuable works
of art in their house; I never saw the equal of a buffet in the dining-
room, while a buhl table in the drawing room beats any at Warwick
Castle. I shall not have enough money to buy any of the things
however. I must economise strictly; I have only ten shillings over what
will be taken up in the tour. The ticket cost 30/– and Father took 10/–
which only left £4–10–0 for an eight days' trip and the hat and other
articles have already come out of it. Mr. Corbel is not in Dinard but
in a place about 60 miles off. The Lefevriers inhabit the house the other
side of the road: the Chaignons send all sorts of messages for Bob; it
took me nearly ten minutes to explain all about the Brigade to them;
it was about the first thing they asked me. They also send dittos to you
and the other nippers. Poor Hall is not 1st in Locals after all. Love to
yourself. (Don't do any work at all). To Father and to all the other
worms down to the smallest. Just off to post. Ta Ta.

DINARD

Monday, 6th August, 1906

DEAR MOTHER

Here goes another letter full of nothing! Since the last was written
very little has been done by the most important person in Dinard. I have
visited the old Church of St. Lunaire and it is most interesting. The
architecture is wonderfully plain (Norman) about 1000 A.D. There is
absolutely no sign of "Long and Short" work, although the masonry
is rubble. It contains seven magnificent tombs. One of a Bishop has an
effigy in full canonicals, except the tunic; he has the usual Maniple,
Chasuble, Dalmatic, Stoles, Alb, but no Tunic at all; it is rather
peculiar I think, must ask Streatfield on return. The Pastoral Staff is
very good, and he has his hands crossed at the wrists; I wonder if this
is a sign of Continental Work? There are two sepulchral slabs in low
relief of a baron and wife about 1350, these are on the floor but a little
worn. The knight wears cyclas etc. and the lady resembles Mrs. Malyns
as Arnie calls her; No. 11 in my room. Under Ogee canopies are two

excellent effigies of a knight and wife (5), about 1500, still very clear and good; the knight resembles Brome from Holton No. 15; and the lady is dressed as Mrs. Adderbury No. 9. They are both most interesting, but I will not bother you with details except to remark that the mail collar of the knight, just above the tabard, is excellent.

On the other side of the Church S. Transept is an effigy of the same family as the other civilian, of Pontual, only this time it is a daughter who is represented, with the pedimental head-dress, and other garments to match. I was much struck with the sideless côte-hardi worn by the lady of 1500 (5); it is the most highly developed manifestation of it that I have ever seen. The coat was reduced to a narrow band of ribbon, running down her front. It is one of the finest churches that I have seen, considered with regard to its monuments. I have seen the Kerrys who appear comfortable, and also I saw Mr. Kempshead who was most astonished to see me: he has given me valuable directions about Corseul, and other places. I have bought 16 postcards of Breton heads, bodies, and legs in weird costume. I hope they do not invent them for the sake of the photographer. There are about 400 more postcards of costumes; how many shall I get? Now, Mr. Kempshead says, no advantage greater than a halfpenny per £ is ever got when changing money. The rate is practically par. I am off to Mrs. Clark, and possibly Fr. Fabel: the Fletchers are here; I saw Mr. Fletcher behaving in rather a loud manner on the beach. Your postcard has just come. I am rather surprised about the Morris; it should not have broken like that. Tell Arnie I am not coming back for a long time; not for weeks: there are wolves quite close to a part which we will visit on our tour (close means forty miles). It appears that there are a number of mountains about, and the country is quite wild; the wolves did a lot of damage last winter. I cannot promise to kill one for Will. Two or three of the Chaignons are wearing Arnie's pinafores, and the other things were much appreciated. M. Corbel is not in Dinard, but the Lefevriers, all except the Mr. are: all this morning I have been wrestling with the tyres of Will's old bicycle here, I removed three outer covers (without the one minute removers), took out and exchanged 3 inner tubes; changed two valves, tightened a chain, and adjusted the bearings of a wheel, all in two hours.

Please give my kindest regards to Father and the rest and DON'T WORK TOO HARD: do nothing rather than too much; you are worth more than the house; love to all: hope you are all well: I have not been bilious yet; don't expect to be. A flock of sheep disappeared in the sands round the Mont {Mont St. Michel} this spring and so I will not try to find them. Ta Ta. Love. love, love. love. love. love.

NED

LE CLOS BRIANT. DINARD
Monday Evening, 6 August, 1906

DEAR FATHER

I have decided to give Mother a rest now from writing letters, so I am writing to you; but please don't answer this; letter-writing is a bore. I posted Mother's letter so late that I fear she will not get it till Thursday, although there is just a chance of its catching the boat, since it was so foggy this morning that it could not start. This afternoon I have paid a succession of visits. I went to Mrs. Clark, and took my washing, giving her one list & keeping another myself (this item is for Mother). Mrs. Clark knew me at once from my likeness to Bob. She is very anxious to be remembered to you, and would like you to come to Dinard: she offers you all her house, and will sleep herself in the shed: at present Dinard is rather empty: prices have risen too much I suppose: she said that it was twice as dear as it was when you were here. Her "baby" who was ill when you were here is now 13 and quite strong: she has another of eleven, also a boy. From Mrs. Clark I went on to the Chalet du Vallon, which appeared the same, only I did not go in, but proceeded instead to the Frères school at the door of which I met Frère Fabel. The recognition was mutual. He asked dozens of questions about all of you, and was quite distressed to hear that you had given up photography. He told me that you were a Tory, and that you did not like Mr. Gladstone; he also said that you were the best neighbour he ever had. He would be quite intoxicated with joy if he could see you again; I invited him to Oxford, and he seems inclined to come. His school was sold on Wednesday, and next Saturday they will know whether the Abbé or another man will get it. If the Abbé wins, Frère Fabel will remain in Dinard. He was very interested in the state of affairs (religious) in England. He is well up in the High Church Movement, and knows Father Maturin (A Cowley Father) who is now a Roman Catholic, & at Dinard, I think. He considers the High Church Party as too High for the Church of England, and said that his opinions differed from theirs in no way, except that they were Catholics and he was a Roman Catholic. He was hugely amused at their calling themselves Catholic. He was much interested at hearing of the Benedictine Abbey lately inaugurated in Yorkshire by the Ritualists, (which is not Mirfield), and was anxious to know the relative strengths of the different sects. He was very interested in the Education Bill of which I gave him a history and an abstract, and was very specially inquisitive as to the probable action of the Lords in connection with it. He was also interested in Mr. Burns, and so I gave him a history of that individual, and my comments upon the probable influence of the Labour Party on the future history of the Parliament. In fact we discussed the political situation of the present, with special bearing on the Church of England, and its disestablishment. He also asked for an account of Oxford, University, customs, manners, etc., and I gave him a mighty account. He has a St. John's pupil at Dinard, I think he called him Cameron: I imagine he would like a photograph of an undergraduate, and one of St. John's if he has not had one already. He also wished to be remembered to all of you. From him I went to Mrs. White at the Villa Nahant, and saw her: she thought I was Bob at first: but we soon cleared matters up between us. The Villa is let to the Nobels, the builders of the *Kashima*, the new Japanese battleship. The White's were interested in the Unemployed so I gave them a history of the movement, for it is undoubtedly engineered. Mr. White has no sympathy with them. He comes from near High Wycombe, and was very surprised to hear we were at Oxford. They offer you a little house down near their gate. They say that Dinard has changed greatly. The Hôtel des Terraces has been burnt down and rebuilt; a new large hotel The Royal has been made just beyond the old Casino, and the Third Casino is being built. The Vicomté has many houses on it. Do you remember the mysterious death of Mlle Rochard, in England in a tunnel, some months ago? The cause of her falling from the train was never found out. She was the only daughter of the Count Dada whom you have mentioned to me. The Count is nearly out of his mind. Mrs. Hopkins is dead; the Whites say you knew her. They wish to be remembered to you, they also asked about Kate. They say that Toby Purvis is quite white-haired, and looks as old as his mother, who is getting very frail. After the Whites I visited Mr. Lewis: he remembered you, but not me; of course. He will have finished a painting in 15 days and wants me to go up and see it; he looks just the same, and enquired after you, and your bicycle with great affection. When 49 he took to cycle-racing, and holds the 12 hours champion-ship of Brittany: I have verified this. He also asked several questions about my bicycle and was decidedly interesting. He would not shew me the unfinished painting, but remembered the sea-weed-gathering picture perfectly. The one of the forge which you will remember he promised to show us, if it was successful, was hung at the Salon; but he did not seem quite satisfied with it. Frère Fabel told me that Mme Fécélier was quite well in the evening, but during the night woke up and died in a minute, almost instantaneously. I will get more details from the housekeeper when I have an opportunity. I see M. Fécélier nearly every day, but have of course not done much in the way of talking. The road to St. Briac is vile; a cart-track.

Tuesday afternoon I hope to visit Corseul, where there are very interesting remains of a Temple of Mars, and also Gallo-Roman sub-structures. It was the Capital of the Curiosolites whom Chimp will remember in *Cæsar*. Mr. Kempshead advised us most strongly to go to Montcontour. The old manor-house is now the hotel, and the landlady told Mr. Kempshead that she could not charge him less than 100 francs per month, but that would include everything. After dinner there he declared that he had no wish to explore Montcontour, although it contains no house more modern than the sixteenth century. We will if possible go there, as it is on our route. Mrs. Kempshead declares that those cider jugs frequently run out, and she has advised me to make certain of the glaze before buying them.

Your next letter if any should be sent "Poste Restante, Paimpol" where we will stay Saturday and Sunday. I will send a postcard off each night from our stopping place, but on many occasions these will be blank. It is not worth paying 1½d. extra to say "all well", that is to be understood from the card. This is my last letter to Oxford: the next will go to The Rossett. The weather out here is beautiful; there has been no rain for six months, but they expect a break up soon. I have not written to either Bob or Will, since I did not know how to describe their situation: but I have sent a p.c. to Ruby Strong and have begun a letter to Elsie. Scroggs {C. F. C. Beeson} starts tonight, but you need not be uneasy about us; I have had no difficulty at all in understanding what is said, and people have no difficulty in understanding me. I was given a bad 5 franc piece at the Bank but they will have to take it back today. I hope you are feeling less stiff from your fall, and that the other two are quite right. Love to all.

NED

DINAN

Thursday, 9th August, 1906

Rode with Scroggs to Lehon today, after coming here without incident except a puncture on quay which I mended while the "permit" was obtained. The scenery of Rance from the lock to Dinan was magnificent; we rode of course along the towpath which had excellent surface, free from flints. Lehon is very interesting: the ruins are of course very ruined, but the whole is instructive, as an example of a Norman castle, without any later additions. We climbed all over the remains, and I got stuck on a tower, and had a 30 ft. climb down a wall. It was quite safe, and impressed Scroggs greatly as did our "dejuner" at the Grand Hôtel de Europe in Dinan. Menu was Sardines, Cold Meat, Eggs, Hash, Fowl, Salad, Desert: what will the Dîner be? I had some of everything!

Lehon Abbey (more properly a Priory) is splendid: the Church is fine, but too much restored: the effigies in it were very interesting. One was to a female, Tiphaine du Guesclin, daughter of the famous Constable; who was so named after her mother. The effigy lay on the North Side of the Presbytery, and was most remarkable. She died in 1417 the widow of Jean V de Beaumanoir. She was dressed in a *jupon*, which buttoned down the front with 22 circular buttons; the button-holes were yet quite clear, slightly puckered round her waist, which was exceedingly small, and tightly drawn. The front of the jupon terminated in a tassel, with large bow. The jupon closed quite close round her neck, forming a low collar like the modern military tunic. The sleeves (no man's jupon ever had sleeves), were fairly full and descended to the wrist; underneath it was seen the edge of the vam-brace. She wore genoullières, with square plates beneath them, jambs and sollerets, of three large and heavy laminated plates. She also had rowel spurs, and her feet rested on an eagle expansed bearing a shield (billets or) on the front, held in its beak. The eagle was very faithfully and clearly drawn, and the claws drawn very true to nature. At the sides of the effigy were six other shields, bearing the billets or; the arms of her husband the count of Beaumanoir. The eagle expansed is the badge of the Duguesclin family. Her hands were bare, and finely shaped. Her head was resting on a cushion, with a corded tassel at each corner; her hair, confined by a narrow fillet alone, flowed in two curls one outside each ear, while the rest was cut short and parted regularly down the centre. Her face was perfect, without any mutilation, and exhibited the calm repose and angelic purity which the mediæval sculptor knew so well to blend, with a certain martial simplicity and haughtiness. The figure is carved from white stone, and is yet perfect; it is about five feet six inches in length, and, in its combination of female dress and armour, is so far as I know unique. Opposite her on the other side of the church lay her husband assassinated in 1385. He is chiefly remarkable for two gigantic curls, each supported by a sturdy angel. He has a beard, and wears jupon gorget pauldrons, brassarts, coutes, and a large sword. His feet of six lames were resting on a lion. He bore a shield with nine billets or. Two almost identical figures of Lords of Lehon (14th cent.) were interesting as having slipped off their gauntles, & coifs de mailles, just as Septvans {a brass} whom they greatly resembled. One of them had his feet covered with scale armour. They wore surcoats, and demi-jambs. A Prior of the 14th cent. has a beautiful canopy, *and has his wrists crossed*. Raoulin de Redon wears a Tabard, quarterly. Two ladies of about 1440 complete this wonderful series, and one of these effigies to a lady was the most perfect example of artistic merit that I have seen in effigies. It would have adorned the Parthenon. Her face was perfect, and her dress most beautifully arranged: I am going out to try to obtain photographs of these effigies, and to explore the furniture shops: no time for anything more.

GRAND HÔTEL CONTINENTAL. PAIMPOL

11th August, 1906

DEAR MOTHER

We have got here to Paimpol, after a lovely ride through driving rain, and over heavy roads. The scenery was beautiful from St. Brieuc to Lanvollon. From Dinan I went to Corseul, and found on the way a most beautiful Roman temple, the Fanum Martis, from which the Capital of the Curiosolites took its Roman name. The ruins are down a by-road with poor surface, and many turns. Although we did not

know if we were on the right track, and had no directions, still I
walked straight to it! My bump of locality must be enormous. The
ruins comprise three sides of a hexagon, and are about forty feet high.
The walls, about 4 feet thick, are built of stone, with a lavish amount
of mortar, and a slight admixture of Roman brick. The ground all
round is strewn with pieces of brick and tile. The facing of the ruins of
the walls is formed of small blocks of stone, each exactly a cube, and
laid with the most precise and mathematical certainty. The courses are
perfectly level, and the whole is more regular than a brick house, or a
chessboard. The blocks are about half an inch apart, and the total effect
is excellent. I will try to get a photo of it next time I visit it.

From Corseul we went to Montafilant, a Norman Castle, whose
moat, now rather swampy, we crossed by a narrow bank only a few
inches wide, with water-jumps. The remains are now much ruined,
but the old well is still perfect: we pulled up a bucket of water and
drank it, for the sake of the association. After Montafilant we lost
ourselves in a maze of by-roads, for about two hours: Scroggs had a
dust-slip, but was not damaged. We had lunch at Plelan-le-petit, and
paid 3¾d. each: for this sum we had cider and soda-water, four poached
eggs, bread, butter, biscuits etc. On the whole the meal was cheap.
From Plelan we rode to Jugon, and walked a hill of two miles long:
it was terribly exhausting. From Jugon we went to Lamballe, and had
dinner on arrival. Lamballe Mr. Kempshead had recommended for its
furniture, but I saw nothing to equal a very pretty little box at Dinan;
the costume of Lamballe is rather unusual; I have a p.p.c. of it. Lamballe has a wonderful church Notre-Dame, situated on the highest
ground of any round about. We ascended the tower and the view was
splendid. The tombs in the church were especially interesting; although
the Norman nave was good. There was a rood-loft, absolutely perfect;
a little reading desk is situated in front for the gospeller. I sent a postcard of one door (N) of the church: there are twelve pilasters on each
side, and the whole is about 4 feet deep. It was very remarkable. From
Lamballe we trained to St. Brieuc, a dirty town with a flamboyant and
Renaissance Cathedral, containing excellent tombs. At St. Brieuc we
had dinner, and were very much amused by the comments of a ?
in front of us; he did not know that we knew enough French to understand him, and was covered with confusion when he happened to see
us laughing internally. They are most amusing; sitting down to the

table, squaring their shoulders, and attacking "Course 8" with the same ferocity and sternness as they did the first.

From St. Brieuc we rode up a beautifully engineered road, up hill for 3 kils. The views into the valley were perfect. We went through Lanvollon, in which church I found two little medallions of rather nice stained glass, put away in a loft. I will try and get them from the Curé on return. At Coetimen we saw a château, and at Lanleff a most interesting round church of very early Norman date. The capitals had crossed lines scratched on them to about $\frac{1}{4}$ of 1 inch deep. The Church, (ruined) was nearly a facsimile of that at Cambridge, but it was ruder, and had a little apse about 5 feet deep, as a chapel to St. Amtong. The chancel was destroyed. From Lanleff we rode here straight; arriving quite late, owing to the badness of the roads. I cannot write any more just now.

{About 21 words partly illegible}. Love to all.

HÔTEL DE FRANCE. LANNION
13th August, 1906

DEAR MOTHER

Have got here all right after a pleasant ride through beautiful weather. We stayed Sunday at Paimpol, and saw Ploubaylanec and Beauport. The situation of the first is perfect;—the architecture of the abbey at the latter better still. The refectory of the abbey is the finest vaulted hall I have yet seen. The style is 1st Pointed (E.E.). Visitors are "rigoreusement defendus" from entering the abbey which lies in private grounds, and so we were forced to enter by the back door. We thus lost the best view of the "ensemble". At Paimpol on Sunday night about eleven we were disturbed by the continual tooting of a motor horn, and yells of "feu." A fire had broken out in the town, and for an hour, (which was all the duration of the erif {"erif" or "fire" spelt backwards}), we were deafened by the most awful row I ever heard. Everyone yelled! The people in the bed-room next to us began to knock down chairs and scream.

Three buglers and two drummers sounded the "reveille" for an hour and a half, and the motor horn still tooted. Firemen rushed about dragging engines and yelling, no one kept cool, and the result was that the fire burnt furiously without anyone doing anything but dance and rave deliriously. I never saw such an instance of incapacity. In the morning the hotel presented a great bill: larger than they said it would be. The result is that our expenditure is 8/– per day instead of 6/– up to the present. We were also robbed shamefully at Treguier today, when at "dejeuner", a meal in which S. {Scroggs} delights.

Treguier has a beautiful cathedral, with the best cloisters I have ever seen. I will buy some post cards if my money allows it. Till now I have spent some 36 francs on hotels, and stamps are to be counted as well, also post cards. We have only had two punctures, both in Scroggs' tyres. One in St. Malo, mended by myself, and one outside Lamballe mended most excellently by myself. Yesterday my brake wire (back) broke. I rode here applying my foot to the wheel at hills, and took it to two shops which had no suitable place. At last I found a practical workshop, and got a *mécanicien* to assist me in mending it. I hope all is right now. They charged 4 francs which was cheap, considering that we were two hours over it. There was a lot of soldering to do so that I could not do the job alone. My bicycle decidedly surprised them. I gave the man who helped me 1 franc for himself, since I kept him an hour over time: we have only spent 1 franc in tips besides this;—we have thus introduced quite a reform.

The foliage and flora here are semi-tropical, plants I have never seen before flourish in the open air. It is quite a common sight to see old women spinning in their cottage doorways. Would you like a spinning wheel? The children flee in terror when they see us in our cycle capes; such articles are unknown: I have only seen two French lady cyclists, and one was in rational dress. There is a St. John's man staying in this hotel. I do not know his name, only he rather resembles Thompson, except that he is almost bald. Tomorrow we go by Tonquédec, a wonderful château, to Guingamp. At this place there is a church with 5 naves, and the thickest circular pillar I have ever seen. It contains the stairs of the rood-loft, and is gigantic. Father would have enjoyed the Cathedral of Treguier: it was magnificent, mostly flamboyant, but very massive: nearly all the pillars here are very massive, except the Norman, which are octagonal and very thin. I got your p.c. at Paimpol; thank you very much for it: I hope you will all enjoy yourselves. Take gentle rides at first, gradually increasing in pace and length. We have sent cards of Ploubay to Mr. Cave. Scroggs wants me to go out

with him so I cannot continue: keep yourself well, and let me know
the local & Ewelme results: both were out before S. {Scroggs} left
Oxford.

   . . . my love: I think . . . his.

Love to all NED

HÔTEL DU COMMERCE
GUINGAMP
14th August, 1906

DEAR MOTHER

    Have arrived here from Lannion after a beautiful day. We rode
straight to Tonquédec. The word Tonquédec means the well-guarded
place, and is applied to the château which stands on a hill overlooking
a most beautiful valley, the course today of the Guer. The château
dates from about 1260, and has had a most eventful history. It is nearly
a trapezium in plan, that is an irregular polygonal figure. It is surrounded by ditches, and parts of the moat are yet full. Hills surround it on all
sides, and the country near is thickly wooded. The first door is ogival
and was defended by a drawbridge and portcullis. The hinges of the
drawbridge yet remain, in the form of stones hollowed out on the top.
This door stands in the centre of a sort of demi-lune or rabelin with
walls about five feet thick and the door is flanked by two semi-circular
towers, with latrines of peculiar form of which I will speak later. To
right and left of the door are embrasures for cannon, pierced about
1660, although the whole of this wall is a later addition. The towers
are, like others, hexagonal within; one is still used by a family of three.
Within this entrance one fronts the main gateway of the castle. This
façade is formed by three semi-circular towers, and one circular. The
gateway is about six or seven feet above the ground, and is an ogee
arch. It had a drawbridge and portcullis. The semicircular towers are
perfect to the machicoulis, a height of about 50 feet. The masonry is
well cut, and the whole, in perfect preservation, is perhaps the finest
entrance to a castle I have ever seen. It is most imposing. On the left
side is a semi-round tower, now terribly destroyed, which once flanked
that remaining perfect on the right. The sides in front are about 12 feet
thick, and the form inside is square. It contains a Perpendicular fire-
place and is entered by a shouldered door. The great circular tower on

the right is more interesting. It stands about 70 feet high, and is some 40 feet in diameter (inside). The walls are about 12 feet thick at the bottom, and decrease to about 9 feet only. The tower is perfect and is entirely detached from the rest of the castle, except for two low walls which connect it with the remains of some domestic buildings. The tower was entered by a drawbridge on the second story some 150 feet above the moat. It was thus a separate fortress, and could be cut off from the remainder. It had a turret with conical roof on the top; but this is much ruined. The machicoulis are still quite perfect and are

each formed of 7 stones arranged thus.

They are all mathematically precise. The tower is ascended by a newel staircase, has most of its mouldings renaissance, and bears the remains of a latrine on the face. It contains many windows and fire-places. The courtyard within the principal entrance is much encumbered with debris to the depth of about four feet, through which project foundations of walls. The remains of the chapel are on the right but they are meagre: a small perpendicular aumbray and a piscina are yet visible.

On the left of the courtyard was the great hall, which had two windows deeply set in alcoves. One of these alcoves had a cupboard in it. Is such a fixture not unique in domestic architecture?

The grand fire-place at the end of the hall was about seven feet wide and four feet high; the mantelpiece was entirely composed of one enormous stone. The hall must have borne a great resemblance to Kenilworth, for beneath it are large vaulted cellars with barrel vault, just as there were in the Warwickshire castle; this Tonquédec is much finer, and is far the best I have seen. The vault has four entrances, and a fifth practicable for a cat. The hall had no latrine, but further along was another, communicating apparently with one on the wall, and thence to a *drain*. This must be most unusual. There is a semicircular tower still perfect on this side, and on it I impaled myself when climbing. I tore my face with thorns and have ruined my beauty. It was a very tricky place. The machicoulis are perfect here, as elsewhere in the castle. Next to this tower a wall leads across to the tower by the chapel corner; this tower has a beautiful latrine, of whose interior Scroggs

made a sketch at my request. I enclose it, numbered 2. It projects from
the wall as in that on the keep enclosed (number 1), and looks like a
sentry box. It has a little window and is fitted with a seat with large
hole. The debris fell into the moat. The keep had three, one for
each living room story. They were placed diagonally like this.

Scroggs made a sketch of the outside of the best preserved. They are most
interesting as improvements of the Norman variety, which was just
a little crude. The keep was the most interesting piece of work I have
seen. It was a perfect circle, and was hexagonal inside, and pierced by
15 openings; four of which were fire-places. One fire-place had rather
nice engaged columns, in Perpendicular style. The keep was on the
end of the triangular hill on which the castle was built, and it was
about 35 feet diameter (interior measure) with 14 feet walls, narrowing
to 10 feet. It was ascended by a newel, and had a walk round the top
above the machicoulis. The keep was quite detached from the rest of
the castle, and was entered by a door on the third story: this door had
a drawbridge, whose sockets remained: this pont levis fell on to a
pillar about 30 feet high, and seven or eight feet square, situated midway between the keep and the walls. From this pillar a bridge led to the
wall of the castle proper. Each bridge was about seven feet long, and
the place would have been impossible to enter, covered as it was by
hoards and loopholes. An enemy would have had to make two bridges
before he could reach the door. The drop to the ground was about 40
feet. My nib has given out. I will get another soon. The keep is ascended by a newel, and has a walk round the summit. The view up
and down the valley is perfect. The river, quite narrow now (30 feet
wide) flows at the bottom of a very precipitous hill, too steep to climb
without difficulty. Just below the castle there is a very pretty water
mill, with underground passage communicating with the castle. The
passage cannot be entered, because, say the local inhabitants, the spirits
of the Huguenots who died in the castle blow out the lights of any
adventurer. The castle was a great stronghold of Cardinal Richelieu.

The rocks about the castle are granite of a reddish tint. The view of the castle from the exterior is perhaps the most perfect of the many perfect parts of this wonderful fortress.

Throughout the whole enceinte there is not one stone of the main walls out of place. And the castle has not been restored! Some of the durability of the masonry may be due to the placing of flat slabs of thin oolite, or other stone with lateral grain, between the different large stones. The mortar is thus not much in evidence, and the whole is a homogeneous mass of solid rock. Whatever the cause, the result is wonderful. Every machicoulis on the circuit of the walls seems in its original position, only the battlements are gone. Tell Arnie I saw a brown squirrel run up the wall, and he went right up the keep to where Scroggs was sketching: when Scroggs moved he jumped to the main wall. He was a very good jumper. The squirrels about here are very large and carry their tails like the foxes do theirs straight out behind. We had dejeuner in one of the embrasures of the gateway: our dejeuner was an innocent one; nothing had to be killed to feed us. Milk, bread, butter, was our total. Price 4d.

We were on the whole some four hours in the imposing ruin: we had serious thoughts of staying the night; but finally rode on to Guingamp, where I wrote the first part of this letter, in which I lessened the glories of Tonquédec by attempting to describe them. I would have given a great deal for Father's Camera there. I bought some post cards, which I will enclose to illustrate my account. In the general views the keep is the low circular tower at the far end. From Guingamp (uninteresting place) we rode to St. Brieuc, and then to Erquy, where we slept. Erquy is a bathing town so called, with enormous quarries of rose-coloured granite. We walked all over the quarry cliffs after eight, and the wind being high we enjoyed ourselves much. The cliffs were about 400 feet high, and commanded a good view. From Erquy, we rode to Château du Guildo, near Ploubalay. At Erquy when returning from bathing, I rode a measured half-kilo. on the sand in 40 seconds exactly. There was a gale behind me, and the sands were perfectly level and very fast, but still 30 miles per hour was distinctly good. I have never gone faster; of course my high gear was the one I rode. Father would like to come to stay at Erquy for a week, to do a little speed-work on the sands; he would not do it anywhere else, for the roads, like most Breton ones, are vile. The Château du

Guildo is most interesting and has large remains, but I cannot descend
to it after the inimitable Tonquédec. It

> "Lichen bearded grayly draped
> "With streaming grass appeared, low-built but strong.
> "The ruinous donjon as a knoll of moss,
> "The battlement o'er topped with ivy-tods
> "A home of bats, in every tower an owl."

I must mention however that one of the latrines here had a drain,
leading to the river, and thus the Tonquédec example has a parallel.
From Guildo we rode to Dinard, and Scroggs is staying at the Hôtel
des Etrangers here.

I am quite right, and am fit to ride 100 miles per day for a month.
We will probably visit the Mont in a few days. So far I have seen
nothing in the souvenir line that I liked; not even cider jugs: except
that box at Dinan. I intend to return there soon to have another look.
It rained the evening we were there, and all the antiquity departed
from the furniture exposed to sale. It's all in the polish! I don't like
Dinard; it has a misplaced ambition to become a watering place like
Bournemouth which it will never perform.

DINARD
Friday Morning {August 17th}

With reference to my luggage. My silk shirt was a blessing. It took
up no space, and every day I used to roll it tightly round my other
articles, and it used to hold them all in place. Thus my luggage was
never larger or longer than my carrier. Father will be very interested
to learn this, for the carrier is a small one. It went through the trip
excellently and my baggage gave absolutely no trouble. I carried two
pairs of socks and wore a third. Next time I would only carry one pair
and would not trouble to bring a sponge. A spare pair of trousers is
useful and in fact necessary: also a spare shirt. A coat is quite useless if
a cape is carried: by this means the weight can be reduced to practically
nil. I had plenty room for a camera, and wish I had brought one. It is
very strange that the Local results are not yet out: the Kerrys told me
a lot about them the day we crossed. Was it not extraordinary that my
tour this year ended on the 16th of August, my birthday, just as my
tour last summer to Norfolk did? I have mended three punctures only

this trip; last one it was four: I can now polish one off in about ten minutes, as I have quick drying solution. Tomorrow Scroggs is going to Mont St. Michel, and I expect I will go with him. This afternoon we think of looking at St. Malo and possibly St. Servan. I will keep this letter open till Saturday when Scroggs starts for England. I will send it with him and so you will have it quickly. . . . We went over the "Tour Solidor" at St. Servan. I will send you an account later. At St. Servan I became extravagant and purchased myself a birthday present for 4 francs. Ruskin's *Stones of Venice*. I had no prose reading with me, and one can have too much Spenser. The new acquisition seems most interesting architecturally, I expect Father will like it. (Give my love to Florence, and tell her to keep you strictly idle and quiet: no work. I am glad to hear that you are feeling better: by all means become quite well before you return: this trip is intended to set you up.) Is Father going to have wood rims and Constrictors on his new one? Fixed gear and fixed wheel, North road bar, etc.? It would be best. I hope Will has been successful with his barrow (if it is a barrow, let me know more about it). Hug and tickle Arnie for me: I am off in ten minutes to the Mont. The weather here is cold and windy; only had about three hot days since I came here.   Love.

NED

16th August, 1906

MY DEAR WILL

Your letter has put me in a fever heat of expectation: but:— what is it you are going to dig up? Your letter bristles with inconsistencies. You think it is a Roman or Celtic camp (the two things are absolutely opposed to each other) and then you proceed to say that it is a mound on some rising ground. If it includes a mound, say 40 feet high, it is a Saxon or Danish fortification, with probably an interment or two on the top; if the mound is 10 feet high or less, and is about 30 feet in diameter, then it is a barrow, as you said in the former part of your description, which has a lamentable lack of exact figures. You next say that you cannot see traces of vallum or fossa, which are both terms to be applied to a Roman camp, and not to a Celtic, Saxon, British, or Danish erection. These last three or four possibly might have *mounds* and *dykes*, but you see no traces of them. If the mound is

British it will be closely encircled by its fortifications, (if it ever had any). If the mound is Saxon, the encircling lines of fortification may be half a mile away. The bayonets Florence describes are bronze spearheads, of a very early pattern: they might point either to an encampment or a burial, probably the latter, if no great quantity was found. So far all that you have told me which stands is that the mound is round. If I had further details I could advise you where and how to dig: a camp would not be worth excavating:—you might dig over half a mile of ground and only find a spear head: a burial, if a low mound should have a trench cut through it, from S.W. to N.E., on the level of the ground. Keep all flints, except the whole mound is flint and gravel, and by all means keep all bones; if you find human bones, do not disturb them, but dig round them, to find if they are male or female, and to recover the whole skeleton if possible: the skull is the most important part to determine the date. Any bronze implements found, should not be disturbed at first, but try to trace the haft, which will have shrunk to the thinness of a pencil. You will find this very difficult but the result will repay it. If the mound is small sift the earth you throw out—Frank and Arnie can help in this while you and Bob dig. Work very carefully, so as not to break any tender article: if the mound is large, you should begin in the same way from the top, and work down until you are sure the strata have not been disturbed: i.e. if you find pure clay with no admixture of earth, you may be certain that it has not been moved. You may discover the whole mound to be natural (you say it is "unnatural," most archæologists use "artificial") in which case only the upper three feet need be dug supposing it is a large mound. You see I am trying to advise something for every case. In a small barrow 4–8 feet high, the articles would probably not be more than two feet from the body on each side: to search further out is an energetic course which occasionally repays itself, but not as a rule. It might be worth while trying to obtain some of those "bayonets." I think they are preserved in the village, unless those preserved are real bayonets, dating from 60–70 years back. They will probably not be so old as the civil war, although it is possible that they might be. I should advise you to find out where they were discovered, and why they dug there, and at what depth they lay. You should be able to draw conclusions from the answers to these questions. Let me know how the matter progresses, and unless it is very light soil, use small spades. Keep an accurate account of your progress, & mark on a plan where each important article is found. You have my best wishes for success. Don't give up at once if you don't find anything. Digging is an excellent exercise.

DINARD
Monday, 20th August, 1906

DEAR FATHER

I think it time that I dedicated a letter to you; although it does not make the least difference in style, since all my letters are equally bare of personal information. The buildings I try to describe will last longer than we will, so it is only fitting that they should have the greater space. On Friday we went to look over the "Tour Solidor". The plan as you will remember is two circles, joined by connecting walls. Each circular tower is polygonal within, and the floors still exist in their old places, only wood has taken the place of stone in the vaulting. The tower is ascended by a newel of great width, with the base of the central shaft moulded. This I think is always a sign of Perpendicular work. It was built in the 14th Century by Jean IV. The walk round the top is sloping outward, and the spaces between the machicoulis have been filled up, but it is still very interesting and commands a good view. A most striking and novel feature were the form of the latrines, which were here exposed to the air, and were in the form of truncated pyramids about 18 inches high. Inside they were neatly plastered, and dropped sheer into the sea. There were three of them round the top, and two more on the other stories. These latter had drains. The top storey (I will work downwards) had four rooms, one with a magnificent hooded fire-place. A curious feature of the place was that each room, however small, had its Perp. fire-place even the little seat for the sentry, cut out of the thickness of the wall, near the gateway, and not more than three feet deep had its little chimney and grate. It is an eloquent testimony to the changes which had taken place since the Norman times. The loophole windows let in enough light by which to read, on a sunny day, when the walls are as thin as these (only about 4 feet). On the second floor counting from top (four rooms) there are two good fire-places, and a curious piscina (I suppose the room was the chapel). On one of the floors a chess-board had been carved by some prisoner of an intellectual turn of mind. The vaulted stone roof (destroyed) sprang from corbels about three feet below the level of the present ceiling. On the next floor below the windows three different lots of iron bars one outside the other. Two rooms had erections like scaffolds in them, with notched poles by which to ascend. They were evidently sleeping bunks. On the next floor, still descending, there was a room with a drain made from an aumbry and a magnificent hooded fire-place; perhaps the best I have ever seen.

This floor had 4 rooms as also had the next, the ground floor. One room had a cupboard; and a latrine opening into another room was joined to the sea by a drain. The tower was entered by a drawbridge and defended by a portcullis. The whole is about 70 feet high, and bears the arms of Brittany on the face. On Saturday S. and I rode to the Mont, it is distinctly fine in parts: I will not say what struck me the first time, but will reserve description till third or fourth visit. All the nave is being restored, and the roof is therefore off; a fact which rather disfigures the rest of the church. The piscinas are horrid; tall, thin, about 16 inches wide, and eleven feet high. They are very ugly and ill proportioned. We both decided to leave the omelettes and do a little serious work while there. Scroggs came back from Pontorson by train, but I rode, and thereby saved 3 francs 50 cent. Another 50 cent. and I will have paid for my Ruskins. I like his style and subject intensely; his is most interesting. I am exceedingly glad I bought them for I now have some conception of the right way in which to study architecture, and how to draw the truest lessons from it. Father will be entranced with it.

Have you any objection to my cycling to the Mont and back some moonlit night? I hear the views over the sands are sublime. The insides of the buildings on the Mont are lovely; the outside is decidedly badly proportioned, with its dumpy spire, and flat masses of unrelieved masonry. I was horrified with the exterior.

Will write again soon: accept the usual salutations and wishes as said. Love to all. Success to Will. Visit Haddon Hall if possible.   N.

DINARD
Tuesday, August 21, 1906

DEAR BOB
This letter is to be dedicated to you, for no reason whatsoever, except that you will know the places described. This morning I saw

Frère Fabel, from him I went to the Black Prince's Château, opposite
Mrs. Clark's, but will defer description until I have thoroughly
explored the interior. The exterior is delightful, with its two round
machicolated towers, capped with conical roofs. I did not go inside,
but Toby says that very polite people are sometimes admitted; he said
the same of the Montfort Priory, opposite the Villa Nahant, on the
beach. I visited this next, and spent a long time in the chapel. It is
private property and belongs to two old people, who let me in to
examine. The chapel is Perpendicular, built in rather English style: the
wooden lintels to the doors gave it almost an air of Godstow chapel.

The Priory, founded in 1324, was a location of the monks of the
Trinity, a body who collected money for the ransom of Christians
from the Infidels. The two Sires de Montfort Oliver and Geoffroy,
had gone on the last crusade, and when returning from Acre were
captured by the Algerians and enslaved. Their ransom was paid by the
Trinity brethren, and this priory is the result. The secular buildings
are now inhabited, and turned into stables, and the chapel is the only
ruined part. It is small and of an oblong shape. The East End is of
course the most interesting. In the place of the High Altar there is a
medley of stones, in the form of rude steps, and on the summit is placed
a most interesting statue of the Virgin and Child. The statue is about
3 feet 6 inches high, and portrays the Virgin seated on a stool or stone
seat. In her lap she is holding the Child, who is in the act of giving the
Benediction. Both figures wear crowns, and are both in the most
excellent preservation. The Virgin holds an orb in the right hand, and
holds the Child with her left. She is wearing the same form of head-
dress, the veiled, as Lady Cressy, the lady whom Mother dislikes on the
screens. The statue is hollowed out at the back, and had I should think
been in a niche. On the North and South sides of the chancel repose
two beautiful effigies in granite, under the most graceful Perp. tracery,
on the outside of their tomb recesses. These figures, the two Lords
Montfort, date from about the beginning of the fourteenth century, or
a little earlier. I will describe that on the North, since that on the S.
has lost its feet, and owing to the location of a wasp's nest beneath it
I was not able to examine it with the care which it required. It seemed
the same in all but the folds of the surcoat, and the form of the cushion
beneath the head. The effigy on the North is life-size, and rests beneath
an elegant canopy, which has been plastered inside, and painted a dull

reddish-brown, inclining to crimson. The figure wore complete chain mail, and a surcoat; although he and his brother visited the East their legs are not crossed. His gauntlets are slipped from his hands, as his coif is thrown off his head. This fashion seems universal in France, and points to undoubted French influence in Septvans. His hair is curled over his ears, and confined over the forehead by a fillet. His cushion and feet are supported by angels, two on each side. A baldric sustains his shield, which bears rather peculiar arms on which I will consult Scroggs. His sword is supported by another belt, and his feet by a lion and angels. He wears pryck spurs, but his knees have no plates over them (a sign of early work). On each side of the slab on which he lies, about half-way down near his waist there is placed a hand, clenched. If they are not gauntlets, which they can hardly be, they are most mysterious emblems. I will correspond with Scroggs on the point. Midway up the chapel there are two piscinas of most eccentric forms. They are about twelve inches square, and the basin of one of them is about two inches wide, four inches long, and three deep. In fact it represents a little box sunk in the stone. The other piscina has a basin of six inches wide and half an inch deep, terminating at the back in a drain. The pan of this latter is circular, of the former a rectangle. Each had been plastered and painted a dull red. The remainder of the buildings were unimportant, but enclosed a stone dated 1196; this stone is supposed to have come from an earlier priory which stood on the spot. The place was most interesting.

I went to Fougères today. The ride was very pretty, and was the longest I have had yet (total about 114 miles or more): I was very pleased with my bicycle: no punctures. Rode the high gear back but could not do so going because of head wind. It of course died away quite calm at 5 o'clock. I saw a winnowing fan—they are very handsome articles; the one I saw might have been the model for those of Septvans, and would do beautifully for a waste paper basket for my room. Your (or rather Will's) letter just come. Will must be more exact. If the ramparts have clear principal and Decuman gates the camp is Roman: if they are circular then it is Celtic. Don't dig if Roman. I will consult Woolley on return. If we go in Easter we will work together. Gather all details you can about shape of mound, ditches, etc. and step the distances. Also note direction of Road (impossible to tell if Roman or not, since Romans used Celtic pathways). Write everything down *on the spot*, and I will refer to Woolley. Bring some pieces of tile; they are *most important*. Better not work until he has been consulted. Fougères in exterior is sublime, the inside is not. Off to Mont St. Michel tomorrow with the C's {Chaignons}. I will ride.

Scroggs wrote hastily, and told me I got a first with distinction in Scripture & English; but said nothing more. I hope you got that enormous letter that he sent off. The C's are much amused at my vagaries in matter of riding. They cannot imagine how I go so far. I will write letter on Friday but will not promise anything tomorrow. Don't know what time I will return. I have to revisit St. Brieuc and Château de Hunaudaye, and then I have finished for the present.

Saw a pretty piece of Breton pottery at Dol which I will buy tomorrow if we agree in price. Good-night for present, will post this tomorrow. Love to all: Not at all tired 400 miles to date.

DINARD

Friday, 24 August, 1906

DEAR MOTHER

I am so delighted to hear you are so much better, go on and improve: I think we must take a cottage on Boar's hill for you: mountain (!) air seems to set you up at once. So glad Florence has kept you quiet: don't walk too much: cycling is a much better exercise. I wonder if Father has his bicycle yet. Everyone over here wants you to come back. Mr. Fécélier was speaking so nicely of you yesterday: you were "capable" "aimable" etc. If possible you must come to Carnac next year with me: it is quite cheap: rail to Vannes, and ride only about 30 miles in the week we are there. I am planning a trip. Toby and I went to Langrolay a great beauty spot on the Rance, half-way to Dinan: the chestnut woods were exquisite. Toby is very fond of the place.

My ride to Fougères was very pleasant: part of it lay through woods where it was deliciously cool; (it was the hottest day of the year, I never felt such heat before). There is great difficulty in getting a decent drink in France: milk is not obtainable anywhere, and eau de seltz only occasionally. The result is that one gets very thirsty, and the only fruits are plums and pears, their apples are uneatable: I have not had a good one yet. I upset myself with too many plums on Wednesday. Effects visible today. I intend to visit Mr. Lewis this afternoon: Toby says he never enters Dinard at all: he is quite a recluse.

Fougères castle is splendid, outside. I have attempted a plan, which is not very correct. There are some thirteen or fourteen towers round the outer walls and three of them are circular and enormous. They are

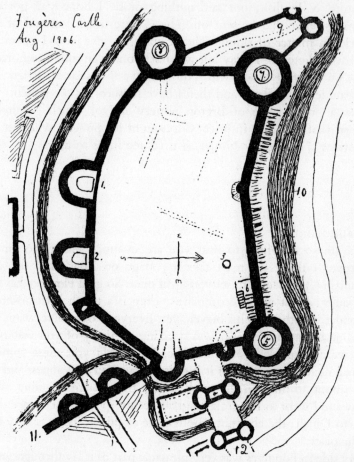

quite perfect in every detail, since they have been lately restored: one is now undergoing the process, which seems to be very carefully done. The walls are exceedingly thick, and the gateway with six towers and three drawbridges must have been impregnable (the walls date from 1173, but the mouldings are all Renaissance). On the plan 1 and 2 are two huge semicircular towers called Raoul and Vrienne, each of whom has a turret on his or her top, 3 is the well, and apparently the only one: 4 is a gateway (St. Sulpice) with museum (of stuffed birds) 5 is the chapel tower; the entrance is on the top storey and has a Doric portico, 6 is the stairway up to the ramparts, which are all machicolated, 7 and 8 are two large west towers with turrets on the top (75 steps to top of 7 from the ramparts, three good halls with late fire-places, dungeons etc.), 9 is a ravelin with gate at end; this part later than the rest; 10 is a branch of the Nançon acting as moat, which later on divides (or divided) into two, one part of which flowed along before the city wall (11). Twelve is the present entrance. I have some excellent post cards, of the place, which describe it much better than I could. Inside the castle is all destroyed; it is nothing but a shell, though a glorious one. No finer exterior exists I am certain. There are fields, orchards etc. inside. I ate a glorious feast of blackberries: they were enormous, as large as mulberries and in great profusion since the Bretons will not eat them. They say that the crown of thorns was made from bramble. One is supposed to have a guide to go round the castle, but by coming at the dinner hour I escaped that appendage. I shall certainly return there next year for another examination, and I shall bring a camera with me: Father's one if possible: it is a paradise for a photographer. I got a long letter from Will last night and a p.c. from Father. Thank them very much: I am glad you got the budget from Tonquédec. I suppose I should write now to Polstead Road: you will be returning soon, as I hope I will: I have finished except for two rides. I look at all the shops of china and curios, but all the pretty things are so dear that I want to settle all things before I buy: it would be unpleasant to have to change that sovereign at the last moment. Bathing here is most unpleasant from the crowd, and in the little bays I have damaged myself on rocks. I had been reading there on a cliff seat I constructed for about 5 hours on Sunday afternoon, when I woke up to the knowledge that the tide had cut me off; of course I had chosen a place where the cliff was climbable (?), but it took rather long with all my books in my hand. I will call on Mrs. Bell & the Monteiths today or tomorrow: they were out last time. I have to write to Scroggs and to two of my boys {of Sunday School}, so I will leave this open till the evening: the evening has come, and I have not visited anybody; I took a bathe instead. To fill up this rather mixed letter I will give you a sketch of one of my days here. I wake up at 7. and get up at 7.30.

At eight I take "petit dejuner", and after inspecting my bicycle I read and write till a few minutes to twelve. At twelve I go out to the garden, till dejuner, generally about half past. In the afternoon I go with the Chaignons to the "plage", ride, or do other trifles. If I bathe which I do when possible, it is about six or seven, when the crowd have gone. If I am going for a ride I rise at 6.30, and breakfast at seven. If I intend to start from St. Malo I take the bac at 7.30; for St. Servan I leave by the bac at 8. Returning from the ride I cross about 7.15, or 7 o'clock, by the last steamer. I alarmed all the family most terribly by going to the Mont {St. Michel} without a hat: it was a cool cloudy day with a high wind, but they were excessively alarmed for my safety.

Mrs. Kerry said this week that a great many people were returning by the *Vera* on the 31st. If so I will not come that day. As I have a tourist ticket I can break my journey at Winchester, and I would rather like to do so, since I have not seen the Alfred statue, or Westgate. If all is agreeable I would choose to arrive in Oxford about four o'clock, giving me about four hours in Winchester.

Saturday Morning. Cold today, strong S.W. wind threatening rain: will stay at home today and visit. I hope those two walkers {Bob & Will in North Wales} will have fine weather for their tour. If they do not, matters will be rather miserable. Am going now to put *two* more repair bands on my front tyre; wish I had not allowed myself to be talked over by Jim {a cycle repairer} about it. He said most confidently it would go 800 miles, and here it is gone at five hundred, and decent tyres are unknown here.

Evening. Have seen Mr. Lewis again; he was most kind and hearty: not finished his picture yet; wants me to return in ten days. In the meantime I am to tell Father that he is now 62, and that five years ago he gained the 12 hours' amateur record, unpaced, of West of France; his distance 301 odd kilos. has not been beaten yet. He intends to race in a 200 kils. race at the end of next month. I have verified his statements, and found all correct. He is certainly wonderful; I should be pleased if Father sent him a message; he is exceedingly proud of himself. I like him very much, he is very good-natured: when he heard of my Fougères ride he declared I was very strong and that I had inherited Father's talent. The thermometer was 42 (Cent.), and it was the hottest day in the year, being a record for the last 16 years. I am beginning to be proud of myself. Mrs. Bell I saw for a couple of moments; she sends messages to you all, as do Mr. Lewis & Mme Chaignon. Mrs. Bell said that Madame Fécélier was in the highest spirits the evening of the day she died; she played with the children, and afterwards sang Dédé to sleep. About eleven o'clock at night she called Mr. Fécélier to come, and said she was suffocating; 20 seconds later she was dead. It was her heart which was wrong, as I thought. I may add another page to this letter before it starts. I have a lot to say to you all.

I am very surprised at the speed with which your letter re the Local Results {Oxford Senior Locals} came. You posted it at 9.10 a.m. at The Rossett; and it arrived at 9.30 tonight (Saturday). The result is on the whole not as good as I had hoped, although I am quite satisfied with the Eng. {First place in English}. I wonder whether there is any profession in which a knowledge of one's own tongue is of the slightest use. There is no hurry over the responsions; the examination is easy, and there is a Local exam. next year. In the Divinity I had hoped for more. Polit. Econ. is not surprising; I expect we both made asses of ourselves. It seems impossible to obtain black bread for Hall here, I must try Rotheneuf. It's ten o'clock: Good night for the present. I have only two more envelopes left, so will not write many more letters: may borrow one or two from the Chaignon's, so don't be alarmed at the mourning. By the way in the English my essay on Physical Culture in 2000 A.D. evidently went down: I wonder who got it.

My front tyre has three repair bands over it; with canvas inside to match. The tread of the tyre split down the middle: I am not sure if it will last me to Hunaudaye. This will I expect have to be your birthday letter (there's enough of it). I hope you will have a very happy day. I have not bought any china yet: everything of any use is exceedingly dear, and I don't want to buy an ornament. Your cider jugs with the handles on the top are not very elegant: I will buy a couple, but cannot promise to waste any money on other things. There are any amount of imitation antiquities over here, and some few real ones, but I will not requisition my packing case till next time. I will meanwhile read up my subject. You have not said how many costume cards you require: I have 19 now. It seems that the terrible erections come from Normandy, and views of them are not obtainable here. The Breton ones are usually in good taste, but the Norman ones are certainly ugly. I would not recommend them even if it was possible to obtain them. My latter ten post cards or so are much better than the earlier ones.

I am becoming discretionary. Must stop now for the present. Will start again later. Have started again. I cannot make out when you return to Oxford. You are at The Rossett for 17 days, and you went about the tenth. On the whole I'll send this letter to Oxford and chance it.   Yours

NED

DINARD
Sunday, 26th August, 1906

DEAR MOTHER

As I was sending off your letter it began to rain here, so perhaps I will not manage Hunaudaye after all. I would not like to return before Saturday, since there is a great "pardon" at Dinan that day, which I would like to see. Either Monday or Tuesday would please me best. Will write in a couple of days and let you know. This afternoon was lovely,

"The day was fair and sunny, sea and sky
"Drank its inspiring radiance, and the wind
"Swept strongly from the shore, blackening the waves."

I went to my seat on the cliff and read; beneath this projecting rock the sea

"On bare black pointed islets ever beats
"With heaving surge."

As I have started giving quotations you will have to endure more, or burn the letter. Really the spot is singularly beautiful. It is just beyond the Château, and lies at the head of a little bay. On either side rocks project nearly to the low tide level, and in front lies an islet, very fantastic and jagged in outline, with its lower slopes covered with seaweed, which when washed by the water, heaves "like a maiden's hair". I reached there before two today and stayed till seven. I think an August afternoon is the best time of the year

"I love the close
"Of Autumn's sunny day
"When gently from each leaf and flower
"The daylight fades away."

Fougères (See p. 28)

Fougères (*See p.* 28)

Also is it not your opinion that

> "The day becomes more solemn and serene
> "When noon is past"?

The morning always seems to me to give the impression of modernity of incompleteness;

> "There is a harmony
> "Which through the morning is not heard or seen
> "As if it could not be, as if it had not been."

While walking about there before continuing my reading I fell into a little lake, between two rocks, and I wet all my legs. It was

> "A still salt pool, locked in with bars of sand
> "Left on the shore."

From my reading desk

> "I see the waves upon the shore
> "Like Light dissolved in star-showers thrown."

And I hear the waves,

> "Climb and fall
> "And roar rock-thwarted under bellowing caves
> "Beneath the iron-bound wall."

Before I had left the place the sun had set and the simile

> "Like pageantry of mist on an autumnal stream,"

was exactly fulfilled. The mist rose heavy and thick

> "A death-white mist slept over sand and sea
> "And rolling far along the gloomy shores,
> "The voice of days of old and days to be."

But before the sun actually departed

> "The wind had swept from the wide atmosphere
> "Each vapour that obscured the sunset's ray
> "And pallid evening twined its beaming hair
> "In duskier braids around the languid eyes of day."

Here is another for you, also appropriate.

> "With shifting ladders of shadows and light
> "And blurred in colour and form
> "The sun hung over the gates of night
> "And glared at a coming storm."

Then later

> "Twilight ascending slowly from the east
> "Enwrapped in darker folds her magic veil
> "O'er the fair front and shining light of day."

Later on however there grew

> "The shallow rifted glooms
> "Of evening and the moanings of the wind."

As I left

> "After the sunset down the coast he heard
> "Strange music, and he paused, and turning there
> "All down the lovely coast of Lyonesse
> "Each with a beacon star upon his head
> "And with a wild sea light about his feet
> "He saw them, headland after headland flame
> "Far on into the rich heart of the west."

Really about five lighthouses can be seen over

> "The rising world of waters vast and deep."

As I was returning I lingered about admiring

> "Till the moon
> "Rising in clouded majesty at length
> Apparent queen unveiled her peerless light
> And o'er the dark her silver mantle threw."

You really must excuse this battery of quotations, but I have got into the habit of quoting any appropriate lines to myself, and this time I thought I would put them on record. The scene really was perfectly lovely; each of these lines might have been written to suit it; as well as many other phrases I remember, but I will be merciful and let you off with

> "The beams of sunset hung their rainbow hues
> High 'mid the shifting domes of sheeted spray."

The sea was of the wondrous blue met with sometimes here, and all was perfect; *there was no one else there*. This last makes such an addition to one's enjoyment of nature and her prodigal loveliness; all this scene was reserved for me alone: it is a wonderful surpassing thought on which to reflect. I can only wish my mind was more receptive and my emotions more deeply affected. Nature contains that spirit and power which we can witness but not weigh, inwardly conceive but not comprehend, love but not limit, imagine, but neither define nor describe. Nature is incomprehensible, fleeting, and yet immortal, and a love for it and its impressions are both ineradicable. *Next morning*. My Ruskin is better than ever. I will have him bound in Oxford, or will bind him myself. It gives a most masterly exposition of the meaning and method of Gothic, and he simply smashes the Renaissance styles. No wonder they are going out of fashion after this book. Father will devour it with avidity, and start for Venice next week. I wish I could go with him. By the way how did the last two elections at Cockermouth and Exeter go? Did the Unionist or the Liberal get in? I have found another envelope, so I will write two more letters after these; one perhaps on Wednesday and one on Friday. After Friday expect no more till you see me. I hope you are still feeling well in Oxford, it is a glorious place, but its climate does not agree with you. By the way I believe I am as strong as M. Chaignon; I will try him some day. People here say that I am much thinner than Bob, but stronger, and have a better accent. Still Bob's fatness is much better than my muscle in their eyes, except for Mme Chaignon who got a shock when she saw my "biceps" while bathing. She thinks I am Hercules. Good-bye for the present; love to Arnie and others.

NED

DINARD
August 28, 1906

DEAR MOTHER

As is visible from the plan annexed, I have been to Hunaudaye and treated it fully. It only took two hours to reach there, wind strong behind. The visit has left me in a painful state of doubt as to whether Tonquédec is eclipsed or not. The Château of la Hunaudaye is on a slight eminence in a valley, and was once enclosed by a moat, which is now only partially filled. The enceinte is in the form of a pentagon,

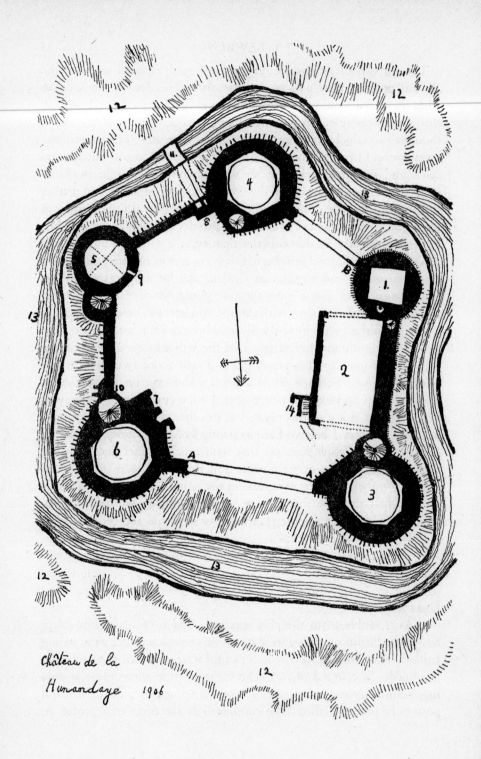

Château de la
Hunaudaye 1906

and is fairly regular. Two large towers form the base, and one the apex. The lesser angles are defended by smaller towers. I will begin with the West one, merely saying beforehand that the masonry is regular and good, but has been damaged round the windows, and in two places A—A. B - - - B, the wall has been totally destroyed. The small tower, No. 1 in plan is some 50 feet high, and while circular outside is rectangular within. It contains five stories; fire-places exist on three of them. The tower is entered on the 1st story by a staircase leading up from the outside in the thickness of the wall. This staircase is connected with a newel in the outer wall of the castle, and this newel in turn at the top has a passage conducting to one of the smallest newels I have seen, which leads to the battlements. These staircases were entered by crawling through a nearly buried doorway, and then, in pitch darkness, stumbling over blocks of stone to find a way out. On the dust of the steps no footmarks except my own were visible, and from the state of the battlements I can believe that not many others ascend. The last stairway has steps only about five inches in height each, and is very fatiguing. The machicoulis are perfect, and it is interesting to note that one of them was turned sideways to avoid a projection into the newel staircase within. A part of the parapet is left and is ornamented with a trefoil niche. The walk round the top is inconveniently narrow owing to the turret with which the tower is finished. The top storey of the tower contains two windows and a fire-place with circular arch. The windows contain seats of the usual kind. The chimney, of the other floors, is fronted (i.e. on the inside face) with small thin red tiles, which abound everywhere. They were in nearly all the grates and fire-places. The next storey (2) is entered from the newel by a large door, and contains two large windows with seats, which were once plastered pink, and a great fire-place with very debased arch. The whole of the interior of the château had once been plastered and painted pink. A square-seated latrine opens on the right from the entrance. On the 1st floor there was also a latrine, not worthy of special mention. The floors of this tower had been of wood and had long since perished. The arrangement of staircases is I think peculiar. I have placed two on my plan. The hall numbered 2 on the plan has lost both ends, and is a late annex to the rest of the castle. It is about 60 feet long, and was divided into two stories, entered by a light and graceful staircase of four flights of shallow steps. At the top of the staircase was a pilaster with pseudo-Ionic volutes, and there were arabesques, and mouldings showing Chinese and Egyptian influences. The date would be about 1750 or thereabouts, and the general effect was pleasing. The hall to which it gave access was lit by two windows on each side. Beneath this stairway is the commencement of a passage, communicating I should think with tower 3 which was octagonal within and had walls of about 15 feet thick. It contained six stories whose floors have all been destroyed. It is ascended by a very wide newel of shallow steps, with moulded base. There are numerous fireplaces, latrines and enormous windows: a passage ran from this tower to No. 6 in the middle of the wall now destroyed. This tower (3) is the fellow of (6) and each is crowned by a modern chimney, which detracts greatly from the general effect. The great batter with which the towers are built also takes away from their grandeur. No. 4 tower had been joined to (1) by a wall through which a breach has been made. I have not succeeded in getting any good or any at all, history of the place. All I know is that it was built in 1378. This tower (4) is hexagonal in the interior, and has its pink plaster perfect in two alcoves. It was one of the most important towers but its newel only has the few top steps left, and so I was unable to go over the whole. I managed two of the six stories. The tower is about 80 feet high, and perfect to the machicoulis. The ground floor has two windows, doorway, latrine etc., and the others seem much the same. There were on the whole 28 openings in the central part of the tower, a number which will give an idea of its size and form. The great gateway is next to this tower and is marked in my rather haphazard style as 8. It is about 6 feet wide and was entered by a drawbridge of great length, the cup-stones for which remain. By the side of the large gate is a little postern about 2 feet wide, also with drawbridge: this saved moving the enormous pont-levis that the large door must have had, since the little one was large enough for ordinary purposes. Both archways were pierced with holes, to drop missiles, but neither had a portcullis, which is I think an unusual omission. Tower 5 perhaps the oldest part, is the most interesting. It was of four stories and the two upper ones are vaulted, although the top vault is broken in the middle. The lower is entire, very flat, and quite plain. I have marked its ribs on the plan. The door is decorated and the walls, of from 8–10 feet thick are pierced by four openings, three inches wide on the outside, but two feet wide on the inner. The masonry is of early character; and the lowest five feet I would consider Norman. I imagine the place must have been the chapel, for on the jambs of the door and the edges of the windows there were most peculiar carvings, all I imagine of sacred subjects. On the entrance doorway, inside face, (marked 9) there was a series of these works, executed with a certain naïve skill and a good deal of power and realism. The lowest one was a saint, holding an ear of barley, standing beside a church (?) tower with spire. Above this came a figure standing and another in an attitude of adoration. The third above was a male with crozier (or two handed sword?) digging it into the ribs of a prostrate figure on whose stomach he was standing. The vanquished tried to fend off the crozier with one hand. The victor seems to be pouring water on the beaten one from a pitcher. Is it a case of forced conversion? Next to this sculpture is the figure of a woman standing on a pedestal holding a child, to whom a well dressed man with a beard, offers an image. It cannot be the adoration of the Magi, or at least such is my opinion. The man making the offering seems to be wearing a jupon. The next scene is the crucifixion with a figure standing each side. The cross is a double one ╤. The skull and bones are prominent in the foreground. This bas-relief occupies the apex of the arch. Descending the other side is a saint, then St. Peter with a six-foot key, two more draped figures and a bust wearing a high-horned cap, then a half figure displaying a large cloth on the centre of which is a human head with long forked beard. Other figures, unrecognizable to me completed the list. On the side of the door were heads with ruffs etc. & one in chain mail. On one of the windows was a spirited crucifixion, and another couple of figures, one with long sword the other incomprehensible. The other arches had been walled up about 1500, but figures had been carved on them also as I ascertained by thrusting my hand between two blocks. It was very difficult to make notes on them, because of the darkness which was intense and because I was clinging with teeth and eyelids on a ledge about four inches wide, half way up the tower. The sculptures had been done with care, and at a very early time, certainly not later than 1420. I think I must be practically the discoverer of the little carvings, since they are not in a place to which the ordinary antiquary would attain. If the room was not the chapel (there was no sign of piscina or altar, and the room was circular) then it might have been the guard house, and the carvings might have been done for amusement. They are all by the same hand. This letter will perhaps be finished tomorrow. It is eleven o'clock now and I ought to have thoughts on Hypnos. *Next morning.* The upper story of this tower contained an excellent fire-place, the finest in the castle, with capitals to the engaged columns of stiff necked foliage. The general design was Perpendicular, and was effective. A latrine lay to the right of the entrance passage, there were three windows and at the side of the fire-place was an undoubted cupboard. The tower was ascended by a side tower with newel staircase, just as the others. It was impossible to reach the third story, since the staircase was destroyed and also the walls of the tower, about two feet above the broken vault. I have a fair view of the exterior of this tower in one of the only two post cards I could obtain. All the photographers live in St. Brieuc, and that is why I wish to visit the place. There are shops full of nothing but post cards. Tower 6 on plan, the sister tower to No. 3, was octagonal within. The ground storey was entered from the outside near the letter A in the plan. The actual entrance to the first storey was from 7 and comprised a vaulted archway with passage. The walls of this tower were very thick, but I foolishly took no measurements. The first floor had two windows with seats, and a peculiar stone, perforated, occupied the lower part of the opening. It is too small for a cannon, and I cannot imagine its purpose. There were others like it in the building. The fire-place of this floor was rather well designed, though very plain. A latrine opened from one side of the room, and was fitted with a seat the facsimile of that at Tonquédec of which you have the sketch. On the third storey of this tower, besides the usual windows, there was a latrine which I could not reach, and a fire-place of ornamental design, which had been built up with solid stones, and only a little hole, shaped like a piscina, left. The hole, towards one side, was about twelve inches high, and came to a sharp point, in an arch. I was unable to reach it to make fuller examination, although I tried to do so, but the ledges for the floor beams are not exactly ideal for a promenade, and the wall had no chinks to afford hand-hold. The fourth storey had a delightful fire-place still perfect. In general effect this fire-place matched that in tower 5, but in detail it was inferior. The fifth and sixth floors contained nothing worthy of notice. The newel at the side of this tower, by which it was ascended, was of magnificent workmanship, with each step about five feet long, one foot deep at the outside, and six inches high. I was able to run up it with the greatest ease. The base of the shaft was of course moulded, and the steps underneath were hewn to a regular curve. On the wall by the side of the tower at the spot marked 10, there had been latrines and other constructions: two or three stones with nicely carved niches remain. This tower seems from its work and design to have been intended for the habitation of the lord and lady of the place. It contains many little refinements which the other towers lack. I have now been all round the castle, and have got back to where the wall is destroyed. It had been about ten feet in thickness. The moat round the castle marked 13 in the plan, still contains water at one part. It is now very much filled up with rubbish, and is a little muddy. A deep drain has been cut to empty it of water. This drain flows from nearly opposite the drawbridge, and leads the water to another pond beyond. The aspect of the castle seen from the banks beyond the moat is very grand and picturesque although it is not the equal of Fougères in the first nor of Tonquédec in the second. Inside it is, I think, on the whole more interesting than either, and it would have been much more interesting if I had had a ladder to reach various portions which are inaccessible in the ordinary course of things. The room with the sculptures is most fascinating. Just imagine the delight of going round a four-inch ledge in semi-darkness, and trying to write notes on sculptures, only half seen. A friend with a candle would have been a useful adjunct. In future I shall have to add matches and tapers to my kit. The number of picturesque pieces and excellent views in the castle passes belief. If I had had a camera I would have expended three dozen plates without taking the same part twice. One thing the castle lacks, one cannot get a general view of it. From the high towers the trees get in the light, and three of the towers are practically of the same height. The banks outside are not high enough to see over the walls which are almost all complete to their machicolations. I shall certainly return there next year with a camera or two. By the way the corbels comprising the machicoulis are unusual. Some of them are nearly six feet long. Of course one half of this is buried in the wall, but the rest projects. There were at times some five piled one on top of the other, to make one machicouli (?) and two were never put abreast. They were about 12 or 15 inches apart, and so the top of the tower simply bristled with them. I cannot say that I have put the right number in on the

plan. In tower 1 I have put far too many, but the others are fairly right.
One piece of my plan requires explanation, namely the round ring
inside each tower. It is intended to show the thickness of the wall in the
lowest part where it was circular. The hexagonal or octagonal forms
did not arise till the ground level had been reached. The others were
cellars. You will observe that I have not planned it to face the North.
I thought the place looked more symmetrical when it sat on its longest
side. On the whole my drawing is correct, and is not more than a few
feet out in any part. If it errs at all it is in making the place too wide,
but I do not think this is the case. The road to the castle is good, and
the whole ride is exceedingly easy and pleasant. I am very sorry that
Scroggs and I missed it on our tour, but it was inevitable, and on the
whole I think we saw enough. If you have no objections you might
pass this epistle across to Scroggs when you have read it. By this means
it will save an extra letter to congratulate him on his Locals success. He
really did marvellously well. What a pity he passed Responsions, it was
all waste labour, unless it enabled him to get on so excellently in the
Locals. . . . There is a great pardon at Dinan on the Saturday next, at
which Botrel will supervise the production of some of his works. I will
ride up and see it if I can. I am going to St. Malo this afternoon to get
post cards and engage a berth. I will take this letter across with me and
post it there when I hear, but I expect it will be Monday night. The
moon should be good then. My total mileage is about 600 miles now,
and I have had about six or seven punctures on my own machine. . . .
I expect Woolley will have started for his excavation-days now. He
ought to be successful. I wonder what those walkers {Bob and Will}
will think of their tour: it will at any rate prepare them for a cycling
tour soon. The Chaignons declare I will kill myself if I don't eat more
meat; they say all vegetarians fill an early grave, although I'm not a
veg. out here, no Frenchman has any opportunity to be. I find I have
left out a page on one of my other sheets, so I will go back and fill it up.
After the first two pages of sheet three, kindly go on to sheet four. By
the way the machicoulis, vaults, and newel staircases in the plan were
put in for Scroggs' benefit. He grumbled at their being left out in the
Tonquédec plan, I have hopes he will be satisfied with this. I am not
going to be bothered putting in windows or other things like that.
As it is the present plan took an hour to make and another hour to
draw. If he wants anything more put in he has got to become typog-

rapher himself. I'm not. (By the way its a delightful sensation writing to two people at once, or rather two sets of people) I can gird at the second set as much as I please. Scroggs was such an ass on the tour: he flatly refused to believe he had speed-legs, and then one day he rode 8 miles in half an hour (from Guingamp to Château-Laudren). I argued the question with him every day, but he would not be convinced. I expect he believes in his powers now. If not I will take him for a spin or two and we'll do 18 in the hour. I don't care what he says then. The Chaignon family have contracted his supposed name from Scrog-Binty to Kronprinz, and then it remains. I have not enlightened them as to the full extent of his sonorous title. By the way you know those annoying post cards which don't cover the whole sheet? Well I have discovered how to deal with them. I pencil over the lower part, either to a plain grey or else in continuance of the subject; the effect is really excellent, if the p.c. is unglazed. If it is glazed you have to rub it with a paper spill to make it shine. I intend to patent my device. Have not heard from you for some days which shows that all is right. By the way this letter will be too stout for the 2½d. I expect. I will find out. When at Oxford, go down and look at St. Peter's to see if they have finished there or not. Bring back any corbels you can, if any are obtainable. As this letter is intended for a second person there will be no private or family messages in it, although there have not been anything of the sort in any letters of mine up to the present. Enjoy yourselves and don't work too hard. Will I finish 1,000 miles out here? At present it is nearly 650. I want to run out to Granville this week, but must hurry up. No time to spare. Will return on   Boat arrives at Southampton about 8 in the morning, be in Oxford about 4 or 5. don't quite know when, since have no timetable. Expect me   evening.

NED

DINARD
Friday, 31st August, 1906

DEAR FATHER

Your letter came last night, thank you very much for it, I am sorry you have had more trouble with your teeth, I hope it will be all over soon. What a pity Mother has got ill again, from your letters I had supposed she was quite well. Yesterday I took a long ride to Lanvollon, and purchased those medallions of glass. I rather like them;

and hope they are good. The price was rather high, but it must come from my birthday money. I have enough to come home on, so you need not send any to me. I have spent rather a lot this year I fear, but I have certainly seen a lot. I rode back from Lanvollon with those medallions on my back. They weigh about 5 lbs.; and are 18 inches or more in diameter. If they are 14th Cent. they will be worth their money, but I will not say what I gave for them till I know what they are. They will look excellent in the drawing room windows. I found them being kicked about in the tower gallery, and have certainly rescued them from destruction. My bicycle went splendidly yesterday, except for the front tyre bursting; (A little trick of its which happens too often to be amusing): I mended all up including repair band, in half an hour. The tyre begins to have a distinctly bulbous look. It is practically impossible to get a beaded edge tyre out here, except for an enormous price, all the French tyres are wired on. I am not in the least tired today from my ride, I must be getting into wonderful condition, for I rode the last 15 miles in under the hour, (it was getting rather late) and finished perfectly cool and fresh. I shall have to try for the Bath Road Hundred next year. This will be my last letter. I am sorry my letter was so much overweight. I expect the next one will be also; still you will appreciate them more if you have to pay for them, I often think that it is demoralizing to have too much given us free: I am sure a 24 page letter is cheap at 5d., only works out to a fifth of a penny per page, and you get the plan thrown in. In ecclesiastical architecture this province is hopeless. Every church is entirely modern; if it is not Flamboyant or Renaissance. Very rarely one comes across a tiny scrap of Norman, but it will be all perfectly plain. Enriched Norman seems unknown. Tréguier Cathedral was a fine building nearly as fine as Merton Chapel, but it is the best church in the Côtes du Nord. You will find absolutely nothing interesting here in your line. Of course an effigy will repay me for a modern church, but you are not an admirer of them. I have sent you an account of everything which I thought worth writing about, and I have seen nearly all the best things in the province, speaking of Gothic work. There are interesting Roman and Prehistoric articles which I know nothing of. Across in Normandy matters slowly improve, and the best Churches are the furthest East. The devastating wars of the Vendée etc. destroyed everything here. The League struggle also raged very fiercely around Dinan and Guingamp. A motor bicycle would be very useful for getting away to the antiquities round about. The Côtes du Nord province is one of the most uninteresting in France. Next year I would like to stay in Dinard a fortnight and then tour for a month, from a centre like Moncontour where I could live for 100 francs for four weeks most royally according to Mr. Kempshead. The Chaignons all admire my glass immensely. M. Chaignon offered me 20 francs for the two, but I mean to hang them in the drawing room. They represent I believe two angels since both figures have wings. The colouring is very vivid and harmonious. You will not like your first view of them, but they will grow on you. I regret to say that I won't be able to buy any more presents for anybody, except Arnie's balls. I'll send him one post card but it is rather a useless thing to do. I have a post card to spare. Tell Mother I am going to pack my windows in my shirts but I will take care to wrap them in clean paper first. They are very dirty. I'm going to wash them. My leg muscles are like steel now. I expect I'll delight Mother when I return. I'm as brown as a berry. Have been unable to bathe every day. On my rides I always start sharp at seven, and return at 8 also don't like bathing on St. Enogat plage too great a crowd about. I bathe in a little bay, but it is only good when tide is nearly full. I can swim in the Assyrian style now. I think it is good, although very confusing at first. Will not send this letter overweight, at least not if I can help it. Ta Ta. Could not find a pretty cider jug anywhere, all with top handle ugly. Have purchased a most artistic Breton Vase: really very pretty hope you will like it. Give poor Arnie my best wishes. I'll tickle him on Tuesday. I have a post card or two for him, but they are not good, I could not get animal ones anywhere. I have met such a lot of bears on the road here, the gipsies have dozens, I nearly ran into one. Also I have seen dozens of balloons. They send them up often round here. In Dinard there is a dog (a brown Pomeranian) who sits on his mistress' lap in her motor, and wears goggles. He looks very funny. Accept my best worms Arnie and have all ready to hug me on Tuesday. I've quite a benevolent look now, my beard is so long. Love to everybody, & best wishes for Mother's recovery.   NED

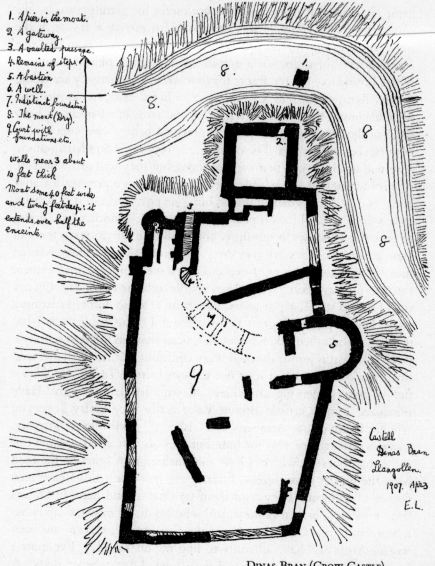

1. A pier in the moat.
2. A gateway.
3. A vaulted passage.
4. Remains of steps.
5. A bastion.
6. A well.
7. Indistinct foundations.
8. The moat (Dry).
9. Court with foundations etc.

Walls near 3 about 10 feet thick

Moat some 40 feet wide and twenty feet deep: it extends over half the enceinte.

Castell Dinas Bran Llangollen. 1907. April 3 E.L.

DINAS BRAN (CROW CASTLE)
LLANGOLLEN
1907. *April 3*

Ruin of fortress on conical hill, 910 feet above the Dee, about one mile from Llangollen. Length of castle is about 290 feet, and breadth about 140 feet. The entire crown of the hill was occupied with buildings. On the North side a deep trench has been cut in the rock, since on that side the descent is not precipitous. On the West the rock falls away sheer to the depth of about 70 feet. On the South, the descent, though not so rapid, is still very difficult to surmount. The date when the castle was constructed is unknown, but it was the capital of the Principality of Powys in the 8th Century. In the 13th Century its lord, Griffith, sided with Henry III. There are the usual stories of a British origin, but a twelfth century date appears more probable. Apparently nothing is known of its destruction.

The remains are fragmentary, but the walls are of great thickness, and the mortar rivals the Roman in its hardness. There would appear to have been a square keep, and two outer courts, but little can be decided with certainty from surface indications. A vaulted passage still remains entire, and the arch is very flat. The remains of two latrines or chimneys, probably the former, are to be seen in the wall of the keep, where it joins the E. wall of the castle proper. These openings do not communicate with the interior of the keep, and are destroyed about four feet from the ground. All other arches in the building are rough, pointed arcs.

CARNARVON CASTLE

April 1907

A. *The entrance*

Has remains of a statue of Edward over the gateway, with Perp. canopy, direct shape. The gate towers are about 120 feet high, and the actual wooden gates about 14 feet. There were formerly 4 portcullises, and numerous holes in the ceiling for dropping missiles etc. There are remains of three guardrooms, and over them two fine bedrooms with handsome fire-places: over the archway is an oratory, and a room for hoisting the drawbridge and portcullis, above all being the governor's hall, lighted by three good Perp. windows, and half a dozen loopholes. This part of the castle is not now open to visitors. Turning to the right on entering; the site of the walls dividing the two courts is passed over. There has been a gateway, about 10 feet wide with two portcullises, and two guardrooms. The dividing walls were about 8 feet thick. The length of the inner, or royal court was some 70 yards, and it contained banqueting hall, kitchen and buttery, and three bedrooms and a hall, attached to the wall between the Well and Eagle Towers. Of these buildings the banquet hall was 100 feet long, forty-four feet

wide, and 40 feet high. The roof seems to have been of wood, and was
supported on a row of corbels, on a level with the lower of the two
galleries, which traverse the South wall of the hall. At the S.E. corner
of the hall, once beneath a raised dais, there is a postern gate leading to
the harbour; the whole hall filled the space between the Queen's and
Chamberlain's towers. The kitchen and buttery, between the Entrance
and Well towers, were vaulted, as at Conway in the banquet hall. The
kitchen possessed a trough or sink, connected with the well by pipes
in the wall. At present the sink is raised about 6 feet from the ground.
At the end of the building are two circular ovens. The buttery contains
nothing of interest but a staircase and passage in the wall to the guardroom at the entrance. The hall with bedrooms further down the court,
is now almost entirely destroyed. It contained a good fire-place, with
round chimney and a two light window with window seat. There is a
latrine further up the court. Tower B. The Well Tower, is, all except
the basement, closed to the public. In the basement (octagonal) it has a
postern, communicating with the moat, with single portcullis. It was
approached from the outside by a flight of steps. It was pierced with
no fewer than 22 openings. The well, in an anteroom, is now blocked
up. There were four stories in the tower and a turret containing a
newel. Next to this tower is now a plain wall, some 40 yards long,
and lower than the rest, being only some 26 feet high (inside). It
is pierced by six loopholes, a latrine, and a win-
dow. One of the loopholes in the battlements is
rather skilfully defended.

Then comes C, the Eagle Tower. Has two doorways into the
Royal court. The one on the right leads, to a postern opening on
the river, through two small rooms: it also communicates with the
interior of the tower, and with the door on the left. This latter leads to a
newel staircase, leading, by 37 steps to a small anteroom, from which
runs a narrow passage, in the thickness of the wall, to a small room on the

{The middle sheet of the letter is missing.}

The covered galleries through the walls are also most interesting.
In the royal part of the castle they are about 12 feet high: in other parts
about 7 feet high. They exist only on the river sides of the castle, and
they always have numerous loopholes towards both the outside and the
inside. The narrow passages round the tower are only lighted by slits

Mont St. Michel (Telephoto 15 miles away) *(See p. 57)*

Mont St. Michel. Cloisters (See p. 57)

about 9 inches wide, and not splayed at all. The loopholes are about
6 inches wide on the outside and splay inwards to about 7 feet wide.
The passages in the walls are about 4 feet wide: those in the towers
barely 2 feet wide. The extraordinary number of steps and staircases
in the towers is also a matter of wonder. Nearly all the rooms are on
different levels, and all are entered by two, three, or four steps, and
there frequently is the same number to descend, before the floor is
reached. The stairs are in great part unnecessary, and seem intended to
improve the muscles alone. The Eagle Tower alone must contain some
hundreds. The small turrets on the top of all the towers are a distinguishing feature of Carnarvon. All are octagonal, and contain newels,
ascending to the very top, and finishing abruptly, without any covering. The sculptured parapet figures are amusing, especially as restored;
a portrait of Lord Roberts with 18th Cent. dragoon helmet being
rather strikingly incongruous. The mouldings of the castle are all as
plain as possible. There is no ornamentation in any part, except for the
statue on the great gateway. Everything else is absolutely flat. Any
distinguishing marks that can be observed are Early Perpendicular,
pointing to the end of Edward III's reign. The shouldered arch is much
in evidence in all the passages and corridors. The moat, surrounding
the Castle from river bank to river bank, is disappointingly small. It
is only about 30 feet wide, and the same deep, although dwarfed of
course by the walls behind it. Of drawbridges, although we know
that they did exist, we have absolutely no trace.

Section of wall: military side.

Military side wall.

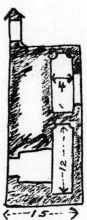
Royal side.

H.L.—4

Harlech was very interesting yesterday: the chimneys above the gatehouse were bound together in a cluster of four and tied together with a cable-moulding. Each was round, and projected some four feet above the wall. (This is not for you to read, it is only a note to refresh my memory.) We have had beautiful weather so far this trip, and the best thing seen yet has been Carnarvon Castle. If Bob has not arrived by 6 he may get a later train. Perhaps it would be as well if you did not lock the outer door. Hope you enjoyed yourself in London, and have seen all manner of portable, self adjusting, and self respecting horizontal & parallel bars.   NED

CHEPSTOW CASTLE

April 1907

Chepstow is built on the slope of a steep hill, running parallel to the Wye, to which it drops on one side almost perpendicularly, to a depth of 60 feet. This cliff forms one defence of the castle, and a deep ditch has been drawn around the other sides. This ditch must have always been dry. The highest part of the castle, that furthest from the present entrance, is the barbican, a strongly defended court, separated from the rest by a ditch, crossed by a drawbridge resting on a pier in the centre. The entire length of the bridge must have been about 24 feet. The gateway of the barbican has had three portcullises, and doors, which still remain. Above the gateway is a room in the tower, for the purpose of working the portcullis, and for defence. This room could be reached only from the battlement walk, which ran round the barbican on the landward sides. The defence towards the river was only a slight low wall. There was another tower in the barbican called the Watch Tower. This can now be entered only from the wall at the first storey, but it seems probable that a lower door has been blocked. There would appear to have been a postern looking S. but it is now walled up. It will thus be seen that two drawbridges were necessary before entrance could be had to the castle proper, through a plain gateway, without any portcullises. This opens on a court, called the 3rd Court, about 45 × 20 yrds. The curtain wall on the south is here about 9 feet thick, and has many loopholes. The gatehouse is all destroyed, as are all the buildings that once stood in the court. The windows alone remain in the outer walls. Many of these windows are round headed, and astonishingly like Norman work. It seems however more probable that they are Perpendicular. The East side of this is closed by the so-called Keep, which may embody portions of the original Norman structure. It is about 30 yrds. long, and there is, between it and the river, a narrow passage, floored with the natural rock. Except for an archway thrown across half way down, this passage has been open to the air. There are seven windows looking up the Wye, and four from the hall, with four smaller ones above, all Perp. The hall has been a magnificent room; the capitals and corbels are beautifully carved: there does not seem to have been a fireplace, except perhaps in the dividing wall which has perished. Ten feet from the ground there are four rows of flat bricks, either Roman or Mediæval. The entrance must have been by an outside staircase. There is a newel in the S.E. corner, and all the windows (a row of roundheaded ones) to the S. have been blocked. An archway, without defences leads to the middle or second court. On the S. are steps to the walk along the battlements. Half-way along this is a small semicircular tower, containing nothing of interest. It was ascended by a newel staircase. The court measures some 50 yards long, and 40 wide at one end, 20 at the other. There are no buildings in the court, except some nine massive buttresses, supporting the curtain wall. At the

{Second sheet missing.}

{Enclosed with letter from Monmouth}

CAERPHILLY
Sunday.   April 1907

DEAR MOTHER
    Here I am at my last Welsh Castle, and I think, in most respects, my best. Before going on with it however, I had better tell you what I have done since I wrote from Tenby. I left that place about 12 noon next day, rain and other things delaying me. I had a miserably wet uneventful ride to Kidwelly where I slept (Carmarthen Castle is not worth looking at). Kidwelly on the other hand is splendid. The state of it is good (just ruined enough to be interesting), and although quite plain, it is very large, and strong. I did not draw a plan, because it was wet and late, but on my next visit I will have much photography & planning to do. Specially remarkable features were the ovens, and the dungeons. The ovens were circular in shape, about 8 feet in diameter,

and with low vaults (some 3 feet high). In front of the door was a fire-place and chimney: this seemed the only apparatus for heating. There had been two such ovens in the castle: one is perfect the other much damaged. The dungeons were under the gate tower. Two were of the ordinary kind, the third was conical, like the Treasury of Atreus, or one of the old fashioned straw bee hives, with a way in only from the top. The depth must have been about 10 feet, and the place always pitch dark and very damp. There are records of many deaths in it. Tell Arnie that at Kidwelly I stayed at the Pelican Hotel, where the prices charged me were only ⅔ of those given in the C.T.C. handbook. The landlady (quite young) I overheard talking about me, and describing me. It really was awfully funny, for I could not help listening to it. The family council ended by deciding that I would probably "be" something, rather a pointless conclusion I think. From Kidwelly I rode on here, (78 miles) through Swansea and the heart of the coal district. It was the first fine day I had had since I left Bob so I enjoyed it, in spite of a 40 mile an hour gale ahead. Today is glorious, and matters promise well for tomorrow. I expect to return on Thursday at 5.25, in time for tea, "porridge please", but don't be surprised if I am a little later. Gloucester Cathedral is I believe very fine.

Caerphilly, to return to more important subjects, is magnificent. The Horn-work is most interesting, and the outworks could not be excelled, either for preservation or attractiveness. There are no good photos to be obtained, and there have been none at any time or at any castle I have visited. The conviction has been continually growing stronger upon me, that I must tour round this part again with a camera. Details which interest me, such as the moulding of a chimney piece, or the shape of the flue, even the vaulting of a room, are always neglected by the professional p.p.c. maker. So Father, if willing, may have an opportunity to "pass-storm" in the autumn: my gear is too high for such pastimes (I find there is a pun in this sentence, please excuse it as unintentional). After ten days in Wales I ought to be able to sum up all the character, habits, peculiarities, virtues, vices, and other points of the Welsh people. I am sorry I cannot do this yet. They seem to me to be rather inquisitive; at the same time they appear honest; I have had no extortionate bills (which reminds me that I have over £3 in hand). I have come to the conclusion that two meals a day with a glass of milk at one o'clock, suit me better than three. At any rate I have always felt fresh in this trip in spite of very hard journeys, and the number of castles has not palled on me; I am fresh for any amount more, and could continue for months, I also feel stronger as the day goes on: with my luggage left at home I could do 180 miles in the day with ease. Talking of baggage reminds me that I have thought out an economy in weight. My low, wide, handlebars spread the cape in such a way that in a shower or storm of rain only the toes of my shoes get damp. If the rain is very hard my ankles get splashed, but I have not had occasion to change my trousers at all, even after 6 hours in the rain. Therefore it will be seen that a change of trousers is not necessary. A nightshirt is useless if a spare day shirt is carried, and so the grand total of luggage required for a fortnight's trip is a pair of socks, a dayshirt, a sponge, and a cape. It is worth taking a fortnight's tour for a result like this. Had better stop writing here, it's getting late.   NED

Tell Arnie I have not seen any decent post cards this trip: none that he would like.

MONMOUTH
Tuesday Night. April 1907

DEAR WILL

My last letter was sent, I fancy, from Caerphilly so I had better continue from there. I left it on Monday morning, and rode through Newport, to Chepstow, of which you will have an account enclosed. Near Newport I passed the site of Caerleon; a huge tumulus only is now left. (By the way Yniol's castle is founded on Caerphilly which Tennyson visited). (See *Geraint and Enid*). Chepstow contained beside the castle, a very early Norman nave to the Parish Church. It is little spoilt by restoration, and has a most peculiar effect on the visitor. It is like standing between two high walls of stone, placed very close together. One of the Town gates also remains. From Chepstow I rode up the Wye, a very pretty road, winding along the banks of the river. The tide unfortunately was a little low, showing rather much mud bank. Tintern is only about 5 miles from Chepstow, and I got there about 6 (30 miles). I went to a C.T.C. house, which proved dear, but was quiet, since the landlady was deaf, and her daughter dumb (and deaf). In warm weather the house would be a delightful place to stay; (there is a most eligible waterfall for bathing at the back of the house). There are only half a dozen cottages near. Tintern Abbey is certainly the most beautiful abbey I have ever seen. The church is in wonderful preservation, and most interesting. The tracery of the windows is most delicate, and graceful. The East window is the prettiest one I know. The West is later, and a little too florid. The conventual buildings are well preserved, and at last I have found a hearth on which a fire used to be lighted. Even in this case there was a chimney above it, but the actual fire was unenclosed. There are two magnificent encaustic tiled floors, one very early. No pottery seems to have been discovered in the excavations. From Tintern I rode today to Monmouth, and leaving luggage and mudguards there, I rode to Raglan. The castle was most picturesque, and very remarkable. Nearly all was 16th Century work, and the castle was composed of a palace and a fortress, divided from one another by a moat. In the Norman times the fortress was the dwelling house: in Edwardian times we have the mansion within the castle, and the Tudor period divides the two parts. The palace in this case is uninteresting except from its association with Charles I. It contains some nice Renaissance work. The fortress part is much more remarkable. It is a huge hexagonal tower, surrounded by the moat, a piece of water about 30 feet wide. The moat had a walk round it, with statues of the Roman emperors. The tower (Fairfax blew down $\frac{2}{3}$ of it) was some 60 feet high, and had walls about 10 feet thick. It was ascended by a newel stair, with large square windows (Late Perp.) and loopholed embrasures for cannon. The Parliamentarians bombarded it for 6 weeks, and did not chip the corners of the masonry, (except that they blew away the battlements). They had only 20 pounders, to reduce the only fortress in England which resisted. This would seem as if the strength of the Roundheads had been somewhat over rated.

Fairfax promised in the treaty of capitulation to preserve the buildings intact, and as soon as he got in blew up the Tower with gunpowder, and gutted every other building of importance. Raglan is not architecturally interesting, but it certainly offers most wonderful opportunities to the artist, and photographer. When I got to the moat I simply sat down and sketched: you know it takes a lot to make me do that. Monmouth itself is a quiet old town, with scanty remains of a castle. I asked some people where the castle was, and they didn't know! Poor Henry V! He was born here. The bridge is the most interesting part of Monmouth. Half-way across there is an embattled and machicolated gateway, pierced for one portcullis. It must have been used as a

watch tower and chapel, and affixed to it is a latrine, of the same graceful shape as those at Tonquédec. I expect the others are at London so I
am writing to you. Expect me on Thursday as before. I hope the
Brigade {St. Aldate's Oxford Church Lads' Brigade} has prospered
exceedingly.   Yours

                                                                NED

                                                            EVREUX
                                        Sunday, 11 *August* 1907

DEAR MOTHER
        Father is out, and so I am at last writing to you. I would have
written before, but was so busy taking photos, etc. at Château Gaillard.
Beauvais was a wonderful place, and I left it with great regret for
Gisors which was disappointing, (a large castle, but all the towers
locked up), from Gisors we came to Petit Andelys. The Château
Gaillard was so magnificent, and the post cards so abominable, that I
stopped there an extra day, & did nothing but photograph, from 6.0
a.m. to 7.0 p.m. I took ten altogether, and if all are successful, I will
have a wonderful series. I will certainly have to start a book. Some of
them were very difficult to take, and the whole day was very hard.
I think Pt. Andelys would be a good place to stop at. The hotel is cheap,
and very pleasant. The Seine runs near the back door, & the bathing
is excellent, from a little wooded island in the centre of the river.
There are plenty of hills within sight, & many interesting places. Also
the scenery all along the river is exceedingly fine. Long strings of
barges pulled by a steam-tug pass the hotel occasionally, and the whole
place is over-shadowed by the hills with the ruins of the Château.
I have talked so much about this to you that you must know it all by
heart, so I had better content myself with saying that its plan is marvellous, the execution wonderful, and the situation perfect. The whole
construction bears the unmistakable stamp of genius. Richard I must
have been a far greater man than we usually consider him: he must
have been a great strategist and a great engineer, as well as a great
man-at-arms. I hope Mr. Jane will emphasise this in his book. It is
time Richard has justice done to his talents. From Pt. Andelys we came
on here, where there is a fair cathedral, with the most exquisite stained
glass, all old, and of a glorious scheme of gold and red. The effect is
magnificent, and makes a poor building look splendid. Our further

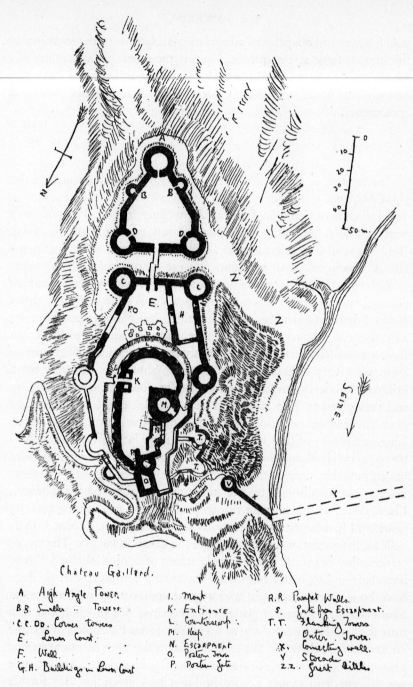

Chateau Gaillard.

A. High Angle Tower.
B.B. Smaller " Towers.
C.C. DD. Corner towers
E. Lower Court.
F. Wall.
G.H. Buildings in Lower Court

I. Moat
K. Entrance
L. Counterscarp.
M. Keep
N. Escarpment
O. Postern Tower
P. Postern Gate

R.R. Parapet Walls.
S. Gate from Escarpment.
T.T. Flanking Towers
V. Outer " Tower.
X. Connecting wall.
Y. Stocade
Z.Z. Great Ditches

V. Le Duc.

movements are doubtful. Father will probably reach you in Jersey about the 21st or 22nd. It would be much better if, instead of writing to Mt. St. Michel, you wrote to Poste-Restante Coutances. We will reach there about the 19th and you might give any further directions you pleased in that. Only write a little, but send something, or else Father will be anxious. He is fearing for Sir William Herschel. I am thinking of leaving Father on the 20th or so, and going South to Fontevrault. The trip would take me about 8 days, and I would call for letters at P.R. St. Malo. These letters would tell me whether you were continuing in Jersey, and if it was worth while my coming to meet you there. I could then return to England direct, if inclined or wait a week in Jersey. I expect you are now at Miss Wright's, and in love with my marvellous box. If you feel it is worth getting then please order a new one, I will pay the cost. It should not be more than 10/– they tell me. It will be so interesting to find out what the box is, for it quite beats me at present. Tell Miss Wright that her shirt is going on excellently: the washing has been quite simple, & quite satisfactory; in fact the only superfluous piece of luggage I have is a pocket hand-kerchief, which so far has not been employed. Also the little woollen vest has had no calls upon it. I really think I am approaching the solution of the baggage question. Stockings only are a little heavy. Ask Miss Wright how that could be improved; I mean by detachable feet etc. Kind regards to Miss Wright & Nelly, & love to self & worms. Will try to get A. some more stamps. Ta Ta. NED. ᘯ.

Father is very well, hardly any neuralgia. He is having déjuner at present.

LE MONT ST. MICHEL

26 *August* 1907

DEAR MOTHER

Here I am at last about to spend a night at the Mont. The dream of years is fulfilled. It is a perfect evening; the tide is high, and comes some 20 feet up the street. In addition the stars are out most beautifully, and the moon is, they say, just about to rise. The phosphorescence in the water interests me especially: I have only seen it once or twice before, and never so well as tonight. The whole sea, when oars are dipped into it, seems to blaze, for several feet around. I rode here from Dinan, getting Frank's P.C. in St. Malo on my way. As you do not say you want anything, I will not bring back more than a cider-jug for Arnie. It is just large enough to hold all the cider he will ever want, and is a reddish-brown tint. (This news is for him). I am bringing it because there are none of the stamps which he wanted to be bought. With Dinan and the Rance I am entirely in love. The Rue de Jersual, from the old bridge to the "place," is perfect: the river is most lovely. Above the town it becomes very quiet and peaceful, like the Thames: lined with Aspens & Lombardy poplars. When you add waterlilies, willows, and an occasional high bank, crowned with a quaint farmhouse or château, you have a fair idea of the characteristics of the stream. With its bathing, (excellent they tell me) its boating (they have some of Salter's boats) and its beauty, I think it should suit the entire family. Suppose we transport ourselves thither some Autumn? Since I left Father (to return somewhat on my travels) I have had a very wonderful time. It began at Fougères, which I saw by moonlight, and a more exquisite sight I have seldom seen. That castle is quite above and beyond words. It pollutes it to mention any but Château Gaillard, Pembroke, and Caerphilly in the same breath, and I am not sure but that Fougères is the finest of them all. The Tour des Gobelins is six stories in height, and circular. It stands on a granite cliff 80 feet high, and in the moonlight had a marvellous effect. It set off the strength of the Melusine, a tower near, with an enormous expanded base. The talus shoots right out like the Keep of Château Gaillard. Beyond the Melusine, after a hundred yards of machicolated curtain, come Raoul and Yrienne, two wonderful chefs-d'œuvre of the military architect. They are semi-circular bastions, projecting some 70 feet from the wall, are over 80 feet in diameter, and more than that in height; neither has a window or projection in the face, and over against them leans the Spire of St. Sulpice the most crooked, and the thinnest in Bretagne. I would have given anything to have been able to sketch or paint these things as I saw them. I really must return to Fougères soon, and do justice to the whole. The neglect in which it has been left by the guidebooks is abominable. From Fougères I glided S.E. to Le Mans, to photograph the effigy of Mrs. Richard I., Berengaria, in the cathedral there. The Apse and Nave of the building were splendid: the former especially. From Le Mans I rode to Saumur, via Le Lude, a most splendid Renaissance Château, unhappily private. Saumur itself is still in parts as Balzac painted it in *Eugénie Grandet*, though the main streets have been rebuilt. The Castle is a military storehouse, and the

photos of Fontevrault were not as good as I had wished. I slept that
night at Angers. On the stretch one of the small nuts holding the bolt
that joins the chain fell off and the bolt, fortunately striking the crank
& making a noise, was almost falling out. Angers was a very quaint
town, spoilt by electric trams. The exteriors of the castle & of the
prefecture were interesting (nothing at all inside), and the cathedral,
roofed as it was in domes, was a new style for me in architecture.
From Angers I rode the next day, through Lion d'Angers, where I was
asked for my "permit", to Rennes, and so on to St. Malo & Dinard.
The vineyards were quaint but monotonous. At Dinard I tried 5 hotels
& all were full. As it was by then 8 p.m. I went to the Chaignons, &
strolled in whilst they were at dinner. When I spoke & revealed myself there was a most enthusiastic scene: all yelled welcome at once,
they insisted on my staying to dinner, & sleeping there, and, whilst
sending all sorts of messages to you, told me that I was always a friend
there: that I was always welcome & was to come in whenever I could.
They were quite upset at the idea of my going off next day. M. Corbeil
was with them, & collapsed when he heard where I had come from.
I have given them a topic of conversation for a week. Deux cent
cinquante kilomètres, Ah la-la, qu'il est merveilleux. Deux cent
cinquante kilomètres. The Lefèvriers were in Dinard, but I did not see
them. Next day I went on to Lamballe, meaning to go as far as
Guingamp. It however began to rain heavily, so I stopped, & made a
careful study of the Rood screen in the Church there. Next day I
photod it, and the time taken (3 hrs. to focus) should ensure a present-
able result, better than the vile p.c. I sent you. Next day (by the way
the Chaignons, & the Lamballe people, complimented me on my
wonderful French: I have been asked twice since what part of France
I came from) I went to La Hunaudaye, & took 4 photos. In the evening, at Dinan, I wrote to M. de la Brière asking him to take steps for the
preservation of the Château. Nothing like making his society of use.
In Dinan I got into conversation with an English artist, rather a noted
one, staying at the same hotel. He gave me a lot of very useful hints.
Tomorrow I am going to ride into Granville. I expect to reach you
with my £5 note unchanged, but will get rid of nearly all my French
money. If need be, will give some tips, and buy old furniture. That
Box at Dinan with which I was so charmed last year is going at £5,
so the woman told me. I will return next year & get it for 3. I am glad

Father is not off till Thursday: we can compare notes. Also that you have a nice place. When I get there I am going to take a complete rest. This week has been rather hard.

NED

23 July 1908. *Thursday evening*

DEAR MOTHER

I am beginning a letter to you tonight, which I may not be able to finish at this sitting, but you'll get it in the end. I had better begin at the place where Will left me. The roads were bad to Winchester, gritty, but quite supportable: in some extraordinary way I took the wrong turn at Whitchurch, and found myself at Andover. As a result I had to go on from Winchester by train, to catch which I had to wait an hour; fortunately there was a Socialist meeting. The passage was fairly rough, & there were many "accidents" down below. The boat was full, but as the decks were deserted that did not concern me. We got into Havre about 8, and I left at once for Rouen, by our old road along the Seine, through Lillebonne. They were going to perform *Brittanicus* in the Roman Theatre on the Sunday! I would have liked to have heard that. At Rouen I sent you a p.c. and left for Les Andelys which I reached about 6.30. The place was as charming as ever, and the English had not yet arrived in their scores. I made a plan of the cellars next morning, and in the afternoon rode to Gisors. Next morning I mended punctures, & made a really superb plan of the castle keep (xii Cent.) on paper like this counting one long side of the oblong as 5 feet. It is not a bad idea I fancy. Leaving Gisors about 1 o'clock I made for Beauvais, but what with head wind, & most furious storms of rain & hail I had enough of it in an hour, & turned due east, reaching Compiègne late. There I discovered a good & cheap hotel, & stayed over Sunday. Next morning I had a great treat, in the shape of a ride through the old royal forest to Pierrefonds, of which doubtless you got a p.p.c. As you can see it is a considerable fortress (xv Cent.), but you cannot tell that inside: there is not the least sign of anything of the sort. One finds only a Renaissance palace, covered with the richest carving (statues of Caesar, Charlemagne, Viollet-le-duc etc.) and with a series of the most grotesque gargoyles I ever came across. I sent you a dragon today:—he is in reality about 15 feet high, and everything is on a like scale. There are galleries, & magnificent flamboyant windows. Napoleon III handed the Château over to Viollet-le-duc to restore, and he has left it as he thought Louis D'Orleans would have liked. Although a little too late to please me, it was most interesting. I arrived at an unearthly early hour, & so had the privilege of being led over it alone. Some of the rooms (decorated in the old style) are very handsome. From Pierrefonds I bumped over execrable roads to Coucy. This was better even than Pierrefonds:—for one thing, it is xiii cent.—another its keep is 200 odd feet high (it used to be vaulted, when it must have been overpowering: the revolutionaries wanted to destroy it, so they exploded half a ton of powder in the basement. The tower didn't break (walls 20–30 feet thick) but it acted like a barrel of a gun, & sent the vaults into Mars and Jupiter)—and there are splendid remains of 4 other towers, a great hall with two tiers of cellars beneath, and domestic buildings:—besides the town has almost complete walls around it. On the whole I made a note of Coucy as a glorious place.

From Coucy I (on Tuesday) went to Provins, near Paris. This has a most puzzling xii cent. keep, and remains of town walls. I was in & around them for hours, and came to the conclusion that the architect was making experiments when he built them. On the walls is a square tower turned inside out & cut in half: the keep would have been amost incapable of defence, & yet in spirit it is half a century ahead of its time. It ranks with Ch. Gaillard in importance for my thesis. From Provins I rode through Troyes to a little place near Bar-sur-Seine. There I gave out late, & today started at 1 p.m. and rode to Montbard (an interesting tower) and thence here, which is a tiny village about 15 miles from Vézélay "the grandest Norman church in Europe" (or outside it I presume) the guide-books all sing in chorus. I'll let you know tomorrow about that. I hope to reach Le Puy just about as I said & Carcassonne also: further I cannot yet say, for a tourist (French) whom I met said there were 2 inches of dust in Lanquedoc on the roads just now. For myself I'm riding very strongly, & feel very fit, on my diet of bread, milk, & fruit (peaches (best) 3 a 1d.: apricots 5 or 6 a 1d. if very special; cherries don't count—I wish you were here; but no apples or pears or plums). I begin on 2 pints of milk & bread, & supplement with fruit to taste till evening, when more solid stuff is consumed: one eats a lot when riding for a week on end at any pace. My day begins early ('tis fearfully hot at mid-day) there is usually a château to work at from 12–2, and then hotel at 7 or 8. I have no time for sight-seeing: indeed sometimes I wonder if my thesis is to be written this Nov. or next, I find myself composing pages and phrases as I ride. The roads have been almost uniformly bad, but the hills all rideable. My back tyre is in a bad way: I failed to repair it with bands etc. so changed it to the front, (couldn't get a new one, though I tried hard at Troyes), filled all the holes full of cement, & rode this afternoon on it with some success: still it has run away with a fortune in repair bands already, not to mention stopping & solution. Otherwise nothing is lacking in my equipment. The country hereabouts is idyllic. Besides my cherry-trees (which it appears are a feature of Champagne, not Burgundy) there are quantities of wood, & rivers. All is very green, except the crops which are only now being cut (harvest late this year they say—too wet). The carts are pulled usually by oxen, of a bilious white colour (rather amusing to see six great solemn beasts pulling a little load of straw), and the high roads are infested with dogs, whose duty it is to bark at all tourists, above all motorists, & people in knickers. I don't think there is anything more to tell. I expect you will be crossing to Jersey tomorrow (Friday): if it's like today you will feel as if you're crossing a mill-pond on a "primus" cooking stove: which reminds me of Will afloat on his walnut-shell with Henry & Co. {on the Norfolk Broads} I wonder if they will be congenial companions? Frank has doubtless secured his 1st on the excellence of his Westward Ho paper ("Eastward Ho" is all *my* cry), and Arnie has engaged a seat in Form No. I of the O.H.S. Let him carry on our tradition: "no games." As for yourself and Father don't be anxious about me: if my tyre *does* sob out its life prematurely I'll buy or hire a French wheel & tyre. If anything else happens I'll do my best to mend it, & I'm fairly handy. Money I have sufficient for present purposes (your notes are as you placed them) though it does go apace, & goodness knows where: I believe it's these great dinners in the evening. Will you if you write to Carcassonne tell me what is happening in Turkey: the rubbish here that they call newspapers say one day that movements are taking place among the people, & a revolution is taking place, or that all is calm, and the sultan drank tea as usual at 6 o'clock on the terrace: I see today he's proclaimed a constitution and his intention to withdraw it: do let me have some solid fact if there is anything in it: it might well be important.

Closing time.   Ta Ta   NED

AIGUES-MORTES
Sunday. 2 August 1908

DEAR MOTHER

I had better begin from my last letter before Vézélay. This I found superb but rather in sculpture than in proportions. The carvings were the finest early work I had met with till then: since (?) you'll hear. From Vézélay I rode to Nevers, arriving on Friday. It is a quaint rather than beautiful town, with a good Renaissance ducal palace, & a fine cathedral. I telephoned from here to Dunlop in Paris for a new tyre, which after anxious waiting arrived all right on Monday: since then all has gone like a marriage bell in the way of punctures, and I am generally happy. The cost was however immense:—with telephoning: carriage: fitting etc., it cost nearly 20/–: result is I'm afraid I'll be short later on: in fact I am rather disgusted with my cost to date. The hotels all charge 2 f. for bed, & at least 2 for dinner (I don't like going to any but fairly decent places, alone, with money). My litre of milk staggers them for breakfast, (I always order it the night before, and it is amusing to watch their efforts to convince me I'm mistaken "Monsieur does not mean a litre: it is too much" etc.), but not sufficiently to persuade them to charge less than 75 c. to 1 f. result 5 f. are gone by the morning: add some fruit or milk in the day, post cards (now total over 100) & postage, repair-bands, solution, tips for show places, an occasional bath etc. and you have a fair 7 f. per day: I had really hoped to do it cheaper. 6/– a day is absurd for one. (I have changed a {£5} note quite successfully by the way: pocket proved admirable).

From Nevers I went by Moulins to Le Puy. Tell Father I had a 20 mile hill up into Le Puy. Part of my ride was up a superb gorge, with river foaming in the bottom, & rock & hill on each side: it was the finest scenery I have ever come across: truly the Auvergne is a wondrous district: but *not* one for a cycle: I'll take a walking tour there some day I hope. The volcanoes (all extinct of course) are queer, being plumped down all over the country, without any order or connection. They are very diverse in material (sand, rock, etc.) & look ugly. At the same time the needle of which I sent you a p.c. is an impressive peak. It rises from the town of Le Puy, where I was delightful to get 3 p.c. from Will & you & 1 from Scroggs; at the same time I am disgusted at what I fear was my mistake in antedating your departure for Jersey: but a trip like this upsets one's idea of time. In the Auvergne

by the way there are few if any trees and in parts to make a garden
they have piled the stones from the ground in a wall around it. A
garden our size would have a wall 5 feet thick, & 4 feet high so made.
From Le Puy I rode up for 10 miles more, (oh dear 'twas hot!) consoling myself with the idea that my sufferings were beyond the conception
of antiquity, since they were a combination (in a similar climate) of
those of Sisyphus who pushed a great weight up hill, of Tantalus who
couldn't get anything to drink, or any fruit, and of Theseus who was
doomed ever to remain sitting:—I got to the top at last, had 15 miles
of up and down to St. Somebody-I-don't-want-to-meet-again, and
then a rush down 4,000 feet to the Rhône. T'was down a valley, the
road carved out of the side of the precipice, & most gloriously exciting:
in fact so much so that with that & the heat I felt quite sick when I got
to the bottom. I slept that night at Crussol, a fine xii. c. castle on a
500 feet precipice over the Rhône. Next day via Valence to Avignon,
glorious with its town walls & papal palace, (Popes lived there 90
years, & built an enormous pile) & passed thence through Tarascon
to Beaucaire, which I saluted for the sake of Nicolette, into Arles. *The*
thing in Arles is the cloister of St. Trophimus: it is absolutely un-
imaginably fine with its sculptures & its proportion: all other architecture is very nearly *dirt* beside this Provençal Romanesque, when the
scale is small (Provence has never done anything big in anything at all).
I have seen the three best (almost the only 3) examples at Arles, Mont-
Majour, & St. Gilles, & am absolutely bewildered. The amphitheatre
(Roman) at Arles is magnificently and gigantically ugly, as everything
of that sort must be: Nimes is I believe better (that is for tomorrow).
From Arles I rode to Les Baux, a queer little ruined & dying town
upon a lonely "olive sandalled" mountain. Here I had a most delightful
surprise. I was looking from the edge of a precipice down the valley
far over the plain, watching the green changing into brown, & the
brown into a grey line far away on the horizon, when suddenly the
sun leaped from behind a cloud, & a sort of silver shiver passed over
the grey: then I understood, & instinctively burst out with a cry of
"Θαλασσα, Θαλασσα" that echoed down the valley, & startled an
eagle from the opposite hill: it also startled two French tourists who
came rushing up hoping to find another of the disgusting murders
their papers make such a fuss about I suppose. They were disappointed
when they heard it was "only the Mediterranean"!

Mont St. Michel. Cloisters   (*See p.* 57)

Mont St. Michel. Cloisters (*See p.* 57)

AIGUES MORTES

From Les Baux I descended to Arles, & thence to St. Gilles—Aigues-Mortes. I reached here late last night, & sent you a pencilled p.c. It is a lovely little place, an old old town, huddled along its old streets, with hardly a house outside its old walls, still absolutely unbroken, & hardly at all restored or in need of it. From it St. Louis started for his crusades, & it has seen innumerable events since. Today it is deserted by the world, & is decaying fast: its drawbacks are mosquitoes, (a new experience for me, curtains on all the beds), and the lack of a cheap hotel. It is however almost on the sea, and exceedingly pleasant, (above all if one could get acclimatised quickly to these brutes, I'm all one huge bite). I bathed today in the sea, the great sea, the greatest in the world: you can imagine my feelings: the day was lovely, warm, a light wind, & sunny: the sea had not our long rolling breakers, but short dancing ripples, the true ἀνήριθμον γελασμά.

"And from the waves sounds like delight broke forth."

The beach was hard sand as far as the eye could reach, and sand rippled like the waves themselves: t'was shallow, and all most lovely, most delightful

H.L.—5

"I love all waste
"And solitary places: where we taste
"The pleasure of believing all we see
"Is boundless, as we wish our souls to be:—"

You are all wrong, Mother dear, a mountain may be a great thing, a grand thing, "but if it is better to be peaceful, and quiet, and pure, pacata posse omnia mente tueri, {Lucretius V. 1203} if that is the best state, then a plain is the best country": the purifying influence is the paramount one in a plain, there one can sit down quietly and think, of anything, or nothing which Wordsworth says is best, one feels the littleness of things, of details, and the great and unbroken level of peacefulness of the whole: no give me a level plain, extending as far as the eye can reach, and there I have enough of beauty to satisfy me, and tranquillity as well! *that* one could never have in mountains: there is always the feeling that one is going up or down: that one will be better, will see clearer from the top than from the valleys; stick to the plains Mother, & all ye little worms, you'll be happiest there. But for my bathe—that was a lovely time. I hope I'll "hear the sea breathe o'er my dying brain its last monotony"; on such a day as this, and also at the time of the setting sun. It was as warm as may be pleasant, and the water refreshingly delicious: I felt that at last I had reached the way to the South, and all the glorious East; Greece, Carthage, Egypt, Tyre, Syria, Italy, Spain, Sicily, Crete . . . they were all there, and all within reach . . . of me. I fancy I know now better than Keats what Cortes felt like, "silent upon a peak in Darien". Oh I must get down here,— farther out—again! Really this getting to the sea has almost overturned my mental balance: I would accept a passage for Greece tomorrow:— and there I am going to Nimes:—I suppose it cannot be helped: well I am glad to have got so far. The heat is great, I was almost going to say excessive, especially between 11 & 3. Everybody wears tinted glasses (even the children) & stay within closed blinds till within 3 hours of sunset. Now (9 p.m.) all the world is awake and in the streets, killing mosquitoes: fruit I find almost a necessity, but only pears & peaches procurable, & dear: however I am a disciple of Blake

"Abstinence sows sand all over
"The ruddy limbs & flaming hair

"But desire gratified
"Sows seeds of joy & beauty there."

So I take plenty & keep cool & well, albeit copper coloured, &
I think thinner: I will write again next Sunday at any rate if not before:
till when, expect a couple of p.c.'s only. Shall get to Carcassonne on
Wednesday I hope: and may all be well there just as here: love to all:
                                                           N.E.D.

                              CARCASSONNE. *Thursday, 6 August* 1908
DEAR MOTHER
    Today has turned out most wet, so I will spend some time in
beginning a letter to you. Paper is precious you see, so I will write very
small, & Frank or Arnie must read it to you. I wrote last from Aigues–
Mortes. I rode thence to Nimes where the amphitheatre proved fair,
no more: the "maison Carrée" was a little gem of a temple, in time
stained marble, of pure Greek style. I never saw a handsomer little
place; it makes one marvel what the Parthenon must be. From Nimes
I rode to Agde ('Aγαθη πολις it was) with a wonderful church spared
by Andrea Doria when he sacked the town. The building is all fortified,
with wonderful machicoulis all round. It has a front seat in my thesis.
All this part of France was sown with Greek colonies, and the women
of Arles still retain the type. They look very splendid in little Phrygian
caps of black cloth. I have post cards of a couple for your collection.
It is interesting to find local influence still so lasting. Agde to Béziers
was my next stage. This was the headquarters of the vine troubles last
year, and was celebrated for the massacre it witnessed in the wars of
the Albigenses under De Montfort. The town had been taken, and the
Crusaders wanted to kill the heretics, but there were many Catholics
in the town as well. What shall we do? they asked the Legate, Peter of
Castelnau. "Kill them all," said he, "God will recognise his own," and
some 8,000 were butchered in cold blood. Pleasant people those 13th
cent. Crusaders!
    From Béziers I rode to Narbonne, and so to Carcassonne. This place
is absolutely indescribable. It is of all dates: much Roman work: much
Visigothic, a splendid Saracenic tower, some Carolivingian work, and
mediæval of all sorts to the end of the 14th century: *nothing later* except
a very little modern restoration. This makes it the most interesting

& most valuable object-lesson in military architecture (for at all periods it was a first-class fortress) and it happens also to be wonderfully picturesque. An artist in black & white could obtain most marvellous effects (there is no colour in the building, & no creepers or plants) and there are some fine photographs to be bought. I have 24 post cards, and some of those giant p.c.'s. They should be framed when I get back. Also I have a superb plan, showing the different periods of the buildings. In fact I spent 5 francs on getting about the place, & getting views. When it clears today I'll go up there again. It is quite small, (about a mile round) but every inch has two lines of defence, with a fine castle in the inside of all. This, they say, is early twelfth century, but that's all rubbish. It is late in the century, or else early thirteenth. All the same there is much of the twelfth for me; so much that I cannot satisfy myself upon it: in fact could only do so by carting it back to Oxford, & fixing it on Brill hill. From it there are glorious views both over Cevennes & Pyrenees, but I do not intend to go over either. It looks as though it has cleared up, so I'll go off & see, merely remarking that the water-jugs here are superb: large green pitchers, shape of Jersey milk-cans with two handles, one of which contains a spout. A special joy in Carcassonne is that one does not need a guide with one, all is free & open except some of the towers: there there are guides, but no fees. Photography is allowed, but there is not much to do; I have got them all I think.

Sunday.   CORDES, *near Albi*

In the end I took 4 photos. one of which is meant to be pretty (the only one so far this tour: all the others are of technical points in architecture). I will not write anything more of Carcassonne. It is as impossible to describe it as it would be to illustrate it: I have some 40 photos. which will prove what I say. I got your p.c.'s there, a letter from Father, & a p.c. from the Broads, {From Will} all well there evidently, but bathing is not for that climate: it is for this: convinced I am.

From Carcassonne I rode to Toulouse, through torrents of rain, coming down not in mere stair-rods, but in scaffold-poles: all the roads were an inch deep in a few minutes, the vines & other crops are a total loss; the fruit has doubled in price, everything is flooded, or rather was. They certainly can teach us something in the way of thunder-storms, though the local papers refer to it as a storm of unparalleled violence, a never to be forgotten deluge. I was drenched in a minute (it lasted 30) and dried in an hour, for the sun came out afterwards with burning force, and the wind was furiously against. It took me just seven hours to reach Toulouse (70 miles). Toulouse is a horrid modern manufacturing town, with only one old church, but that a beauty. I fancy I sent you a card of it from Rabastens, where I slept. As it is in the Department of Tarn, which is "ultima Thule" to the Gauls, I don't know if it will ever arrive.

Next day (yesterday) I rode to Albi, where the Cathedral disappointed me, inside: the sculptures of which I had heard so much were Renaissance, & certainly second class: there were however yards & yards of them; 'tis wonderful they managed to do so many. The whole place is covered with paintings, (Italian xv. Cent.) and is generally tawdry. Outside it is marvellous, and reminded me much of a beer-barrel, or a huge series of beer-barrels, piled round a blanc-mange mould. It is all of rose-coloured brick, and one of the most strikingly original buildings extant. I shall never forget the enormous swollen bulk of the apse, rising quite suddenly out of a little market square. The people, even the houses near it, looked infinitesimal, like a colony of ants. The architecture round Toulouse is most peculiar, all of red brick, which looks queer to our eyes, though the brick in half a dozen centuries takes on a most exquisite tint. There are never pillars or arches in the naves: they are vaulted in one spring, and are really only huge halls. They are then plastered & painted. Windows are almost lacking, and even the smallest is shuttered & heavily stained to keep out the sunlight. In the dwelling houses they never open the shutters, and the doorways are closed all day by a curtain. Everything shuts up between 11.30 & 2.30, at that time I pass through village after village without meeting a soul. I have however forgotten what a mosquito bites like, since I left the marshes of the coast. Aigues–Mortes is celebrated for the ague in the winter: it is such that no decent people will live there after September: for miles the country is covered with stagnant swamps, so that not even the little black wild oxen (which they hunt on horseback) can exist. At the same time there are swarms of strange animals, flamingoes, bustards, even the so-called ibis: of this latter I roused two. They come to France for the summer, & return to Egypt for the winter.

This place Cordes is the most picturesque town I have come across in my travels. It lies in Tarn, which is a district cut off from the rest of France, by dialect, geographically, ethnologically, and even climatically. The people are utterly unlike French, & cannot speak it. (I can't make head or tail of the patois, and a Frenchman can only understand a little: it takes 3 years to learn, my French landlord told me). The country is one of rolling hills, & poplar filled valleys, with fearful gorges where the Tarn goes through the mountains. A boat can descend most of it, if the boatman knows the rocks, & they say it is one of the wildest trips in the world. The cliffs (often 400–700 feet high) in places approach within 60 feet at the top (there are even natural bridges) & the river at the bottom tears along at 8 miles in the hour; in semidarkness. This sort of thing, with waterfalls and rapids, extends for 60 miles. The villages (no towns) are of course all lighted by electric light, though generally smaller than Begbroke {village near Oxford}. Hotels only exist occasionally, and at each I am the only guest; (apparently I have to bear the whole expenses of the house as well: I am ruined in pocket & in health too if this continues); their food is weird and wonderful, (*omelette aux pommes de terre* yesterday and other articles unspecified & indescribable), the bread tastes like . . . can you imagine leather soaked in brine, & then boiled till soft: with an iron crust, & a flavour like a brandy-snap? It takes me a considerable mental & physical effort to "degust" a mouthful: milk has not been heard of lately, butter has a smell like cream cheese, but a taste like Gruyère, (thank goodness for the Roquefort, 'tis the district, and its strength would make palatable (or indiscoverable) a cesspool), and in fact a dinner for me is like an expedition into Spain, Naples, the North & Antarctic regions, Central Australia, Japan etc.: one never had such thrills, such nerve-shattering expectation and such galvanic shocks for 3 francs before: let anyone feeling dull or blasé come to a Tarnais Hotel for a week: there is no fruit, the water tastes highly suspicious, & there is nothing else but wine: I was feeling desperate (soda water is unheard of), when I met, first a plantation of melons, & second a pastry shop, bristling with *choux à la crême*. Still such a diet has its disadvantages, on the scores of price & wholesomeness. I hope to be out of the department tomorrow. My water-drinking is the subject of general amazement, by the way, far beyond what I had thought possible: the hotel people after I have asked for it, bring me everything else they have in the place first, and I heard last night the servants talking to the people next door, telling them there was an Englishman there with a strange hat, who drank water, and liked it better than wine! The neighbours flatly told them it was a *blague*, humbug, and the patron had to be called upon to convince them. People never seem to have thought of water as a drink, they regard it much as we would regard oil or a hair-wash: useful, certainly, but for cookery, or for cleaning: nothing else. Certainly the Tarn is a district to be revisited, but on foot: it is too hilly for cycling. You may wonder what it was that brought me here: 'twas partly the learning it was the most backward district in Western Europe, and partly because of its picturesqueness. I wish you could get an idea of this place Cordes: I have not talent to give one. Imagine a valley, formed by the space between four ranges of hills: in the middle of this place a hill, about as steep as Mont-St. Michel, & a matter of 400 feet high. Cover this with houses, all over, and you have a fair idea of the general view. The house-roofs are almost flat, & of red semicircular tiles:—

Inside, the streets (two streets paved) are so steep that one can only maintain one's balance with great difficulty, & a strange horse cannot mount. Join these streets by narrow alleys of flights of broken, irregular stairs alternating with tiny squares of gravel about one house (say 20 feet long) each way. In places throw archways over the streets, or make them run under tunnels for 50 yards, put in 8 or 10 fortified gates of the xv. & xvi cents. and fairly complete town walls, built over & round with a tangled ram-shackle mass of hovels and ruined cottages. Let every other house be of stone, and of the xiv. cent, with charming Flamboyant windows of two lights, divided by exquisitely carved pillars & shapely capitals of a bunch of vine leaves or other naturalistic foliage. Half these windows are blocked up with a mass of broken tiles and mortar; over the others are worm-eaten shutters with splendid iron-work, & hinges of the Renaissance time. Between the windows are string courses, often carved with grotesques of animals with human heads, hunting scenes etc. The roofs project a couple of feet, with gargoyles grinning down into the middle of the tiny streets, only a matter of two yards wide. These houses are usually of three storeys and are mixed up with modern houses (modern for Cordes that is), perhaps of the xvi century with transomed & mullioned windows & square-headed or ogee doorways. The market hall is xiv, the church xv. cent. Some of the houses are in ruins, others tottering. There are only 3 straight ones in the town (these are now the Mairie), all the rest lean backwards & forwards, or are shored up by a stable, or a buttress thrown across the streets to a similarly affected house: and so two sick men support each other. Some are of brick, plastered, or have been plastered, for it has usually fallen away, revealing blocked doors & windows, niches, & sculptured blocks built into the later work. All the wood-work is old & weather-warped, much of it quaintly carved, with all sorts of dilapidations. The streets are all grass-grown, & full of piles of dirt & rubbish: there are no drains, hardly even surface ones, but the sun quickly dries a little damp, & in winter the rains will carry all down to the bottom of the hill. Every wall is hung with grass & creepers, all the house windows are full of flowers, growing in rusty tin cans or earthenware jugs, broken & worn with use, & with half their brilliant glaze worn off. Each house has its little trellis of vines, and each is a subject or half a dozen for a painter. The colouring is simply unequalled. One could stay here for months, painting every day, supposing one escaped fevers or other trifles of that sort. A visit here is a glimpse back three centuries, to the time of hand-looms (weaving is the great industry here; wouldn't Mr. Binney like it!) and threshing floors. A roller drawn by oxen & a winnowing fan do the works in this respect. I could go on with the Tarn all night, but must stop now. All is going very well (fewer tyre troubles, 34 punctures to date however, in 1400 miles), & nothing wrong, except financially. I hope you are also enjoying yourself; though in a less strenuous manner: this has been a very hard, but a very instructive tour. I expect Will will have reached you {from Norfolk Broads} when this gets there. Hope he got on well. As for the future, about Friday I should reach Castillon & Saintes a matter of 8 days later, but 'tis all a bad district for hills. From Saintes 8 days more or indeed a few less should put me in Loches, I expect it will be: Redon is improbable, since I don't suppose Scroggs will come. Write a p.c. to each place & hope for the best: I may possibly get there. For the present, ta-ta.

NED

By the way, I go from here to Najac, & so to Cahors: thence to Fumel, Montpazier, & down the river Lot to Castillon. From Castillon to Peregueux—Limoges, Angoulême, Saintes, Niort, Poitiers. This might be useful to you, if you can find a map.

When you {return}, will you send timetables of boats from Granville & St. Malo from Sept. 4 to the day you leave? Also fare.

CHALUS (HAUTE-VIENNE)
16 *August* 1908
{His twentieth birthday.}

DEAR MOTHER

Here goes for another Sunday letter, the fifth altogether I think: there should be only two or three more. I wrote last from Cordes. After paying a "largish" bill, I rode to Najac, over huge hills: I don't think there was a mile of level road in the whole 30. However there I found a splendid xiii cent. castle entirely unrestored, a town as picturesque as Cordes if not more so, (the streets were not paved, but cut in the solid rock, houses often likewise), and a splendid xiv cent. fountain, with a basin xii feet across & 3 deep, all of one stone

From Najac I rode x miles downhill to Villefranche, & then xxx splendid level miles to Cahors, the birthplace of Clement V, and other people. A bridge there is of the xiv cent. with archways & portcullises, machicoulis & loopholes: very interesting & very pretty. That night was mosquito-haunted, till in the end I wrapped a towel round my head, & so got a little sleep: however I can appreciate Æschylus'

αἰθηρ δ' ἐλαφραις
πτερυγιων ῥιπαις ὑποσυριζει.

'Tis a glorious description, and that word ὑποσυριζει is unapproachable: Æschylus spent a night in the Hôtel de la Gare, Cahors. After making this discovery I tucked up my tail & fled to Fumel, where I found Bonaguil, a castle of the middle xv. cent. most interesting: provision is made everywhere for cannon: and at the same time the old methods were not out of date. It is so perfect that it is almost ridiculous to call it a ruin: all the vaults, stairways & some of the roofs are perfect. From Bonaguil I waded through hills to Montpazier, where I slept, in a huge room, with editions of Chateaubriand, the Corneilles etc. a glorious Renaissance window, & splendid polished floor, old carved furniture, good pictures etc.: all comforts desirable, and for 1 f. 50. The Hôtel had a fine carved Flamboyant doorway, or rather two of them: the entrance hall was cobbled with white & red stones, & the staircase was handsome: people pleasant also. In fact it would be a place for spending a month with a reading party, or something of the sort. The country is that of the Agen plums, for our prunes: they are very good, & not worth selling in the shops: of delicious green plums I could get more than I could eat for 1d. Who said they were unwholesome? I ate 126 one day, & rode 90 miles: next day I breakfasted, lunched & dined off them: in fact didn't stop eating all day: no ill effects: this miserable district here has nothing but walnuts, maize & bad apples: tons of tomatoes everywhere of course. For plums they charge 1d. a pound: it is a great change from Agen. Montpazier itself is a little old town, perched on a hill. It was built about 1270 by the English, one of the Bastides they then erected every-where in France. They are rectangular towns, more regular than an American city, with arcaded market-place in the centre. Montpazier still keeps the formation though many of the houses are rebuilt: it is a little place fast going to ruin: the registrar with whom I spent the evening, (& rode the next day), said that in 6 years there would only be 300 people there at present rates: it was a town of 4000 people 50 years ago. Next day I rode to Castillon, seeing Pujols, an important xii cent. castle, on the way. Castillon itself gave its name to the battle that finished the 100 years war. I found there 3 p.c.'s from you: am glad all goes so well: but for bathing go South: even this place is too cold, though I cannot walk with comfort without a hat. In the Medi-terranean one could be in the water all day, and feel just right: at least I was most happy there: try & persuade St. Helier's to get some sound books. I am going I hope to be at Saintes on Tuesday, and Loches about a week later: you might send there a list of what you would like me to bring back from Normandy, the Granville district. I will also call for letters in Falaise about 5 days later: but don't trouble about that unless you have something special: at present I thought of bring-ing (or sending) two second-hand brass cans, (if possible) say at 13 f. each. The real things are much dearer than the one we got last year. If you prefer new ones, say so to Falaise or Loches: or if you would like less: or large ones or small ones: that we brought last year was a medium size: they run from nearly the size of the Jersey can to that of a good sized bucket. Also if there is anything else—? Granville has also those Isigny butter jugs, which are rather quaint there are no cider jugs there, or at least very poor ones). From Castillon I rode to Peri-gueux, via Montaigne. This was the great man's estate, and the tower which contained his library is still extant. The château itself is rebuilt

(they call them chastels in langue d'or pronounced just as we would).
It was most interesting to me to visit the scenes he describes. Perigueux
has a Byzantine cathedral, of the same date and style as St. Mark's at
Venice: I think I sent a p.c. that night from St. Yreix, to which I went
via Hautefort, Bertrand de Born's castle (of this a photo. for Mr. Jane).
From St. Yrieix I rode to Chalusset (hills galore) and then through
Nexon here. Chalus is the place where Richard I got the wound that
caused his death. There are two towers, on opposing hills, from which
the arrow is said to have come (either would be a tremendous shot)
and a rock on which he is said to have been standing (this is quite
probable, if he wanted to keep his feet dry, all the rest is a swamp).
The local antiquary stands out for a third tower, between the other
two, and close to the rock. His evidence seems however doubtful:
Richard at any rate did not die here, but near Poitiers. It was his
foolishness in going to banquets and riding steeple-chases with the hole
in him that killed him. There is nothing else to see in Chalus. You say
I should have a lot to tell you: indeed yes, but so much that I can never
remember it, and indeed I am getting used to my surroundings. It
seems quite natural to walk about in the heat of afternoon with us at
10 p.m., and listen to the cicalas: they make a sound rather like a
grasshopper but sweet. On the terrace round Montpazier it was glorious, with hundreds of them singing in the trees in perfect time with a
chorus of frogs in the meadow, and with a full moon lighting up the
county like day for miles around, so that I could see the lights gleaming
in the windows of Le Château de Biron, 15 kilometres away. It was
the reflection of the moonlight, for the château is uninhabited. Everything is absolutely different to what I am accustomed, & yet the
transition from Normandy to the Midi & back again has been so
gradual that I have not been struck by it. Here in the Limousin things
are more normal. There is one thing I do loathe about this part, the
dogs: each has his district round his house, and if he leaves it, the whole
town is awakened by the most horrible howling. The dog may be shut
up indoors but he will go perfectly mad with fury, and his excitement
spreads all round: at times last night there must have been 100 dogs
on the go at once; (the Hôtel has four). I sleep lightly now-a-days
& was four times disturbed by the racket. And all through the day-
time one has never an instant without noise: my brain would go if I
lived here long: hydrophobia is very common: I suppose the weather is

responsible, but 'tis unpleasant to have a beast the size of a small donkey (everybody here drives donkeys: few horses) chasing one for 4 miles as hard as he can tear: (this was yesterday; fortunately it was downhill, so I won easily) what would he do if he caught one up? he cannot be taking such a run in the heat for exercise or amusement. Do you know the fat Frenchmen which are such a feature of Dinard life have all disappeared down here: everyone is as thin as possible: I suppose it is the heat:—at any rate I am copying them. It is a nuisance, but milk is unobtainable, even in the morning: I have therefore at times ordered eggs, for which they charge a lot. This has swallowed up my little economies so that a new tyre would put me short: therefore I wrote for a pound or so to Loches. If you want many things, you might send a little more to Falaise, in case I have to get a tyre. But for this however I will manage quite right. How can people live with these dogs? As usual I have run away with my paper & must come to a stop without the usual messages, apologies to all. Let them be taken as read.

MONTOIRE. NEAR VENDÔME.
Sunday. 23 August 1908

DEAR MOTHER

Here goes for one more Sunday letter: I don't suppose there'll be another one this trip: however I can't quite make out how long I'm going to be: the last 3 days have upset all calculations.

I wrote from Chalus, and next morning I rode to Montbrun, a most charming little castle with xii cent. keep: it is really, architecturally a most important place. Thence with a disappointment or two (this sounds nothing but it meant 30 miles wasted) I reached Angoulême & passed on down the Charente to Cognac, near Saintes: being Monday I rode powerfully: on Saturday there are always hills & a wind against: funny, isn't it? At Saintes next morning I got your p.c.'s visited Taillebourg (a great failure) Tonnay Boutonne (worse) and so through to Niort which was magnificent; nothing could possibly have been more opportune or more interesting for my thesis. The castle is composed of two Norman keeps, each square, & quite ordinary inside, but outside each has a tower at each corner, & a little turret in between;

so—

The corner towers are quite solid: in fact as I learnt at Loches, they

are only buttresses. Loches is so— regular flat Norman

buttresses, but with a semicircular projection down the middle of
each: and at Montbazon, where we have the second stage so—

The Niort people simply ran the two corner buttresses into one: I
think this will interest Father, & so give it contrary to usual habit:
you'll excuse it I know though it is talking "shop". From Niort I rode
towards Poitiers, turning aside at Montreuil Bellay, which castle
Richard I is supposed to have built. The doorway bears an inscription
in, I think, Arabic characters:—it has never been translated: I hope my
photo will be clear enough to be read, but it was in a very difficult
place. From Montreuil I worked into Parthenay (head wind, hills every
kilometre etc. etc.) which is a charmingly quaint place, and the home
of the romance of Melusine: the beautiful lady who turned into a
snake every now & then. Unhappily the castle which her spirit used to
haunt has been most barbarously destroyed: therefore the "roman de
Partheney" must remain unillustrated. From Parthenay I rode to
Bressiure but found nothing worth study, either there or at Cerizay:
result I found myself that evening Thursday, near Thouars, and next
day reached Chinon about 12. Chinon is very fine indeed, (the French
Windsor for its associations & place in history) but much destroyed.
What there is, is of the xiii & xiv cents.: as it was not therefore useful
to me I proceeded to Loches, arriving on Friday evening, six days
before I had thought possible! I can't imagine how I did it: the result
may be my reaching you a little earlier, or my doing a little more out
here. At Loches I found letters from Will & Scroggs & p.c.'s from you:
the last was dated the 18th just after my p.c. had come asking for
money I expect. If you sent it to Loches it will follow me to Falaise:
if not I'll get it there direct from you. Falaise pretty quick in about
4 days or 5 I expect, but cannot really say, lately I have quite outrun
all my designs. The 5 or 6 castles to come, if important as they sound,
should delay me 4 days at least. Loches, to continue was splendid, a huge
Norman keep in excellent preservation, & its corner buttresses with

little colonettes as per plan. There is also a church with very fine Romanesque W. door & narthex. Yesterday I left Loches which by the way, Chimp {Frank}, should be celebrated as the residence of Rupert Holliday, {in *Cornet of Horse*, by G. A. Henty} and rode through Montbazon, the second keep with round buttresses, to Tours. Here I would not stop, even for the shrine of the blessed Martin over whom Gregory waxes so triumphant, but came right on to Montoire where I am writing at the present moment in the cheapest bedroom of the only hotel in the place. This may conjure up visions of distressful poverty & wretchedness in your mind but cheer up: I'm paying 3 francs a night for it, and it contains two or three tables half a dozen chairs, wardrobes etc. etc. Bed has spring mattress (box spring) & all "modern comforts" as the advts. say: still I prefer my polished boards of the "midi" to extra pile carpets, & extra piled bills. No mosquitoes, thank goodness, but alas no cicalas! Montoire has a rebuilt church (which has the impudence to call itself restored), a Norman keep unrestored but also uninteresting, & two kilomètres off the finest feudal ruins in the valleys of the Loire, Loir, Indre, and Cher, or so the prospectus says. They really are very good.

Tomorrow I run up & about in a very small compass of land, seeing castles: then I take a lively sprint through Orleans to the gates of Paris (or Etampes ἁπλῷ λογῳ), and so worm my way against what I hope will be a less furious W. wind to Falaise & Grandville. If you're in any doubt about what to do with your money, send it to Dinard: with a speed leg such as I unearthed last week I could be in Jersey tomorrow. I have not a ghost of an idea how long I'll take. Do you know I am among my own people at last? There are English servants at the hotels, English notices in all show places, all the world takes tea at 5 or 4 p.m., English visitors in every ruin, English goods in every shop? 'Tis worse with Americans than at Stratford on Avon: at Chinon a party of 13 looking round the castle was composed of 12 twangs & myself: it is an awful state of affairs, for as each twang bowed to the guide at the exit, he left 1 f. in his "itching palm". Could I have done less? (I didn't so the question has only an academic interest:—yet such proceedings are not productive of economy). By the way did the "old age pension" scheme get through? If the English nation has accepted such an impudent pauperisation of all its old wasters, & penalisation of all its old workers, then . . . I'll become a young Turk. Really with the facts of history & political economy staring him in the face no man above vote-catching tactics should have hesitated about it for a moment. I have bought a copy of Hérédia's *Trophées*, really fairly printed & produced, though of course unbound for 3 fs. Hérédia is a living French poet, & a great one, almost the only man today whose works will survive him and really they are wonderfully good. At present in about 7 years they have run through 38 editions, & he refuses to print any more! Really he must be a man well worth knowing. What do you think of this

	"La Terre maternelle et douce aux anciens Dieux
From a description	"Fait à chaque printemps, vainement éloquente
of the present state	"Au chapiteau brisé verdir une autre acanthe
of a temple	"Mais l'Homme indifférent au rêve des aïeux
in Greece.	"Ecoute sans frémir, du fond des nuits sereines
	"La Mer qui se lamente en pleurant les Sirènes."

Could anything be more perfect artistically? This is half of the first piece, & the others seem as good. I am promising myself great pleasure in reading them, since the Bodleian has no copy, and the Union has had its stolen. Well now Mother dear once more my $2\frac{1}{2}$d. worth of paper is filled up, and I have such heaps & heaps more to tell you of all the beauties of the rivers & the sunsets and the buildings I have lately seen. But the bell is going for dinner (3 f. this is not starvation at any rate) and I must hop off or I won't get two helpings of soup & haricots.

```
               - - M - - T - - W - - Th. ┐
┌ - S - - - - - - - - - - F - - - - - - - - - - - - - ┘
└ - - - Sunday - - - - Mon. - - - - Tues. - - - - Wed.
```
NED

LAIGLE
28th August 1908

DEAR MOTHER

This is Friday night, but if I could get this letter off tomorrow night you may get it before Wednesday, since I am now so close. I feel quite at home in Normandy. From Montoire I rode by way of Lavardin, which is magnificent mostly of the xiii & xiv cents, with excellent carving, to Mondoubleau which the guidebooks called ix cent. Really it was an enormous keep of the latest xii: the interesting part was the doorway, which I planned. The tower leans at such an angle that I easily climbed up the outside face! From Mondoubleau I went to Vendôme, a very poor place after all the froth that the guide books have covered it with, is blown away, and thence to Fréteval, which is almost incredibly concentric but xii cent. all the same—a marvellous fortress. Next day came wandering round byroads, culminating in a splendid run up the Loire to Orleans, which is all monuments and P.P. Cards of Joan of Arc, the cathedral is however good in spite of it. I slept at St. Lyé, a hamlet. Next day was a gale or half of one against: I saw Etampes, interesting xiith & arrived late at Chartres very tired.

I expected that Chartres would have been like most French Cathedrals spoilt by restoration, so I slipped out before breakfast to "do" it. What I found I cannot describe—it is absolutely untouched & unspoilt, in superb preservation, & the noblest building (for Beauvais is only half a one) that I have ever seen, or expect to see. If only you could get an idea of its beauty, of its perfection, without going to look at it! Its date is late xiith & early xiii cent. It is not enormous; but the carvings on its 3 portals are as fine as the best of all Greek work. Till yesterday I would put no sculptors near the Greeks of the Vth cent. Today the French of the early middle ages *may* be inferior, but I do not think so: nothing in imagination could be grander than that arrangement of three huge cavernous portals, (30 odd feet deep), of gigantic height, with statues everywhere for pillars, bas-reliefs for plain surfaces, statuettes & canopies for mouldings. The whole wall of the cathedral is chased & wrought like a Florentine plaque, and by master hands! You may think the individual figures stiff—the details coarse—everything is hard & narrow I admit, but when you see the whole—when you can conceive at once the frame *and* the picture, then you must admit that nothing could be greater, except it were the Parthenon as it left the hands of Pheidias: it must be one of the noblest works of man, as it is the finest of the middle ages. One cannot describe it in anything but superlatives, and these seem so wretchedly formal that I am half tempted to scratch out everything that I have written: Chartres is Chartres:—that is, a gallery built by the sculptors to enclose a finer collection than the Elgin Marbles. I went in, as I said, before breakfast, & I left when dark:—all the day I was running from one door to another, finding in each something I thought finer than the one I had just left, and then returning to find that the finest was that

Lamballe. Rood Screen (*See p.* 59)

Holy Water Stoop. Dinan

in front of me—for it is a place absolutely impossible to imagine, or to recollect, at any rate for me: it is overwhelming, and when night came I was absolutely exhausted, drenched to the skin (it had poured all day) and yet with a feeling I had never had before in the same degree—as though I had found a path (a hard one) as far as the gates of Heaven, and had caught a glimpse of the inside, the gate being ajar. You will understand how I felt though I cannot express myself. Certainly Chartres is the sight of a lifetime, a place truly in which to worship God. The middle ages were truer that way than ourselves, in spite of their narrowness and hardness and ignorance of the truth as we complacently put it: the truth doesn't matter a straw, if men only believe what they say or are willing to show that they do believe something. Chartres besides has the finest late xvi & early xvii bas-reliefs in the world, and is beautiful in its design & its proportions. I have bought all the picture post-cards, but they are of course hardly a ghost of the reality, nothing ever could be, though photography is best for such works. I took a photo myself of Philosophus, a most delightful little statuette, about 18 inches high: if not fogged, (I forgot to lock my camera, & somebody has fiddled with it), it may give one an idea of how the smallest parts of the building are finished with as much care as the centre-posts of the main doorways, and if Philosophus were of Greek marble there would be photographs of him in every album, between the Hermes of Praxiteles & the Sophocles of the Lateran. He is great work. I also tried to take a photo. of the masterpiece, the Christ of the south portal, but that cannot be worth looking at. I expect I will burn my photos. of Chartres as soon as they are visible. Yet perhaps with care & time, one would get something worthy from a photograph. We must return there (I would want assistants) and spend a fortnight in pure happiness.

{On a picture postcard of the Rue du Jerzual, Dinan, addressed to Mrs. Lawrence, 2 Polstead Road, Oxford.}

Friday evening (4 *Sept.*). {Postmarked 1908}

At Dinan now. Will very much admires: we are wondering if you went across today, not a bad time. Wrote however to St. Helier's & Guernsey. Return to Oxford Tuesday night. Monday in Jersey. Are taking it easy & spending royally.

NED

Monday night, 21 June 1909. {On board P. & O. S.S. *Mongolia.*}

We arrive Gibraltar early tomorrow: so I am scrawling this tonight: it is only in case Arnie hasn't got all the Gib. stamps: if he has he can exchange. Nothing whatever has happened: I caught the special train with 27 seconds to spare, & found only about 40 people with me: most of them 1st class passengers: the boat is therefore nearly empty, and thanks to my Arabic Grammar I haven't had to speak to anybody yet—except a Jerusalemite (? Jebusite), with whom I talk wonderful Syrian at mealtimes. There has been no wind, and so no illness on board: but very cold. Inform Will parts of Spain are visible (by day-light): not distinguished in any way. Will you look on the second shelf in the Photographic Shop, on the right, about half way down, & you will see my red cloth wrapped round a packet of Cristoid films (or two packets & an envelope rather). These I meant to put in the Linen Cupboard or other dry place: the other shop is too damp for any length of time. There is a packet of plates in my top long drawer (bedroom) which might be stored also. We only stop at Gibraltar a couple of hours.

NED

P.S. Palestine Syrian wants to come with me on my trip: which is consoling but I would have to pay for him. Will would like my table in the saloon anthropologically: a French girl, & a German male, a Swede, two Spaniards, an Indian of some sort, an Italian, an Arab, and a Greek. Swede, & Hindu talk English: to all the others I translated a notice about the landing at Gibraltar: the Spaniards didn't seem to know much about my version of their language. Greek swore I wrote like Demosthenes, but "steam tug" I'm sure has no classical equivalent.

P. & O. S.S. *Mongolia*
Wed. night. 23 June 1909

These people (poor Arnie!) don't keep crested notepaper: tell him it's not my fault. Of course nothing has happened since Gibraltar: it is very pretty indeed in the bay—nothing at all in the town itself, except the Rock dominating everything: like a faint reminiscence of Beauvais from the "grande place". Also the Sierra Navadas looked attractive: they are very wild & jagged, but the colouring is splendid. We reach Marseilles tomorrow morning, & stay 24 hours. On average this boat does 360 miles a day (24 hrs. of course), & P. Said is 4½ days from Marseilles. Boat rolls like a turnip, but nobody has been ill: an officer said in 18 years he had never known the Bay (Biscay) so disappointing! I can't say anything else. I do nothing all day but Arabic.

NED

Next letter from Beyrout in about 10 days probably: unless I have to wait in Port Said for the Syrian boat, which appears probable.

Let me have the results of the Exams. when out: E. F. Hall, Miller, Richards etc.

Get Will, (if he goes to France with a bicycle) to write well beforehand to the C.T.C. for their special Customs ticket (or Father should . . .). It will save him in ignorance of French some embarrassment, and costs nothing. If they try to press on him a number plate at the same time, let him refuse. No Gendarme would expect one on a traveller for a moment; and if he's touring let him *always* see his bedroom, and get its price before he decides. The C.T.C. foreign handbook in Father's room is fairly up to date. He should carry a repair band in his pouch, *and valve tubing*.

P. & O. S.S. *Mongolia*
Tuesday, 29 June 1909

There really has nothing happened since Marseilles. I wonder if you got my p.c. In case not give Bob my condolences: at the same time it keeps our family free from the taint of scientific learning. I settled with my Sunday School boys before I left.

From Marseilles we passed through between Corsica and Sardinia—both looked attractive though it was a little late in the evening. Next day we passed Stromboli—smoke capped—and the Straits of Messina. Charybdis still maintains a remarkable current; the ship was deflected a good deal from her course. Messina, the town, looks in a very poor way; but it was too dark to make out details. Then past Crete, to this morning when we have just sighted Egypt. I have not been able to get anything positive about the Beyrout boats. There may be one in the harbour, in which case this letter will be unfinished. If not I may have to wait till Sunday (I'd go to Cairo or somewhere). A sea voyage is a monotonous waste of time for me. One feels disinclined to work, though I have managed a couple of hours talking and some 6 hours reading (of Arabic) daily. Without it I would have perished, or over-eaten! Some photos. of Mecca may arrive for me some day—preserve them please. The weather has not been at all hot so far, though it is getting better that way.

Boat on Thursday. In Beyrout Saturday Morn. Mail just starting. This is a complete set of stamps tell Arnie

10 Milliemes = 1 Piastre = $2\frac{1}{2}$.

PORT SAID
Friday, July 2, 1909

DEAR MOTHER (the rest are understood)

I am still at P. Said, for yesterday's boat by which I should have gone to Beyrout was full up of a large party of Russian pilgrims: the next two boats start on Sunday night. It is a nuisance for P. Said is not a lovely place, and if I had had the 5 nights clear I could have gone to Cairo, or to Damietta or somewhere interesting. The above is a very glorified version of my hotel. Concerning P. Said there is not very much to say. It dates of course from the time of the Canal, it is growing enormously rapidly. It is divided into two parts, separated by a "plain" 200 yards wide. On the E. is the European quarter (European is a mixture of Greeks, Italians, French, Armenians, Turks, Russians, Germans, Spanish, Portuguese, & English (very few)). In the native town they have all the other native races on earth. I have got hold of a most cosmopolitan Abyssinian (he calls himself (and his country) Ethiopia) who points out all the types to me, and enlarges on their qualities. So far there have only been three genuine desert Bedouins, but hosts of Jews, & Orthodox Greek priests, Coptic women, and Turks, Berbers, and Hindustani.

The Abyssinian talks eleven languages, & amongst them Arabic perfectly. I can make myself understood in it, but cannot, except rarely, follow a long conversation. The Abyssinian has been over all my ground in Palestine & Syria, and tells me that everywhere it will be cooler than this, and I don't feel this hot in the least. The thermometer is fairly steady from 81 at bedtime to 89 at midday: a very slight variation don't you think? In Port Said there is great bathing, on a very rough, shallow beach, of glorious sand: there is no end to the sand, one finds it all over the streets & in the coffee, & in the beds. The water is so warm that the bathers can loaf about in it for hours: in any case if they were cold, they would only have to stand in the sun for half a minute. The light is incredibly strong: anything in the shape of artistic photography absolutely impossible. I have bought a colour screen, which I will use permanently, in the hope of softening down some of the contrasts. For food in this place the Arabs seem to depend almost entirely on bread, water melons, and grapes, & this with figs, prickly pears, and ordinary fruits will be my diet in Palestine, according to my Abyssinian (he was educated at the American College in Beyrout). Do you remember Mr. Schor; a Jewish lecturer in Oxford many years ago? He lives here it appears: the Abyssinian knows them very well. Inform Will that an Abyssinian looks a cross between a Greek and a Hindu, but with crisp curled hair, like a negro. Their noses are however straight & their mouths good; from our point of view. They seem to be largely in the police & coast guard in Egypt. I went up yesterday to look at the Canal: it is wider than I expected, nearly 200 yards I should say, but the soft nature of the banks makes it necessary to grade them very gently, so that there is only a narrow strip in the middle for a boat to pass along. When two boats meet, one of them draws into the bank, into a cutting called a station, which occur at regular intervals. All ships carry searchlights at night, it looks very pretty. I do hope I will get off next Sunday, for this is a horrible place, & I want to be beginning my tour. I believe though that I have to remain in quarantine for some days at Jaffa, on account of some illness in the town.

Sat. I am definitely starting tomorrow, so that is most satisfactory. At the same time thanks to the Abyssinian I have seen far more in P. Said than I would ever have done in the ordinary way. Tell Arnie I eat water-melons every day, (they cost about 1d. each bigger than footballs), & peaches & apricots & grapes. All drinks from coffee to water have lumps of ice floating about in them, and ices also appear at all meals. The heat is nothing at all to grumble about: I don't know when my next letter will be: it is rather soon to write from Beyrout unless I have something to tell you. Still I will at any rate write in a week or two. I sent p.c.'s to Florence & Nellie from Marseilles: others later from Syria.

NED

BEYROUT
Tuesday. July 6th, 1909

DEAR MOTHER

I reached Beyrout about 6 this morning, and Cook's man put me through the Customs most excellently: they have ways & means! Today is most delightfully warm, & the bay of Beyrout lovely. From Port Said we steamed in 18 hours to Jaffa: then up the coast from Cæsarea to Haifa (Carmel) then past Acre, Sidon, Tyre etc., here. Beyrout itself is picturesque. Today I have spent in visiting: the Consul got a wire last Saturday saying that 2 Iradés have been posted to me: they should arrive shortly, but the Turkish P.O. is irregular. Then to the American College which breaks up today. The tutors (young Americans) have been taking walking tours in their summer holidays for years, exactly as I propose to do. On Thursday I start with a party of them (5) down the coast: we may keep together for a week or more. The country is quite quiet. Beyrout opened an electric tram service today: but the streets are too narrow. Mr. Parfit has moved out to the mountains 6 miles away for the summer. Letters from Gib. are very slow: I expect you got the Marseilles one first. Strange wet weather sounds! Here even English people don't talk about the weather. Saying "Fine day" for 6 months they found monotonous. Richards has done well: I am writing to him. I will, I expect, be gone from Beyrout about a fortnight: so I will get any letters on my return. After you get this one you may write (for any time up to a month) to P. R. Aleppo. I may get it: after that again Beyrout. I will sleep on Thursday night at Sidon, on Fri. at Tyre, & on Satur. at Acre. Then next to Haifa & Athlit (just south). From Athlit to Haifa again; by train to Beisan & up through Tiberias to Safed. Then to Banias & from there to Sidon & Beyrout. Any map (if you can't find any of mine) will show these places, and it will give you an idea of my movements for the next fortnight or 3 weeks. Don't worry about the heat its only comfortable, or about the food, for nobody eats meat hardly, with bread of various kinds, water-melons by the score (its merely ordinary to eat a whole one), figs, pears, peaches, plums, apples, grapes, prickly pears, cucumbers, apricots, & others unidentified.

I am setting out to enjoy myself, as everybody, from the Consul downwards, tells me that travelling is as ordinary as in Europe. Cook has a permanent camp at Petra, the brute! Tell Worm that this letter is going by the English P.O. There are also French, German, Austrian, Russian & Turkish Post Offices. Will he let me know what stamps he wants of these? I can't get him complete sets of all without bankruptcy, & they are all different apparently. You will find this letter hard to read I expect: but there are sufficient young eyes in the family to manage it. Thank Will for his letter, and for most excellent quote from *Theocritus*. I brought it out with enormous effect in the College Common Room this afternoon: a reputation as a classical scholar is easily gained. My Arabic is getting fairly fluent: all Beyrout fruits & drinks are covered with snow brought down each morning from Hermon. The sun does not however rise till about 4 & it is dark at 8. Quite a short day to us when you take out the 3 middle hours. I have bought a sun-helmet & a water-bottle. Such a disjointed letter but one cannot compose fluently, with a hesitating nib. Tell Arnie the streets are full of camels, donkeys, & mules, & of millions & billions of dogs. The Consul here has asked me to keep in touch with him, in case local governors are obstreperous.

Safed

July 17, 1909

Dear Mother   *Arabic all right.*

I am writing to you quite unexpectedly, as an opportunity has presented itself. From Beyrout I walked to Sidon, along the coast-road: seeing very little of importance, except the Arab site of Jonah's coming ashore from his fish. Being a carriage road the walking was easy, & I did the 30 miles to Sidon quite easily in the day. One of the Americans fell ill, & so their tour was postponed. At Sidon I spent the next day (Sat.) sightseeing, & antiquity hunting (tell Will I was offered a very nice little terracotta head (about 4 ins. high) for £2). The American missionaries to whom I had introductions, have a splendid collection of seal rings (Roman & Greek) & a few statuettes. Then I walked inland to Nabatiyeh, & from there to Banias, & from there here in about a week. There were no troubles or incidents, (except the charring of my finger-top in a magnesium flame) & throughout I found the people most hospitable. The roads in Palestine are awful: either they are basalt, or limestone, in huge blocks, often a couple of feet high, & with smaller ones strewn about at random. As the whole country is made up of these stones it is a little difficult sometimes to distinguish the road.

When one has found it one proceeds gaily by jumping from one stone to another, & as they are all angular, & some of them tottering, progress is painful. Occasionally however I found a road made of little stones no bigger than my fist or even of dust, & then I made good way. The country is fearfully hilly, no level ground at all, except in the L. Huleh plain. The roads are never at rest, indeed climbs & descents of 1500–2000 feet into valleys (usually dry) & up the most scorching hillsides are regular things. So that walking any distance is hard work, my average is only about 20 miles a day, & the people here think that good. I have not been footsore at all, & my clothes & baggage have been quite satisfactory. I approve of the food: it consists of a very dry, thin, wafer-like bread, flexible, tough as leather, and in cakes of 2 feet across usually. I can manage one at a meal, if with plenty of milk (I drink a lot of this) or leben (which is horrible). Up country one cannot get much fruit beyond figs, & grapes: still pomegranates, cucumbers, tomatoes, & prickly pears are fairly common. Water of course is abundant, & good in all this mountain district, but everything is terribly brown: an olive tree is a delight to the eyes.

I sleep variously—one night at a Greek priest's, three nights in native houses (or on top of them), one with a doctor (Syrian, from New York) & the rest in the open air. I like the latter best on the whole. Today I am spending with the London Jews Soc. Missionary & his wife: I may stay here till Monday, as there have just been important discoveries of passages in the castle mound here, which I am to explore with him and Dr. Anderson after dark. Therefore you may picture me to yourself as living in the most civilised surroundings, in an English family. "She" comes from Abingdon. They are most hospitable, indeed all the missionaries have been.

I will be back in Beyrout in 10 days or quite possible 15: don't expect a letter till it comes, when I will tell you something of my tour: this has been intentionally a personal letter, & is only to fill a gap in time. So far I have enjoyed myself greatly, except for 258 flea-bites on my right fore-arm. Remainder in proportion: fearfully dirty places.

{This letter was written while he was resting during a bad attack of fever.}

HOTEL VICTORIA. BEYROUT
2 *August* 1909

DEAR MOTHER

I have now got back to Beyrout, in my former quarters, & therefore the first part of my work out here is finished. I think after all it will be best if I simply send you a very long account of everything that has happened in the last month, just as it occurs to me now. Of course there will be a tremendous lot missed out, to be remembered later on in scraps as occasion arrives: but on the whole it will give you an idea of Northern Palestine in summer. At the same time, Will, no purple patches for me: I never relished them myself, except done by a man like Ruskin: and also after a month's walking I am not quite inclined for any gambolling. Likewise, as I don't know whether you may not like to lend this production, strictly personal stuff will be banished to the last sheet.

First of all it is hot out here—not unbearable, and at times under the shade of a tree, near running water the climate is almost pleasant: but generally it is too warm. The temperature is not very high; of course I have not much means of finding out, but in Beyrout itself it is settled at just under 90° day & night: that is what makes it trying: with a cool evening one could enjoy the heat of the day: but there is hardly any variation to be discovered. Inland, up the mountains, it is cooler, though when one gets among large rocks one is stifled: they seem almost to give off a vapour, or heat-breath, that is horrible; add to that a sirocco, a wind that shrivels every green thing it meets, that blisters one's face & hands, & makes one feel that one is walking towards some gigantic oven; and you get an idea of vast possibilities. Round about Galilee and along the Jordan Valley is the hottest part of the country, & at Tiberias, where I stayed a couple of nights, it was 106° & 105° at midday in the back of the hall of the hotel:—and that felt cool as an icehouse in comparison with the outer air! (there was a block of ice melting there all day). After that Will will not be disgusted to learn that the Lake of Galilee, & the lower Jordan are lukewarm at all times, and that near Tiberias are hot springs, rising at 180° degrees. However this should be enough for the climate: it has not prevented my walking about and sightseeing as I chose nor have I had to take a siesta at midday, though

it is a habit that residents in the country soon fall into. I left Beyrout
not long after the beginning of July, & walked straight to Sidon (30
miles or so). It was very pleasant, along the sea-shore the whole way;
beginning with sand-hills & mulberry plantations; (for all N. Syria
battens on silk-worms): it gradually improved to olive yards, &
finally arrived at sterility and empty sarcophagi, at Heldua, a famous
place once, & now so freshly, for there I first tasted native bread &
leben. Native bread is of two kinds, one, with small loaves, about 6–10
inches across, circular, & of double thickness of material: it is lumpy
outside, but not thinner than cardboard of some stoutness, & when
fresh very good. Everybody likes to eat it hot, & when I get to a house
in its district & ask for a loaf (proffering a half-penny) the woman goes
out at once with her tray, made of straw closely woven, so as to be
quite stiff, about 2 feet in diameter, slightly concave, on which are
loaves already mixed up but not cooked, & in about 6 minutes she is
back with the whole thing ready, sprinkled with grains of sesame &
cummin, is it? I forget. At any rate bread No. 1 is good, when not dry.
I think you saw a loaf some years ago at the {C.M.S. Centenary}
Exhibition in Oxford. Bread No. 2 is more doubtful. It is light grey
in colour, deepening to brown, very large, sometimes up to 3 feet
across, & of course circular. It is very thin, quite as thin as ordinary
brown paper, tough, & pliable, almost leathery when fresh, but when
dry becoming brittle like a cheese biscuit or oatcake (it really does
rather resemble oatcake, though not one third as thick). To bake it they
plaster it against the side of the oven, so that on the surface it is lightly
dusted with clay. To eat leben, or burghul (boiled wheat) with it (the
regular thing) one tears off a small part of one's loaf, & doubles it up
into a spoon or poke-bonnet shape:—this then makes a splendid dipper.
Leben is when fresh rather thin and lumpy: when old it gets like cheese
(cream-cheese that is) and has a distinctly acid taste. In colour it is pure
white, with a sourish smell. Everybody tells me that it is quite distinct
from butter-milk, not nearly so good, & some of these informants
were Irish & Scotch women, who may be trusted. Leben certainly is
not worth much, though it is nastily-refreshing if one is hot, and makes
the bread go down. So far I have not found a European who approves
of it, except some Americans of Sidon, who were accustomed to eat it
with equal bulk of sugar, almost like crême goûtée: I tried it so, and
it was palatable. Now I am on the food question I had better go

through with it. On the march one begins with breakfast; (by the way this diet is only my lunacy, and the native habit: no other European would think of it): if I have slept the night in a native house then it will be "Haleeb" ordered overnight. The people do not usually take this, since it is fresh milk, (boiled, or heated rather, they fight shy of it cold), with quantities of sugar in it. They prefer their milk soured as a rule: though some take haleeb. With this will be eaten a sheet of bread No. 2 (the more common variety). If I feel thirsty after it they bring me a bowl of prickly pears, & cut them open for me till I am satisfied. Prickly pears are the cheapest, most plentiful fruit, very refreshing, above all in the cool of the morning, &, with all the rind cut away, the prickles are never happened on. Then at midday I eat another sheet of bread (usually brought with me from stopping place; No. 2 is not bad dry) next a spring, if there is one: if not it is consumed on the march, moistened with an occasional drop from my waterbottle. Sometimes, but only in exceptional country I can get figs, or even grapes or water melons: when I can there is great feasting: nothing is more refreshing than to march for an hour up a dusty road, eating the melon in one's arms: it is as pleasant as loitering in a country lane in England: here we have water-melons football size, streaming with juice, for 2d. I wish there were more places where one could find them. Grapes are very sickly things mostly: though not the best sort, long banana shaped, green ones. These are rare. Figs are very small & poor: pomegranates hardly ripe: tomatoes one can often get, & they are refreshing, when they are cool: cucumbers very plentiful & pleasant. Apricots of course are finished, & apples only cultivated & very badly near Beyrout. Still one can get along in Palestine for fruit. In the evening I get, either bread & leben, or more rarely haleeb. Sometimes I have to join in the native burghul, which is wheat, boiled in some way I fancy, but very greasy. One could not eat much of it, without a river near at hand to help it down. There are I believe other native dishes, but not among the peasant class at this time of year: I at least have found none, though the priests (native Arabs) give me stews & meat-messes of divers sorts. Nobody drinks anything but water, except coffee, for visitors. When I go into a native house the owner salutes me, & I return it and then he says something to one of his women, and they bring out a thick quilt, which, doubled, is laid on the rush mat over the floor as a chair: on that I squat down, & then the host asks me four or five times how my health is, and each time I tell him it is good. Then comes sometimes coffee, and after that a variety of questions, as to whether my tripod is a revolver, & what I am, and where I come from, & where I'm going, & why I'm on foot, & am I alone, and every other thing conceivable: and when I set up my tripod (sometimes, as a great treat) there are cries of astonishment and "Mashallah's," "By the life of the Prophet," "Heavens," "Give God the glory" etc. etc. Such a curiosity has never been seen and all the village is summoned to look at it. Then I am asked about my wife & children, how many I have etc. I really feel a little ashamed of my youth out here. The Syrian of 16 is full grown, with moustache & beard, married, with children, & has perhaps spent two or three years in New York, getting together enough capital to start him in business at home. They mostly put my age as 15, and are amazed at my travelling on foot & alone. Riding is the only honourable way of going, & everyone is dreadfully afraid of thieves: they travel very little. However; meanwhile the women have been getting my evening meal, served up on one of those large straw dishes I mentioned: (the "charger" for John the Baptist's head is translated by this in the Arabic version) then they pour water on my hands from a pitcher (they have spouts like Breton cider jugs— I'll bring one home) and if very polite, will offer to wash my feet. The next thing is bed, which is the same quilt as that on which I am sitting, laid either in the house, or outside on the roof of an outbuilding or veranda. Another quilt on top acts as blanket & also there are pillows. These quilts are of course far too hot for a European to stand, since they are stuffed with wool, & feathers & fleas (in about equal quantities I fancy), so usually I lie on both mine, and hope for the best. One goes to bed soon after 9, & gets up at sunrise (about 4.30). Dressing consists of smoothing one's hair, and moistening one's hands & face in the stream from the pitcher: then on the road after bread & leben. Sometimes the people of the house will take money for one's lodging, sometimes not.

The houses are usually of one storey, built of mud, with door and unglazed window, shuttered in the daytime. The floor is of clay, very often of two levels, the upper for humans, the lower for animals, with mangers in between (the animals are usually goats: sometimes cows; or even a horse). Over the floor are laid rush-mats, of long reeds 5 feet long & an inch across. There is no furniture except a few little stools, of wood & rush (about 8 inches high) a large chest, often inlaid, with bone or mother-of-pearl, and the straw dishes hanging on the walls. There will also be a large, bed like recess, for holding the quilts: in better class houses the room will be situated above the stables, and so at the end will be a kind of veranda, or terrace: the roofs of the dwelling rooms are not usually used. When they are pieces of mud drop all night through the brush & poplar poles that hold them up. The people are pleasant: very childish & simple of course, & startlingly ignorant, but so far quite honest. Very many of the men in all the mountain villages have visited America, & they love to display their English before their fellow-villagers. Once or twice they have tried to overcharge me excessively, but to their minds every Englishman is a Croesus: so one can hardly blame them. They usually wear baggy trousers, & short coats, or shirts, with a sash round their waist, but further from the coast they approximate nearly to the Bedouin dress: for head-gear, sometimes the fez, sometimes the keffiyieh, the black coiled rope of the desert Arab. They all carry revolvers, some of them guns, & you see them ploughing in the fields, or eating at home in a belt of 150 cartridges: enough for a campaign: however I had better get back to Sidon. All along the coast of course I skirted the Lebanon; from underneath a hill in Palestine looks entirely barren: from on top one finds that it is all terraces and has been cultivated: now all the corn is cut so that all day one walks over varying greys, and browns, & whites, & reds, never a touch of green, except small thorny oaks or at times a fig tree where there is water under the surface: one does so rejoice in a spring! There was nothing interesting on my road, except the place where according to the Arabs Jonah was cast ashore. Sidon was interesting its streets are so narrow, & all built over above with houses: some were so narrow that 2 men could only with difficulty pass, and in others I had to bend even my head to pass: no wheeled vehicle can enter the gates. There are two castles, one standing on a mound of purple shells: neither very interesting: it is astonishing to see the number of antiquities dug up continually in Sidon: the neighbourhood is a perfect treasure ground. I was offered a small, perfect, Anadyomene (2nd Cent. B.C. probably) for £60; the lucky man bought it from the finder for £5! There are other nice pieces of carving, and terracottas, much glass, & dozens of seal-stones (many forged) however those do not appeal to you. From Sidon (this letter is getting too long) I had a

long hot walk over waterless hills to Nabatiyeh, the Metawileh (Xtian)
Headquarters in the hills. It is near the elbow that the lower course of
the Litani makes: as the town was in fête I had the usual things to look
at, the people in the shops chaffering over infinitesimal sums, sweetmeat sellers, the icedrink man who sells syrups, crying out "Take care
of thy teeth" or "Refresh thy heart," "This for a metallick" ($\frac{1}{2}d$.), or
the man with plain water in a goatskin with brass spout, then the fruit-
sellers, "if an old woman eats my cress she is young tomorrow"; and
funniest of all men with woman's ornaments crying "appease your
mother in law", and then as you are looking on at this comes a hoarse
gasp of dahrak (your back) and a porter crashes into you with a fresh-
killed sheep on his back, or a load of charcoal, or perhaps a camel loafs
through the crowd with its bell round its neck giving notice. If anyone
neglects this warning they are knocked down like ninepins: camels
seem irresistible. They are extraordinarily common at this season for all
the corn of Bashan & the Hauran & Esdrælon is coming down to the
coast, & all the nomads, who draw to the Jordan in summer for its
water, hire out their stock to the farmers. It is very sweet listening to
the ringing of the varied bells of a caravan of half a hundred camels in
a valley: all the roughness of the tone, and the growling & grunting
& cursing of the animals themselves is lost at a little distance. They
have horrible faces, and keep up a running flow of apparently the most
fearful language as they walk: a camel always looks discontented, and
apparently never misbehaves. However I can't discuss the town life
this letter, or nobody will ever get to bed (from a strict sense of duty
to an absent brother of course). At Nabatiyeh I got a guide or chaperon
or whatever you like to call it (male!) to go to Banias whose people
have the finest castle, and the worst reputation in S. Lebanon. First of
all though we went to a splendid castle Kalaa't el S'ch'k'if (perhaps you
had better call it Beaufort) a fine fortress (early xiii) well situated above
the Litani about 1600 above sea level. The view was very good up and
down the said sea coast, and along the Litani gorge for 20 miles. A
stone I threw from the chapel windows fell spattering after two re-
bounds into the river 1600 feet below. Across the low foothills & plain
of the Jordan springs to the E. we could see Hermon, still with snow
in its valleys, and the mountains of Bashan and to the North half the
Lebanon. Southward hills near Safed and Nazareth rather blocked the
view. Still even so it was fine and very refreshing to catch a breeze, &

find a spring of water on the top. We had then to get down to the river, which meant dancing down a goat path for an hour: the worst of it was my man proved to be a wonderful singer, the best of his district, and there was an echo in the gorge. He yelled all the time like a Syren (of the modern sort). Still just before we got to the bottom the sun managed to join (it only shines there at midday) so I had a delightful bathe. The river was shallow (up to 5 feet deep) with a raging current and full of rocks. No swimming was possible; one just hung on a rock and waved about in its eddy like a fish's tail. Still it served to wash the dust off. The banks of course were all oleanders so that generally the colouring was satisfactory. Unfortunately the water was very cold.

We then climbed the other bank, fortunately only about a thousand feet high and slept for the night in a village near the top and next day reached Banias, (Cæsarea Philippi), on a hill above the plain of Huleh, the swampy lake North of Galilee. There is level ground intersected by numerous feeders of the Jordan which really rises from the lake, for some 5 miles to the N. of the water. Tell Arnie that pelicans are common, & ugly, and that jackals are too numerous to trouble much about. The Arabs call them 'ibn Wawi, sons of owls, from the noise they please themselves in making at night when one wants to go to sleep. Every stone has got its lizard on top or underneath, but scorpions and centipedes are rare, and snakes not very common. Of the other animals I have seen several herds of gazelles in the hills, and a few badgers & wolves. But Palestine is not a very inviting country for anything living. There is an ever-present plague of flies and everything in the world that bites. However we went across the plain with great joy for it meant soft roads & green fields until we reached Banias a small enough village now, but with a wonderful spring (you will find admirable descriptions in *The Crescent and the Cross* by Warburton or in *The Land and the Book* by Thompson) "purple patches" both of them. Over the spring which rises in a hidden cave is a niche with Greek inscription mentioning Pan, who certainly might have had a hand in such a lovely water supply. Of course with that & the heat the vegetation is entirely tropical, and most delightful, after four days complete barrenness. The town was formerly fortified, but mostly Roman & Arab work I fancy: on top of a hill about 700 feet high however above the town is a much finer fortress. The view is extraordinary, one of the finest in Syria according to Baedeker, who drivels as usual architecturally. . . . Still it is a castle 500 yards long, on a spur of Hermon, and has got in one place rudimentary machicoulis like those of Château Gaillard, so I was very satisfied with it. I got all over the place, and at last set fire to the brushwood in the inner court which burnt all the morning. Still in the evening I profited, by seeing the building as a whole, as no other person can have done for 20 years— it was simply choked with rubbish. The owner was a little surprised but did not expostulate, as it was a courtyard inaccessible to anything but a mountaineer or a spider. He had never got to it (entrance on the 1st floor of course, & the walls elsewhere still intact). It must have made a jolly bonfire from a distance, for there was a space of 30 yards square of old thorn trees. Banias Mother will remember from Matthew xvi or Mark viii and other places. To read such extracts on the spot is certainly much the best way: it may be that the Transfiguration took place on one of the neighbouring spurs of Mt. Hermon: of course though that is not known, but it would be a very pleasantly appropriate place.

We went downhill again through the olive groves into the village after tipping the owner of the castle, and then found the villagers very anxious to murder my man, as he was a Christian & they were going to make a foray in that direction soon. However we cleared (they would not have ventured to touch him as long as he was with me for fear of the consequences) (international), to Tell-el-Kadi a mound about 3 miles off. It is about 30 feet high & crater-shaped inside & now quite deserted, but with plenty of real trees, and such a spring! cold as ice, (my water-melon cracked when he got in) & splendid in scale: it makes at once a pool about 4 feet deep & 60 feet across (and very pretty it is too) from which rush forth two wide streams, uniting almost at once to make a river the width of the Cherwell but infinitely faster, & about 3 feet deep. It is glorious, a river springing full grown from a pine grove. It is absolutely deserted without even an Arab tent upon it, and historically well it is the Laish of Judges xviii, & subsequently Dan, which should be enough for most people. What a weird story that of those Danites is: I can understand them being confident to surprise the Sidonians: anyone would live carelessly in Tell-el-Kadi except for the malaria. Indeed Dan must have been used to surprises for Abraham came up with his kings there, and later on it

Vezelay. Door from Northax into Nave *(See pp. 61 and 63)*

Vezelay   (*See pp.* 61 *and* 63)

was again captured. It is a lovely place. From Dan we passed to the site of Abel-Beth-Maachah, where Sheba was finally run to earth by Joab, & then over a rocky spur into a delightful valley with gardens, running streams, etc. There I enjoyed myself greatly for that was one of the hottest days of all. Then in the evening up 2000 feet to Hunin, where we slept. The castle there was trifling in strength but as for fleas! I wanted to plan a loophole in one tower, so stayed in it for about 10 minutes, & then found myself fairly black with them to the knees. The Arabs say that the king of the fleas lives in Tiberias, but I can guarantee that he has summer residences elsewhere as well! Next day I went on alone to Tibnin (borrow *The Land and the Book* if you want a purple (very purple) account of the defiles) where the castle might have been worse, & then struck South intending for Safed. On the way I had refreshment at the springs of Kades, Barak's native place, and then a terrific climb up from a valley & over undulating country into Safed, itself on a hill 2700 feet high. In the day's march I went up & down the height of Mt. Blanc—and Palestine is all like that: a collection of small irritating hills crushed together pell-mell, and the roads either go up & down all the time, or wind in & about the rock of the valleys, & never reach anywhere at all. Nobody ever built a house except on a hill-top or half-way up, the path is only a piece of land from which the smaller stones have been pushed; all day one steps from one sharp rock to another which is not only tiring to the feet but to the brain also for one has to be continually on the alert, to find the best place for the next step, & to guard against slips. As a result one is soon satisfied with that sort of road. The alternative is a field path which is much better; these paths are very easily made & have an odd trick of dying away in the middle of a square mile of thistles from one to three feet high of a blue grey colour & very hard. To walk through them for any length of time is rather painful: one acts as pincushion. I got in the evening to Safed a large town but without a hotel: still I tried the English doctor (of the Hospital of the Jews Mission) & he gave me a most admirable reception. I stayed 4 nights & thoroughly refreshed myself. Mrs. Anderson (their name) comes from Abingdon & has 4 children out here. They were exceedingly kind to me. I wanted plenty of water for washing of all kinds! He is very anxious to get a young medical colleague for he is *slightly* overworked (with about 250 out-patients a day and a big hospital full of better specimens

& half a hundred other things besides). From the castle (good) $\frac{2}{3}$rds of the Holy Land is visible. I had great sport in an underground passage that is being excavated: xiii century work I think.

From Safed I visited Chastellet, now called the bridge of the daughters of Jacob for some unknown reason: it is the main link with the beyond-Jordan Arabs & crosses the river just below Lake Huleh. I then walked down the Jordan Valley to the lake of Galilee & home past the site of Chorazin—all thistles for miles. Next day I got going again and descended from Safed to Tell-Hum (Capernaum) from which there was a beautiful view across the Lake. The place itself has ruins possibly those of a synagogue but those have been walled in by the Franciscans so it is pleasanter to sit under the oleanders on the actual shore. The view is not grand, the hills on either side of the lake are not high, & to the S. is a level part the Jordan Valley, but they are very pleasantly broken up, with plenty of light & shade, in a brown purple tint. The lake itself is very blue & always moving: never quite calm, as seen from Capernaum there is not one dominating feature in the whole—it is just a pretty little inland sea, without sign of human occupation. The water is lukewarm, but quite fresh & wholesome swarms of fish. There are of course no woods or trees only oleanders everywhere. From there I walked along the plain of Gennesaret to Tiberias. The plain is very fertile & very highly cultivated, & the lake gives abundance of water: it is the best place I have found yet in Palestine. Imagine walking on a grass path (real grass green) by the water's edge through oleander shrubs, which sometimes meet above one's head, & were all in bloom: the actual beach where the grass does not grow in the water, is of a beautiful white sand—altogether charming. This lasted for about 3 miles, then I reached Magdala, & had to stumble along a rocky path for an hour into Tiberias. Tiberias is a hot dirty, not unpicturesque old town, with a lovely port, where the fishermen loaf about all day: the circuit of the walls is interesting. Then I walked down the lake-side to its Southern end where the Jordan leaves it, & down the river valley for miles. It was a fair road, but it is such a comfort to *know* that the country was not a bit like this in the time of Our Lord. The Renaissance Painters were right, who drew him and his disciples feasting in a pillared hall, or sunning themselves on marble staircases: everywhere one finds remains of splendid Roman roads and houses and public buildings, and Galilee was the most Romanized province of Palestine. Also the country was well-peopled, and well watered artificially: there were not 20 miles of thistles behind Capernaum! and on the way round the lake they did not come upon dirty, dilapidated Bedouin tents, with the people calling to them to come in & talk, while miserable curs came snapping at their heels: Palestine was a decent country then, and could so easily be made so again. The sooner the Jews farm it all the better: their colonies are bright spots in a desert. From the Jordan Valley I climbed about 2000 feet to Belvoir a castle, & then in a straight line went through Endor to Nazareth seeing Nain on my left. There is nothing outstanding in any of these except the village spring at Nazareth, a most uniquely interesting spot. I think I sent home a couple of postcards of it. From Nazareth I went past the plain of Esdraelon to Harosheth where Sisera's Mother looked out of the lattice, and pictured her son dividing up the spoil. What a glorious poem that is! The plain was very good; so fertile, & all the people of the villages engaged in harvesting & threshing: they take tents out & live in the fields, while strings of camels & asses carry the corn to the threshing floors. When the straw has been broken up & separated from the wheat by the flint-studded sledge they fling it into the air & winnow it, & then each man stamps his heap of grain with a large sign so that no one can take away from his pile undetected: & there are a thousand other things they do —— I could write hours longer than you could read, if I haven't done so already! From Harosheth I crossed the back of Carmel, over the place of sacrifice, (one of the loveliest views in the world perhaps in spring), where the Druses still celebrate Elijah's {sacrifice}, to Athlit, & so to Haifa. Then to Acre, so quaint & unspoiled a town, to Kala'at Ka'arn, to Scandalium, to Tyre, to Sarepta, to Sidon, & so back to Beyrout. Tomorrow I hope to start N. up the coast to Latakieh, then inland to Antioch, next to Aleppo, & then across the Euphrates to Edessa & back again by train from Aleppo to Beyrout & home. I will try to send a line from Aleppo, in about 3 or 4 weeks, & perhaps a wire before starting back. NED

4 *August* 1909

Time has run rather short—so must be brief. All has gone very well; spent some £8 so far in Syria: also in P. Said more of course. Will be all right that way, barring accidents. Clothes most satisfactory: stockings not holed once yet speaks well for boots: luggage as comfortable as to be expected. Iradés arrived: am Professor of University & Artist: have written Lord Curzon. {Lord Curzon as Foreign Secretary & Chancellor of the University obtained the Iradés for him.}

Sent Canon {Christopher} p.c. {from} Nazareth: no chance on Aug. 20 {Canon Christopher's birthday}. Arabic difficult: but sufficient so far. Castles very disappointing.

I hear M. Blèriot has got across {the Channel by aeroplane—the first to do so} & that Mr. Latham {the Airman} has been taking baths: I envy the latter more for its 93°. I don't know, as I said, if I will write again to you. If Aleppo Consul is able to send I will, & also if country beyond is disturbed, because then I'll go to Damascus, Palmyra etc. But if I go N. I fall rather out of line. If I don't get another chance till just before return I will send a wire, with one word "retournant". That means, all well, & if there is a number after it, it is the probable date in October: ... if I come overland that will be all, unless I wire from Dover. If I come by sea: a letter from Marseilles: the latter the cheaper: if it is after term (Oct. 9) you will inform college: (the Vice-Principal—or Rev. W. Hawker Hughes) *not* Mr. Poole, except by courtesy: Health has been very good except touch of malaria at Safed (not noticeable) have walked on average 22 miles a day: longest 36. many rest days: no signs of disturbance anywhere between here & Aleppo. You may write to Aleppo after *receiving this*; *for a week*. Love.

NED

By the way: if I am feeling tired, even if it would make me late at college (they will excuse) I will come long sea: for the rest & sea air: the rush across France is a racket.

This is a terrible scrawl: but I have had to hurry: don't be nervous about me: I can't see any cause for uneasiness. Tell Mother no smoking so far: but a mouthful of brandy (ejected!) by mistake: people are asses to drink such stuff.

{BEYROUT.}   *August 5, 1909*

DEAR WORM

I'm going to stay one more day in Beyrout, and then going N. Tell Mother I have sent a long letter to her, which will reach you soon. It went yesterday, but by a longer road than this one I expect. It will

tell you everything I mean to do. Father told me you had been top of
the Form, that is *very* proper! Did you get any prizes? These stamps
cost a lot, so take care of them: they are the Turkish set. The other 3
(10 paras, 20 paras, & 1 piastre) are of the Austrian Post Office: there
are also English, French, German and Russian post offices here, all with
stamps. As they are going to do away with them soon, I will buy sets,
while I can. These post offices used to be necessary, for till a year ago
the Turkish Post-Office was very bad. Remember that 40 paras make
1 piastre and that a piastre is worth from $1\frac{3}{4}d$. to $2\frac{1}{2}$; in the shops they
only count them as $1\frac{3}{4}d$. In the Government things, (railways & post
offices) they are worth $2\frac{1}{2}d$. You would be amused at the Turkish
money: gold is never used, only a thing about as big as a 5/- piece
worth 3/6 of silver, and then a copper cart-wheel worth 6*d*., and 10
little things like bronze 3*d*. pieces which go to make this cart-wheel.
So if you carry much Turkish money with you, you must have a
porter to carry it. Once I had 25 bishliks (the 6*d*. cart-wheels) in my
pocket at once, & I felt quite off my balance. I must stop now: offer
my worms to Mother, Father, Bob, Will, & Frank, when you see them,
and take great care of Mother: I want her to get quite strong, so as to
be able to come out here for a trip with me in a couple of years. I hope
you are happy in Jersey: try "Prosit" to drink if the water is still bad,
but the newspaper says that you have been having a lot of wet weather:
it sounds so funny to me out here, because it is never wet or dull.
Still then I expect Madame Pierre's well will be full. Loud worms to
yourself.

NED

TO BE READ ALL BY HIMSELF

SPECIALLY WELL WRITTEN.

The 3 + 2 duplicates are "new constitution" stamps & are only in
use for 2 months, now obsolete.

TRIPOLI (TARÂBULUS)
August 13, 1909

I have quite unexpectedly got an opportunity of sending you a line,
so I will take it, though there is nothing special to tell you: still you
may be glad to have additional evidence that I am all right. I did not
leave Beyrout till last Friday 6th & then I went N. to the Nahr-el-
Kelb, the Dog River, which has the inscriptions of Esarhaddon,
Ramases, Shalmaneser, Marcus Antoninus and many others. It is

wonderful to think of 14 inscriptions Egyptian, Babylonian, (Nebu-chadnezzar II), Assyrian, Greek, Roman, Arab, & French on the one promontory: all these people had used the rock road cut in the face of the cliff. The river itself is large & cool. Then I went further N. (by the way I passed the place where S. George killed his dragon) to Jebail, crossing the river Adonis the one which at certain seasons runs blood-red. It used to be the centre of the Adonis worship. Jebail is of course Byblus, & I stayed there 3 or 4 days with Miss Holmes, the American missionary. She was most exceedingly kind in feeding me up, & as she had plenty of books & a marble-paved hall, with water ad lib. and trees (real green ones) in her garden I was very happy. I think I ought to tell you about the American mission, for it is doing much the most wonderful work of all in Palestine. It is Presbyterian, & has most brilliant men at the head of it. They recognised that at present conver-sion of Moslim was impossible. They have opened schools all over the country. In these the instruction is given in English, & includes many very important matters. In Beyrout they have headquarters, a College or University (which confers diplomas) some 800 strong, with a teach-ing staff of nearly 200 young Americans (they come over for 3 years each, though of course there are senior men, & Professors). Here the chief study is Medicine, & Pharmacy: but Law, Agriculture, Dentistry, and teaching are now commencing. Nearly every educated Syrian in Beyrout has been through some part of this college, & all through the country one finds the leading men in the village its graduates. Thus English is a common language in Syria, & in 10 years no other will be needed. The influence of this college has promoted emigration to America, & I don't think there is a village in N. Syria where one of the people has not been to America (they never stay more than a few years). These men are all eager for reforms in Syria, & dissatisfied with the government, so that the secretary of the government of the Lebanon (a high Turk) said to me—"the recent reform of the constitution in Constantinople (i.e. the revolution) is entirely due to the American mission." They have so educated the country (without touching on politics) that public opinion rejoiced in reform. They have colleges all over Syria, & Asia Minor, & in Constantinople (mostly self-support-ing) and in all of them the religious side is emphasised: also every school is a mission station (they are usually boarding schools). From Jebail I went to Batrun, with a little castle, & then to Mseilha with another, & then to Enfeh with a third, & then to Tripoli with two or three, where I am now. Tomorrow I am going into the interior, circling about till I reach Latakieh. There is no news about myself. I am very well, & very hot, my clothes are all well, & my stockings still unholed, & my boots look as if they have hardly been worn. My last three castles have been very good. Salaams & love to all.

NED

TRIPOLI

15 August, 1909

DEAR FATHER

I have been thinking, & getting information here for 2 days about the next part of my trip. It will take me at least 3 weeks to go to Aleppo (there are 15 castles in the first 125 miles) and from there to Edessa another week. Then to return will take 10 days, to Damascus. Altogether it will take till the end of September to do this piece. Then I should go to Kerak & Shobek, two important fortresses on the Dead Sea (it will be cool enough down there by then) but that would entail my being home very late. To miss these would be a pity, & Kerak is near enough to the railway to make it accessible from Damascus in 3 days: Dr. Bliss (who did the excavations of '92–'98 in Jerusalem) told me that it was the most interesting castle in Syria and Shobek (Monreale) is only two days further. If I went to those two I could not return before October 20: and now that I am in Syria, & have seen so much of it, I would be extremely sorry to go back without managing at any rate a glimpse of Jerusalem, & Judea. You see I have not really been further S. than Galilee, & that leaves Palestine proper almost untouched. This will give you an idea of how it is: my wishes are of course evident; this is a glorious country for wandering in, for hospitality is something more than a name: setting aside the American & English missionaries, who take care of me in the most fatherly (or motherly) way:—they have all so far been as good as they can be—there are the common people each one ready to receive one for a night, & allow me to share in their meals: and without a thought of payment from a traveller on foot. It is so pleasant, for they have a very attractive kind of native dignity: but I mustn't enlarge. If you feel able to give me long enough to finish my preliminary (I hope) survey of the country I would be delighted, & have enough money to do it: only Mother would have to resign herself to getting only a small packing-case from Damascus. But if you think I have done enough I will come back direct from Damascus, without Kerak & Shobek: I would then reach Oxford in the first few days of term. The summer is rainless here till early November. Will you answer please as quickly as possible to Aleppo (H.B.M. consulate) or if this letter is delayed, as is quite probable (i.e. if it takes more than 12 days) to Poste Restante, Damascus. If you are in doubt please write to both. This letter must do for Mother's birthday as well I am afraid. I hope the rest in Jersey may have set her up again. Tell her I have not bought her silver teapot yet! If I do I may come home steerage! But seriously they don't make tea out here if they can help: and I don't think she would much fancy the Damascus silver work: it is mostly filigree, & I think a little finnicking: also it would be hard to clean: but I have secured for her a splendid laver (a tall brass jug with long spout) in a brass bason: good, fairly heavy work: decidedly graceful in mine eyes so if she doesn't like it it won't be wasted! NED. Please keep enclosed prints.

LATAKIA
29.8.1909

DEAR MOTHER

Another chance for a note: this time hurried. I wrote last from Tripoli. I went thence to Aarka, & then to Kala'at el Hosn, passing one night on a house roof, & the second in the house of an Arab noble reputed, as I was told next day, of the highest blood: a young man very lively, & rather wild, living in a house like a fortress on top of a mountain: only approachable on one side, & then a difficult staircase. If you keep this note I can tell you all sorts of amusing things about him later: name Abdul Kerim. He had just bought a Mauser, & blazed at everything with it. His bullets must have caused terror to every villager within a mile around: I think he was a little cracked. Then I got to Hosn, which is I think the finest castle in the world: certainly the most picturesque I have seen—quite marvellous: I stayed 3 days there, with the Kaimmakam, the governor: a most-civilised-French-speaking-disciple-of-Herbert-Spencer-Free-Masonic-Mohammedan-Young Turk: very comfortable—. He sent an escort with me next day to Safita, a *Norman keep, with* ORIGINAL *battlements*: the like is not in Europe: such a find. Again I slept with Kaimmakam & Co. (Co. here means fleas) and next day I went on again with a huge march, to two more castles, and a bed for the night in a threshing floor, on a pile of tibn, chopped straw, listening to the Arabs beating out their Dhurra in the moonlight: they kept it up all night in relays, till about 2 a.m. when they woke me up, & said they were all exhausted, would I keep watch because there were thieves, & I was a Inglezi & had a pistol: I obliged thinking it was humbug of the usual sort, (every village distrusts its neighbour), but they told me in Tartus next day that there really were not thieves, but *landlords* about! Isn't that charming? These dear people wanted to hide the extent of their harvest. Next day as above I went to Tartus, by another good castle: then struck far inland, (through a country of flint & steel & handmills, to Masyad, the chief city of the Assasins country: & then to Kadmus, another of that gentry's strongholds, where the "Old Man of the Mountains" himself lived: (I slept in his château) & so to Aleiha, to Nargat a castle about as big as Jersey I fancy: one wanted a bicycle to ride round it: to another Banias to Jebeleh, & here to Latakia, all well. Monday I want to get off to Sahyun & then in 4 or 5 days to Antioch, & then to Aleppo in 5. I hope there to hear from you because Bob's going to Germany is in the nature of an experiment: he will have better food than I have—last week only bread & that bad: this is a considerable town however, with native restaurants. I have got to like leben. No smoking yet, though here every man woman & child does: Latakia tobacco, which Father knows all grows here: the peasants dry & smoke their own, all in cigarettes: I will have such difficulty in becoming English again, here I am Arab in habits & slip in talking from English to French & Arabic unnoticing: yesterday I was 3 hours with an Orleannais, talking French, & he thought at the end I was a "compatriot"! How's that? I may manage a pencil scrawl from Antioch: but you may be happy now all my rough work is finished successfully: & my Thesis is I *think assured.* *Iradé invaluable.*   NED

ALEPPO
September 7th, 1909

DEAR MOTHER
    I arrived here all right yesterday, but found no letter from you: I have wired to Beyrout in case you mistook my directions: I hope nothing has happened. I wrote to you from Latakia: on the Monday

I went from there to Sahyun, perhaps the finest castle I have seen in Syria: a splendid keep, of Semi-Norman style, perfect in all respects: towers galore: chapels, a bath (Arabian) & a Mosque: gates most original: & a rock-moat 50 feet across in one part, 90 feet in another, varying from 60–130 feet deep: there is a cutting for you! And in the centre had been left a slender needle of rock, to carry the middle of a drawbridge: it was I think the most sensational thing in castle-building I have seen: the hugely solid keep upstanding on the edge of the gigantic fosse. I wish I was a real artist. There were hundreds of other points of interest in the buildings. I stayed there two days, with the Governor, who was most obliging & then came on here by forced marches, 120 miles in 5 days which no doubt Bob or Will will laugh at, but not if they had to do it stumbling & staggering over these ghastly roads: it took me 13 hrs. of marching per day, & I had an escort with me (mounted) so I lost no time. By the way it is rather amusing to contemplate a pedestrian guarded carefully by a troop of light horse: of course everybody thinks I am mad to walk, & the escort offered me a mount on the average once a half-hour: they couldn't understand my prejudice against anything with four legs. My trip was part of the time through very lovely country, almost English in parts: & also up rocky defiles, *packed with ruins*, Xian, of the fifth & sixth cent. mostly: massive basilicas and pandocheions and lauras: private houses a few: tombs in abundance: inscriptions were all in Greek: in parts of my journey I seem to have been the first European visitor.

At Harin I found a Crusading castle, too ruined & rebuilt to be valuable, with underground passages that would have rejoiced the rest of the world: I explored them with candles, followed by a very reluctant escort, swearing it smelt "jinns": ask Arnie what a jinn is: I certainly smelt a lot of things: but did not see anything. The passages went to water-springs etc. From Harin I paid a flying-visit to Antioch, to see the walls; miles long: the modern town is not one-tenth the size of the old one. I did not enter it, but broke away E. in a hurry here: over about the worst road on the face of the globe (or anywhere else on its body). Aleppo is European, with a decent hotel: much washing, for I hadn't had a bathe for 10 days (or any other kind of wash!).

I am afraid I have to drive from here to Urfa (Edessa) which is going to cost me about £7: so bang go my proposed purchases in Damascus:

I'm very sorry—but must make haste: wish the letters had arrived. Telegraphing is such slow work out here, & there is no telephone. Why can't somebody invent an occupation for flies? they have too much leisure: all this district is plagued with them & mosquitoes. By the way I took the escort abused above because I was shot at near Masyad: an ass with an old gun: I suppose he was trying it. At any rate he put in a shot at about 200 yards, which I was able to return rather successfully: for his horse promptly bolted about half a mile: I think it must have been grazed somewhere: at any rate he stopped about 800 yards away to contemplate the scenery, & wonder how on earth a person with nothing but a pistol could shoot so far: & when I put up my sights as high as they would go & plumped a bullet somewhere over his nut he made off like a steeple-chaser, such a distance was far beyond his old muzzle-loader. I'm rather glad that my perseverance in carrying the Mauser has been rewarded, it is rather a load but practically unknown out here. I complained of course to the governor of the district: who was furious, & sent out all his police at once: he agreed with me however that the man simply wanted to frighten me into money-payment: no success for him. I am now of course far beyond any disturbed country & there is no chance of a repetition of the joke: which is why I tell you: it is not very sensational I fear. I hope to reach Damascus in about a fortnight, but of course that depends on Urfa: I hope all is well at home: & that Jersey came up to anticipation: but I can't say more, being in ignorance: my last letter was dated about July 16! and no newspapers here.   NED

ALEPPO

September 22, 1909

After all I am coming home at once, for lack of money. Of course you could send me more but I'd want new clothes, those I wear at present shall be left in Beyrout, I'd never get them past the sanitary inspection at P. Said:—new boots the present being "porous", I've walked them to bits at any rate, & my feet lately have responded to it. They are all over cuts & chafes & blisters, & the smallest hole in this horrid climate rubs up in no time into a horrible sore. I can't imagine how many times I would have had blood poisoning already if it hadn't been for my boracic: but I want to rest the feet now or there will be something of the sort. To undertake further long walks would be imprudent, for even in new boots these holes would take long to heal. Then I would want a new camera, for alas! mine has been stolen. It is a most terrible pity: taken from the carriage at Seruj on the way back from Urfa, while the coachman I left on watch was asleep. This Ramadan is a horrible business. I have been working in the Consulate here, and at the Weli & the Serail & the police offices & writing to the local governor at Seruj: so there is hope of its recovery: or there would be if it wasn't Ramadan. Except for this & a runaway when the carriage was upset (no damage to any of us 3) my trip to Urfa was delightful & I found there the only 2 beaked towers in all N. Syria. I hope my photos will be clear. They were the last I took. Another reason for getting back is the weather, the last few days have been very wet:—the rains commencing early this year—& one couldn't walk here in rain. Altogether I am a little tired, & just getting out of my 4th malaria none of them serious fortunately: I would like to stop, & if I had money & knew what the college would say I certainly would. But I can't afford to telegraph them to find out. Will you say I will be back on 15th or perhaps 14th by Orient or P. and O. long sea—it will be pleasant to have 14 days with no sightseeing nothing to do but eat. By the way it is remarkable that all this 3 months on most unaccustomed & most changing food & water my stomach has never been upset. That is the great bugbear of the European traveller in Turkey. I suppose my exercise etc. [I have walked 1100 miles] is responsible for my health. I find an absurd canard in the Aleppo paper of a week ago: my murder near Aïntab (where I didn't go). I hope it has not been copied. The hotel people received me like a ghost. Mr. Edvard Lovance sounds like me. Tell Will I have got about 24 Hittite seals & congratulate Arnie on his bicycle his tumbles & his handwriting.

The P.O. had my letters here after all. They thought no apology necessary for their former mistake; but I got one after a little work. Am glad you are all right, & that Jersey was pleasant. "So warm" indeed come out here & revel in 106° in the shade. Must finish now. Will spend 3 days Damascus (not a penny to spare) & then leave Beyrout 30th. Miss Holmes has offered me her purse: so I'll borrow if I run short at last. But not if I can help. Salaams.

NED

Tell Father I am sending by this same post a letter to Sir John {Rhys}: saying I have asked him to go & tell the college (I expect the Vice-Principal or W. Hawker Hughes) I'll be late, but that I thought I'd let him know what I had done also. *Sir John does not like to be bothered with college matters*: & won't care if I am early or late; probably won't know. I had hoped to spend a week or ten days in Damascus, & work up the details of town life in the East into a letter such as I sent you on the country Arabs. This will I expect now be impossible. But if I can I'll do it, since it is only by that one can get a general idea of the East. It will be a mere shapeless, disconnected mass of course, but valuable for reference. Unless I write this I won't write again. A letter to Marseilles may find me but not unless important please.

Le Petit Andelys
August, 1910

Dear Mother

     Frank is very satisfied with his exam. results: (which are really very good.) His speaking of French whatever his writing is no great success: & I don't like trying to correct him, since I am little better myself. The name of a French Curé (near Perigueux) has been given me—he takes English students at a reasonable cost. I got Mr. Hutton's letter {one of the Examiners in the Final History School 1910} all right: have answered him pointing out a few weak spots in the thesis. It was good of him to write. Miss Holmes please let us know of at P.R. Valognes, Manche, if not to Caen. I am interested in her of course. About cash:—I hope to finish at Cherbourg with nearly £5 to spare. Frank has told you what else happened. We have had very few punctures so far, & good roads, winds, & weather. Also our days have been very short. Beauvais is finer than ever: & is now marked with a white stone, since there I found worthy French-printed books. The sculptures of Rheims are almost perfect, it is not a Chartres, but wonderful all the same, I have got what p.c.'s I could get: none worthy of course. Gisors I liked: Frank didn't. He is enjoying this place, because it has a river and steam tugs, & an English family: so we will stay over Monday & let him get a little more of it. There is very safe bathing: & some

boating in flat tubs of boats. The country here is altogether lovely: &
the views more & more necessary: if I stayed very long I would take root.
I sat up in the castle this morning a little after Frank went to dejeuner,
& read below the keep. The colours in the water below me, & the
sweep of the river under the cliffs were superb. Is there any chance of
Will getting here this year? I can assure him he will find it repay any
pains. The view has the same effect on people as a forest or a church:
they talk in whispers. The book I had was *Petit Jeha de Saintré*, a xv
Cent. novel of knightly manners—very good:—I have wanted to read
it for a long time, but the Union Copy was so badly printed that I had
not the heart for it. Now I have found (for 1 f. 25) a series quite nicely
typed on fairly good paper. So far I have only got 4 volumes, because
they are rather much to carry: it is altogether glorious to have found
good French books at last. I can read Molière & Racine & Corneille
& Voltaire now:—a whole new world. You know, I think, the joy of
getting into a strange country in a book: at home when I have shut
my door & the town is in bed—and I know that nothing, not even the
dawn—can disturb me in my curtains: only the slow crumbling of the
coals in the fire: they get so red & throw such splendid glimmerings
on the Hypnos & the brass-work. And it is lovely too, after you have
been wandering for hours in the forest with Percivale or Sagramors le
desirons, to open the door, & from over the Cherwell to look at the
sun glowering through the valley-mists. Why does one not like things
if there are other people about? Why cannot one make one's books
live except in the night, after hours of straining? and you know they
have to be your own books too, & you have to read them more than
once. I think they take in something of your personality, & your
environment also—you know a second hand book sometimes is so
much more flesh & blood than a new one.—and it is almost terrible to
think that your ideas, yourself in your books may be giving life to
generations of readers after you are forgotten. It is that specially which
makes one need good books: books that will be worthy of what you
are going to put into them. What would you think of a great sculptor
who flung away his gifts on modelling clay or sand? Imagination
should be put into the most precious caskets, & that is why one can
only live in the future or the past, in Utopia, or the wood beyond the
World. Father won't know all this—but if you can get the right book
at the right time you taste joys—not only bodily, physical, but spiritual

also, which pass one out above and beyond one's miserable self, as it were through a huge air, following the light of another man's thought. And you can never be quite the old self again. You have forgotten a little bit: or rather pushed it out with a little of the inspiration of what is immortal in someone who has gone before you.

NED

We are both so delighted that Lancresse is satisfactory. It was such a gamble. Please try so far as is possible to rest yourself. We are of course all right. F. a little saddle sore: but we have not ridden 40 miles any day since we started: as a rule only 20 or 25.

CAEN

September, 1910

I have bought Arnie a great envelope today, so he will have his 25 stamps. I am afraid I have nothing else to tell him: for I spend my time in walking up & down streets and in looking at churches. I have a map of the town, & I go up & down each street marked on it. I have finished them all today & there is not one profitable digging: so that about 20 miles of walking has come to nought. Of the churches, I spend 5 or 6 hours a day in one or other: there are five I like specially, & I know them all fairly well now: one is best in a morning light, another at midday, & I like one best in the evening, after the lamps are lit. It is called l'église de St. Jean & Arnie would be amused to climb its tower, & look over the parapet at the top, for it is seven feet out of the strait; he could (perhaps) slip down one side into the street; & the other overhangs in rather a dizzy manner. Will you tell Frank that I am staying in the same hotel.

Tell Mother I am glad the can will do. I left Will to go to Chartres and Amiens with a very doubtful back tire. He should not have started with such a thing. I am going to St. Germans near Paris to look at a museum. I am writing this in St. Sauveur, a church I like very much: it is so quiet: it is getting dark now, so I am going out to the banks of the Orne, to see the river-mists rise round the spires of St. Etienne, the Conqueror's great church, it is so pretty, I wish you were with me to admire it. I will get to Petit Andelys today week: so you may write the day you get this: after that I don't know yet. Expect me back for the prize-giving anyhow.

N.

{Second Voyage to Syria}

MESSAGERIES MARITIMES {STEAMER}
December, 1910

There does not seem much chance of our getting into the Piræus before this evening but I am writing now in case we should be up to time. I sent you a letter from Naples but as there was no time to go ashore I had to entrust it to a boy to post & one can never tell what will happen. Please let me know if you got it & if it was sufficiently stamped for I sent off another letter by the same way. Naples is wonderfully beautiful,—far finer this time than last, for there was a mist that toned down the factory chimneys, & the ugliness of the further shore. So that I really enjoyed the place, & think it quite as fine as Beyrout. There is more of the bay about it for one thing. Naples is nearly land-locked, & Beyrout only a depression in a long straight shore. However,—we left Naples in the evening, with just time to look at Cape Palinuro before bed. I kept still my four berth cabin in lonely state. Next morning when I came on deck we were at the opening out of the Straits of Messina with on the left the extraordinarily barren shores of southern Italy cut into rocky folds & flats of lava, very clear in the sun, & on the right a long line of grey mist where Sicily should have been, with Etna rising out of it black for some thousand feet, then a snow-cap, streaked with ridges of rock, & finally the blackness of the crater-top above with a dark steam rising from it all round: a very charming sight. By mid-day Etna had disappeared, & we saw no more land till we got up this morning, when the S.W. Capes of the Peloponnese were dim ahead of us. These have not yet become very visible, which is the reason of this letter. I am improving the shining moments as Dr. Watts might almost have said. In case you do not get my Naples letter I will repeat that the boat is slow, very slow (11 m.p.h.) but comfortable. That the food is much like French hotels, and abundant, petit dej. when one gets up (you really do get "up", & not "down" on a boat), a huge meal at 10.30 and dinner at 6.30. Most people find the delay between the two big meals an empty time, too long to wait, but of course it suits me perfectly. I have a very comfortable four berth cabin to myself with unlimited facilities for reading in bed, which is

Provins. The Keep *(See p. 61)*

Castle near Lannion

important, for deck & saloon lights go out at 11 p.m., a very primitive custom, and 1st & 2nd class passengers (not 50 all told) share the deck in common: so that there is space enough to ride a bicycle if one felt so minded. This is absolutely all that can be said for the present except that I have no great love for Greeks, judging from present samples. There is very great doubt what time we reach Athens; some say midnight, which would be a horrible tragedy, & involve my entrusting this letter also to aliens to post: and if it didn't come Mother would no doubt feel unquiet: yet the sea has been quite calm up to the present, and the boat has not presumed either to roll or to pitch, and the sun has shone most gratefully, so that at Naples the heat was quite unpleasant: one manœuvered to find a shady spot with a draft or breeze. This last page I am really going to keep for some views on Greece—Peloponnesian Greece of course:—Athens is not to be judged by a layman. *Later.* It seems inevitable that we get into the Piræus after dark, which is a terrible pity. However we are now off Cerigo, to the S. of Matapan, and the coast is most enticing. Cape Matapan (to Arnie for details) is very lovely, red & grey, sunset colours, over the face of a lofty cliff & the ground slopes back behind it into a wooded valley, dotted over with three or four white-roofed villages, shining above the trees; And then behind this valley there run up again great hills, very high & steep & brown, with terraced vineyards in their hollows & on the top a gorgeous looking town, with walls and square-towers red-yellow in the sunlight. There were very few houses within the walls, & the whole place looked desert, but it was about 8 miles off, & I could only see it through my camera. No field glass on board could make out so much, & yet its image was quite clear on the glass in a magnifier with which I have to focus. That was with the magnification of 18 diameters, and the deer-stalkers only give 15! A very good camera outfit I think it must be.   N.

We are now creeping up the narrows between Asia & Mitylene, having left Smyrna this morning; the weather is glorious, with a spotless sky, and sea of glass, but unfortunately the heat-haze blots out all the detail of the shores.

We pass the Troad shortly, but will see nothing of it; Tenedos though will be fairly visible, and Mitylene, wooded to its hill-top, with towns & villages & castles on its seaward slopes, is satisfactory. I

stopped my last letter on the night before Athens, & shortly after the
ship anchored off Ægina, continuing an hour before dawn, so as to get
into port in the early morning. It was too dark to gain more than a
ghostly silhouette of Ægina, but Salamis was clear and very large in
the half-light, & as we approached there gradually detached itself on
the main-land from the mists a grey hill with black bars like cypresses
upon the top. Just as we entered the Piræus the sun rose, & like magic
turned the black bars to gold, a wonderfully vivid gold of pillar and
architrave and pediment, against the shadowed slopes of Hymettus.
That was the Acropolis from a distance:—a mixture of all the reds &
yellows you can think of with white for the high-lights and brown-
gold in the shadows. Of course I got ashore at once, & plunged into
the intolerable cesspit of the Piræus: the place is a filthy drain for all
the dregs of the capital, its only virtue that it saves it from being a port.
Before you reach Athens you pass through green fields & over small
streams, that effectually wash away the taste & smell of the sea. The
rail lands you in the midst of a very modern looking town of squares
& gardens, with a character partly French but not wholly European or
Asiatic; too bright for the one & too clean for the other. It was above
all things quiet, the quietest town imaginable, with few trams, & those
slow ones, no motors or bicycles & very few carts. The streets are
usually asphalt-paved, & there seemed hardly any dogs to bark and
fight. Even the vegetable-hawkers shouted like men, not like jackals
or fog horns. Everywhere were palm trees & mimosa, with green
lawns. I had to go back through the town to reach the Acropolis, &
chose therefore to wander into by-streets, that I might come out at the
Theseion; and the further I went the stronger became a curious sense
of unreality, almost of nightmare. Here was a town full of people
speaking the same tongue & writing the same character as the old
inhabitants of 3000 years before. Some of them looked like what we
know & hope the old Greeks were, others of them are visibly of the
class of metirs or βαναυσοι or freedmen, whom Aristotle so loudly
scorned. The Athenians to whom he appealed were never more than
a handful, a little party who held by themselves walking in the gardens,
& looking out dispassionately upon the world around them: they had
heard (as I did) tousled black-haired women calling loudly for their
children Gorgs or Aristomenes, & they had seen (as I saw) the two
women up the street hurrying breathlessly along, tiring their hair, to

meet the procession, of priests in vestments this time, but still the same undercurrent of back-biting and slander, and ill-natured comment of the neighbours. A cabbage-seller passed me, before just such a sausage-stall as one had looked for in the street of Victory that leads to the Temple of Theseus, driving his ass, & chaffering with Demosthenes, a fisherman. It was all out of Aristophanes or Juvenal, all in keeping, so that it seemed quite natural when I walked up a little hill, & passed under the pillars of the temple. It stands today as perfect as ever it was, with the added beauty of the stains & hollows with which Time has endowed its stones. When you have passed around one of the angles of its cella wall, you see framed between two pillars the sunlight on the steps of the Propylea and the pediment of the Erectheum. The rock of the Acropolis is very large & high and steep. The quiet was really almost uncanny, as I walked up the shallow valley below Mars hill, & along the processional way to the gateway of the citadel. There were no boys to bother one, no loud bellows'd leather sellers, only a misty sunlight in which all Attica, Phaleron, Salamis, Eleusis, and the distant Peloponnese lay motionless, "drowned in deep peace", below the rock platform of the Wingless Victory. To get there I had to climb up the white marble staircase of the Propylea within the entrance gate. There were no porters, no guides, no visitors, & I walked through the doorway of the Parthenon, and on into the inner part of it, without really remembering where or who I was. A heaviness in the air made my eyes swim, & wrapped up my senses: I only knew that I, a stranger, was walking on the floor of the place I had most desired to see, the greatest temple of Athene, the palace of art, and that I was counting her columns, and finding them what I already knew. The building was familiar, not cold as in the drawings, but complex, irregular, alive with curve and subtlety and perfectly preserved. Every line of the mouldings, every minutest refinement in the sculptures were evident in that light, and inevitable in their place. The Parthenon is the protocathedral of the Hellenes. I believe I saw the Erectheum, and I remember coming back to look again at the Propylea, and to stand again beside the Niké Apteros: but then I came down again into the town, & found it modern and a little different. It was as though one had turned from the shades of the ancestors, to mix in the daily vocations of their sons: and so only this about Athens, that there is an intoxication, a power of possession in its ruins, & the memories that inhabit them, which entirely prevents anyone attempting to describe or to estimate them. There will never be a great book on Athens unless it is one by an enemy: no one who knew it could resist its spell, except by a violent attack upon its spirit, and who can attack it now of artists, when Tolstoy is dead? He, and he alone, could have uprooted Greek culture in the world. I am coming back by Athens I think next year to stay a little time. For the present I am only confused with it: I do not know how much was Athens, and how much the colouring of my imagination upon it.   N.

Saturday. December 10, 1910

This letter will go off on Monday, and will inform you that I am still in Constantinople: in fact that I have taken firm root there, and mean to make a comparatively long stay. The reasons for this are of course first and foremost the loveliness of the Golden Horn and of the Bosporus; 2nd the miles of Greek walls that defend the city on the landward side, four miles of them, and triple all the way. Then there is St. Sophia, which I have not seen yet, but which must be very glorious, and (not least or last) the Imperial Museum, which should (by report) be a very storehouse of wonders. These are reasons enough to convince a household of reasonable beings, but Mother will not be satisfied with them, I fear, so for her benefit I will add that the engines of the vessel have at last finally broken down, & that there is no other boat at present leaving here for Syria. There have been engine troubles enough since we left Marseilles:— the utmost speed to be coaxed out of them was a bare ten miles an hour, & every day or two they would stop working suddenly, usually choosing an inconvenient moment when we were coming out of harbour, or ramming a headland. Still we got here this morning all well & happy, and lo & behold about 3 p.m. (when we were due to start at 4) there grows out a rumour that repairs are in hand: & then that we start from here next Friday. There is a Russian boat which leaves on Tuesday, but it takes ten days to reach Beyrout, & this thing hopes to do it in four: and so for the reasons on p. i (before Mother's two) I am going to live on board in hope. The Company is shabby: by its regulations we pay 8 francs a day while we stay here, & if we go on by another boat (except a Messagerie one) we have to pay for it ourselves. However I have plenty of money, & am really going to learn Assyrian grammar. On Monday

I will wire to Miss Holmes, since we should then be in Beyrout by schedule. Constantinople hotels are very dear:—much dearer than living on board. My companions in the misfortune (which I am suffering with my usual fortitude) are three French-Canadian priests, en route for Jerusalem. They talk broken English and being country clergymen are pleasant enough. We had a mighty argument one night (about a week back) on the infallibility & general excellence of Popes: I rather scored through a sufficient knowledge of history, & thereafter there has been religious peace: in fact they have avoided the subject, which is good, for they are really happy as they stand in their belief, & have besides no case to argue. I went up to the Embassy this morning, & arranged to have my Iradés renewed: so that is well settled: it was not really necessary, but a clean paper will look much better. Constantinople is most beautiful from every point of view, & besides is clean (very, now, being all garnished & flavoured with disinfectant) & full of interest in the people & artistically. I will have to buy a cheap guide-book of some sort to help me round it, though I found my way everywhere today without check. I remember great parts of it from my reading of Gibbon and Porphyrogenitus and Cecauminus and the rest of the party.

Will would probably enjoy by the way, the fatuousness of the "Embassy" of Leo. Is he aware that the dedicatory snakes of, I think, Salamis, are here somewhere? I go to look for them on Monday. The boat is most centrally placed (in the entering in of the Golden Horn by the Galata bridge) & having it to ourselves is most comfortable. We are now debating whether we shall dine first-class or second: I vote for first for the chairs are more springy:—and First has it. I must go & have a wash first.

Monday. It is really great good fortune to be stopped here in this way, for the cholera has ceased to all practical purposes & it is warm (though not hot) & fine & today is Bairam with Cannons firing all round, & all the people feasting in the streets. I have bought my guide-book (a very good one for 3 francs 50) & am going to *do* the place thoroughly. Will write again at the end of the week: a very lovely place this & most interesting.

　　　　　　　　　　　　　　　　　　　　　　　　　　　　N.

Enclosed stamp is for Arnie. It is a 10 piastre (about 2 francs 20 centimes) given me as receipt on a telegram. But it is a post stamp too.

MESSAGERIE MARITIMES STEAMER
Friday night. December 16, 1910

I.

I think I ought to write at length about Constantinople, to give you
a last news before we start. The engines are now in repair and we leave
on Saturday (tomorrow) afternoon. It has been a very pleasant week.
As for the town, I have not tried to sightsee, but have gone each day
to the old walls and have worked at them. Still I know something
about it, for to reach the walls means a walk of four or five miles
through the town each way, and as the walls are four miles long, to
reach my various daily sections I have, at one time & another, passed
across every part of the modern town. If Athens in its quietness stood
for sleep, Constantinople may as well stand for life and activity. It is a
very large place, fully the million inhabitants they give to it, and they
herd together in low wooden houses in a very warren of tortuous lanes.
There is hardly a wide street in all Stamboul, (which denotes the old
town, in opposition to Para and Galata, the quasi-European quarters)
and the only open spaces are before the mosques: not that all the 480
have open spaces near them, but the larger ones. You may imagine
how wonderful it is, after stumbling along such alleys in a press of
people for an hour and a half, to issue out of a gate built by Constantine
into a quiet country air, and the greenery of the innumerable cypresses
among the tombs. All the wall is bordered outside with cemeteries of
crowding tomb-stones, with carved turbans painted blue & red &
green, from the Sea of Marmora to the Golden Horn. The cypresses
which are everywhere in groves give a great feeling of peace, and of
stillness to the air, and as well their shade is very welcome. Hunt's
painting in the Ashmolean though over-bright like all Pre-Raphaelit-
ism, is fairly faithful in its general tone. The town walls you will not
want to know about, but they are so manned with historical associations, and so remarkable for preservation and design that really in my
mind they far outweigh St. Sophia and all the other remains of old
Byzantium, the Salamis pillar excepted. The Beautiful gate, a Roman
triumphal arch walled up, through which the Turks say their Christian
conqueror will ride, the Constantine gate with a clear-cut Latin
inscription of his, the triple lines of wall, the great moat, and the loopholes and chemin de ronde are all noteworthy. The picturesqueness of
the whole is above most such walls, which is saying a good deal, for if

there is no ivy or creeper, yet there is grass enough and ozier, with a continual relief of cypresses and painted tombs. I took a few photographs, more with a desire to make a good beginning of my camera than with any hope of doing good: one of them might be pretty but the most are technical. I have found a Roman portcullis which carries me back six hundred years in that respect. The later Normans can only have reintroduced an older invention. I wonder why the Greeks do not mention it . . . (Procopius). There are Greek walls everywhere in C.P. mostly as foundations with an aqueduct or two, 89 odd churches now become mosques (nothing wonderful) a splendid cistern or two, and the remains of a palace. After these you have to go to the Imperial Museum for old stuffs: it has been closed all the week (Bairam) but will be open tomorrow morning when I will visit it, too late to write about it. After the walls you have to jump to Turkish xvi century mosques for features of interest. I do not like them much. There seems to me to be a crudeness, an incapacity, a smallness of conception and design about all their art. The Turks, when they get a glorious broad wall-space and a deep porch, which should rightly be bold sunshine and shadow, will insist on fretting the wall into little confectionery-arcades, and on fitting up the porch with bright coloured tiles. The result is you get a façade all of a neutral strength, looking generally flat. To their eyes these petty mouldings are delicacy sublime; but they certainly do not suit my taste. There is a lack of sense of form, combined with a perfection of detail, of ornament which I think runs through most things oriental. The early Arab work is as fine as the Mediæval . . . but Turkish art in Constantinople is of a period of decadence. These are of course only private opinions and a little hasty. It may well be that in a little one's eyes get trained to seize detail in the mass, and retain it. If so these mosques and palaces are great, because their detail is unquestionably perfect. The colours of the tiles are splendid, and the arabesques and the intricacies of the inscriptions. I wish they had not had their prejudice against the human form and the animal. Their inspiration is often dried up for lack of root. Modern Constantinople is better than the old: everybody (except the women) lives & works & eats in the open, and the markets and shops are burning with movement and colour. To walk down the great fruit-market at sunset, when each man's basket of oranges or apples is lit by a candle fixed in among the fruit, and when they are all redoubling their efforts to rid themselves of their stock before the evening prayer is a regular orgy of activity: the fruit I avoid for cholera's sake, but besides them are sweetmeat sellers with splendidly-varied stalls, and bread-shops, and the vendors of coloured and perfumed drinks, and the red-leather shoe shops, and a whole street of copper-smiths, creating most glorious shapes of cauldrons & basins & ewers in a deafening clatter of hammer on metal. Most tragically the French invasion is beginning to swamp them here also. The brass work is more often than not machine-pressed, & frivolous in design. It is only very rarely that one sees a new piece with any dignity. The copper is better, but there too is a growing inclination to burnish away the hammer marks, and to make vulgar the traditional types. When I buy (which is as soon as I have Turkish enough to bargain) it will be the old pieces that I will search out, the handiwork of the generation before last or even earlier, graceful and yet most solid pieces, exchanged while still sound for more modern shapes. They melt the old stuff down for the good quality of its metal, but some day collectors will be longing after it for it is as beautiful as the very ancient and in its plainness to my mind at least, superior. In the beginning of the xviii Century the craftsmen had still sufficient leisure to engrave their pots: but in the beginning of the xix century they rely on the shapes alone, with their glorious clothing of hammer marks. I saw a jug in copper about 18 inches high, narrow necked, and round-bellied, beaten out of one sheet. The handle was broken off, but it was one of the noblest pieces of furniture imaginable. Beside it was one of the good modern works, one of the large basons in which Turkish delight is boiled:—a pan 6 inches deep and nearly 2 feet across: a small bath: but they make them all sizes. If I had bought the jug fitted it with a handle in keeping, and added a bason of bedroom size, it would have been a toilet set in keeping with my xv Century roof. In another shop there was hanging to the rafters a *bronze* water-pot a matter of 2 ft. high by a foot wide, a ravishing work, that must have gone back three or four centuries, and I have no doubt now going as old metal, because it is not engraved and inlaid with silver. It is really disgusting. However they will be valued someday. I am going to pick up some Turkish. Beyrout prob. Wednesday. I wonder how that demyship has gone.

N.

What happened to Mr. Bonar Law at Manchester?

II.

Saturday Morning. We leave at 3.0 p.m. today.

We are still very happy on board, the three Canuck priests, a young French-Egyptian avocat, & myself. There are huge discussions every night on most things of heaven or earth . . . the avocat loves disquisitions and two of the clergy are talkative: one of them, though is intelligent and well-educated and he and I and the captain sit aside and hold the balance of the dispute:—I supply the paradoxes, and also act agent provocateur if they flag in their activities. Are any of Democritus' works extant, or can I only carry on a tradition? It is huge fun at any rate, for the avocat is such a bromide. Amongst the crew exists an ultramontane, a legitimist, and a Bonapartist-military-despot-man. We had a grand saloon-night last night, with them all up and in the wrangle together. I took the chair and summed up at 11.5 p.m. to the effect (in a hurricane of applause) that "there was much to be said on all sides". In French it sounded well and was not beyond the truth, since their spirits were still combative though their voices were weak after four hours of disputation:—not a dull moment, though occasionally they showed a disposition in the heat of the argument, to disobey the presidential ruling. They are really modern Attic nights and have made our stay at C.P. generally enjoyable.

I find I have not said enough in the rest of the letter, on the extreme loveliness of the town. It is quite impossible I fear to give you any idea of the life and bustle and general disorderliness of the streets. In all old Stamboul there is not 20 yards of straight street. The whole place is one maze of narrow ill-kept ways twisting and turning between crowded booths, and cafés, and memorial fountains, with every now & then a sudden stop before a blank wall, or the vine-hung gateway of a mosque, through which one can see a gleaming marble pavement in a courtyard silent with worshippers. These stray mosques are really very grateful in the general rush of business: they always have a wide cloister before them, paved with white marble, and the arcades filled with merchandise, deposited there by those on a journey for surety. Over all is usually a vine with clusters of green and yellow leaves and a brooding sense of the cooing of doves. I don't suppose there are doves in every mosque but one always feels there are, for the imams walk about quietly like the people with stockinged feet, and there is no word

spoken louder than the low mutter of their prayers:—that is until the
muezzin climbs up his candlestick and yells like an old clothes-hawker
gone cracked. How on earth such an artistic people as the Arabs undoubtedly are can have endured such cacophony for long, passes my
imagining: I was told at Damascus that they had there arranged their
muezzins so that their voices chimed like the notes of a piano, but if so
what a piano! The pottery here copies the forms and glazes of the xv
Century in England. There are the same lamps and money-boxes in
green & brown-yellow, and jugs with applied masks. They are made
about 5 miles from C.P. and on my return (I'm coming back this way)
I will go out and watch their processes.

I have been trying to make my curés understand a little of the joy
and pleasure of the Orient. I took them for a walk through the market,
and showed them how to make Kamreddin, and how to iron a fez,
and all sorts of things, but they did not really seem to care. They were
always talking of *quel salété*, of the dirt & disorder of things, of the
lack of shops and carriages and what they were pleased to call con-
veniences (which are more trouble than they are worth). They seemed
too narrow to get outside their own civilization, or state of living,
except the one who is more educated than the rest. Is civilization the
power of appreciating the character and achievements of peoples in a
different stage from ourselves? Let Will send me some reflections upon
the topic. I will write next from Beyrout.

N.

JEBAIL
Dec. 31, 1910

Two letters arrived together: have sent a long letter to Green
{Leonard Green}, giving a conspectus of Syrian political geography;
send him my Thesis, & Stevenson's book (bound in red, on the lowest
shelf but one in my large bookcase) if not already gone. Thesis when
it comes back, if soon enough, for without it he will make nothing of
the photographs: and there is a map in it also: he must be in a hole, for
there are no books at all on the subject. I got a letter from Mr. Warren,
asking me to report my movements: I will answer. One from Snow:
I will answer, also to Mr. Hogarth, & Pirie-Gordon: no talk of Corvo,
no real opportunity. A letter from Mr. Jane—will reply: have refused

the *Wide World*: written to Mr. Poole: don't show Mr. Hogarth any more letters of mine, please! He can write himself in a way that makes me despair! Miss Holmes knew what a Demyship was:—a sort of fellowship.

How did Will meet Sir John {Rhys}? and what happened? My acknowledgements of Kerry's package. I am returning a small note from a bulbul wrapped in ass's skin. Please thank Chaundy also. Mr. Cave you have probably told: no more, but Florence, to whom I sent a p.c. lately: ditto Miss Wright. I have written 16 letters, and about 70 p.c.'s since I left! You have no idea how they mount up when one is away. Money is holding out: a note still unchanged. Will be short before long I hope. Modern Greeks are not really statuesque, except one or two rare exceptions: Hamdry's great sarcoph. the "Carian" is not very good: the drill used to excess in its carving, & so result rather worm-eaten: still the figures are good. The best thing in the museum is the sarcoph. of the weeping women from Sidon. I did not see the Cerigotto: too busy for Museums: you know there are the tegæan heads & the Eubuleus as well there. Must write to Mr. Hutton: Books satisfactory. This is all in your letters: will you tell Miss Kemmis that her rug is half done? looks splendid, but is held up, for they cannot get wool just the shade of brown-black used: they have to wait till the right sort of sheep offers his fleece, & then all well: a man in Beyrout is on the look out for them. It will be pretty. Am very sorry Bob has failed again: still there is always a third opportunity, & he is in no hurry to get into practice. Doesn't he feel that he would work more freshly or with more variety, if he read a little, or took up some other subject as well. It is one's spare time that is most fruitful. Still that is his affair: I would suggest a longer day. As for Arnie I don't know what to say, except that I expected it! I told Miss Holmes he was a likely chance. Inform him that it is the result of doing the ordinary work, but having interests much wider and deeper, which enable him to illustrate & appreciate all he meets with that is good. He will probably find this a rather large pill to swallow: but let him read *Kim* by Kipling. I enclose such $2\frac{1}{2}$ stamps as have come my way: also Arabic Numerals, which he will find on Turkish stamps.

Miss Holmes is writing to you to say all is well with me: that went off last Tuesday, so you may get it first. She is flourishing, & her school: I came in for great Xmas festivities, which I kept out of mainly: Arabic now, with a little Antiquity: some 5 good flint saws: much prehistoric pottery. Father should really come out here. Today, midwinter, has been roasting hot, with a glaring sun, & clouds of flies & mosquitoes. We can pick ripe oranges in the gardens, and roses and violets in Miss Holmes' patch (facing N.): everything is green and flourishing, for there have been two or three showers since I landed. Still the heat, & the perfect calm, and the exquisite twilight effects are nearly equal to summer's. I need a sun-helmet, really. It is very sandy soil, & they say a golf-links is preparing on the seven miles of sand-dunes below Beyrout. I hope he is better in Wales, but it is not much good asking after his health, since all things will have changed before I get the reply: you must wire if it is to be of use. Seven letters tonight: and some p.c.'s. Gave Miss Holmes Mrs. Abbot's scraps: she was very pleased with them: also with other things. Express to Arnie my sense of fitness that his scholarship should be recorded in vellum: for without my books he would never have got it: 14/- was exceedingly reasonable: let me know what Richards thinks of the parchment end-papers to the hollow land. Will report on Mrs. Rieder and Noel later: quite satisfactory: she likes Morris, & Marot, & les Aliscamps, and Daudet.

JEBAIL
Jan. 10, 1911

Your letter just come: Dec. 22. . . . will write to the Canon {Canon Christopher} . . . later. Arnie shall have coins. I have collected some half dozen already. Some duplicates will come: for Μενων. If Cristoid films are out of date, or making, you must choose another sort, but get Cristoids if possible: flat films, cut, $\frac{1}{4}$ plate, in any case not Kodoid. Arnie's jackal may be difficult: there are heaps of them howling round the house every night, but they seem to cling to the bushy part of their tails: however I will ask Abdullah about it. Arnie will enjoy Greek. I enclose Will two or three inscriptions; the seal is curious. I would be glad if he would ask Leeds about it and let me know: the man wants to sell it. I have bought, for 3/1 an Arabic prayer book of 1145 A.D. small, but very well written. I want it as a model to learn writing from. The modern hands are unsatisfactory.

About money: I have enough for present purposes (I don't know how much, and it would involve a search to find out). So it doesn't much matter. I enclose you Cook's paper: put in what amount you please; if it is equally convenient send me enough, at a lump, for my July–September wandering (£8-0-0) and my return (about £16-0-0) for expenses must be past paying for now. Miss Holmes is perfectly suited with a cheque, for her bank takes all such & settles them as in Europe. I am returning Cook's paper filled up: I don't know what you will do with it, if anything: but it seems fairly safe to send it back. I have no pen at all which is readable. Time out here is quiet: get up about sunrise, (6) and bed soon after 12 or 1. It is a little chilly in the evenings, too much so as to sit up late. Fine weather the last fortnight. I do little beyond Arabic, photographs, and receive visits from antiquity-mongers. But the manuscripts are the best things. Of modern books I have only a *Koran* and an *Antar*: neither to be understanded yet. I have learnt how leben is made: it will all come on to you next letter when I have time. Mr. New's little drawing is very lovely: I'll send him a line to say so. About Arnie's Greek: let him bear in mind that it is a living language, and that nothing in it is without significance: above all it is the antithesis of everything "natural", the most *artificial* of all things in art and life, and literature: artificial in a neutral sense. Will please explain these utterances. I am, according to Miss Holmes, eating well, & sleeping well: she sends you this for your material comfort. If it is so wet & cold in England you and Father are no doubt in distress: please emphasize on him the desirable climate further South: then as soon as Arnie is grown up you will get away. We get *The Times* here so I am up to date. Take care of yourselves: England is an unrestful country, and the risks of life & health very much greater than here: I wonder if Winckworth will come out? Only six weeks off now.   N.

{JEBAIL}
14 *Jan.* 1911

Richards has written to me. He has made some changes in the matter of the hut: it is to be given to a contractor in part, apparently: however that he will write to you about. The pressing thing is to get the roof, and conserve it. Can you send him £30, if it is at all possible, when you can? Give him notice if it cannot be yet, saying when you will be able to pay it. He is going to learn line-process etching of a city firm, and is short of cash. Delay the remittance you proposed in your last letter to send to me, until July, if this would help you at all. Dr. Warren wrote asking whether he should pay quarterly or half-yearly, and I told him I didn't care, but that he might ask you. The chances are that you will have something coming in from Magdalen therefore before the summer. About the other matter, the suggested advance from Father for building purposes, that is entirely for his judgment: if he feels inclined to do it, of course it would make matters much easier for the press. If not we will have to wait. You know that Richards & I decided last meeting that he would continue teaching for the present, whatever the fate of the demyship: we thought it would be wiser, since my power of earning the demyship depends on my health, and my ability to spend it on the press depends on my getting a salary, digging, next year and the year after, or on my getting "Richard." It is a great battle of the wits, creative, on his side, for he is doing the work, and utilitarian on mine, for I am to provide the materials beyond his keep. It will be a comfort when we get through into smoother water with the whole thing. {Leonard} Green has written to me. Apparently the thesis might be useful to him even after Jan. 17: so please send it to him if before Easter it returns from Mr. Barker or Mr. Jane.

It would be a distinct kindness if Will went down to see him (Mr. Jane) occasionally, on pretexts such as Green's request might afford, or even a letter from me. He lives so much alone, and is so short of money (not his own debts either, but other people's) that he gets very much despondent, and visitors who talk decently encourage him. And he is too interesting for it to be an ordeal. Will no doubt is busy with Mods. work. I am hoping for him to wipe Mr. Powell's eye (or both eyes). If he has specialised rather on the humanist side, so much the better for himself. I recommend him *The Stream's Secret* by D.G.R. and possibly *Sartor Resartus* if he is not disgusted with it already. Tell Arnie that Abdullah has asked in the Suk for a wauri's tail, and that they hadn't one: but he offers to cure me one if I will get it for him: so I have a revolver by my bed, and the household sits up in turn to look for one that comes most nights & eats their chickens & rabbits. Tonight there was great excitement for a hyena arrived about eleven, and began to crunch bones just behind a box: then he came out, & we all had a good look at him: a handsome beast, too. They were very anxious for me to shoot him, but he wouldn't have been any earthly good to anyone. I wonder how many shots I will have before I get this tail?

For the rest Arabic, and Assyrian, and a good deal of French with Mrs. Rieder: no antiquities this month: I may have more time later on. A sirocco yesterday that blew off some of the school roof, and windows, etc. Today the sea front for a hundred yards deep, is clouded with spray, all up & down the coast. The waves are rolling on the rocks like thunder.   N.

Miss Holmes fell upon Mrs. Abbot's patterns with rapture . . . many thanks returned for them.

JEBAIL

Jan. 21, 1911

Thanks for copied letters. So you are at Barmouth after all! or was it only Father? I could not make out much of the postmarks. Please tell Arnie that I shot at the wauris one night, and that they ran away forthwith, before I could pick them up. So his tail is not yet, for they have not come back.

Today, though, we have snow all over the hills, which will drive all the animals into the coast-villages. So tomorrow, or tonight all will be well, perhaps. But they are difficult to hit. You read Winckworth's letter I hope. He is not coming out, for Mr. Hogarth has secured a cuneiformist. So that I will not have any responsibility this year. I am very glad of course, for the Arabic will profit thereby. Isn't this ink vile? After all Father had better not come out here. It can be very cold, and wet, and only two houses in all Beyrout (and none in Jebail) have fireplaces, or heating apparatus. So he would be rather put to it to keep warm (ice $\frac{1}{2}$ inch thick). I hope he is better this winter where he is. Is all well in the family? The last three letters have said nothing upon this matter, which may be good news, but of an insubstantial kind. Please remember that my anxiety (there being 6 of you) is necessarily many times greater than your own. Two sides to all arrangements, and I have written manfully, despite the ink. By name Will and Arnie & Mother are excepted from any implication of censure, and Father, since his ink weighs so heavy in the post (not but that his letters are the best . . .): but has Frank or Bob forgotten so soon how to hold a pen? or is the frost checking their flow of ink? or have their "swans" migrated? Salaams.   N.

P.C. by this post to Florence.

Am gathering coins for Arnie: a shield-bishlik, some nahasis (of Damascus) & double nahasis and a silver half-bishlik. Others when occasion offers, & stamps when I visit Beyrout. The tail will be sent as soon as it is offered me & cured.

N.

Will you try to send me out Stevenson's *Crusaders in the East* the book I suggested be sent to Green? I find myself shaky on the import-ance of Atharib, Ezaz and the other frontier towns of Aleppo: and he is the only authority compact. I would like the book at any rate in June: as much before as possible. If Mr. Hogarth has no Carchemish address to give send it to Miss Holmes: she will forward it Turkish post. The Jebail office has just begun to transmit foreign parcels.

Jebail

22 January 1911

They have just found your note on the floor where it had dropped, & hidden itself. So you must have another sheet. Am glad Arnie saw Harlech. The group of the chimneys over the front wall are what I remembered chiefly after my first visit. The second time I was with Bob, & remember fairly well.

We had snow this morning, which covered all the beach to the breaking of the waves: such has not been for 40 years. Miss Holmes thought the wire was good news: but was very excited to know. Mr. Parfit does not live at all in Beyrout: but comes down on Saturday for the Sunday services only: I cannot go up to Ain Anub (his schools) for they are 8 hours drive from Beyrout. I will write to him, & will try to arrange a Sunday in Beyrout in February: when I am going North. Shall be interested to hear what Jesus Coll. does. You must offer to return the money, and if they refuse give them a silver mug: which Hall or Prys-Jones would arrange for Will. It should be about £5: but the odds are 1000 to 1 against their being generous. The film matter is getting serious. Father will be rather puzzled to know what to do with the "house" if it is left on his hands: tho' I am glad it is to be concrete. Miss Holmes very ungrateful if she complains of me: for I have mended (on average) 2 things a day since I entered the house, & broken nothing. Mrs. Rieder is literary: which is a comfort to me: she

Carcassonne (*See p.* 68)

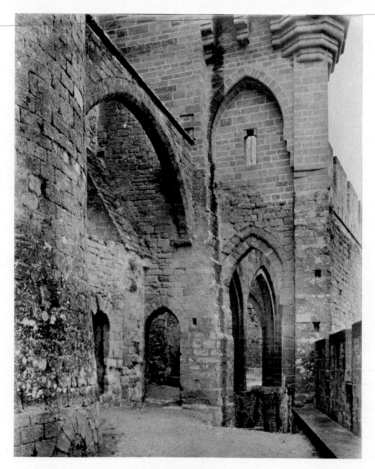

Carcassonne (*See p.* 68)

has introduced me to Daudet's shorter pieces: all very good, *printable*. Don't give Mr. Hogarth anything for me, if you can help. Arnie will prove a serpent if he does not get the senior scholarship next year. Tell Father not to write overmuch: it is no great pleasure for him and for what else has he five sons? I told you Mrs. Kemmis' carpet was half-way only. It sticks there, still. Am making a careful survey of the castle, & reading Arabic with Miss Fareedah (who is wonderful) & Omar, Miss Holmes' protégé. I will have to reward them both somehow, since payment is impossible.

N.

JEBAIL

Jan. 24, 1911

Letter from Father, including Mother's copy of Richards' huge letter. The post comes in one night, late, & letters have to be answered by next morning at 7 a.m. This means that there is not much time for consideration. However:—Richards and I work together of course, and approve what each does for the other. If we are to preserve the utmost elasticity in our relations, we cannot be bound by a written agreement. We must (if such agreement exists) inevitably go outside and beyond it whenever we feel inclined: so that there will always be a contradiction between our theory and our practice. At the same time perhaps an agreement might be useful (especially in the case of one of us dying or retiring): the unfortunate dispute over the Morris firm's reconstruction makes one afraid of one's constancy, so that it might be better for this reason if the agreement gave all things to one of us. By that means the other would have no possible ground of public complaint in case of a rupture:—and while we are agreed formal arrangements are only foolish:—Then further I would feel uncomfortable if we held equal shares, for after all it is Richards' energy & inspiration & design. My part will have been only to have furnished the money. To rate this as important would be to stultify our ideals in the outset. As far as I can see therefore all legal documents (leases and deeds and the rest) should be in Richard's name only: the money (if you are able to provide it) should be a loan to me, unconditionally, or as you please: and it should go (in theory only) from me to Richards independently. You can, I think, quite properly lend me money as an advance on my demyship, while to send it to Richards direct would leave you in about the position of a mortgagee. The matter is one for you to settle: it is purely a money matter, and I know nothing about such things. In any case I would not like a clause giving me possession on one year's notice: say 7 to 10 years to Richards, and 6 months or a year to others: but the house would be better entirely in his hands, save for my having the refusal of it if he should clear out or die. You might encourage him to make a will, somewhat in this direction: so long as he does not run into lawyers, & their bills.

Let the occupier of the house always have the duty of repairs and the right of alteration. The place is being put up as much for my use as for his: so that it is not a normal transaction. He is spending it as I hoped & intended he would, on a cause which we both have rather at heart. If the attempt succeeds one can hardly question the wisdom of the undertaking, and the matter of the furnishing of the money will look a little trivial. If it fails (and I think it will not, with the new copper-wire idea) then I will probably occupy the house, if (or until) Richards' home affairs come to a head. The thing to do before that is to take away materials for any possible dispute: and that I cannot help feeling is for me not to appear anywhere in writing. The rest is left to your judgment: please do not tie us up too much. Richards knows (or has forgotten) that the demyship is held for four years, if Magdalen is satisfied with my movements. As the conditions side with my inclinations it should be a fairly safe consideration. There cannot be any fixed hours of work. We both feel (at present) that printing is the best thing we can do, if we do it the best we can. That means though, (as it is an art), that it will be done only when we feel inclined. Very likely sometimes for long periods I will not touch a press at all. Richards, whose other interests are less militant, will probably do the bulk of the work. The losses (if any) will be borne by us both, according as we are in funds (we will approximate to a common purse): the profits will be seized upon as a glorious opportunity to reduce prices. You will see, I think, that printing is not a business but a craft. We cannot sit down to it for so many hours a day, any more than one could paint a picture on that system. And besides such a scheme would be almost sure to interrupt *The Seven Pillars of Wisdom* or my monumental work on the Crusades.

If you think fit you might send this letter to Richards. It will give him my point of view about the matter more fully than before, and besides the last sentence is meant especially for his instruction. He wrote to me for present expenses, which is why I asked you to send him £30. He will not need my pressing to be economical. I cannot send away all the demyship, and if the house costs £250 it will be quite the limit advisable. It will do without fittings very well for a time.

All here is quite right. I will try & write to you by the next post:— on Sunday that is. Tonight it is late.

N.

I have exhausted my envelopes!

JEBAIL
Jan. 31, 1911

This letter goes more particularly to Will. Ordinarily they are to be taken as delivered from the second-best chair in the Morning-room, with Mother perhaps as principal listener: but this one is for Will, not as a reward for writing so often and satisfactorily (which would be to attempt a return in kind) but because his last letter was heavy with the sense of responsibility.

Mr. Jane's review was splendid:—though written with personal animus. I wonder who the man was. It will increase the circulation enormously but will not tend to soothe the Press, or make his work successful as a text-book. I have written to him: of course you could see that the reviewer was either hair-splitting or blundering in his criticisms: he did not so much as grasp the central idea of the argument.

We get *The Times* foreign edition: so have been quite up to date. The "Anarchist" troubles have been acute, evidently. They will find out soon that they were burglars! I don't think Richards told you anything without my justification: except that I did not give him enough data. I told him all I knew & we could think of in our time: but we are so busy always when we get together. I will write to him about the length of the house. He is only trying to carry out what he believes to be my wishes, though I asked him to consider his own ideas only. A 40-foot hall would be more beautiful that's all. I hope he will give up the idea so far as it is inconvenient.

I am not as sanguine as himself about the early start of printing. His own enthusiasm is enormous, and a little catching: so with him I lose

a little of my (inherited) Scotch caution. It would be very splendid if
he had made a beginning on the final stock of type by my return: but
he will be kept busy with the building first. Your character of him
seems to me very apt and fairly complete: though I must say I think
some of the "snobbery" which gives such an unpleasant conceit to his
judgments comes rather from lack of understanding, than intentionally. Richards is exceedingly narrow in his outlook and interests, and is
too apt to condemn generally where he does not find the particular
colour and cast of thought that appeals to him. He is not at all intellectual, but an artist to the finger-tips. The lack of spontaneity is only
evident in matters such as King's Stephen & Hewlett. As soon as you
get him on what he thinks really good he loses entirely his critical
sense, and becomes a most fiery prophet. He has said things to me of an
intimacy & directness which are beyond anyone else I have met.
Altogether though he is a most complex and difficult personality, and
I do not think he will get any better on acquaintance. He is quite in
earnest about the printing: just as I am. I fancy we each of us trust the
other entirely in that, without any great love, personally. But he will
do his best for the press, and I also, so that only a little savoir vivre is
necessary to make a very satisfactory partnership. I am most fortunate
to have found a man of tremendous gift to whom craftmanship is at
once a dream and an inspiration. You will remember that it is the ideal
of not over-sentimental beings which usually realize most completely
their aim. They may not be very high ideals but they come into practice so far as an ideal may without disappearing. I think even Mr. Jane
would be satisfied if our association produced the best book of modern
times. We hope no more than the wages of creation, and the meat &
drink promised with them in Ecclesiastes (3). To do the best of anything (or to try to do it) is not waste of opportunity:—and to be
keeper of a Museum would not be my best any more than to teach
history: I want something in which I can use all these things instead of
being used by one of them.

    Your poet is interesting. Though how a "decadent" could be much
use I cannot understand. There is certainly no place for the professional
poet, qua poet, just now: but we can all present poetry to others in
different ways. Do not worry overmuch over work. The main thing
is to spread yourself at present, and for that you will probably find
history best. Read as much in the originals as you can: whenever you

can appreciate the mode of thought of another age or country (or even person) you have gained a new world. I am sorry to hear of Father's cough: but your weather has not been worse than ours this week. I never saw such storms: and no way of heating the house either. I hope he will find relief soon from it: he was so well the last two winters.

Good for Lang. The *Iceland Journal* will be a pleasure. If the coming reprint of the 1611 Bible is satisfactory in paper & print & price please get one. The facsimile would be best, if it is not on glazed paper. We will want one for our reprint in any way.

The "wauri" has not yet put in an appearance: or his tail.

BEYROUT

Sat. Feb. 18, 1911

Am come down to Beyrout with Miss Holmes & Mrs. Rieder: Mr. Hogarth comes on Monday. The "Third" was in Beyrout yesterday (he is really the second) looking for a piano: so we are not going to rough it in Carchemish. The railway line is blocked between Beyrout & Aleppo; no trains for a month: snow 30 feet deep for 7 kilometres: it may be free this week: if not must go round by Haifa & Damascus: or across country from Iskanderon.

Last days in Jebail were very busy: which will explain only p.c. last week. Mrs. Rieder got up a sort of amusement-book for Miss Holmes, unfortunately the day before her own birthday: and both were in the way of being festivities, and in both I had a lot to do. Besides that I worked harder than usual at Arabic (my eyes have recovered all right) and also I finished the mending of the things in the house. I am going to the Brit. P.O. now to ask for parcels: their parcel-post comes in today, & if I am going to get my films it will be this morning. Such a pity the Cristoid people have given up. The photo. of the castle with the stairs & the beehive (really the weli of an excellent Mahommedan) is Markab: and another photo. of a castle much on the same scale (above) is the same place. My Syria films are all labelled in the lower edge (right way up in Indian Ink: with name of place & subject (i.e. in this case Markab S.W.)). Markab is about 40 or 50 miles N. of Tripoli on the coast. The other photo. is of Carcassonne: you will find a similar view in my postcard packet. Tell Green to read the labels on the films: he has written to me. Davis is of course an extraordinarily queer creature; all over crotchets, clever, but with an over-developed sense of his own superiority ridiculously over-developed. Mr. Jane cannot ask him for anything without putting his back up: Davis likes the reputation of knowing everything: and I expect he will not return the thesis until he has read up all the other books on the subject. His decision will be very interesting: though of course my rather knight-errant style of tilting against all comers in the subject will ruffle his hair. I must I suppose do without letters from you for a bit: you evidently (by your last letter) had forgotten our date for starting diggings: and you probably missed Mr. Hogarth therefore. At present Aleppo has been for days without a post (for the Haifa route is continually being washed out, & Alexandretta has no mail system) so you must not be surprised if you also do not hear from me. I will go N. with Mr. Hogarth though: so you need not fear what may happen to two such people. Miss Holmes has had influenza: & is come down here for 3 or 4 days to rest. I stayed with her just 8 weeks exactly: and she says my washing was not worth counting as an extra: that is ambiguous as a compliment, but except for collars it was as at Oxford. She always loses a little (about 2% on cheques from England: but it is perfectly simple to cash them. She has been exceedingly kind to me all through: Mrs. Rieder also: Tell Arnie I did not get his "Wauri": perhaps at Carchemish. They only came one night at Jebail: & I missed that shot. I suppose they were frightened off. Today I am going to look up Cook's (many thanks for money, they have sent me their receipt & directions) and the Consulate (where my Iradés are): and the Post Office. Horrible weather today: more snow. It is fine enough at Aleppo, but there is a dearth of provisions & no charcoal, as the trains are held up. The Lebanon can evidently be unpleasant when it likes. If Mr. Hogarth has left no address write to Aleppo (Brit. Consulate) for the present: but I hope he will have. Leeds will want to consult him sometimes. No other news: I may pencil in the rest of this before posting it.

Tell Snow I am going N. now: he may like to hear. Also commiserate Frank on his ankle: such troubles take a long time to clear up: let him take refuge in reading. Have bought a Shakespeare: tell Arnie there are no Russian Stamps Austrian only, & German, which enclosed. Campbell-Thompson: the "second" is to be married in Aleppo this spring. He wants a house and a piano for his bride.

Films come next week: have arranged they be sent to Aleppo. I go on Tues. (if D.G.H. comes) to Tripoli, drive to Homs, & go up thence to Aleppo by Rail.

L.

DAMASCUS
Sunday, 26 February 1911

Snow began to fall again on Wednesday night, just after I had closed my letter to you: also a storm blew up, and they said that the boat would not start for Haifa. We waited till Thursday, and then went to see the director of the railway: he told us that all the work of clearing the path had to be begun again. As the wind had dropped Mr. Hogarth thought it best to try for Haifa: he would have gone over the hills, but for old Gregori, his Cypriote head-man, who is 60, and not very active.

We had a pleasant enough passage, with the sea fairly rough. There was a great glare of sunlight, but we managed to get a good view of Sidon and Tyre, and Acre, and the other places I knew. Haifa was reached at midday on Friday, and we walked up in the afternoon to the monastery on Mount Carmel. Mr. Hogarth is paying my expenses to Aleppo: not those of the trip out to Beyrout from England, however. He has been very interesting indeed so far, especially on Arabian geography. I saw Dr. Coles at Haifa. He knows nothing more about the purple dye than I do: but there are plenty of the fish alive, and he will help me when I make experiments. From Haifa we took train for Damascus. It ran at first along the plain of Acre at the foot of Mount Carmel, which on the East side rises very suddenly from the level ground. That was before dawn, so that even when we passed over the Kishon we hardly were in a mood to appreciate. Still I did rouse him up to look at Harosheth, Sisera's town: now it is only a mud village (which gave me a loaf of bread last time, but grudgingly: it is very poor, and dirty), but he more than shares my admiration for Deborah's little ode, thinking it one of the best things in the O.T., so that went down very well. After that the sun rose, as we came across Esdraelon, and we both thawed out very happily. We had a carriage to ourselves, and were otherwise most comfortable. Nazareth of course was only visible in the shape of the great convent on the hill, but Mr. Hogarth

does not like it any better than I did: I think, if Mother comes to
Palestine that we will just look at the view of the village from the
hill-top: it is then no uglier than Basingstoke, or very little, and the
view from it, southwards over the plain, is beautiful. Then in the
evening, when the dusk is beginning she shall walk down to the well
in the village, and so find it free from the very parasitically unpleasant
natives of the place. After she has had a drink we will go back to the
tent, and she will have been spared a disappointment, and been given
an endurable memory in its stead. Tabor looked uninteresting this
time: it had not the glory of being the only green thing in a sea of gold.
Esdrælon looks best in summer, when they are reaping the corn. Last
time I saw it the whole plain was chequered with the brown and gold
of stubble and ear, and lined red, where the paths were trampled
through the fields. There is not a hedge or a wall or a house in all the
twenty miles, but in their place were black tents, and cooking fires,
and long strings of camels carrying the corn to the coast from the
threshing floors. These floors were always marked by little figures of
men and women (for the air was wonderfully clear, even to showing
the chaff and dust clouds from the flails and fans), and occasionally a
field would also be marked likewise by a field of reapers, with scattered
figures after them tying up the sheaves, or gleaning what had fallen.
That was lovely from the hill: much lovelier than the spring colouring,
though that is lovely also in a strongly marked division of red and
green: green for the young crop, and red for the soil fresh-ploughed.
I never saw before any ground so red: unless later the Hauran was
redder. The colour was a rich crimson lake, without any stains of
brown. After Beisan we ran along the Jordan valley, which was no
more lovely than in autumn, until you look into the grass, and see red
and blue flowers. The train waited a little while at Semakh on the Lake,
and then began to wind up the Yarmuk valley. It twisted up it for three
hours, so that often and often we could see the engine and last van of a
short train on different sides of our carriage: it crossed the river half a
dozen times on bridges, with wonderful lava and basalt walls all over
red and blue anemones above on each side a thousand feet or more:
once there were some palm-trees even, and always splendid views: our
speed hardly ever passed xii miles an hour: at the top we passed a large
waterfall, and then crossed the "red-lands" of the Hauran, supposed to
be the richest corn land in the world. Mr. Hogarth of course knew all

the country by repute, and by books, and we identified all the mountain peaks and wadies and main roads . . . do you know we saw the
pilgrim route, the great Hajj road? Doughty is the only man who has
been down it, and written what he saw. Do read his account of it: we
crossed it first near Muzerib, and again to the North. The mountains
were all snow-covered & drifts were lying in the water-courses: but
at Deraah all was sunny, and we had a French *déjuner* in the Buffet,
where Mr. Hogarth spoke Turkish & Greek, & French, & German,
& Italian & English all about the same as far as I could judge: it was a
most weird feeling to be so far out of Europe: at Urfa and at Deraah I
have felt myself at last away out of the Renaissance influence, for the
buffet was flagrantly and evidently an exotic, & only served to set off
the distinctness of the Druses & their Turkish captors. The Lejah, the
lava no-man's land, and the refuge of the outlaws of all the Ottoman
Empire lay alongside the railway for an hour or more: it is almost
impassable, except to a native who knows the ways. There were villages
in it, the "Giant cities" which Porter talks about. We got into Damascus
late, & tomorrow we go up to Aleppo. Mr. Hogarth has just come in
with news that a wash-out of 2 kilometres has taken place near Homs,
so our pains at getting here are apparently wasted, we may have to
wait in Homs till it is repaired. At any rate we are going up to see.

ALEPPO.   *March* i., 1911

I have got a bundle of letters here today & yesterday, the Stevenson,
& down to Father's letter of the eighth. I'll send you off a line tonight,
for the days are rather busy in getting things. We reached here last
night, over a snow-covered line from Damascus: nothing of note.
The second man is very much alive: pleasant though. We will get on
all right together. Mr. Hogarth has £1700 still unspent: that will carry
us on for 9 months digging: it is possible that I won't get back this
year: especially if digging starts again in March: but it is more likely
that the B.M. will refuse to continue. In any case I will stay as long as
they will have me. We are going to be very well fitted up in stores:
Mr. Hogarth has a huge consignment of things coming out (9 sorts of
jam: 3 varieties of tea, and other things in proportion), and more is
being got here. I expect to go across soon with Thompson & begin a
survey of the ground. Thompson has a complete Shakespeare, Mr.

Hogarth a Dante & some French novels, & I a complete Spencer. I am looking forward to the *Golden Legend*, when it arrives. The Stevenson will be invaluable. I had not expected it so soon. As for the tin cases of the films, I won't carry them. Aleppo is indescribably dirty just now: the streets are like mud geysers when a carriage plunges into them. I saw one this afternoon drive over the edge of an embankment, & disappear to the top of its hood. The horses were got out. A mule kicked a bucket-full of the compound into my face in the suk: and I was plastered all over & temporarily blinded by it. I am revelling in the bazaar here of course. We have got 35/- worth of pistachio nuts, & as much more of Turkish delight, & Arab sweetmeats. The Thompson man has a weekly parcel of books coming out. I can commend the example: only that they would be a nuisance to bring back. If we do decide to dig on into November however I may ask for a Francis Thompson and a Rabelais and a Vergil or Lucretius. There is no need of any of them now. It seems likely that I will take particular charge of the pottery found: that would be a business very much to my taste. By the way I picked up ridiculously cheap in Damascus a little blue red and green Rhodian vase that Mother may like. It is a drawing-room piece though comparatively late as Rhodian pottery goes: pretty all the same. If we dig till November I will not do any wandering this year, beyond the minimum required to satisfy Magdalen. I will ask Mr. Hogarth what that will be. Jesus of course will not require a cup now: they are all tho' to be of one established model: you know I do not give what I think good to other people, unless there is a chance of their liking it too! C/o British Consul Aleppo is the best address. Not a bad plan to write {Aleppo, in Arabic characters} in the left hand bottom corner opposite "Aleppo": but not really necessary.

The post is still disorganised with Beyrout yet snowed in. I cannot, and Miss Holmes & Mrs. Rieder could not, think of anything for Omar & Miss F. as presents. Fountain pens one cannot write Arabic with. I am sorry Wink. {Winkworth} is not coming: but Mr. Hogarth himself takes no salary. . . . Am sorry to hear you have been unwell to the extent of Dr. W. "Remember it is better to keep well than to get well": your advice recoils on your own head for I am a valetudinarian compared with yourself. Thank Will for his letter: the Aleppo button is the effect of a fly: I only hope I may be able to cover it by a beard if it comes. Frank's letter is a great success: also his repairs of the lamp. I wonder if he will find the acetylene acceptable: it cannot be relit or run on small charges: or could not. His revolver practice sounds excellent. I hope he tries to shoot without taking aim. The only practical way is almost to throw your bullet like a stone, at the object: you can do that in a flurry. The M.S. was Arabic: a Greek [- Church] service book. The revolver was the Mauser. Bicycle must be treated delicately I fancy. The frame whipped under me in France the last tour so that it had to be trued in Rouen. The barring of football may be a blessing in disguise. Father's letter I will answer later when I have had a little breathing space: but he is right in that but for the wonderful chance of the oak we would put off the hall a year or 6 months. A letter from Florence arrived.   N.

CARCHEMISH (JERABLUS)

March 11, 1911

We have got here, & this is a hurried note to go off by the returning camelmen. We left Aleppo Thursday: this is Saturday, nothing of note on the journey except the flooded Sadjur: which was easily crossed tho', at a ford. I had no camera ready unfortunately. Mr. Hogarth drove & walked & rode: Thompson rode & walked: I walked, except of course over the river. Not much yet of course to say about this place. The mounds are enormous: but I'll send you a photo. or drawing later. We only got in about 4 o'clock: and have been unpacking since: eleven baggage horses, ten camels. . . . The head-man of the village, who is also the agent of the Liquorice Company that I ran into last time, has put the Co's house at our disposal. It is a big, stone-built, one storied place, with a court-yard adjoining: the roof will be good for sleeping on later in the year: at present the thermometer is 40° with a gale off those N.W. summits of the Taurus, that, snow-clad, were in view all this afternoon. We have bedding enough, good hap, for a host. The village is about ¾ of a mile from the site, & the river: on high ground, so there is no possibility of fever in the hot weather, when or if it comes: snow here a few days ago: no skating on the river, worse luck. As for the place: there is a high plateau in the corner N. of the Sadjur and W. of the Euphrates: this is some 500 feet above the river. We started on that this morning & then dropped gradually from foothill to foothill until we reached this village. It is a little place, of about 40 houses, very clean and fresh-looking, being all quite new, with a very fast-running spring on one side. I thought (and Mr. Hogarth said) that there was nothing but river-water in the place: as it is "the most delicate fabrics may be washed without damage": the water is quite clear, fairly cool, and good-tasting. Its situation puts it out of the way of defilement. The mound is about $\frac{3}{4}$ of a mile N. of the village: the river about $\frac{1}{2}$ mile to the E.: and it bends round until it washes the edge of the great "Acropolis" hill. Our unpacking was a lively sight: heaps & heaps of baggage animals of all sorts; horses mules, donkeys, camels: about a dozen of our men, and perhaps 20 villagers, who swarmed out of their houses when we approached, & as soon as we had approved the house, all turned to under the orders of the little overseer, and cleared it out. It was full of camel-hides, & corn, poplar-poles and lentils. The last were impounded for the benefit of the expedition. I cater to some extent. . . . I want to go to bed now: we have had two very rough nights, and it is very cold. All quite well: I like the second-man Thompson, very much.

N.

Jerablus
March 20, 1911

Have got a letter from Father–Will–Mother: & cuttings: with another letter. Glad all well. May Mods. be profitable. Sports are only a "divarshun" besides it. My eyes got tired easily with the horrible Arabic type in common use: and with the cuneiform on top. So I gave up reading altogether, that they might be fit for the strong sunlight we expect out here. I thought I had told you that: for it limited my learning of Arabic very seriously. Still I can get on here with what I have: and my eyes are perfectly right again. Nothing more to say I fancy: I have not written to anyone for a long time: for we are rather busy out here. Tonight it is quite impossible to write properly, for it is already late, and we get up at sunrise of course. Still I will tell you a little of the place till the light gives out. We have got the Liquorice Company's house, of which there is a plan overleaf: it is one storied, stone-built will probably be cool in summer. Very cold now, at any rate. I have the large bed-room: also used as store-room: about 45 feet long: but narrow. Garden all round house. Thompson has been planting seeds flower & veg. no results as yet.

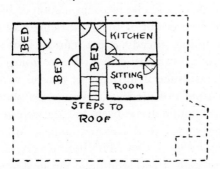

We have two servants at present: with one of their wives on the way: probably when Mrs. Campbell Thompson eventuates we will have another. Much eating & very civilised, with about £80 worth of stores: and meat etc. on the spot. Unlimited (goat) milk. I hope to make a little vellum from their skins later on. Village of about 40 houses: on rising ground half a mile from the river: good spring (a little warm) coming up in the middle of it: women weave excellent coarse cloth. All people serfs of one Selim Touma, ex-muleteer, & now liquorice-magnate. He is decent towards us: and the piled-up liquorice in the back-yard makes a delicious smell. Also all the men in the village, & the neighbourhood (to no. of 100) are in our employ. The mounds (about $\frac{1}{2}$ mile across), on the banks of the river, are about 15 minutes walk from the house: there is a large central one, & walls round it, & a probable town-site: if we ever have leisure I will send a drawing or plan. Work begins at sunrise (6.0 a.m.) we breakfast first & walk down a little later.

Thompson is surveying the site, & will be to the end of the week. Mr. Hogarth does the writing up of the results: I do the squeezing & drawing the inscriptions & sculptures, & (with the great Gregori, of the *Accidents of an Antiquary's Life*) direct the men. Work goes on (with an hour for lunch) till sunset. Then home: write up journals: & catalogues: feed, & go to bed. This week has been extra busy putting up shelves, & fitting doors, windows etc. This I have done mostly, being handiest. In digging we began where the Museum people had left off 30 years ago. We uncovered a great entrance staircase, with some Hittite slabs on each side, much damaged: now we are rather puzzled with things in general. Lots of miscellaneous bas-reliefs (mostly ugly) have been got out: but till today we have only had few (50) men, & of course as usual there is a huge accumulation of big stones on top. At any rate there is no doubt of the great richness of the site. Some 8 or 10 Hittite inscriptions already, & the staircase is of a late city, with infinitely older work buried beneath it. We are going below it shortly. We have 5 cameras (mine is in order of course, with the films Mr. Hogarth brought, but not used yet, no time for photographing) but many of the slabs found have been too defaced for photography. These I have been trying to draw on a large scale for reproduction: this has been a big business. One lion's head is very fine work, artistic-ally: also a god or king. I will send drawings next week perhaps if on Sunday there is breathing space. The men chose that day for their rest, though they are nominal Mahommedans. The Kaimmakan of Biredjik has had warning from C.P. that we are precious people: so there are proclamations going out into all the country that we are tabu: and he has bothered us with what almost amounts to a garrison of soldiers: we have a small camp in our courtyard and not one of them has both gun & cartridges: they share the glory of those things. The district is exceedingly pretty, from the model-village with its spring to the Euphrates, & the plain of Tell Ahmar, & the Taurus, snow-covered, to the North. The whole affair till now has been ideal, or would be if one had time to think about it.

Mr. Hogarth is a most splendid man: has read, & still reads most things, & likes talking about them, & the people who write: he knows Hewlett: the objections seem mistaken in his case: at least D.G.H. gives him a clean bill. Thompson, the second man, is not an archæologist, but a cuneiformist . . . : very good fun, & very pleasant: knows a tremen-dous lot about Semitic languages. He expects to be married out here in the Autumn. There seems a little doubt whether we will stop digging at all: but that you will hear (from Leeds via Mr. Hogarth) in June before I do. We are expecting Professor Sayce, & Miss G. Bell (whose book, *Between the Desert and the Sown*, you might like. I am expecting a parcel of films, which has got to Beyrout at least.

                                                                        N.

8 wild boars turned up on Friday at a village over the river: all the people turned out & shot them: a fearful riot . . . & powder burning:

Excuse this paper, & general appearance of letter. It is being written
on the mound, in a dull day of digging, with an empty pen. The pen,
by the way is a very distinct comfort out here. Today we are moving
great stones: the remains of walls & houses are buried about $\frac{2}{3}$ of their
height in fairly clean earth, but the upper few feet are filled up with
rubble, and small rocks, with the ashlar masonry and concrete of the
late Roman town. Whenever we break fresh ground dozens of these
huge blocks have to be moved. Some of them weigh tons, and we have
no blasting powder or stone-hammers with us. As a result they have to
be hauled, prehistoric fashion, by brute force of men on ropes, helped
to a small extent by crowbars. At this moment something over 60 men
are tugging away above, each man yelling Yallah as he pulls: the row
is tremendous, but the stones usually come away. Two men out of
three presume to direct operations, and no one listens to any of them,
they just obey Gregori's orders, and their shouting is only to employ
their spare breath. Now they are raising the "talul", the curiously
vibrant, resonant wail of the Bedawi. It is a very penetrating, and very
distinct cry; you feel in it some kinship with desert-life, with ghrazzus
and camel-stampedes. (Meanwhile the stone has slipped & fallen back
into the trench, and Gregori's Turkish is deserting him). Whenever he is
excited he slips back into Greek in a high falsetto voice, that convulses
our hoarse-throated men. To-day is a lovely day, in the shade of the
diggings as I am at present: outside it is a little warm, with the usual
streaming sunshine everywhere. We have had no rain since we came
to Carchemish, but generally sun, with often after midday a gale from
the North that drives the workmen off the top of the mound, and
tosses up the dust of our diggings and dump-heaps in thick blinding
and choking clouds all across the site. If one can struggle up to the top
of the mound and hold on one can look over all the plain of the river
valley (a very narrow one to the N. wide to the S.) up to Biredjik and
down to Tell Ahmar, and over it all the only things to show out of
the dust clouds are the hills and the tops of the tells. There might be
no river except when a side-shift of the wind splits the clouds, and
shows it running brown underneath. It still is not in flood, but is very
swift, and cold with the melting snows of the Taurus. We look out
for the hill top above Andiamar every morning and see them each time

with more & more lines and black spaces on their white. Before very long I expect the ¾ of a mile of river-bed will be one unbroken race of water. That will be the time when our mound looks best, but at all times it is very impressive rising about 100 ft. direct out of the river very steeply as all those North Syrian mounds are. I have taken a photograph or two, and will try a drawing, when I have leisure enough, if ever that will be. It is not that there is much to do, of course: for most of the day we are not in the least necessary, and in those times I play with the pottery, which Mr. Hogarth has handed over to me as my particular preserve. Our house is half a mile away, and so we cannot all go back there and amuse ourselves, or work as the case may be during digging hours. Somebody must be within call of the diggers and so I am usually down here, with just sufficient interruptions to make writing or sketching not worth while. As soon as these Northern hurricanes stop, however, we intend to give up our house, & camp out on the mound. Then we will have time to do things. At present our evenings are filled up with the odd jobs that might have been done in the day, squeezing & copying inscriptions, writing up pottery & object lists, journals etc. Also it gets cold after sunset, and we go to bed early (about 10 or 11 as a rule), to avoid it. In the matter of food all goes quite easily, except for the Haj's quite inadvertently emptying a curry tin into a pilaff! It was like eating peppered flames, and the other two are now crying aloud about their livers! That has so far been our only little hardship: I learnt a little about Syrian foods from Miss Holmes' servants, and this has come in usefully, for the Haj is not original, except in the matter of cakes that are half custard and half rubber sponge. Of course he has no oven which makes matters a little complicated. I am now building him one, out of a water jar. My power of sleeping through anything, which I acquired in my little house by aid of late hours and a telephone bell is standing me in excellent stead. I am the only one out of the three who gets any sleep at all at night. Mr. Hogarth is always getting up, to chase cats or rats or birds or mice or dogs. Everything comes in and out of the window holes, and the light sleepers suffer. The only time I woke up was when a cat scratched my face, entirely without provocation so far as I am aware. We are tired of the village bread (the thin cloth-like galettes) and still more of the bread so made out of English flour. The villages all live on barley-bread, but the Haj tried to use our home flour, and

Niort (See p. 76)

Chartres (*See p.* 81)

the result was a sheet, not of paper or cloth, but of wash leather or thin indiarubber sheeting. It is very tough & holds water, and most elastic. Mr. Hogarth's teeth refuse to eat it, and so he is brought very low. Thompson can just get through it: I flourish, but the others got tired of seeing that, and have made arrangements with the Commandant of Biredjik to supply us with mule-loads of the soldier's bread. This is thick, brown, whole-meal stuff, rather like the ideal bread of the Limousin, but darker in colour, and without the very slight sourness of the French stuff. By the way "whole-meal" does not mean that it is like Veda bread, or the English "whole-meal". Sometimes we have Euphrates fish: the small ones taste of mud, and are more bony than herrings: and thick bones that choke a cat. The larger ones are much better. Another year we will have a sailing canoe, or something of the sort: it will be splendid to go down the river to Bassorah. This much is being written on the great mound, with the main branch of the river some 200 yards wide at my feet. The men behind, digging in the top of the tell have got down about 10 feet, through an Arab strata, into a Roman one. This means cement and big stones, and slow work: but they have found a very nice little cup of early Arab ware, probably 11th Century. At present they are pulling up stones from the bottom of their pit, in a mist of "Yallah's" and "Issa's." The last is curious for they are all nominally Mahommedans. They can do nothing without noise. A man has just put off from the island across the near branch of the river, to swim across to us. Their antics on the inflated skins are more curious than beautiful. The skin itself is goat or sheep: (though a man came across the other day between two wild-boar hides): very perfect vellum in appearance. I hope to buy enough to bind a Xenophon and another book or two, if I can find a new skin, for they have the bad habit of rolling them up tightly when dry, which lines them with cracks. The method of preparation must be most interesting. I cannot pretend to understand it yet, but in some way the skin is taken off whole, but for the head & lower legs, and the hair is stripped from it, & it is cured, without lime, or vegetable stupes and fermentations. I hope to get to know about it: and to get a few of the skins, at 6d. each! Worth 5/– in England, you know, if such natural-coloured vellum could be got out of Italy. The legs are tied up with sinew, and the man inflates the skin through the neck, until it is as tight as he can blow it (42 blows, to be very precise in a biggish skin): then they lie down on it, face down, in the water, and paddle across with hands & feet. Being light, the current catches them little. They take their clothes across as well, on their backs. My faculty of making & repairing things has recently demonstrated how to make paint (black & red) for marking antiques, how to render light-tight a dark slide, how to make a camera-obscura, how to re-worm a screw (difficult this without a die), how to refit a plane-table, and replace winding mechanism on a paraffin lamp. Also I have devised a derrick, and a complicated system of human-power jacks (out of poplar poles, & rope, and Arabs) which have succeeded in setting an Ishtar on her legs again. The Romans or Assyrians had broken her off at the knees, and the men could not shift the slabs back again, with any delicacy: so Mr. Hogarth & myself set to, and with our brains, & the aid of 90 men, put all right again. Before this there had been 120 men playing about with the ropes quite ineffectually.

Digging results will appear in *The Times* as soon as Mr. Hogarth gets back. They have been meagre, and not very satisfactory to date: but it is like Pandora's box with Hope always at the bottom: and we are not nearly at that yet. I will send drawings when I have a quiet Sunday. The women here weave very beautiful cloth: and sell it at about $1\frac{1}{2}d$. a yard: it is thick & coarse, like grey sacking: the probabilities are that I will bring home a bale: also enough camel-hide to bind my Doughty, when I get him. The book will be necessary, for I must know it by more than library use, if ever I am to do something of the sort. Mr. Hogarth thinks my idea of patronising the Soleyb, instead of the Arab, promising, both in security, & novelty. They are an interesting people: however no hurry about that, with Carchemish & military architecture and above all the necessary Arabic first. There is one thing I think I will get you to do: this piece of country is all rock, & very hard on one's boots. Will you get down to Gillman, & order another pair of boots, as before, only with slightly thicker soles: nails as before; leather boot laces. When these are made will you send them to Miss Holmes, and a letter asking her to be good enough to pay the Customs charges, and forward them to the Consul at Aleppo? They cannot be sent direct: as the adventures of my films, still held up somewhere in the country, go to prove. There is no hurry about them: it is only in case I am able to do some walking out here, if we knock off here before the rains. It would be appreciated if Will asked Blackwell's to write to

Jean Gillequin, publisher Bould. St. Michel Paris, ordering the 3 volumes of the Rabelais in his 1 f. 25 collection (*La Renaissance du livre*) to be sent to me c/o Consul. Aleppo. But not if you think books unnecessary! This letter is only an interim scrawl, to be strengthened by a heavy letter in a week: I hope by then to have heard of Mods. We get weekly post from Biredjik. All very well.   N.

JERABLUS

11 *April* 1911

. . . Mother is right about a letter having fallen through: I sent off one from Beyrout just before embarking for Haifa. In case it never appears I got the films & was very glad of them, and saw Mr. Parfit on the Sunday: he sent the usual messages, and came up to Aintab (close to here) a week ago. He meant to come across & see us, but did not feel too energetic, & was rather hurried: so I will not see him again till I get back to Beyrout. Just now we are expecting Professor Sayce, & Miss G. Bell, and Meissner Pasha (who is the Bagdad Railway). Arnie must not run to win the Cup: if so he deserves to lose: the things you get by trying after are never worth the things that, if too set on the end, you will pass over by the way. I would be very glad for him to get the cup; but later on I want him to learn to laugh at it. A. T. P. Williams (Jesus College) has written to me asking for the Thesis. He may have it, if Mr. Barker does not object. He is his tutor. Williams is in for History this year: but I don't suppose he would find much call to mention architecture. I think Frank is quite wise to give up the idea of a profession of the learned sort. All his tastes are in other directions, so far as one can see. Of course the Army is not one and the same in all its branches (thank goodness!) and he can choose a decent side of it. At the same time if he could get a Channel Islands scholarship it would be much the easiest & readiest & cheapest way to a commission.

There are always the University ones going for competition, of not an unattainable standard, and to have been at Oxford would make the way much easier for a man of small means. Poor Father! his sons are not going to support his years by the gain of their professions & trades. One a missionary: one an artist of sorts and a wanderer after sensations; one thinking of lay education work: one in the army, & one too small to think. None of us can ever afford to keep a wife: still the product of fairly healthy brains & tolerable bodies will not be all worthless in this world. One of us must surely get something of the unattainable we are all feeling after. That's a comfort: and we are all going for the same thing under different shapes: Do you know we illustrate the verse about heart, soul, mind, body? Will Arnie prove the strength that will make it all perfect & effective? Frank's toes can (like other candidates) be operated on. Consult Dr. Gibson if you do anyone. He knows the dodges of the red-tape fence. But let him in any case try for the Scholarship unless Mr. Cave says it is not worth the continued preparation. The ordinary route into the Army is less pleasant than by Oxford & the O.T.C. Glad you sent Miss Holmes her cheque. She is doing a hard work, under great handicaps. If Will wants a little preliminary breathing time he might do far worse than try his hand at her boys' school. There is such need in Syria for taste, as well as good will. . . . I hope to go back to Miss Holmes for a visit when we finish digging (end of June). I left a portmanteau there, & have a bag here: I'll walk down slowly (2½ months perhaps). Weather just now perfect. Euphrates in flood. I forget (after 6 weeks) what my reference to Harosheth is: it stands at the entrance of Esdrælon.

Digging is tremendous fun, & most exciting & interesting. The results so far are not nearly enough to justify a second season (I'll write about them soon) but the thing is (as I have said perhaps) like Pandora's box, with Hope in the last spit of earth. I have had some good pottery lately. Mr. Hogarth returns next week: he hopes to get to Oxford about Mid-May, & shortly after will publish interim report in *The Times*. I'll ask him to let you know when. He has been most exceedingly good to me all through: taught me a tremendous lot about everything from digging to Greek erotic verse: He'll help in my Meleager: whom he enjoys also.

N.

The dig will probably last another 5 weeks: after that we go to Tell Ahmar for trial pits: then to Harran, and after back to Aleppo: about end of June: write there c/o Consul, till June 6.

CARCHEMISH
Sunday about April 16, 1911

Letters came in yesterday: one from Bob & you: glad all well. The idea of writing to you in the evenings is impossible I fear, because the others go to bed so early, and I cannot get off without waking them up: & what with pottery & photography, & a good deal of drawing & painting that I do there is little spare time before 11 p.m.: Sunday is our only day without digging. Mr. Hogarth goes off this week. As this dig has proved a failure to the present (tho' there is still hope of one part of the site) he is going to try & persuade the B.M. to apply for Tell Ahmar. That would be a couple of seasons dig in two years' time, at a mound only a few miles from here lower down the Euphrates. He would not come out to it himself, & the place would be left to Thompson & myself. Thompson is not a digger, so the direction of that part would be my share (as it is going to be now). Mr. Hogarth suggested that a season or half a season with Petrie in Egypt might be valuable experience: and of course it would be. Digging in any case would be always a thing I would try to do, & the more I know of it the better. The question is whether this season or next, & I would strongly recommend this season, when I am out here ready. Petrie starts in Nov.–Dec. which is about the time I will be free in Syria: and I would go straight to him till Feb. or March. Then either to Syria again, or back to England as seemed best. That is in the probable case of our not having a second season here. Of course if we do this would be the necessary course: and that would mean my second spring occupied: otherwise I would spend next Feb.–July castle-hunting.

. . . Mr. Hogarth takes this letter to Aleppo with him. He leaves tomorrow (Thursday) probably with Professor Sayce. Of late we have found a chariot relief (our 4th) a figure adoring sacred palm, and two slabs of warriors holding captives & heads. They all come off the side of a street, which had been lined with them, but the depth of earth was not enough to save them from the Persians & Romans who have destroyed everything worth having on the site. So far it has been very nearly a failure as a digging, simply from that lack of small objects: there are still faint hopes of a second season, in a part of the site that we have not yet explored. Mr. Hogarth has recommended us to try it fairly exhaustively, and we have reduced the number of our workmen in expectation of Gregori's and his going: so that there will be best part of two months work here still. My camera has of late been doing quite good work, taking sculptures, that Mr. Hogarth may give a fair idea to the Museum of what we have got. He is sending out more films. No more time now.

This is intended to give you a rough account of a day on the digs: and it is being written on the top of the mound, with the Euphrates wide in front of me to the North. The river is flooding higher and higher, and all day long we hear the heavy crashing of its banks, as the waters eat under them and they fall; add to this the rushing of the river over the rocks on which Chesney's steamer struck (his *Euphrates Expedition* might interest you) and the continual rolling and grinding of the small pebbles in its bed before the oncoming water. I do not know what we would do in this place, without the Euphrates, to look at. Now about our work. We get up about 6 at present, of course later on it will be earlier. After breakfast we go down to the site, at which the men have been under their overseers, since about 5.30. The mounds are about $\frac{3}{4}$ of a mile away from the village, and their shape is like the plan enclosed. The large mound is, as you see, right on the river bank, and is about 90 feet high on that side. I hope to make a drawing tomorrow (Sunday) of the acropolis as it looks from the N.W. But one's Sunday is usually very well taken up with other things. Some of our digs have been at the foot of the mound, in what must have been the Royal Palace. Others have been right at the top. At present we are finishing off these top pits, by carrying them down 30 feet. There is nothing much on top, but huge Roman foundations, carried right down to prehistoric strata, with late Classical column-drums, and scraps of entablature: all very large in scale. The building cannot have been much less than the great temple at Baalbec. So far we have found nothing Hittite but a scrap of steatite cup in all our digs on the top. That and a brick stamped with the name of Sargon are the results of 3 weeks work. Much of the mound is made of unbaked brick: it was once the Hittite fortress, but I fear the Roman barbarians have destroyed everything upon it. The men dig till 8.30, have a half hour's rest, and then go on till 12, when they knock off for an hour and a half: after that they work till 5. We have dinner about 7 or half-past, according to the mercy of Haj Wahid, the cook-cavass.

While the men dig we loaf: which resolves itself into copying inscriptions, measuring depths & levels, & photographing. For the last I have 5 cameras, none much good but my own. . . . While we are at work on the top of the hill there is very little to do, as at present; so Thompson & I have divided the day, working each a morning or an afternoon at the house on our finds, or at the digs, alternately. I have control over the pottery, and if we had found a Hittite piece I would be quite content with digging: however, we may possibly get on to a Hittite stratum in the lower ground after a fortnight. To the present we have found nothing Hittite but large sculptures, & fragments of such. Never a Hittite stratum, or even a Hittite building. For all this place so far has taught us about them we might as well never have come.

We have about 80 men now, and two overseers. There were 120 when Mr. Hogarth & Gregori were here, (for Gregori see the *Accidents of an Antiquary's Life*) but these men are not good enough to handle so many. They get about 8 piastres a day each (*c.* 14 pence) and are very content with it, since the local wage is 6. However it lets us pick & choose, and they all work very well: pick-men, spade-men, and basket-carriers. Of course there are no wheel-barrows. The most pleasing part of the day is when the breakfast hour gets near: from all the villages below us on the plain there come long lines of red and blue women & children, carrying bread in red-check handkerchiefs, and wooden measures full of leben on their heads. The men are not tired then, and the heat is just pleasant, and they chatter about and jest & sing in very delightful style. A few of them bring shepherd's pipes, and make music of their sort. As a rule, they are not talkative: they will sit for minutes together at the house-door without a word: often coming out in the morning we have found 100 men grouped outside, wanting work, and have not heard a sound through the open window just above! The only time they get talkative is when they are about half-a-mile apart. A little companionable chat across Euphrates is a joy—except to one's ears near by, for sound carries tremendously in this region, and they bawl with their raucous voices. However not even Sheisho and Berkawi, two Kurd brothers, and the last in our employ, can talk over the noise of the flood at present: the other men gave up trying some days ago, and so the valley is at peace.

Will asks after the ethnography of the place. I am afraid I do not know what it is. There are Kurds, a few Tcherkers (of course heaps in Membidj), Turks, and Arabs. Will it do if I take a few typical heads, of our workmen in their varieties? They are mostly quite willing to be photographed. Thompson has been making frantic efforts after local folk-lore, but without result. These peoples' trilingualism makes them ignorant of all languages, and very limited in expression. They can seldom frame a sentence in Arabic, without Turk & Kurdi words creeping in. Their Arabic accent is vile: almost incomprehensible after Jebail and Mosul, which is to Thompson & myself. Some of the work-men are rather fine-looking fellows: all of course are thin as sticks: and the majority small: there was no one within an inch of Mr. Hogarth's height: indeed the majority are hardly more than mine. Many shave their heads, others let their hair grow in long plaits, like Hittites. Today, Saturday, is pay day, and we knock off at 4, instead of 5, to give us time to get them paid. Each man, or nearly each man, gets an extra every week, according to the value of his finds. This little gamble appeals to them immensely.

This week we have been quiet, after the over-rush of our seven visitors at once the week before. Miss Gertrude Bell is expected, but has not yet seen fit to come. The country is very green now, after several days of rain this week. The harvest they say will be in 5 weeks time: it may interrupt us, for quite probably we will dig for another 6 or 7 weeks. The heat here they say is never excessive, on account of the amount of wind: often after midday there springs up a great gale from the North, and West: very strong usually, and one which makes digging on the top impossible. Then we adjourn to the low country. But for that the weather now is the most perfect you can imagine.

As to your last letter, from Ventnor: we are about 70 miles from Aleppo: and get our post about once a week from Biredjik, 5 hours off, when we send for it. It is irregular, for I was 3 weeks without a letter. Don't expect much from me:—and then you may be satisfied with what you get: remember you are six to one. I suppose Arnie tied in the Sports with someone else? You talk of a six months' arrangement with his cup. I hope the chinless one does not come out. There would be nothing for him to do. We might possibly find work for an archi-tect, but for no one else: and he would be a horrid incubus. I am glad Mr. Barker has got my Thesis over. Now one is in the country one has hopes of improving it. . . . I will probably want no more clothes this winter: you see if I stay out it will be to go to Egypt, and I can get summer things for that in Beyrout or Cairo. But there is no hurry about it. The customs expenses of getting things out are heavy. 5/- that last parcel. The Morris book is going to be bound in vellum, from one of the skins on which the men swim the river. It is a funny sight just now, to look at a family (2 women 3 boys, & a girl) coming across: quite a little fleet of inflated skins. It is about a ten minute passage: the river runs, crosswise for half the way, at 7 miles an hour: very brown, with creamy foam all over it; but dark blue further off, when the sun is shining. Must go round the trenches now.

1911

I did this this afternoon (Wednesday May 3) and so I will send it off with the letter & map I wrote last week. You will excuse the badness of the drawing for the sake of the information it brings. The thing in the middle distance is the great mound. You are looking right at the end of it, and so get no idea of its length: but it shows you how it stands from the little valley. Behind the mound (on the top of which is one of our dump-heaps and a workman with his basket) is the Euphrates, with an island in the middle, and hills on the far bank. These are about a mile away so you see they are fairly high. The smudge before the mound is a poplar-grove, irrigated by the little canal built up alongside it: it hides the low stone building of the mill: but you can see, like a shadow along the mound 20 feet above the water the little irrigation canal of the plan. It is cut into and built against the rock. Below the trees is the little side stream (nameless) which runs into the Euphrates at this point. It comes from a large spring about a mile up, and its lower part (as you see) is now fairly full of water, due to the flooding of the great river. Below the copse is a grass field, running up to the mill-stream, and thence to the wall of the city. Just at this point is the N. gap mentioned on the plan. This side of the little stream is a bamboo-patch, an outcrop of bare rock, and then a field of young corn, cut up by two water-channels. Then a little space of stony ground, and a path (to Biredjik) through it rising to the hill-side of which I sat. The very dark object in the foreground is the far bank of another water-course. A square stone, with holes in it in the foreground is a Hittite tomb-monument. There may have been a statue, or a stela, in the socket. All this near hill-side is covered with such stones, & pieces of carving, with two inscriptions. They point to a Hittite cemetery having preceded the Arab one now on the site.

Nothing to add to letter: last Sunday was very wet all day. We have got our Imperial Commissaire relieved of his duties: he had bothered

us to our wits' end since Mr. Hogarth went, with impossible requests,
& illegal demands, & interferences. However now he is going back
to Constantinople, & a clerk from Aleppo comes to take his place.
The dig will go peacefully now: no new finds. Mr. Hogarth has some
photographs of the house & antiquities & village: he will show them
you if you ask: . . .   N.

Of course you keep this drawing to yourselves—and people like
Florence if you think it would interest her.

CARCHEMISH

May 16, 1911

Two very rough tracings of "Museum" drawings enclosed. Was
hurried, & had no time to make better copies.

I am writing on our roof, about 7.30 in the evening: we knocked off
work at 5, as usual, and gave the workmen a dinner (of meat, &
parched corn) before the house. Then came up here. There have been
no great incidents: today the sheikh of the village, a black-bearded,
rather quiet & picturesque young man, rode up to a group of women,
washing by the spring, on his horse, and picked up one young girl, his
first cousin, whom her parents had refused to him. He set her before
him on his horse, and galloped out of the village, offering to shoot
anyone who stood in his way. All the men were digging with us, so
escape was easy. Thompson brought the news down to our digs, and
there was great excitement: the relations of the girl caught horses at
once, and rode off to try & find the sheikh. They have not come back,
but matters will probably be settled by a money payment. Then Sunday we had a double marriage between the two villages of Jerablus,
upper & lower: the whole people turned out, the men afoot, or on
horse in such as had them, the women perched in threes or fours on the
humps of Camels: everybody in the most brilliant colours, new or
clean, with the sunlight soothing down all too violent contrasts. The
two bodies met in the middle of the cornfields, after about a mile:
there there was a violent dispute over precedence, to see which bride
should advance first: finally one came out (not ours) on her horse, and
was at once ridden down & captured by the horsemen of our village:
and then ours was taken similarly, with a mighty firing of guns &
pistols, and the hu-hu-hu and violent tahleel of the women. The
grooms sit at home, in their houses, waiting for the women to come

to them, & come they did in a great triumphal procession, everyone galloping or singing or shooting: the dowry carried before them on an ass in a great painted chest: and till late at night there was dancing to the music of hand-clapping, and shots being fired, and chanting to the pipes of such as were goat-herds or shepherds. We sent a present to the man who was our workman, and all our salaams. On Saturday an old Mullah came to the trenches in the afternoon, beating a parchment drum, with a little boy to carry a head-veil on a stick as a banner before him. The men all threw down their tools & baskets, to lie on their faces in his way. Then he walked on their backs, muttering various phrases. They said that their sinews would be made strong at his touch. Later he married the couple from Lower Jerablus. The weather tonight is curious: all day there have been heavy clouds and occasional gusts of wind, with once a dash of rain: now there is a smell of thunder in the air, and a grey mist is creeping up the river valley towards us: we have a very lovely view from our roof, across the flat plain that was the battle-ground of Carchemish to a huge "tell" over the river, and others at long intervals to Tell Ahmar a day's journey off. This last mound Mr. Hogarth is going to try to dig—or get permission to dig—. Further down are sharp limestone hills, "one like the blade of a knife" said Shalmaneser, with Kala'at en Nedjur, a great Arab castle of the xiiith Century, on one of the first peaks. The Euphrates turns a great bend, six or seven miles down, so we have a wide stretch of water, two or three miles of it, to look at, with the little mound that was the out-post of Carchemish to the South, thrown up against it. Just below we have a poplar grove, and over it is a wild crowd of bee-eaters, sweeping about in the wind and the dust-clouds, with their shrill cries. The little village spring is led into this grove, (and causes it): if the village was a little older (it is only 4 years since its foundation) we would have plums & apricots and other fruits, for quite a large orchard is planted down below. There is bush grass all the year round: and there will be mosquitoes, or there are, since we heard one tonight for the first time.

We are now beginning to clear up our small objects, with a view to closing the digs in three weeks. The Museum has asked that everything be photographed, to spare the expense of sending a man to Constantinople later on. So I am glueing up pottery (we have no proper cements) and trying to fit pieces of terracotta, and inscriptions. There are about 150 photographs to be taken, and mine is the only real camera we have. Mr. Hogarth is sending me films from Beyrout. I have some very fine pots, one in particular, pebble-polished, which is unique (and a nuisance, in 147 pieces, and only about half of it remaining). Thompson is not a photographer. Of large things (we have not yet found any small Hittite) we have got a very interesting basalt relief, about 5 feet high, semi-mythological, a doorway prophylactic slab, of two lion-headed human figures, hustling two human-headed figures with bull's legs: a scrap of this is still missing, with the lower half of one of the lion-headed ones: we hope to find it in a new trench we are opening out.

Then we have a small relief, again in black basalt (which is much the best material we have, being sharp in texture, & not friable in damp or heat, though brittle) of a lion, winged, but with a most curious human head, with the horned cap & two long plaits of hair that distinguish the Hittites of this place, apparently growing out of the back of the lion-neck. I have seen something like it somewhere: Thompson never has, so the motive of it is not Assyrian at any rate. I hope to send a tracing of my sketch of it before long.

Then from the top of the great mound, at the end shown in a letter to you sent off a week ago, we found 18 feet deep, a sort of pedestal in basalt, that may have carried a statue or a copper bowl. It was composed of a round base of stone, rising from the backs of two very stylistic lions: curious work, but powerful. Near it was a basalt votive altar, of a style rather common here, with four lines of close-packed Hittite linear inscription on it. Of course we can make nothing of it, though Thompson hopes that he has a clue or two in the very large inscription in relief, with the heads & hands upon it; that we found a month back. I hope you may have seen a print of this, from the photograph of mine that Mr. Hogarth took back to Oxford with him.

I am borrowing money of Thompson, to buy things in Aleppo with, & for my trip to Urfa: the money I have was hardly enough, & one cannot send Cook's cheques by post. So can you send him £4 to 13 Cheyne Gardens Chelsea S.W. (R. Campbell Thompson) in an envelope to await his arrival (in mid or early July)? His father lives there. Thompson is a fortunate man: he is getting his expenses, and a pound a day, so he will clear £150 this season. I hope we have a second! but it is highly doubtful. Tell Ahmar cannot be till the season after next.

The country out here is very quiet: there have been no religious troubles, or suspicion of them for a year and a half: and Ibrahim Pasha, the Kurd chief of Kiranshehir, was poisoned a 9 months back by the Vali of Aleppo: so there is complete peace. We finish here perhaps in 3 weeks or so, and will then go down to Tell Ahmar for a week: to look for pieces of a big inscription there, & to squeeze others: also there is a piece of cuneiform for Thompson. After that I must look at Kala'at en Nedjur, for nobody has dated it yet, or planned it, and from there I hope to go over the Mesopotamia plain to Harran, & back to Biredjik & Tell Bashar by way of Urfa. Please go on writing therefore to Aleppo (Consul) till early July, and probably longer, if as I fancy I explore principally this north part of the Latin Kingdom this year. I expect to reach Jebail in late September, and will probably be passing through Aleppo in August.

Euphrates is still high: and there is a plague of locusts: all the grass of the mound is full of them. We have got our Imperial Commissaire dismissed, for a general nuisance: so are happy, & great in the repute of all the country-side.   Salaams.   N.

CARCHEMISH
May 19, 1911

Letter just now (Father's & yrs. on Arnie's birthday): I am going to scribble a few lines about it at once, since if I put it off I don't know when it will be done. We are getting busier & busier: let alone the ordinary work on the mound I am photographing everything, & piecing up pots: and as well trying to repair a centrifugal pump-engine for our new Commissaire, who is a local gentleman. I don't know much about machinery, & nothing about centrifugal force: however it is going on. Cameras too are a nuisance: I have had to mend a shutter: (not mine). About letters: quite likely some of mine have dropped out (I have sent two lots of plans: of the palace steps, & of the site) some of yours certainly have: we can tell how irregular the post is by observing the gaps in the series of Thompson's newspapers: on average we get every other one. Then one always feels a letter in Turkey a sort of privilege—and at Biredjik (our post town) they cannot read Frank handwriting: we get all sorts of people's letters, including those of most of the missionaries in Euphrateria. This uncertainty must make you feel quite assured if a long time passes without news of me: for if an accident does happen you will get news by wire (from Consuls, who have your address) before my preceding letter has arrived. People don't disappear quietly in this country: we knew that Mr. Sayce was on the way (by rumour) the day he came, though he was driving direct from the station of Aleppo in a 3 horse chariot! And all the local people knew his history & reputation, a little inexactly perhaps, but that only to be expected. Therefore if you get no letters for a couple of months remember the Turkish post-office and read something interesting instead *The Agonists* perhaps. I am most anxious to get a report on that.

Miss Thornton was at Sidon: I believe she is at either Beyrout or Safed now: I was introduced to her two years ago, when I was out here: but have forgotten her. But all Syria has heard of me;—and of us.

What is the dog's name? Wrote once to the Canon {Canon Christopher} will write again this week: but cannot give any account of the digs, for that is against the rules. Thompson will not say more about them in his letters than that they are continuing. I allow myself a little more licence in your letters: but do not say a word to anyone else. The drawings etc.—you will not allow into anyone's hands, who knows anything:

About Mr. Jane & Will. The longer he goes to him the better: if he goes at all. Mr. Jane is not a crammer, or a superficial historian, either of which would be Mr. Barker's opinion. But of course Will must agree with his tutor. Do let him beware of text-books, or of doing more than the minimum (which Mr. Jane can lay down) in subjects that do not appeal to him.

About Frank: he might go to India: but has he the remotest interest in such a life? he would get exploring & shooting in smaller places (Nigeria, Malaysia) without the ghastly social boredom of India—and cheaper. The pay, even of the regular army will soon be enough to live on, in the more modest regiments: the rates will be raised as the next reform.

In any case Oxford if he can: though unless he is an Engineer (well paid) it should be history & not mathematics. Has he considered what an officer is when he retires? the narrow specialization makes him quite unfitted for anything else: if it leaves him even with the tastes for it. This seems to me the fault in the matter. The military man is as much

stamped with his mark as the schoolmaster or the clergyman. Of course
Frank may not object to a certain finity of idea: but he will lose some
of his originality in the mill.

I fear Father is right about us & our careers: but this idealist disregard
for the good things of the world has its bright side. And to say that he
had 5 sons, none making money, would be a glorious boast—from
my point of view at least.

Very many thanks about the roof. It is very precious to me, as a
remain of antiquity that cannot be replaced if destroyed: so I have an
advantage over Richards who only feels artistically: I have two counts
in my favour. Thompson only thinks scientifically out here. If a stone
or a pot cannot be turned to use;—cannot be published as a thing that
he has used or improved, it is worth nothing to him, though it may be
a splendid piece of potting, or a magnificent relief. Yet to my mind the
pleasure of a thing for itself is one of the best things we have. The
personal element ruins them. Have found nothing this week except a
Byzantine wall foundation, a scrap of lion-mane, and a Roman bronze
coin. There goes £40! You are right that the place & our hopes in it
collapsed suddenly: the afternoon that we dug down in our palace-
court & found virgin rock 5 feet below. The digs might almost have
been given up that night. Probably 3 weeks more. Am not going to
carry more than my camera in my tramp.

                                        Salaams.   N.

                                                        CARCHEMISH
                                                      23 *May*, 1911

We have just heard from Mr. Hogarth. He suggests 6 weeks more
dig. So go on writing to Aleppo for a long time: till mid-July at least.
The prospects of a second season are a very little better. This week we
have found a Hittite seal, and proved that the great wall in the "palace"
down below turns at a rt. angle after the end of the chariot relief
procession. It is this latter idea which is cheering: there may be something inside, and in any case the wall does not end abruptly. We were
only feeling along the one side of it: and cannot do much more this
year, because of the stone-heaps that have massed up.

I am writing now in a Temple, (or palace) on the N. end of the
mound: the part showing in a sort of sketch I sent you. We dug down
to it, & Thompson was disappointed in what he found: but now he is

Chartres. Philosophers (*See p.* 81)

Chartres. The CHRIST of the South Portal (*See p.* 81)

getting more hopeful. I don't suppose though that we can touch it again this year. In it we found the little lions I sent last week, and a memorial altar, with four lines of linear script. I think the building is by far the earliest Hittite thing we have found. But that remains to be proved. There remain the foundations nearly everywhere, and in places one stone above them. So it is really a find. The pottery in it was early. Thompson as a cuneiformist has no care for buildings or pottery, or sculptures. He wants tablets in cuneiform: and we have found none. So he is a little disappointed generally. But we have not done so badly on the whole, in large objects: and I think this building might provide the small ones.

I told you we had got rid of our first Commissaire? Now we have got rid of our second; and are hoping that the third will not last out very long. You see the finds are not at all encouraging (a week for a single cylinder seal!) the village is a very poor one, without the amenities dear to the "cultivated" Turk, and the power & opportunity of the Commissaire (thanks to our attitude) nil. So they have a very poor time: and since the first one left under such circumstances (and has had such a time since leaving, with the Government after him for the money he got on false pretences) they are all very low, & reverent to our excellencies. We are all Beys here, you know.

Miss Gertrude Bell called last Sunday, & we showed her all our finds, and she told us all hers. We parted with mutual expressions of esteem: but she told Thompson his ideas of digging were prehistoric: and so we had to squash her with a display of erudition. She was taken (in 5 minutes) over Byzantine, Crusader, Roman, Hittite, & French architecture (my part) and over Greek folk-lore, Assyrian architecture, & Mesopotamian Ethnology (by Thompson); Prehistoric pottery & telephoto lenses, Bronze Age metal technique, Meredith, Anatole France and the Octobrists (by me): the Young Turk movement, the construct state in Arabic, the price of riding camels, Assyrian burial-customs, and German methods of excavation with the Baghdad railway (by Thompson). This was a kind of hors d'œuvre: and when it was over (she was getting more respectful) we settled down each to seven or eight subjects & questioned her upon them. She was quite glad to have tea after an hour and a half, & on going told Thompson that he had done wonders in his digging in the time, and that she thought *we* had got everything out of the place that could possibly have been got: she particularly admired the completeness of our note-books. So we did for her. She was really too captious at first, coming straight from the German diggings at Kala'at Shirgat, where they lay down gravel paths, wherever they want to prove an ancient floor, & where they pile up their loose stones into walls of palaces. Our digs are I hope more accurate, if less perfect. They involve no "reconstruction", which ruin all these Teutons. So we showed her that, & left her limp, but impressed. She is pleasant: about 36, not beautiful, (except with a veil on, perhaps). It would have been most annoying if she had denounced our methods in print. I don't think she will.

That is the finish of our news. Euphrates has fallen, nearly to normal: the weather is hot, with thunder, & showers occasionally. The harvest is now going on: all barley, no wheat in this district: just alternate crops of barley, liquorice, and fallow. They reap it green, & let it dry cut.

No more trouble from the men: since the high dispute of Monday fortnight the days have gone as smooth as oil. Of course we got rid of some 30 of the ring-leaders, which "pacifies" the rest.

I forgot to say that Miss Bell left us two Merediths', the Sandra Belloni series: great joy to one half the expedition at least. She is going back as quick as she can (from Baghdad & Diarbekir), and so had done with them.

They prepared their inflated skins for swimming by rubbing into them salt & flour (barley-flour): it is interesting. The hair is scraped off with a knife. I have had the goat-skin that wrapped up the mens' feast-meat so treated, and propose to bind a book or two in it. It is really very good stuff, & to have a book in the skin that one used to cross the Euphrates on would be a pleasure. If I had thought of it I would have got a tolerable looking *Xenophon* before I left Oxford, for the purpose. But if we have a second season it will be the same thing. Crossing the river is a matter of 20 minutes, and about a mile. Thompson, using crawling & trudging strokes in swimming cannot advance a single inch against stream, or even hold his own; he goes down steadily at about 1 m.p.h.: and at a fast trot when he swims with the current. It is such a pity to think of a huge iron girder bridge across this river below us. They expect to be four years building it, and that will mean a town of navvies, and all these beautiful villages spoilt: not to mention that they will sack the ruins for stone.

I am going to take a few photographs now. Have taken them. My camera is proving a good one: and the telephoto has been used several times of late: It acts (at a couple of miles) rather better than the naked eye.

Last week we dismissed the son of Sheikh Ibrahim; a village worthy; the old man came into our kitchen next day, & told Haj Wahid (who sends his salaams to Father) that he was going to ensorcel Thompson & myself & Haj Wahid, & our overseers, if his son was not put back. The Haj came to us a little perturbed. He thought it might be best to use force on the old man to dissuade him, and it really was serious, for a case of illness in the expedition would have put us under his thumb. So we told Haj not to mind: that you made a wax image of the man, with one of his hairs in it: that you said certain words, & stuck a pin through the heart at midnight: or warmed it over a charcoal fire, and as each drop spluttered & fell, a day would go from his life. Haj rushed out, and pulled one of his last hairs from the old man's head: and then triumphantly told him what was in store. The old man begged his peace of us, swearing good conduct for all our lives, and offered us a hen: (refused), but the request for peace was granted, and a hair (not *the* hair I suspect) was returned. Our renown advances in the Arab-speaking world. In case former letter does not get through: I have books & films of last parcel: all very good.

We have a large beast, like an 18 inch chameleon on the mound. I am trying to photo him for Arnie: such a quaint insect to look at, a small crocodile, almost.

N.

CARCHEMISH

May 29, 1911

Letter about Prof. Petrie come in: am glad it appeals to you: you will find out more about it & our chances from Mr. Hogarth than I know. I fear a second season is a little less than likely. Have found this week only a second Hittite seal: and some walls of unburnt brick. Am not going to write more: I develop tonight, which means a hour's work: and have been making notes of the pottery & photographed objects all the evening: we are taking all the small objects now a days: at least I am taking them.

The Rabelais has come: a beautiful little edition & a great joy: very many thanks for the quickness of it. Thompson is one of these unhappy mortals who cannot or will not read French—but there he is a scientist. . . . All goes admirably. No more mosquitoes: a good deal of rain, which has interfered with the picking of the harvest. There is not a sickle in the place: you tear off the barley at its roots.

Our new commissaire is a gem: we have not only no trouble, but actually help & encouragement. The past month now looks like a nightmare: we sleep soundly now: do ditto!

Why did Bob join the anthropological Soc.? He can never be an anthropologist, or even a scientist, for he has predilections & opinions. I wish this house did not overflow with mice & rats & birds. Very many thanks to Father for his care of the roof: it is a great joy to feel that my coming out here has done no harm. I will not write to Sir J. Rhys: it would be too long after Lady Rhys' death, & would look officious.

We expect to have cleared up in a month: then a week at Tell Ahmar: and I am off to Harran & Urfa. Miss Bell asked me to photograph some things in the first of these two places for her:—however I will send them to Mr. Hogarth—don't mind.

Frank had much better the Sudan or some such place than India: not only is there a chance of advancement, but there is less "white glove" nonsense about it. In India he is always dancing on the skirts of society: out in the wilds he has a chance to do something: whether administrative, or anthropological or linguistic—or merely naturalising: at any rate something non-military. For these special posts a good degree is necessary.   N.

CARCHEMISH
June 8, 1911

Have just heard from Mr. Hogarth that we go on till August: that is splendid news, though it probably means no second season. He writes that Will called to see him but found him engaged: he will write to *The Times* in the next few days, but the Coronation press of news may hold it off till afterwards.

I will reply to Will's of the 18th since it is the only letter I have had lately: rather a gap just now! If he studies European history from the French point of view it will be fresh & valuable.

Place-names are against the Teutonic element in E. Britain and also the little stories we have from Gildas etc. of the methods of the actual conquest. There was not overmuch welcoming. Had Britain accepted the Celtic church it would still be Catholic: do you really expect a history don who is abstract and constitutional-political to understand the mysteries of tattooing & the origin of the impi? I have recently read an attack on Chaka as only the reorganiser of the Zulu system.

The literature clause has been put in operation two or three times (I had leanings therewhither myself). Of course the ordinary history man thinks it a joke: but you would be safe with Mr. Hutton & Baskerville among your examiners: they are above the common scientific stock. In case I forget later, Baskerville is a quite exceptional man, rich, not a student, passionately fond of wandering in Italy & France. The more of such geography (especially physical) and mild architecture you could work in the better. Political poems are the only things not dry in history: do you call *Piers Plowman* dull? or Renard? and if you can read history & Bertrand together you would not dream of following Ezra Pound. If you touch Renaissance France read a little Rabelais (especially *L'Ile Somnante* in book 5) between Villon, Rabelais, & Ronsard (with Clement Marot) you get the flesh & blood side of the Renaissance. The Scaligers don't touch.

What is a nympholeft? It sounds like a sort of newt: don't use these words: your letter on the whole needs a chastening of Bunyan, and perhaps Addison. Don't reply & say they are not alike.

I left my special subject (the Crusades) till the last two weeks of the last term. It was mostly done while the examination was actually in progress in three all-night sittings: Special subjects, if you know all but the facts are a matter of simple cram. I should certainly not recommend doing it (except to know your ground, if it is territorial) before the last term: or the term before the last, leaving the last for revision. If it is a matter like the Crusades two or three weeks are more than enough. Other subjects have more to read: but always read something that throws a side-light on the set authorities (i.e. I didn't touch them till I had read the Armenian Chroniclers, William of Tyre, and the gestes). You are going to too many lectures. The English Constitution did *not* develop out of Domesday Book. If you imbibe all Mr. Barker's lectures thereon, you will not be able to see it didn't. But it takes three terms to do so: give him up after the first term: you get nothing new from him, because it mostly comes from Pollock & Maitland (which don't read) & besides everybody goes there, so it is no use repeating anything he says: everybody else does. A. L. Smith is an institution: he delivered those lectures on Aristotle the year before his eldest daughter was born, & since then he has polished their style, while new interpretations & texts have passed over his head. He is an excellent joke, but you will get more out of Mr. Barker's book in ten minutes: Mr. Jane is very good on Aristotle. Don't make the mistake of over-much political science. I went astray on Utopia & Campanella and Harrington on S. Augustine:—and forgot Maine, whose errors I had to evolve out of Mill's political economy when the paper appeared. There is only one paper on polit. Science, though classical dons forget that in their joy at finding a common ground between Greats & History . . . do treat Aristotle historically; and Hobbes as a joke. Wakeling of B.N.C. is very useful (schools point of view) on Hobbes: and amusing too. Oman is a monument: and one doesn't need to look at such things over long. Hewlett certainly has the courage of his convictions: but he is not a Greek, but an Italian of the early Renaissance: the time when they believed in Pan. I want to see Brazenhead. It may be another early work: one felt (in New Canterbury's) that one had not all the story there.

I can't imagine a man writing on Ch. Gaillard without reading le Breton: and to the Stubbs! It was a gross insult to the society. I fancy there are echoes of the siege in Reynard the fox. Atkinson is to be admired: did he know you were there? No one knows how the outwork at Gaillard was breached: I fancy (against V. le Duc) that the angle tower was mined over the filled up moat: or that the moat was later made larger.

Mustn't argue over Chandos at this distance: but the Prince was not a {next word not clear} (cf. his conduct in home politics). Of course Chandos was a sort of general: he knew how to win a fight, but he dissipated the energies of the English, and was a good deal responsible for the collapse. The Prince fell away at the end with that illness of his. A friendly (or at least neutral) Pyrenees was essential to Gascony: which excused downfall of Trastarnare. What did Chandos do in Aquitania but make Bordeaux disaffected, & the seigneurs all out of hand. The Prince found his hardest work crushing the independent lords.

Digging is not good: though we have a fair bag of photographs for our book. Professor Petrie seems a most exciting individual: no regularity but disorder continual. Homer result curious: perhaps the dear old philologists regard a unitary theory as an exploded one: but there will always be the fight of art & science over it. What on earth personal news is to write? I shave three times a week, and yesterday darned a hole in a sock—nothing more: remember we are only exist-ing, & digging. No more over that Thesis: let it grow a little worthy dust. Richards thinks little of everything else: I fear a great reaction of disgust when our first book is out. He is not fully prepared for its bad-ness. Rabelais here: Plough Inn a scandal.

CARCHEMISH
June 13, 1911

I fancy about a week has passed since I wrote, though it seems to me I do little else all the evenings: of course there is much developing and pot-mending and writing up of notes to do.

About our digs. Mr. Hogarth said "Go on two months" which will take us into the grapes and water-melons: we have just arrived at the apricots. Thompson has given up testing the site (perhaps a little too soon) and so we are concentrating on the three best points we have found. No results to date or next week either, since it takes long to get down through the surface earth. We have got a very interesting base of a column in basalt, Hittite, and I think unique: and a poor sculpture or two: one, the lower half of a man holding a lion-cub by the hind legs, I think I mentioned. In pottery no results, beyond a pocket of Hellenistic amphoræ: and some of the very best of the little terracotta figures of horses that have been so frequent on the site. We have now about 200 of them: quite a reasonable stud.

Euphrates is falling continually, and every day new shoals & islands appear: the current runs about 3 miles an hour, which with the stream 10 feet lower than before is not so bad.

We have been a good deal disgusted with the locusts. They have been in great plenty, but small in size: yet it was horrible to see them everywhere so thickly that the ground seemed to take flight before one's steps, and their continual singing made one's ears hum as though they were deafened. I don't think I have ever seen a more detestable beast: one would almost have killed them with pleasure, but the winds did that without our help. For three days the river was full of their bodies, and I could not take photographs for the air was silky in texture with the shimmering of all their wings. I have picked up a dead one for Arnie, and if he dries nice and sweet I will send him along by post. Singly, like human beings, locusts would be nice enough: in millions they are intolerable. There is no leaf or green ear left in the fields on which they pitched: but they were strangely irregular, and so the losses are not total, even in corn, and the liquorice is unhurt. With the metayer tenancy in force however, very little of the village harvest goes to the common people.

Of other things there is really nothing to say. The weather is getting a little warmer: about 86 just now (9 p.m.). No mosquitoes to speak of, but heaps of sandflies which bite of course, much worse.

The house is so full of fleas that I have carried a bed down to the mound, and sleep there for comfort's sake. It is very pleasant in the moonlight, to look down, on one side to the rushing Euphrates, & on the other to over the great plain of Carchemish, to the hills of the Salt Desert on the S. Our diggings are certainly in one of the loveliest spots in the world: and in one of the most memorable.

I slept up here the other night after developing till past midnight: we had a little sleep, both of us, and were then roused by a rustle, which grew to a roar as a great white thing leaped through the hole near the roof which does duty for a window, right out towards my bed. Thompson was up at once with a fearful yell; and all his spare hairs on end; and we both grabbed the same revolver at the same instant, and tried to fire. But it was only the newspapers which we had stuffed in to keep out the birds and bats, and which a sudden puff of wind had flung into the room. We were just in the full force of this discovery when Haj Wahid (who sends salaams to Father) bounded in with the kitchen hammer in one hand and a rifle in the other, while our two zaptiehs came thundering at the garden door, to learn what was the matter. Thompson's yell was the cause of all that & of the wondering requests of the villagers next day. He is a restless being at night, always getting up to souse the stray cats that come & sing by his bedside in buckets of water. He is nice about his water, and will not put two cats in the same pail. We have now (good fortune for me) got rid of meat eating. It kept on being bad, & any little thing upsets Thompson: so now a chicken once or twice a week, a fish or two from the river: but there is rice, and bread & leben which are better.

Mohammed Jasim (a great man this) slays fishes in the river with his sword: and brings down doves, and hoopoes, for his pot, with stones. The hoopoes are glorious birds, and now being full-fed of flesh meat their plumage shines, and the crests on their head ruffle and perk to see their mates. They are pairing, & to attract the females sit on great rocks and blow their beaks: at least it makes a noise like a snuffle.

Today I cured a man of compound scorpion-bite by a few drops of ammonia: for that I have a fame above Thompson's as a hakim: and as a magician who can conjure devils into water, from my mixing a seidlitz powder for the Haj, in the kitchen before visitors. Am now going to scribble a very short line to Florence, and then to bed: the walk down of 15 minutes, in the gale that *always* blows, is just enough to cool one off.

Salaams.   N.

CARCHEMISH
June 18, 1911

To-night is not the night of the going of a post, so that I can write in complete ease. At the same time I have nothing to tell you about, except that today we found a very nice little bas-relief: the upper part of a thunder-god, in basalt. On Sunday too we walked out to a village near, and saw a lion's head, and part of a memorial altar, inscribed in linear script.

One of our rare smiles developed on Friday. Our new zaptieh is a poor creature, a little unpleasant even, at times with his constant malingering. His object of course is brandy, which we never give, since once it was known we did so, we would have all the people in the country-side besieging our house for a drink. However we had got rather tired of him, and when he produced a preposterous fever we promised him medicine. We called him into the kitchen and Thompson gave him to hold a glass with one half of a seidlitz powder dissolved in it. Then with one finger on his pulse he recited in a solemn voice the Hebrew alphabet and the "House that Jack built", waving a scroll of cabalistic figures. As he finished I poured in the other part of the pow-der. The zaptieh gave an awful yell, and dropped the glass, leaping backwards, and in a twinkling the room was cleared of the crowd that had been gaping upon us. Many hid themselves behind the corner of the house before they felt themselves safe from the devil visibly striving in white smoke to void himself from the water. "Am not I your friend, your raffik?" said the zaptieh. "Why did you give me that from which I might have died." "What have I done to you that was not good?" (Many things, but he did not know.) The village was awestruck, but rejoiced that their bully was brought low.

By personal example, and the strictest orders we compelled our two water-boys to take each half a glass, and ever since they have gone about delicately, feeling their limbs, and shaking themselves, in terror lest they be changed to mares or great apes. "I drank some of that sorcery," said Dahoum on the works next day, "it is very dangerous, since by it men are turned suddenly into the forms of animals." (This from a boy of 14 years.) So for the third time we have worked miracles, and even to Aintab and Membidj the fame of our nigromancy is gone abroad. The seidlitz powder now foams a tall man's height from the glass, with a noise like a dust-driving wind.

Our people are very curious and very simple, and yet with a fund of directness and child-humour about them that is very fine. I see much of this, for I sleep on the mound and start the work every day at sunrise, and the choosing of new men so falls to my lot. I take great care in the selection, utterly refusing all such as are solemn or over-polite, and yet we are continually bothered by blood feuds, by getting into the same trench men who have killed other's kin or run off with their wives. They at once prepare to settle up the score in kind, and we have to come down amid great shouting, and send one to another pit. There is no desire to kill, and public opinion does not insist on vengeance, if there is 50 feet of earth between the offender and the offended.

Then there is always rivalry of pick-men and shovel-men, with the mere basket carriers. Those who have *cosmas*, picks, are the aristocracy of the gangs (the κοσμηφορας λαων) and below them come the shoveller (*Karuk*). To be a basket man is to be of the masses. Each day there is a riot between those who have by force or cunning advanced a rank, and those fraudulently sent down and this business we have to adjust.

And then there is the case of the good and so privileged workman, who brings each day a new one of his seven brethren and 49 cousins, all afire to work (our wages are so good) and the case of the man embroiled with the overseer, both parties calling Allah to witness that the other is entirely in the wrong ("And if I did strike him with a pick-handle," said Abdo Jadur, "where is the harm? Is he not the son of my sister's aunt at law?"). There is the water-boy to abuse for dead locusts in the water, or for lack of water, or fouled water (and our Arabs drink a half-pint every 45 minutes as a rule): and one man has to be ammoniated for a scorpion bite: (ammonia is an instant cure) and a second has cut his head with a falling stone, or his foot with a tool. One day we counsel a man moderation in the buying of his new wife (he, Suleiman son of Hissu, wanted to give £12 for a town-bred girl, when a first class country article could be got for £2); another day we bail out of prison a man who had many years before stolen a sheep from Tell Bashar, or cast out of the village an Armenian tobacco-seller, not free of suspicion of dealing in antiquities. Every day nearly there is something, and yet all together they amount to nothing. You asked for personal news, but what is there to tell? Thompson has had a little more fever lately: I have had none since Mr. Hogarth left.

Next day.

Letter come from Father: two of mine (one to you) and five of Thompson's letters were given one week to Mazloum Bey, our first Commissaire, to post. Report says he threw them in the river, afraid that some complaint of him was in them. At any rate they have none of them got through; Mazloum was dismissed next week.

This will show you how easily (by the miscarriage of two letters) you might remain six weeks without news of me, tramping; please don't let me hear of anxiety, unless you get a wire that something has happened. And that you will get immediately anything happens. This is a country where facts are not hidden but proclaimed (large) from the housetops. No excitements, about strikers or anything else. We can do anything we like here, for our great wage makes us trebly sacrosanct: and we have the force of the 100 best workmen within five miles behind anything we wish to do. I don't live a mile from Thompson: only sleep: I don't go down from the house till 11 p.m. and come up at 6 a.m. to breakfast.

I don't think £3 of wood is extravagant, even as a speculation: I can guarantee we will use twice as much as he has thrown away! A modern contractor has a curious rooted objection to dry rot, which is harmless in the outside of a log.

Are your injections for bronchitis? If Dr. Gibson thinks them worth trying they probably are. Somehow the idea sounds hopeful, though one live one would be worth a million dead. I don't want anything but boots. Perhaps this message will get through: and as we are digging here till mid July (at least) I may not want even boots. But that depends, and I am quite likely to winter out here. Rabelais I read every night: a most profound comfort: I have no plans yet, except that for the first month after the diggings (August) I will wander to Harran, Urfa, and Aleppo. After that depends on what I feel like: but I will arrive in Damascus or Jebail in mid or end September. The cold begins just after that here in the N. This is all: for I have three or four letters to write. I have heard lately from Hall. Send me Finals results as they come out: he is very anxious about them. When does Bob come out again? How is Arnie taking to Greek: καν ἡ ϱηδ θις ἀνδ IF νοτ ὑι νοτ? I will present him with a Parnassus Homer for the next Second of May.

By the way did my account of the festivities at the top of the Acropolis on that date suffer drowning at the hands of the miscreants? If Will took the Crusades as a special subject, it would well pay him to spend the next long vac. out here: he could get a very full view of the Latin Kingdom in three months and with me on the spot he would not have to spend time over Arabic. Two would wander near as cheap as one. Let him consider it with Mr. Barker (to whom salaams from Carchemish in the county of Joscelin of Tell Bashar). If he sees Mr. Hutton tell him I am still going about: I am now going down to the site:

CARCHEMISH

June 24, 1911

Have had orders to clear out as soon as possible: so in a fortnight we will shut down the digs. By the terms of the telegram from the British Museum they are so disappointed at our results that there will be no second season. It is a great pity for we had on the strength of our former orders, just begun important clearances. We will leave the site like a warren, all disfigured with rubbish heaps and with all the work only half done: altogether about the most unsatisfactory job that one can imagine.

So in a fortnight we will go down by boat to Tell Ahmar, and after three days there I will walk across to Harran, up to Urfa to Biredjik, and back to Aleppo by Tell Bashar and this place. This will be a walk of about a month, for there will be several days each in Harran & Urfa.

I got letters June 1 and 8 yesterday: about June 1. Anxiety is absurd: if anything happens you will hear it by wire: I am well known in this district. The man-headed lion is in basalt, & as sharp as the day it was cut. The drawing was traced from a drawing on a camera ground-glass. Lots of our letters have gone astray, including Thompson's great report to Kenyon: we now suspect one of the men who carried them to Biredjik. He would so save money on stamps. When away by my-self I cannot write oftener because there are no post-offices. On this next tramp for instance there is only Urfa & Biredjik: and they are only two days apart, so I will only write from one. People seldom or never get ill out here: fever is not a serious ailment: it only at the worst involves resting half a day; small-pox I should be proof against, & typhoid is rare *in the country*: one is much more likely to get it in Aleppo, or even at Jebail. Neither Thompson or myself has been in any way unwell. Best wishes to Bob. Cheque for £4 enough at present. If I take more the last minute I will let you know. He will be back about July 26.

Have found nothing for a fortnight, except some small scraps of Arab pottery, & a classical moulding. There are pots worse than the pebble-polished beauty: but all large scale work: much too big for white of egg, I'm afraid.

It's two years since I lost that other camera: and it was at Seruj which is miles away. The Aleppo people knew nothing about it.

The eloping Sheikh was the donkey boy's enemy: and the girl was quite willing to go: her relations (who are amongst our men) are very much distressed at the affair. For second cousins to marry is a terrible disgrace. The sheikh is not back yet, but will probably be able to return soon, on a money composition. We did not get a photograph of the wedding: it was spread out on such a scale that it would have been hopeless. The donkey boy mentioned above (Dahoum) is an interesting character: he can read a few words (the only man in the district except the liquorice-king) of Arabic, and altogether has more intelligence than the rank & file. He talks of going into Aleppo to school with the money he has made out of us. I will try & keep an eye on him, to see what happens. He would be better in the country, only for the hideous grind of the continual forced labour, and the low level of the village minds. Fortunately there is no foreign influence as yet in the district: if only you had seen the ruination caused by the

French influence, & to a lesser degree by the American, you would never wish it extended. The perfectly hopeless vulgarity of the half-Europeanised Arab is appalling. Better a thousand times the Arab untouched. The foreigners come out here always to teach, whereas they had much better learn, for in everything but wits and knowledge the Arab is generally the better man of the two.

I am not living in a tent: it is much too hot for that. I am only sleeping on the top of the mound. The river is swift, but quite pleasant for bathing: I have been in a few times: but at present it is not really warm (c. 90°). There are mosquitoes here about the house in plenty: on the top of the mound never, for the wind drives them off. I have written to the Canon {Canon Christopher}.

June 8 letter.

I fear I will eat no beans from Oxford this year. Will you get Will to add a copy of the *Agonists* to my library, if he has read it, and approves. Brazen-head must be procured in the Tauchnitz from France. Glad you have joined the Architectural {Society in Oxford}. Prof. Petrie is always good. Prof. Sayce is nearly 80 years old. You have been wanting to go to Minster Lovel a long time. The road to it after Witney is pretty. Many thanks for boots etc. I expect I will be quite ready for them when I reach Jebail. The report has been delayed. It is just as well that Arnie does not work too hard: there is such a thing, well known in the family, as overdoing it. I heard of Lady Rhys' death from you, from Hall, & the papers {Three lines omitted}: I will winter either in Jebail or in one of the villages in the plain here: the latter would be the more interesting: and certainly as comfortable: an empty fireless marble-lined hall does not add to one's natural heat. If I can find some-one here to teach me Arabic I will probably stay. We are such kings in the district that it would be a pity to spoil all our good work by abandoning it finally. It is quite extraordinary to see the difference our stay has made in the workmen. Will write as soon as I have settled this point. Petrie of course not needed now.

L.

TELL AHMAR
{July 12} 1911

We have been here about four or five days working out a cuneiform inscription and photographing & squeezing things Hittite. Now it is

all over, and today in the afternoon I am going off towards Urfa. The
men here say it is best to go along the carriage road as far as Seruj
(about 2 days) and then take another road south. This route I may vary
of course as I get later information. This village is one of the poorest,
& quite the stupidest I have seen.

Thompson is carrying this letter in to Aleppo and will post it there,
so you will get it quickly. After this you will not even expect another
till I get to Urfa, in about a fortnight: from which to Aleppo is about
a week in the post: so you see there is no hurry about that. Therefore
allow three weeks after you get this letter, & then if none comes allow
another ten days (Biredjik or Aintab). If that fails also it will be ten
days at least before I write again from Aleppo, for I am going from
Aintab or Tell Bashar back to Jerablus, to cement in place three pieces
of a large basalt relief that I put together, but which is in the nature of
things rather crazy. Thompson is sending out the cement from
Aleppo, and our overseer, and the water-boy (the two men of brains)
will do the work with me. Now about photographs. I have taken
about 200 for the Museum with the three cameras I have used: of
these all the quarter plate of the sculptures & some others are with my
own camera. Thompson is going to ask Dr. Kenyon, the director of
the British Museum to let me have a set of proofs of these, since
naturally I am interested in seeing them. If he consents (it is against
custom) Thompson will either send them c/o Consul Aleppo, or to
you. If they go to you, as I hope, you will recognise the parcel: open
it, & look at the photographs yourselves, but don't show them to anybody else on any account. So don't let anyone say they have looked at
the things: after you have looked at them, send them out c/o Consul
Aleppo or to Jebail if they come within August.

If in September hold them to hear from me if I am coming back this
winter or not. All the same the first week in September treat as August
that is address to Jebail c/o Miss Holmes. By the middle of September
you will know for certain if I come back or not. Will you ask Mr.
Jane to find out for me if anything should bring me back to England
this winter? I have written to him twice, but heaps & heaps of letters
have gone astray: Did you ever get two large bundles of plans &
drawings of Carchemish? I am anxious for you to see the photographs
for they will tell you all you want of the site: the book (which will
come to you in 9 months time) will be interesting: but please remember

to send out the prints to me afterwards, noting on the back any you would like me to preserve. There are ten or 12 photographs of work-men: of these I hope two sets will be sent: the negatives are B.M. property: but the prints are Will's—his set & mine, & I will send accounts of the men represented: the young boy who is turning up his eyes horribly is Dahoum, the boy with whose father I may stay this winter: the boy can read & write, & so would be the best teacher of Arabic in the district.

{The next month's Diary starts from here.}

JERABLUS
July 29, 1911

{This letter was written when he was almost dying from dysentery —Mrs. Lawrence.}

I am sending in a man from here to Biredjik tomorrow, so I will send a line to you. From Biredjik I went up to Rum Kala'at: from there to Nizib, and thence to Tell Bashar and Jerablus. You will find most of these places in the map in my Thesis if that sorely battered book is in peace. I have nothing very new, nothing very good: the castle of Rum Kala'at yielded some new points, mostly Arab: it had a most enormous moat a perfectly appalling thing: . . . It cut off a mountain from a mountain along a col like the coupée at Sark. I am very well, and en route now for Aleppo. I got a letter from you here which Thompson sent up three weeks ago from Tell el Hamra. I am probably going now to stop wandering in Ramadan. I dare hardly ask for food from a Mohammedan house, and Christians are not common enough. I have had the pleasant experience since a week of being the best Arabic scholar in all the villages I entered. In every single one, except Rum Kala'at someone knew a little Arabic but I knew more than all: the people were all Turks & Kurds; a few Armenians and Yezidis. Rum Kala'at was my Northern point.

This is nearly all I can write: the man is waiting anxiously—his own business, and I cannot delay him. I have the luxury of clean clothes, and am overhauling my stores. Thompson gave me free run of all the spare stores of the expedition, & as a result I am fitted out like the Swiss Family: only I have no embroidery silk or sugar mill.

L.

Hautefort *(See p. 75)*

(See p. 104)

Safita. The Keep

On P. & O. Liner
Early in December 1911
Monday Afternoon

There is such a crowd on board that I am writing in the cabin: the boat is nearly full, and so all seats are more than so.

An easy journey this: Calais passage smooth, Paris easy, and also the run down to Marseilles. Since we left there we have had bright sun and smooth water, but with just enough of wind to make the heat comfortable. I have not worn my helmet at all, because there are awnings all over the decks. That may not be so on the little boat to Beyrout of course.

In London I bought three collars, a pocket full of bullets, etc. Doughty told me that *Adam {Cast Forth}* was written about 5 years ago, though the idea had been in his head since Arabia. He is well, though not as strong as last time I fancy. I also saw Mrs. Doughty. He gave me a letter for Bessam, his old protector of Kheybar, whom I heard of in Damascus last winter.

I wrote you a p.c. from Marseilles saying I had forgotten some things. I want you to send them in a parcel to Beyrout (B.P.O.). My Baedeker to Palestine and Syria, my map of North Syria, by Blankenhorn, mounted on linen, and folded between marbled-paper back and front: and a police or other very loud whistle for Gregori. He had a police whistle years ago, and still talks of it.

The map I have shown to you in settling where Jerablus is: it has been in the Morning-Room, the Smoking-room and Father's room. There is no saying where it is now. It has a Stanford's label on the front. I should be glad if you would send off these things first. {The next five or six words are not decipherable} . . . but they will be heavy enough for one parcel. If they don't reach the minimum, though, add Mackail's little translation of the Greek Anthology from my house.

I'm now roasted and must go on deck.

Also I want prints (2 each) of the Sheikh of Harran and the photo of four friends of him: I put them out, and then forgot them: also I want another stud with curly top. All these things together to Beyrout please. And from the Hall drawer two automatic cigarette lighters—these for our zaptiehs.

I'm posting this on board, to make sure of its catching the home mail. If I stay in P. Said any time I will send a p.c. but it is always possible

that I will only tranship. A most lovely day today but exceedingly
hot. Nothing happened. I wonder what's the news of the war: no
wireless on board or at least a wireless and no operator.

ALEPPO
Wednesday, Dec. 13, 1911

This will be only a scribble, for I am lying in bed writing it. Don't
imagine I'm ill;—it's only cold; and bed is an unaccustomed luxury.
I left P. Said on Thursday, and had an ideal voyage; as far as Beyrout
on Sunday: I landed near mid-day; packed the Jebail stuff into a box;
left it with a friend of Miss Holmes'; saw the Consul; and left at 1 a.m.
by the night train for Damascus. Got there by 10.0 a.m.; saw the
Consul and Mohammed el Bessam, delivered Doughty's letter, and
then took night train for here. Accordingly I arrived last night, just
in time to catch Mr. Fontana and Wilkie Young, and arrange a carriage
for the next day. That has now begun, and I am writing this in the
early morning before I start. I am feeling exceedingly well, very much
better than in England. The sun is warm up here but the wind very
cold, and the night also. No rain or snow so far this winter, so the roads
are choked with dust and the country unploughed. Now then about
money. I am going to run short soon; this carriage trip is going to be
dear and already I have spent £5 over my estimate. You'll have to
send me more. I expect to be away six days now, and will then go
down to Jebail. I leave Beyrout on Jan. 1 for P. Said, and I can of course
borrow from Miss Holmes then, but I would rather not. If you can
send me £10 to Cook at Beyrout; it will probably mean a wire, but
he has codes which make it easy to do. If you find that very expensive
send it by post to Cook at Cairo, on whom I will call in the evening
of Jan. 2. That's enough for that:—by the way Cook of Beyrout knows
me perfectly well—tell that to the Head Office; my name is enough
for them. Am off to Jerablus about midday; and am taking Haj Wahid
with me. We hope to arrive tomorrow evening, and will find 12 tents
of Germans on the site. I fear buying will be impossible, for the railway
obviously means business. I have found two Hittite seals for Mr.
Hogarth already, and will hope to get more. I had no customs troubles
anywhere: in Beyrout I was not examined at all.

I must get up now, and as I have a great deal to do, I shall have to
leave the rest blank. I feel as though I had been travelling for weeks and

months on end, and it seems quite strange to me. Only, here I am in my own Arabic country, and am looking forward immensely to seeing the men again: if only those Germans are neutralised somehow. At any rate we have turned them off from the big mound: new plans are being made for a bridge to the South—which will be almost harmless. This is better than I ever hoped.   N.

Write to Cook at Cairo—post there only takes six days if you catch the mail: I'll make him forward them to Heliopolis or wherever we may be.   N.

> BARON'S HOTEL, ALEPPO
> 19 *Dec.* 1911

I hope you got my letter from Bab {East of Aleppo}. This one is hurried: I am just off to Biredjik.

I went to Jerablus last week: saw the old owner, and he told me it was sold. That evening he offered it me for £100: it seemed it wasn't sold. He says $\frac{2}{3}$ are his still. Salem Touma, the local magnate claims $\frac{1}{2}$. Habib Touma, head of Touma company claims $\frac{1}{3}$, and an Aleppo merchant thinks he has brought the lot. Where we come in is not very plain. Some say we have $\frac{2}{3}$ some $\frac{1}{3}$. We have a deed in our hands of the old owner's selling it to the Touma people for £120. It is properly executed, but both parties deny it.

Mr. Fontana & myself can make nothing of it: such a hopeless tangle of unknown boundaries, mortgages, etc. you never saw or heard of. To get to the bottom of it I am off to Biredjik to forage in the government archives. If I find anything definite I'll be the only person in the country who knows.

Jerablus was most delighted to see me: there had been a rumour some time ago that I had died in Aleppo, and they had sent a messenger to the consul to find out. The consul had gone across then and told the Germans that the site was ours and that they were not to touch it. As a consequence of this & of Mr. Hogarth in London & Berlin, the engineers have had orders to leave the site entirely alone; not a sod or a stone is to be touched, and the railway has to pass around it to the South, where it will do absolutely no damage. I saw the Germans there, and they were rather unpleasant creatures, so I am glad. The village loathes them already. The old sorcerer came and wrote a most

delightful letter to Thompson, regretting his not coming. Most of the
village heard of it and sent salaams to him by me.

In case my former letter failed, please send £10 to Cook of Cairo
for me. I am getting short with all this travelling. If my former letter
was in time, I'll get it in Beyrout from you: otherwise Miss Holmes.

Icy cold here: but fine and sunny. I took Haj Wahid to Jeralbus with
me, and will take him to Biredjik. This will ensure great comfort on
the way. At Bab last time he prepared soup, fish, meat, vegetable,
omelette, and a sweet: all this on one little spirit lamp, in the room of
a khan. This new Biredjik jaunt will take me till Christmas Day: it is
possible that I may find time for a couple of days at Jebail before going
to Professor Petrie. My boat to Egypt leaves on Jan. 1. Such running
about you never saw. I'm exceedingly well, and have forgotten very
little of my Arabic. There is no doubt that this part of the country is
glorious: I feel on my native heath, and am on the pitch of settling in
a new Carchemish as Sheikh. But this is only a dream, I fear. At the
same time I'm going to find out the owners of that site, if I can.
Carriage is heralded downstairs: Salaams for a week. Am taking Consular dragoman to Biredjik with me.

BARON'S HOTEL, ALEPPO

Dec. 28, 1911

This I am writing in Aleppo: I hope to leave here early tomorrow
morning for Beyrout. If I can I will go up to Jebail for a night: my
boat leaves on Jan. 1 for Port Said. I should get to Cairo on the afternoon of Jan. 2. Heliopolis that same night, or next morning.

I am writing now, because my time in Beyrout will be too hurried
for letters: you see I have about a dozen pounds of pottery with me,
which I must pack in small boxes, and send off through the post. Also
I have to take my ticket, and go up to Jebail: altogether rather a lot. I
will post this letter in Beyrout.

I wrote you last after Jeralbus, and before Biredjik. I went over in
two days to the latter, with the Consular dragoman, and Haj Wahid.
Going over it was exceedingly cold: but fine: there we had two days'
wet weather. We managed to find out how much was our share of the
Kala'at, how much Hassan Agha's: Salem, the liquorice person, has
none at all. The Kaimmakan did his best to hide all things from us, but
we got all we wanted nevertheless. Still I have written at length to Mr.
Hogarth on this matter, and it is mainly his affair.

Coming back on Christmas morning the driver topped the carriage over the edge of a little bridge into a stream. We were fortunately walking in front at the time. The mess was horrible: one horse quite out of sight, one, with its leg pinned under the mass, the third dancing on the other two trying to get out. The coachman was heaving frantically at the head of the submerged animal. Haj Wahid groping about in the inside of the vehicle pulling out rugs and quilts and coats and baskets all sopping with mud and water. A minute later his foot slipped on a patch of mud and he plunged head-first into mid stream, holding the dragoman's umbrella. In doing this he lost his tobacco-box. Lots of things we never found: they went floating away down-stream till they sank. However we got out more than we expected: the carriage unhurt, the horses also. Our lunch disappeared—we had only a walnut apiece and water unlimited—and we had a drive in pouring rain (for it rained all the time) in a sopping carriage full of mud-drenched blankets and quilts to the next village. It took us hours to get the carriage out. The bedding we borrowed of the sheikh was rather too populous for comfort—altogether it was the most memorable Xmas I've had. Probably at lunch time you were wondering what I was doing—well, I was fishing—I am none the worse, nor are the others. I paid Haj Wahid extra, for he did tremendous work. Without him we would be there still. Today I hope to buy some Hittite seals: I have nearly finished my Consular business. Mr. Fontana has been most splendid throughout. I have borrowed £10 of him, and spent it all on the way to Biredjik nearly. I hope to get through all right. If not will borrow in Beyrout or from Miss Holmes. I got one very nice seal on the road back—just after our bathe, and we met two very pleasant Aghas in the villages where we slept on the way: but all the same there were too many unpleasantnesses for enjoyment. In Biredjik especially we had a very great deal of bother with all the officials. Still it is a pleasure we managed our work so completely.

{Concluded at} BEYROUT

Jan. 2, 1912

In case of doubt, this is my third letter: previous ones from Damascus and Aleppo. I will repeat my money request once more. Please *wire* £15 at least, if possible £20, to Cook in Cairo, for me. I have borrowed from Miss Holmes £5, from Mr. Fontana £10, and spent it all. I will be very short my first few weeks with Petrie.

Mrs. Rieder has come here with me from Jebail. I went up there on Sunday afternoon, and left yesterday for here so I only had one night. My steamer goes at 5 p.m. today. Miss Holmes has had pneumonia, and is ill still: it began about 3 weeks ago. She sent regards to all & everybody, and is writing to you herself when better. Noel is much better this year: That nervous trouble has disappeared ——. I got two letters from you, Arnie & yourself of Dec. 7. I forgot the slides: if you have given them to Mr. Hogarth, & they can go with the stores, all well: but if too late for that, please send direct to Beyrout for me —or rather, if not yet gone, send c/o Fontana H.B.M. Consul Aleppo. I don't want them till the digs start, but then immediately: so Mr. Hogarth must not bring them out when he comes in April.

M. Roberts is deteriorating in ingenuity.

Arnie { Greeks don't write a bit like us: all their letters now a days are joined together like this   Kufir a.b.c.
I don't know: it's the same as Arabic, only more primitive.
Will ask for Russia P.O. on return.

Also letter Mother Will Father Dec. 13. Parcel of course not yet arrived. Photos. all well. I hope at his house you saw Mr. Hogarth's rugs. House plan not really needed. Am feeling exceedingly well now: much better & stronger: Have no spare time now for wauri's, and Thompson's cartridges no use without a gun! Glad rug good. Miss Fareedah away. Masefield's *Ev. Mercy* I've read: good certainly. Will you enquire at Blackwell's for the last novel (Spanish) of {word illegible} and send it to Mrs. Rieder. She doesn't know its title, but it is the last: he's dead now, last year only I think.

Great rumours of wars and annexations:—not to be believed yet, but such a smash is coming out here.

Go to Ashmolean & see my new seals: am sending them today to D.G.H. Also strigil for Will: send this to Young {repairer in Ashmolean Museum} for preservation.   N.

                                        BRISTOL HOTEL, CAIRO
                                        Jan. 6, 1912

Got here Thursday: boat delayed by quarantine and storms. Found money (£20) at Cook's: very many thanks: obviously some letters got through.

Had two days search for Prof. Petrie, and only found him tonight.
He has been ill, and is staying in a hotel near Cairo. Heliopolis where
I had hoped to dig, is not to begin till March: so I am to go to a place
called Kefr Ammar and dig prehistoric tombs. My address (in Roman
letters) will be

KAFR AMMAR
Upper Egypt.
I have put the Arabic in a circle.

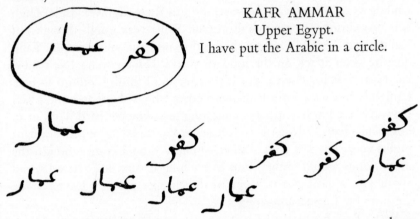

: here
are lots of specimens for you: write them together as in the cartouche.
Arnie may know the letters K.F.R. A.M.A.R. backwards.
I will be there till Jan. 30 probably: in any case you
cannot write very long: but this post (off tomorrow)
won't be long getting there.

I have had, as you will see, a couple of days in Cairo: met a most
admirable artist, a friend of Brangwyn's. He says Brangwyn designs
carpets: so I'm after him.—by the way Mrs. Kemmis' rug will never
be finished. Miss H. school is rather shaky just now. Mrs. Rieder has
promised not to write to you about the things you bought:—on
condition that I would thank you sufficiently. This hotel has a dining
room like the Hall of the Volsungs: two great Branstock's grow up
through the midst of it, and wave their tufted heads in the sun over
the roof. A very pretty idea. Cairo is good, with most glorious Arab
architecture: I haven't seen the Egyptian museum yet, but the Arab
one is glorious. I am learning about tiles. The streets of the town,
though, are a disappointment. I had expected something better than
Aleppo, which was perhaps presumption. By the way Kafr Ammar is
about 50 miles S. of Cairo on the Nile. There is a man called

Wainwright digging there: and P. Petrie is expected (or hopes) to go there in a week.

By the way I mentioned storms in the first sentence of the letter:— they delayed the boat only—I had fine weather. Have been 2 days in Cairo and bought nothing—but Blackwood's *The Centaur* which I am sending you. When read please send on to Richards (Woodside. High Rd. Woodford Green): it will interest Will: very good, though not "all the way" enough for me: but at the same time more reasoned and definite as an attack on the modern world than anything I've read— bar Morris. What else to say? It's 1 a.m. and I think I will go to bed. I am only just back from Professor Petrie, who is about an hour away. He was exceedingly cordial—interesting too, which is hard work in an hour and a half. Weather here wet yesterday: today beautifully warm: nights cool, but not cold. Father certainly should come, though the dusty winds would bother him. Everything is very dear: here I spend about 11/– a day! and it is one of the cheaper places. I leave for the diggings on Tuesday morning.

Write Kafr Ammar till Jan. 22 or so: depend on Brindisi mail.

N.

KAFR AMMAR
Thurs., 11 *Jan.* 1912

Have been here some days (3 to be exact) in great content. One Wainwright, excellent person to be described later, is lord of the digs. We go out every morning about 8 a.m. after breakfast, and look at tombs. About 15 men and 20 boys are digging for them: they find them in sand and flint soil, the edge of the great desert of Africa, where it dips down in flats to the cultivated lands bordering on the Nile. They scrape this soft sand with hoes—one's feet sink in it each step— and where they do not feel rotten stone at the tool depth, they hollow out. In a few minutes, if they disclose a rectangular form of 4′ by 3′ 6″ they know they are at the top of a well-tomb. They then dig down from 8 to 15 feet in the same soft sand, filling of the shaft, and at the bottom find a room, or two rooms, still clear of debris, unless the roof has fallen. In these rooms are piled up three or four mummy-bodies, in rotting coffins with great store of bead-nets along their length, and amulets, and sometimes pottery. It is all of Harka period—about 700

B.C.—and so not very beautiful, but there is also to be dug—next week
—predynastic tombs, and things of the first dynasty.

It is a strange sight to see the men forcing open a square wooden
coffin, and taking out the painted anthropoid envelope within, and
splitting this up also to drag out a mummy, not glorious in bright
wrappings, but dark brown, fibrous, visibly rotting—and then the
thing begins to come to pieces, and the men tear off its head, and bare
the skull, and the vertebræ drop out, and the ribs, and legs and perhaps
only one poor amulet is the result: the smell and sights are horrible.
Digging here is very unlike our Carchemish work—and very much
easier. They have nothing of our complications of depth, or of levels,
and fragmentary {one word not clear: "rests" or "nests"} of cities or
civilisations. I shall be glad to be back in Syria—and should be now,
only for the present beauty of the weather and the misty sunlight,
magnifying the palm-trees, and making the pyramid of Illahun, our
neighbour greater than many mountains. Also we see the Nile two
miles away, with the brown sails of boats passing up and down its
sluggish length. Our house would make you laugh. We spend our
days stringing beads, or copying painted texts of the book of the dead,
until the little room is more ancient than modern, and until you cannot go in or out without brushing past mummies or statuettes, or tomb
pottery. Even our very firewood comes from 24th dynasty coffins, and
our charcoal brazier first performed that office in the days of the fall
of Carchemish. At night jerboas perform triumphal dances over my
body, and mosquitoes are the orchestra.

To be earthy—I'm very well, and eat well, and sleep still better;
W. believes in food, lots of food, and food hot: and the digging is so
very different from ours that it will occupy me the three weeks I am
here: Mr. Hogarth was quite right in arranging for no longer: I'm no
body snatcher, and we have a pile of skulls that would do credit to a
follower of Genghis Khan. These men are less squeamish than our
fellows. Salaamat.   L.

KAFR AMMAR
Thursday, Jan. 18, 1912

Prof. Petrie has now come—and in his camp everyone writes
pencilly—this explains that. I got two letters from you, with Mr.
ffoulkes' one. My letters to you have obviously gone wrong: though

20 days seems unduly so: of course the quickness of the P. Said post, and the slowness of Beyrout throws things out. You only talk of Bab though. I hope my week later one will get in:—from Aleppo. In any case if you do any wiring, let it be to British consul—Beyrout or Aleppo—Jebail has no telegraph now, and as a matter of fact they did not know there where I was, for my Aleppo letter to them miscarried. The things for Mrs. Rieder & Miss Holmes I sent to their agent in Beyrout to be forwarded. This was not done till Jan. 2:—I was 30 days without letter from you—. My shortage of money arose from the second journey to Biredjik which became necessary as explained in letters: I bought nothing for self—only for Mr. Hogarth. I hope he will like his seals. The news about *Sigurd* is splendid. You didn't say how you liked it: put it in either morning room or my house if it's Will's now, and let Arnie read it. Tell him it's the best poem I know. Am sorry to hear of illness: hope all clear now.

Mr. ffoulkes' book might be sent—book post—to British Consul Aleppo. It's quite small and will go for $2\frac{1}{2}d$. Book-post is gloriously cheap. *Sigurd* I must leave till I return I suppose. I wrote about slides from Beyrout: if not gone by now send British Consul Aleppo. In case Beyrout letter fails know that I got two there You—Father—Will—Arnie. I don't like Egypt or the Egyptians—after Carchemish & the Carchemisians:—and I don't like Mrs. Petrie. He is interesting—but so intensely self-centred and self-standing. Argument etc. is ludicrous between them, for either's opinion is rooted against all winds that blow. I like him exceedingly, but rather as one thinks of a cathedral or something immovable but by earthquake. He is a quite inspired archæologist—and I am picking up hints of sorts all day long. Very little of his methods applies to Syria as yet. The styles of digging are so utterly dissimilar and the things dug and the earth you dig them in. This here is ghastly work—too easy, too monotonous, and mostly body-snatching—not one tenth the joy of ruin exploration. I'll not become a digger in Egypt at this rate. I hope to send you some prehistoric pottery—hand polished with a surface like silk and a lovely blush of red in parts—by one Wainwright to Oxford. He is one of Mr. Petrie's permanent assistants, and is interesting, though in a simple sort of way. His voice cracks also but he is not self-complete. He is coming to Oxford in April for work and I'll ask him to bring them up: not at all a formidable person: you may even like him.

They call me here es Shami—the Syrian—and cannot go about to understand me. I am digging on the Laxdale and Burnt Nial, Orderic Vitalis, Canterbury tales, Daudet, and Richard Yea & Nay:—a very tolerable selection of the light sort: we start at 7 and stop at 5 and do some night-work, mostly development—the weather is warm and sunny without a drop of rain and nearly windless—which is as well with all the Sahara unbroken lying W. of us.

Salaams to all the world.

N.

KAFR AMMAR
Friday, Jan. 26, 1912

I am leaving P. Said on Feb. 2, Friday, for Beyrout by the steamer that goes direct. So I will only be 19 hours at sea. That probably means I leave here on Tuesday, for I want baths and things in Cairo before going down to sea.

I got your 13th letter on Thursday: I'm glad you got my Beyrout letter: yes it was a very funny Christmas: though why you should be very anxious about me I don't understand! About money: you suggest a cheque to Miss Holmes: but the B.M. {British Museum} now owes me £48, and I don't want to have too much over. It only leads to spending. It would be better if I left Miss H. till I got up to Aleppo again: I should have enough for that, for at A. {Aleppo} I hope to find credits for me in the Bank for housebuilding. I've written to Mr. Hogarth about this. In any case don't send money for me to Miss Holmes at any time, or wire to her about me, because she has no bank nearer than Beyrout, and no telegraph and it takes a day (and costs 5/–) to get up to her. Also post between Beyrout and Jebail takes often a week. It's better in all cases to wire direct to B.P.O. Beyrout, or to wire to Consul.

About the site: I don't think Hassan Agha is a rascal: it's only the coming of the railway that has raised golden hopes in all the country side. It's quite certain that we have now the truth about the site, we have copies of all documents enregistered. The Germans expect to take 4 years over the bridge, and of course they are raising prices, but our employment of only local workmen will save us many of their food difficulties. As it was, last month, when they told me that in three days they had only been able to get three eggs out of the village, Haj Wahid went out at once and brought back ten in about an hour:—only you see, they were for my use. Did I tell you the village sent a man in on foot (4 days) to Aleppo, to ask at the Consulate if I had arrived well after that attack of dysentery last summer? And the messenger didn't ask if we were coming back or anything else. You'll see my pottery and seals—in time—in the Ashmolean. Miss Holmes' committee which promised to buy her property has failed to do so, and the leases of her boys' school are running out: also she has been a little too hard lately on Miss Fareedah, who has nearly broken down. As I wrote the Table Cover has not (or had not) arrived. I'll tell you later what its judgement is. And I have not yet settled with Mrs. R. {Rieder}. Dr. {A. G.} Gibson isn't very dear: remember F.'s {Frank's} share of the insurance money was £10. About my journey up the Nile: left Cairo 9.30 a.m. arrived Kafr Ammar 11.15, seeing nothing of the river but an arm near Cairo, and that through a girder bridge. Egypt is not to be ranked with Syria for a moment: you have only to think of fellahin—and ours are Bedu. All the difference in the world. These are such poor fellows.

You know it has been the gradual realisation of the barrenness of Egyptian art after the Pyramid time that has removed all my wish to dig things Egyptian. Fortunately this is nearly all prehistoric, which seems the best there was in the country. I find very distinct influences of Mesopotamian art in the carvings of this cemetery: not in the pottery. Prof. Petrie agrees, and has suggested that he pay for a tentative dig in Bahrein (vid. Strabo I think, or some early geographer on the Phœnicians) or any other point on the Arabian coast I settle for. It appears to me that Bahrein (with authority of Strabo above) is the most likely half-way house between Mesopotamia or Elam and Egypt. A dig there would be excellent sport, and as it is an English dependency, not very difficult, and one could carry off the stuff. I will enquire of Mr. Hogarth before closing with the idea. Write next to H.B.M. Consul, Aleppo.

Am quite well but very dirty: people in this camp wash only twice a week and never change their clothes. It is certainly the most uncomfortable place imaginable: but I like the professor very much indeed. He has been with us a fortnight.

BRISTOL HOTEL, CAIRO

Jan. 31, 1912

I got your letter yesterday (Tuesday) just before leaving the camp. I'll answer it first. The later grave digging, after the Professor came, was not objectionable: the bones were bare, not mummified, since that was unknown in the predynastic times. I enjoyed the last fortnight very well. Professor Petrie was there all the time: he was very nice: Mrs. Petrie was not. The G.P.O. has certainly made a mess of things: you were exceedingly wise to go to Mr. Hogarth with the slides: I hope he'll send them in time! His fault if he doesn't.

The British Consul in Aleppo has proper arrangements made with the B.P.O. in Beyrout to forward all his parcels: anything else would be ridiculous. Good thing you didn't send overland P. post: that means Turkish post, and a general doubtfulness of delivery. I would probably never have got them—certainly not without sending an agent to the Beyrout Customs to frank them through. Book-post at least should be simple enough for the compass of the G.P.O. authorities. Things by that go direct and cheaply, to any point in Turkey to which you can write, without customs examination. I'll write to Leeds and appease him: I am not (second thoughts) sending the book, not because it is not good, but because it is not good enough. Read it if it falls in your way, *The Centaur* by Algernon Blackwood. I have read it three times with profit, and have left it behind me, of intention, literally and metaphorically: incomplete, that's what it is. The strigil is still in Beyrout. I was too busy letter writing and packing to find a box for it. I hope to send it this week.

Mrs. Rieder never gave me the name of the author: her fault therefore: I'll ask her this time. Don't send cheque yet: I'll wait to see if I have credit in Aleppo at the bank: have money enough still. Hot here with mosquitoes: have had two malariæ since I came: Petrie camp too primitive for words. Sorry you ill: Father too it appears. Don't serve tables. Vincent may have the Thesis—though he doesn't want it—that young person's politeness puts him to excessive pains. His ideas of History are too crude for any exam. at present above the Locals. He has no idea what it is. The discovery opens up a new world of ideas when it comes, as it did to me after a couple of hours' talk with Mr. Jane. Times of letter-writing worked out exactly, as above, I got your letter yesterday.

The Petries refused to take anything from me for living expenses, as we had arranged: also they very kindly pressed me to return any time I pleased, and he has offered me help to £500 for Bahrein. I think all this is deserving of a subscription to their fund:—so will you (at your convenience) send £2.2.0 (two guineas) to

The Hon. Sec.
British School of Archæology in Egypt.
London University, Gower Street.

With a note saying "please apply to benefit of Ashmolean Museum Oxford. Publications not required." This means that Mr. Hogarth gets £2.2.0 of antikas, and we are spared a very dull volume describing the digs. The volume is worth about 4/3: so that it's better value to take antiquities.

I've brought away with me from the digs two prehistoric pots: about 7000 years old each. I may send them, but am more likely to bring them.

Arnie's letter has just come to light. He wants an Encyclopedia, not a brother to look at. If I come home via P. Said I'll try to get Abyssinian coins: not Maria Theresas: can't carry them with me now: besides I probably won't be given any. The three-tailed flag I haven't seen: if I do see it I'll pull it down and pocket it for him. Is it Abyssinian and do they hang it over Consulates? I can't get Aby. stamps: at least I've never seen one, or an Aby. P.O. I live in hopes.

Am going out now, to buy cigarettes! Not for myself, but for one of Petrie's men, who starve for tobacco down there, since the Professor doesn't admit smoking as one of the accomplishments of a gentleman. They begged me to send them some. About Egypt in general, all I can say is that it is a tolerable enough place, with pretty colours in the air. The country has not the subtlety of curve that you find in Syria, or the immensity of space, for all the time you are in a narrow green valley, or on the edge of a stony desert. You are not able to see both at a time. The Egyptian people are horribly ugly, very dirty, dull, low-spirited, without any of the vigour or the self-confident independence of our men. Besides, the fanaticism of the country is deplorable, and the treatment of the women most un European; most of the Petrie workmen have several wives, and have had many more, and one could not stand or work close to them for a few minutes without catching fleas or lice. Nor could one talk to them with the delicious free intimacy of the men of Carchemish. They either got surly, or took liberties. They were frenetic, and querulous, foul-mouthed, and fawning.

Cairo is glorious. I have spent in all now six days here, and have been four times to the mosque of Sultan Hassan, once to the bazaars, three times to the Arab museum, twice to the Khedival library. Sultan Hassan is amazing. I must come back to see it again some time, and as well to go out to see the Pyramids and the great Museum of the Egyptian things. But the real matter is that the Arab architecture, faïence, and manuscripts are so fine that one has no time for sight-seeing. There are 300 mosques in the city!   N.

ALEPPO
Feb. 10, 1912

Got a letter from you, suggesting large writing: Here it is!!!!!! I came up here, by way of Damascus on Thursday; spending two nights and a day in the train. In Damascus I bought a cylinder which I think is Hittite, and today, here, three more.

Now for your letter. "Sigurds" are flocking in! but don't get more than one, unless you want to give one away. And do let me know how you like it. I hope it is not kept carefully: a good book like that should be put in the best place where it may have the widest influence on the lives of the people it meets. Mrs. Rieder wasn't bothered a bit: and they cannot send for parcels. I told them it was there. I didn't see McNeile. You are evidently having a lot of rain. It is quite fine here, and warm. Cold only at nights. Hot bath in hotel. Am glad Will has got a rise. Probably another next year: Am glad too that F. {Frank} is still shooting. Let him do a little revolver work: it is harder than a rifle to learn, and more often necessary. I'll ask about stamps tomorrow, or when I get near the Post Office. There is only the one for the town of 300,000 people, and it is the other side of the bazaars: it takes an hour to reach through those packed streets. Rugs are all upstairs in the Hogarth house. Have paid Miss Holmes £4, and will send the fifth when I can. Have not sent the strigil: no time to get to the Post Office in Beyrout: so it is still in my bag: Woolley expected about March 10.

Now about affairs. The Turkish Government wants to buy the site of Carchemish: but it hasn't any money just now. So all is yet hung up. Mr. Hogarth has communicated with Constantinople (Embassy). I got a line from him here; saying they were sending money, but none has come. As I arrived with only 16 piastres, counting on him, I have had to borrow of Mr. Fontana. With this I am filling up my spare time buying antikas: and I will continue so, until the funds arrive. Aleppo is an inexhaustible field of Hittite. Meanwhile the house is not begun, and it is Feb. 10 and Woolley is due in a month. Not my fault at least, if it isn't ready! Haj Wahid and I today bought (for myself) a camel-hair mantle, such as Bedouin sheikhs wear: Baghdad made: very warm and beautiful. With this, if I sat on the North Pole, it would melt: so it will be invaluable for next month's tent-life.

Aleppo is a splendid place to spend a week in, and I have the consulate and its books whenever I please to borrow. Mr. Fontana is really an excellent consul to have in a good place. Have lent him the Anthology. I got a very cheerful letter from {Campbell} Thompson: he is gardening with his wife. All the curio-dealers of Aleppo are calling all day at the Hotel: simply a queue by the time I have finished breakfast. And they go away so easily content! I have only bought 12/- worth this trip. Mr. Fontana promises unlimited money (enough to build the house, if I like but I don't—that's the B.M.'s affair) and I like hunting antikas: so all is smooth. Am well.

Salaamat.　　　L.

ALEPPO
Feb. 20, 1912

Kenyon has sent me a draft for £50, so I hope to be off tomorrow for Jerablus. The weather is fine, and not over-cold. Last week was pouring wet. We are taking four loads of stuff to Jerablus with us: three mules and a donkey. So that you may imagine our comforts. We hear encouraging reports of the village people from two carpenters just back from the German works. Everybody is expecting us. There is great local jubilation at the ousting of the railway from the Kala'at: everybody regards it in the light of a triumph of England over Germany. It really is a triumph of archæology and history over commercial expedience. In either case it's very good.

Got a long letter from Will yesterday about his visit to Cambridge. Interesting, and I should think amusing. He was over-fortunate in his host. It might have been a mathematician with a passion for fossils.

Kalaat el Hosn (See p. 104)

Kalaat el Hosn (Arch Machicoulis) (See p. 104)

Kalaat el Hosn (Crac des Chevaliers) (*See p.* 104)

What a queer time Rolfe must be having. He is obviously a little queer.
That persecution mania is a harmless form of insanity (c.p. Blake and
Mr. Jane when morbid). Don't be like a don. If you joined to it the
encouraging bonhomie of an examiner you did pretty well—for a jest
—but drop it in private life. I wrote & asked you to send Mrs. Rieder
a little Masefield & Galsworthy. And will you send Miss Holmes a
cheque for £1..1..0 = a guinea. The remains—tell her—of my debt.
I hope to do the rest of the year on nothing. By the way how does the
family like *Sigurd*? Has it wooed father yet?—for it will—. Read
Richard Yea and Nay in Egypt for the ninth time. It is a masterpiece.

{Ezra} Pound has a very common American affectation of immense
learning in strange things. Funny thing about D.G.H.'s daughter. He
is only 50 years old, and Courtney no younger. Glad Mr. Jane has a
crowd. Got Mr. ffoulkes' book—a week before your letter, and Green's
articles. Not very good; I should not have published them. Mr. ffoulkes'
little thing is very pretty and very interesting.

Fontana (Consul) is head over ears in the Greek Anthology quotes
it in office hours, sits up o' nights cherishing it, and (for all I know)
sends his best pieces to the ambassador in place of dispatches. Salaamat
to the people. I go to bed, & thence to Bab on the Euphrates road. It
was Mr. Fontana who lent me money to go on with last two weeks.

JERABLUS
Feb. 25, 1912

I have nothing to do, so why not write? I think I sent you news of
the arrival of £50, and my proximate start. Well, I got off on the
22nd, leaving Haj Wahid and the muleteer with about an hour's
packing, to follow later. I walked all day, to Bab, about 30 miles, and
went to my old khan, and waited: no signs of the mules. About 6
o'clock I sent the khan boy out, to buy food, and about 8 went to sleep:
about 9.30 they woke me up with the tidings of Haj's arrival. The
muleteer's man had disappeared mysteriously in Aleppo, with the
money that the muleteer had given him to get changed, and they had
had to find a new man, and more money, before they could get going.
The result had been that it was past one before all was ready, and the
muleteer had refused to start on an eight hours' journey so late. In the
E. you know, they like to arrive in the early afternoon. However Haj

pushed him out, and they reached Bab as I have said. Next morning I was up first and I went out along the road for the Sadjur: I met nobody of interest, till I got there (its a river—the one I fell into last Xmas) and found there a German engineer in a carriage firmly stuck in mid-stream. The horses would only stand on their hind legs and look foolish, and there was no help at hand: so I consoled him by relating my adventures of December—from the bank—and by telling other stories of people washed away by sudden floods, or by the swift currents of Syrian rivers. Then, in about an hour, more carriages came out, and by a second team of horses he was saved. I only met two parties that day who knew me not. They both abused me as an Italian ('talian and Talaman—Italian & German, are the same out here) and apologised profusely when they learnt I was English. In all the villages I have acquaintances. In any case to get a good reception out here all one has to do is to stand at the entering in of the village, and lift one's voice in declaring oneself English. If you say German expect a shower of stones.

Well, let's see, the Sadjur. I crossed by the foot-bridge and struck out, for Tell Ker, with an Armenian of Urfa, who didn't care what or who took the Government, so long as they ousted the Turks. He was more bitter against the Mahommedans than anyone I have met out here. At Tell Ker I sala'amed the sheikh, and walked W. to Nukhé, where Sheikh Suleiman was an old acquaintance. I had hoped for a Hittite pot from him, but alas! it was only Roman. So I left it. Sheikh Suleiman fed me excellently on parched corn, leben, and grape-sugar, with tea and coffee: he loves tea. Next morning I ate again, and then left him, for Tell Ker again. Thence I crossed to Halman, Kundariyeh, where I bought two good seals, Yusuf Beg, and lastly Kekledji: thence to Jerablus, with a train of about 30 would-be employés. Haj Wahid turned up a little later, minus his donkey, stolen in the night. We pitched a tent, and slept. This morning the workmen came along (twenty-two of them) and we began to dig foundations. I laid out a great room 23 feet by 14, and eight smaller ones by tape and compass, when lo! up comes old Hassan Agha, still grumbling, and proposes to be our tent-guard. This was refused, promptly but gracefully. He then mentions airily that the government had offered £200 for the Kala'at, but that he had refused the offer, since he liked us better, and hoped we would buy it off him. He could let us have it, at a sacrifice for our sakes, for £180. I happened to know that the Gov. were expropriating him for £17..10..0 so I told him I would think his offer over, and tell him. Then he became violently angry, and said the offer only lasted for 5 minutes more. I had him turned out of the place. Next came the lieutenant in charge of the soldiers here: he, poor man, was very apologetic: his duty, he said, was inter alia to look after the Kala'at. He was quite aware that I had a firman to dig: but had I an order from Constantinople to build a house. I told him that Kenyon had the permission of the Ottoman Museum, and that the Kaimmakan was aware of that. He said: "Quite so, but that Kaimmakan is gone." Result was that I agreed to stop the digs while he telegraphed to Constantinople. Perhaps in two or three days (I have ten days to build the house) we may begin again.

Up came next the German chief engineer: "Would I give him stones for their houses?" I would be delighted, but I couldn't: not until the Government let me go on. He agreed entirely; and was exceedingly polite. He has evidently had orders to behave himself better. They will, I believe, move all the surface stones from near our digs, for us, and we will be able to go straight ahead. So far so good, and it is a favour to them as well. Who said an "entente" with Germany? It is an achieved fact, and Lord Haldane still tarries on the way.

N.

ALEPPO

March 10, 1912

Got here on Thursday night from Jerablus, and found Woolley just arrived. The B.M. has forgotten to give him credits at the Ottoman Bank, and so we are very badly off, and have had to borrow £100 from Mr. Fontana. We have sent camels to Jerablus with our stores, and got off Haj Wahid and his family. We intend to go on Tuesday ourselves. The country is quite quiet, now that all the Italians are expelled. Woolley and I went to the Marcopoli (the big dealers) and bought seven of their things (Hittite) the day before they were expelled. So we got them cheap (£35). You will see them by May in the Ashmolean.

Walking over the country I bought two most wonderful Hittite tomb-groups of pottery: the finest in existence, & in the bazaars today a third. Got a letter from you on Thursday. Glad if F. {Frank} gets something: but no use saying so. Will would do well to go with A.T.P. He will quite likely be Fellow himself some day. About the house—no permission came, so I could not put up a stone: Woolley is very annoyed at the Museum, and has wired and written so.

There are to be many seasons more of digs at Jerablus. Don't be nervous about us if anything happens in Syria: Englishmen are safe with the Milli-Kurds: and a rising is not yet due. When the Italians strike for Constantinople we will come home—but that won't be till after the digs. This is a stupid note, but I am very busy—and rather tired.   N.

BIREDJIK
March 17, 1912

Have come up here with Woolley to fight the Kaimmakan: we have done it: threatened to shoot any man who interrupted the digs, whether soldier or not. The Kaimm. collapsed and sends strict orders to allow us to do our pleasure: he was trying to get a month's salary out of us illegally, for an unofficial commissaire. A very great pleasure. Woolley came out exceedingly well: he explained that he was not declaring war on the Turkish Government, but on Biredjik only. We are very well amused. This is all I can write now. Your letter (or Father's) came shortly ago. They ask about Henry's present: give him anything not too useful. Am off back.

N.

All very well, but fearfully busy! digs not begun yet.

BIREDJIK
March 20, 1912

Small writing: have only this piece of paper.

I am writing once again in Biredjik to which I have come back, without Woolley, to buy the roof-beams and stuffs for our house. I have written very little lately, and that hurried, but you will allow for the amount of work that falls on me with Woolley a stranger to the country, and the language and the antiquities. I have to act interpreter for him, always, though he is fairly fluent in Egyptian: I have to do the bargaining, and keep the accounts, for he does not know the coinage: I have to choose the workmen, for he does not know them, and to settle our plans, for he has no idea of what we can get in the country and what we cannot: and to coach him, meanwhile in things Hittite. Besides, we have had a lot of work with the government, and there he was without experience, and at first deceived. I had to act adviser there also.

On the whole therefore, we have been well employed. May I say that our accounts for £176 odd spent in Aleppo and on the way, came out right to within a half crown? And I spent £70 of it one day in the bazaars!

Woolley is getting on very well—goes down with the workmen, is dropping Egyptian hauteur and ruling-race fantasies, likes Syrian cooking and sweetmeats, and (*mirabile dictu*) our dialect! It is a pretty hard piece of work for him. He has accepted all my pottery theories of last year, except the least definite and most difficult. That even I would reserve in some points, and he has determined to keep an open mind.

Only two of our old workmen of last year have preferred nine piastres with the Germans to 8 piastres with us. The others we found had left in good time, and were awaiting us. It is satisfactory to be running with one's old gang. They are exceedingly good fellows. Woolley unfortunately has brought two Egyptians with him, to take photographs: he refused to believe Mr. Hogarth's assurances that there was not enough work for them: result is that they are loafing, and the men are getting a little disgusted at it. The Egyptians stand very much in awe of them. I wonder what you think of our diplomacy, as explained in last letter? It really was too funny for words to hear Woolley explaining to the Kaimmakan, that he did not mean to declare war on the Turkish Empire, but only on the Kaimmakan of Biredjik: and that he was very sorry that the little corporal at Jerablus would be the first victim, since he had a real regard for him. He would prefer if the Kaim. would come personally to lead the attack. The K. simply collapsed and promised all we wanted: and visited us yesterday in Jerablus to placate us: we have his leave for all sorts of illegalities now. There has, of course, come no sort of answer to my wire of three weeks ago to Constantinople about the house-building. So we are building the house and have wired again, saying that it would be convenient to have permission before the house is finished. You would have liked our home-coming two days back triumphant from Biredjik.

The men had lined the town walls under arms, at our orders, to repel attack, and when they learnt of our success they fired salvoes of bullets excitedly into the air with wild yells: while the staid Haj Wahid pulled my Mauser from his belt (he was commander in chief in our absence) and sent ten glorious shots through the kitchen roof—which has had to be darned in cold blood—for it is a goat-hair tent. The irony of the matter was that the Kaimmakan was just coming down the river on his message of apology—and his cavalcade met an excited troop of Germans, rushing down to see the fun, under the belief that the attack had commenced.

What more remains to say? We are well, very well, and as yet cordial: we have books, and pistachios, and six kinds of soap—if not seven. We eat a lot, and sleep a lot, and talk a lot: and I have for the second time, assimilated Thompson's *Mistress of Vision*. It is very good. We sleep by the ropes of the camp, and we rise with the dawn and we tramp with the sun and the moon for our lamp, and the spray of the wind in our hair. I read much Meleager, some Meredith, Rossetti, and Shakespeare.

You speak of a wedding present for Henry: get him something a little more than useful, with my best wishes: or if this is too vague, write out here, and I will bring a carpet back with me. I hope Will will get to Andorra with A.T.P. I got a letter from Mr. Jane the other day: he flourishes.

So Mother reads *Sigurd*! I want to know whether it is the most beautiful book any of you have ever seen: and what she thinks of the telling of the tale: remember the tale itself is Norse, and it is perhaps the most near to us of all the Norse tales—the one we can best assimilate and enjoy—better of course, if one knows a simple people, as I happen to know the Arabs.

You will like my camel bells: I met a camel caravan swinging down the spice market in Aleppo to the booming of two huge iron cylinders under the belly of the foremost: and I stopped the line, and bought the bells, and walked back to the hotel making a noise like a caravan from Baghdad Oah Oah, and the people parted in the narrow ways to give me passage. And now we call the workmen out of bed with them. Goodnight.

N.

CARCHEMISH
April 6, 1912

Just got Mother's letter written from the Smoking-room during house-repairs. It has come out to us in a day of driving rain and hail, with furious wind, and my huge camel bells ringing a day-long peal before the blasts. Carchemish is very beautiful these days:—and today we found the Hittite level in the mound-top, a pot-burial, and two sculptures. So we are very happy. I told you, I think that we had been prosecuted for various causes by the ground-owner: his case collapsed, because his witnesses refused to give evidence: the village is so wild at his treatment of us that they have driven him away to the town to live. He has, of late, been quite outrageously dishonest: in any case we have finished with him now. The Kaimmakan, who was egging him on, has received a tremendous reproof from Constantinople, and came to us with apologies, dreadfully scared.

You would like our stone-house, with its wood-beamed ceiling, flat roof, Roman-mosaic floor of birds and trees and gazelles and peacocks, and Damascus tiles on the walls, the beaten-copper fire-hood, the beaten-copper bath, the basalt pillars and door-mouldings. It has eleven rooms (two very large) and is very massively built. I hope to live in it this winter.

I'm glad Mr. Hogarth is coming out shortly: we have such quantities of things for him to see: just now we have in hand ten packing-cases of Hittite tomb-pottery, all perfect pieces, with much bronze work, all brought from villages near at hand, and all going to the British Museum and the Ashmolean. None of it comes from the digs of course, and to add insult to injury, we have presented all our duplicates and inferior pieces to the Turkish government. Our coffee-cups, sugar-bowls, and soap-dishes are of the finest Hittite work, and must also go to the British Museum, if they survive the season intact. I'll bring you some as well. As for heat and cold—I'm always warm, and stalk about the site in a camel-hair cloak like a Sheikh of Baghdad. The colour is a red-brown: the texture thick, not very soft: but very pleasant to the touch. Woolley is very jealous of it all. I hope to have some p.p. cards of the site next week. The Germans are very friendly now, for we are allowing them to clear away our dump-heaps of last year and this year free of charge. As we want to dig under them in the near future

we are doing ourselves a good turn as well. The railway is too far
away to disturb us.

As for money, I have lots: about £40: in hand: or to be in hand
shortly, when Mr. Hogarth pays me for our seals. We have a very
splendid collection.

Woolley gets on most excellently here. He is fresh enough from
Egypt to see the glory of the country and the people and the customs:
I don't think he will ever settle down in Egypt again. The men are as
good this year as last: splendid humorists: Bedouin for ever!

Please give me your opinion of *Sigurd*: or Frank's or Arnie's or
Will's, or Bob's or Father's.   N.

JERABLUS
April 16, 1912

A scrambled letter only: I am still moving my mosaic pavement, and
as well had a pleasing experience this morning, when Woolley agreed
to my breaking down the door of the government antika store of last
year, and bringing out the things. The old Commissaire had refused
the key to us and the new man, and by Ottoman law we had right to
enter the room as we pleased: so we did: I picked the locks, with great
neatness, and a zaptieh to hold my lamp. That pleased me because after
all I was breaking some one's else door. Our poor little Commissaire
of this year was dreadfully shocked, and is telegraphing to all the chief
towns in the Empire: no matter. Coal strike is ended according to the
Editor of the *Debats*, who visited us this afternoon. We have many
strangers this year, coming over from the Railway works, and they are
all amazed at our friendly relations with our men, and the way they
work for us. It strikes them as such a contrast with the German works
and their continual rows and ill feeling. Our men feel the difference of
treatment very acutely, and we are driven wild by applicants for work.
Woolley is thawing down from his Egyptian aloofness splendidly, and
the men are getting to like him immensely: also, in all he has done so
far I approve most exceedingly: so that we are well agreed to date.
Will is now coming back probably: I hope he got to Carcassonne: let
him get Dunsany's story of the man who never got there. It is good.
How does the house like *Sigurd*? not the poem only, but the book?
The poem I am not afraid of. I think I mentioned to you I was three

weeks without a letter: so do not expect better than you give. Am very busy this year. This pavement is a huge undertaking: about 34 square meters to be moved for one room—say 480,000 tesseræ. We are finding some fine sculptures and a poor inscription or two: but at present all is so indefinite that I am not going to enlarge: besides it is late. You ask how I am—all well—it is not cold now—97° today in the tent at 9 a.m. —and yet just cool enough for pleasure. We are buying peacocks for the Kala'at.

CARCHEMISH

Sunday: about 20th April 1912

Got a letter from Will from Carcassonne, and one from Mother—death of Mrs. Kemmis—today. Sorry to hear Father has a chill again (thermometer here is 99° at my side on the table): glad Will enjoyed himself with Williams: their snow-storm must have been amusing: Carcassonne gets its real distinction simply to my mind because it is so new and fresh: it is a mediæval fortress, and not the ruin of one; it is the fellow of the castles out here, and (with Aigues-Mortes) a stranger in Europe. Saissac I have visited—xiii Cent. and very fine—I wonder how Will got back from Carcassonne. I'd suggest the Rhône valley. Tell Mother I cannot write a journal: let me give her yesterday's doings—Up before dawn, and to the mosaic pavement with a couple of boys, to glue cloth over it, and pick up: all glueing work has to be done in the cool of the day. This was about 3 hrs. work. Breakfast was about 7. and after it I wrote an Arabic telegram, and deciphered a bill and a letter, for Woolley. Then I paid a flying visit to the digs to take off all the men up to the village with me, where I opened the doors of Salem's house again, and brought down 90 loads of stones and pottery. This made it about 10.30, and till midday I had to be on the digs, planning a new great gate and staircase, and making a restoration (to scale) of a great basalt lion from pieces that we found. The lion was 15 feet long. From noon till one we rested—that includes lunch, and the tying up of four or five men wounded, and the interpreting of Woolley's orders for the afternoon to our overseers.

Meanwhile Dahoum (water boy of last year & this) had filled the inside of part of our courtyard with the pottery and stones that we had brought down in the morning, washing and arranging them roughly. I spent till 4.30 labelling & arranging these things, and setting them in

our store room in the new house. From 4.30 till 5.15 I helped Woolley
pay some of the men who wanted money (we have run short again) and
then went up to the other end of the little valley to see a stone newly
suspected to be inscribed. I returned to the mosaic pavement (it now
being after sunset) where I found the boys waiting for me, and we
glazed and cut it till about 8 p.m. Then I sent them away, and walked
back to the camp, where I found Woolley in difficulties with a number
of men whom he could not understand. Our commissaires then came
in, and asked for money etc. after which we ate, and I had only to write
up notes and clean a few objects before bed, which happened about
eleven. I should mention a hunt for a lost donkey after dinner: it had
strayed away in the dark. If I wanted to write up this day in the evening,
I would point out

 i. That it had no salient features, which could be shortly put.
 ii. That a full account has taken a page and a half, and I have
   forgotten half that I did.
 iii. That your letters nearly all require answering, and that I have
   been writing this letter now for an hour and a half. A sense
   of style is not always blessed.

No more possibility of trouble from the Kaimmakan: he has had
very strong orders to behave. Old Hassan Agha, the owner of the
Kala'at is still suing us, and we still refuse to attend. I'll write to Miss
Holmes. My regards to the Canon {Canon Christopher}, if he is still
alive—your letter seems to make it unlikely: I'm glad he is in no pain,
but the helplessness will irk him.

Our house is all finished but the mosaic pavement, which is proving
a very difficult business: we have used all the glue of the province. I'll
send you post cards of the house when it is finished and in occupation.
Woolley moves into his room tonight, and I move up to the top of the
Kala'at as last year: weather is now quite warm, even at night: at
midday it gets up to 105° in the shade. Salaamat.

{CARCHEMISH}
April 29, 1912

A very hurried note, waiting dinner: I fancy a post goes tomorrow
and I have not written lately: am working day (and half the night) on
the mosaic pavement, of which about half is now in place and looking
well.

The part down is a vase in a decorative circle, with sprays and fruits of a tree: in the foliage are two peacocks, a pheasant, a glossy ibis, and some ducks, geese and doves. The whole about 15 feet by 12. I got it down in one piece, but in parts tesseræ were missing, and we had two days' work fitting them in. The other half is a little larger, with a design of gazelles and birds, with a large orange tree. Altogether a difficult business; there are about 144,000 tesseræ there, weighing over a ton.

I send a photo of our house—or a piece of it—looking down the bedroom wing through the main gate of the courtyard. An open door at the bottom beside a passage leads into the mosaic room (which is large and fire-placed): behind it is the antika store-room, which is largest of all: there are also dark room and bath room, rooms for us, Mr. Hogarth, Gregori, the Egyptians, and Haj Wahid's wife, and a kitchen. Cost £75: but the mosaic takes at least ten of these. The man in black and white in the bottom of the quad is one of Woolley's Egyptians—poor creatures they are, here.

Later. Am going up now to the mosaic (it is Wednesday) for my third night this week: we go up about 6 p.m. usually, and work till 11 p.m. then again at dawn, for the glue goes wrong in the heat of the midday. You will hardly expect letter-writing now! I got a letter from you on Sunday: Father was ill, and was reading *Sigurd*: let him try it in the ordinary type from the Union and see how much it loses as a poem. *The Well at the World's End* was lovely. Don't promise blue rugs too hastily. I looked over all the shops in Aleppo last month (Feb.) and failed to find one. Blue is the most difficult colour in the world. I expect to return almost at once after the digs: the war will I hope excuse me to Magdalen any wandering this year. I do not feel inclined for it. The only pity is my Arabic, which is going forward painfully, but still evidently. The break from season to season spells ruination to it, and it is a thing which I value as much as anything I'm doing. I manage an hour every day at it in the early morning with Dahoum and a dictionary: which is a lonely alliteration. I should like to get out here in the winter if the Museum would agree, as site-guard (the Germans want supervision) and stay over till the spring. For this I had a fire-place built and cold weather arrangements made. Also I would like to bring Dahoum back with me for conversation purposes: Woolley says I will probably be needed in England in the Autumn.

I am afraid I haven't got the money though for a servant in travelling: —and I don't know what a wild Arab would think of Oxford and 2 Polstead Rd. The others have come—so I am off.—

Salaamat.   N.

CARCHEMISH

May 5, 1912

It has been quite a long time since I wrote, & then only a card. You know we have been finding a very great deal, and the need of having it all written and photographed up for the April report to the Museum, has left neither of us with spare time. The report went yesterday, and today is Friday, with less even than usual to do. Got a letter from Mother from Sidmouth, and one from Father & one from Bob . . . nothing in particular therein. . . . I have acknowledged the second £20 cheque before, lots of times. . . . Mr. Hogarth sent me £25. . . .

The bull's head in the Ashmolean was bought by us here for 20/– from a village about 8 hrs away, whose people knew me before. It was a drinking cup, and only the rim is missing. There is one, not so good, in the B.M. from Cyprus—we don't know what that one is, except that it is probably late Hittite (900 B.C.) and came from a tomb.

Have bought nothing lately. I am sending you a few photographs, spoiled prints: please keep then strictly to yourselves . . . you see, we have no right to show them to anyone, much less to send them to other people, and I am sure the B.M. would object. At the same time our finds this year have been so very fine, and it is so doubtful whether you will ever see other photographs of them, that I will put these in. Woolley has promised me the loan of a selection of our official prints if we are in England together, and if he can carry off a set he will do it. The B.M. is a little more sensible that way than it was, for Mr. Hogarth has now got all the Carchemish material with him.

I send a bull-base, the pedestal of a statue, in basalt, about 4 feet long, very good work. This was behind a large slab on the staircase.

In another part of the site we uncovered a long line of black & white slabs, of which I have already written. They turned round a corner, with lines of foot soldiers, to a procession of captains, each with his arms, but in clothes of peace: and these were walking to meet a king & queen, the other side of an inscription, all whose children, playing with knuckle-bones and whip-tops were walking after them: finally there was a nurse, holding a baby, and leading a wild ass on a string. There was another slab also of musician & dancers, but out of place and early work. We lately found the rest of a huge laver in basalt carried on the backs of a pair of great bulls, about 8 feet long, fronting the door of a little temple found last autumn. This is now complete (we had before, the tail end only) and we have spent two days reconstructing it in its original position.

Now it is harvest, & we have cut down our men to 100, and next week start in on a graveyard, hoping to find something dateable.

Woolley and I may come home by way of Asia Minor, Trebizond, and Constantinople leaving here about June 15, and getting back about August 10. I shall rather hope to find you somewhere other than in Oxford: though it will be a very short visit, and a busy one, with much work to be done in London.   N.

For Arnie.

Euphrates is Frat . . . canoe is shahtur, "boat" . . . Alexandretta is escale; in Aleppo they call it Shanderooneh: Shaderiyei is Alexandria.

N.

CARCHEMISH

May 11, 1912

Letter from Mother (Oxford) and Will on April 27 arrived. I see Pirie-Gordon is recovering {from} his anaemia. Has he become agent generally for the Duke of Beaufort?

Please send the boots out to Miss Holmes: nothing more at present wanted. I will write if need be. If any of you likes to wear them for a little please do: they are more likely so to escape the Turk customofficer. But the duty is charged only on the declared value. Address Miss Holmes, Jebail: not B.P.O. Beyrout. My old, last times' tramping boots are to go down the Euphrates in a few days' time: quite worn out. I shall be sorry to see the end of them.

Will may like Galsworthy's book (1/-) on Shakespeare: it is written from a very fresh standpoint, though he rather obscures the merits of the plays by considering them as dramatic works. It always seemed to me that the rather unworthy humour was Shakespeare's concession to theatrical demands. The poetry, if anything, unfits them for presentation, since one cannot find a man worthy to do anything more than think of it.

I have been reading a good deal of Shakespeare lately: some Dante: more Spencer and Rossetti. Generally I take down a vol. of the *Acta Sanctorum* with me to the mound. The *Roots {of the Mountains}* are as good as ever: not many books will be read 6 times by me, unless they have a little more than prose in them. The Rabelais will be a consoler: one wants something o' nights with a little more thought in it than Shakespeare. Richards seems to have been a little cavalier: still he always is, so it doesn't much matter. I may hear from him shortly.

Many thanks the family for writing so often of late. I think I have done as well on my part, though of course I have less to say. If Mother writes every Thursday, then some letters went wide in the three-weeks gap. Of late I have got a letter by nearly every post. Has Will noted Hewlett's new book on Brazenhead? *The Times* and *Spectator* commend it highly: if it is a modern work, & represents a return to his old manner it will be of some interest, stylistically. We should have a Tauchnitz ed. of it, when published. Hewlett always seems to me to demand green in his binding: but as you please. *Artemision* should be in blue or crimson and white: the latter for preference I think. Brown end papers. Euphrates is going down, slowly.

The Soleyb (Solubbies they never are: it is a confusion of the word for Crusader with the tribe name: due to Blunts etc.) are not gypsies (Nouri) and deny all connection with them. They are pagan, and by common consent the original, pre-Arab, inhabitants of Arabia. They go on foot, often, by preference, since some have wealth and baggage-camels: are great hunters of gazelles, hospitable simple folk, in no way fanatical. They are much despised by the Arabs, who as you will see in Doughty are feather-brained & rampol-witted. He always has a good word for the Soleyb, but told me he thought their mode of life would be very primitive. Yet the Arabs are low in the scale, and I think travellers generally are inclined to see the Soleyb through their glasses. A Mohammedan race in the place of the Arabs naturally tells many ill tales of subject heretics (cf. the Irmailiyeh, Assassins, of Syria, and the wandering aborigines (Haddad) of the Sahara you quote.) Neither people is to be despised, when set along the Arab: but the fanaticism, & the blood-feeling makes the latter worthless as judges. You see this in the Arab Chroniclers of the Crusades.

I am not trying to rival Doughty. You remember that passage that he who has once seen palm-trees and the goat-hair tents is never the same as he had been: that I feel very strongly, and I feel also that Doughty's two years wandering in untainted places made him the man he is, more than all his careful preparation before & since. My books would be the better, if I had been for a time in open country: and the Arab life is the only one that still holds the early poetry which is the easiest to read. The Sahara is not Semitic, in atmosphere or in its past. However, no hurry about that: know only that the Soleyb have no touch of Gypsy blood in them (they would not mate with nouris for the world) and that nobody but Doughty has met the real ones: (and Zwiemer, but he is hopelessly untrustworthy). Burton's were pinchbeck. They never touch Egypt or Sinai; but wander among the Aneyza, as far as Resafeh: sometimes a few will come into Damascus: more to Baghdad (from which I would start): usually they will only trade with towns like Resafeh, through the agency of half-nomadic Arabs. A spring & summer with them (which is what I was thinking of) would be a fresh experience: but I have no intention of making a book of it. I would not even go down in Arabia proper: the S. Mesopotamia is much like it, without the great difficulty of access. So there would be no map: no inscriptions: and I do not like the modern habit of wrenching all legends into the purpose of anthropology. Will might have any folk-lore I bring back, if he will produce it decently, without connecting them, by an analogy of parables, with the 5 nations, the Bushmen, & the Hadendoa. I am sorry his Mods went but haltingly. The Examiners as Mr. Jane explains are only human: sometimes only machines. There is more scope in a final school such as History where traditions are less formal. I fully expect Theses will be frowned upon: partly my fault, in straining the statute far beyond what ever was intended. Simple pieces of secondary work were supposed. Yet there will always be room for a good Thesis: though they will be less essential to a good degree than was prophesied my year. Remember a family tradition will be found if your subjects have novelty & purposefulness. I should not write a thesis on any part of the French Revolution, if I were you. It is too complicated a subject to handle as a beginner, and annalistic work is worse than useless. No one has any idea what caused La Vendée, simply because its growth was as natural as a buttercup's. However you may be in Mr. Jane's hands. I warn you that he and Mr. Barker will be an ill-matched pair to drive. The only way to run them is to keep your own line between, & utilise such of each as harmonises which is exhausting, but very profitable. It will mean your reading much less than I did. Do persuade Mr. Barker to let you off the waste of time of lectures. Mr. Jane's tuition would be a great joy to you: it is not filling, but intensely stimulating. He will give you the minimum of pertinent facts, and leave you to mould them to your purposes. Don't hesitate to argue with him. He does not know till it is challenged, half the reasons which make up his mind. Mr. Hogarth's approval of my visit to the Soleyb was a little qualified. He thought it a good idea, for my purpose, but had no wish to share. Borrow's philology is a modern laughing stock: he had Romany on the brain, and any statement of his, in the absence of confirmation, is a strong counter-proof of itself.

The digs are cheering up a little: today we got a good little pedestal, on the backs of two basalt lions, and a memorial altar, with four lines of close-written Hittite linear inscription. Tomorrow we begin our last hope, the trial pits on the remaining section of the site. If they fail we close the digs for good and all. It has been very hard work lately. We have to be overseers, moving the big stones, and with ropes & crowbars only a five-ton block is a ticklish monster to handle: also we are doctors, curing wounds & scorpion bites (the latter instantly with ammonia): then we had a strike, engined by the village sheikh, who wants to be overseer of our men, that he may levy toll on their weekly pay: also great troubles from all sorts of pseudo-claimants of the mound, from the Vali of Aleppo, local gentry, and above all our Imperial Commissaire. Him however, we have now got either stiffly reprimanded, or recalled. So that for a little we may be without worries. Digging in Turkey is not all joy: the actual work is splendid, but not the being protector of-the-poor-and-enemy-of-all-the-rich-and-in-authority which that involves. What with police, and feudal gentry, and shifty tricksters in the village the path has been a little thorny. Our donkey-boy till last week was only getting 15 of the 45 piastres we pay him: the percentage of the sheikh accounted for the rest: since he was a boy & helpless.

N.

{On a Post Card with photograph of the house}. *May 12, 1912*

A piece of our house: got a letter from Will about it this morning. Give my salaams to Mathews. Tell the family we are going to dig here

Aleppo. Citadel Entrance (*See p.* 105)

Safita. In the Keep (*See p.* 104)

Sahyun (*See p.* 106)

Kalaa't el S'ch'k'if (Beaufort) (*See p.* 94)

Sept.-Dec. this year, and I'll not come back till after that; I'll spend the warm weather here, in the house, which is built for heat. Mr. Hogarth is here, and has heaps of money for four years work. All very well. Mr. Hogarth has brought the parcels.   N.

CARCHEMISH
20 May 1912

A letter (April 30) came last night: Glad Arnie got to the B.M. but he must have wanted a guide! A camel is not at all comfortable—and the Zoo camels are not theluls—riding camels. There are eleven camels with six baby ones just now eating the thistles on our lawn. Glad Arnie has gone up a form. Rug does not sound good enough: I may send something from Aleppo: next year I am to be comparatively wealthy if we dig 8 months: (Mr. Hogarth proposed 15/- a day and expenses which with the Magdalen money would give me the £200 I want to save at once), and I can afford to spend a little. I am going to borrow £20 from Woolley in a month: to be repaid by you in England for me: I am not coming home this summer. I have not written much lately, I don't know why. I'll send a photo of the mosaic floor soon—but there is only half of it in place as yet. I am too busy to take the other half so we have buried it till after the digs this month. We stop in 13 days. I made the hood {for the fire-place} & bath.

Old Hassan Agha has lately got me condemned to pay him £30 and half the antiquities we have dug up, and to refrain from digging till he gives further permission—all in a judgment of the court at Biredjik which has no authority to order me to do anything, since I am English. Of course nothing has been done or attempted. You needn't be afraid of Hassan: he is only trying to prove that it will be less trouble for us to pay him the £170 he asks. He is not going to annoy me seriously, but is sedulous in pin-pricks.

Mr. Hutchins should offer his stuff to Leeds for his Millenium {Exhibition of Oxford Millenium}: it is too much work for Leeds to do. I will want things for next year—or rather for September which is to be our next year—but no hurry. In any case don't send things to Jebail, for that is so far away: everything to H.M.B. Consul Aleppo. Is anything being done with the piece of Morris tapestry I have? And when will *Sigurd* be free? He must come out.

Mr. Hogarth is very keen on my learning Arabic, and quite agrees (knowing the house) to my plan of living out here the summer. I had meant to come home for a month and then return for the winter, but he has had £5,000 from a private source to spend here, on condition of the B.M. producing £2,000 more: that means about 4 or 5 seasons digs of 4 months each—say till 1914 winter. After that he has money for two more big sites. All this I think is not public information. At present I expect to get home in December. If one of you wants a trip let him or her come out. Woolley has sloughed all his Egyptianity and become enthusiastically Arab: indeed nobody could be other in this village except the Germans. I enclose a photo or two. Mr. Hogarth has gone away with packing cases of Hittite pottery and bronze and seals: go to the Ashmolean Museum soon and see them: it is the best year they have ever had in things Hittite. Mrs. Rieder is returning to France: at least I think so, from a letter of Noël's that I got. But we have not written for months. Salaams to the world.   L.

CARCHEMISH
June 2, 1912

Got two letters tonight. 1st asks about pottery. Tell Leeds your pot (cooking one) was found in the Civet Cat site {East side of Cornmarket St. near Carfax} in connection with pottery of Elizabethan or just pre-Elizabethan wares: I should have put it in the first half of the 16th Century. Arnie's cooker was found with bellarmine jugs, and probably is Carolingian: from the High St. site behind the Masonic Hall.

Second question is about Turkey in Asia—no—Syria is the place: Turkey in Asia is only a Post Office name and repellent to all sense of decency.

I'm not getting one every week: but I get two every three weeks or so. Shall be glad to hear of Doughty's poem: he sent me a very lovely photo of himself with recommendations to study early Bedouin poetic tradition. Says they have many good verses in their camps. I don't want poor Henry's sugar tongs to last a life-time! Please tell him so, if you have not done so already. Mrs. Whitelocke has obviously had a bad time: good she is recovering. I repent me about Richards: I haven't sent him a letter since November! Of course I haven't heard from him. Thanks to my salary proposed for the Autumn I hope to put ourselves in a semi-satisfactory position. Glad Will took Leeds to Mr. Hutchins.

Mr. Hogarth has had all sorts of rumours of wars to war with: he was here six days. I got the acid: but I cannot wander much this year: there is so much work in this camp to do. I am quite well—and strong.

2nd letter. Picture post cards obviously are not over good: I have sent you several but they don't seem to have penetrated: now all my prints go off into a dirty cloud of dust in the water. The thermometer bulb on a negative glass in the printing frame this morning at breakfast (8.30) was 136°. So you won't get any more photos.

The pavement is Roman, and about the 3rd Cent. A.D. It was found outside the Kala'at about half a mile away, and a lot of it is still there, to come down when the digs stop. At present we cannot afford the time. Woolley considered the design of the mosaic so important as to make its preservation a matter of archæological necessity:—and the owner was fast ploughing it to pieces: so it had to come somehow: I brought a ton of it at once, in a huge roll like a steamer funnel.

I am much more busy now than I was: am taking and developing (and sometimes printing) from 12 to 20 photographs a day. Woolley gets on well with the men, but so far as possible I take what I can of that from him and he runs the actual dig. The men are splendid fellows. Gregori is with us: I sent a photo of him, I think. I did raid old Salem's house, but he was our enemy long long ago: since last year: but a very harmless enemy now. As for old Hassan: he is very happy for we have promised him compensation. But good heavens don't you know that no Turkish officer or policeman or government official can lay hands on an Englishman, or enter his house? Much less imprison him. There would be a warship in Beyrout if any one in Biredjik only insulted us. The commotion in Aleppo at the illegal judgment against me in Hassan's suit was tremendous: leaders in the local papers etc. Don't bother Mr. Hogarth please. If there was anything serious he would never tell—and there isn't. I don't blame anybody if I don't get letters: the proper mood is one of gratitude if anything gets through: our newspapers come through about one in three. Probably Broad Camden press is Mrs. Vincent's: Coomaraswamy's: but he doesn't print books like *Sigurd*: I won't come home this summer: will write for necessaries soon.   N.

CARCHEMISH

June 1912

I'm going to write you a note at odd times today, since I have sent you such very hurried cards lately. However, it may console you to know that I have not written to anyone else but the Canon {Christopher} for weeks. It has been quite impossible to do so. No letters from you lately—but in war time all things may happen to posts: and when I wait three weeks usually I get two letters together.

About what we are doing here—we have just found five reliefs of mythological subjects: not very good; the real feature of this year has been the sculptured fragments found broken at the foot of the great staircase of last year. I have numbered them to 800 so far (the less interesting pieces I leave plain) and the photographing all these and the copying and squeezing of the inscribed ones, and the fitting of all together means quite a large piece of work. A room full of basalt pieces weighing from one lb. to a cwt. is rather an unmanageable sight: especially when the room is 40 feet long. We have made up a number of figures of the greatest interest. Pottery this year has not been very good—that is from the site: our tombs are of course magnificent in this respect. We have found no buildings this month. Our first month found the very poor Sargon fort I described:—Mr. Hogarth thought it good, but it was quite barren of pottery or small things. Our second month found the great carved entry from the river with the colossal lions and the staircase, of which I sent you Woolley's postcard sketch. This of course was a very great restoration.

This last month is blank architecturally, only for the finding of a door-lintel in basalt carved with a winged disk in relief. This is (other than columns) the first Hittite architectural ornament identified. From outside we hear of many carved and inscribed stones. After the digs I will load up a donkey with squeeze-paper and camera and go and copy them. In my three months here I will have a good deal of leisure, though I have to cement the floors of two rooms, and repair the mosaic pavement, and tile the bathroom, and glaze and waterproof the roof of the dining room: not to mention fitting up pottery and stones. You may be seeing Mrs. Rieder shortly: I got a letter from Noël giving an address in Paris! She is interesting and very simple in her tastes: you will not find her exhausting. I'm delighted to hear of two servants again—please go slow now. We find four not too many here, and yet don't allow any dusting: to tell the truth we haven't any dusters, and if we had they wouldn't cope with a diurnal dust storm: one must just cultivate an admiration of grit.

Heat is not much yet: about 96° just now in the room and 140° in the sun: mosquitoes have appeared in the German camp so they report, but have not yet attained to us: of course our house is rather high up, and far away from water: I am sleeping as ever on top of the great mound, where it is still quite cold at night.

I am putting in this letter any spare photographs I can pick up: I told you, I think, that Woolley's Egyptians had run away: so I have the doing of all their sort of thing now, on this very inferior Aleppo paper: the heat makes the surface gelatine melt away, and confuses all the lines of the image. We have decided that we cannot do it all ourselves next year, and so I have the training of a boy—Dahoum of course—as well to see to. You have no idea how hard it is to instil elementary optics into his head in imperfect Arabic. He will put plates the wrong side out. However all these are little worries, which are working towards my improvement in Arabic: I hope to be fluent—though still incorrect—by Xmas.

I'll want soon two pairs of stockings, and a pair of boots: they must be sent by parcel post to Consul Aleppo: I cannot go to Beyrout for them: no hurry . . . but you might order them: as last time. Salaams to the world.

N.

JERABLUS
Sunday, 1912

We have now stopped work here, and are digging some Hittite tombs five miles away: we walk across two or three times in the day (sleeping there in turns) and so our work is not much lightened. No letter therefore this week: we dig till Saturday next: and then have four days or so to clear up here and then go in to Aleppo together. We spend some days there (three or four) and then Woolley goes home & I go to Jerablus, or elsewhere: I don't quite know yet, but somewhere in Syria—— Am writing in our dark room while Dahoum is developing: I'm supposed to be changing plates! The photography has become a very difficult problem in the heat. Yesterday 112° in the

shade: but very comfortable all the same: 8 visitors last week: all in
pairs! What will it be like in Sept. with the railway here.   N.

No post yet come; so don't expect answers to questions.

ALEXANDRETTA
June 20, 1912

Have just borrowed £20 from Woolley: this leaves me about £50
in hand: so that unless in stress of circumstances I will not want more
this year: one never knows. Woolley is going to Constantinople and
thence to England, and the arrival of this letter will mean that he is
back. There is no need to repay the money to Woolley: I'll pay it him
back in October: it is only in case of interesting antikas turning up:
I'm merely sending notice in case I forgot later: keep the letter
therefore.

We left Jerablus on Saturday last (today is Thursday) and have been
driving ever since. We avoided Aleppo since there had been a cholera
case there and quarantine was declared. Our route took us along part
of the new railway, which is most extraordinarily irregular: rails are
at times 4 inches out of the plane: the public opinion ascribes this to
the loss of the railway of all the experienced Italian gangers when they
were expelled: at any rate it's awful: they only venture to put very
slow trains along it—about ten miles an hour—and all passenger traffic
is confined to a little tiny motor car that carries four people. The rail-
laying has reached the Sadjur; about 6 hrs. from us: and they expect it
up to us in August. Besides this I saw the site of Ezaz, which explained
its importance—the only defensible site for miles—must go back there
and photograph—and Bagras. We skirted the huge lake of Antioch,
beating a way through the packs of mosquitoes, and then climbed up
a hill-pass to Beilan. Alexander had taken this route so we felt at home.
Then we climbed up 2,000 feet to see Mr. Fontana the consul: he lives
all the summer on top of a huge peak beside a spring where he has
built a little house, and sits meditating. Quite a nice library, including
a Lucretius. My passage in that on music was new to him and pleasing.
He was a little astonished at my idea of living the summer in the village,
but accepted it as a good one. It seems that the rumours of the pro-
English sympathies of the Jerablusi men is rising in Aleppo. The railway

company has recommended its engineers a little modification of their
attitude towards the Arabs "with a view to mollifying public opinion".
That is copy our very excellent selves. Thermometer here, hot place,
113° in shade. And the Fontana house is wrapped half the day in a veil
of grey mist, without glimpse of the plain, and he walks in an overcoat.
This is 9 miles away.

Alexandretta is a horrible place, but Catoni our consul has promised
to put through our 15 packing cases of pottery for us: so we had to
come. I have been all day packing and making packing-cases. Woolley
caught a steamer at midday. It is now dinner time, and I must go off
there: the Hotel gives no food and so I dine with the Committee of
Union and Progress at Catoni's suggestion. There is no need to dress!
I got a letter from you on Sunday: one about Arnie's going to the Zoo.
Sorry Mother has been ill again. Am going up towards Aleppo tomorrow, and hope to reach there on Sunday morning. This driving is
horrible. I'll stay a couple of days in Aleppo packing pottery and fitting
out in photographic things for the summer: then up to Jerablus and a
quiet month there while I move the other pieces of the mosaic pavement. Then a little touring to squeeze and photograph some Hittite
stones we have news of: that means a donkey and a man with me:
weary work!

Salaams to all.   N.

BARON'S HOTEL, ALEPPO
June 23, 1912

There is a sort of feeling of blessed peace in the air at the ending of
my immediate digging work. Woolley is off and I am my own master
again, which is a position that speaks for itself and its goodness. I came
up here in two nights and two days from Alexandretta, and find that
there are six boxes of antikas to pack—nearly a day's work! It is a
nuisance: I am also buying all my things for the summer, which is a
big work in a place like Aleppo with no Arab to do my bargaining:
and to crown it all I am going to write to you, and so waste my last
precious moments.

You people, six in a house, and all England to wait on you, take
virtue at the thought of one letter a week—and expect me to make
adequate response! My only revenge is to write very small and very

long at longer intervals: and so the mass of my material outweighs yours, though the expression is slighter. If you seek a meaning in this paragraph you will find it when I do not write next week.

To come down to Aleppo:—I was wandering about this morning—at church-time save for the unfortunate existence of Greenwich—with an odd Englishman who clung to my side as the stronger vessel, since I had called for breakfast in the hotel at five minutes to five and convulsed the staff—and when we had been afoot about ten minutes and I had shown him all the beauty spots of the town and its bazaars, then I began to notice that his attention was wandering: he was not concentrating on the spectacle provided by five dancing dervishes drinking tea outside their convent and so I asked him what the matter was: and he said: "I was wondering how many times you have been to Aleppo, and I was wondering how many times you have been in the bazaar, and I was wondering how many purchases you have made, and how many people spoke to you": and when I had satisfied him on all those points he said: "When I was trying to buy that embroidery in the silk bazaar, and wanted all your attention, nine old acquaintances greeted you with all signs of returning gladness, and six new ones were presented." And just as he said so one of the dervishes got up and said: "Did you not travel with me in the train last year?" and a muleteer and carriage-driver called out together "Salaamat, effendi!" and Haj Wahid's sister, passing, asked me of the health of his wife. I have not seen that Englishman since, for the consular dragoman drove up just then, and begged me to come to the government with him. And yet I think not six people in Aleppo know my name! Baron the hotel keeper told me laughing at lunch time that nine people had called to see me with antikas up till then: It is now evening, and I have not seen him to ask him for more modern figures. Such is fame and a famous servant, and the power to know ancient things in Aleppo. I find all Aleppo preoccupied with Jerablus thanks to the newspaper reports. Baron says five people came just after lunch, and that his head waiter had seen about fourteen more.

I have made the day responsible for my doing no work: and have got through six iced rose sherbets and three ices, in a lounge along the bazaars: and a man has left me here in the Hotel a most lovely Damascus tile, cracked across but perfect, for 12 piastres: imagine an Aleppine leaving antikas on approval: the compliment is too vast and too intimate for your full comprehension, but it is one of the finest I have been paid, and tomorrow I'm going to have the tile:—with a piece of quite useless embroidery I saw, which is too beautiful to leave: and after all—let's give it as a present to somebody, or we'll use it as a towel or a dish cloth or something, anything. It is very lovely work, though not so decoratively-effective as our hot-weather waistcoats at Jerablus.

Did I ask you for more stockings? I want at least three pairs of normal ones, and one of white wool: isn't that luxurious? Please send them soon by parcel post to Aleppo. I bought 24 lbs of glue today in the market as a little bit of practice to get my hand in for what is coming tomorrow and the next day, and then I am going to racket once more across to Jerablus for the last time before the railway serves and lie down to rest a week of Sundays. I have been on my feet for four weeks, and they are beginning to show signs of wear!

No letters from you last week here, but no matter for concern, for the Ottoman Post, never very robust has been knocked dizzy by the stress of war. It does the most eccentric things these days, as when it sent us to Jerablus the entire Armenian correspondence of Aintab: we got a bundle of letters that turned us pale, and then found that only 5 were ours and the other three hundred theirs. I really feared that by some horrible chance all my correspondents, regular and occasional, had seized that post to display their activities. They hadn't—yourself and Mr. Hogarth were the bill.

It seems the Turks suffered a defeat the other day somewhere: *soit*: it won't hurt Turkey.

What does Will mean by talking of being arrested as a motor bandit? I don't know the brutes, but I'd like to know what he did to look like one: he seems to have ill-luck in France.

I seem to have been months away from Jerablus, and am longing for its peace. You know there one says "I don't want to talk" and there is silence till you break it, or "I want to be alone" and twenty men post themselves around you out of sight that not even a hoopoe or an ant may cry out and break your rest. Our men have gone back to the bridge-builder to work or 20 of them have: and the last day when I said "I want to bathe" the gang log-rolling at the river's edge got up and went away to leave me untroubled water. Their foreman simply raved and I roared, till the engineer came along and roared in sympathy, and gave orders that river work was to be stopped while I bathed, whenever I expressed a wish. Great is the Kaiser and D. G. Hogarth, who got out of the august-and-would-be-Macænas-presence a promise that if it came to us and the railway, the railway should go to the wall! Really this country, for the foreigner, is too glorious for words: one is the baron of the feudal system.

N.

BARON'S HOTEL, ALEPPO.

June 24, 1912

You really have no complaint to make of the amount of my correspondence this week: three letters in 4 days: take notice it is not going to last. I have bought things all day in the bazaars, till I was altogether sick of the smell of them: they are all corrosive sublimate, calcide, and carbolic, in the frantic efforts of the authorities to find the cholera germ:—who is obviously not in the bazaars! By the way please send out quickly by post (letter is best), two dozen Gillette safety razor blades: I am nearly run out, and there are no more in Aleppo. They are light and will travel easily enough. I had plenty, but Woolley ran short and I came to his rescue.

Today I was at the government, and got letters to the Governors of the towns I hope to visit this summer: the vali described me as a Professor of the University of Oxford, who had made excavations at Jerablus, and was now travelling for pleasure: that I was an inestimable person, whose worth archæologically and intellectually they (the Government) were quite unable to express in words: and that by my diggings I had conferred benefits incredible on the Ottoman government in particular and science in general. *Therefore* all Kaimmakans, Mutessarifs, Mirdirs and government officials are to see that I am well lodged, well fed, provided with transport, with guides, interpreters, and escorts, if I express a wish: If I desire to travel without these accompaniments I am to be permitted: and tidings are to be sent to Aleppo that I have arrived, that I am being entertained, and that I have departed satisfied. So I cannot use these beautiful letters except upon need. I don't want to make a progress, but a tour. However I have also got the ordinary official recommendations, which all important travellers carry: and these I will present first and watch their operations. It is rather quaint that a person of my superlative attainments should

travel with a donkey and a boy to push it. But the world is full of
inconsistencies, and undoubtedly my virtues are greater than my purse.
By the way one clause in my documents particularly charges the
military and police authorities to carry out all my orders. If I wish, I
can with them conduct a campaign or perform excavations.

Today I bought such a lovely piece of Aleppo work for Haj Wahid.
He asked me to bring him a cloth of gold head cloth, and gave me £2
for it, and it proved to be a most lovely weave of rolled gold over
silver wire entwined in scarlet silk: the most noble material I have ever
handled: it's about 5 feet square and local stuff: one man and his son
alone of all Syria know how to make it, and just make a living out of
selling it to cavasses for their head-bands: no one but a cavass may wear
it by police rule, and oh won't Haj Wahid be proud of himself! it is
perfectly royal.

What more did I buy? Printing paper, hypo, developer, toner, plates,
candles, chisels, sheet copper, rivets, knives, cartridges, watch chains,
potatoes, quinine, hydrochloric, bismuth, corrosive sublimate, seccotine, arnica, vaseline, Arab clothes, silks, books, boots, glue, sacking,
hemp, naphthaline, gauze, writing paper. . . . I don't know how much:
but it was very much: some of it is for Woolley and some for the expedition and some for me and some for Haj Wahid, and for the Hoja and
for the men at Jerablus: It was a huge buying: and besides I went to the
government and chattered French and Arabic and English till the
French consul remarked "Our compatriot has a great knowledge of
languages": I have not been in such linguistic form for years, and it
was all good much of it Rabelaisian: as for the Arabic, it is almost
fluent when I am on ordinary ground: my grammar is atrocious (Arabic
is exceeding difficult there) and I slur over all my inflections of necessity:
with a larger vocabulary and a simpler grammatical scheme (i.e. a
nearer approach toward the Bedouin Arabic) I'll get on easily in two
years time. And as Mr. Hogarth said "One who knows Arabic is never
at a loss". I had a joke today with my hemp: I bought a huge bale for
packing a plaster mould that rests at Jerablus to be finished: and sent
it up to the Consulate: the dragoman was more than puzzled as to
what it was, and sent the cavass to ask me: I was in the upper part of
the house, and sent word that it was probably the hair that I had just
had cut off, and that if it looked like that would he send it up: and up
it came in due course, with the chancellery staff to admire this greater

Absalom: it was splendid for the bale weighed 28 lbs. and was larger than the donkey that brought it. I had to cut my hair because at our last stop before Aleppo the khan was unutterable, and I didn't find that out till rather late: I was so full of beasts that I insisted on having my head washed and cut as a final move towards demi-godness.

Armenian patriarch (Arm. Cath.) has just come, to know if I will interfere at Biredjik in favour of his church. Our notorious move in the matter of our Biredjik agent's debts has got over the country and the Biredjikly Armenians reported us to him as possible helpers. Who else would have got debts from the Committee of Union and Progress? Besides the Kaimmakan made a public oration condemning us: however I wrote all that. I think I have managed the Patriarch's affair for him here in Aleppo: I saw the authority concerned at dinner this evening, and he promised to put it right.

Salaamat.   L.

{CARCHEMISH}
June 28, 1912

A very hurried line. Last week's letters missed the post. So it will come with this. We are frantically busy at last squeezing inscriptions before sunrise, and writing notes after sunset, and developing till all hours: only an eight days more.

Nothing new turned up: except that we may buy the site. The old Agha here is forcing the sale with a view to getting it for his debt-interest, & selling it at high price to the Bagdad railway. The old man who owns it does not like this system, & has implored us to buy it for £30 ready money. If he gets this of course he will have done fairly well: for his debts are fully covered by the value of his other land. It is just that the railway may start from this piece across the river, & if so would buy it.

We have written to the Consul in Aleppo: if he recommends favourably, & Hassana't does not repent his offer, I will be $\frac{2}{9}$ owner of Carchemish. It will never be worth much, but if it is our land our workmen can move on to it, and live out of the clutches of their sheikhs & mukltars, for Haj Wahid (who sends salaams to father) would live here as our representative, & take what rents & harvest he could get. There is the seigneural flour mill as well.

If the men were living on their own land they could sell their

labour (which is necessary) to the effendis for what it is worth: instead
of starving as at present on 5*d*. a day. The policy of all the landlords
about here is to get their men heavily into their debt by fictitious
interest (our effendi lends at 1,930% per ann.) and then exact forced
labour. But they could not pursue them on our land with a man like
Haj Wahid on top: Haj is absolutely honest, & has the greatest dislike
for the Government & the effendis. Also of course it would be to his
interest to attract men. All very well: weather beautifully warm: no
mosquitoes, except in the village: where I don't sleep.   N.

A lot more of our letters have fallen through: a dishonest letter-
carrier we fancy.

CARCHEMISH
July 14, 1912

5 letters from you! Whatever am I to do? Answer them in turn—
   i. Thursday June 4. No letters from me: complaint set right in next
post: Ottoman post is either drunk or disorderly: it is wonderful any
letters get through: no printed matter does. The postman in Aleppo
(there is but one) has been seen to set fire to all the printed-matter
letters in his bag in the post-office yard before setting out to distribute.
They are so heavy you know! Will's sprain: I hadn't heard of it, owing
to regrettable loss of all your May letters! It is almost laughable sometimes when one considers the trouble we take to write: Mr. Hogarth
liked our purchases, and paid me here for them: Don't send Doughty's
book: it will only go astray.
   ii. June 11, Father's— Nice our reports to the Museum going astray:
and we sent such lovely photographs & plans to them! Hope the B.M.
will pay me! I'm spending it beforehand: but they won't pay me for
this summer—next digs only.—Our people are Arabs & Kurds and
Turks: those who wailed on the bank when I started out to swim the
river at night were Sheish, a Kurd and a splendid sheep-stealer, the
only man in the two villages who will swim the river in the dark,
Dahoum, who is mixed Hittite and Arab, being of old local family
(possibly a strain of Armenian in him) Ahmed Haji Aissa, Aneyzeh
Arab, Bedouin, and Yasin Hussein, a Turk: we talk six languages on
our digs you know, letting alone French & German to visitors! nothing
if not pantaglot. The house is comfortable, but noisy with 3 children

& two women: Mrs. Haj Wahid has just added a girl to the two previous. No need for double doors: a curtain is better! We have our copper-hooded fireplace. Have now three resident doctors, but only German by position: two are Armenian—not bad men. Ask Bob what harm it does people to have enlarged spleens: and if he had one, what would he do with it? (one of the men is so).

iii. Mother's June 11. The house is big, but the photo is a wide-angle one, and so exaggerates—no gates! Can you see the camel-bells? The walls are about 2 feet thick: all stone.

Gregori is a most splendid man: that photo of him sitting on the column-base smoking is very good of him: only Gregori only speaks Greek, and I cannot reply to his remarks: he is to return in September: and is invaluable with the men and the big stones.

Dahoum is strong and I think honest: but I knocked him up over the pavement. He gets sleepy very soon at night! Hamdosh is not beautiful but very powerful: his shirt is European, of the sort manufactured for Arab uses. No need to send Woolley a cheque: you might send me £10 to Aleppo (cheque) in about a month. I may want to buy stuff in September there. I packed all the pottery boxes in Aleppo (14 cases) and have just finished here two packing cases full of plaster casts: it will be fun to go to the B.M. and say "my casts"!

Wainwright had nothing of mine after all. They are with Miss Holmes—two early jars.

iv. Mother. June 18. Leeds has written me about his Millenary {of Oxford Exhibition} difficulties!—

v. Father. June 18. Not much work now: have cemented the floors of two rooms, and done other work in the house, plaster-casts, mended pottery etc. nothing important: bought some good things. I expected the Insurance policy to end. Woolley had great difficulty to get on a company at all. They don't like archæologists. He pays a huge premium: I shall let mine slide: the Universal suffrage vote will be good, as enfranchising the stay-at-home sons of the middle class, and the lodger—two heavy conservative classes: it won't be radical. Frank shoots too much! It is a useful trick out here only!

vi. June 25. Mother's. Mrs. Rieder was a curious case: am glad you didn't find her exhausting. (May I point out you got 2 letters & a p.c. on June 11, and 3 letters & a p.c. on June 25: and I had none from June 4 till July 14?) Merely a lesson in patience. Today it was 149° in

the sun, 132° in the shade, 114° in the room: the Euphrates is 89°.
Bassett's paid you a flying visit indeed! I wonder when that phrase
will become exact! Quiet place Miss Wright's! This place would not
suit you with the insects. Sand flies are awful in the rooms: no mosquitoes. Haj Wahid is with me here: I put glue over the mosaic pavement, on coarse sacking, and then prized it out of the concrete with
chisels in a long roll like linoleum that weighed a ton. It came from
just outside the Kala'at in a field. I don't think I want anything but boots
for next year: Dahoum eats rice: and as much of anything that he can
get: but he won't come to England this summer: I am going off to
Seruj and Urfa for a few days to look at inscribed stones lately found
there: so no letters for some days:

Salaams.   N.

Write always Consulate Aleppo: I am going to take several little
trips this year, but this will be my centre.

July 16, 1912

Have no time to write this week, but have just got a chance to send
a note by Biredjik:—I have no postman now, you know. All very
well, and family particularly on the mend; the establishment became
ill of one accord—and I nursed. The enclosed photos. are untoned,
and strictly family—*pour rire* in fact. The large head I snapped of
Dahoum, one day he was too ill to spoil my effect by immoderate
laughter: it gives his (uncommon) Arab type of face very well.

{To his small brother}

{JERABLUS}

Ancient beast

July 21 {1912}

It is about a year since we wrote letters to one another: suppose we
do it again? It doesn't cost anything but time, and of time do you
know, I have mints just now. This is the first time for years and years
that I have been able to sit down and think, and it is so precious a
discovery: and one that so many people want to take from you.

Just now I am in Jerablus, and feeling matronly. Also I am house-
physician, for you never saw such an establishment as mine has been
this week. There are seven of us here—six Wahids and myself. First of
all I had malaria—a short spell of the usual two-day sort. Mrs. Haj
Wahid got a new baby, and turned very ill. Haj's boy fell down and

broke his head to pieces and had to be tied up; Haj himself went drinking and collapsed with internal troubles of sorts. So I brought in Dahoum to help Haj's mother in the kitchen, and he ungratefully produced malignant malaria (autumno-æstival) and raved his head off for three days until he nearly died. I had to sit on his chest half one night to keep him in bed. The little Armenian doctor did the main part of the work (he's our consulting physician) and now Haj and Dahoum are convalescent, and more trouble than ever. This morning, when I woke up, Dahoum, (who can just stand), was trying to sweep out the big room with the hold-fasts of the tables and chairs, and Haj Wahid was feeding his donkey. I have to watch them all day to keep them in bed.

Mrs. Wahid has to go to Aleppo for an operation, much to the disgust of Haj. I had a mighty battle with him to get consent, for operation is anathema in the eyes of the doctors of his religion, and he wanted to save the money for a new one. He is angry because he has two daughters now. Nice people these . . . they think Father the most miraculously fortunate man—in fact they suspect him of female infanticide. In a few days therefore I am to be alone in Jerablus, for all the others (but Dahoum) will be in Aleppo. Nice place Aleppo though too hot just now, and there is scarcity of water, for the crocodiles. They line all the canals you know, and swallow the water as it comes down from the river: everything in Aleppo loves water. Even the hippopotami sit all day on the kerb with their feet cooling in the gutters, and when sunset comes they boom for very joy, till all the valley is giddy with the sound. We have nothing like that here in Jerablus, which is a country place without hippopotami: but we have frogs who croak in chorus old, old, tunes that Aristophanes taught them, and iguanas who sup in king's sepulchres. And talking of sepulchres I bought such a lovely one last week: a crematory urn, a glazed jug of Babylonian work, some Hittite terracotta horses, and bronze fibulæ: one of our first finds.

I have turned school-master, O tumult, and taught up to 11 times table a class whose average age was about seventeen. Then the house became a hospital, and I put an end to the local education authority. It was sad for they did so want to learn twelve times: It was a very wonderful school everybody who got a table right got a lump of sugar each time. We finished two large tins! I took a class of four

(*See p.* 105)

Markab (Nargat)

Note by T. E. L.   'A sort of beehive, underneath is a Sheikh's tomb'.

(See p. 108)

Urfa. Triangular Tower

(See p. 108)

Urfa Castle

(including our Commissaire) in local history (special subject) and had the mollah of the district to listen to my lectures on geography. They can't make out, why, if the world is really round, the people on the other side don't fall off. All this has stopped now, and the head-master is reduced to writing nonsense to a worm.

The Kaimmakan visited me yesterday, to consult me about the destruction of Biredjik castle. I made him squirm—but they will pull it down all the same: the French bridge-builders have offered them £12,000 for its stones. I hope to have the pleasure of a little talk with them next week.

Von Oppenheim, the little Jew-German-millionaire who is making excavations out at Tell Halaf in Mesopotamia came and saw me one night last week. He came about 5 p.m. (sunset at 7.30) stayed till 11 p.m. then went off to eat & sleep: came back at 4.30 and stopped till 10 a.m. and left with a two-hours gallop to his train: a special, so it would wait for him—We have a train only 16 miles away. He was such a horrible person—I hardly was polite—but was interesting instead. He said they were the most interesting & important discoveries he had ever seen barring his own—. Invited me over to his place by his relay of post-horses—6 days journey in 36 hrs.! Not for me thanks! Have just been interrupted by a spider as big as a whale's nebula: bottled him in whisky for you: such hooked teeth & toes: I took him for a crab when he knocked at the door and said "come in" such a fright: Salaams to the world.   N.

JERABLUS
July 28, 1912

Today, Worm, I must tell you of a battle that took place lately here. About two days ago I was on top of our big hill, watching some men on the island carting sand for the railway cement-works into two boats, when I saw about twenty men spread out into a long line, advancing through the scrub-grass towards them: and in a few minutes this new body opened fire with revolvers. The sand-diggers raced for the river, and tumbled into one of the boats, and were off: only they left two of their number behind: one of these swam for it: the other was captured, and his revolver and clothes taken away. Then the invaders (who were Kurds) took possession of the other boat, and set out to invade Syria.

However the first boat had by then arrived and the men from that, reinforced by many others, lined the banks, and opened a hot fire with revolvers at 400 yards: you could see the bullets splashing up the middle of the river, and the Kurds decided not to try to cross. So they went back and the Arabs jumped again into their ferry boat, and set out for the island. The Kurds tried shooting, but the Arabs made such a furious reply that they began to retire across the island, followed by the Arabs both sides shooting vigorously: the retreat became very rapid, and went as far as Mesopotamia, where about 200 Kurds came rushing down from their village to prevent the attack. Then the Arabs retired to our side, with both boats. Wasn't that a lovely battle? Absolutely no one hurt.

What more, puffet? The railway is not going to do any more digging for a month or so, and not very much even then for a bit, so I am going into Aleppo, and thence will move up to some hilltop, either at Beilan with Mr. Fontana, or in the Lebanon with Miss Holmes and the Beyrout Consul. I won't live with them, because neither is alone, but will take rooms or a house near them: and will go on with Arabic with Dahoum, who is cheaper than local labour, and who can cook and wait very well. He was six months table-boy with the Railway Engineers here. Go on writing to Aleppo. It is good exercise for you, though nothing has of late arrived this end! I have got you such a glorious spider: he is about four inches long in the body, hairy to the point of ugliness, with teeth and horns like a rhinoceros. His legs are very angular very thick and very hairy, with such claws: and his body is wasp-shaped; a beauty if ever there was one, and now he is drinking whisky in a bottle that used to be Carlsbad salts: poor fellow! I hope to find you a scorpion, when one will oblige us near the house, for I have got quite good at picking them up by the tail unharmed. You have only got to grip them each side of the sting from behind. Our scorpions are very miserable little beasts. We have had hardly any snakes this year: next year I don't suppose we will have any: and that is sad, for Sandan the snake used to be great god of Carchemish, before the days of Ishtar, lady of heaven. We have reached the season of grapes, ancient one, and that means many delights washed down with the sauce of the terror of appendicitis. Tell Mother I will write before long from Aleppo or my hill-top.

BEYROUT
August 3, 1912

I went over to Biredjik, & got an attack of fever, and another upon return to Jerablus. This made 3 slight attacks close together, & I judged it prudent, in view of the excavations to follow so close, if I rested a bit in the cool before going up to Jerablus again. So here I am in Beyrout, going out to Jebail, & then probably into the hills. This immediate letter is about money: I borrowed £25 from the dragoman of the Consul in Aleppo, & have spent much of it on antiquities, which were yesterday stolen from me: I have set the consular people after them, but fear a loss. A terrible pity, for there were in the collection (of 25 seals) some 3 or 4 of the finest Hittite I have ever bought. However, still hope [one inscribed seal]. Therefore I am short of money: I know it is not fair to ask you for such in August, but if you could send me cheque up to £30 I would be exceeding glad: my expenses here in Lebanon will be thrice those at Jerablus: and I don't like debts! The B.M. has promised me 15/- a day next digs: good for me: but have I spent it all? The Museum owes me about £10 for work done this summer: so that I am still solvent: but must borrow from Miss Holmes for return to Aleppo. Please send everything to Aleppo: razor-blades arrived, but stolen with the seals, and *all* my soap: Letter in two days: very well.   N.

JEBAIL
August 12, 1912

Have not written you for some days: have been here in delightful ease: Miss Holmes is in the house with me. What news? None: we are hearing of tumults & confusions in Constantinople: but it is very far off, and here there are no disputes: except a difference I have with the Vice-Consul over Marot's paraphrases of the psalms: he comes up to see me at times. What do I do? I eat a lot, & sleep a lot, and when I am tired of reading I go and bathe in the sea with Dahoum, who sends his salaams: "great salaams" he corrects: Also we have dug up the first primitive Phœnician burial on record: it is very primitive: just a man lying on his back in a great 5 foot urn: no objects with him or about him, except some shapeless flints: Have also got some very nice flints— axes & knives and a mixed lot of pottery, more than one period:

Jebail properly worked, would afford a "corpus" of Phœnician pottery of all ages, I believe: The later (*c.* 1000 B.C.) stuff is adorned with striped patterns of the sort of the later Hittite: that is patterns worked into the polishing: very curious analogy. No letters from you of late of course: I don't know if I have any of yours unanswered: Jebail is hot, but always there is a cool breeze off the sea in the day and off the hills at night: I talk Arabic and "rest" at midday. Am learning a little to write Arabic. Miss Holmes offers her salaams: she will write a little to you when the spirit prompts: but the spirit melts in summer. Miss Holmes may visit England (on her way to America) in the autumn. She wants Will very badly! Let him come to no favourable decision without trial. Post goes in a little so I cannot write much more: it is with Arabic pen & ink—a difficult operation.   N.

I wrote for £30 from Beyrout. Did you get the letter? If possible please a cheque to Aleppo: it is to pay debts!   N.

JEBAIL
August 30, 1912

About Mother's birthday I suppose with you: and I am hurrying to write to you as I leave Jebail: I have had a very quiet pleasant time here for about 3 weeks and a half: Dahoum was with me, and I have left in abeyance my question of remuneration to Miss Holmes. I talked to her about it, and she suggested that it be left to you: you know we have lived very cheaply, perhaps you may feel moved to offer her a something for her work. It was very good of her to come down from the hills to stay with me here, and she has made me very comfortable. I have done a little work at digging, & much Arabic. This last week the cliff fell down into the sea below the town, and out tumbled a Græco-Phœnician sarcophagus from a rock-tomb. It was white marble, about 8 feet long & pleasant work, anthropoid but Greek-featured. In the remains of the tomb-chamber on the cliff were apparent jugs & cups—I climbed up, made a plan, and dug them all out myself: finally I bought the lot for a pound: not the sarcophagus of course. I have four or five painted jugs complete, rather pretty, three or four cups etc. a good lot, & all new types I fancy. I hope to get the sarcophagus in a month's time, & will then send the lot to Oxford: of course the government may want it though. If you see Leeds you might tell him something of the sort: I'll forward photographs in due course. For present movements: I expect Woolley will be out soon: and am now going up to Aleppo & Jerablus to get ready for him: have had no letters from you or him since I left Jerablus: indeed no letters from him at all: one came from Leeds lately.

No more news possible: had a fine view of an Italian fleet yesterday: talk of war, which won't be popular here: the Arabs fancy they are winning. Bulgaria looks interesting but that will be an old story before you get this. Miss Holmes has fallen in love with *Sigurd*.   N.

CARCHEMISH

Sept. 12, 1912

I have written a great deal to you all lately, but I think *Will* requires individual treatment. I have in hand a letter from him from camp, which took months on the way: no matter. He had had a crop of letters from me: you are always in extremes: either miserable in a ten-days dearth, or flooded with a bunch. I get mine monthly! I'll answer this letter, to prevent discursiveness:

Imprimis. Dahoum is very useful now, though a savage: however we are here in the feudal system, which gives the overlord great claims: so that I have no trouble with him: he wrestles beautifully better than all of his age & size. Doughty's photo I will enclose, if I can find where I laid it up to preserve it from white ants, our scavengers. *The Clouds* is unequal—though in parts magnificent. I wish he would desert the pulpit. The poet's place is at the altar. Explain to Bob how unpapistical this sentiment really is. You will of course visit us next year on your way out. It is two days and a half from P. Said, and does not cost much. What was Roberts doing in the Crimea? Anarchising or tutoring? or didn't he go there at all?

New's "Towers of Oxford" is a very lovely drawing: a good idea to present it to L.C.J. His schools came out much as expected. Am glad Pascall got a first: he deserved it: The great risk of Pound's poetry is the symbolic for its own sake: He has educated himself on old books and never correlated them. A good poet though. You will like Middleton, for whom I wrote from Aleppo. The ghost ship is an amazing tale —the "pirate ship" (poem) better: read them. The Arab-looking gentleman in a cloak, enclosed (our vice-consul in Beyrout, Flecker) introduced me to him: Of late I have been reading a lot of Spenser, Catullus, Marot, the *Koran*, Simonides, and Meleager. Parts of Simonides are very splendid: also Antipater of Sidon, Tyrtæus, and Hipponax: all in Bergk and the Anthology. I got a Greek dictionary from Mr. (now Canon) Parfit in Beyrout, and have made great play with it. There is one very splendid Meleager, beginning Ευφορτοι ναες πελαγιτιδες ... Ant. xii. 53 and another Εικονα μεν Παριην ζωογλυφος xii. 56, and his elegy on Antipater is splendid: also that verse of Leonidas of Tarentum, when the old man, without his fellows on earth, turns about to join the greater company: or Meleager's epitaph {Ant. vii. 419} δ τον γλυκυδακρυν Ερωτα, και Μουσας ίλαραις συστολισας χαρισιν. You have most of the man there, and he wrote it himself: there is a great deal of the Syrian in Meleager: far more than one would suspect from his Greek clothes and habits and turns of speech. Clement Marot has many excellent things, though it is rather a silly jest to talk of him after Meleager and Antipater of Sidon. Also I have re-read for about the sixth time Baerlein's novel of the Crusade of Children, that you criticised in Oxford. It is very good, very vivid: I don't think the man could do better with his talents and occasions. I suspect him of not being English-born. In Beyrout I read *Renny* by Hewlett: one smells the craftsman too much: I think Hewlett is finished. A letter to come in a week to the family.

N.

CARCHEMISH
September 12, 1912

A letter to Bob! Why? I don't know: perhaps because he wrote to me. I think I'll answer his letter for a joke.

Imprimis: you know after all, I feel very little lack of English scenery: we have too much greenery there, and one never feels the joy of a fertile place, as one does here when one finds a thorn-bush and green thistle. Here one learns an economy of beauty which is wonderful. England is fat—obese. Osney Abbey, if preserved in accord with Henry 8th's original scheme, would have given us one of the finest cathedrals in existence: and please *Trill* mill stream: Bob begins to show a technical interest in men's bodies. Well, on the whole the district is fairly well. The village has just had a big dose of small-pox, but nearly all the adults had had it, and I had all the children inoculated (primitively, by the way, with virus from a patient) at once. Result no losses, except two grown-ups before I got back: and of the 30–40 children down at once (!) not one is marked on the face. It would have made a row if anything had gone wrong: but it didn't, and a lot of people died in the district, which makes our record more creditable. These professional details are for the Hakîm. Tell no one that I practise medicine without a licence!

There has lately been a slight recrudescense of cholera in Aleppo, but obviously the germ is getting tired, since only about one in five of the unreported cases prove fatal. The reported ones all die, for the Gov. puts a sentry before the door, and will let nobody in or out, except the government doctor, who is a Beyrout-trained chemist.

Now to depart from the province of the physician: no—please tell him I broke two ribs in Jebail one evening, and that nothing came of it, beyond a slight local stiffness for a fortnight. They were not important ribs, only the little measly ones low down, and I fancy one doesn't really need those in civilised conditions. At any rate they are mended up again all right (one a little crooked), but not enough to grumble about. I wish I could think of something else for the last page of the letter. Yes: let the Hakîm take note that a strong wash of carbolic will remove certain forms of skin irritation: also that ammonia neat will reduce the inflammation of a bruise or boil. All these little hints are golden. This is absolutely all our medical notes that require transmission to the family at present. I am preparing an exhaustive report on the nature of malarial attacks (disputing the Ross theory) but am at a standstill for lack of material: I have had no dose of malaria for a month: nor has Dahoum, my second document in my research work. I am filling him full of arsenic (not on my own of course: Dr. Altounyan prescribed). N.

Mrs. Wahid is well again—or nearly . . . N.

CARCHEMISH
Sept. 13, 1912

Letter of Aug. 27 just arrived: will answer it, & send you it at once by return of messenger. You got a line from Jebail from me. Miss Holmes' house is a fair one, & Jebail pleasant: but of course much hotter than Carchemish, & not so healthy an air. I went for sea-baths simply: now I am enjoying the Euphrates more than ever! England is seldom or never suitable for bathing: even at Jebail (at 96°) it was often too cold for pleasure.

Am very glad Father's cough is gone. Dr. Gibson or another? It is good to hear of your having rain. Ours are due in a few weeks also. The whole country is waiting breathlessly for them.

I don't know what Miss Holmes thought of Dahoum: she never grasped his Arabic properly, but I am more than ever struck by the beauty of it over the horrid noise that the Beyroutis make. Miss Holmes of course is worse than most, for she loves the harsh gutturals and mouthed consonants. As the Jebail people speak it, however, it is one of the ugliest languages on earth: whereas the Jerablus is very like a deep Greek: a Greek without the 4 "e" vowels. However, I think it possible you may hear that tongue this winter—and until you do you won't be interested in it. Dahoum had seen the sea: he was more interested in his first pig!

I am feeling perfectly well, and have always said so: there is a sort of pessimistic fatality which leads you to suppose I am usually ill out here. I cannot imagine why! I sent you those photos untoned, especially knowing that they would be nearly invisible if toned! No fear of the world seeing them! But burn them better. I must see Miss Wright's pot: but such shapes were in use till modern times. I hope to have about a fortnight in England at Xmas: possibly even more, to three weeks or so. It depends on how long we interrupt the digs, which depends on the weather. I left Miss Holmes about 10 days ago. I am afraid no "open fellowship" for me: I don't think anyone who had tasted the East as I have would give it up half-way, for a seat at high table and a chair in the Bodleian. At any rate I won't. I fancy Mr. Snow sent the notice. It is quite without significance. I am sorry you should have troubled with it.

My seals were stolen from my bag in the luggage van of the train between Aleppo & Beyrout on my way to Jebail. Nothing else but a razor, soap, and a pair of socks went: no loss and no damages. Nothing has been heard of them as yet. You might send another razor, if you will, by Parcel post to Aleppo. What is your objection to Continental Parcel post?

Tons of quinine here: or at least a matter of 4,000 grains. I got your cheques: many thanks. The £10 for Miss Holmes will be abundance.

This summer has been one of the pleasantest I have ever had: I don't share your opinion of it at all! Next year you may come out to see how pleasant it can be. Remember we are heaps colder than Jebail. We have beans, plums, & pears: not so savage you see! Also quinces, cacti, peaches, grapes, pomegranates, apples, melons, cucumbers, lemons, figs. How rapidly Oxford must be changing! Leeds has made a profit on the exhibition. Arnie needed that bicycle. Have written to Mr. Jane.

N.

Have just wired to Woolley asking date of diggings! Got tired of waiting for him.

CARCHEMISH
About Sept. 18, 1912

Today is Sunday, and a man whom I know is going to Aleppo tomorrow, to the Consulate. So I hope this letter may reach you. Very little has happened: the usual stream of Teutonic visitors, very dull specimens, has poured in every afternoon, and to all I give tea, and talk about the Hittites, and Roman mosaics for they nearly all prefer the pavement to the pottery! Of course just now the pavement is the main attraction, for the remainder is in process of being moved, and the whole air is full of tesseræ. I got a handful in my bed the other night. We are moving about a quarter of a million altogether this time, in batches of 50,000 at a time. The Hoja and Dahoum now do nearly all the lifting, having learnt very cleverly, with special tools that I designed and had forged at Aleppo. It is coming up beautifully. But I can understand how it is that this transporting to another site, for walking on, has been done only once or twice before. It is far too difficult.

Besides I have carved a great sun disk, with crescent moon, & wings, on our stone door-lintel—the dining room door that is. As I had no chisels I carved it with a screw-driver and a knife. It is a Hittite design and use, and looks very fitting. It was admired exceedingly by my last-but-one batch of Teutons, as a genuine relic. Besides I went to Beredjik & back afoot in 16 hours, and saw the Kaimmakan and the captain of gendarmerie, & of the troops, & bought numerous things. As nobody in the village has ever been & returned in the day, it is considered a great feat.

You know from my former letter how the Railway tried to steal our town walls for their embankment, and how we stopped them:—it seems that in return the company has refused free transport of the antiquities to Stamboul. So there is really at last a hope that we may be able to keep them here till the end of the digs. The convenience, in the matter of fitting broken fragments to sculptures, would be enormous. I would like to send an official letter of thanks to the company! They would be wild.

The village is over-jubilant at the defeat (as they regard it) of the chief-engineer. He, stupid man, made things worse for himself, by boasting before my arrival of my impotence against him, and by blustering after the arrival of the prohibition, of continuing by force. Two local attempts to shoot him came to a head last week. Both missed! But they will get him in the end. His own staff have sworn to have him!

What more? Nothing: I swim miles every day, and take photographs and carve, and patch mosaic, and sleep a lot, and eat a lot. None could demand more. Also I have found a most lovely epigram of Mnasalcas, which I will offer to Will in due course: it is too much work to dig it up just now, with the man waiting at the door. All well in district: no illness left.   N.

BARON'S HOTEL, ALEPPO
2nd October 1912

Am in Aleppo—come in to see Woolley,—and the day after to-morrow we go to Jerablus. These three days have been frenzied rushes & bargains for antiquities (we have spent nearly two hundred pounds) from before breakfast till after dinner in the evening. One gets so tired of talking bad French and worse Arabic!

As for our finds—firstly there is a polished steatite statuette of a woman tiring her hair: and it is perhaps lovelier than any small Greek statuette known: I have never seen its peer in any museum; a very simple draped figure, well-preserved, Hellenistic in style, we paid £50 for it, and you could probably add a couple of noughts to find its true value. Then we bought a hexagonal Arab coffee-table (of the mother of pearl & wood type) in early faïence of Rakka for £10, which is worth about £150: and are in treaty for two others: also many bronzes, some Hittite pottery, & good seals. I picked up two little Bokhara rugs for a trifle: they are valuable though only about £30 worth: but very

pretty. Aleppo is very full of things:—and we are the first buyers for
nearly six months. Woolley has brought out a deal of money to speculate in antiquities: and he is in fair way of making about 300%. I am
more modest, because I have still scruples about engaging in trade!
Also I have little money to spend: somehow the temptation to make
money is so very nauseous! Perhaps at Xmas I'll buy you some trifle,
and you shall only keep those you really want.

I got a letter from Llandrindod Wells from Mother: one from Will.
There seems to be supersession in your mind that I am "suffering"
from malaria: nothing further from the truth. I don't suffer at all, and
have not had fever for a long time. I got the cheques: many thanks:
they came in time to pay bills that I had in Aleppo: and now I am making 15/- a day: a very curious feeling: I don't like that also, but I felt
incapable of refusing what will make me semi-independent.

As for Jebail I had a pleasant month of book-reading. Of course it
was very hot, but the sea was pleasant: and Carchemish was unpleasant
from Haj Wahid's drinking. He was of course not my servant, but the
Museum's site-guard, and I was only lodging with him: it was exceedingly expensive. Next summer I will put up two or three rooms in the
lower village (cost under a pound a room) and live there. Anthropoid
means human "shaped": the sarcophagus is like the sort of mummy-
coffin that has a face carved on it. None of our things, casts or pottery
have yet reached England, so the B.M. is still without a Hittite collection. They have promised us a special room—which will be full in
six-months time. Mrs. Wahid is better—only for nervous troubles: she
howls at the top of her voice if anything displeases her—and all the
babies do the same: we are going to build them a house far away from
ours this month.

Today I saw the loveliest painted lacquered & gilt ceiling that I ever
dreamed of: it is really indescribably lovely, and the owner only asks
£400 for it: it is such a thing as has never been seen or heard of outside
Aleppo: and 154 years old: glorious. I wish Will could have seen it:
we hope to get it to South Kensington or to some place like Lord
Carnarvon's.

It is nearly midnight: so pity me & go to bed: N.

I should also say I have bought (with the Hoja & Dahoum) all our
stores for next season here in Aleppo these three days also! A month's
work. . . .

You will not (I hope) have expected a letter from me these first days
of the dig. What with accounts to make out, men to see, visitors,
disputes, and a mosaic pavement in addition to the ordinary work of
excavation, I have had little time to compose anything worth writing.
And even this is the first copy, which I must send you for lack of time
to revise.

We got to Carchemish on Friday, and the men lit a huge bonfire on
the top of the citadel, and fired about 300 shots that evening in our
honour. It was the biggest noise ever heard in Jerablus since the defeat
of Pharaoh Necho by Nebuchadnezzar in 614, and was seen and heard
from Biredjik & Tell Ahmar, and inland for nearly eighteen miles:
The Germans were rather upset about it, since the Arabs tried to shoot
one of them about a fortnight ago, and a Basje sheikh of 4,000 Kurds
had two days before offered to the government in Biredjik to wipe out
the railway settlement. He stipulated that the English excavators should
be left undisturbed!

The Kala'at was glorious in the blaze and the Euphrates became a
twisting river of liquid gold. We wanted 200 men this year and have
written every other man who came to us. The railway works (which
were before undermanned) are now suspended, while the chief engineer wires to Aleppo for labourers. The man in charge of the Bridge
works had assured me of the utter impossibility of our finding more
than 50 local men (and those the wasters): I told him we would have
300 men the day we came: and at the bonfire that night Woolley gave
away 11 boxes of 25 cigarettes each: one to each man. I told you of
my row with the chief engineer when he began to take away the walls
of the Kala'at. Well, to return that compliment we took all his workmen, down to his grooms, his night-watchers and his carriage drivers
and masons. Then we sent back those we found unsuitable. He was
rather crushed. The weather is cool in the evenings, and over-hot at
midday: and we have so many men, & so many calls, that we have
no time to enjoy it. However the cheeriness and good spirits of the
men are incomparable. It was amusing today, when time went at the
end of work, to see the two gangs of 100 racing across the rocky
ground to see which should be first to lay down his tools in store.

I have got your parcels from Woolley, excellently preserved. The quinine only overstocks an overloaded market—but the studs and stockings are precious. I have bought a little carpet (3 feet by 2) which is lovely: and Woolley has its fellow: we saw them by accident in Aleppo.   L.

ALEPPO

October 15, 1912

I am in here trying to raise a loan of money, for the Museum has failed us with its funds (paid over to it in July by Mr. Hogarth, and asked for twice or thrice by telegraph from Woolley) and pay day is three days ahead with only £40 in hand. And unfortunately Aleppo is very disturbed with the Government forcibly levying transport animals, and scouring the country for reservists in hiding, and so nobody has any money in hand. The job is not a pleasant one:—at least though we have sent a wire to the Museum that should cause them to send us something soon.

Now about other things. We went on digging in a Hittite room found two seasons back, and in half an hour had uncovered the two jambs of a doorway in black basalt, with long and perfect Hittite inscriptions. After our great stone of the Hogarth period this is the best inscription yet discovered here, and we are correspondingly glad. Also to find them in place as door jambs is an important piece of evidence architecturally.

In many other little ways we are making forward, though the size of the operations we have tackled is becoming more than a little oppressive. The whole of Hittite history is in the melting-pot—or the craftsman's mould—out here. We have 200 men this year, (three overseers) and corresponding difficulties. Not the least is the business the Government is giving us with its frantic levying of every able-bodied man as soldier. They visited the Euphrates bridge works and decimated the workmen, and entirely broke up the construction of the station: they have only old men & boys left. Thereupon we ventured a risk & forbade the police & soldiers to set foot in the Kala'at, offering our house as temporary refuge for runaways among our men. So far we have not lost one, but it is not quite a secure game to play. We also recovered the village donkeys which had been impressed.

I forgot to tell you that our light railway has failed to arrive, and

that our stores are delayed en route. So that we are living literally &
completely on the country, and have no photographic supplies. On
the whole you will see that I am going about to earn my salary. I got
a letter from you lately, when you had been a fortnight without news.
You will probably have had some by now. The bank sends its letters
by courier to Beyrout (whence it is 8 days, or even 7, to England): but
the province of Aleppo is jealous of Beyrout, & forwards its post overland as far as Constantinople. That makes a delay of about 5 days for
English letters, but is of course about on a par for Turkish internal
posts. No matter. I don't know anything else to talk about just now—
and besides I have to go up to the Bagdad Company to see about
transport of stores when they arrive. They have fallen out with us
again: stupid creatures these Germans are. Their line is bad: yesterday
I left Jerablus at 3 p.m. stopped (with the train) six hours at a wayside
station because the telegraph line was cut, and reached Aleppo at 3 a.m.
and at 6 I was in the bazaar. It is now 3 p.m. and I must go off.

N.

CARCHEMISH
Oct. 22, 1912

Woolley will go into Aleppo tomorrow, if the Railway succeeds in
getting into order again. A thunderstorm of two days ago lifted out
the temporary bridge over the Sadjur, and left them lamenting. And
only about three days before, when I was nearing Jerablus on my
return from Aleppo, the engine dropped its forepart off the rails,
because they were spread, and skated along on its belly, cutting off
bolts and sleepers, and twisting up about 250 metres of line. That made
one more delay added to the many they have had in laying the metals.
Now for news. We are digging out a room in the palace of the great
stairs, and finding many interesting things: and I have been doing some
copper-work in the fire-place, grinding the mosaic smooth, and building
chimneys and waterproofing the roof, against the rain now overdue.
The weather is become ideal—cold at night (when we sit on Bokhara
carpets before a wood fire in a stone & copper grate on a mosaic floor,
and read beautiful books):—almost any good book is welcome.—hot
at midday, when we go bathing with a frolicking company, but always
with a fresh-blowing wind. All the country is of one colour, a murrey

brown, but very subtly beautiful. As for our troubles, we carried the day in the matter of military service: the two railway sections lost numbers of men and are crippled: we did not lose a man. There were rumours and panics, and they say 200 men slept out in the digs (and seventy in our house, which is immune of the Ottoman police), and all the villages stabled their asses and horses with us, but the patrols scouring the district passed not within gunshot of the Kala'at, except the day they paid a friendly call to drink coffee and smoke a cigarette. This has much enhanced our prestige.

What else? Nothing: we dig and dig: and doctor our men and settle their disputes and talk with them about all things in heaven & earth. I am gathering a store of Arab News and notions which some day will help me in giving vividness to what I write—and by the way I did write something (I have forgotten what, but something very short and simple) for the man who wrote to me about a Jesus College magazine: you will know whose it is if he prints it as I suppose I should subscribe to the production. We have again no money, having paid out over £100 last Thursday: if the Museum has left us still without any funds it will be a black look out for Woolley; though the little money-lender-banker who paid for last week's work would like to pay for next week's also. He takes about 12%, and offered to lend me on note of hand up to £1,000.

I bought in Aleppo a very handsome beaten bronze plate in the manner of the Italian–Arab platters in the Fortnum room in the Ashmolean:—very good work, though worn. We are pleased with this in our living room: it, with the mosaic peacocks and gazelles, the Bokhara rugs, and a strange cement-&-Roman-pillar table that I made (and the Copper hooded fire) make a good beginning in the furnishment of our room: we hope to line it with Hittite bas-reliefs (trial casts!) and are buying any cheap (and pretty) Damascus tiles we find: if we could only venture to set out the Arab glazed pottery we bought in Aleppo we would make it very fine: but it would be too dangerous from the Expedition point of view.

This letter contains no news, but after all only is it the more evident that there is none to give. Haj Wahid has dengue fever, but is better today—and about 60 of the men are down with it also—his wife is quite recovered her health again, but the baby is very weak and ill: we are building a new house for it (and the other two elder ones) to howl in at pleasure: for there is a wide space in between as safety zone. Also we are building a store room, two stables and a huge warehouse of antiquities: so that before we leave here we will have a large colony of buildings under our care. We of course are architects and head masons: no one can complain of the monotony of our daily occupations: if only our stores had come and our light railway!

N.

Hope to send a P.P.C. or two—of Dahoum's work—showing what & where we are.

CARCHEMISH
Nov. 4, 1912

Again I am writing to you out of season and without cause: there is no post going today, and none tomorrow I suppose, and it is days since one came: but as I have not written to you for a week I am going to, simply as a pious demonstration. I got a letter from Will asking about Arsenic treatment. In *chronic* malaria quinine has merely an encouraging effect:—as a preventive or palliative it is ridiculous. I gave Dahoum doses of quinine up to 20 grains a day for a fortnight, and his fever attacks came on all the same. Then started the arsenic (in August) and he has had no trouble since: before that he was never long without trouble in the shape of high fevers and headaches. Chronic Malaria comes irregularly: the three day variety dies by quinine: you don't give arsenic for that though you may strychnine. In any case your man should ask a doctor (preferably continental) before starting to poison himself; and should guard carefully against diarrhoea the first few days. Dahoum is still taking about a gramme of arsenic a day: & quinine gentian carbon sacch. and Loadacum mixed with it: His was a specially desperate case.

Our news here is nothing: our stores are between Port Said and Alexandretta: our light railway also at Tripoli, Beyrout and Alexandria: an oven at Trieste, and sheer-legs & block in Marseilles. If we had photographic stuffs we would be quite content.

Yesterday wolves came into our farm-yard at the back of the dining room and went off with our two sheep: so we have hired two noted hunters to go & kill them: they have dug a deep pit, and sit in it with a carcase before them; but only jackals have come so far to sniff about,

(See p. 108)

Urfa Castle. The Moat

(See p. 106)

Sahyun. Moat

(See p. 108)

Urfa. Beaked Tower

for there has been a great deal of shooting tonight all round, and no doubt the wolf is scared easily by reports. I wonder what one would say in England if one had bullets singing over one's courtyard? Or it one's cook put his revolver on to cook an omelette? Our house is getting formidable in size: a new stores-house, a stable, a magazine, a harem, and a wash-house are now added, and a w.c. is building. We are very amused with the latter—the pit has a 49 foot drop! and it is vaulted in a hipped dome with pendentives: all in mud brick. Our roofs leak furiously, because we will not put mud over in Arab style, till we get waterproof paper from Aleppo to go under it: and to get things from Aleppo takes about a fortnight. However there are only three of our 16 rooms in this state: the others are mudded and are water-tight. We have been making quince, pear, and apple jam this week—all quite successfully: also finding some very good pottery (nothing large but mud-brick walls) in the digs, four cylinder seals, and some bronze-work. And besides we have bought some pottery and a sculpture from outside the digs: the sculpture seems to be a Roman descendant of a Hittite goddess (seated on two lions) and is rather an interesting piece therefore. On the other hand we are only buying from a photo which Dahoum went & took of it and it may be Hittite: very unlikely the latter.

No other information that I can give you would in the least interest you. They say a war has broken out with Bulgaria and is finished already. Which may be true or not. I think Bulgaria has every possibility of finishing off Turkey (if the powers let her) because the Turks are such helpless stupids: however you will know better than us what has come to pass. I hope books are on the way for winter evenings: Salaamat.   N.

If the Museum does not send more money shortly we shut down works at the end of the month! Bankrupt!

CARCHEMISH
Nov. 10, 1912.

I wrote about a week ago: but no matter I'll write again. Our last novelty was a letter from Mr. Fontana, prophesying the fall of the Turkish Empire, and apparently he has some justification for his ideas. You will know what has happened, and we only get news by backstairs and in delays: still I think it is obvious that the Balkan states have the better of it. Posts and telegraphs have come to an end, so far as Aleppo is concerned: Fontana hopes to send these to Beyrout and Egypt: all boats have stopped coming except French warships arriving in Beyrout. The really serious affair for us at the moment is that the B.M. frightened at the prospects, has written to say that it withholds the last £550 that Mr. Hogarth gave it for us this year: by paying out our salaries and travelling expenses we can just meet our bills in Aleppo: but we must stop work this week for the most part, and borrow afresh from Mr. Fontana to get home! We won't come yet (indeed with the possibility of trouble in Beyrout it would be silly) but will sit out here and look on at what is going to come of Turkey. You must *not* be alarmed at a cessation of letters from me for about a fortnight: or even more.

You will note in the papers the date at which communications with Asiatic Turkey are renewed by mail steamers, and expect letters about ten or twelve days later. Till then all I write will accumulate in the hands of our consuls. I hope this gets round to warn you.

The Armenians of the N. intend a small demonstration to show Europe their claims to separate treatment: don't jump to the idea that we are in Armenia and revolting or being revolted. We are in Jerablus (and probably camped out) digging the tombs cut in the rock behind the lower village with the ten or twenty men we can afford to employ. And we can find the wages of these men for another six weeks. That will give us time to receive Mr. Hogarth's answer to our cheque (we have drawn bills on him) and relieve the situation. We give up the Museum in disgust. Mr. Hogarth payed them over £1,200 for our use this season, and they send us (in slow relays) £650 and then write (in the middle of the season) that they intend to hold on to the remainder of our credits! It is very good business for them, but we are insolvent. However the weather is warm and pleasant: our house roof now water-tight and mudded over, our mosaic complete and waxed to act as a damp-course; Kurd carpets, a huge boat-load of olive-tree-roots for firewood, and a scientifically constructed hearth with stone pillars to flank it on Hittite column bases, and copper back & hood to refract the heat. All this makes us delightfully comfortable. Eleven boxes of stores Mr. Fontana found arrived one morning, and sent up by a cavass (the celebrated Fattuh, of Miss Gertrude Bell): so we have loganberry jam, and wheatmeal biscuits and linen sheets and shortbread: and everything possible photographic and chocolate and asparagus and medicines to stock a ship: not to mention the eleven pound tins of curry-powder in stock, which we feel to be a great stand-by. You will be glad to hear of 10 tins of Cooper's marmalade. Our jams this year are from eleven firms, and our stores in all from 19 countries: origin has to be given for customs purposes: did you know that rubber sponges were made in Russia: we have those with caviare from that country. Cerebos salt got through this year labelled chemically: salt is here bad, and a government monopoly.

Got a letter asking if I was Flecker's "archæologist". He wrote the poem about ten years back about one Beasley a don at Ch. Ch. I wrote and asked you for Middleton: no doubt that letter failed, and I will be back before the reply to this reaches here: many thanks indeed for the Doughty: Go on writing to the consulate at Aleppo: though much of it will be waste labour.

N.

CARCHEMISH
Nov. 14, 1912

Letter from Will enclosing one from Roberts: I think the latter is worked out now: one never knows though. Got a razor, & a Doughty as per last letter: many thanks: Order me any clothes you like as per last measurements: but I won't bring many back with me, and can just as well see to them myself on arrival: you know the cold of December is a very mild heat compared with the Syrian winter, where the thermometer rises to 90 in the shade at midday, & falls to 35 at night. There is really no need to get me anything at all as yet: boots all right, and I have stopped wearing boots lately so am set up for life (nearly). I'll come home very light (unless I have a colossal lion-pedestal for the British Museum) and very quickly, perhaps by Brindisi if the boats serve: and will not stay in England more than a few days: perhaps a fortnight in Oxford, and three or four days in London, where we have to squeeze inscriptions in the B.M. Then out here again as quick as possible: you have no idea of how much there is to do here, with tombs being plundered and buildings destroyed every day in the districts round about.

We stop digs today week, being penniless: and then tour for a fortnight (we have to call—a return visit—on the big Kurd chief in Mesopot. whom I wrote about.) thence home about Dec. 24: probably: I would have brought Dahoum and the Hoja with me, but alas, we spend our salaries next week on the dig! All very well, and flourishing. On second thoughts don't bother about clothes. Have two suits still.

N.

Have found nothing yet this year but two basalt long & perfect inscriptions. Town gate next week.

CONTINENTAL HOTEL
PORT SAID
Sunday: about Jan. 19, 1913

You see here I am still: I landed on Tuesday: and was told of a Messageries steamer on Friday: so went inland, to return on Friday and find that the steamer had gone away from Alexandria direct to Syria: some special chartering they said: so I am to leave only today, and will not be in Beyrout till Wednesday, Aleppo Thursday, Jerablus Friday: and our poor little Commissaire has been looking for me since the 15th! However:—I went up Egypt on Tuesday night (sleeping in the train) to see Professor Petrie: spent Wednesday with him, sleeping with one of his subs. on a dig a couple of hours to the South, and got back here on Friday morning, sleeping in the train. I was lucky to find Mrs. Petrie not there: the Professor was as usual, though with a worse staff and poorer graves than last year.

Only one of his people had ever been on a dig before, and that was the little man with me part of last year: and he had been entrusted with a big piece of work to the S. by himself. Unless two or three huge shafts he is clearing prove fruitful it will be a very lean year for them. But these shafts are huge pits dug in the gravel, forty feet across with brick steps down one side, and at present still going down. They have pushed one of them to 25 feet. Of the prehistoric cemetery they have now cleared rather over a thousand graves. There are stacks of pottery lying all over the earth there to be thrown away. But nearly all of the type of yours, and of course none so good. By the way Petrie thinks now that they are to be put in the first years of Mena, the 1st king of the 1st dynasty: that is, in the short period when he was consolidating his kingdom, before conquering all Egypt. The two Egyptian photograph boys, whom Woolley brought to Carchemish his first season had advertised our glory and savagery and state. The contrast of the palace at Carchemish with the wattle & daub huts of the Petrie encampment certainly gave ground therefore. And the poor people afraid to turn a dealer out of the camp by force for fear of prosecution for assault! I had a look at the Cairo Museum: found a very wonderful little Hittite cup there labelled Persian! and got them to open the case to let me handle it: this involved a carpenter with a hammer & screwdriver because the keys were lost. They refused at first to bother themselves, but repented when I declared my intention of doing their duty myself. A little implied vigour carries one so far in Egypt one finds: I believe one could Turkify as one pleased without active opposition.

Time to stop off: all well so far: I wonder how the Beyrout Customs will welcome me? We paid them £3 last month.

N.

BARON'S HOTEL
ALEPPO
25 January 1913

Got back here last night from Jerablus: all is quiet and satisfactory there: a train runs there & back taking about 6 hrs. each way, though schedule time is 3½ hrs.: still it is a comfortable set of carriages. I had to cash a cheque in Beyrout, and will get the next one paid tomorrow, for I had to provision Jerablus with money loans.

I am just going out, so that this letter is only so to speak to mark time. I hope to write to you on Monday with news of some general interest. At present there is absolutely nothing. I did not of course see the Holmes' in Jebail: as I wrote from P. Said my programme carried me direct from steamer to train in Beyrout. None of our men have been bothered by military service—and they were delighted with the post cards.

N.

BARON'S HOTEL
ALEPPO
2 *Feb*, 1913

It is about a week since I wrote to you & you see I am still here: the Beyrout line behind me has been blocked with snow, but I hope to get down there tomorrow. I am going to Alexandretta to see after our cases which are delayed there. The consul has asked me to go down, & there is deep snow over the Belila route, so that I have to go down to Beyrout & up by steamer. Here in Aleppo are snow-drifts, & ice & hail & sleet & rain: very seasonable!

Got two letters from you the other day: one contained cards: thanks! I don't want any more, or any Magdalen ones: ... You suggested my bringing 4 carpets home: but do you know how hard they are to find? I have been wandering all over Aleppo for a week, have seen hundreds, & only liked *two* both very expensive £38 & £11. I am trying to cheapen these: but you must remember that it is very hard to get them cheaply: the little Bokhara you have was a very exceptional find.

There is nothing to buy in Aleppo, pottery or seals or anything ... except though that this afternoon I was offered a huge silver chalice like a tureen on a stem of mediæval Byzantine work (say 800 A.D.) with greek dedication to a church of S.S. Sergius & John. I was really tempted to throw away my salary of this year upon it ... you know there are so few people have Greek chalices on their side-boards! I am sure this letter will be illegible but it is so bitterly cold that I can only write from my elbow. I hope to get Arnie a pair of Kurd stockings. Aleppo quiet politically but as pessimistic as it can be. Armenians are arming frantically. Will write when next possible: expect to be ten days away.   L.

KHEDIVAL MAIL LINE STEAMER *Tewfikieh*
8 *February* 1913

I have come down from Aleppo to Beyrout in a snowstorm: at Beyrout I found blazing sunshine, and no steamer for Alexandretta for three days: so I went to the consul, and he sent me up in a cruiser, the *Duke of Edinburgh*, which was quick, and comfortable, and big, & quite interesting: I had Dahoum with me and he was most impressed, &

impressed everybody on board. They all made him offers to come
with them permanently, and took him all over the ship and feasted
him. His remarks on what he saw were very funny: sometimes very
embarrassing, for me who had to translate. They blazed off big guns,
and searchlights, and had drills and parades and sports for our benefits,
and were anxious for the state of inner Syria. And when we got to
Alexandretta they sent ashore boats by night, and took off all the cases
of antiquities which had been resting in Catoni's house since June.
Therefore I profited by the time I spent with them and am grateful.
The boxes were put on another little cruiser, and sent off to Beyrout,
where they will be transhipped to a boat bound for England. The
Museum will be pleased to get them I hope: if they aren't Mr. Hogarth
will, for his lot is included. Leeds will let you know when they arrive,
I suppose towards the end of next Month: 16 cases: . . . In Alexandretta Dahoum saw a box in a shop in the market which he thought I
would like: and I did and bought it for a trifle. It is of ebony, inlaid
with ivory in floral patterns, about 24 inches square, and with about
two dozen drawers in the front. One side is hopelessly ruined, with all
the ivory and lacquer split off: the top & front & two ends are perfect.
If one puts it against the wall it is a first-class piece. I should say of early
Renaissance Italian, but it may be Eastern. I'll have it photographed
when we reach Jerablus and send you a copy to be consulted upon.
It is most exceedingly handsome, and looks very precious.

I am now on board a little coast steamer, going down to Tripoli,
and thence it will be only eleven hours in the train to Aleppo. I will
avoid all that freezing Lebanon, and the discomfort of a midnight
start.

In Aleppo I want to try again to cheapen the carpets I wrote to you
about: indeed unless they get much cheaper I cannot buy them at all,
for with all this wandering about my stores of money have been
melting away: fortunately a lot of it I recover from the Museum: . . .
and meanwhile I will borrow, and hope for the coming of Woolley: if
the Museum doesn't dig, and doesn't pay me a retaining fee, I'll be
ruined. Still they are presumably paying me 15/– a day since Jan. 8 . . .
that would be £22, and would also be welcome.

My canoe {sent out by Salter, Boatbuilders, Oxford} has reached
Beyrout . . . and Aleppo too I hope by now. Will write next from
Jerablus: so expect a slow post.   N.

I wonder what today is—and I have no idea at all: so much for living
in backwoods. I got letters from you the other day . . . and don't think
it needful to subscribe to Mr. Hughes' portrait: . . . What else? . . . the
palace of Ibn Wardani has many strange scents about it, as I wrote:
it is famous all over North Syria, and my description is more like the
rumour than the reality: I have received many cards, and the bill of
Shepherds was right . . . and my canoe has been 3 weeks in Beyrout,
waiting till our agent there can find a spare moment to put it on the
train for Aleppo, and I have bought 6 carpets, two 16 feet long, and
am short of money therefore . . . and I don't know if we will dig or
not this spring, and so I don't know if I will come back or not this
summer . . . what other queries were there? Congratulate Will on a
scholarship {Casberd at St. John's} . . . and not on a blue in prospect
{in running} which *is* a blue prospect . . . and F. will probably *not* go
to Jesus on an emolument. I am more likely to go to Baghdad on a
canoe.

Apropos of rifle shooting this afternoon I put 4 shots out of 5 with
a Mannlicher-Schonauer carbine into a 6 gallon petrol-tin at 400
yards . . . very good that.

Now all is peace, and I have been wandering up and down: . . .
forming a very beautiful collection of Hittite seals . . . small but very
select, and with some nice pieces of Roman bronze and glazed pottery
as side-lines . . . also I am in treaty for other carpets in the villages.
Meanwhile I am making all day tarpaulin for our roofs, which leak,
and repairing the house, and white-washing, and getting all into trim
for a season in a week's time . . . and perhaps all quite needlessly!
Salaams to Arnie from the men here . . . they rejoice in his socks, and
all wear them themselves ostentatiously.

                                                                    L.

We have now been digging two days:—and it feels like ten. I wrote
to you last from Aleppo:—and by the way eat that halawi in my house:
Campbell-Thompson doesn't want it. In a batch of seals sent lately to

Mr. Hogarth was a duck-weight, which should go to Mrs. Rieder, who is coming to England shortly—Mr. Hogarth will send it up.

I am glad Will got Ezra Pound: & that he was a success: sounds a very curious person: I think the *Goodly Fere* is by far his best thing . . . though some of the Provençal canzoni run it very close indeed. Indeed the *Yearly Slain* may be better . . . No matter.

In Aleppo we bought a lot of stores, and some antiquities, though not many. Then on the way out we stopped at the Sadjur to visit Deve Huyuk, the village whence had come the bronze bowls, glazed pottery, & fibulæ of which I had written to you. We had sent the Hoja out to supervise excavations, and on our arrival we bought quantities of things (in fact everything in the village) and were able to split them up into tomb-groups, and date them therefore scientifically. As a result we found that they were of about 550 B.C. that is, in this district, Phœnician in origin & not Greek, and therefore of very high interest. We have about 20 bronze bowls, and many fibulæ, ornaments, beads, some mosaic glass, Greek red-figure pottery, etc.

The Baghdad Railway is ceasing operations here . . . because of lack of funds: so we are shining in contrast, with our 200 workmen. I am teaching the Hoja and Dahoum to paddle . . . the canoe is a never-ending cause of gaping to the villages and the Germans, who have never seen its like. It got here without a scratch. This being early in the digs, & light railways being the order of the day, it leaves me nothing for writing: in a week may write again.

N.

We dig till July: could you send me a straw hat of Panama style (roll up) by Continental parcel post, or by letter post?

N.

CARCHEMISH
March 13, 1913

Today is Friday, which is our Sunday, and we have had five lots of visitors. So that there has been little time for the usual oddments of leisure. Add to this a gale from the North, which swept my canoe down stream like a galloping horse, and splashed great gobbets of water over us, till we nearly swamped, after doing the fastest mile on record in the Euphrates. I have never even in Carchemish felt such a wind. The canoe rocked and plunged, and swirled back & forth. It was bitterly cold.

Now about other things: the enclosed little print is the very nice box I bought in Alexandretta; we have filled it all full of the little things we continually want, and don't want dirty, and it takes us æons to pull out all the drawers and find them again. It certainly is a mistake to have a 30 inch chest with about a dozen drawers of all shapes and sizes and besides some of them have false bottoms, & little trays beneath for money. The back is ruined, with all the veneer and ivory gone: the front fairly good, the top a little damaged, the ends as good as new. Ask Leeds if he can recognise from the very poor photograph, what the thing is:—it looks like Italian work to me, in style, but one never knows.

I also enclose prints of the sarcophagus of Jebail, which might also be given to Leeds: he may like to keep them, as he has the pottery, or will have some day.

Got a letter from Bournemouth lately from Mother, in which Arnie was ill: he is probably flourishing now like a upas tree.

We have lately had the good fortune to tap a cemetery about 20 miles away, of Syro-Phœnician period, full of very nice bronze bowls, & beads, and spears and fibulæ, with some nice pottery. I may have written to you about it; in any way it is still going on, and we are getting very nice things out of it. You say you are sending me £20 which will be seasonable, if it comes.

Digs are now a week afoot, and we have not yet set the Euphrates ablaze: I am digging out the S. gate of the town, Hittite and Roman work, but mostly Roman. Woolley is clearing a part of our Hittite temple or palace about the triumphal stairs:—only what we really are is navvies, struggling to get our light railway into running order. I have half a dozen letters to write, and no time to do it in: so here endeth.   N.

BARON'S HOTEL, ALEPPO
23 *March* 1913

I have heard nothing of you for a fortnight:—not your fault or the Ottoman post, but the fault of the letter-carrier between Aleppo & Jerablus: a very stupid business, because the missing letters contain very important papers, & we have lost all trace of them. I hope there weren't any cheques for me, by the way; nobody else will cash them but they will be destroyed, & I'd like £20 or so just now. At Jerablus we dig furiously, & we are inundated by visitors: it makes our day very difficult: we start in the morning early as usual, when it is too cold to do any writing of notes or planning or photography: and then about 10 a.m. comes one batch of visitors, and about 3 p.m. a second. They are usually foreigners or distinguished people, or people with introductions:—and we have to show them all over: such a dull set!

About finds: Woolley has been all week cutting & banking a line for our light railway, (the earth-dump line): it has involved careful grading, and the building of two bridges, one stone, & the other pile & trestle in wood: a considerable matter: so he has done no digging properly so called.

I have been clearing out the S. gate, interesting architecturally, being well preserved, with good polished walls in stone, & a flagged pavement scored with wheel-ruts: late Hittite:—The tragedy is that it is only defensive, with no more sculpture than a (or two) horrible lions, standing on the inner edges of flanking towers: we have dug out one tower, and found one lion, badly battered in Roman times when it had stood in the street, and without a head. It had been about 12 feet long poor beast, but is now sad-looking. I think I will cover it up. Gregori has not yet come, nor news of him, since we lack a post: I hope he comes soon, for the absence of him is hard on both of us. Dahoum sends his salaams. He is working very well this year in photography:

Salaams to the rest.   L.

CARCHEMISH
March 28, 1913

I got a letter from you the other day . . . congratulate Frank on his exhibition: and Will on a half blue: I hope neither will be annoyed if I say that each was to me unexpected. . . . I thought Will & Frank both too busy with more serious things: F. I suppose goes up in October: and there will be the usual heartburning as to whether he is to live in or not. As a social being he would probably prefer to. In case he lives at home, he must have my little house:—it is for the reverse

reason . . . I had it that I might be quiet: Frank that he may be noisy
. . . and it speaks many things for the catholicity of the place, that it is
equally adapted for each. As for Will, a half blue is a half blue, and as
such is over in one race—say five minutes— . . . he will not find it or
a degree of the smallest use to him in the sort of work he proposes:—
any more than blues or decorations would have been to me. Abroad
such trifles are in their proper place:—and you know most English
things are such trifles. We call ourselves a great power, and our neighbours great powers, and go fiddling away our money and minds and
minutes on absolute balderdash. Germany is going in for armaments,
England for insurances, and all of them for nonsense . . . consider the
suffragettes! Still—I got a cheque for £20 from Mother, with injunc-
tions to spend it on myself, so I bought a Greek seal of a resting athlete,
a Phœnician bronze bowl, and some other little things, including a
new head-cloth, and have still something in hand. The seal is pretty,
and if I can remember I'll seal this letter with it. About carpets:— . . .
I haven't bought any more lately: and I don't intend to sell those I have:
Mr. Barker may have a choice certainly: though I won't promise first
pick to him or to anyone else: we will see first how many will go in the
house . . . a plain carpet with a couple of nice rugs is cheaper & prettier
than a great coarse English carpet of strips sewn together.

Today is Friday, so in the morning we planned the S. gate, & in the
afternoon Woolley & I went up the Euphrates in the canoe: we disturbed heaps of wild duck & snipe, and some eagles. We are using both
ships this week for the export of the first part of our Phœnician collection: Lately I bought a couple of pieces of Roman glass for you:—
a saucer & a bottle: both nice clean pieces.　　　　　　　　　　N.

Have been for last two days digging out about 300 fragments of an
ivory casket of middle Hittite work; good style, & preservation.

CARCHEMISH
18 *April* 1913

It seems the month is more advanced than I had thought. However
you know we only date by the *Punch* which comes to us erratically,
and sometimes that throws us a week out. Today is Friday, and as there
is a great wind blowing, we are sitting indoors writing letters. This is
about my sixth today.

About an hour ago we bought a splendid bronze axe-head, decorated, from an early Hittite tomb: I have bought you another couple of Phœnician bronze bowls, and some other little trifles: . . . We have been overdone with visitors lately . . . the Fontanas stayed three days, and after them came two other lots of Europeans & Americans: it is rather a confusion to our work. This month has been a very full one. On the stairs we got a very fine sculpture of a double-bull pedestal: about 4 feet long:—it was in basalt, and the bulls' heads came out in the round beyond the pedestal front. Otherwise the sides and top of the stairs were blank: Another slab found lying loose in some Roman rubbish showed two bull-legged demons grasping a palm tree: this was in basalt, and quite tolerably good work: not interesting though, since we had duplicates. Then in front of the stairs, in a temple courtyard, we dug out half of a great basalt laver, which had been bronze-lined, and which rested on the backs of two bulls: this had been in front of the temple door: we found its base in place, but under a great mass of Roman concrete, which we have had to blast with dynamite. Then on the other side of the roadway to the stairs we found a long line of carvings: a camel-man, two slabs of winged human monsters attacking winged horses, one of two men killing a third, one of two bulls striking a tree, one of a lion attacking a bull and gazelle, one of two demons with four wings, one of a lion attacking a country cart (the cart of which Mr. Hogarth has a clay model in the Museum) one of two minor deities killing a lion, one of a ποτνιος θηρων, and two of marching soldiers: the line is still continuing: the slabs are mostly complete, in good condition, & good work. Each about 4 feet high only. A sphinx-lion (you had a copy) and a slab of bull & lion demons came from the line in the Thompson year.

We have found no small objects, but I have managed to piece together a long inscription, picking out the fragments from a pile of nearly 4,000 pieces.

I enclose a snap (very poor, but the lighting is impossible) of the floor of our sitting room in position. I took it one day when we were whitewashing & so the room was empty.

N.

Hat came, fits, & is very useful: thanks.

L.

CARCHEMISH
{26 *April* 1913}

~~No letter this week:~~ this is in reply to one asking for news!!!!
Woolley is in Aleppo, drawing money, & Busrawi and 9 other chiefs
are looking at me writing, & there is no news, and no time for any.
The duck-weight is for Mrs. Rieder: I have bought one a little smaller
this morning for you.

NED.

CARCHEMISH
April 26, 1913

Got two letters yesterday: one holding a cheque for £20, in reply
to a letter of mine stating non-receipt of your former cheque: all the
same the first one came, and I acknowledged it duly, even sending an
account of what I spent it on! This new one I will hold over for the
moment—or send to Akras, my banker in Aleppo, to be put to my
account. He is a consular dragoman, and is doing all our money affairs
this year. You complain of our keeping Friday—but would it be quite
considerate to make 200 workmen miss their day for the sake of the
two of us? Especially as they are not sophisticated enough to have heard
of Julian & Gregorian calendars, or the "first day of the week" theory.
. . . Today Woolley has been in Aleppo, drawing money. He went in
in state with 9 great Kurds, for Busrawi, and his great enemy Shalim
Bey took it into their heads on Thursday to come down "accidentally"
to our house and meet there, and make peace between each other. It
is a three generation old feud: Woolley cemented the alliance with
chocolates, and a photograph, and the whole lot went off to Aleppo
with the largest lunch-basket on record, to pay a call on the British
Consul there. What poor Mr. Fontana will say to 9 Kurds I don't know.
The diplomatic career is not a sinecure in Turkey.

News here? Two new slabs, which bring this month's lot to 15.
Not bad that, especially as they seem to be working up to a great gate,
and that the inner part of the palace is well preserved. Our digs are the
richest British Museum dig since Layard's now. . . .

I enclose you two photographs of a lizard: he is of the sort which
grows a yard long, and in colour is mostly violet and green, with
yellow and red-brown reliefs. He refused to sit to the camera at all.

Also a snap of our sitting-room door, taken to illustrate our night watchman, the great Kurd . . . who is really most excellent sport. Euphrates is still in flood: the boatmen said my canoe couldn't shoot the railway bridge without upsetting, so I took a Miss Campbell, staying with us, through to prove my side of the case. But the current is too swift to get back without a strong crew. Tell Arnie the Arabs pronounce the i as am ai, or ŭ, though always with a constriction of the throat like a slight swallow. I regret to hear of influenza troubles in the household: one way to avoid them is to avoid cold baths, and take plenty hot ones. As for summer proposals: I hope in July, August, to go up into Asia Minor: to get to England early in September, and to stay there about two weeks: possibly coming out here later with Will: we should be digging again about September 20. I hope this idea will please you. Salaams to all.   N.

CARCHEMISH

June 4, 1913

It is quite a long time since I wrote—and this will be only a scribble: because we are digging tombs, and have absolutely no time. Digs on the site stopped about a fortnight ago, and we have been clearing out cremated burials ever since. With them are bronze bowls gilt, copper brooches and fibulæ, pottery plain & painted, seals, scarabs, and gold things: with a lot of miscellaneous stuff: a very fine collection on the whole. One silver boss, inscribed and decorated, is one of the best Hittite things known, and one scarab, in hæmatite, is the best Hittite flat seal I have ever seen. Now we are digging a strange place of shallow stone circles, and graves of Greek type, with painted pottery very like the stuff from Crete. With it are many flint knives, and a great deal of very curious stuff. We cannot either date it or explain it as yet.

The weather is beautifully cool, (we have not had a hot day yet), and the river still in flood: we have only bathed twice this year. . . . Digs will probably close in about a fortnight:—and I will stay out here at least a fortnight after that, looking at two or three inscriptions, and hunting for seals. After that I may come back for a little while:— say in Mid-July, to remain on into August. ·

On the other hand, the Turkish Government wants me to do a dig at Rakka for them, in Arab glazed ware. This would take about a month, and would be a tremendous opportunity, for they offer me a representative collection from the results, and it is rare and beautiful stuff. I have accepted this, and it remains with them to find the money, and settle the date. I offered either July, or August from the 10th onwards: meaning to go to you either after or before: on the other hand they may find difficulty at the present moment in getting together the money required. So you see, there is no telling you when I come back: if possible it will be to Oxford: if you go away as usual about August 3, and come back say Sept. 10 that would be exactly right, so far as I am concerned. We have a good deal of work to do in London & Oxford, on the stuff sent home this year: so that I can always put in a week at that after you have gone off for the sea, or before you get back thence. So use your pleasure only in this matter. Will is probably in schools now: sympathies.   N.

CARCHEMISH
June 11, 1913

Some little time I fancy since I wrote . . . and a little more since I heard from you. By the way, what meant an isolated sentence in Will's letter that "Father was still in Ireland"? Why go . . . to such a place: perhaps he had desires to sign a covenant. As for work here: it is finished in so far as the multitude of men is concerned . . . we have now only got Dahoum left to us, and are working at pottery and photography.

In our last few days we stumbled upon a neolithic pottery kiln, and spent four or five days clearing it out. We dug it in squares, since the ground was nearly solid pottery, washing and sorting the fragments ourselves, and then having all the preservable pieces labelled by Dahoum according to their squares and now we are packing them to come to England to be looked through and made up into complete pots by Young {repairer in Ashmolean Museum}. There are about 11,000 fragments, and there must be about 20 complete pots amongst that lot: we collected together three or four such ourselves. It has, as you may imagine, left us busy. Then we have been clearing the grave objects, with a view to a good deal of work upon them at once: (they must all be photographed up complete before we go) and also we are rearranging our Museum, and working at stone-fragments,

Rum Kalaat (Main Gate)

(See p. 176)

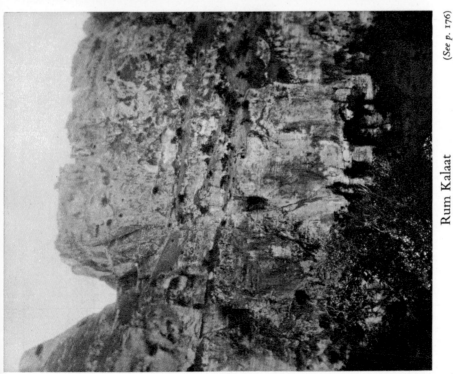

Rum Kalaat

(See p. 176)

Facing p. 256

Rum Kalaat (*See p.* 176)

Biredjik (*See p.* 176)

& squeezes of inscriptions. Busy, therefore, to the exclusion of ease. Occasionally a visitor drops in: we have had 36 in the house this season, sleeping, many of them for two or three days . . . besides lunches and casuals innumerable.

As for future movements . . . we will finish here in perhaps six days: then I have to travel a little . . . down to Rakka in Mesopotamia, and to Abu Galgal, and elsewhere: that will take about a fortnight. Then to Aleppo for a little time, and thence to England, say about July 12 or 15 . . . to stay with you till you go away, then a week in London, and then out here for August 12 to begin work at Rakka, if the Turkish Government can make up its mind to the effort. As for Will's finding a ticket to India from P. Said in September: it's possible though not certain. In any case it would only mean waiting a week. They make a lot of fuss about the Autumn rush to India . . . because they want to appear fashionable.

Salaams.   N.

CARCHEMISH
June 15 {1913}

Woolley went off yesterday, and the resultant feeling is one of a most perfect peace: it is midday, everyone is asleep, and the only noise near me is the ticking of a watch on our great table. Last letter from you was May 27: things come slowly this year. You were getting photographs from me of this year's slabs:—they are very fine, as you say, and you know most of them. Mr. Hogarth says they are the best things found archæologically for many years. "Kenyon is lyrical." . . .

Father seems nervous about canoeing: but what harm is there if it does upset? There never has been any danger yet (there cannot be much with a square-rigged sail, running before the wind) of our overturning, except intentionally, and then it is quite easy to right her again and continue. It is not like being capsized a day's journey out at sea: one simply tows the boat ashore here. You seem to have had photographs of our big room: the tapestry looks extraordinarily well: only today I had a couple of the directors of the Baghdad line admiring it. Daisies are all over: we could only get them from an island in the middle of the river, and they only last three or four days in water: we used to send the canoe over twice a week to bring back a few armfuls.

Now there are strange blue flowers, and some lovely yellow things: while I have struck out a new line in convolvuli and vine-tendrils, on the mantel-pillars: rather pretty, as my visitors today said.

The mosaic floor is certainly not worth transport to England: it weighs tons (you know our room is really very large, though it didn't appear so on the photograph) and in Europe is probably not worth a £5 note. However it makes a very handsome floor . . . 9 colours, most of them bright ones. I may bring you a little yard-square panel of fishes, if I have time to chisel it up.

As for Asia Minor, it is off this year, for lack of time: next year we hope to make some arrangement with the B.M. about our travelling money. It is absurd that one should have to come home, to draw one's salary and keep for that fortnight.

About the summer . . . well, you know, I can only be a very little time in England, and Miss Wright's would suit me very well. If I came away with you (improbable, unless you go away early) I would only sit quiet . . . one gets enough here of running about.

The footsoldiers sent home are really Hittites: we have many of them. Details of their armour are curiously Greek (not Roman). The lion pedestal of two years ago is quite the same style as the bulls, but much less good work. The baby holding a stick, we are assured by distinguished physicians, is wonderfully life-like. Woolley is no sailor . . . I am . . . No fever this year to speak of among the men; and of course the season for it is past: there can be none now till September or October. Arnie seems to have been a trouble to you in the point of view of health: perhaps I'll bring him out here next season: it is quite impossible, here, to imagine any earthly need of being ill. Personally, you know, I feel that all precautions and specifics cure or prevent their particular evils, simply that the way may lie open more smoothly to other difficulties. As for a poor appetite, which in Arnie Father deplores, it is a thing to be above all thankful for. If it were himself who felt no desire to eat, would he not rejoice aloud. To escape the humiliation of loading in food, would bring one very near the angels. Why not let him copy that very sensible Arab habit, of putting off the chewing of bread till the moment that instinct makes it desirable. If we had no fixed meal-hours, and unprepared food, we would not fall into middle-age.

Mother remarks with pride of 95° in the greenhouse on Sunday afternoon: the thermometer on the little stone table beside me, in our darkened sitting room, without glass in its windows, and with a water-sprinkled floor is 109°. And yet it is only a pleasant, healthy, warmth. I expect to start for Rakka in two or three days, and thereafter to return to England about July 12.

N.

CARCHEMISH
June 21, 1913

Have had an unexpected delay here; which has prevented my getting down South to Abu Galgal . . . A stray English consul turned up, bound for Diarbekir . . . empty, but meaning to be pleasant, and a very bodily person: he went and swam all over the Euphrates, "crawling" about, dived off the German construction bridge, to the horror of M. Hoffmann who thought it a suicide . . . and did many strange things in four days here. He loved shooting also, so I let him have as much of that as he desired . . . and as he couldn't shoot with a pistol he was rejoiced to learn it: (Got very good too, though to the end erratic) . . . he had a small battery with him.

Frank will approve of 5 shots out of 7 on a medjidie (about a 4/– piece) at 25 yards with an automatic colt, which was the best score of the meeting: of late I have been getting quite sure of eggs at 25 yards, & medjidies, but even so, it was a good score, fast shooting without dropping the hand. Also at 500 yards we got (he 5 out of 10 with a mauser pistol, I 5 out of 5 with a Mannlicher carbine) an orange box with some certainty: and finally at my 1,200 yards range (which is the longest I have set out) he got 4 out of 15 on a metre square target, and I 3 out of 10 . . . Obviously it is Frank & not Will who should come to Carchemish for a visit.

I will start back in twelve days, & get to England I hope about July 15 . . . I'll come to Oxford, and if you are not there, will look for the key of one door, in Mathews, the insurance office in St. Aldate's. I have work in Oxford which will keep me a week there.

Salaamat.   N.

Hope to bring 2 Arabs with me this summer.

N.

BARON'S HOTEL. ALEPPO

25 August 1913

I got to Aleppo last night, driving up from Alexandretta. We had
to wait one day only in Alexandria before a cattle boat left direct for
Syria . . . and as the nearest boat for Beyrout was not till after four days,
I jumped at the chance. However that means that Will is not expected
at the hotel in P. Said. Cook in Beyrout on the other hand knows he
is coming. Owing to a strike there are no Italian boats for the moment.
That may possibly mean an extra delay for him in P. Said. However he
won't see this letter. I got all my luggage through in safety, without
giving the customs-house in Alexandretta any work! It is rather fine
to have passed from England through Holland, Germany, Austria,
Egypt to Syria without opening a bag! I got a sheaf of letters here from
everybody: including one (of June) from you. . . .

Today I have found five very good pieces of Hittite work:—seals;—
for which I fear tomorrow I will pay £14. Mr. Hogarth will groan.
The Arabs will go on tomorrow to Jerablus: I will follow on Wednesday probably. All is reported at peace there, except that the Railway
people put up some sheds once again on our ground, and were expropri-
ated by Haj Wahid. The engineers deserve a medal for their per-
sistence in incurring defeats. The bridge has been found unsafe:—
some anglophil insect has eaten away the piles by the water's edge, and
you can scoop the wood away with both hands! They are considering
a metal sheathing as an antidote.

The Turks are going to levy more soldiers as soon as Ramadan ends:
that will mean acute local difficulty, I'm afraid. However we will see
what we can do.

Baron von Oppenheim, the German excavator, has had a cart-load
of cases seized upon the road near Aleppo: nineteen large boxes, which
are being telegraphed upon to Embassies and foreign offices in clouds:
we know not what will become of him—but if he gets them away
intact it will make our road for the future more interesting. We are
very fortunate to have had no check so far in any of our forwarding
departments.

Aleppo is hot: the village will be probably hotter: still there is always
the river, which is a standby . . . and after all, so soon as the fast ends

(in a week) I'm going down to Hamman, to dig out the cemetery I told you of.

The cost of exporting your bicycle from England to Alexandretta came to 3s. 8d.: which cannot be considered as a ruinous expense. This is not a letter, but a series of jottings unconnected and in isolation; put down each by itself, in a very unambitious mood. On the way out I came to know the early work of Swinburne better than before. He is quite good after all, though alas, like Browning long-winded to the extent of ultimate boredom. On the steamer however, where all passengers yawn their way along the decks between meals, he was very well. I have five other letters to write, so that a certain modesty is only befitting: I'll leave this letter at that.   N.

I have been fortunate in finding a very good little lot of Hittite seals at tolerably reasonable prices . . . it is also unfortunate, for Mr. Hogarth has exhausted the Ashmolean grant for this year, and so I have to carry their value locked up till March or April. I'm afraid I'll go smash after the demyship ends. The Turkish government is taken with a sudden craze for collecting mules: it tours the city and when it sees a good-looking mule it puts it in its pocket, and promises to pay for it later. Possessors of mules are miserable . . . and I gloat over ourselves, who possess only one mule, and that not a good-looking one . . .

Salaams   N.

CARCHEMISH
August 29, 1913

You see I have got here at last after spending a couple of days in Aleppo. It is Ramadan still for another three days, and till that is ended there is nothing to do. So I have carried the canoe up to the house, and am occupying myself in cleaning & varnishing it for next season's work. The scraping over shoals and rocks, and the heat and sun are not easy on the paint. Everything in our camp is well at Jerablus. Haj Wahid's wife sends her greetings to you. Her children flourish: all but the younger bitten by a scorpion two weeks back . . . and who is yet a little upset over it. Scorpions, you know, are sometimes fatal to young babies. Its hot here,—86° in the room just now,—but nothing to speak of, and the nights are wonderful. The weather is cloudy with strong winds. I have never seen the Euphrates so low.

The Railway company had a fight the other day—no one hurt—
with some Turkish Effendis . . . the matter has left a good deal of sore-
ness behind it on both sides. It is unfortunate, for of late the Germans
had been behaving much better to the local people. It is curious that a
strong conviction of their own superiority should lead the engineers to
act as though it was in danger. As it is they only succeed in being disliked
and despised as boors.

The Hoja and Dahoum entertain large houses nightly with tales of
snakes as long as houses, underground railways, elephants, flying-
machines, and cold in July. I have not yet had the chance of hearing of
anything ludicrous. You know those two are too sophisticated to be
comic in their relation:—they usually say the just—if unilluminative—
thing. My luggage is just arriving: which means that post goes out.

N.

CARCHEMISH
Tuesday Sept. 9, 1913

Well, I have been to Hamman, and further South, and have come
back. The Government had been showing a little misplaced activity in
suppressing illicit digging, and so the people of Hamman were too
nervous to allow me to work on their cemeteries. Further on I found
in Mesopotamia a new Hittite site, a little fortress dominating a ford
over the river . . . with early graves at the foot of it, and many promising foundation-walls, etc., showing. The place is called Kara Kazak,
and is on the Euphrates about 10 miles below Tell Ahmar . . . altogether about 35 miles from here, Southwards. I hardly expect you to
find them on any map in your reach. On the trip I saw nothing to buy.
I am going in to Aleppo on Sept. 14, with the expectation of having to
wait there some few days for Will. His boat was due I fancy on the
10th at P. Said, and he may have to wait there a little.

I saw one rather melancholy thing on my trip down the river. The
Arabs at Kala'at en Nejm, a very large and splendid Arab mediæval
castle on the Euphrates, had dug out a pit in the old xivth Century
town: it was full of pottery and glass, of the xvth and xvith Centuries
which they broke and threw away in their hasty hopes to find gold
or treasures at the bottom of the hole: so that in the earth piled round
the pit that they had thrown out, were fragments of enamelled cups in

terracotta, and of about twenty vessels in mosaic glass, with fishes and snakes and birds worked in colours in relief. Each of these glass vessels would have been worth from £500 to £1,000 if brought complete to Europe. If I had gone to Kala'at en Nejm 2 weeks earlier we would have all been very well off for a little time! I don't suppose such another store house of Arab glass has ever been discovered in history.

No news to tell you:—Jerablus is at peace with itself just at present, after the little troubles of last week. The Railway is still unable to use its bridge, but has hopes to repair it quickly. The old Kaimmakan of Biredjik came down here ten days ago, and I sent for him to the house, to talk to him: he came delicately, but this time suffered no harm.

Have had very heavy expenses here this last fortnight, and have had to borrow money off Haj Wahid: there was a case of abduction put on to me by the Consulate which cost a good deal to hunt down:—and I deported some undesirables from the village back to Aleppo at my own expense. However, the B.M. owes me money now.

Nothing to tell you: all well.   N.

No letters yet!

CARCHEMISH

Sept. 21, 1913

It seems quite a long time since I wrote to you:—I don't suppose it really is, since I have been knocking about the country, and so made the time seem long. However Will wrote from Aleppo in my place a few days ago.

I don't know what really there is to tell you. We have been here a few days, and Will has boated and bathed a certain amount, and found the country pleasant. Also I have now quite a tolerable choice of books, and so the staying here has not been too dull for him. Yesterday all our visitors departed together in a cloud so the place bears little resemblance now to a hotel . . . I rather dislike having it so over-full. Still Will enjoyed them, and the one who is left, one Young, a Lieut. in an Indian Regiment, is a decent sort of person. He is going with Will this afternoon with the son of Busrawi (who came in to accompany us) to spend a couple of nights among the tents. The Hoja and Dahoum are both going with us as servants on our side:—so all should be quite easy. The house is uncomfortable for them, since we are rebuilding the roofs all along it: the dust and noise are unfortunate . . . but they have been sleeping every night on the hill top, and there it is most pleasant.

I have picked up some small saddle-bags very cheaply in Aleppo . . . they make good cushions, stuffed with chaff, and will do well to give away to people:—besides being rather less valuable presents than full-sized carpets.

Will perhaps told you of a splendid carpet that I have at last managed to buy from the Kurds of the further bank. I have been trying to get it for two years, ever since I first saw it, and now have managed it for £2.10.0. It is in poor condition, but exceedingly lovely. All of it in dark colours, mostly red and blue, with the leaf-pattern of the little blue rug that you seem to have retained for your room . . . but very old, perhaps over the century, and very splendid. I cannot satisfy myself whether its colours are more splendid, or those of the Morris tapestry hanging beside it . . . for I am using it as a table-cloth, its being thin. At present it is just 10 feet long, but it used to be longer: the ends are cut, and sewed up in leather to prevent its fraying. It is far better than any carpet Mr. Hogarth has in his house.

Weather is exceedingly hot . . . no wind day or night and many flies: these little discomforts rather interest Will, who has no experience of them as yet. Well, on re-reading the letter it appears that there was nothing but the carpets to talk about. Our visitors were Dr. Altounyan of Aleppo—a very good man—his daughter and son who are English . . . another doctor called Ussher, med. mis. at Van: Lieut Young, who remains a week with us: Bonham Carter, who is legal adviser to the Sudan Gov. and a man called Lamington of the Board of Trade: all of them quite pleasant.

Our Commissaire paid us another visit, since two truck-loads of antiquities were captured before yesterday on the Railway, belonging to von Oppenheim, and the Turkish Government feared that some of them might have been stolen by him from our digs. Needless to say they weren't! Oppenheim is an ass to have his things taken so, and not very virtuous to take all these things from his excavations: still they all enhance our credit.

Salaams,   N.

BARON'S HOTEL, ALEPPO
30 September 1913

I have come down here now to Aleppo to meet Woolley, who is due tomorrow: I expect you will have heard from Will after his having left Carchemish: he went off I think quite easily, and got away from Aleppo also. I did not come any of the way back with him, since there was a house-party in the place, and I could not very well leave them. In the East it is not so easy as it is in Europe to go away for a few days and leave one's house standing:—or find it standing on return. However my last visitor went yesterday, and today I have been sitting quietly in the hotel taking stock of my effects. I have some Hittite seals . . . one good carpet . . . and a presented rug or two, all bad. It is heartrending to have to return good equivalents for a foul new carpet: yet it is what one has very often to do. News of here:—none. Of late I got two letters (the only two I have had, by the way) one from Mother from Ireland, one from Father. It seems all is well. By the way which carpet, if any remains with you? I could not understand from Will: and it is rather a matter to be provided for next year. Will Father, if it is not a difficult matter, send me a cheque for £20 by about the beginning of next year. I think I may be a little short then. At the same time it is not necessary, and if Will's fitting out has caused a shortage I can carry on till June without difficulty. Another letter has just come from Cork from Mother. I am glad she has found Ireland unfortunate. I think that what we cannot help knowing of its history, that it is a sort of duty of English people to avoid it.

You are obviously interested to hear what the Arabs {the Hoja and Dahoum} think of England. Unfortunately they are too intelligent to be ridiculous about it. They describe it as a garden, empty of villages, with the people crowded into frequent towns. The towns wonderfully peaceful and populous, the houses very high: the tube railways are to them a source of stumbling. They tell the villagers that Syria is a small poor country, very likely to be coveted by us tree-lovers . . . and that the Arabs are too few to count in world-politics. All of this is very proper. They also estimate the value and quality of the food they ate in England: . . . and feel relieved at their discovery of the true end of the collecting of antiquities. Concerning ourselves, they praise Will and Arnie . . . Mr. Bell and Sir Arthur Evans: in this order. They were very pleased to see Will again in Jerabîs. Both went with him to Busrawi's camp.

We are to have a third man with us this year, one Reitlinger, who is unpaid: indeed I shouldn't be astonished to hear that he paid something for the honour of our entertainment. I wonder how our queer, half-insane house-keeping and conversation will strike him. It speaks well for my pen-powers that with less than nothing to say I should take two large pages to realise it. Possibly you will get two or three little trifles in cylinder seals shortly from the Ashmolean: any of these which do not appeal in particular to you, please send to Mrs. Rieder with a guarantee of verity. I have asked Leeds to send you what he does not want . . . and in the last lot I bought there will be some things not fit for the Ashmolean. . . .

L . . .

CARCHEMISH
October 3, 1913

We are short of note-paper, and our stores have again been made a mess of by the Stores. So economy decides that unstilted letters be written on sermon-paper. You get more for your money so, wherefore I expect no protests on your side.

About things:—I learnt accidentally in Aleppo by the loss of a local letter that my one-before-last letter to you never reached the post. That I fear will have plunged you into mourning—but it was only a dishonest messenger. I wrote from Aleppo again, while waiting Woolley. He came on the first, and we stayed two days in Aleppo, occupied in buying potatoes, carpets, and a light railway. I found very little to tempt me, except a little Baluch rug about five feet long, old, of dark red, dark brown, and deep blue, of the finest wool, silky as velvet, and superb in preservation. It is far finer than the little Bokhara rug in the Morning room, (and cost a little more) and it will be impossible to leave them in the same room, since they are like to extinction. The new one requires a bright light, if possible glaring sunlight: and this is the most beautiful piece, (except one) that I have ever seen. That one is Altounyan's blue Baluch: mine is a red one. Understand though that the early Persian piece I bought in the village here is a far better piece . . . the Baluch is an exquisite miniature, and the Persian

a great work of art. Woolley also found two fine things in Aleppo . . .
one a very large camel hair piece: one Kurdish, in pale and very
beautiful colours. Then we came out here, and today began work on
the house: you know I raised the roofs and put in order the old house
before Woolley came—now we are to have a third man here, one
Reitlinger, in a fortnight, and we are adding therefore two spare
rooms, and as well as 40 foot store-room for antiquities. This makes
our house cover a great deal of ground. This plan is all out of proportion, (our sitting room is twice as large as any other) but gives the shape
of things.

The new rooms are 10, 11, 12.

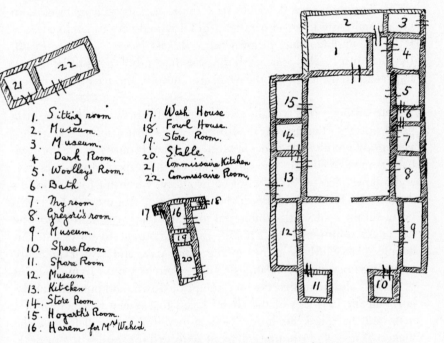

1. Sitting room
2. Museum.
3. Museum.
4. Dark Room.
5. Woolley's Room.
6. Bath
7. My room
8. Gregori's room.
9. Museum.
10. Spare Room
11. Spare Room
12. Museum
13. Kitchen
14. Store Room
15. Hogarth's Room.
16. Harem for Mr Wahid.

17. Wash House
18. Fowl House.
19. Store Room.
20. Stable.
21. Commissaire Kitchen
22. Commissaire Room.

We have not begun digging yet, but had to cut away a little earth
to bank up our railway line, and found out a new line of sculptures
in basalt, running in two directions. We have come upon the point of
the right angle of the corner, about six inches away from the end of
our work last spring! It will make our season a burning success if we
find nothing else . . . but I'll talk more about them in my next letter,
when we have run a little way up and down the line. However it is

good to be reassured of the continuance of the sculptures. There is not much other news: everything is quiet here.

Woolley heard of Will from the Khedival boat, and from the Scotch doctor at Tiberias {Dr. D. W. Torrance} and other people. I do not know if he got to Jerusalem or not, but I expect to hear from you about that. I cannot imagine what else to tell you about.

We are having warm weather in the midday, and an icy cold at dawn . . . which is a flippant mood of the weather, and one difficult to agree with.

I asked you lately to try and find me a book, if reasonable in price, the Greek Anthology recommended by Mackail in his collection of Select Epigrams. He describes it, I think, as a French edition, with Greek and Latin texts on parallel pages. I would very much like it. . . . If this is unobtainable, please send a *Richard Feverel*, and *The Egoist*, by Meredith . . . by post . . . but not if the Anthology is to be found. Paper-covered books, by the way, go cheaply, and pass the Customs easily.

Our sitting room is really rather delightful now: we have a little good pottery (Turkish, Arab, Roman, and Hittite) some glass trifles, very good woodwork, and a few fine pieces of bronze; on the floor we have some exceedingly fine carpets and on the walls a Morris tapestry, and a large piece of Arab wool embroidery: I mustn't forget Dodd's drawing of Dahoum {done in the Ashmolean, August 1913} a really beautiful piece of work which gets more pleasant with familiarity: he has never summoned up, himself, enough courage to show it to his people. Hassan Mahli came up the other day, and saw it suddenly pouncing upon it; ("Wullah," he said); "here is a most living likeness of a cow" and he turned the picture upside down, and pointed out the horns in the two legs of the chair! I said that it was the picture of a man, and he shook his head "God is merciful, and will forgive the maker of it" . . . Dahoum collapsed with delight outside the door.

Bed-time, and tomorrow we have to get 200 men to work upon the hill top, and in the lower palace: so no writing tomorrow. I'll send again in a few days.

                                                                    N.

CARCHEMISH
October 16, 1913

Got a letter from Father yesterday (Sept. 15) enclosing a cheque for
£20 . . . which was most welcome, as we were just beginning a
serious attempt to recover some of the enamel glass I mentioned to
you before. We have one beautiful piece . . a tumbler with Arabic
inscription in blue: red glass bead-border, and gilt scroll-work above
and below. The neck & ornamented part is complete, though shattered:
the bottom of the glass is missing, but we have hopes of recovering it.
The present value is very little . . . but if we can only get up a complete
piece we will be happy. There are heaps of people, incidentally ready
to pay huge sums for Arab glass. It is the rarest art object in the world,
and one of the most sought after. If we had been able to gather up all
that was broken that day in Kala'at en Nejm, we would have been
tolerably well off. Professor Petrie had not in all his collection one single
piece for which an amateur would have said "thank you". Collections
of purely scientific interest (Egyptian or Hittite or Roman things) are
of very little money value. It is the pretty things that matter. Don't
go to Ireland, even to play golf. I think the whole place repulsive
historically: they should not like English people, and we certainly
cannot like them. I wonder how Bob will like hospital work in London
. . . it is not so hard as Percy Cave made out!

You would feel a certain pleasure out here, shooting. We are digging
on the top of the hill, and yesterday, looking up from a pot-burial I
was digging, I counted about 30 wild-duck (in four bunches) swimming about the river below: that is, in open view of the whole country-
side: they are much more common in the reeds and brushwood of the
islands . . . when one takes the canoe through, one disturbs them on all
sides: one day last week, when two people came to us, and we had no
meat for them, I shot two in about ten minutes—with a pistol of
course, as we have not got a gun. With a pistol one must hit them in
the head, which means not more than 20 yards away as a maximum.
And we don't put them up first. Snipe are also very common: but not
worth shooting with a heavy bullet. You could also have swan and
pelican and goose, with lots of mallard. We have not killed any of
these:—only the two ducks, and that because we needed meat. So
don't condemn us as sportsmen!

This season we have not bought any antiquities at all: so that there will be no need for us to export any antiquities. At the same time we do it better than von Oppenheim, I think. Woolley goes in to Aleppo today: to meet Reitlinger, the third man who arrives here on Sunday next. He is 25 and has black side-whiskers: we are both wondering what sort of person he will be. Now we have just been interrupted by visitors—the worst sort that want to see everything in the hour and a half between trains. Germans too, this time. Nothing else to tell you.

In the digs, early Hittite graves, and slabs turn up regularly. The procession of servants of the seated goddess has stopped short abruptly, and behind them comes a gate which is interesting: it has been of cedar wood, and we are getting out the iron bands that tied it together, hinge pieces, and a door sill & very fine long Hittite inscription in relief characters: rescued by the builder of the new building.

Post goes.   N.

CARCHEMISH
October 21, 1913

DEAR WILL

Nothing especial to say. We have been at work about a fortnight . . . striking out beyond the King's gate we found the return of the buttress only six inches from our limits of last season: a slab of drums and trumpets, heralding a seated goddess. The lady is followed by 15 servants, carrying either a mirror or a sistrum & fillet. After this seven men carrying on their shoulders gazelles: these slabs alternate basalt and white limestone. Then came a break, which turned out to be a door, flanked with huge inscriptions in Hittite. By some strange fortune the door had been rebuilt, and new inscriptions, in basalt put up by some acquisitive monarch. So we got not only the new inscriptions, in their places, but the old slabs turned face downwards and used to walk upon. A great find, the greatest we have ever made.

Besides this, we have added an outer courtyard to the house and built on two or three large rooms and a store for antiquities. I persuaded Young in his week here to spend his spare time carving gargoyles for the better adornment of the house. He managed in limestone an ideal head of a woman; I did a squatting demon of the Notre-Dame style, also in limestone, and we have now built them into the walls and roof, and the house is become remarkable in N. Syria. The local people come up in crowds to look at them.

Two more good carpets have come in, Woolley took one, and I took one: no other news.

The Hoja and Dahoum send greetings. . . .

Got back Baedeker, and a letter from you from P. Said: am glad you got about as easily as you did. Tiberias was a place worth seeing, wasn't it?

Nothing more: since post starts at once.   N.

(If you want anything Aleppine, please command it.)

{This letter is evidently from Carchemish but is not dated.}

No time this week either: all perfectly well, but we are in a perfect mist of photography: camera's snapping all day.

Enclosed instead a stamp for Arnie: they are on sale in the Turkish Empire for one month only . . . but none are to be got in Aleppo: this one our Commissaire gave me.   N.

BARON'S HOTEL, ALEPPO

1 *Nov.* 1913

Got two letters today: one posted in London, one from Oxford. It is not necessary to send to London to ensure a letter's arriving in time! I got your cheque which I keep on repeating in each letter in order that the fact may arrive. [you feared I might have been anxious at not hearing from you . . . but really I should have been rather ashamed of myself for that!] Will had I think quite an interesting tour: the Tiberias water isn't very aperient! it was only that he was getting tired. We have finished the roofs for the moment . . . it needs a little mud plastering in a month's time, after the rain has made solid what exists at present. The house is quite large—seven bed rooms not counting servant's—but most of it is taken up by the four large store rooms for antiquities. It would reach about to the top of the {Polstead} road perhaps from your front gate: I sent you a plan of it a few letters back.

We have put on since a couple of side-houses. I never developed the photos I took with the Kodak: . . . they were I thought, too little valuable. Of late in Jerablus I have managed to take a couple of very good photos . . . one, of some bronze objects, was really first class. There is the misfortune that only Cristoid films stand heat. . . . About getting letters regularly . . . it seems very unlikely. There is some difficulty with the Government, which protests that there is a bi-weekly post to Jerablus, and with the Railway, which protests that there isn't . . . so far the advantage is with the Railway, which refuses to carry anything offered. We hope to get something arranged in a few days—meanwhile letters are being sent to Urfa or somewhere . . . at least we never see them.

Here is a letter of Mother's of the 15th which says that she sent off two on the 14th . . . one of the latter got through. This one is about carpets . . . the Barker's came off well! You did quite right to give them both. . . . The long thin one in your room you may now give away (or give away when I am about returning) since I have a new one worth twenty of it . . . a really fine one. You really, you know, have not got enough carpets . . . there are about ten in the house of the pre-Syrian days which are unworthy . . . however I have not even tried to buy any lately—except a little one for Leeds or somebody (not good enough for you), Persian and quite pretty, which Dahoum bought in a village for 1/9 and presented to me in triumph. No book from Mrs. Rieder . . . at least none for some months: don't bother her about it though.

Leeds doesn't think Mr. Hogarth is going to give you any seals: he likes even the poor ones we sent to him. Now about other things . . . in the digs we have been finding masses of slabs:—one nice one of a stag with heavy antlers . . . one of a lion pulling down a bull . . . one of praying sphinxes . . . one of a man carrying a hare . . . one of a winged lion, one of soldiers . . . also a pedestal of double lions, like that in the Museum, but three times the size, and with it the colossal seated figure of a god, with his name written on his robes, that once sat on the backs of the lions. Coarse work, but interesting. Also there is coming out the finest small sculpture we have ever found . . . all broken up, but we can repair it: . . . it must have been a row of figures about a yard high, but in basalt carved and polished in exquisite style, and most beautiful in expression . . . better perhaps than anything from Egypt, and far finer than anything Assyrian. We have the heads of six figures, and pieces of drapery and the hand of one figure. The

T. E. Lawrence
(taken by B. H. Liddell Hart)

T. E. Lawrence

slab had been broken up by the Babylonians, and the pieces used by the Romans to fill in the concrete of their foundations.

No other news to speak of . . . by the way, I have asked several times for a copy of the edition of the Greek anthology in Greek & Latin, recommended by Mackail in the preface of his edition of "select epigrams from the Greek Anthology". Frank could get it from Black-well's, and I would very much like it, if not too costly. You have never mentioned it in your letters, which encourages me to think you never got them. No news. . . .   N.

CARCHEMISH
Nov. 25, 1913

Got a letter from Father today enclosing cheque . . . many thanks: £12 English make about £13 Turk. I have not written for a long time, because we have been exceedingly busy, and finding absolutely nothing. This last rather a blessing because at the end of last month we found a large Roman wall cutting across our great gate, and all the lowest course of foundations was Hittite:—that is the Romans had smashed up the Hittite slabs, and built them in. In the end we pieced together about a dozen sculptures, and having measured them in and out, have arranged them in the shape of a great double gate, with inscriptions and lions on each side. It has been a very difficult piece of work but very successful. Only we have been kept at it from morning to night. Even now it is bed-time and I am only sitting up because we have got a huge fire burning and so the room is comfortable. Tell Mother that Dahoum has brought me an Arab wall-hanging for her. It is about 70 years old, in blue and red and cream, and rather beautiful. I will give him something from Aleppo in return from her, so she need not bother over it. I am going to bed now.   N.

You might send me any letter of Will's which is good. . . .

CARCHEMISH
Dec. 4, 1913

Digs ended this afternoon, which is timely, since we are having very difficult weather . . . a day of rain, a day of fine, and a day of icy cold alternate just at present. The rain has been very heavy: the first time all our roofs leaked all over like sieves: a new roof always does—and when it stopped, which was after 24 hours, we had to strew mud & chopped straw all over them, and roll it in with a stone roller that we had fortunately dug up. The next day's rain, and the later days have run off harmlessly. The French railway to Beyrout has been washed out twice lately: the first time it was repaired in eleven days, during which the post both ways was held up, lacking means of bridging a gap of two kilometres. Then a rich Aleppo merchant placed a horse at the disposal of the P.O. and service with Europe was resumed. The line is cut now.

The snow effects on the hills to the North are wonderful . . . with us we have not had so far very heavy frosts. The sun has always managed to thaw the ice by midday. Our plans may interest you. We have built a new store-room for stone-fragments, and are going this winter to spend a month or so sorting them . . . now at once we are going over to Busrawi's for a couple of days: then to Aleppo for the same, and back here about the middle of the month to settle down. In January we will probably go about a bit. I want to go down towards Antioch. . . . Woolley may go to Egypt. In March we begin work again . . . the last season if we do not get another grant.

The last days have given us two very large & very fine inscriptions: in some ways the best we have. I got a letter the other day enclosing a card of Professor Petrie's, and his report . . . also a *Punch*: the previous letter had contained a cheque.

We have just bought 5 tons of fire wood . . . olive tree boles, . . . which burn most gloriously. Our fire-place is looking quite well, and serves its intention. We are very busy copying inscriptions.

Tell Arnie that a Government official in Aleppo has presented us with a young leopard from Asia Minor. It will only eat meat, but is otherwise good-looking and serves us as watch-dog: nearly everybody keeps clear of it. Nothing else now.   N.

If Will sends you any letter of interest, you might send it out to me.

N.

CARCHEMISH
Dec. 10, 1913

Day before yesterday we went over to Busrawi's house, and slept a night with him, returning here late last night. Not for any special reason, but simply to return his call. We saw a Hittite sculpture in the round, and a couple of reliefs, that when safe we may try to send to London. Incidentally he gave me a big carpet to send to Will:—but as it is modern work I will sell it in Aleppo where it will probably fetch £10, as it is very thick and strong . . . Persian and buy him the return present with the proceeds. In this country presents are usually tragic things, since they are unusually new and bad, and one has to give good things in exchange. This rug I suppose is not 30 years old. I will not bring many rugs home with me this year: this one of Will's I'll sell:— and I have a beautiful old one, one for Leeds that cost 1/9: and a little Persian thing with peacocks on it in bright colours that Dahoum bought for me when he went down to Tell Ahmar: about 150 years old, thin but pretty:—and of course the wall-hanging which is a present from him to yourself. He has been liberal lately, sending also two little saddle-bag pieces to Mr. Bell.

Digs are ended, as I think I told you: we found nothing particular the last few days: but the season as a whole is the richest we have had: between twenty and thirty sculptures, and three large inscriptions: which were the longest and best we had. Very little small stuff though.

We have had the usual crop of visitors . . . but Miss G. Bell passed straight through from Beyrout to Damascus for Baghdad, and will not visit us till spring. Nobody else peculiarly exciting came.

We had fun two days ago putting a stronger collar on our leopard. He was in a box, but too wild to catch, so we made a hole in the side of the box, and stuffed in sack after sack until he was wedged so tight that he could not move. Then we took the top off the box, collared him, and let him loose again. He is not very sweet tempered, but not yet half-grown. He will make a most splendid carpet some day, if the Zoo don't want him.

Gregori has gone off to Cyprus. We are going in to Aleppo to-morrow for two days, and then out again here till the new year, trying to piece up some of the sad fragments in the store rooms. We have now three huge rooms each about 35 feet long, full of stone fragments packed two and three deep. The librarian of the Royal library of Munich, who saw them a few days back, said it was the saddest sight he had ever seen. He was an amusing man by the way: called when we were out with two or three railway engineers: and finding a fire and books and a decent chair (none of which exist in the railway houses) said good-bye to them, and sat down and read till we came back in the afternoon. He said ours was the best (in quality) of any small library he had ever seen, and that it showed on the face of it natural genius in selection: he would not go away! indeed in the end we had to lend him four books for his night's reading in the German camp: one German, one English, one Greek, and one French: he wanted to take a latin one, but feared he would be greedy. We heard from the bridge engineer that he sang our praises all night over there. It is a pity that Will is not with you to hear that my Heredia was the crowning virtue of our shelves. He borrowed one of the new Meredith's Mother sent out this season: and has promised us three or four rare editions of mediæval German poetry from his own collection: the amusing part about it is that we only have about 150 books, which have to represent eight languages!

A cold wind from the north is turning everything into ice in the village and the Kala'at: in consequence nobody is doing any work. We are sitting indoors writing letters and watching our room being hung with Arab tapestries for the winter. We are putting a black goat-hair tent-cloth over the mosaic on the floor, and scattering over it rugs here and there. The whole effect is going to be rather nice. You did quite right I think in continuing the Petrie subscription, it is not a very heavy matter. I am answering his card to-day.

Afternoon

Busrawi has just sent in three more carpets as presents. They are not pieces I like, but fortunately Woolley likes two of them, and the third, which is rather hard, we will try to sell in Aleppo. My taste is entirely in favour of soft carpets, with colours a little deep & rich. The hard things one generally sees are to my mind detestable. You know even if I did bring home with me half a dozen rugs or so, you need not keep any of them. They are cheap & valuable presents:—or one can make people pay for them. Mr. Hogarth told me he was ready to buy one or two from me.

Incidentally, we were offered £60 for one of ours three weeks ago: however it is one rather falling to Woolley's share. No letters lately . . . we have now arranged a daily post with Aleppo, each way. That makes communication much easier with the world, though it still takes four days to get anything from the town. {The next few words are not decipherable} . . . on a railway with one train a day in four hours should take three days and *petite vitesse* ten days is a mystery only to be explained as the effect of German organization. I got a letter from Will two days ago on his return from visiting a monastic school: quite a good letter describing his run across India. He seems not too favourably impressed, which will probably mean his getting very fond of it. I only hope he will not send you Indian wood-carving or stuffs, since they are most of them too awful for words. Will has taste, though, and probably will not mess things up too much. We went hawking at Busrawi's camp: and shot at glass bottles. I broke four in four shots with a Colt at 60 yards: which is good: for the rest of the world out there could not hit them at 20 yards. Tell Frank this.

N.

CARCHEMISH
Dec. 17, 1913

I got an insurance paper from you about a week ago, and sent it off at once. I signed three or four papers of the sort in Mathews' before I left: please remind him of them. About news here:—absolutely none. We are working over our many thousand fragments of carvings, trying to make out which is which, and to group them again into sculptures fit to photograph. It is a most awful job. It took four men just three hours to carry the fragments of lion about fifty yards—from one store-room to another—and there over a thirty-five foot room the pieces were lying three and four deep over the floor and the three shelves that run round the room. You will appreciate the difficulty of picking out of this pile (which takes half a day to turn over) the particular claw or ear or scrap of jaw required to complete a broken lion in the excavations. And it would require a genius to tell which is lion hair, and which human hair, in the tangle of tiny fragments, many of them no bigger than a penny: some of them weighing three or four tons. We have got together the figure of a charioteer in magnificent style:— as good as fine Greek work—about two feet high, and we only need the chest and beard to complete a colossal statue of a standing god in the round about seven feet high. We have also the pedestal of this god— two large lions—and the problem before us is how to set him up. Seccotine is not much use with half-ton blocks, fitting too close for cement: and drilling holes in basalt for setting in cramps is too slow work (and too difficult) to commend itself. I'll complete this letter in my next. **N.**

CARCHEMISH
Dec. 26, 1913

This is only a scrabble of a letter, since we piece sculptures, and copy inscriptions, and photograph slabs, all night. We are labouring now at double speed, since we got a wire from the B.M. asking us to do the archæological part of a survey of Arabic Petræa (Gaza—Petra) undertaken by the Palestine Exploration Fund. So we go off in two days for Jaffa . . . not knowing in any respect more than I have told you: a letter should be at Cook's in Jaffa for us, telling us where to go: if not! . . . In case of finding everything a hopeless muddle we can get our own part right, since we are taking down the necessaries and Dahoum with us to make arrangements locally. The survey is being done by R.E's. I got a letter from you the other day, sending one of Snow's, and a cutting of motor 'busses and photographs of the Jesus fire. I hope the College will now have the common sense to get rid of the ceiling of the Hall. It is really an opportunity. Will you send, addressed to R. A. Fontana Esq. H.B.M. Consul Aleppo, a new book of Flecker's, just out at Max Goschen's called the *King of Alsander* (6/–) and also the edition (Oxford) of Morris' work 1856–1870, published by Milford at 1/–. Write my name inside each book (in pencil) but don't put it on the address. I got a letter from Flecker the other day; he is in a Sanatorium in Switzerland, writing many poems.

On Xmas-night we took so many flash-light photographs that the Germans, living a mile away, walked across, thinking it was a display of fireworks. The engineer who bothered us has gone, and the present ones are exceedingly polite and friendly, and are taking away all our waste heaps of earth & stone, to bank up their river wall. Have eleven more letters to write tonight! **N.**

ALEPPO
Jan. 1, 1914

Today great festivities in Aleppo, as being new year: in our case it is important also, since we got today a letter from the P.E.F. {Palestine

Exploration Fund} telling us what to do. They want all place names, in Arabic: plans of places, dating of places, flints, photographs, and squeezes. This should be a very fair employment for two months: as we go from Egypt to Akabah on the Red Sea, by Petra, to the Dead Sea: all Arabia Petræa and Midian in fact. There are a party of R.E.'s with one Capt. Newcombe as commander: camels. We return here to Jerablus for March i to dig. Letters still to the Consulate in Aleppo. We know nothing of addresses or posts down South. I expect very few, since the place is all absolute wilderness. Not even any Arab tribes there: empty, they say. In any case kindly don't worry if no letters come, since we are with a party of about a dozen people. I return a letter of Will's . . . congratulate Arnie on his scholarship. It is a very excellent proceeding. About news here:—none. It is cold, sunny, with the streets like butter soused in oil.

I have bought you a silver milk-jug about 7 inches high, good shape, and beautifully hammered, (not chased, but very pleasing) . . . about 100 years old, but probably Aleppo work. It cost about 16/- (the weight of the silver, and 1/- for the workmanship) and would have been £10 in England, judging from what I have seen. Only, unfortunately the metal is rather thin. When I can find the sugar-bowl required it will complete the set, unless I knock up against a really good tray, which is little likely. Beaten silver is dear in England, since it is only the most highly-paid craftsmen who can do it. Also it is always sold at a fancy price. On the other hand out here they used to like beaten silver, but are now all buying enamelled iron: so the jewellers are always glad if they gain a shilling or so, to avoid the trouble of melting down the old stock. In any case I won't spend much on the stuff, since a table with too much white metal on it is ugly. I will write again, probably from Jaffa, where we will hear what the main body of the expedition is doing: or it may be from Gaza, which is actually the starting place. I wrote to Sir John Rhys about a fortnight ago, congratulating him on the fire. We are trying to find squeeze-paper here. T.E.L.

AT SEA
Jan. 4, 1914

I wrote to you from Aleppo, saying that I would write again when it became possible. Well, we ran down to Beyrout, getting a letter and a telegram on the way, which showed us that we must catch the first steamer to Jaffa, and then run down quickly to Gaza, and after seeing the consul there, go inland to Beersheba, and thence as local advice directed. There are a certain number of R.E.'s thereabouts, beginning the survey. We are obviously only meant as red herrings, to give an archæological colour to a political job. So here we are tonight between Haifa and Jaffa on a Khedival steamer, hoping to make Jaffa by 6.30 a.m. Only the wind is blowing so hard from the W. that all on board prophesy an impossible surf. In which case we go on to Egypt. So look at the post-mark and stamp on the letter, and you will be wiser as to our present movements than I now am. We have Dahoum with us, and are warned that we may have to ride camels some of the time: otherwise we are as ignorant of our supposed work as we were at first. I sent off from Beyrout to Mr. Hogarth a little cylinder seal: of prettily veined stone. I hope he will send it up to you and that you, if it seems to you worthless, will hand it on to Mrs. Rieder. It is Persian, about the time of Darius, or a little later perhaps. Now I want to go to sleep. There is no saying when I can write next: certainly not for a week or so.   N.

Got ashore: & going off today at midday for Ashdod.

BEERSHEBA
Jan. 9, 1914

I wrote to you quite lately, on the steamer: afterwards we landed at Jaffa, and a couple of hours later were in a carriage and driving South over the Philistine plain towards Gaza. Of course at first our road was all through orange groves:—miles of them, with eucalyptus and acacia trees in lines to mark out the different people's estates:—also much cactus. Philistia as a whole is enormously rich . . . wonderful soil, very deep and clean, sandy. There is no stone about, which of course explains partly why the P.E.F.'s diggings at Gezer were such a failure: they could never have had any sculpture. We slept at Ashdod, after looking at Gezer on our way: and our sleeping place was a very dirty untidy one at that. Next day we passed Askelon, which has great Crusader ruins and beautiful gardens;—reaching Gaza about midday. At the Consul's there we found letters, from Captain Newcombe, under whom we were nominally to work, telling us that he had sent us ten camels, and that more would follow: he wanted to know how much luggage we actually had. We wired back that we had one donkey load. He expected us fully prepared, a complete camp; and the P.E.F. had told us that he would provide for us. As a result I suppose we have neither squeeze-paper nor camera nor instruments but the bare minimum we brought with us. We went out at once into Gaza—(which is a picturesque little Crusading town of about 20,000 people: a fine xiith Cent. church) bought ourselves tents, camp outfit, hired servants, etc. (all on credit, since the P.E.F. had sent our money to Jerusalem) and started off next day, here, by carriage. We slept here last night, and will sleep tonight also: tomorrow Capt. Newcombe is to arrive, and thereafter we will go out into the desert. So this is my last letter for a little. With tents and our own men we may be comfortable and can certainly do as we like. Beersheba is a village built about ten years ago on the site of the old place. There are many deep wells: but the whole country is a desert of earth and gravel. We have found many Greek inscriptions, some quite interesting: and a Syriac one or two. These will all serve to amuse the P.E.F. The Turkish Gov. is exceedingly shy of us, and is doing its best to throw all possible difficulties in our way. Today we discovered masses of Greek tomb-stones under a sofa in the Police Station: after they had solemnly assured us that they had none. Fine cold weather . . . all well.   N.

SEBAITA

January 17, 1914

Today is Saturday, and as we have nothing to do tonight, I'll write to you: in a few days' time we may be able to send it off. I fancy I wrote last from Beersheba. It was a modern-built place, of no interest, though we found about twenty inscriptions, including a Hebrew one, most of them in Greek. While we were in Beersheba, Captain Newcombe, who is making the survey, turned up. He had been warned by the P.E.F. that we would bring about 15 tons of baggage with us:—and so was agreeably astonished to find us with one fair donkey-load between us. We had bought two tents and a cook, and crockery and table and bed things with camp furniture and stores in one afternoon at Gaza, though, so that a couple of days later we were ready to set out.

The first stopping place was called Khalassa about 15 miles S. of

Beersheba. We found there a very much ruined Byzantine town, at one end of a great flat sandy plain, full of wells and cisterns, but not very well cultivated. It had been very rich, of course, to support such a town (perhaps 30,000 people), and had been important as one of the halts on the road from Gaza to Akabah. We copied a lot of inscriptions and made excursions to ruins round about: all of the Christian period, most of them very uninteresting. The Palestine fund, of course, wants to find sites illustrating the Exodus, which is supposed to have passed this way ... but of course a people 40 years out of Egypt could hardly leave much trace of themselves in their later camping grounds ... any more than could Abraham or Isaac.

We went to Rehoboth, supposed to be the same as Isaac's well, and were fortunate enough to find near by pottery in a fort-like ruin, dateable about the time of Solomon. Which is interesting, as it is on his road from Elath to Gaza. No doubt he put a guard house there. It is the only really old thing we have found yet. The Well at Rehoboth is nearly 300 feet deep, and not old in masonry-work. I don't suppose it is really Isaac's Rehoboth.

We are about 20 miles S. of Khalassa, in a place called Sebaita, which somebody called Zephath. The ruins round our tents are all Byzantine, of about 500 A.D.: ... things like churches, baths, town halls, khans, and gate-towers. All these towns were destroyed by the Arab invasion of 650 A.D. The churches are interesting in plan, but not beautiful. We are making a plan of the town (which is about 600 yards long) and putting in the better houses: also taking many photographs: a very dull job we have on the whole. The houses are fairly well built of dry stone, with arched doors and roofs, ceiled with thin slabs of stone. They had no timber here you know, which hampered them in building. Every house has a rain-water cistern, since there is no spring within 20 miles ... and the 20 mile one is Kadesh Barnea, to which we move off next week.

After we have finished the buildings here, we want to search the neighbourhood for a possible site for Zephath ... because it isn't much good identifying a Bible site with a town no older than Christian Greek. Our camp moves about on eleven or twelve camels: very slowly. We are sufficiently comfortable: nights cold; and days very hot: all well.

N.

El Auga

Jan. 24, 1914

We came over here yesterday, from Sebaita: after staying there about a week, planning the town, and the churches and houses, and the public bath. Sebaita was in some ways the most desert place we have seen: since there was no water and no soil for miles round: only a ruined town of white limestone in a gently rolling upland of red flints, spread over a bed of chalk. The place was obviously only the settlement that had grown up round three great monasteries. A hermitage on a hill about 3 miles away had been published by a traveller as Zephath, a hill-fort of the Amorites! Auga isn't much better than Sebaita: it has some tamarisk bushes round about it: and a little land that could be, if anybody wished it, ploughed. The ruin is on a hill-top, a Byzantine cathedral and a castle: but the government has destroyed them both, to build its police-stations. At least nine years ago they pulled the old houses down, and that looks as though some day they meant to build! It is a pity, because the fortress has been interesting.

I got a stray letter of yours which the Beyrout P.O. had sent to Gaza: contained a request for the murder of our leopard: well, I told you long ago of his death while eating a sheep. We never got his skin. The country here is full of gazelles.

Longmans have published 2/- editions of some of Morris' prose romances. You might send out *The Well at the World's End*: and *The Glittering Plain* and *The Sundering Flood*: and *The Wood beyond the World* if these are not in the volume of Morris I asked for from you about a month ago. These new ones are little books, and easily sent. We stay here two days, and then go down to Kadesh Barnea (Ain Kedes) for a week: after that I go down S. to Akaba, on the Red Sea. I told Akras of Aleppo to send you the rug that Busrawi gave for Will: it should arrive in Oxford in a few weeks time, with much to pay on it for carriage. I gave Busrawi return presents. After this no letters for some time. All well here: hot & cold weather: nothing at all to eat.

N.

Talked today to an Arab who had never before tasted an egg: and who thought it a nasty tasting thing.

KUSEIME

Jan. 29, 1914

We got last night to this place: the border station of Egypt towards Turkey. I wrote to you lately from Auga, the corresponding Turkish post: we set off from there Southwards, finding on our way the great Shur road, used by patriarchs at times, between Beersheba & Egypt. It turned West from here to Ismailia on the border of Egypt. We got early ruins at Bir Birein on the way: Rehaibeh, our former find, was on the same road. Many gazelles and pigeons, some of the latter we have eaten, when short of food in the camp. You know this country is without any vegetables or eggs and fowls, has almost no sheep or goats, and the people here have had no crops for four years: so they haven't any bread either. When the milk season starts in a fortnight or so we will be easier.

We had an amusing time yesterday: Two days ago we sent our baggage camels on ahead of us, and went ourselves along the old Shur road. We told the baggage to go on four hours and then camp: that we would come in about sunset, and that next day we would get to Ain Kedes before midday. As it happened however we delayed on the way very long with some early ruins to plan, and an attempt to stalk a gazelle (you see, we want meat, and I couldn't make sure of so small a mark at much above 100 yards with a pistol). We had food with us, so slept out that night in our cloaks: two of our camels went mad in the night (they all do, one way & another, this month) and bolted: our baggage men had taken another road, and were alarmed at our non appearance: they warned the Egyptian police here, who sent out to look for us (Woolley, self, & Dahoum) and found two wandering camels: result was wild telephoning all over the frontier: 20 of the 25 camel police here at Kuseime were wandering over the hills all day & a night: the Turks were wandering over their hills: about 40 Arabs were arrested & brought in as hostages for our reappearance: and meanwhile we were sitting quietly in Ain Kedes, wondering where in the world our tents had got to. We came straight over the cliffs, being on foot, by a road no camels could pass, so that none of the searchers could find us. Finally after midday, finding no tents coming, we walked up to this place, and were received with enormous relief. Some of the searchers are not back yet. They were just going to report our strange disappearance to Cairo! They had found our camp, with the remains of our camp fire, (we kept up a huge fire all night) and that was all. It shows how easy it is in an absolutely deserted country to defy a government. Ain Kedes is a very poor place: it cannot possibly be Kadesh Barnea. At the same time the country round about may be. We will look into the matter in the next few days, while waiting the coming of photographic stuff from Cairo. After that I am going down to Akabah: I may write to you in a week or so. All perfectly well.

N.

KADESH BARNEA
Feb. 6, 1914

I sent you a letter quite lately, indeed this one is quite likely to catch it up on the way. Nothing else has happened. We are camped in a lovely valley, full of running water and trees, and standing corn. We have a pool big enough to bathe in: and the spring (from Limestone) is the only good water between Egypt & Syria. Kadesh itself is a filthy dirty little water-hole, and we more than sympathise with the disgust of the Children of Israel when they got there. On the other hand, when they got here (which is only about 5 miles from the Kadesh spring proper— they stayed 40 years. I will probably stay here another four or five days, Woolley will leave a day earlier. In the valley we have dug out the top of the walls of a fort that must be about the period of the Exodus: probably Amorite work: curiously early pottery, all very rough. Nobody had seen this place before us, so we are really rather pleased with ourselves. We got some tombs of the same time . . . but nothing in them but bones. The last tomb dug up had no head on its body! Pottery all hand-made. The Governor of Sinai (an Englishman) turned up this afternoon, and we are making him post our letters on to Egypt: so that means you will get this very soon. He has given us permission to dig in our fort, so we hope to clear one room by tomorrow. From here to Akabah is about four days or five days: I expect to get there about the 15th and if I stay four or six days in Akabah I should get up to Maan (on the Hejaz Railway) about the 23rd. That would put me into Aleppo on the 1st of March, which is our date. Can you send me two woollen sweaters, rather large (since they shrink quickly) of soft wool, fairly thick. One with collar all round, (not open in front:) the other open in front, collar elsewhere. Post them to

Aleppo, H.B.M. Consul without my name on it. Then there will be
no trouble at the customs. Nothing else wanted, I think. Carchemish
will be cold after this burning sun. Dahoum sends his salaams to
Mother & to Arnie.   N.

Ask Frank to send out to Carchemish a copy of Keats, (1/- or 1/6,
so long as it is not Everyman's) and a copy of *Sigurd*, by Morris: which
is best second-hand, from Blackwell.   N.

PETRA

Feb. 25, 1914

I am writing from here, since I cannot hope to write as I pass through
Damascus in a couple of days time, yet may be able to post a letter.
I wrote to you last from Kadesh Barnea, and thence rushed down to
Akabah, bathed, and looked about the bay, then rode up the Arabah,
across to the Egyptian frontier, and back to Mount Hor, and thence
here. Tomorrow I start for Maan, and hope next day to get a train for
Damascus. I am due in Aleppo on March 1: and don't want to be
very late.

This place is very pleasant after the waste country I have passed
through since leaving Kadesh. It is a running together of narrow stony
gorges, between great cliffs of red sandstone. And up and down the
cliffs, all over are great rock-cut tombs. Of the town ruins there is very
little remaining: it has been all washed down and buried by torrent-
bursts. But the tombs all stand undamaged, though the soft sandstone
has rubbed away in very curious patterns. The rock is a dark red, with
veins of grey and black, very narrow and regular running through it.
So you get strange effects of colour, like surface ornament, everywhere. Some of the tombs are enormous:—that is their fronts are big,
spreading over half a cliff, with only a couple of tiny rooms behind
cut out of the rock, for perhaps twenty bodies at most. Some are Greek
in style, some more Egyptian. There is almost no fine work: the beauty
of the place lies in the contrast between the green oleander and the red
of the sandstone, and in the queer way in which without plan the
tombs are dotted over the cliffs of the valleys. Also they have many
of them great bold lines of columns and architraves. It is quite cold up
here (3,000 feet high) and we have had a good deal of rain. There are

two English ladies staying here for a couple of days: nothing over much.

The Turkish Government now repents itself that it gave permission for the survey to be done: so the Kaimmakan of Akabah sent with me a lieutenant and a squad of soldiers to make sure that I did their country no harm on my march. However I learnt that their orders were not to let me out of their sight, and I took them two days afoot over such hills and wadies as did for them all. I have been camped here for two days, and they are still struggling in from all over the compass: the first was ten hours after me: and the last is still missing. It is a country of awful crags and valleys, impassible for camels, and very difficult on foot. The lieutenant has gone home.

N.

DAMASCUS
Feb. 28, 1914

Have got to Damascus at last, after a delay of two days at Maan, waiting for the train to come up from Medina. The Turks on the Hedjaz line, thinking their own genius sufficient unto the working thereof, sacked all their foreign mechanics: and now at times engines are scrapped, at times they blow themselves up, and at times they come in punctual. Mine was of the class that come late:—it was 13 hrs. behind time on a 28 hrs. journey: and I got very sick of waiting for her.

By the way the two English ladies whom I found at Wady Musa are curious people {eight words omitted} one of them, Lady Evelyn Cobbold, improved vastly. Would F. look her up at the Union, and let me know what she is? I expect she's in *Who's Who*. I borrowed a lot of money from her, since our post arrangements broke down, and I went for three weeks (and am still going), on money that I borrowed from my policeman, and from Captain Newcombe, and from Devey the Consul here, and from this lady. By their united efforts I managed to get my servants paid in Maan (all except Dahoum, who by good fortune doesn't want any) and to get a 3rd class ticket here. The train fortunately was not over-full.

Today there seems to be great excitement in Damascus, over the deaths of two Turkish aviators. They gave them a great military funeral, which nobody else but the Consuls attended, and (most

horrible desecration) buried them in Saladin's tomb. If I had been a
Consul I would have seen them burnt first.

Tomorrow is Sunday, and I want to rest and do nothing.

Then on Monday I must go up to Aleppo, and we will start digging.
I expect that there is rather a bulky post waiting me up there. Incidentally I have of course lots of money—potentially—if the Palestine
Fund pay up soon. My shortage is only a local one, and will I hope end
on Monday morning. I cannot hear what has become of Woolley. He
has never reached the Hedjaz line. Petra was marvellous. When I wrote
to you from there I thought that I had seen everything— . . . but the
finest building and the most beautiful piece of gorge was on the way
out—or in, as you like it—and it was I think the best thing I have seen
in all my goings about. Mother must try and see it some day, when she
gets stronger.

At Maan, after protestations of utmost anxiety to serve me, the local
authority arrested all my camels and camel-drivers: I took up Dahoum
and cleared out the police-patrol, and led them all defenceless to the
Government house, with their rifles under my arm: a huge jest;—
. . . Everybody apologised profusely ever after.

N.

CARCHEMISH
March 8, 1914

Well I get a cheerful letter from Father & Mother on coming back
to Aleppo: My last letter had been in the end of December, when Arnie
was being X-rayed for a damaged leg . . . the new one of Feb. 16 had
operated on him for appendicitis after an attack of measles. What
happened to him in between Xmas and Feb. 16? There is lots of time
for Mumps and Whooping cough. Please give me all possible news:
perhaps it would be better if Bob wrote, since he has the professional
touch. I presume from the fact that there have been no letters since
Feb. 16 that Arnie is going on flourishingly, however even good news
is worth writing down you know. If I left you eight weeks without
letters you would have telegraphed to every Consul in the Levant.
I return two letters of Will's, which came with the December letters.
I was in the Akaba district, and couldn't send off letters, since the
government was much against us. They refused even to send or deliver

telegrams for us. From Damascus I ran up to Aleppo by the midnight train, and stayed only two days in Aleppo: there was nothing to buy or see in the town, and it was very wet and muddy. This place is wet also, though only showers between sun-shine, and owing to the fact that our house is on the high-land the ground round about is always dry: also it is all beautiful green grass, and that colour is a pleasure after the desert of Sinai's continual brown and yellow. I wish we were digging Petra though.

We have a short season this year:—only a little money: we are not digging yet, since we have to wait a new permission from Constantinople. I expect in a couple of days time it will come. I got from you in Aleppo a pile of little books of Morris' . . . which is a pleasure. More to follow I fancy.

Mr. Hogarth comes out shortly: he has raised a new grant for the digging, and is coming out to consult with us on the spot. Today I am asphalting the roofs of the kitchen & store-rooms which were leaky.

The Hoja & Dahoum have brought up for us three or four old carpets that were in the houses of their relations. I'll take one or two of them, I fancy, since they are extremely cheap, and also beautiful. One in particular, a very bright piece of colour, you will enjoy in your room. Give away the long thin one that came last. Keep the little square one: it is valuable.

N.

CARCHEMISH
March 8, 1914

You mentioned in a letter I got in Sinai a new wax, which set hard: you had forgotten the name, but thought you could get some. Will you have a try, and send out a little by post here: white would be the best colour. It might be invaluable for cylinder seals, to roll them out on: or for little moulds. I expect the stuff can come by post.

N.

Enclosed photo is of our workmen dancing: it needs enlargement to be really good.

N.

DEAR WILL

I have been all round the Turk–Egypt frontier. . . . Gaza–Akaba in the last two months, and did no writing. I'm not going to write to-day either.

I decided in the end to send the red rug Busrawi gave you to England. It has not gone yet, but will go off with some others I have in a few weeks. Mother will probably like it, since it is very new and strong, very glossy and very bright. To me the mixture of red and orange is too hot. Still it's not a bad piece.

I have bought several more locally but nothing old . . . and no more Greek or Roman stuff. {Six lines omitted.}

You interested me greatly in your account of the cloth of gold. Could you send me a little piece of the best quality made? I want it to compare with the Aleppo & Baghdad fabrics. Any of your Indian family people would know what was best. There are no carpets in India . . . and their wall hangings are usually stamped with yellow figures of tigers ramping.

Lately we have discovered beaten silver work (old . . .) in the private houses in Aleppo: coffee pots and drinking cups and basins: some of it very good . . . and some of it very cheap. I hope to buy half a dozen of the decent things. Hoja and Dahoum send their salaams to you. Tell Young if you see him that he owes Busrawi a bamboo cudgel.

Your translation of Meleager was exceeding good: though I don't like translating him: his matter is not separable from his form.

N.

We began work today at last, after a most wearisome delay. The Museums between them had muddled the affair of our new permit, and so we couldn't do anything new. As a matter of fact we spent our time in putting up a great many of the large sculptures that had fallen out of place in the period succeeding the destruction by Nebuchadnezzar. So that the time wasn't at all wasted. I got some letters from you the other day: Arnie better, which is as well to know. Dahoum offers him his consolations: and wants to send him a lot of jackal skins. I don't know what the Customs will say to a consignment of furs: however I'll send them (the boy got them in Gaza) on spec. There are about twenty or so, I think. Arnie & yourself can make coats of them. Will's carpet is still in Aleppo. I cannot send it yet; Akras lost the last chance of sending it, when stuff went down to Alexandretta from us . . . and it isn't worth while sending it alone on a mule. I got from you the other day a volume of Keats and a *Sigurd*. Both very excellent works. The article in the I.L.N. {*Illustrated London News*} and letters by Mr. Hogarth have between them extracted enough money from the former anonymous donor to carry on the digs here for five years. So that we are preparing ourselves and our house for a long stay: water-proofing the roofs with asphalt, cementing floors, getting a couple of tables and chairs and table-cloths and things: the delay in the permit allowed of most of these things. Nothing else of interest:

N.

CARCHEMISH
March 27, 1914

A lot of letters from Oxford lately, including one from late Miss Jane. Dr. Cowley of the Bodleian also, we expect here tomorrow: Mr. Hogarth is due next week. Altogether, a very local gathering. Of news:—very little. We started work on the 21st and have been since blasting away a great Roman cement foundation to clear between our digs and the Euphrates. The Altounyans came today: Dr. & Miss . . . the Fontanas left this afternoon. We had also some rather amusing American ladies for a week end and a medical missionary from Aintab and his wife. Before the digs the German consul stayed a night, and the Austrian & Italian are coming as soon as we are free. You see, the house isn't really a large one, and we cannot handle many people at a time: besides it wouldn't do to have all sorts of people together. The Austrian consul, who is a very good designer, has made us for 24/- each some very fine armchairs in black wood and buff leather cushions: they are built on very straight lines, and go very well with the colours of our wall-hangings. Also, of course, our floor is jet-black. Did I tell you of the box I bought in Aleppo, of chestnut wood, decorated with corner pieces and lock-plate in pierced bronze. It is about six feet long and two feet square, with very handsome handles in heavy metal. It weighs rather more than a porter can carry! The old sheikh of Dahoum's village brought me his grandfather's carpet the other day, as a present. It is only a prayer-carpet, about five feet long, but very beautiful. No other acquisitions lately.

The Railway company here has just had a strike of workmen: so we lifted from them a long piece of line and a number of light trucks, and carried them into our fortress. We have them now all in use, and as a consequence are working much faster than usual. As we tell them the longer their troubles last the better we will be pleased. Our position against them has been greatly improved of late, for the German consul employed us officially to make peace for him on the Company's behalf, between the engineers and the Kurds. We made the Company pay damages to Busrawi, and got from him guarantees of no further violence on his side.

We haven't found anything as yet, but we have managed to piece together half of a great lion out of a mass of fragments of our first two years: the beast must have been very interesting, since he has a cuneiform inscription down his back. If we can only fit a Hittite inscription down his middle we will have a beautiful bilingual: however as yet the head, shoulder and body of the lion to the hinder quarters are missing: and all the rest is battered out of shape: nobody but ourselves would know what it was. However we have found for it its old place in the digs, though no piece was found anywhere near about: it stood on our great staircase, and has been magnificent.

Would you like a long string of Roman amethysts? They are cheap in this country, where the Romans stayed so long, and not ugly, as stones go. We hope to get our Sinai book published at midsummer: have written about half of it already between us. It will be very dull. I went to Akaba, & Woolley to the Dead Sea, in the hopes of covering more of the country. We neither of us found anything. I paid my ladies {met at Wady Musa} their debts in Damascus: I had to borrow a note from the other one also, (a Lady J. Legge) to square matters: Woolley and I are now trying to do accounts. The carpet is still in Aleppo. Offer my regards to Arnie, tell him I was offered £20 for my canoe yesterday: and refused it. We bring flowers from Mesopotamia in it twice a week. Heard from Will the other day. No books from Mrs. Rieder lately. Expect to stay six weeks or more in England this summer: but will be at work in the Bodleian on "Sinai" mostly. Dahoum sends Arnie his congraulations: his brother has just been married, which has cost him a lot of money. Otherwise all is peace.

N.

BARON'S HOTEL, ALEPPO
1 *April* 1914

Another letter from this beautiful hotel, whose face you must be getting to know by heart. I got a letter from Father the other day, in which mention was made of Arnie's getting better: and of Mr. Hogarth's coming out. He got to Carchemish yesterday, and I saw him at the station. No time to say anything to him. I came down here for money, and tomorrow I am going back. Any news? Well, only our visitors. The Altounyans, Fowles, and Cowleys. Dr. Altounyan is the best carpet authority in Aleppo. He priced our sitting room at about £350 in rugs. Which is not bad, for nearly half of them are mine . . . not the best one though. You will next year have as good a floor as Mr. Hogarth . . . which means the best in Oxford.

The Cowleys turned up, and Busrawi sent them a sack of truffles, a lamb and a horse-load of clotted cream in copper tanks, and of cream cheese. They were amused exceedingly by the patriarchal character of the gifts. We have got them also Busrawi's muscians, to give them Kurd songs. Some of which are rather wonderful. It is so quaint to have Cowley {Bodley's Librarian} here looking as exact as he does in Oxford. Mrs. Cowley is quite pleasant.

We have received the thanks of the Turkish Government for settling the Kurd-German dispute of last week.

You asked once about milk & sugar basins. Payne said he would and could get them when I wished. I did not order them, being a little short of money: even the teapot was not cheap! Next summer perhaps. I got yesterday three books from Mrs. Rieder, sent up from Sinai: also a letter from you, about measles. Am glad the Jesus roof is to be opened. It would have been criminal to have missed the chance of the fire. Posts have lately been irregular, since the Alexandretta mail has been twice plundered by Turks. I got a letter from Miss Jane: nothing said.

About Akaba . . . Captain Newcombe was actually turned out of the province . . . sent across the frontier under escort . . . a few days after I left. So I only got off just in time. If I had been sent back into Egypt it would have meant a deal of trouble and delay. Incidentally it would have troubled the Turks. There is no news of Miss Holmes in Syria: she is said to be on a lecturing tour in the United States.

Dinner time . . . I have to go over to the Consulate tonight.

N.

CARCHEMISH
April 20, 1914

Mr. Hogarth went yesterday, and only the Fontanas and their children and nurse are left . . . so that I have a little more time. We have had more visitors than discoveries lately. I told you of the Cowleys, and of Professor Porter of Beyrout. A little later we had Dr. Mackinnon of Damascus, and two Anglo-Indians: also four or five of the Americans from Beyrout came up for a couple of nights. We were a little put to it to hold them all in the house: since of course Mr. Hogarth had his room, and the Fontanas are a party of six, and we are building a new room or two on the house as well. So we are in a muddle everywhere. We are not trying to find antiquities much this year . . . only preparing for future work.

Your last letter mentioned a telegram about the little row here in *The Times* . . . There was a dispute about wages, and some Kurds threw stones at a Circassian who was trying to kick them out of the office. And then the Circassian shot a man, and all the other Kurds near by threw stones at him . . . then three or four people fired from the German side, and half a dozen of the Kurds who had revolvers emptied them, and then ran away. The one Kurd was killed, no one else at all hurt: the Company has paid compensation to his relations, and the whole thing is over. The Company tried to make a great fuss of the affair, but failed hopelessly . . . because it was a mere trifle. Post goes now.

N.

CARCHEMISH
23 *April* 1914

No reason at all why I should write to you tonight: there is no news and no prospect of any. Mr. Hogarth left three or four days ago, and the consul and his people yesterday. Today we have three American ladies from Aintab:—but they leave tomorrow, so that doesn't much matter. Your sweaters came a week ago. They were stolen from the post near the Beilan hills, and rescued with difficulty. Many thanks. You mentioned once a new book, a grammar of Kermanji (Kurdish). I want a copy very badly. Please order and send out by book-post. You and Arnie seem to have been at Bruges a few weeks ago. I'm glad you are moving about:—but you know I don't think that I will ever travel in the West again: one cannot tell, of course, but this part out here is worth a million of the rest. The Arabs are so different from ourselves.

I wonder what there is to say. The river is in flood, and is tearing away the staging of the bridge-builders in great gobbets. The roaring of it and an occasional crash is filling all this house tonight, as there is no wind to listen to. I was across in Mesopotamia today, looking at a village whose buying is under consideration. The English and Austrian Consuls, with the head of the liquorice business, have proposed to us a confederation for the buying of a Euphrates village . . . and we suggest one called Beiluna just over the river from Dahoum's village. It is quite small, only three or four square miles, but very good land, and quite undeveloped. Much of it is uncultivated since Roman times. The flowers are now out over the plain, for today is our first sunny day after a week or so of rain . . . and the whole place looks fresh and proper. I am afraid there has been delay in the sending off of Arnie's jackal skins: the V-Consul at Gaza has been ill, and we have not been able to get anything out of him for weeks. We cannot even close the accounts for the P.E.F. whose book we are still writing in spare moments. Is there anything you want from Syria this year? You might say in your next letter, since I will be coming back a little after that. We have not over much left in wages this year. It has been a very expensive season. Mr. Hogarth has bought from me two carpets I didn't want, and two others I did. So that is quite satisfactory. There are all those needed for your room left over.   N.

CARCHEMISH

May 4, 1914

No news as yet: last week we found a good relief inscription of about 400 characters, broken but quite a nice piece. Also a column in basalt with a large linear inscription down the front: good style, but short. These are the first monuments found this year.

We also got a huge god-head, about two feet high, in bad style, and much damaged: many cylinder seals, and best of all a bronze greave, in very good condition, of a Hittite soldier. I think this is one of the most interesting things of all found in Carchemish. It came out in the West town gate, which seems well preserved. We have been digging it since Mr. Hogarth went away.

No news other. We had a number of visitors—Wainwright of Egypt for ten days, a digger who thought of coming here permanently once, but now cannot: and two majors from the Gordon Highlanders, one of whom was quite pleasant. In the last two months we have been alone to dinner just four times.

Our new sitting room is now finished: quite a pleasant room. We intend it mainly as a place to put visitors in when we want peace. Also it will do for the other people (architects and otherwise) threatened for next season. No more news of your skins. I have written again to Gaza about them. One of the troubles of this country is the delays of action when one is not there oneself.

N.

CARCHEMISH
May 8, 1914

Today being Friday, everything is at peace except ourselves, and that is because to our misfortune all the people of the bridge and railway make holiday, and come around to see our latest things. It a little wearies us: however at times we have amusing visitors. Since last writing to you I think the Graceys and their children are our only house-guests. They only stayed one night passing through, so since Wainwright left we had had two evenings with no-one but ourselves in the house. It does feel so curiously quiet.

We found a sculpture of a demon with horns and bull's legs this week, and a lot of little things of interest such as cylinder seals and the like. We have found a large room with good stone pavement and are clearing it, with hopes. I am sending you with this some photos. of the sitting room:—the old one, that is. It is of it in its winter dress, with the mosaic covered by Arab tenting, and its cupboards carpet-filled. Only the lighting of the room is very bad for photography, since there is only a door and a little window beside it, and two small windows at the end of the room. So the place is full of cross-lights, which however beautiful to look at, are not much use in photography. I have scribbled notes on the back of these prints, behind the things worth looking at, and I don't think its worth while saying anything else about the stuff. We have enlarged the house a good deal this year:—another sitting room and a huge antika store, and a stable and charcoal store . . . and wash-house. So I will take another photo of it later on and bring a print back with me. It is now about as long as to the top of the {Polstead} road from your gate, and a little wider than the space between the houses. I heard from Will the other day . . . and from you again from Ostend. You ask again about the railway row, which was about the 20th of March, not the 30th. We settled it at the request of the German consul, by paying the relations of the dead Kurd £70 in blood-money and giving a tip to Busrawi for future good-conduct. It was a very small row—any number of worse ones pass unnoticed every week —only by some ill chance it got into the newspapers. Stupid nonsense: we refused decorations from the Turkish Gov. They are such expensive things! I want a copy of that Kurdish Grammar: buy it please and keep it for me. No other news: N.

CARCHEMISH
May 8, 1914

I think perhaps, there being nothing to do, that I will write to you again. Today is Friday, and we have taken things very easily; enclosed are a couple of prints of our sitting room from each end: the ink pot please note as an incense-burner from a mosque in Aleppo . . . the flower vase next it on the table is Hittite and Bronze Age: on a little side table of a Greek column, and a Byzantine hearth-stone are a late Hittite stone bowl (usually full of roses, but now with oranges inside: and a three-legged cooking pot, early Hittite, with daisies inside. There is a large chest in the end of the room near the little window, Aleppo work, carved with human figures, and birds and vines, with lion-feet: and the tiles of the fire-place are Damascus and Aleppo.

In the other photo, showing the door, you can see the Persian box I got at Alexandretta, with a glazed Turkish water-pot on top, and in the window-sill, a Roman water jug, with Arabic copper drinking cup: and I fancy that a Phœnician three legged basalt mortar is on a little table by the window, with forget-me-nots inside it, growing. The Morris tapestry is very dark in the photo: it in reality looks most wonderfully well. It always amuses me when our European visitors (after seeing some priceless Arabic textiles we have) walk up to the tapestry with a gasp, and say "Oh, what is that marvellous stuff?" It is such a satisfaction to say that they sell it in Oxford street at so much a yard.

Incidentally, I have for you a quilt of old Aleppo weave, in silver and coloured silks: old, and now becoming rare, for they burn them all to get out the metal, when they tarnish.

These photographs enclosed make our room look very small: really it is quite a fair size, and well lighted, but the small windows throw very fierce lights on to the whitewashed walls, & bury all the rest in shadows. You seem interested in the history of your first cheque: it was handed (in its letter of course!) to a transport director of the Railway for delivery to us, and he kept it and other letters in his hands for two weeks before delivering them. Got a letter from Mrs. Rieder and a book & some papers lately: I'll acknowledge them in a few weeks time.

Today there was a gale from the S. so we put a mast and sail on the canoe and went splashing. Rather amusing, and it had the usual object: we went to the island, & uprooted armfuls of daisies, & put them in buckets in the house: daisies have such a smell that they keep off flies. No news, & nothing probable.

N.

CARCHEMISH
May 17, 1914

Another Friday, and therefore another letter, with the old difficulty of a life too peaceful for tidings. Few visitors of late thank goodness:— all the last two batches Americans:—but Captain Newcombe and his Sub. Greig expected now every day. I have wired congratulations to Mr. Jane, and will bring home amongst the rugs one that will do for him if his engagement results in anything.

Today and yesterday were warm and sunny: as there has been so little new stuff in the diggings coming out I have been filling up gaps in the photography of the old . . . however that doesn't interest you. Today of course was workless: in the morning we slept later than usual, and then I riveted up a set of points on our light railway till midday. In the afternoon read a little, measured up a building, worked at the plastering of a broken relief, bathed, and shot a little at 200 yds. Now I ought to be reading, but am not.

Our new room we have made rather pleasant, with a few rugs on the walls, a dado of hemp-sticks, and curtains of red leather:—walls whitened with powdered chalk:—It is a long room, about 35 feet long, but not very wide. It is impossible in this country to make a very wide room, since the roof-poles are not strong enough to cross a large span. I have also laid out for myself a sitting room:—in protection against rumours of third hands next season.

I wish I could think of something interesting—no news of your furs by the way— Your bicycle has met with many misfortunes. It has run into all sorts of people and things, and many parts of it have been broken and bent. But it still runs quite gaily, with innumerable punctures. I am to bring it new tyres in the Autumn. Dahoum has a passion for high speeds, and this country and its roads are not yet educated thereto. However it is a very useful thing, and we use it a lot in sending up to the station etc. . . . He only uses it between the home villages: has done no touring yet. Please get me a copy of that Kurdish grammar published lately.   N.

Should start back about June 10: and reach England about June 22.

CARCHEMISH
June 1, 1914

This is just a scrawl, to say that we stop work on Thursday next, and no long time later will start back. I have to go to Stamboul, and spend a couple of days there:—which will require time in the getting back: but you may look for me about the 25th or so. I may telegraph if I am much before or behind that time:—but I think not.   N.

Wax arrived yesterday, & I used it all today—it worked admirably.

CARCHEMISH
2 June 1914

We stop work tomorrow and are going to leave here very shortly.
I am not going to Constantinople I expect, or at any rate not yet, but
down to Baghdad first and down the Gulf to Bahrein, and so round by
Egypt. A Captain Noel is boating from us down the Euphrates, and I
have seized the opportunity of going with him to halve the expense of
seeing Baghdad. It is good fortune in a way, though I am sorry in
another, for it will delay me another fortnight or so. I expect to be
back some time in the first half of July. Am glad you got that Kurdish
Grammar. Soam is a very good man.

By the way a London firm are going to send you a number of drills
with a bill. Please keep them for me.　　　　　　　　　　N.

{LONDON}
15/11/14

DEAR WILL

I am going out to Egypt probably, at the end of this week, on
special service. The Turks may do something in that direction, so if I
were you I'd stay either there or in India. . . . In Belgium there is less
scope for untrained people.

If Egypt falls, there will be trouble all through the East. I notice that
you expected trouble in Delhi, if Turkey came in . . . but I think there
won't be any unless some great man starts out on the warpath . . .
and such people as the Nizam of Hyderabad & the Agha Khan (if he is
really anybody great) know about as much of Turkish misrule as we
do. The old Col. Nizim el Mulk, when I saw him was most splendidly
anti-Turk.

Keep your eye on Afghanistan . . . there may be trouble there,
though the Amir is out with a good deal of his army.

The Khedive is coming out against us . . . but declines with thanks.

Nothing doing, I fancy either in the Caucasus or in Sinai till spring
. . . hope not, since I want time to look round & polish up my Bedouin
dialects.

I'll give you an address in Egypt when I get out there (long sea!) . . .
Don't do anything in a hurry.　　　　　　　　　　N.

CAIRO

21 *January* 1915

Address

INTELLIGENCE DEPARTMENT
CAIRO

I hear from home that you are attaching yourself to some regiment
in India: I wish you had been in Egypt, though there isn't any job I can
actually offer you, since you cannot speak Arabic. Can't you get on a
regiment that will come here later? This show in Egypt will be rather
a pleasant one I hope. Turkey is crumbling fast.

More news when I next write. For the last 6 weeks I have been stuck
in Cairo, in the office from morning to night, making sense of the news
brought to us, and asking for more. Also writing little geographical
essays. It doesn't sound exciting, but it has been far and away the best
job going in Egypt these few weeks. The people at the Pyramids or on
the Canal have had a very dull time.

Not much news from home: things seem to be moving quietly
enough, over there.

Belgium has become a very unpleasant place. I don't want to go
back there now!

G. is married, & settled down to a comparative peace. His pan-
Ottoman feelings must be now much encouraged—but so long as
things go quietly his sort won't have much scope.

I expect Young is in the Persian Gulf by now, talking Arabic &
Persian, & doing great things. If not salaam him from me.

N.

INTELLIGENCE OFFICE
CAIRO
12/2/15

Well, here goes for another empty letter: my bicycle is here: very
many thanks for getting it out so quickly: I wish the W.O. would send
out maps equally promptly. You ask about the other people in the
Office: well Newcombe and Woolley you have heard of. There is
Hough ex-consul at Jaffa . . . pleasant and nothing more: there is
Lloyd, an M.P. (I should think probably Conservative, but you never
know) who is a director of a bank, and used to be Attaché at Con-

stantinople. He is Welsh, but sorry for it: small, dark, very amusing . . . speaks Turkish well, and French, German & Italian: some Spanish, Arabic & Hindustani . . . also Russian. He is quite pleasant, but exceedingly noisy.

Then there is Aubrey Herbert, who is a joke, but a very nice one: he is too short-sighted to read or recognise anyone: speaks Turkish well, Albanian, French, Italian, Arabic, German . . . was for a time chairman of the Balkan League, of the Committee of Union and Progress, and of the Albanian Revolution Committee. He fought through the Yemen wars, and the Balkan wars with the Turks, & is friends with them all. Then there is Père Jaussen, a French Dominican monk, of Jerusalem. He speaks Arabic wonderfully well, and preceded us in wanderings in Sinai. We praise his work very highly in the *Wilderness of Zin*. He is very amusing, & very clever: and very useful as interpreter. . . .

There is also Graves *The Times* correspondent, and very learned in the Turkish army organisation. I think that is about all. We meet very few other people, except officers on business . . . see a good deal of them, from General Maxwell downwards. He is a very queer person: almost weirdly good-natured, very cheerful, with a mysterious gift of prophesying what will happen, and a marvellous carelessness about what might happen. There couldn't be a better person to command in Egypt. He takes the whole job as a splendid joke.

The Turks are off for the time being. The troops that attacked us last week were from Smyrna (Turks) and from Nablous & Jerusalem & Gaza: there were no men from Aleppo, and very few from Damascus: our prisoners are very comfortable, and very content here: when they have been a few weeks in idleness they will be less pleased. Lady Evelyn Cobbold turned up, on her usual winter visit to Egypt. . . . I am to have dinner with her tonight.

Dr. Mackinnon {Medical Missionary of Damascus} is here: he is doing medical work, and Dr. Scrimgeour of Nazareth is looking after the prisoners: Cox {Army banker} is being paid 15/– a day for me: so I hope that my account there will be clear: There are no carpets in Cairo that I want to buy: you don't get good ones under £50 here: so don't expect anything at present . . . perhaps when I get back to Carchemish?

N.

MILITARY INTELLIGENCE OFFICE
CAIRO
20.2.15

The Seven Golden Odes of Pagan Arabia or *The Moallakat*: translated by Lady Anne Blunt, & put into English verse by Wilfred Scawen Blunt: published at the Chiswick Press 5/- in 1904 probably. Can you get me this book? I expect it is out of print:—but if so Blackwell would get a copy very easily, as it is a well known book. If you get it, please send it out to Intelligence Department, W.O. as above. No news this week: we sit still, & maintain an appearance of miserly inactivity: The hotel cost 10/- a day, which is not dear for Cairo . . . and all of us & all General Maxwell's staff are living here so as to be available by telephone at any time: we have our private wire to the hotel. We have all to stay here & that is why they pay us £400 a year . . . or a little less, as it seems to work out. I heard from Will, who is consumed with a wild patriotism. I am afraid that I don't feel strongly enough. So far as Syria is concerned it is France & not Turkey that is the enemy . . . but I wish I could give it to Germany in some way, for the shameless way in which she dragged Turkey into the war. I don't think any nation has ever done in high politics anything quite so . . . {the last word is not legible}. I have written to Mrs. Rieder. Campbell Thompson has gone to the Persian Gulf.

It is no use my sending you news: only I don't think things are going well: it seems to me that attention is so fixed on the Belgian front that our interests in the East are being sacrificed. It will go against us very heavily some day.

Could you see if Stanford, (Long Acre) can sell you a map of North Syria, by Blankenhorn: it is about 20 years old, but very good: cost about — 10. —. If you can get a copy, please post it out to me, folded up.

Arnie did not ask me for any postcards I think . . . tell him to write again. I will be in Egypt some time yet.   N.

MILITARY INTELLIGENCE OFFICE
CAIRO
4.6.15

I haven't written since I got your wire as I was waiting for details. Today I got Father's two letters. They are very comfortable reading:—

and I hope that when I die there will be nothing more to regret. The only thing I feel a little is, that there was no need surely to go into mourning for him? I cannot see any cause at all—in any case to die for one's country is a sort of privilege: Mother & you will find it more painful & harder to live for it, than he did to die: but I think that at this time it is one's duty to show no signs that would distress others: and to appear bereaved is surely under this condemnation.

So please, keep a brave face to the world: we cannot all go fighting: but we can do that, which is in the same kind.

N.

MILITARY INTELLIGENCE OFFICE
CAIRO
{Not dated}

POOR DEAR MOTHER

I got your letter this morning, & it has grieved me very much. You will never never understand any of us after we are grown up a little. Don't you ever feel that we love you without our telling you so? —I feel such a contemptible worm for having to write this way about things. If you only knew that if one thinks deeply about anything one would rather die than say anything about it. You know men do nearly all die laughing, because they know death is very terrible, & a thing to be forgotten till after it has come.

There, put that aside, & bear a brave face to the world about Frank. In a time of such fearful stress in our country it is one's duty to watch very carefully lest one of the weaker ones be offended: and you know we were always the stronger, & if they see you broken down they will all grow fearful about their ones at the front.

Frank's last letter is a very fine one, & leaves no regret behind it.

Out here we do nothing. There is an official inertia against which one is very powerless. But I don't think we are going to have to wait much longer.

I didn't go to say good-bye to Frank because he would rather I didn't, & I knew there was little chance of my seeing him again; in which case we were better without a parting.

T.E.L.

MILITARY INTELLIGENCE OFFICE
CAIRO
16.6.15

Well, here's another week gone, & nothing has happened or is happening, except an occasional Turkish feint on the canal: it's very hot here, with a Khamsin blowing so that we have to keep all doors and windows shut. The shade temperature outside the office is 115° just now. Yesterday was 112°, but it cools down to 95° or 100° at night; it has gone up to 117° now: it must really be rather like the Persian Gulf, and yet it doesn't feel at all oppressive.

We are very busy just now. I don't really know what with: there is a lot of telegraphing to do, in cipher, which takes a long time—and we have other work, & besides I have 6 maps in hand being drawn.

Wainwright passed through yesterday, going to England. He had been digging in Egypt for some weeks.

Tell Arnie to get out Collignon's book on Greek sculpture. There is a beautiful frontispiece of a head in the Louvre.

T.E.L.

MILITARY INTELLIGENCE OFFICE
CAIRO
23.6.15

I got a letter yesterday asking for more details of what I am doing. Well, drawing, & overseeing the drawing of maps: overseeing printing & packing of same: sitting in an office coding and decoding telegrams, interviewing prisoners, writing reports, & giving information from 9 a.m. till 7 p.m. After that feed and read, & then go to bed. I'm sick of pens, ink & paper: & have no wish ever to send off another telegram. We do daily wires to Athens, Gallipoli, & Petrograd: & receive five times what we send, all in cypher, which is slow work, though we have a good staff dealing with them. Newcombe, one Macdonnell and myself are Intelligence, Captain Cosens, Lord Anglesey, Lord Hartington & Prince Alexander of Battenburg do the ciphering & deciphering with us: that's all we are:—with a Colonel Clayton who does Egyptian Foreign Politics in command of us.

We do no internal work: have nothing to do with Egyptians, or police or anything of that sort. That's all done by the Ministry of the

Interior. We have only war work:—European Turkey, Asia Minor, Syria, Mesopotamia, Arabia, Sinai, & Tripoli:—we all dabble in them all. One learns a lot of geography, some people's names, & little else.

The Dardanelles show is looking up a little. If they please it will not take much longer now. But it's a great question what their intentions are. I'm dreading the end of it, as no one can guess what will happen afterwards. No news from Syria: the country is quite at peace.

N.

Hope Bob gets through.

N.

Military Intelligence Office
Cairo
3.7.15

There is nothing happening here except great talk, and the continual supply of all sorts of things to the Mediterranean Expedition. It seems to me that that particular job is nearly finished. No news from Syria that matters. Most of the Syrian troops are in Adrianople watching the Bulgars. Syria itself is very quiet; corn cheaper than it has ever been, and sugar and paraffin unobtainable. No coal; Gold is plentiful in the country, & the Government has not ventured to issue notes. The young men have nearly all gone on military service. Oppenheim went to Jerablus on the 15th. I fancy not with good intentions. Everything here very hot and unpleasant. Map-total is now 140,000, and still growing. I'd like Will's job of teaching musketry better than this continual weariness of bricks without straw!

N.

Cairo
27.7.15

Mr. Hogarth turned up yesterday without warning. He will take over the Anatolian section of our office on the spot: we hope that he will be able to stay here for a bit. Though I suppose he must eventually go to the Dardanelles. He seems very fit: I have hardly spoken to him yet.

There is of course, nothing happening here, or likely to happen. Reports, & ciphering & drawing maps all day. The Dardanelles show will end soon:—Syria is quite quiet, though the Armenian villages in the North have been broken up, & the people scattered to various districts. No massacres, however, as yet. I can't think of anything else to say:—The hot weather, as Father is interested in it, will end at the end of September. It's not very hot now—and besides I am never more than about 5 minutes in the open air.

MILITARY INTELLIGENCE OFFICE
CAIRO
19.8.15

This is only a scribble. I've just got back, & there is a post going. Athens was very hot, & glare of sun very bad. Otherwise not dull. I was in office there from 9 a.m. (when shops opened) till 7 p.m. (when shops shut): so I bought nothing, & saw nothing:—except the Acropolis from the window. Letter by next post: I have a great lot to do today.

N.

MILITARY INTELLIGENCE OFFICE
CAIRO
31.8.15

I'm going to write only a little, as Macdonnell has gone to the Dardanelles on a visit, Newcombe has been appointed to a R.E. Company there, & leaves on Friday, & everybody is working hard to clear things up for his successor, who is a Colonel Parker, nephew of Lord Kitchener's, and an authority on Sinai and not much else. In any case there is nothing to write about. Jimmy Strong turned up about 6.30 one night, but I only saw him for a few minutes. He looked very well:

Today is Mother's birthday, which is why I am writing: I believe there is a post out also. For the next one there will probably be peace. I gathered from Father's letter that you had nearly all of you, been unwell. I hope it was not really serious? They say that the weather has been very bad in England lately. Salute Arnie from me. Ask him to search at Blackwell's for a copy of *The Twilight of the Gods* by Richard Garnett, & if it's not dear, to send it me. The book must be out of print long ago, but is probably common.

The Dardanelles expedition wasted a great chance it got. I don't like the look of things up there: and the worst is, it was such an easy business till we blundered. We are two to one there, as compared with the Turkish forces, & they have no more trained troops to send.   N.

I'm not going to write much now, as I have a trifle of malaria, & a lot of people are jabbering away a few yards off. The weather is now changing very fast. At midday it is warm, like an ordinary summer day in England, and at night it gets cold. That I think is probably why the fever caught me. However I haven't had any for a year now, so there is not very much harm in it. I hear from your letters (a bunch of about 3 weeks supply came yesterday) that you are all well again, & that Arnie is going back to school. That will seem odd for him, but he will be comforted by the expectation of a new disease to interrupt him once more. It's hardly worth trying to go on, is it? I find I have a balance at Cox's, of some £60 or £70 so far as I can reckon it out. Would it be any use to you? I cannot well draw on it here, as you lose a lot in exchange, so I have a local account on which I live: therefore the other one isn't really any use to me.

Mr. Hogarth is in Athens just now. He worked in the office here for 6 weeks or so. I expect he'll be back some time or other. The Gallipoli business is dragging, & will go on dragging, till somebody who knows his mind interferes. It's been very badly done so far.

No news of Syria: I'm afraid a lot of men from our neighbourhood have gone to Gallipoli lately.   N.

I haven't anything to do:—or rather I have a lot which I am not going to do;—so I'm going to write to you. It's very difficult to do that, for all one's work here is writing, & I have a nausea of it. There seems to be very little to write about. I go to the office every morning, run out to Giza to the Survey Department usually for an hour or so

before midday, and go back to the office again after lunch till about
6 p.m. I knock off then, because it is almost dark, & I want to ride home
without lighting up. There is usually a little to do there before dinner,
& after dinner telegrams in cypher come in from Medforce or Athens,
or Russia or London or India at any hour of the night. Then at 6 a.m.
the messenger from Alexandria turns up, with papers from the Residency:—and that is the next day's work, which is exactly like to-day's.
The work consists in finding out where the Turkish army is:—that is,
to know at any moment where each of the 136 regiments is: how many
men are in each, who commands it, and what artillery is round about
it. Then we have to tell anybody who wants to know what any place
in Turkey is like: what the landing places are, what the roads are like,
if the people are friendly or not, and how long it would take to get
reinforcements there. Then we have to try & find out what is happening politically in the interior of the country, & how the harvests are,
& who are the local governors, and things like that. There are other
things also. At present I'm making a directory (a sort of {one word not
legible here}) of the tribes of N. Arabia: and publish a little daily paper
for the knowledge of Generals, India, Medforce, Aden and the Home
Department, in which we tell them what we think they ought to know.
Sometimes they don't agree with us. In addition I have maps to settle:
not the actual drawing, of course, but the style of it, the colours to be
used, & what is to be put in or left out. That is the most interesting part
of the work, though I am very fond of my army. Following it about
is like making a map of the movements of a fly before breakfast. All
our work is to do with Turkey. We never touch any other part of the
world: & Egypt never comes into our horizon at all {five words
omitted}:—which is as well. . . . That's all, for I'm going down to
headquarters to see Colonel Parker.   N.

                          MILITARY INTELLIGENCE OFFICE
                                          CAIRO
                                     {Not dated}

Another letter as there is nothing at all doing, & no hope of it. . . .
It's getting hot again: we had a week's cool weather about 92°–95°.
Today it's up to 105° again. However it affects one very little. I haven't
finished any of my maps—except the Gallipoli one, and that I cannot

boast about very much. The machines ran for 56 hours doing it, and they had to have electric fans all round the motor to keep it cool!

We are sending Dowson, head of the Survey Department up to Gallipoli to see the staff, & try and settle some of our differences. I don't think it is very interesting up there.

Did I tell you the wooden bridge at Jerablus had been washed out? The stone and iron one has been damaged also. Good business: ——
I haven't anything else to say. Only there is a post going, that's all.

N.

{CAIRO}
19.10.15

Another empty letter: I really don't know what to write about: there hasn't as a matter of fact, been anything to write about for months. No. I'll send you a copy of my new map of Gallipoli. It's for sale here, & probably the W. O. will publish it at home: but not for a little time, as they have to make the plates by photography. There are 12 printings, & they have not been all very good.

Woolley is beginning to walk about again: on crutches that is. He has been a long time ill: it was a compound fracture. Many thanks for the book by Garnett. I wonder what Arnie thought of it? I don't think I require anything for the winter:—except more clothes which I will get here.

The Near East is all sitting quiet, watching affairs in Salonika: when that is concluded, it will all start in again. There is going to be rather a busy winter in the Levant. I am pleased on the whole with things. They have gone against us so far that our govt. has become more reasonable, and the final settlement out here, though it will take long, will I think, be very satisfactory. We have to thank our failures for that: and to me, they are worth it.

N.

GENERAL HEADQUARTERS
THE FORCE IN EGYPT
CAIRO

25.12.15

I'm writing just a few words this morning, because it has surprised me by being Christmas day. I'm afraid that for you it will be no very happy day; however you have still Bob and Arnie left at home, which is far more than many people can have. Look forward all the time. Everything here is as usual, only we had a shower of rain yesterday, and it has been cool lately. I am now living in the Savoy, which is the new Headquarters: the staff has been somewhat increased, and we have more to do: most of it is fiddling little work, but some of it is interesting.

Address me Intelligence Section G.H.Q. Cairo, as before. I must knock off now as a lot of people are waiting for me.   N.

{Probably CAIRO} 28.12.15

No time to write anything this week. We are just in the midst of changing our office for the third time: horrible din, & deadly confusion of papers.

Newcombe turned up yesterday: he is not coming into the office again though, but stationed on Canal. Perfect peace here, except on the West, where there is a little war going on: not serious. Very busy.

T.E.L.

GENERAL STAFF—INTELLIGENCE SECTION.   GENERAL HEADQUARTERS
                                            THE FORCE IN EGYPT
                                                CAIRO
                                              4.i.16

Another blank week. Reconstruction of Staff here is still going on. The latest idea is to turn us all out in favour of the Medforce Staff. We'll see. In any case I expect now to stay here for a time at least. No signs of Turks near the Canal; indeed they are not working very hard at their preparations. On the West the little flare up seems nearly over: a damp squib, the Senussi. I can get no news of Dahoum: indeed I am afraid to send & ask. Most of the men (and boys) from that district have been sent to Constantinople, where they still are. Few have been in firing lines as yet. Had the Arabs been a little more interested in the things of this world they would have been a nation by now: Your last mail this time went swimming. I hope there was nothing important.

Very cold here today: no fire-places in Egypt. {five words omitted} I'm longing for touch with decent Arabs again. There is a very heady old Shammar, and an Aneyze, and a Beni Temim townsman from Boreida, who comfort me. Miss Bell is doing great work for me. N,

GENERAL STAFF—INTELLIGENCE SECTION.   GENERAL HEADQUARTERS
                                                THE FORCE IN EGYPT
                                                    CAIRO

                                                    18.1.16

Only a line again this week: I am most busy writing a sort of newspaper article on weak points of the Baghdad Railway. Not much news.
The reconstruction has gone over our heads, and passed off leaving us
in the same place exactly. I do not know if it is all finished yet or not.
Anyhow apparently I am to stay out here for the present. I don't think
there is much chance of my getting off for a time . . . we are supposed
to have an afternoon off a month, but in practice we never get it oftener
than once in 3 months. The rest of the week we are on 9 till 1.30.
2.15 till 8.30: 10 till 12: the rest of the time one spends looking about,
& running out to the Hotel for meals. The work is very interesting:
mostly writing notes on railways, & troop-movements, & the nature
of the country everywhere, & the climate, & the number of horses or
camels or sheep or fleas in it . . . and then drawing maps showing all
these things.   N.

Please congratulate Bob on getting all his compulsory exams. over:
I expect he will now go in for quantities of voluntary ones, just to
prevent himself feeling queer!   N.

GENERAL STAFF—INTELLIGENCE SECTION.   GENERAL HEADQUARTERS
                                                THE FORCE IN EGYPT
                                                    CAIRO

                                                    24.1.16

Tomorrow is mail day, and as that is always a frantically busy one
I am going to write to you before going to bed. Nothing much happening this week. The Medforce are now gone away from Cairo, which
is a comfort: one could hardly move about for generals: we had 108
in Egypt! There is no real signs of the Turks' coming on. Of course
they can see that it would be lunacy now we are so well prepared: just
in the first moments of joy, when the Germans joined hand with the
Bulgars, & the blockade of Turkey was ended, they thought about
conquering Egypt. Now they have got sensible again. It is very difficult for them (for lack of camels) to bring more than a small force down.
George Lloyd, who came out with us, came back a short while ago,

and worked in the Office for a fortnight. A man called Bolland, who is in the Sudan Agency, as a sort of secretary to Clayton, told me today that his people are living at 228 Woodstock Road (new-comers) and suggested that you might like to go & see them. I didn't undeceive him! Miss Bell is going to India for a week end in a few days time. Mr. Hogarth still in London.   N.

GENERAL STAFF—INTELLIGENCE SECTION.   GENERAL HEADQUARTERS
                                                      THE FORCE IN EGYPT
                                                              CAIRO
                                                       January, 1916

A huge scurry this week. I have left writing till too late. Miss Bell went to India yesterday. Have been very busy lately working at the camel-trade in Arabia, and on several other points. Will try and write a letter next week. This week my head has been a compost of wool and pulp; horribly cold weather.   N.

Staff re-organisation ended: we stay as before, but have to do more work: one new man is added: name Deedes.   N.

I don't think I ever told you who "we" are
  (i) Colonel Clayton—Chief.
  (ii) Capt. Deedes—Suspects.
  (iii) Capt. Cornwallis—S.W. Arabia.
  (iv) Capt. MacDonnell—Tripolitania.
  (v) Capt. Graves—Turkish Army.
  (vi) Major   —Censor {Major Engleton or Engledon—the writing is
                                              not clear.}
  (vii) Capt. Beaumont—Censor.
  (viii) Major Hennessey—Suspects.
  (ix) Woolley—French Fleet.
  (x) Major Garvice—Alexandria.
  (xi) Major Barlow—Suez.
  (xii) Colonel Jennings-Bramly—Ismailia.
  (xiii) Armbruster—Enemy trading.
  (xiv) Rider   — ,,   ,, .
  (xv) Capt. Hadkinson—French Fleet.
  (xvi) Capt. Stirling—Port Said.
  (xvii) myself—Maps.
There are a lot of others;   N.

{Cairo, Savoy Hotel}
21.2.16

Post is going tomorrow, so I'm going to write now. Nothing to say, as usual. Newcombe is back in Cairo for a few days: he may be going back to the W.O. for a few days, though I shouldn't think so. He will probably be made a Colonel shortly. We are changing office tonight, so that everything is in a royal disorder. Each time we change we get more and more rooms: here in the Savoy Hotel, which is Headquarters at present, we now have 15 rooms, not counting little rooms. I have now got quite a decent room to myself, and have decorated it with a map of the Caucasus about 15 feet long (the largest map I have ever seen) one of Syria, about 12 feet high, and the beginnings of one on Egypt, bigger than either of these. It is rather amusing work publishing and drawing maps. We are up to 1,000,000 now, actual sheets, (mostly Gallipoli) of a total of about 600 different maps. The Egyptian Government handed over its Survey Department to us—or rather Dowson, Director General of Surveys, handed it over to us, and the Government agreed—so that there are about 1,000 workmen and a very large plant (second only to Southampton) at our disposal. The cost has not been what one would expect: paper etc. about £28,000: and expenses of staff etc. about £75,000. Egypt pays the second, War Office the first. There is a very great deal in hand just now. I wish I could send Arnie some of them. However you got the Gallipoli, which was a very pretty map. I have a lovely little 500,000 of the Turkish Empire in hand just now. It will take about six months to do. Also an Arabia (two months) which will be an important thing. I wish there was some news to tell you: there is heaps as a matter of fact just now, but it is not for publication. We seem to be fixed for ever in Cairo: all efforts now are directed to organizing the office so that it continues after the War on its present scale. They will have to find a substitute for me! We have got a little man called Deedes in our office now: he is an ex-Turkish Gendarmerie instructor, captain in the English Army, and a very excellent man. I like him best of the bunch. I'm going to bed now.   N.

{Cairo}

16.3.16

I didn't write last week, as I was too busy. We have now become Medforce Intelligence, as Force in Egypt is abolished. It makes no difference so far as I am concerned. I'm writing to Mr. Jane. I see his brother is dead, which will upset him.

I'm sorry Dr. Whitelocke is ill: it must be horrible to be in a hospital where one of your relations was a doctor. I hope Arnie will be pleased with his drawing lessons. If one has the power to make one's hand put down on paper what one pleases, it is most excellent. Drawing is one of the few things in which one need not excel to give pleasure. An amateur musician is a disaster in a family, but drawing does no harm, so long as it is not hung on a wall, and one is lost without it. Also you appreciate the shapes of things much better, if you know how to represent them in the flat. Tell Arnie to keep up an interest in sculpture. It is finer far than flat work, much more difficult to do and to appreciate, and gives one complete satisfaction where it is well done. I would rather possess a fine piece of sculpture than anything in the world.

Only 7 of us work in the Savoy. The others are all over Egypt. Egypt has always some cold weather every winter: the country is so unfitted for it that it strikes one as an offence, and much colder than it really is. It is hot now.

No news of Aldridge. Alexandria and Cairo are very far apart, & I don't meet people, as I never go out, and can do nothing for them. I have to write to Mrs. Rieder now. There is an extra post this afternoon, and the office is for the moment empty. Things in the Near East are going better than they have been since we came out, I think. There is some faint prospect of the result of the war being good when it does come.   N.

{Cairo}

20.3.16

I am going away, for a month or 6 weeks, to consult with some people, and suggest certain things. Is this vague enough? I hope to meet Miss Bell shortly, since we are much on the same tack. Letters will not be forwarded to me, as I am to be so little away. You must expect a break in my letters of at least three weeks, & possibly longer.

N.

Father's letter received. I would rather a separate account was opened
for Will's money, as he asked me to arrange some things for him. If
that is difficult then {the next (?) two words are not legible}.

                                                                    N.

                                                    {On S.S. *Royal George*}
                                                    End of March, 1916

We are in the Straits now.—Bab el Mandeb—with a splendid Arabia
on one side, and a dull damp Persia on the other. I wonder why Arabia
is the best-looking land, however you see it. I suppose it is the name
that does it.

We have been about ten days at sea, and have perhaps two more,
I suppose. A comfortable-going ship, where they leave one alone, and
easy water. Rather cold some days, but generally mild and pleasant.
There hasn't been much to see. A long-continued line of Arabian hills
on the left, some Red Sea Islands, no more than rocks, and Aden, which
is a jagged rim of coloured cliffs sticking up out of the water . . . no
beach, no flat land, but very beautifully coloured, and striated, with
deep polished ravines. From the sea it was splendid, but it would be
hot to live in on the sheltered side, where the little port is.

Flying fish are little things like minnows, that splash off the water
like a flung stone. They look pretty at night, when it is phosphore-
scent, for then they leap away from the ship in jagged flights, splashing
out constellations of stars.

I won't write to you from Basra I expect. I will be very busy ashore,
and will make my way back probably by the boat which would carry
the mail. Unless I have fortune to return at the same time as the flag-
ship, in which case I will go twice as fast. We will take about twelve
or thirteen days this trip.

I hope Bob is better. Diphtheria seems to be a very unpleasant ailment: however you will not be sorry to have him sitting at home for
a bit.

Tell Arnie that Heredia (in my house) is a man who paints pictures
in words as perfectly as ever they have been done in colour. Let him
get fond of Hypnos. There is more in that little head in the bronze
room than came out of Phigaleia. If the Ashmolean is still open let him

try and understand those broken heads by Scopas. It is an education which takes time.

I expect Mr. Hogarth is in Egypt now. I want to bring Gertrude {Miss Bell} back with me, and our Arabian office will be complete.

N.

{On a Leyland Liner}
May 18, 1916

We are at sea, somewhere off Aden, I suppose, so before it gets too late I am going to tell you something of what I saw in Mesopotamia. You must excuse the writing, because the ship is vibrating queerly.

I went off, as I told you about March 22: the transport I went on was the *Royal George*, a comfortable Canadian liner—and we got out to Kuweit without any happening of note. At Kuweit—which is a wide inlet of the sea, with low sand-dunes round it, very desolate, but for the town which is neatly & regularly built—we transhipped on to a fast mail-steamer, the *Elephanta*, of about 6,000 tons. This took us across the bar at the mouth of the Shatt el Arab, & up to Basra in the day. The joining of the river and the sea on the bar was very visible, as it was a quiet day. The river came down in a grey-green flood, and stopped abruptly in the sea, which was a heavy blue. You could have straddled anywhere, one foot on each water. The line was not straight though. It ran up and down irregularly as the tide pressed it, and you could follow it for hundreds of yards each side of the ship.

The bar is about 18 feet under high tide, but it is really only a cushion of liquid mud, and ships plough through it. It looks odd to see the propeller churning in stuff like chocolate cream. After a few miles of bar you get into the estuary of the rivers. It is about $\frac{1}{2}$ a mile wide shortly after, and at high tide the banks are marked only by rows of palm trees, for all Mesopotamia, to Kurna, is under high-tide level. The salt-water does not go so far up, but its weight in the mouth banks the fresh water up for three or four feet at Basra. The palm-trees get flooded every day, with a mixture of salt and fresh water which seems to agree with them. If the people want to keep the water out of any part they throw up a little dyke, three or four feet high, and as many thick. This is water-tight, for the alluvium is most rich clay. They get a double crop off the land, by sowing barley or wheat between the palm-trees.

We went up to Basra—60 or 70 miles from the sea—at top-speed, about 18 knots, and the river was never less than 300 yards wide. Generally it was a good five hundred. There was only one single-track place, where the Turks had sunk three German ships in a line across the stream to block our passage. The current slewed one steamer round, though, just as she was sinking, and so there is still free way. On the way up we passed—at Abadan—the depot of the Anglo Persian Oil Company. You will remember the petrol wells in Persia in which the Admiralty bought a controlling interest, and whose protection was the first object of the Mesopotamian expedition ... well, they bring the oil down about 150 miles across country in a pipe, and refine it here. It is mostly reserved for warships. It looks odd to come opposite a bare space in the palm groves, and to see there, banked up a little from the stream, workshops and villas, iron-roofed huts, and oil-storage tanks. It is a very large plant.

A little way above Abadan, on the Persian side, is the mouth of the Karun river, a broad and very swift stream, full of silt. The town of Mohammerah lies nearly at their joining, but you can see very little of it, as there are palm-groves between it and the Shatt el Arab. You do see however a country house of the Sheikh of Mohammerah, prettily built in a half-European style of yellow brick. In the whole river-valley, from the sea to Baghdad, there is not a stone as big as your finger-nail, and so the building material is either mud, or bricks of river mud, burnt lightly in a fire of reeds to a pale yellow colour. This brick disintegrates slowly in water, it is so soft. The Sheikh of Mohammerah is nominally a Persian subject, but in reality independent, and allied to us. He is very wealthy, and has lent us his river-palace at Basra as a hospital. We are fortunate in having big native friends on each side the river, for the Sheikh of Kuweit, on the Arabian bank, is also our ally. The father, Mubarah, began the friendship, but the son, Jabar, now reigning, seems quite anxious to maintain it.

I don't really know what to say about Basra itself. You know you have got there by the crowd of ships in the river, and by a few houses along the shore:—the town lies some two or three miles up a side-stream, deep enough only for small boats.

However our headquarters are on the bank, and there are usually dozens of row-boats and launches along the shore . . . no wharves, no piers, no signs of a port, no roads;—no one would ever dream that we had been in occupation of the place for months and months. When I landed it was pouring with rain, and dark. The officer who brought me off got a lamp, and we slid over the top of what seemed to be a bank of soft soap and toffee for about three hundred yards. Then it got better, for they had thrown some clinkers on the mud: so we stood upright (how my shoes resisted remaining in the tacky glue of the first part I don't know) and passed down a garden into the headquarter house. It was water-tight, and I found Miss Bell and Campbell-Thompson there, so that was well.

Next day I had a lot to do, so walked about and saw the place. The river side (where we were) is still all palm-gardens, in which rows of palms set as close as their heads allow stand in about six inches of water over a soil like blanc mange. You can stick a stick into any part of Basra about ten feet into the ground. There are houses built on little embankments in these gardens, where the consuls and rich men used to live, and paths about ten feet wide, on banks staked at the sides to about two feet above the water, join house to house. You follow these banks up the side stream to Basra (they become quite a broad carriage road some way inland because the level rises a little) which is a small very simple Arab town, with a covered bazaar in which there was nothing native that appealed to me. Trade with the interior is cut off, and Basra itself is not a place with any industry but boat-building. Round about Basra proper there are a good many other settlements which are counted in it as a rule; and these lead you out to Zobeir, a town about 8 miles from the river, on the edge of the Arabian Desert. This lies a little high, and is used as a summer residence by Basra people, because its air is clean. The people of Zobeir are Bedouin.

The native boats give a character to Basra. They are everywhere, for you use the creeks and canals and side-streams as roadways, and shop or pay your calls in a "Bellam". A bellam is a sort of gondola, thirty or forty feet long, about four feet wide, and shallow. Two men work them, either by sculls, or by poling along with a light bamboo. They are not very heavily built, but are much more clumsy than a punt. In the Euphrates lakes they use a sort whose prows are often six feet above the water, but the Basra sort are nearly flat. There is usually ten inches or a foot of freeboard. The bellam is the passenger boat . . . and the Mahaila the cargo boat. Mahailas sit on the water like the scooped third of a melon-rind: they perk up in front and behind, and

in the middle are nearly flush with the water. Their sides have the most
lovely curves, and the sheer up of the strakes to the stem and stern
post is very beautiful. I wish I could send you a drawing of one. They
have a single heavy mast, raked forward, and on that a great lateen
sail. When they are coming towards you they look like that wonderful
drawing in the Yellow Book (or is it the Savoy?) of the Vikings sailing
into the cave of the dead men. Unfortunately they give them only a
spiked prow not dragon jaws.

I only stayed three days in Basra, as the G.O.C. and all his staff were
up at the front. The people at the base gave me some biscuits, ten
loaves, ten tins of jam, ten tins of beef, and put me on board a little
paddle steamer that had been a ferry on the Irrawaddy. Downstairs she
was all engines, and the top was a flat deck partly sheltered by an
awning. The front $\frac{2}{3}$ of the deck was occupied by about 150 territorials:
behind the funnel was a smaller space, in which sat about ten of us,
who all had ten tins etc. Each side of the steamer was tied a 100 foot
steel barge, loaded deep with firewood and forage and stores. These
were intended partly to increase her carrying capacity, but more to act
as buffers and protect the paddles when we charged the bank.

We started in the afternoon, and shortly it began to rain . . . so we
went to bed. . . . We also went to bed whenever the wind was too cold
to endure walking about, and when it was not either wet or cold it was
both at once. As there was no cabin bed was a valise on the deck. If
you lay on the open deck you only got wet when it rained: if you lay
under the awning you avoided the thick of the shower, but endured a
persistent drip for hours after the rain had stopped. However it was
dry inside the valise. The men had no valises, but enough waterproof
sheets to make a sort of tent. So they could be either dry and cold, or
wet and warm, and their tastes seemed equally divided. I censored one
man's letter home, in which he said "We are in the tropics, and this is
the old Garden of Eden. I am glad to say that so far I have not felt the
heat!" Pneumonia was the prevalent disease at the time, so I don't
suppose he had!

It took us six days to reach the front. The first night we anchored
near Kurna, which is a mud village just at the fork where the Euphrates comes in. The Euphrates is the old colour but only about $\frac{1}{5}$ the
size it is at Jerabis. To this point the Tigris is about 500 yards wide,
and runs slowly. Above Kurna the tide is not felt at all, and the river

for two days runs strongly, winding and twisting in all directions, and from 52 yards to 150 yards wide. The second night we spent at Ezra's tomb, which is a clump of trees and a few mud houses, and beside them, just on the bank, a domed mosque and courtyard of yellow brick, with some simple but beautiful glazed brick of a dark green colour built into the walls in bands and splashes. It is the most elaborate building between Basra and Ctesiphon.

The third night we tied up at Amara, a town built I think by Abdul Hamid, all on one harmonious plan. It stretches regularly down a long river front for a mile or so, all of yellow brick set in dark mortar, with deep shadowed door-ways, and fretted windows, and much pleasant ornament on parapets and walls. In the middle of the front is the entrance to a high brick-vaulted arcade of a bazaar, in which you could get all that a poor Arab wants.

After Amara there were little places like Ali Shergi and Ali Gharbi, and Sheikh Saad, between which we spent the fourth and fifth nights. The river had been made small between Amara and Kurna because some large irrigation canals took off on the East bank: north of these it widened out again to three or four hundred yards, but still ran rapidly.

As for the country itself I should think it would be one of the hardest in the world to describe. As far North as Kurna you see only rows of date-gardens, which are simple enough; just light green sunny tree tops, and under these straight regular rows of brown stems hardly distinguishable in the shade. After Kurna though you run out into open meadow country, which you might be able to write about if you were on the spot—and if the precise spot was not the windy deck of a steamer full of people wondering when the next rain storm was coming down. To the west as far as your eye could see (with mists in foul weather and mirage in fine this is not far) the country looks like a shaggy Port Meadow {between the Thames and North Oxford}. It grows a thick crop of coarse grass and reeds, and every few hundred yards is a shallow pool, or a marsh. Not a tree, nor a bush, nor a mound, only sometimes the old waving banks of abandoned water channels meandering away into the distance. When the river rises in April it becomes one water-splash in which the course of the river is indistinguishable, for the whole country is below high-flood level. There are rice fields in the swamps, barley fields on the banks, and

occasionally a mud-walled river-garden of palms or apricot-trees.
Near Amara there were some willow-trees. We saw some wild boar,
and jackals, and everywhere quantities of water-birds.

On the East, sometimes thirty or forty miles away, and sometimes
only ten or twelve, you can see the long steep parallel ridges of the
Persian hills. They were thickly covered with snow, and it was from
them that the biting winds we had blew down. The country houses
are either of mud, when the owner is rich, or of mats. For security they
prefer to build the mat houses on a patch of dry ground in the middle
of a swamp. When such is not available they often put up four straight
walls of mud brick, with a round tower at each corner, to enclose a
space of about 100 yards each way, and then they huddle the mat huts
within the yard thus made. The style of these reed and mat huts is
curious. Of course they have plenty of giant reeds. They stick two
parallel rows of them into the ground about 12 feet apart. Each row
will be some 20 feet long, and the reeds are put pretty close together.
They then bend down the heads of these reeds till they meet in the
middle and are tied there. So you get the framework of a kind of tilt.
They scale over this with two or three thicknesses of small plaited mats
of stripped cane: and at each end of the tunnel thus made you bed in a
standing row of great reeds, and cover these with a wall of mats.
There your house is . . . very cool and sun-proof in summer, but damp
and cold in winter.

The Arabs here are wonderfully hard, much rougher and poorer
than our Jerablus men, but merry, and full of talk. They are in the
water all their lives, and seem hardly to notice it. I shall not soon forget a flood perhaps twenty miles long and wide near Ezra's tomb,
where the river had drowned both its banks for as far as one could
see . . . and in the middle, walking up the hidden bank of the river
to their necks in water, were three men pulling a laden mahaila up
stream. They must have pulled her ten miles wading and swimming
thus, and the nearest place they could hope to reach dry land would
be another ten miles ahead. I do not know what English people would
have made of such a job.

The steamers have their own way of navigating this river. There are
mud banks in it, but so shifting that experience is no help to you. You
go ahead hard, and keep a sharp look out. When you run aground you
back engines, and if that is insufficient you put out a kedge and warp

off. Then there are the corners. These are legion, and many of them hardly as wide as the length of the ship. So you charge full tilt sideways at the outer curve of the bank. Your barge runs into the clay edge with a tremendous bump, and a loud crying noise: sometimes it is pushed right out of the water, and skids over the grass. On board people fall down, and there is a succession of crashes as boxes and baggage topple over. The current presses you on, boring you into the curve, till your barge slips off, and you find yourself floating again. The paddles dash forward, hurl you into the other side of the curve (bump again), and the current again peels you off, and you steam away up or down the next straight reach. The banks are so soft and smooth by the constant repetition of the process that no harm is ever done, so long as the paddle steamer is stout enough amidships not to crack between the pressure of her barges. We had an extra-savage bump once, when the men were standing to attention being served with tins of tea out of a bucket. All those who had tea sat down violently, and poured their tea into their faces. The sergeant with the bucket hurled himself at the rest of the line, and flung it over them. It was too hot for them really to see the point but there was point in the sight of 100 Cumberland territorials unwillingly splashing in hot tea about the decks of a rain-swept river-steamer.

At the front I found Headquarters living in a steamer with good awnings and a saloon! I stayed with them for about three weeks, while Kut fell. We lost too many men at first, in the relief, and then tried too hard in the middle, and before the end everybody was tired out. {The next three and a quarter lines have been heavily blotted out with Indian Ink, either by himself or by a censor; they are not readable.} The weather cleared up and breeded myriads of flies. At sundown the awning over the deck used to change swiftly from grey to brown, as the swarms alit on it to roost. The cavalry sometimes had to ride at foot pace, being blinded.

Colonel Beach, one of the Mesopotamian Staff, Aubrey Herbert (who was with us in Cairo) and myself were sent up to see the Turkish Commander in Chief, and arrange the release, if possible, of Townshend's wounded. From our front trenches we waved a white flag vigorously: then we scrambled out, and walked about half-way across the 500 yards of deep meadow-grass between our lines & the Turkish trenches. Turkish officers came out to meet us, and we explained what we wanted. They were tired of shooting, so kept us sitting there with our flag as a temporary truce, while they told Halil Pasha we were coming—and eventually in the early afternoon we were taken blind-folded through their lines & about ten miles Westward till within four miles of Kut to his Headquarters. He is a nephew of Enver's, and suffered violent defeat in the Caucasus so they sent him to Mesopo-tamia as G.O.C. hoping he would make a reputation. He is about 32 or 33, very keen & energetic but not clever or intelligent I thought. He spoke French to us, and was very polite, but of course the cards were all in his hands, and we could not get much out of him. However he let about 1,000 wounded go without any condition but the release of as many Turks—which was all we could hope for.

We spent the night in his camp, and they gave us a most excellent dinner in Turkish style—which was a novelty to Colonel Beach, but pleased Aubrey and myself. Next morning we looked at Kut in the distance, and then came back blindfolded as before. We took with us a couple of young Turkish officers, one the brother-in-law of Jemal Pasha, the other a nephew of Enver, and they afterwards went up to Kut from our camp in the hospital ships which removed the wounded. The ill feeling between Arabs and Turks has grown to such a degree that Halil cannot trust any of his Arabs in the firing line. {The next three lines have again been heavily blotted out.} After that there was nothing for us to do, so the Headquarters ship turned round, and came down again to Basra. We got there about the 8th and I spent four or five days settling up things and then came away.

This is an old Leyland liner, now a transport. There is only myself and a General Gillman on board. He is from near Abingdon and excellent company: we sit on the deck and write reports and notes all day, and sleep gigantically at night. The weather at Basra began to get warmer before I left, (but 105° was our highest shade temperature), and there has not been any cold day or night on the boat so far . . . indeed the thermometer has not gone below 80°, so that is pleasant for me. I expect the Red Sea will be warm also.

I wonder if in my former letter I told you of the wonderful thunder storm we had at Kuweit? We were on the *Royal George*, and the lightning began about three o'clock in the afternoon.

After sunset it grew more frequent, until by 9 at night it was light-ning almost continuously from three sides at once. There was no thunder and only a few minutes rain. The flashes were like a pattern in lace, an intricate net-work stretched across the lower sky. Their colour was a very intense green, and they made a long crackling noise that hardly stopped. In their light you could see everything near by, up to a mile or two, very distinctly, but the distance less well. The three-fold direction of the light caused a most eerie impression of unreality, like lime-light rather, because we are accustomed to see things lit up from one side only by a steady sky. With these flashes one's rigging, and the shape and position of the ships in the harbour seemed all the time flickering and moving. The storm ended in a sudden dry burst of wind which swung our ship (very high built, about 80 feet above the water) right round like a pivot almost on top of a little sloop, the *Clio*, which had anchored too near us. They had to get up her anchor in a wild hurry (no winch, only a capstan) and dash away: we were within a few feet of over-laying her, and as her masts were below our decks we would have rolled her over and sunk her.

(I wonder if I ever told you about a magnificent storm we had at Carchemish one night Mr. Hogarth and the {Cowleys} were staying with us {letter of 1 April 1914}? It was a very cold week, and after dinner we had all moved round the hearth, on which there was a big fire of olive logs burning: Busrawi had sent in his two musicians at our request. One was an old man, who had been a shepherd all his life. He had a long white beard, and a quiet, weather-beaten face: he played on a pipe about two feet long, that was of a {kind of} reed, but looked like polished brass. Its tone was hoarse, but flute-like, and had a wonderful range: {he goes from high to} very low notes which sound just like the wind dragging over a rocky hill-side, rustling in the dried grass of the valleys. The other is a younger man who plays a two strin-ged {the next word is not legible; it is followed by "and" with one or two other words which cannot be made out}: he is dark, and thin faced with very deep set eyes. I think he is blind: at any rate he has wound a massive turban and head-cloth over his forehead, so that his face is always in heavy shade . . . and he generally keeps his eyes shut as he sings.

They had been playing and singing Kurd war-songs and love-songs and dirges for about half an hour when the storm suddenly broke. There was a torrential burst of rain which hissed down in sheets, and rattled over the shingle in our court-yard like the footsteps of a great crowd of men; then there would come a clap of thunder, and immediately after a blue flash of lightning which made our open door and window livid gaps in the pitch-black wall . . . through which we caught odd glimpses of the sculptures outside shining in the rain and dazzle of light. I remember particulary the seven-foot figure of a helmeted god striding along an inscription towards the doorway:— and the dripping jaws of the two lions of the pedestal which seemed in the alternate glare and shadow of the flashes to be grinning at us through the window. The musicians did not stop, but changed their song for a wild improvisation which kept time with the storm. The pipe shrilled out whenever the thunder pealed and fell down again slow and heavy for the strained silences in between. One did not realise that they were men playing independently: the rhythm seemed so born of the bursts of wind and rain, so made to bind together the elements of the night into one great thunder-song. It all lasted about ten minutes, I suppose, but I think it was the most wonderful time I have had . . . and when it ended it ended suddenly: there was no quiet dragging away of the storm into distance and insignificance.)

There, I have written you a month of letters. I do not know how the Censor will find it in his heart to pass so Gargantuan a bale of manuscript . . . but I'm afraid he will have to pass it, for there is nothing in it to help our enemies—nor is that a fair description of you. Hereafter I will again be nailed within that office at Cairo—the most interesting place there is till the Near East settles down. I am very pleased though to have had this sight of Mesopotamia in war time. It will be a wonderful country some day, when they regulate the floods, and dig out the irrigation ditches. Yet it will never be a really pleasant country, or a country where Europeans can live a normal life. In these respects, and in the matter of inhabitants, it must yield to the upper river, where we are.

I expect to find letters and papers knee-deep in Cairo when I return. The accumulation of two months business and pleasure will be awful to see—so do not look for immediate news of me.

Would you ask Gillman to make me another pair of brown shoes like the last? Also please ask Arnie to send me out two books by Cunninghame Graham, my Aristophanes, and a Bohn translation of Aristophanes. Latter can probably be bought second-hand from Blackwell. I would like my *William of Tyre* (Estoire de Eracles) if the volumes

are not too heavy for the post—and a Lucretius, if I have one. If
Arnie likes any of these too well to part with let him send something
else choice in their stead.

{CAIRO}
July 1 {1916}

Here goes for a letter to you, though there is little to say. The Reuter
telegram on the revolt of the Sherif of Mecca I hope interested you.
It has taken a year and a half to do, but now is going very well. It is
so good to have helped a bit in making a new nation—and I hate the
Turks so much that to see their own people turning on them is very
grateful. I hope the movement increases, as it promises to do. You will
understand how impossible it is for me to tell you what the work we
do really consists of, for it is all this sort of thing. This revolt, if it
succeeds will be the biggest thing in the Near East since 1550.

We carry on much as usual in the office, though Clayton has gone
back to England for a couple of weeks, to talk over things with the
Foreign Office. Mr. Hogarth still here, and in charge of Red Sea
politics.

Tell Father I received his letter of the 14th of June, and will reply to
it when I have time. The last two weeks we have lived in the middle
of a storm of telegrams and conferences, and excursions, and to consider one's private affairs is not possible. The money may have come
very opportunely, for the army here are very savage at being left out
of the Arabia business, and I may have to cut adrift of them, which
would reduce my pay a good deal. I have gone out, with Mr. Hogarth,
to live with an Irishman called MacDonnell, who is one of our office.
He has a house on the island in the Nile, where he normally lives with
his family. They have gone to Alexandria, and we have freedom of the
house. It is a change from the Hotel, and quiet.

I don't really think there is anything else I can tell you. I feel written
out, for now I have two newspapers (both secret!) to edit, for the
information of Governors and Governments, and besides heaps of
writing to do:—and it is enough. It is a very good thing everything
goes on so well. As long as the show succeeds no very great difficulties
will crop up. It is curious though how the jealousies and interferences
of people on your own side give you far more work and anxiety than
the enemy do. I have some very pretty maps in hand, and am drawing

myself one of the country East of Damascus and Aleppo. Thanks to
this war I know an incredible lot about the Near East. Our office is
the clearing house through which every report and item affecting the
Near East has to pass . . . the mass of Stuff is amazing, and it all fits
into itself like a most wonderful puzzle. If we had only begun in
peace time there would have been almost nothing we had not known.

Tell Mrs. Rieder that Dieb her coachman has been sentenced to some
years imprisonment for insulting the Ottoman Government . . . I
think he will be only a few weeks there.   N.

{Cairo}
22.7.16

I'm afraid there is nothing to say this week either. *William of Tyre*,
Cunninghame Graham and Aristophanes appeared duly. Very many
thanks. One does not read them much, but the fact of their being on
hand gives one a sense of security. It's like having a balance in books.
Clayton has got back. Everything here is going excellently, though as
ever there is enough to do. Arnie will be glad to hear I am printing
stamps for the Sherif of Mecca. I'll send him some when they come out.
Of course they are only a provisional issue. It's rather amusing, because
one has long had ideas as to what a stamp should look like, and now
one can put them roughly into practice. The worst is they can only be
little designs, not engraved, so that the finer detail is not possible. I'm
going to have flavoured gum on the back, so that one may lick without
unpleasantness. I saw Kerry a day or two ago, for a few minutes. He is
at Ismailia, with a post and telegraph company, I fancy or motor
cyclist. They have never heard of Hugh Whitelocke here. I think he
must be at Luxor. No news otherwise.   N.

Headquarters
Savoy Hotel
Cairo
16.9.16

Another letter—and as usual an absolute blank. I have come to the
conclusion that as I do nothing but work, and the work I cannot tell
you about, that there is precious little hope of my ever having anything
to say. If you could see Mr. Hogarth some day he would be able to tell
you what I am at . . . but short of this there is no obvious means.

I enclose a stamp or two. We have also got out half-piastre values and I hope to get out the $\frac{1}{4}$ piastre in two days time. I hope to send Arnie a few more later. They may be valuable some day, for I am not printing many, and have taken steps to prevent any dealers purchasing them in bulk. You have no idea what an enormous and profitable affair the stamp trade is. Things in Arabia are not going too well. I hope that they will not go too badly though! The enclosed drawing is very good. I hope Arnie will be able to keep it up. His last letter contained some points of interest.

(a) Lucretius is most of him rather dull, with insets of marvellous fire or beauty, which look the more wonderful for their setting.

(b) Lucan no good at all.

(c) {Seven words omitted} Things are not so bad at all.

(d) I have a "good deal" to do with the Balkans!

(e) No maps of Ægean: plenty of the Turkish coast when you get as far as that.

(f) So called Lemnian Athena head is a very poor thing. Egyptian work never touches Greek. I have a very beautiful Athena seal which I will send you some day.

(g) I fear I cannot get home.

(h) Cheque enclosed will buy you 3 Loebs, and please send me the Greek Lyrics. I am just printing a rather interesting map, showing physical relief, and names, in one. It is done by combining wash and hill-shading in colours. A new idea, and I am pleased with the effect obtained.   N.

{CAIRO}
24.9.16

It is 6.30, and nearly dark, so I'll write to you. There is no post tonight, which makes things more leisured. Not much of interest this week. The affairs of the Sherif are looking better, with the fall of Taif. He has captured there all the civil and military officials of the Mecca province, for they all used to spend the summer there, on the hill-tops in the gardens. If I leave G.H.Q. Egypt, which I have hinted several times lately, it will be to join the Arab Bureau, which is doing all the work of the Sherif's revolt, and in addition is trying to note down and

turn to account all the popular movements in the Near East, from the
Arab Question downwards. You will find evidence of this in articles
in the Press running down the Turks, which have become quite the
thing lately. You know the Turks always feared and disliked the Arabs,
and the Arabs returned it—that's the main thing. The trail is complicated almost indefinitely though by religious and local politics, and
tribal feuds, and ourselves and our allies: so that in all it is a fascinating
study, and we hope to produce a good deal by way of it. I enclose a
few 1 piastre stamps, at last. In the middle is Mekka el Mukerrama
(Mecca the Blessed, a regular phrase, without which Mecca is not
mentioned) on top is Hejaz post, and underneath 1 piastre. Date 1334
which is the Sherif's revolt. The half-piastre looks Chinese, and the
quarter-piastre Egyptian. This is pure Arabic, and I like it rather. I also
send a Turkish postcard. Arnie will remember the picture stamps the
Turks got from England? Well they have finished them now, and have
fallen back on this old thing, surcharged with the new date. It is rather
amusing. That is all, I think. It's getting cold now, though as cold
means only about 80° in the shade at noon, and 60° at night, I do not
suppose you would make much grumble at it on that score. By the
way, the Turks & Arabs use a different calendar: this is 1334 in Mecca,
and will be 1335 next month. In Constantinople 1916 is 1332.

                                                              T.E.L.

                                                          {CAIRO}
                                                          10.10.16

    Post out tonight, and as I did not write last week I must this week.
I noticed from a recent letter that you had not heard of me for some
time. I suppose a post must have dropped out in that sunk French
steamer. Anyway I wrote. I enclose 9 more stamps in this. The half and
quarter piastre are not yet on sale. Have been interrupted eleven times
since last sentence. A telephone is useful but a nuisance. I would like to
know if my letters to you are opened? Two interruptions here. Mr.
Hogarth is due here on Friday, which will be pleasant. He is so entirely
unprofessional that he acts like a breath of fresh air. [Telephone.] Here
is a story for Arnie. Storrs, of the British Residency, went down to
Jidda lately with the Holy Carpet. When there he wanted to talk to the
Sherif. So he went to the telephone, and rang up No. i. Mecca, and

began. In a few minutes he heard other voices on the line, so he told
the Sherif that someone was trying to overhear their conversation.
Sherif, very angry, rang up the Exchange, and ordered all telephones
in the Hejaz to be cut off for half an hour. After which things went
splendidly. The Sherif has a sense of humour, and is doing well. His
weakness is in military operations. Four interruptions. We have added
a new man to our bunch, one Ormsby-Gore, an M.P. . . . seems good
. . . Ismailia come up soon and amalgamate with us. Then we are
nearly 40 strong! There ought to be intelligence enough in the bunch
to down Turkey—but unfortunately half of them are only door-posts
and window frames! Things will go much more smoothly, though,
when we are all in touch. [Telephone.] Arnie should read Spenser as
often as possible: not in large doses (4 more interruptions) but for a few
minutes at a time, and frequently. More interruptions—I think I must
give this up. It is too hopeless trying to write when soldiers keep on
rushing into one's room and throwing fresh papers into one's baskets.
I have three baskets now, and three tables, and they are all about knee
deep. [Telephone]. When they get too bad I go out and see somebody
somewhere else in the building (this place is nearly as big as the War
Office) and come back and tear things up. More interruptions. I'm off.
[Telephone].   N.

P.S.—This evening is worse than usual.

                                                                    N.

                                           ARAB BUREAU
                                           SAVOY HOTEL
                                              CAIRO
                                            18.11.16

This is only a scrawl to inform you what I wired:—namely that I
have got back to Cairo. I left on October 13 from Cairo, reached Jidda
on October 16, left there on October 19, for Rabegh. Left Rabegh on
October 21, by camel; went up to Sherif Feisul's H.Q. at a place called
Bir Abbas, half-way between Medina and the sea, about 100 miles
North of Rabegh. After a few days there returned by road to Yenbo,
and embarked on Nov. 1 for Jidda. On November 4 changed ships
there, and went across to Port Sudan with Admiral Wemyss. Reached
Khartoum on November 7, and stayed with the Sirdar till November

11, when I took train down the Nile to Halfa, then steamer to Asswan, and then by rail to Cairo. At Asswan Hugh Whitelocke got into my carriage, and we were together as far as Luxor where he intended to stay a day to sightsee. Since my return I have been extravagantly busy:— so much so that I cannot possibly write to you probably for two or three days yet. The day is one long series of interruptions.

I have now left G.H.Q. and joined the Arab Bureau, which is under the Residency here. That is, the Sirdar is in charge of it, or will be very shortly. The atmosphere of being one's own master—or at any rate of being with people whose voices are not drowned by their grinding of axes—is pleasant. All very well.

N.

RABEGH

14.12.16

Am in Rabegh—half way between Jidda and Yenbo—tonight, & have just heard that a mail is closing for England. So as I did not write last one here goes this one. I cannot write you details till I reach Egypt, which will not be for some two weeks or so yet. Things very interesting at Yenbo, where is Sherif Feisul, one of the Sons of the Sherif of Mecca. I left there three days ago, and ran down to Jidda, to do a little business: am now going back, to stop a few days. Weather delightful, neither hot nor cold, with beautiful winds.

This letter will probably reach you a little after Christmas. I hope it will not be too wet again. All today I have been discussing Arabian geography & politics, which are the local topics. One has forgotten that there are other wars on.

If that silk headcloth with the silver ducks on it—last used I believe as a table-cloth—still exists, will you send it out to me? Such things are hard to get here now. N.

This is not a letter: only a substitute for a field post card.

N.

UMM LEJJ

16.1.17

I have not written for a fortnight, for at first I was up country hopping about on a camel, and later there was no post-boat. You see we have no mail-steamers, but depend entirely on the Navy for our communications, and they go about their business strictly. However, in any case you know that I am completely well. I have got leave to stay down here a fortnight longer, because things here are interesting, and new. Life in Yenbo was varied, because I lived always on ships, and while there was always a ship, it was sometimes one and sometimes another sort of ship. Some were luxurious, some warlike, & some very plain—but all different. This place you will not find on any map, unless you buy the northern sheets of the Red Sea Admiralty charts (I don't recommend them!): any way, it is about 100 miles North of Yenbo, and is a little group of three villages (about 40 houses in each) on a plain about a mile square under red granite hills. As it is spring just now the valleys and slopes are sprinkled with a pale green, and things are beautiful. The weather is just warm enough to be too hot at midday, but cold at night. I'm on a ship, as usual.

Sherif Feisul (3rd Son of Sherif of Mecca), to whom I am attached, is about 31, tall, slight, lively, well-educated. He is charming towards me, and we get on perfectly together. He has a tremendous reputation in the Arab world as a leader of men, and a diplomat. His strong point is handling tribes: he has the manner that gets on perfectly with tribes-men, and they all love him. At present he is governing a patch of country about as large as Wales, and doing it efficiently. I have taken some good photographs of things here (Arab forces and villages and things), and will send you copies when I can get prints made. That will not be till about the end of the month, when I go to Cairo.

My Arabic is getting quite fluent again! I nearly forgot it in Egypt, where I never spoke for fear of picking up the awful Egyptian accent and vocabulary. A few months more of this, and I'll be a qualified Arabian. I wish I had not to go back to Egypt. Any way I have had a change.   N.

ARAB BUREAU
SAVOY HOTEL
CAIRO

31.1.17

Am back in Cairo, though only for a few days. Left Yenbo about a fortnight ago, for Um Lejj, by sea. Landed at Um Lejj and came up by land to Wejh, which we took without fighting. A landing party from

the ships had practically done the work the day before. I snatched a
week's leave, to come up here and buy some things, before going off
to Sherif Feisul again. As I have not had any letters lately (due to my
moving about, and the difficulty of posts in the Red Sea) I cannot
answer any particular questions. Things in Arabia are very pleasant,
though the job I have is rather a responsible one, and sometimes it is a
little heavy to see which way one ought to act. I am getting rather old
with it all, I think! However it is very nice to be out of the office, with
some field work in hand, and the position I have is such a queer one—
I do not suppose that any Englishman before ever had such a place.
All of which is rather tantalising reading to you, because I cannot enter
into details. I act as a sort of adviser to Sherif Feisul, and as we are on
the best of terms, the job is a wide and pleasant one. I live with him,
in his tent, so our food and things (if you will continue to be keen on
such rubbish!) is as good as the Hejaz can afford. Personally I am more
and more convinced that it doesn't matter a straw what you eat or
drink, so long as you do not do either oftener than you feel inclined.
It has been very cold down there lately: the thermometer one morning
was down to 50° which struck us as rather serious!

The war in Arabia is going on very well: the Arabs are very keen
and patriotic, and the Turks are beginning to get really frightened.
I hope to write a better letter tomorrow: this is only a scrawl to catch
the mail.   N.

WEJH

12.2.17

Here I am, back in Wejh again, sitting in our funny house trying to
write or think or work. I'm afraid there are too many interruptions
for much success. Newcombe is here, and I hope things are going well.
I got a letter from Arnie the other day pleading for more news of what
the Sherifian forces are doing. Well you know, it is not my fault. They
do a great deal, but some people—not themselves—seem to wish to
keep the progress of the campaign a secret. As a matter of fact progress
is difficult. The Arabs of the Hejaz are all for the Sherif, some keenly
enough to volunteer, others less keen, but all well-wishers. Only, they
are tribesmen, and as such are rebellious by instinct. They hate the
Turks, but they don't want to obey anyone's orders, and in consequence

they turn out only as a mob of snipers or guerilla-fighters. They are wonderfully active, quite intelligent, and do what they do do fairly well. They are however not fit to meet disciplined troops in the open, and it will be a long time before they are.

These details will give you a fair idea of the sort of campaign it is. There is a bunch of about 12,000 Turks in Medina and the neighbourhood, clinging to certain important water-supplies and roads South and West of Medina, and surrounded, on all sides except the Railway, by Arabs. The Turks are also holding the Hejaz Railway, which we now threaten from Tebuk downwards, but not as yet in any force. The Arabs proved incapable of taking Medina, held by its present garrison, and the Medina garrison proved unable to advance through the Arabs against Mecca. So now we have shifted part of our forces North to this place, and the struggle for the Railway will probably be the feature of this second phase of the Hejaz Campaign.

The Arab Movement is a curious thing. It is really very small and weak in its beginning, and anybody who had command of the sea could put an end to it in three or four days. It has however capacity for expansion—in the same degree—over a very wide area. It is as though you imagine a nation or agitation that may be very wide, but never very deep, since all the Arab countries are agricultural or pastoral, and all poor today, as a result of Turkish efforts in the past.

On the other hand the Arab Movement is shallow, not because the Arabs do not care, but because they are few—and in their smallness of number (which is imposed by their poverty of country) lies a good deal of their strength, for they are perhaps the most elusive enemy an army ever had, and inhabit one of the most trying countries in the world for civilised warfare. So that on the whole you may write me down a reasonable optimist. I hope that the show may go as we wish, and that the Turkish flag may disappear from Arabia. It is indiscreet only to ask what Arabia is. It has an East and a West and a South border—but where or what it is on the top no man knoweth. I fancy myself it is up to the Arabs to find out! Talk about Palestine or Syria or Mesopotamia is not opportune, when these three countries—with every chance—have made no effort towards freedom for themselves.

I wonder what the censor will make of this letter? It may contain news for him, but I'm afraid precious little to the enemy! However you never know what they will do, and there is a "Hush" policy over the Red Sea and Arabia which causes a good deal of amusement to the Arabs—and to us who are down here.

I hope to be able to send you some photographs of the Sherif and of Feisul and the rest of us shortly. Please wait in peace till then. Incidentally I'm to have no post towards you now for about ten days. Patience!

N.

ARAB BUREAU
SAVOY HOTEL
CAIRO

25.2.17

Back in Cairo again for a few days—till the 28th to be exact. One does run about on this show! But as a matter of fact I have only come up to get some mules, and a wireless set, and a few such-like things.

Affairs are going a little slower than I had hoped, but there has been no suspicion of a set-back, and we are all well contented. I enclose a few photographs—as long as they are not published there is no harm in showing them to anyone. I have a lot more, but they have not been printed yet. They will give you an idea of the sort of country (in the oases) and the sort of people we have to do with. It is of course by far the most wonderful time I have had. I don't know what to write about! What we will do when I get back I don't know exactly—and cannot say any how. Cairo is looking very gay, and everybody dances & goes to races as usual or more so—but after all, there is not, and never has been, war in Egypt.

The weather here is fresh—and in Wejh warmish.

Tell Arnie that I think his drawings try after ease too quickly. There is no point in making lines because other people do. The way is to look at a thing long enough, & try & make up your mind which way you have to twist your point to show up its shape in black and white. It will take a long time to do a drawing, but you do get a certain amount of thought and direction into it—not very much, I'm afraid, unless you are an artist, and born to it. After you have thought out how to do it, then you can get easy, & put polish on. Modelling is better, because there you show things as they really are, instead of recording solids in flat. I don't like relief, for that reason, unless it is half-round, and shows only half the object—otherwise it seems to me only a meretricious sketching. The greatest works I can remember are the battered heads of Skopas, the torso of Poseidon from the Parthenon, and some of the more fluid heads, like the Collignon athlete, Hypnos, etc. Above all, those two wonderful heads.

I got the headcloth safely, about a week ago, in Wejh, together with news that Bob had gone to France. As a matter of fact, you know, he will be rather glad afterwards that he has been . . . and as it will be easier work, and healthier than his hospital work in London. I do not think that you have much cause to regret. Many thanks for the headcloth.

I wrote to {C. B.} Young, and asked him to send me Will's Pindar.

I have now been made a Captain and Staff Captain again, which is amusing. It doesn't make any difference of course really, as I am never in uniform in Arabia, and nobody cares a straw what rank I hold, except that I am of Sherif Feisul's household. Can't think of anything else to say, as have become a monomaniac about the job in hand, and have no interest or recollections except Arabian politics just now! It's amusing to think that this will suddenly come to an end one day, and I take up other work.   N.

{CAIRO}

28.2.17

DEAR ARNIE

Herewith a few $\frac{1}{8}$ piastre Hejaz stamps—a new denomination just going to be issued. The perforation I think better than the old style, and I like the design. What do you think? Inform me if there are any other values of which you want more. Those published are 1 P.T. $\frac{1}{2}$, $\frac{1}{4}$, $\frac{1}{8}$ P.T. Blue, Red, Green and Orange. Also tax stamps, but I don't suppose you care about them. A 2 P.T. is under weigh. It has an arch-&-grill design, and I like it.   N.

Just off again.

ARAB BUREAU
SAVOY HOTEL
CAIRO

12.8.17

This is only a note, to catch what I believe is a post. I'm sending some photographs in hope that they will arrive: of course they are not mine, but some R.F.C. people who had taken them sent me copies. I've sent you a lot, one time and another, but I don't suppose many get through. I cannot send any enlargements, for printing paper is scarce.

Went down to Jidda a month ago, and saw Feisul at Wejh, and the Sherif himself at Jidda, and discussed things with them. Results satisfactory on the whole. I had never met the Sherif himself before, and liked him exceedingly: a very simple straightforward old man, clever enough too, but knowing so little. Upon us as a people is the responsibility of having made him a ruling power, and he is pitifully unfit for the rough and tumble of forming a new administration out of the ruins of the Turkish system. We will have to help him and his sons, and of the sons only Feisul and Zeid will play square to us. Abdulla is an intriguer, and poor Sidi Ali, the eldest son is a religious fanatic, and will be the tool of evil spirits. I do hope we play them fair.

I'm now going back to Akaba to look round at the country there: will start about the 16th from here. The average length of my last five visits to Cairo has been about 5 days! However it is more restful in Arabia, because one feels so nervous of what may happen if one goes away. I cannot ask for leave, as I know there is so much to do down there, and no one to do it. If I asked I would probably get it, but it would not be right at present. If ever things get safe there, it will be possible to rest. You know there are very few of us on the job.

N.

About writing:—please try to realise that one's thoughts for nearly two years have been fixed on one object. We have realised part of the scheme, & the situation is critical but hopeful. In the circumstances one has become a monomaniac, unable to do or think about anything else— and of the one thing I cannot write to you.   N.

{AKABA}

27.8.17

This is written in a tent full of flies at Akaba, and the boat is leaving this afternoon. There is as usual nothing to say. I got here on the 17th of August, and found all as I had left it, except that my milk-camel has run dry: a nuisance this, because it will take me time to find another. I have too much to do, little patience to do it with, and yet things are going tolerably well. It is much more facile doing daily work as a cog of a machine, than it is running a campaign by yourself. However it's the maddest campaign ever run, which is saying quite a little lot, and if it ever works out to a conclusion will be imperishable fun to look back upon. For the moment it is heavy and slow, weary work, with no peace for the unfortunate begetter of it anywhere.

Newcombe is in Egypt ill; (nerves mostly). I've lost sight of everybody else. By the way I have returned to the Egypt Expeditionary Force, and should properly have no more to do with the Arab Bureau: but so eccentric a show as ours is doesn't do anything normal. Wherefore please address me as before, and don't put any fancy letters before or after my name. These things are not done by my intention, and therefore one can hardly count them.

I'm very glad you saw Mr. Hogarth. He will have probably given you a better idea than anyone else could give you of what we are really trying at. It consists of making bricks without straw or mud:—all right when it is a hobby, as with me, but vexatious for other people asked to do it as a job. By the way isn't it odd that (bar school), which was part nightmare & part nuisance, everything I've done has been first hobby and then business. It's an odd fortune, which no one else could say, because everybody else plays games. It was a mercy that I broke my leg long ago, and settled to sit down the rest of my days. Tell Arnie never to use an adjective that does not properly express what he means: slang reduces one to a single note, which is fatal.

N.

Some stamps enclosed.

AKABA
5.9.17

Got a letter of August 9 from you, which shows you never got a letter I sent you some time in July (12th I think) telling you what had happened the way to Akaba. As a matter of fact it was a poor sort of letter, because I was rather doubtful how much to say. Either I said too much, or the ship sank.

I'm now off for a trip inland, lasting for about 3 weeks I expect, so this is the end of letters for the time being: indeed it's only as camels are late that I can write this anyhow. Since July 10, when I got to

Egypt from Akaba I have been to Wejh, Jidda, Yenbo, Akaba, up country, back to Egypt, to Alexandria, up to Akaba again, up country, back, & am now going up again—So you see it is a mobile sort of life, this.

Tell Mother they asked for that twopenny thing she likes, but fortunately didn't get it. {This refers to the V.C., H.M. The King gave him the C.B., Military Division, instead.} All these letters & things are so many nuisances afterwards, & I'll never wear or use any of them. Please don't, either. My address is simply T.E.L., no titles please.

In reply to Father's query, Yes, I have boils, lots of them. They began in March, & will go on till I have time to get to Egypt and be inoculated. Only I am usually too rushed in Cairo to get anything of my own done. Am very fit and cheerful enough when things are not too hectic. Going up country is always a relief, because then there is only one thing at a time to do. Is Elsie Hutchins married? I have had a letter signed Elsie, & think it must be from her. Will you get me Janet's address again, I've lost it. Cheque enclosed for £300. Will you ask Father to invest it for me? I can't do anything out here: Ask him to put it in the most obvious thing, without troubling himself—or keep it, if you want money.

Am off now.   N.

Akaba

Sept. 24, 1917

Writing to you isn't very hopeful, since it is clear that you never get any of my letters. However I'll go on doing it, and some day one may get through. Would you like me to have a weekly telegram sent from Cairo telling you all well? I could arrange it easily enough. It's really a little serious that you should have received no letters between my wires. I sent the second one when I got back to Egypt from a visit to the Hejaz, because I had just had a note to say you had had no letters for two months, or some odd time. By the way have any of my letters ever been opened by censor?

I'm now back in Akaba, after having had a little trip up country to the Railway, for the last fortnight. We met all sorts of difficulties, mostly political, but in the end bagged two locomotives and blew them up, after driving out the troops behind them. It was the usual Arab show, done at no cost to us, expensive for the Turks, but not decisive in any way, as it is a raid and not a sustained operation. There are few people alive who have damaged railways as much as I have at any rate. Father may add this to the qualifications that I will possess for employment after the war! However, seriously, do remember that thanks to him I'm now independent, so far as money is concerned, of any employment whatever, and therefore I'll get back on to that printing-press scheme as soon as I am free. After all, you can't say that I haven't seen something of the world by now, and I can honestly say that I have never seen anyone doing anything so useful as the man who prints good books. So don't worry about my future—and for my present don't put either Major or C.B. or any other letters (past present or future) after my name when writing to me. These sorts of things are only nuisances to a person with £250 a year, & the intention of not having more, and the less they are used the better. I'm sending back all private letters so addressed.

Do you remember a very light dusty-amber silk cloak I brought back with me once from Aleppo? If it is not in use, I would be very glad to have it sent to me. Arab clothes are hard to find, now-a-days, with manufacture and transport thrown out of gear. I got a letter from Bob the other day & news that Arnie has been excused responsions. Also it proves that the anonymous thanks for a carpet was Elsie Hutchins! I'm glad she is married. Do you know I have not written a private letter to anyone but you for over a year? It is a wonderful thing to have kept so free of everything. Here am I at thirty with no label and no profession—and perfectly quiet. I'm more grateful to Father than I can say.   N.

AKABA

19.10.17

Apparently you have begun getting letters from me. I got one yesterday from Arnie suggesting certain things. I'm afraid it is looking too far ahead, but should there be opportunity I would much like the arrangement. It will be quite easy to get the necessary approval if the time comes. A. would come to Cairo in that case, work with the Arab Bureau till *au fait* with the situation, & then take a field job. The Hejaz is nearly closed down, but S. and E. Syria is much in evidence. A. should learn Syrian Arabic, or better still N. Mesopotamian. If from books it will have to be Syrian, as there are no others (except Egyptian, which is bad). If he can get hold of any Arabs, let him pick village or tribal Arabic, not town. He should learn demolition work (explosives) practically, as the theory is very theoretic & does not always justify itself. However the effects of blasting gelatine & guncotton on stone & steel are worth working out, on paper as well as in the open. It is very easy. Fuse and electric firing. He should also learn machine gun work, Vickers, Lewis, & Hotchkiss, and if he has time get a working acquaintance with light Trench mortars, and guns. Of the latter we use field and mountain, & some fancy patterns. It is not worth while his trying to become a gunner, but if he spends a few days with a gunner, or near a battery, it will pay him to pick up how to set a fuse and train a gun. He should be able to ride a motor-cycle and drive a car:—we use Fords, Crossleys, and Rolls-Royces. If he can do some of the above, can write fluently in English, talk a little French, and shoot with revolver & rifle that will be useful enough. Bomb-throwing is a very handy thing. If he makes even a beginning in Arabic it is good. I don't suppose he can get very far, but the further the better.

All books on Arabia & Syria are worth reading—especially Baedeker. What a catalogue of talents! I wish I had them. All very well here. Saw Mr. Hogarth two days ago—not here!

N.

AZRAK
14.11.17

I wonder if you can find this place:—it's out in the desert between Deraat and Amman—and if you do find it you will think it a most improbable place to live at. Living however is quite easy and comfortable here. We are in an old fort with stone roofs and floors, and stone doors of the sort they used in Bashan. It is a bit out of repair, but is improving in that respect every day. I do not know what its postal arrangements are like: at least they begin with about ten days on a camel of mine, and after that the ordinary risks of letters now-a-days. Your chances of getting it are therefore a little thin, it seems to me. I go on writing and writing and it has no effect: every letter I get from you says that you have not heard from me since last time: very disheartening, since writing is always a risk (if our friends get this letter they will pay me a visit) and often difficult. Meanwhile it is restful. I am staying here a few days; resting my camels, and then will have another fling. Last "fling" was two railway engines. One burst into fragments, & the other fell on the first. Quite a successful moment! If you see a note in print saying that "A detachment of the N. army of Sherif Feisul etc." Then that's me .. the rest is anonymous. In case my last three letters have fallen through, please tell Arnie that his plan is excellent. I told the people concerned in Cairo, and either Mr. Hogarth or myself can get it arranged quite easily if the time comes. Personally I don't expect it will, but I always was an optimist. I wonder if Gillman could make me another pair of brown shoes? There may be regulations against export, so he should find out first. I do not often wear shoes, but they come in handy sometimes in reserve. I sent you a cheque for £300 some weeks ago, and asked for Janet's address? Did you get them and if not will you let me know?

There, this letter has been 3 days in writing, & I have done all the rest of the work meanwhile.

T. E. LAWRENCE

THE RESIDENCY
CAIRO
14.12.17

Well here I am in Cairo again, for two nights, coming from Akaba via Jerusalem. I was in fortune, getting to Jerusalem just in time for the official entry of General Allenby. It was impressive in its way—no show, but an accompaniment of machine gun & anti-aircraft fire, with aeroplanes circling over us continually. Jerusalem has not been taken for so long: nor has it ever fallen so tamely before. These modern wars of large armies and long-range weapons are quite unfitted for the historic battlefields.

I wrote to you last from Azrak, about the time we blew up Jemal Pasha, and let him slip away from us. After that I stayed for ten days or so there, and then rode down to Akaba in 3 days: good going, tell Arnie: none of his old horses would do so much as my old camel.

At Akaba I had a few days motoring, prospecting the hills and valleys for a way Eastward for our cars: and then came up to H.Q. to see the authorities and learn the news-to-be.

Tomorrow I go off again to Akaba, for a run towards Jauf, if you know where that is. Mother will be amused to learn that they are going to send me to England for a few days in the spring, if all works well till then: so this is my last trip, possibly. Don't bank on it, as the situation out here is full of surprise turns, and my finger is one of those helping to mix the pie. An odd life, but it pleases me, on the whole.

I got that little cloak all well—many thanks; the Near East used to make all these wonderful things, but the interruption of trade routes and the call of military service hamper it now, and one's needs are every day more and more difficult to meet. I'm an Emir of sorts, and have to live up to the title.

I see Arnie is getting slowly up the obstacles of many exams. They are silly things, terrible to the conscientious, but profitable to the one who can display his goods to effect, without leaving holes visible. As real tests they are illusory. So long as you can read good books in the languages they effect, that's enough for education: but it adds greatly to your pleasure if you have memory enough to remember the why & wherefore of the waxing and waning of peoples, and to trace the slow washing up & down of event upon event. In that way I think history is the only knowledge of the easy man. It seems to me that is enough of didactic.

Mr. Hogarth is here in Cairo, acting as our base of information. He is one of the people whom the Arabs would have great difficulty in doing without. The blank in knowledge when he goes back to England is always great. Pirie-Gordon is coming out, to write popular articles on the Arab war for the home papers—so soon you will know all about it. Secrecy was necessary while the fight was a life and death one in the Hejaz: but since the opening of Akaba the stress has been eased, and today we are as comfortable as any front. As public sympathy is desirable, we must try and enlist on our side a favourable press. Arnie will be content, but must take it as said that it was quite impossible before. This show of ours began with all against it, and has had first to make itself acceptable to the elect. They converted, we can afford to appeal to a wider circle. It is not much use trying, with a J pen, to tell you how we are going to do it.

Many thanks to Father for investing that cheque of mine. When I stay out in Arabia for months on end I spend comparatively little, for the Government buys my camels, & the Sherif pays the men. I have only clothes (cheap things Arab clothes) and personal presents to pay for. On the other hand, when I get to Cairo I have many commissions, from Arab sheikhs, for things they want—and if they have been useful, or will be useful, they get them free of charge! My acquaintances are legion, or the whole population from Rabegh to Deraa, and the burden correspondingly heavy. However they have just raised my pay, by pushing me up the roll of Staff appointments. I'm now called a G.S.O.2.

The French Government has stuck another medal on to me: a croix de guerre this time. I wish they would not bother, but they never consult one before doing these things. At least I have never accepted one, and will never wear one or allow one to be conferred on me openly. One cannot do more, for these notices are published in the Press first thing, and to counter-announce that one refused it, would create more publicity than the award itself. I am afraid you will be rather disgusted, but it is not my fault, and by lying low and simply not taking the things when given me, I avoid ever really getting them. This letter should get to you about Christmas time, I suppose, as few mails have been sunk of late. That will mean that you are getting at least fortnightly letters from me, which should put off any anxiety you might otherwise feel. Mr. Hogarth of course hears of me every few days, so that his information is much fuller than anything I can ever give you.

I'm in the proud position of having kept a diary all the year 1917 to date. It is rather a brief one, consisting only of the name of the place where I sleep the night of each day: and the best thing about it is the disclosure that ten successive nights in one place is the maximum stop in the 12 months, and the roll of places slept in is about 200. This makes it not astonishing that my Arabic is nomadic!

I hope Arnie is getting on with his army subjects. It would be a useful thing to know how to drive a car, but judging from the papers there must be fewer cars in Oxford than in Akaba. He should keep an eye on the illustrated papers soon. They are going to get an occasional photograph from us, to help keep the Sherif (and Feisul above all) before the public eye. The Arab Bureau have about 500 excellent prints, and so the selection may be a good one. Some of them you will probably have already had, as I remember sending you some of the

best. I'm also sending you a sheet of Hejaz 1 piastre stamps. You said
you had not received any of this value. These are of course 1st edition,
and are worth a good deal more than you would expect! Lady
Wingate gave them to me, for of course it is impossible to find them
anywhere for sale.

Here endeth this letter.   N.

AKABA

8.1.18

In this country one's movements never work out as planned: in proof
of that, here I am in Akaba again after quite a short excursion up
country. I wrote to you last from Cairo, I fancy, and prophesied that
I would be a long time away! Tomorrow perhaps we will get off
about midday, to go up towards the Dead Sea, on the East side. It is
beautiful country, but too hilly for pleasure. Today I'm busy buying
some new riding camels, and saddles and saddle-bags. I looked through
the last few letters received, but I don't think there is anything requiring
answer. Newcombe, about whom you asked, has been taken prisoner,
and is now probably in Asia Minor. He was working with the army in
Palestine when he was caught.

Posts have been a little disorganized lately, for the last letters from
England are dated November 9: however one knows that had there
been anything wrong there would have been telegrams about. It is only
good news which is not worth spending money on: you hear the bad
too soon.

This Akaba is a curious climate. On the coast we have a typical
Red Sea winter, which at its worst is like a fine October day, and at its
best is like summer weather. No rain to speak of, not much wind, and
persistent sunshine. If you go thirty miles up country at once you get
into cold wet weather; with white frosts at night. If you go 20 miles
further East you find yourself in miserable snow-drifts, and a wind
sharp enough to blow through a sheepskin. Next day you are in
Akaba again, and thoroughly warm.

I'm sending you a photograph or two with this letter: none of them
are very interesting, but some day we may be glad of them. The Arab
Bureau, to which Mr. Hogarth belongs, has a wonderful collection of
Arabian photographs, of which I want a few published in the *Illustrated*

London News. They include a rather impressive snap of Feisul himself, getting into a car at Wejh, and some of his bodyguard, taken by me from the saddle, as I was riding in Wadi Yenbo with them and him. It would take a great painter, of course, to do justice to the astonishing life and movement of the Bedouin armies, because half the virtue of them lies in the colours of the clothes and saddle trappings. The best saddle-bags are made in the Persian Gulf, on the Eastern shore of Arabia, and are as vivid and barbaric as you please.

One of the prints to appear, showing the Sherifian camp at dawn, in Wadi Yenbo, was taken by me at 6 a.m. in January last, and is a very beautiful picture. Most sunrise pictures are taken at sunset, but this one is really a success.

There, I have an article to write for an Intelligence Report published in Egypt, and much else to do. Don't expect any letter from me for a time now. I'll be very busy, and quite away from touch with Egypt.

N.

{GUWEIRA}
Feb. 6, 1918

Excuse a scrawl: this is only to say that I am here and quite fit: in Guweira, a place 35 miles NE of Akaba. I have come down for a night to see Feisul, from Tafileh, where I have been for the last few days. No news from you for a long time, and no opportunity, I expect, of hearing from you for some time yet. General Clayton has, I believe, wired for Arnie—but I do not know in what terms, why, or what the answer has been. If I hear of him in Cairo, I'll try to cut across for a day or two and fix things up with him. He must spend at least some months there. We had a fight north of Tafileh the other day—the Turks attacked us and we annihilated them. Took 23 machine guns & two guns, all in working order. Our loss 20 killed, theirs about 400. I am now off again, buying camels in the Eastern desert, round Wadi Sirhan and Jauf. Weather bitterly cold, with persistent snow and rain, but not likely to endure much longer. The coast & Dead Sea are warm, but our work lies on the plateau, 4,000 or 5,000 feet up.   N.

Stamps enclosed are part of Tafileh post office, all surcharged Peninsula of Sinai!

CAIRO

8.3.18

Here I am in Cairo again. At Tafileh I had a difference of opinion with Sherif Zeid, the 4th son of the old man of Mecca, and left him for Beersheba. This was about the 22nd. I then went to Jerusalem, Ramleh, Jerusalem, Beersheba, Ismailia, Cairo, Suez, Akaba, Guweira, Akaba, Suez, and got back here last night. I hope to be here four nights.

This year promises to be more of a run about than last year even! As for coming back—no, not possible now. The situation has changed since I came over, and I'm to go back till June at least. One rather expected that, I'm afraid. I thought I had told you that Newcombe had left the Sherifian forces before he was captured? He never came to Akaba at all, but went to Palestine with the British.

No letters from you lately, except a November unit which I picked up at Akaba. By the way after this note don't expect any other from me till about the middle of April, for I'm going up country for a month, on an inspection trip.

They have now given me a D.S.O. {for Tafileh}. It's a pity all this good stuff is not sent to someone who would use it! Also apparently I'm a colonel of sorts. Don't make any change in my address of course. I wonder if you remember Young, an Indian Army officer who came to Carchemish while Will was there? He has just come over to help our thing forward, I hope. He should be the right sort of man: the work is curious, and demands a sort of twisted tact, which many people do not seem to possess. We are very short-handed, and it will make things much easier if he fits in well. Hugh Whitelocke has just joined the Egyptian Army I hear. They say he is somewhere in Cairo, so I may see him, but it is only a chance, as on these flying visits I rush about all day and do very little ordinary speech. It will be a comfort when this gipsy mode of life comes to an end.

However thank goodness the worst of the winter is over. I had one very bad night out in the hills when my camel broke down in the snow drifts, and I had to dig a path out for it and lead it for miles down slippery snow-slopes. One's usual airy sort of white shirt and bare feet are better in summer than in winter. Of course the hill country east of the Dead Sea is very high, and one gets what frost and snow there is, anyhow.

There, I can't think of anything else cheerful to tell you about—

except perhaps that three of my camels have had babies in the last few weeks. That makes me about thirty riding camels of my own, but then my bodyguard of servants is about 25, so there are not so many spare. I never have any baggage camels with me . . . we carry what we need on our own animals.

Here by good fortune are some new photographs just to hand.

N.

AKABA

28.3.18

Well, I foretold a long trip, when I was in Cairo a few days ago, and here I am back in Akaba for two nights. Various things happened to delay my start—and indeed I may have one more chance of writing about a week hence, from further North. News? none. We have lost so much by frost and snow and rain that movement has become difficult, and very unpleasant. There is however hope that the spring is coming. Yesterday was warm, but then Akaba always is. About Arnie. General Clayton asked me about him last time I was in Palestine. They did not wire for him, after all, as another man turned up, who will do for the present, and I knew he would rather not hurry things too much. As soon as I hear from you that he is ready to come out they will make an application for him to the War Office. For it to be successful he must be in the army, and an infantry regiment will be the easiest place, unless he gets a special list commission, which may not be still possible. I do not think there will be any difficulty about it at all, so long as he keeps up with his Arabic. I saw Kerry the other day, and Hugh Whitelocke—the only people from Oxford seen for some little time. No matter: after four years of this sort of thing I am become altogether dried up, and till the business ends I can't do anything else either here or there. It will be a great comfort when one can lie down & sleep without having to think about things; and speak without having one's every word reported in half a hundred camps. This is a job too big for me.

N.

ARAB BUREAU
SAVOY HOTEL
CAIRO

12.5.18

I sent you a wire a week ago, as I passed through Cairo on my way
up to Palestine. Since then I have been travelling at red hot speed, but
tonight have finished. Tonight I am going to spend in Cairo, and I got
here last night. It is the first time for six weeks that I have spent two
nights running in one place. I'll get letters from you tomorrow, and
answer them at my leisure, because I expect I'll be here a week. This
is only a scrawl meanwhile. All is very well, and while we have not
done all we want, we have done all that we could do by ourselves, and
it is not at all bad.   N.

CAIRO

15.7.18

Well, this has been a long interruption of writing. I went off to
Jidda, after the last letter, as soon as I had been to Alexandria (to see the
High Commissioner) and to Palestine, to see General Allenby. At
Jidda I had to stay several days, before I could get a boat back to Suez.
It was an unprofitable journey, and I was not able to get anything done
of my hopes. There were a great many local things however, which I
saw, and which rather changed the outlook.

Then from Jidda we dashed up to Wejh, and thence to Suez: a bad
trip, in a small boat, against a strong head wind. Took us 5 days. From
Suez I came here for a night, then Alexandria, then Palestine, and have
now come to anchor here for perhaps a week. It is very nice to have
finished one part of the show. We begin something fresh next month,
and the change will be a pleasant one.

Having said that much, that is all, I think, that I have got to say.
You know I have nothing doing or to do which does not actually
concern Feisul's campaign, and that I make a rule to write nothing
about. I cannot talk about books because I don't read any, or about
people, because I only meet the Staff who deal with our operations,
or places, because most of them are not to be made public property.
So there you are.

As I'm in the middle of the show, I have to be more careful than anybody else. Mr. Hogarth is coming back to England about the middle of August, and hopes to see you and explain something of how we get on. The communiqués in the press contain the least part of the truth. The two Sherifs down by Medina, Abdulla and Ali, allow their fancy very free play with their achievements, and keep on reporting that they have broken thousands of rails and bridges. The bridges are tiny culverts, and the breaks in the rails only shorten them a few inches. Besides they break usually only 10% of their published figures. The communiqués of Feisul's army are written by ourselves, or at least checked by us, and are more truthful.

One thing they have not brought out, I fancy, and which I can tell you, is that from Maan southward for 100 kilometres there are no Turks, and the 8 stations and all the rails and bridges have been smashed to atoms by us. This makes a break that I am sure they will not be able to repair so long as the war lasts, and thanks to it the very large body of troops from there to Medina are cut off from Turkey, as much as the little garrisons of Turks in South Arabia. Medina is a holy city, and the Arabs do not attack it: it has huge gardens and palm groves, and is quite self-supporting so far as food goes, so there is no definite reason why the troops there should ever surrender. We are not in any hurry about it, anyway, though the capture of the place might be a political gain to the Sherif.

There, I think that is enough talk. If I could think of anything more to say I would prolong it. The W.O. reply to our application for Arnie should arrive any day, and when it comes I will write again. We left it purposely till the vac. N.

CAIRO

19.7.18

This is just a two-word scrawl, as I'm off again tomorrow, and this is midnight. The enclosed photographs are of three of my bodyguards —the people with Bedouin clothes—called Abdulla, Rahail, & Mustapha. They came to Cairo with me once, and appear to have celebrated the occasion by getting themselves taken. All quite good men.

No reply from the W.O. about Arnie yet—but I hardly expected one so soon. Will write from Akaba. N.

{There are no more letters of the war period}.

PARIS
30.i.19

I got your letter yesterday, and will answer it this morning, while waiting up here for breakfast. I'm living at the Continental, which is half an hour's walk from the Majestic and Astoria, the British quarters, and this morning I found a taxi, which is a rare thing. In consequence I have ten unexpected minutes. About work—it is going on well. I have seen 10 American newspaper men, and given them all interviews, which went a long way. Also President Wilson, and the other people who have influence. The affair is nearly over, I suspect. Another fortnight, perhaps. Everybody seems to be here, and of course it is a busy time. I have had, personally, one meal in my hotel since I got to Paris! That was with Newcombe, who turned up unexpectedly. Bliss, of the Beyrout College is here, and proving a very valuable assistant of the Arab cause. Tell Arnie I haven't seen a bookshop yet. I cannot come to England to meet Bob, but if he came to Paris could see him. I'm always in my room (98, at the Continental) before 10 a.m. (unless out at breakfast as today) and after 11.30 p.m.

N.

SEMIRAMIS HOTEL
CAIRO
March 20, 1921

We got here about a fortnight ago: and it has been one of the longest fortnights I ever lived: started about March 3, & went via Marseilles & Alexandria. Eight days out.

Here we live in a marble & bronze hotel, very expensive & luxurious: horrible place: makes me Bolshevik. Everybody Middle East is here, except Joyce & Hogarth. We have done a lot of work, which is almost finished. Day after tomorrow we go to Jerusalem for a week: after that don't know: perhaps home: perhaps I return to Egypt for a further fortnight.

Kennington has gone to Damascus. Can't tell you anything else. Have seen Allenby several times, he's very fit: Kennington drew him, & Ironside & me: wanted to draw Gertrude {Bell}, but hadn't time.

We're a very happy family: agreed upon everything important: and the trifles are laughed at.   N.

Hope Arnie is better.

GRAND CONTINENTAL HOTEL
CAIRO

April 12, 1921

Back here in Cairo for two days: have been moving rapidly since I last wrote. We went from Cairo about March 25 to Jerusalem, stopping at Gaza on the way. Two days later I was driven over by car to Salt, across Jordan, where I met Abdulla, Feisal's brother, who drove back to Jerusalem with me. It was an amusing performance, for the people of Salt & Jerusalem were very enthusiastic & excited, & nearly mobbed the car in their anxiety to welcome Abdulla. From Jerusalem I went, on the 31st back to Amman by car, through Salt. The country across Jordan is all in spring, and the grass & flowers are beautiful.

On this side of Jordan the rains have not been very good, & things are too dry already.

Spent eight days in Amman, living with Abdulla in his camp. It was rather like the life in war time, with hundreds of Bedouin coming & going, & a general atmosphere of newness in the air. However the difference was that now everybody is trying to be peaceful.

On Saturday last I ran back to Jerusalem by car (it takes six hours from Amman) & on Sunday I went down to Ramleh, on the coast plain near Jaffa, where our aerodrome is, & flew with four machines to Amman. Abdulla had been longing for aeroplanes, & gave us a great reception & a large lunch. Then we went back to Ramleh, & I went up to Jerusalem to dinner. Next morning they drove me down to Ramleh, where another four machines took me in to Egypt: and here I have been yesterday and today.

To night I'm off to Jerusalem again, and after three days there to Amman, with Sir H. Samuel, who is going over to call on Abdulla, & who will probably stay two nights. Some of his party want to see Petra, so perhaps after that I'll go down there for a night or two to show them round. That ought to finish my jobs out here. I'll be very glad to get back. Would you tell Hogarth of my movements? I haven't written to anyone since I left, & he may be back by now. I am trying to buy him some bronze weapons from tombs on Philistine plain, axes & daggers.   N.

{LONDON}

15 *February* 1922

S.W. Asia Minor will probably be all in the melting pot in a few weeks: so that's out of the question. Rhodes ought not to be difficult: I don't believe the stories about the pains of going there. That was when they feared the Greeks. The other Greek islands will take you a long time, & you can go about places like Smyrna for the moment: but not shortly, I fancy. Cilicia impossible for English people till we make peace with Kemal. It's possible {Lord} Curzon may start that trick soon, but it isn't easy to do. There is talk of my going to Paris when he does.

I enclose a letter from Bob. If his job in the interior is cancelled it may change your plans about going out there, in a year's time, & enable you to go this autumn. The idea of a fracture in your wrists is more probable. However it must have mended long ago, & the massage should give you back the use of the muscles. I've made up my mind that I'm too cluttered about with objects, & am going to get rid of them: especially the books & pictures. Would Arnie like any of either? I have nowhere to put them, or will have, when I give up All Souls, a decision to which I have lately come. As far as I can I'm going to get down to the position in which I can carry all I have in my pockets—or at least in my hands.

I'm perfectly well, & very comfortable in Barton Street which is quite beautiful. The quiet of so little a place in the middle of a great mess has to be experienced a thousand times before it is properly felt. I will be very sorry to leave, when I have to leave, but it's altogether too pleasant to be allowed to go on too long. The woman who looks after me isn't old: about thirty, I should think, but she's going to get married next month.

Kennington is back at Porto Fino: & I've written to him. His drawings are now on their way to the Colonial Office, to be hung here for the present.

My own plans are still doubtful. I asked Winston to let me go, and he was not very willing: indeed he didn't want it. I told him I was open to hold on for a little till his first difficulties were over (there are new things happening just now), but not in a formal appointment. Probably I'll get leave on the first of March, & not go back again, unless that Paris idea comes further: or some other odd notion. There was a question of me for Egypt, if {Lord} Allenby came away: but that of course I wouldn't accept. I don't think ever again to govern anything.

If I get away finally from the Colonial Office about May my plans are to do nothing for a little, & then perhaps to consider the Air Force. Of course I'm too old to join it, but I think that the life & the odd mind (or lack of mind) there, might give me a subject to write about. This long-drawn-out battle over my narrative of the campaigns of Feisal has put an ink fever into me. I find myself always going about trying to fit words to the sights & sounds in the world outside me. However all this remains uncertain, and will remain uncertain for me till I do it. That's a new course I have: of trying to prevent myself making up my mind till afterwards, when the need of action is over.

Let me know what you yourselves do, please, now & then. It's odd you know how impossible it is to be altogether alone. It's the one experience that humanity has never really worked towards: and I'm quite sure that we can only manage it in a crowded place. The difficulty is to keep oneself untouched in a crowd: so many people try to speak to you or touch you: and your like electricity, in that one touch discharges all the virtue you have stored up. However these things don't really matter.   N.

I'm afraid this letter's very scrappy: but I've answered the points in your last as they arose.

{Bovington Camp. R.T.C.}

22.11.23

A month has passed. This is going to Paoing {in West China}. You told me to write to Vancouver, which I did, no doubt too late to overtake you. Shanghai you did not mention, & I haven't written there. If I had, it would no doubt have been too late also. You are fortunate to miss this November. It has been colder than any other in my memory. No news here or elsewhere. I sent you a Doughty by post the other day: & hope you get it. The postage was dear, & the book is rare, in that edition. Now Cape has brought out a £3.3.0 edition, of the complete book, on quite good paper. The identical print of course.

I am doing a little work for Cape, to fill up my odd moments:

and Buxton (the banker) is looking for 100 subscribers of 30 guineas each, to make possible a private reprint of my book on Arabia. Hardy praised it, & makes me feel justified in giving it so much distribution. Of course there would be no reviews, no copies for public sale, & no profits.

I still see Hardy occasionally. John has painted (at my request) a very beautiful portrait of him. The old man is delighted, & Mrs. Hardy also. It is seldom that an artist is so fortunate in his sitter's eyes.

I've taken a little cottage (half ruinous) a mile from camp, & water-tighted it to act as a work-room for myself. There I hope in future to do my writing, which is becoming more & more a habit. No original stuff, of course: just translations. I hope not again to do anything of my own. It is not good for man to make things.

Nothing else I can think of to write. I hope the journey is not still wearisome to you: but you must be looking forward to its end: yet, you know, these journeys don't really end, till we do.   N.

                                                    {Bovington Camp}
                                                        19.xii.23

Your letter from Shanghai got to me yesterday. I'm glad your trip is nearly finished, & that you have met Bob. Ocean voyages are night-mares in retrospect: & very tiresome experiences. You told me to write to Vancouver:—not to Shanghai: I did. Letters since have gone to Paoing. It isn't much good my writing frequently, since I have nothing to say. Some fellow in the camp took my Brough & crashed it: so that I have not been going about. Trenchard called me up to London twice, & on the first occasion I saw Mrs. D. at 2 Smith Square. She asked for your address in China: & I gave it her. Do you wish people generally to know that you are abroad? . . . just in case I meet anyone else. I saw old Hardy a month ago: he was well, & happy that his new play was over & done. My best address now is

                        T. E. Shaw
                        Clouds Hill
                           Morton
                           Dorset

It's a cottage, a half-ruined cottage, near camp, where I have a room for writing in. A pretty little place, & quiet: among trees, & opening on the heath. I have put some books in it. Did I tell you that John had painted a splendid portrait of Hardy? Let me know if ever you feel the inclination for books or things. I can get into Bournemouth, often now, & buy them for you. They are employing me as a sort of half-clerk, half storeman, in the battalion stores. A quiet life.　　　　N.

{AT BOVINGTON CAMP}

9.v.24

　　There, I've gone out tonight & bought six penny stamps, & stuck one on each of six envelopes. So that in future it will not be so frightfully difficult to write to you. Your papers are ordered, & I hope being sent to you, now. I'll go over to Dorchester tomorrow & make sure.

　　W. H. Smith & Son, East St. Dorchester Dorset, in case you wish to make any alteration or difference in them. Sorry your boxes got so hurt by water. I hope you haven't lost anything irreplaceable. Were the books good ones? I can send you more, as you require them. Little news here. {Lord} Trenchard sent for me, the other day. I went up, hoping to hear something about my getting back to the R.A.F. but all that he wanted me for was to offer me the writing of the R.A.F. history of the war . . . the thing of which {Professor} Raleigh did one volume, & whose continuation Mr. Hogarth lately laid down, after a year spent in working at it. Of course it's a very difficult thing to do, & D. G. H. has been a sick man lately. The diabetes opened the way to all sorts of minor ailments, so that he is now feeling fully his age: indeed I suspect that he will never be quite right again: and in the circumstances he was wise to give up so exacting a job. Of course it is out of the question that I should take it over. I heard the other day from Arnie, who is still in New York, but may come to England next month. He thinks afterwards of going on to Germany and Greece: but if he stays in this country any length of time will try & make time to visit me here. I've just put a bed in one room of my cottage at Clouds Hill, so that he can camp out there if he wishes to be quiet. There are books in the place, & nothing to do. No news at all. A Labour Government is like any other: & this isn't a Government. It's a conspiracy on the part of Liberals & Conservatives to dodge the responsibility of office! No act can be made without the consent of all three parties!　　　　N.

CLOUDS HILL

18.v.24

No, there had been a muddle about the papers. I'd told Smith's to send the bill to me, & they had taken alarm at my khaki (you know a soldier can't be sued for debt) and had decided to wait for cash. It is arranged now, & I hope you will get them regularly: though you are hopelessly far away. You will be careful not to form your opinion only on *The Times*. I've added a *New Statesman* to the order, since that is a paper which does not instantly condemn an idea for the reason that it is new. I forget what I told you when I last wrote . . . that Trenchard had wanted me to write the war-history of the Royal Air Force, & had been hurt by the definiteness of my refusal . . . that Arnie is soon coming to England. I hear very often from Mrs. Bernard Shaw, & Robert Graves intends to call in soon, on his way to visit Hardy. So that things are busy for me. In camp as little happens as ever. I have a quiet place now, live very much by myself, and have no worries, beyond the slow coming of old age:—not so slow this last: I suppose it is the revenge of Arabia for my contempt of its climate. Some changes lately made in my motor-cycle have made it faster & better to ride: but I've only done 3,000 miles this year, so that you may imagine I do little riding.

To date 34 people have subscribed for the private issue of my book. I had hoped for 110 in all . . . but it seems unlikely.   N.

Should you ever need to alter the papers in a hurry: write to

W. H. Smith & Son

Newsagents

Dorchester

Dorset

and ask them to communicate with me . . . that's if I'm sent away from here.

CLOUDS HILL

MORETON

DORSET

18.viii.24

A long time since I heard from you: but every week or so the press is full of floods and rebellions in China, so that presumably there is no lack of events, even in your distant place. I wonder if you ever get our

papers? The Labour Government has just had two successes in Foreign
Politics—a treaty with Russia, & the passing of the Dawes agreement
upon Reparations from Germany. The last means that the world lends
Germany forty million pounds in gold, to repair the damage of the
French entry into the Ruhr. . . . and the French have to clear out
within a year. Also our troops will probably return from Cologne. It
means a return, or the beginning of a return, to peace conditions on
the continent. Arnie came down & stayed a week in my cottage: not
too comfortably, but he is able to look after himself. He was decent to
the little soldiers who went up occasionally to see him. I like him, too.
He's original, & strong-flavoured, & intelligent, with a great deal of
humour & self-sufficiency. Altogether a very complete & excellent
person. He's much older in feeling than I had expected. It comes rather
as a shock to find him quite mature in every way. He went on from
here towards Vienna, & is probably somewhere in Austria or Germany
now. He would spend a second period in Rome, if it were not for fear
of interference from Mrs. Strong: and may go to Greece again in the
autumn, which is already upon us, to judge by the weather.

I found Scott's journals in Dorchester, & asked Smith's to post them
off to you. The book shops of this district are rubbish only, & the book-
sellers haven't an idea of what literature is.

My own reprint makes slow progress. Some six of the coloured
illustrations are in proof, & the first thirty pages of the book. That will
be enough to make the rest easier. It's the beginning, the settling things,
which is so difficult. Subscribers at 30 guineas were hard to find, for a
while, but are rolling in merrily now, at the rate of ten or twelve a
month. Before the year is out I'll have the 110 I need, & the book won't
be within six months of finishing. If I had wished I could have sold 200
copies. However all I want is to meet the bills, comfortably. The sale
of the original pictures will in part repay me for the expense of them.
My revived bicycle seems to have taken over a new lease of life, & runs
tremendously. I don't know what its maximum speed is, but it must
be over 90 miles an hour. Unfortunately the wet season has cut down
my riding: a solo isn't as secure on a wet road as a side-car outfit. Also
I've been doing a lot of proof-reading & correction, for my book.
The Hardys are driving me over to Glastonbury next Friday, to
hear the performance of his last play, *Iseult*, with music by Rutland
Boughton, a local composer, who has made a country orchestra &

opera company, & performs plays there every year in a musical "season". It will be interesting.

No news, I think, from any part of the world lately. I haven't been to Oxford, or heard from Hogarth for a long while. I fancy Arnie went there: but he never talks about his travels or personalities.

There, it's begun to rain again.

N.

I have your salts of lemon waiting a chance to go. The P.O. people said it would be found at once, in an envelope: and I don't want to murder a Chinese postman.

{CRANWELL}

28.xii.25

It's almost the end of the year: so I'm writing again, though there is nothing to say. A letter of yours (October) came lately. I've given up trying to send locks. Clearly someone on the road likes such things. I'm tired of supplying his needs. Let him buy them.

Arnie is leaving Clouds Hill almost at once. Just now he has Florence there with him. It's a bad place to ask a visitor: and a bad time of year. The winter this year is sharp.

No thanks: no money. I am quite right that way just now. How I'll stand a year or so hence, when all the bills of the reprint of my book come in, I don't know. The subscribers (about 100) have paid £15 each, to date. That is £1,500 more due from them. The expenses to date are £4,500. The Bank has loaned the rest, against security from me. To meet the deficit I have sold Cape (for £3,000 cash + a royalty) the right to publish ⅓ of the book after Jan. 1. 1927. And there will be American serial & other receipts, too. Probably I'll come out of it well enough off. Arnie is to have a copy of the subscribers' edition. Would you like one? I propose to buy the liability of Clouds Hill off him so that will be £400 more for his pocket. Clouds Hill is very beautiful, & suits me. Though I will not live there till I have been as long in the Air Force as pleases me. You know I always wanted to be in the R.A.F.

I've sent you a Blackwood article, in which Candler, an Indian journalist has written some butter & sugar stuff about me. Don't worry about that—or me—or anything. People are solitary things (myself especially so) and as long as it isn't true, I don't care what praise or blame I get.

My present name & address are

A/c II Shaw. 338171
Hut 105.
R.A.F. Cadet College
Cranwell
Lincs.

but I may change to Ross in a month or two, so you had better continue to write to Clouds Hill, under any name. The Tank Corps Fellows will forward letters. Everybody up here knows who I used to be. I told them when I arrived. So all the wonder is over. Three years & a half now, my service. So I fit in well enough.

Yes I still have Boanerges {his motor bicycle made by Mr. Brough}: and ride it whenever the weather is good enough. Much snow lately. Arnie has a tiny car: not a good one.   N.

CRANWELL

20.4.26

It is a long time since I wrote: for two months ago I broke my radius and the right arm has not been very fit for paper-work since. I was starting a car, & the starting handle flew back & hit my wrist on the second turn. The tip of the radius was cracked off, & the wrist dislocated. Now they have put it nearly straight again: but it still cramps me badly after a few minutes in one position holding anything small like a pen or knife. They say that in another month it will be quite fit; though I have lost the power of twisting my hand round very far. It goes about half way now.

Otherwise there is little to tell you, which I have not already said. I'm still very pleased with Cranwell, & am doing exactly what I was doing before. So that's well. My bicycle is rejuvenated, & runs splendidly. I had it overhauled while I was in splints, & it is very fast now: though I do not yet feel inclined to ride more than a hundred or so in the day. Your hot weather will be starting soon (and ours, I hope!): I'm sorry you do not like it. I used to find that the heat gave a delicious sense of weary peace to everything within my reach.

My private book is not finished yet. August probably. It has stood still lately, but I hope to start now. Cape is to publish a fraction of the

story in March, 1927. His extra money has enabled me to put more
pictures & luxury into the private edition.

Nothing else.   N.

A letter—illegible—from Menon!

I will reply when I can: but have over 80 letters to write before I'm
up to date.

CRANWELL

6.7.26

I've been waiting for sure news before writing to you: but the Air
Force authorities drag too slowly. So here it is. I'm to go to India this
winter: perhaps in September, perhaps in November, perhaps in
February. It's the ordinary overseas draft, of the R.A.F. pattern. Most
airmen do a turn abroad in their seven years' service. The Mesopotamian term is 2 years, the climate being bad. Egypt is 5 years: India is
5 years. I'm glad I'm not going to Egypt, for there is the risk of trouble
there.

In a way I'd rather have stayed in England: but the warmth, if there
is any, will be welcome: and it is good to be out of England when
Cape brings out that abridgement of my Arabian book. I made the
abridgement myself, & it is a severely plain one, but to sell it Cape
must advertise it, & his best way of doing that will be to rake up all
the old silly stories about me. I shall be glad this autumn when the real
book is finished and distributed. All the work of the little book is done,
already: a good thing, for with this uncertainty about going abroad
I do not want more liabilities than I can help. Your cheque turned up:
many thanks for it: but it is bigger, I fancy, than the money I have
spent.

Florence wrote to me some while ago that you might come home
with Bob in 1929. I hope so: and not to go out again!

They wanted me to go out on a Commission of Enquiry to China,
the other day! I told them I was happily engaged in the R.A.F.

N.

{14 BARTON STREET}

I.xii.26

This is my last free night in England, & I'm writing to you, very
late, in the top of Barton Street, where {Sir Herbert} Baker has let me

stay during this month. It should have been leave, preparatory to going overseas: but for me it has been a very hard month of work on that big book of mine. It is not finished: but every copy is at the binders, so that my share is over. All that remains is to send off the copies, & that my printer, Pike, will do for me. Your copy is to be sent to Arnie, at Highgate. I saw him for a few moments a fortnight ago. He seemed flourishing. A. too has written a book: not so exhausting a one as mine.

Getting it over has been a big relief. I have spent £13,000 on it, altogether, and the responsibility of that has been heavy, since my own resources would not meet its liability. I am reckoning on the abridgement which Cape publishes in March next year to bring in enough to cover my deficit.

Thank you for suggesting my leaving the R.A.F. and living quietly somewhere: but I cannot be quiet, and so the bustle and enforced duty of the R.A.F. is good for me. I wish it was not India—an experiment which has lasted too long, & where we are failing—but that is no great matter. The rank & file have nothing to do with politics.

The leaving England is in one way a good thing. I shall be much more alone in India. Here people I used to know will keep on breaking into my peace: and there are newspapers & news & letters, all of which try to drag me back into affairs. Whereas it is my will to stay clear of everything henceforward.

I cannot tell you where I am going. Tomorrow it is to Uxbridge. Our ship should sail on Sunday, from Southampton perhaps. We disembark at Karachi, about a month later: stay a few days or weeks in the Depot there, & then go up country to our final station. When I get to the end of the journey I'll write to Arnie & to you, & tell you my new address. It should be for three years, but may be for five. I hope that Cape's book will be completely forgotten before then.

Your letter of Oct. 26 has just come: only a month on the way. That has been very quick. Perhaps the Wan hsien troubles have not interrupted the mails as much as I thought.

There: this is not a cheerful letter. The last four weeks I have been wandering about seeing my time drawing to an end, & so I am not able to settle to anything, or rest myself in anything. Once off, it will be all right.

N.

My new address is

11.1.27

338171 A C 2 SHAW

ROOM 2.　E.R.S.

R.A.F. DEPOT

DRIGH ROAD

KARACHI

INDIA

I've only just got here, and cannot yet say what I think of the place. It is comfortable, almost magnificently-built, and cool. I am in room two, with fourteen fellows. It seems a quiet place, though the stone floors & high ceilings are noisy and distant, hospital-like, after the homeliness of Cranwell. The journey out here was extraordinarily uncomfortable, owing to the crowded state of the boat. Smooth seas. We stopped at Port Said, (where Newcombe came on board for me, and took me to dinner with him) and at Basra, where I did not go ashore.

Before leaving England I got my *Seven Pillars* finished, & sent out the early copies to specially privileged subscribers. You will laugh at me to hear that the first went to the King: but he wanted one, & I amused myself by treating him well!

Arnie has your copy, to keep till you instruct him to the contrary. Its completion takes a load off my mind.

I'll be out here, probably, till 1932. If my book is judged a failure I'll be nearly forgotten in England by then.

N.

Your old clock is being sent to Clouds Hill.

24.ii.27

In case my last letter did not get through:—a very probable occasion in these times:—I'll repeat my new address

338171 A C 2 SHAW

ROOM 2.　E.R.S.

R.A.F. DEPOT

DRIGH ROAD

KARACHI

INDIA

E.R.S. stands for Engine Repair Section. To it all the aeroplane engines in India come for their periodic overhauls. I'm not a technical hand of course, so all I do is to walk about and do a perambulating clerkly job. We work too short hours each day, and are bored with an excessive leisure. The camp is comfortable: new, stone-built, cool and spacious. The surroundings are unmitigated desert—great wastes of sand, between sandstone ridges, on which grows nothing but cactus: and not much cactus. Wide valleys of dusty tamarisk wind across this Sind desert, to fall at long last into the Indus, which reaches the sea near Karachi.

Karachi, the town, I have not visited. As a seaport it cannot hold very many attractions: and it is a little Aldershot-like, in having a considerable military garrison. So my leisure is mostly round about the camp, an uninteresting country which scarcely repays one the trouble of walking in it. As time passes I will get here some books to busy myself over in spare hours. After that I'll be independent of India, so far as amusements go.

The time to leave Paoning is while the local people still want you to stay. I'm hoping every day to hear of your safe return. However it is no use talking these things over again. The difference of opinion is too fundamental.

My big book is now all distributed. The Cape abridgement appears in March. Financially I have done well: and all my liabilities at my Bank are now safely covered. Any surplus there may be will be paid to a R.A.F. charity.

The pictures are now being exhibited in London, with a very excellent preface to the catalogue by Bernard Shaw. I will send you a copy, after I hear from you again.   T.E.S.

KARACHI
5.v.27

{Evidently to A. W. Lawrence.}

I wonder if they have reached England by now: or if they have stopped (it would be wise, climatically) for a few weeks in the Rhône valley on their way up from Marseilles. And I wonder in what mind they will reach England, & where they will settle to live. It struck me, thinking it over, that some such place as Dumfries or Edinburgh might please them. London does not care for the things they care about, and the solidity of parts of Scotland might appeal to Bob. Mother, herself, was always Scotch in inclination. You might suggest it to them, as a chance idea of mine. I am sure that neither London, nor any of the usually-considered-habitable parts of England, will suit.

Possibly Mother will be visiting Dr. James, my very adept dentist. If so, please ask her to commend me to him, with the message that his most artificial masterpiece, my mouth, still stands superbly. It cracks nuts. Yes, I'd like to see your book: and can send back the copy, after reading, if that would be a convenience to you. If it stays here, it may lose itself. I'm not responsible for my books: they are at a premium, in camp. No, I have no interest (financial) in the sale of the *Seven Pillars* pictures: and no control over the disposal of the profits of *Revolt*.

Hogarth is one of the three step-parents of *Revolt*. They say it has sold almost riotously. So much the better. I like G.B.S. He is still in the saddle, & able to fight, after 20 years of glory. Few victors survive so long. Mrs. S. {Shaw} is also good. She refuses to be his shadow. Wives of great men have a hard life.

Alonso de Contreras? Never heard of him. His name makes me wish for a copy of *Don Quixote*!

                                      Yours   T.E.S.

                                               {KARACHI}
                                               16.vi.27

I was glad to get your letter at last. I'm sorry you tried to write to me before, but hope there was nothing in the letters which the man who got them shouldn't read. Here the important parts of the address (which you got quite right) are E.R.S., the engine repair section in which I work, and Drigh Road, the village seven miles from Karachi, where E.R.S. is situated. Drigh Road is quite in the country, which here is a mixture of desert and slum. If we want to go to Karachi we have to go by train: but I made up my mind soon after I got here that I would not leave camp. So I limit myself to the two or three square miles of the camp and aerodrome. It was as well you did not ask me to come to Bombay! I will not even go down to the station here!

My work? E.R.S. overhauls the aero engines, after they have done so many hours service in the squadrons on the frontier. They have given me a semi-clerical job, to follow the various engines as they pass through the shops, and record what changes and spares and repairs and adjustments each requires. This is my main job, but it is supplemented with others. We work only five hours a day, and have whole holidays on Thursday and Sunday: except that there are sometimes compulsory church-parades on Sundays. In India the R.A.F. unfortunately is part of the military establishments, so there are many stupid ceremonies and public performances for which we have to turn out and pretend to be soldiers. That causes a lot of bad feeling amongst the airmen.

What else? Nothing to speak of. I came out here to avoid the publicity which would inevitably be fanned up by the sale of *Revolt in the Desert*. In this I have succeeded excellently. There is not enough local press to bother me: and the local people who might try to see me are not allowed into camp, and I never go out. So only the airmen know of my existence, and they are too used to me, as a daily object, to be interested in a reputation which comes to them as a faint echo from the London papers. Very few of them read books: fewer still read any but the English provincial papers which their parents send them. Consequently I am not bothered by anybody at all. The officers steer clear of me, because I make them uncomfortable. It is very good to be left so much alone.

So far as *Revolt in the Desert* is concerned, it has done its job perfectly. My debt is paid off, & the mortgage on Chingford extinguished. Clouds Hill is let, for about 12/– a week, which is good for an unfitted cottage. Pole Hill {at Chingford} brings in £1 a week. So they both pay for themselves, and I have no trouble with them. Richards looks after Pole Hill, and a Sergt. Knowles, of the Tank Corps, after Clouds Hill. I'm afraid neither place would be any use to you. They are both too rough & isolated.

I wonder what you and Bob will do. Low blood pressure is a good thing, in reason: but he is probably tired, and will want a rest. He has been away so long that England will have become strange to him; and that is a pity, for there will of course be no question of his going back to China.   N.

The Kenningtons (two children now) would be glad to see you. They live at Morton House, Chiswick Mall, W.4, near their old home. Also Mrs. Bernard Shaw is an independent interesting straight-forward person, if you feel a wish to go about. I can't think of anyone else. Herbert Baker (now a Sir) you already know. Hogarth is the only other person I write to often.

Yes, I got your letter with the pound note in it. Many thanks. I spent it, of course. I could spend anything: but actually the R.A.F. give me enough for most of the things I want. As I never leave camp and have no motor bicycle my expenses out here are extremely small. Stamps and paper and envelopes are the main items. I wish I could see some way of cutting down the number of letters I write. It is now seldom less than twenty a week, and I only answer three out of five that come to me. Perhaps if I cut down the proportion to two out of four it would ease matters. Ninety per cent. of the letters are about things, business things, of which I care nothing whatever. The other ten per cent. are either to you or Mrs. Shaw, who is very good about sending me books and things (you should meet Mrs. Shaw some day: she is oldish, & plain-thinking, and interesting, and Anglo-Irish from somewhere near Cork. She would like to meet you, because she found me queer, & would like to study my surviving parent! And you would like her, and admire G.B.S. her husband). Enough of letters. They waste my time, & the other peoples. Some day I'll be strong minded enough to stop writing altogether. Till then I'll use up half my leisure saying No or Yes to all the world on paper.

I told you in a previous letter (that's the worst of writing between mails: it means saying everything over & over again: the China letters were terrible that way: half of them never got through, & the survivors only repeated the last one) that your *Seven Pillars* needn't be paid for. It is at the Bank's expense, not mine, and the Bank is now, or will be in November, repaid out of the profits of *Revolt in the Desert*, which has made £4,000 or £5,000 more than is needed to cover my debts. There is no need to make their surplus £4,030 or £5,030, which is all your cheque would do. You must know by now that I do not profit personally by anything connected with the Arab Revolt.

I'm glad you liked Clouds Hill. Of course the cottage has been much changed since I left it. But if I ever get it again I'll soon put it right. The upstairs room is only half-finished. It will some day be as good as its wonderful situation deserves. That heath country is the most beautiful I've seen, & the rhododendrons in Moreton Park climb up the oak trees, like creepers, & hang 50 feet in the air, in showers of blossom.

Graves has finished his book. It is to amuse the young, who can't read *Revolt in the Desert*. I don't care, now I'm abroad.   N.

                                                            KARACHI
                                                            4.xi.27

Please let me off parcels. The duty makes them a real inconvenience. Books came free by book-post: but I get so many that I cannot read the half of them. The camp's electric-light is very poor: or my eyes are failing: I don't know which: but anyway I do not find it possible to read by night: and that is most of the reading time we have.

Mrs. Shaw has sent me Gertrude's letters, which you speak of getting. They are very like her: the eager emotional self. Sir Hugh Bell, her father, to whom she sent them, was a person she liked. They used to exchange letters very often. They have now closed down the English edition of *Revolt in the Desert*: so that is finished. I hope it will never be reprinted in my lifetime: but of course it now belongs to the three Trustees (Eliot, Buxton, & D.G.H. {Mr. Hogarth}) and I have no say in it: it was very good of them to withdraw it for my benefit.

I am sorry to hear of Mr. Hutchins' death: she, I believe, is paralysed. That makes things bad for Louie. I'm afraid Henry will have a hard time of it with the business, now.

I have seen a review of Arnie's book: so it is out. Unfortunately it will not sell enough to pay him a royalty. Publishers take on that sort of book for the dignity it gives them. They make their money on biography and novels, & drop a percentage of it on serious books, for the look of the thing. Of course if it was capable of being a school-book:—but it is too specialist for that. However Arnie does not expect it to be profitable. He has ideas, I think, of writing something more saleable, some day. I wish there was some way of securing him £500 a year, extra.

Chaundry has one very rare & good book of mine: Cavendish's life of Cardinal Wolsey, which you would probably like. Richards keeps all my other books, if ever you want any. There are still a lot of Kelmscotts': though I had to sell my Shakespeare & Dante.

I'm glad Dr. James passes you: he did a very wonderful job, last time, to my teeth. They are as good as new, now. No, I won't pay the balance on Clouds Hill till I get back. The Land Agent there had three years in which to complete the deed of sale. I called on him a dozen times for it: but he was so dilatory that he wouldn't face it. So now I'll let him wait. Not that he has yet done anything. Indeed probably the deed won't be ready when I get back. Then I can pay it (less the £300) out of a *Seven Pillars*. D.G.H. has one for me, & Richards, I believe, another. The two together will be worth at least £400, even in 1930, when I expect to get back.

Arnie has looked after my insurance. I will be able to pay him its amount in a few weeks. The *Spectator* pays me occasionally for unsigned reviews I do for them: only till the royalties of *Revolt* have come in, and paid my overdraft to the Bank, I don't quite know how I stand, financially. I expect I have really far more money there than I think: only I've determined to draw none of it until the overdraft is paid off. It is difficult to run two or three accounts, especially from a foreign country!   N.

{KARACHI}
4.i.28

That is much better: when we do not write so rapidly, our letters have time to reach their destinations and answer their questions: so that we do not need to repeat everything many times. It is not as though I had much to say. Life with me is much the same, from week to week, or from year to year: in camp at Farnborough, or at Bovington, or at Cranwell, or at Drigh Road. One room is like another, in barracks, and one airman is like another airman. We do not have changes or adventures. We stay still, and are physically taken care of, like stock cattle.

I am glad you thought to leave England for a little. They say, in the papers, that it has been cold there, and wintry. It feels improbable, out here, where the climate is hardly varied from January to January, where it is never hot, and very seldom cold. Karachi seems to have struck the mean of the world's climates, and to exist in a perpetual temperateness of heat and sunshine. Yet it is a dreary place, because the weather is too same to have a character. Too long a succession of perfect weeks brings monotony.

Italy, you have chosen: and Rome, of all places in Italy. Now I could have understood some little village in the hills. Did you ever read

D. H. Lawrence's marvellous novel *The Lost Girl* . . . with its pictures of country life, very high up, in Italy? One of the most beautiful of modern stories, told by a master of English prose. You can get a 3/6 edition of it, published by Martin Secker. In such a house as that you might be quiet.

Yes, that sending of the parcel was a pity. I have been much troubled by parcels: the great warm heart of the British and American public seems to yearn over people who write, and they send me incongruous things: so I have my private way of getting the things I ask for: and the Post Office (which in India means the Customs) have my instructions not to notify to me the other things. I do not know what happens to them: perhaps they are sent back as not delivered (but the Stores will have their rules against that, for it would involve them in expense), perhaps they are sold out here to pay Customs charges. Also registered letters are not delivered to me. I found that they were only afflictions. My post is unmanageably great. I have had to make a rule not to spend more than 3/– a week in stamps & stationery, to answer the letters I get: and that means very many letters go without their replies. I cannot answer more than one in three of what I receive, and even what I do write is too much. It taxes my spare time valuelessly: for my opinions and ideas are not useful to anyone else, and it is no pleasure to me to put them on paper. Some day I dream of putting round a little printed card to everyone . . . "Many thanks for your letter, which I should have endeavoured to answer, only that I have determined lately to write no more letters that are not of a strictly business character." It would be a saving of time and tissue . . . but I am afraid of causing more talk.   N.

{KARACHI}
21.2.28

This is only a line. I see from the papers that Eliot, who owns the *Revolt in the Desert*, appears to have sold its film rights. The company will probably take a year or more to make their film: and then a year or more to show it (films do die, fortunately, soon) so I don't suppose that 1930 will be my return-date, as I'd hoped. It will be a year or so later, perhaps. But it's too soon to start even guessing. There is so much publicity about a film, that I very much regret it.

I hope you are now back in England. There's a thing you might send me, after you get back. Bob could find them at any shop. Some DARWIN razor blades, for a GILLETTE razor. I brought out enough to last me for three years: now I'd better have a reserve: say four dozen more. Pass the request on to Arnie, if it troubles you, or if Bob has gone somewhere.

N.

{KARACHI}
23.3.28

There, I have sorted out, in the last three days, my recent letters. There are 132 business letters which I must answer: 26 letters from people I once used to feel with, & whose friendliness has gone on past our separation. I would like to drop them, but am too soft-hearted: and I have thrown away two boxes-full of stuff that did not matter.

My average mail is 20 letters a week: of which perhaps six or seven are of no importance. That just balances my maximum reply-capacity. I can afford two rupees (3/–) for stamps every week, & the little extra which envelopes & paper cost. So if everybody ceased writing to me from today I could be free of back-correspondence in ten weeks at 16 letters a week. Letters take on the average $\frac{3}{4}$ of an hour each, if you add in the getting pens & ink out of my box, & the job of getting them to the post office. So for 12 hours a week (2 a day) for the next ten weeks would see me quit. Only each week there arrive more letters than I can answer. So the problem remains impossible. Also I refuse to waste all my leisure on letter-writing. The letters bore the people who get them as much as their letters bore me, I suppose. Who invented this curse?

I think I shall print a small card "to announce cessation of correspondence" and send it to the 300 or 400 of my regular addresses. After that I shall write not more than one letter per week, & take a holiday once a quarter.

All of which nonsense has well filled these pages, & conceals the fact that nothing has happened here since I wrote to you last. All well. Hope Bob's better, & settling down.

N.

{KARACHI}

13.4.28

Thank you very much for the razor blades. That is two or three years' supply in hand, & should carry me through, however long I stop out here. Fortunately the weather has turned a little warmer, now, so that I feel happier. That chill in the morning & night air is a detestable feeling. Karachi is comfortable, in summer.

Please explain to Menon that the *Seven Pillars* was printed in a limited edition, & at a very high price, just so that it should not be read. I have no wish ever to lend anyone a copy, and I entirely disapprove of other people lending their copies about. Fortunately the book has so increased in value that every copy is now kept under lock & key, and I suspect their circulation will entirely cease. The only reason it was printed was to get the illustrations reproduced. It is not for the public. Explain, please, also to him that I do not leave camp. Incidentally Indians aren't allowed into camp, so he will not be able to see me if he comes up here. People are a nuisance. They will not understand that I have no intention of continuing the acquaintances I had before 1914. That part of the business is finished. I am a different person, now: and live with the Air Force, a class of man that didn't exist before the war. Eliot, my London solicitor, is a very decent fellow, and has done his book business very well. He and Robin Buxton manage the affairs of *Revolt in the Desert* between them. It has been selling fairly in Sweden & Germany, of late: but I hear little of it.

The film is a misfortune, but it was bound to occur, sooner or later. I hope it will be a bad film, I think it will be. They hope to finish it this year, apparently, and are talking of doing it in Palestine! I wonder if they realise how hard it will be to arrange it there.

I have lately read Arnie's sculpture book. It is good. The writing is better than the art-criticism, I fancy. He might have a success with some book on a non-technical subject.

N.

{KARACHI}

26.4.28

This is only a line, to tell you not to write again to Karachi: I have asked Sir Geoffrey Salmond, the Air Chief here, whom I know from

Palestine days, to shift me to some other camp. There is no present need: but I was told some private information, which decided me that I'd better shift before the changes came.

Salmond has so large a stock of stations to which he can post me, that I can't even guess which it will be. Peshawar probably. The insides of the camps are all much the same. So I am largely indifferent. I only hope the place will be generally warmer than this. Karachi climate is like a continuing spring: whereas it seems silly to go to all the waste and trouble of living in the East, without getting the sunlight and warmth which is usually the East's blessing. No other news. I hope that Bob is settling down a bit, and thinking of English work. The advantage of doctoring one's countrymen is that they can tell one what they really think of it!　　　　　　　　　　　　　　　　N.

338171　A/c Shaw　R.A.F.
Miranshah
Waziristan
India
10.7.28

This will be a note only. Very late, & working hard, doing some photography (developing & printing) as well as my office job, owing to the photographer going ill. Your letter to here came on Sunday.

Yes, I think I shall like this place: though they talk of bringing me back to Peshawar. I hope not: this is quieter: and we are not allowed outside the fort walls, so that I have not to imprison myself.

Philby is embittered, by not having succeeded politically. I got all I wanted, & so can afford to be kindly towards him. That angers him worse. A very nice fellow, but queer: very queer. Short of money, now, I believe. I'm glad you met Mrs. Shaw. It's very hard to be a great man's wife. She succeeds with it. I like her. Hope you'll meet G.B.S. some time. He is like a tonic: and very kind. A most sensible, vigorous old man. The Chingford people want to buy all Pole Hill, & exchange it, with the forest people, for some strips of forest, in the village, which they would like to make into roads & things. I do not feel inclined to help them: & I doubt whether they will attempt forced purchase. Don't worry about Arnie's baby. I think Arnie hopes to get his new book adopted as a text-book. They are profitable things.

I'm glad Leeds has got the Museum {Ashmolean}. Lots of people grudged it him.

I'm doing the office job which used to be done by a clerk here: a lot of typing, & that sort of thing. Enough, but not too much for each day. The first date I can come back is the early summer of 1930: and that only if this film gets itself over next year.   N.

                                        338171   A/c Shaw
                                        R.A.F. Cattewater
                                        Plymouth
                                        12.3.29

There, that is the address. I like the little camp. Only 100 of us live in it: the other 50 airmen are natives, and live in the town. The huts and sheds fill the whole of a little promontory (like a petrified lizard's bones) which runs out from a green hill into the Sound, facing Plymouth across about a mile of water.

The camp is comfortable, & the airmen say it is a happy place. So that is hopeful hearing: only everything is brand-new as yet, and nothing has yet settled in or down. The sunlight and the sea's nearness (50 yards on one side of our hut, 30 yards on the other) and the grass, make it lively. To get into Plymouth is a break-neck ride up & down twisting hill roads. Wherefore most people with bicycles ride out into the country, and take a ferry when they want to see the town. Nothing else, I fancy. I hope Bob got his little pamphlet: it was posted on Thursday, in London.   N.

                                        Plymouth
                                        19.3.29

It is not quite so cold, today. The camp still proves itself easy and good. It is so pleasantly tiny, after Karachi and Cranwell. More like Miranshah, but more crowded than Miranshah.

The longest leave we get is from after duty (noon) on Saturday, till midnight Sunday. If you set against that the distance we are from London, you'll see that that amounts to very little. Also there is the *Odyssey* to tackle. I have not touched it yet. It takes so long really to settle down in a new camp. We get a month's leave a year, too, of course: but this I am saving against the fear of a sudden release of that film, with a lot of public chatter.

I saw Clouds Hill. It is as lovely as ever: only chimney-pots on the top, as the sole disfigurement. I have paid for it now: only the conveyance is not yet ready. Four years has that wretched land agent been bungling his business. My job here is going to be given me in about 10 days or so. Till then I just busy myself doing some typing work in an office, helping a clerk who is too full of work.   N.

PLYMOUTH

1.4.29

I have been what they call "Fire Picquet" this last 8 days: that means I have had to stay in camp all the time, with six others. Since Friday we have been almost the only people here: for Easter is our big holiday. I have been working at the *Odyssey*, & have roughed out Book 8. That is good. No other news: the bicycle is getting rusty: so am I, I fancy. If tomorrow is fine I may run out in the evening & buy some stamps & notepaper, both of which are running short. I shall be glad when summer time gives us longer evenings.

This is a noisy hut. It has been pleasant to have four quiet days: and I think I have turned them to good account, so far as Homer is concerned.

This place is good. I like it: but to get to Plymouth (only 300 yards crow-fly) is four and a half miles of bad road! The local papers are making their usual fuss over me: I hope they will get it over soon.

N.

PLYMOUTH

1.5.29.

Here is May, and still it is cold, and nothing has happened to write about. Last week we flew to Calshot, and went over to Cowes in a motor boat. No great changes. Lepe and Langley were much the same, from overhead: a few more houses. Fawley of course is all different, with its oil works. I did not have time to go out of Eaglehurst camp, so saw nothing of the country, except from the air. Back there in July, I expect.

I'm glad you like Málvern, and your house: but if it is as cold as here you will be still imprisoned indoors. Perhaps there is a motor-car which Bob drives about. Most English doctors have little closed cars for visiting their patients. I wonder how long you will stay in Malvern. The Shaws will be there in August, for a festival of his plays at the theatre, and I want to try and come up for one evening, to see the new play: only it will be difficult to get the time off. We are kept very closely at it, here.

By all means take some of the rhododendrons from Clouds Hill. There are only too many of them. I had hoped to put in some red and some white ones, to mix up the colour: and a lot of magnolias, which carry beautiful great flowers. There seems to be some hitch over the purchase. I've given them a week to say yes or no. Tired of waiting, I am. Epping Forest want Pole Hill, to add to the forest. I'm likely to agree to that, as it would be a crime to build streets over it. Only, of course, it means I won't get much money for it: perhaps only about £4,000. Its real value is as building land, for which I don't wish to sell it. However, it will be months before they settle anything.

I've only been three times out of camp since I've been here: twice to London for a few hours, and last week to Plymouth, to eat a meal with Lady Astor, who came here and looked me up. I like her: though she is tiring. If you go to Clouds Hill, see Sergt. Knowles, who will help you, if you want any help. Your Inverness clock is in his cupboard, for dryness sake. I've told Lionel Curtis he may use the cottage, for week-ends, if he likes. The tenants have gone. It is not damaged. The last time I was in London I met Arnie, late at night, near Russell Square. He knew me, & told me about his book. G.B.S. is in the Adriatic, on an island.

If you see Leeds again, tell him I will not be able to come to Oxford till after September, after this Schneider Cup Race. They have set me on to do some of the clerical work for that.   N.

{PLYMOUTH}

4.vi.29

My head is singing like a kettle, after flying to Portsmouth and back today (Schneider Cup Committee meeting). It rained here heavily last Saturday. So I only went over to Plymouth (by ferry) & sent you a wire.

Next week and the week after, and the week-end after that I am engaged, on duty & other things. So my next free week-end is June 29. You will be in Droitwich then, I expect: and it would be better if I stayed that week in camp, and did not go out till July.

I have not done any Homer since the week after Easter. Very busy every day on R.A.F. work.

As yet I can't say what will be my movements in July & August, during the Schneider period. May go up only just before the race (Sept. 7) and spend its two or three days on a yacht, & not visit Calshot at all: or may spend 5 weeks in Calshot. Arrangements will not be settled till July 15th. I will let you know as soon as I know. If we go up only at the last moment I shall not be able to go ashore at all. It would be flying-boat to yacht, & return by air: that's what we did today.

My head is stupid, so I won't write more.   N.

Hythe {Southampton}

25.iv.31

I cannot say how long we will be here. Till we have run the 1st engine of a new type for 50 hours (31 to date) and then till the 2nd & 3rd of the type are running properly in our own twin-engined boat here. It may be 5 days, or a week. Very bad weather is making it both uncomfortable & difficult.

I brought no bicycle with me, because I should be engaged day & night on this work while here. What with adjustments, running-hours, & reports our day is full from 7 a.m. till 10 p.m. So I do not want you to come here. Nor can I come to Clouds Hill. We work every day of the week.

When our boat is satisfactory, we take her to Plymouth, and do 50-hours R.A.F. test of her, on service jobs. After that I shall have some leisure. Not till then. Everything is being done at a rush, because eight of these boats are required to be in commission for the Schneider races, and that gives little time to test 3 different engines & decide which is the best.

I am glad you can use Pat a bit. If I get my *Odyssey* done this year (it is of course held up, now) I shall be able to use him in building my new room.

The estate would not sell the opposite side of the road—but might give me a long lease of it. Knowles' lease runs out in 3 years or so. I want to prevent other bungalows from springing up opposite my patch. It takes the estate months to make up its mind!   N.

{PLYMOUTH}
30.X.31

I do not expect you are still in the cottage . . . but have meanwhile sent to it that photograph given to me by Coster, the London photographer who asked me to sit for him a month ago. Pity it is so large, for I think it is a very good, as a photograph.

I have looked up the Handel records {of *The Messiah*}, and find that your set is complete. Enclosed is a copy of the index, with the records in their right order. I will try & get a cover, somewhere, to hold the eighteen of them together. Meanwhile, better use an old box, to prevent their getting dusty. The more you play them, remember, the better they get, so long as only wooden needles are used.

No news here—except that I have been assured of a further stay at Mount Batten. The camp is still comfortable, so I am glad of that. My boat is temporarily out of order; but as it has been very cold, I am not sorry.

I may try to come to Clouds Hill on Nov. 7 or 8, but it is too soon yet to tell if I can get free.   N.

SOUTHAMPTON
25 *Sept.* 1933

Still in Southampton, but please write still to Clouds Hill. No other address will serve henceforward.

I was there yesterday, for the evening, and lit its first fire in the book-room. No smoke, and little smell of smoke upstairs: while the draught seemed plenty. In fact it burned very brightly, and I enjoyed it for the night was wet, like my clothes.

Not much progress in the public works. The ram is not yet satisfactory, but is being improved. The heating apparatus is at last definitely ordered. Upstairs is due for its second anti-wood-worm poisoning, and all stripped bare for the operation. The bath-room is not yet cemented-round, and the bath waits in the garage for the boiler to be first installed.

The book-room is all finished except for its fender, which I have not yet designed. My books fill one of the two shelved walls: the one on which the dishes used to sit {north side}. The opposite wall waits with empty shelves. Only a remnant of my books have survived their ten year exile: but all the Kelmscotts are present in good order.

That *Odyssey* from China, by the way, never arrived! The book-room window has two fixed side-panes, cemented into the stone frame, and a pivoting centre-pane, in a stainless steel frame. That gives enough light and air to suit me. The other furniture is the window-seat, an affair six feet each way, built up of Bob's former bed and a big box-spring mattress: very comfortable and useful. I propose to move Mrs. Hardy's little stool down there, as a table; and the fender will complete it. What used to be the bed-room, upstairs, I am turning into a work-room, to hold a table and papers and ink and food and probably the gramophone and my clothes. That will make the upstairs sitting room big enough to walk about in.

The staircase has been sheathed in oak three-ply: and the Spenser landscape panelled into the gable, quite successfully. With the finishing of the bath-room, I will have the workmen out of it, and the whole house finished, except for what is reserved for my own hands.

The last five months of the autumn were wild with heath-fires. One would have burned me out, but for the fire-bank and the Tank Corps. It has killed many of those promising young firs between me and the sentry-box on the road at the top of the hill. Gallows Hill is utterly laid waste, and whole miles of heath and wood between Wool and Wareham. As for the New Forest, not for 40 years has so much been damaged. However the late rains have stopped all fear.

I have asked Mrs. Knowles to take all the border plants she can, as my wall-footing operations in the next stage of repair will interfere with them.

You ask me again to get your bank to send you the £80 quarterly: so I shall tell them to do it. As I have explained very many times, they have good technical reasons against it!

N.

This game of writing letters six months apart is like playing blind
man's buff and never touching. However, there it is. By sending a
double letter, one post apart, some of them may get through. By the
way your letters repeat questions that were long ago answered, it is
clear that most mails get lost.

If that goes on we will have to send a telegram to each other, once
a quarter, saying "Well" and no more: for indeed, reduced to its
essences, there is no more to say. However to pad it out I shall answer
your last letter, dated July 29, which you will have long ago forgotten.

I am staying in the R.A.F. for the remainder of my term—that is till
March 1935—so long as they give me special employment that seems
to me worth while. These boats are worth while, I think. If the boat
job runs out, so shall I. It is in my will, and I long for the cottage,
sometimes.

The fast boats have lately been built by the Power Boat Co. but we
are not tied to any firm. The slow boats are always built by Admiralty
contractors. White's of Cowes are doing these last five. Next year there
are to be six slow ones. I do not know who will be chosen to do them.
The seven fast ones are being done by Power. I am now visiting Cowes
and Hythe alternately, Hythe always by bike. It runs well.

I cannot manage any more rhododendrons this autumn, for all my
money has gone on the changes to the cottage. To finish the water and
heating business I will probably have to anticipate my next payment
of American royalties on the *Odyssey*. Until it is all finished I cannot
say exactly what will be the total cost—more than I had expected, but
then I have done more than I meant. Improvements suggest themselves, and it was now or never to put them in. So I have plunged,
rather. All bills are paid, to date, but little remains. Another reason
against more rhododendrons is space—or the lack of it. The shrubs are
growing like wild-fire, and it is becoming increasingly difficult to force
a way between them. Before new ones can be put in, the wild ones
must be cut back: and that I shall have no time to do before I am living
there. I get to the cottage only for a few hours a fortnight: hardly ever
for a night. The place needs living in, badly. I would like to find a
tenant for the winter, but cannot well offer it, without kitchen or bed-

room: and will the water-works be finished? They are so slow, these firms. Even the ram is left undone, half-working and half anyhow.

Mrs. Knowles has voted against more apple-trees, because some soldiers raided her garden this summer and stole all her fruit before it was even ripe. The trees bore a heavy and splendid crop. She is pleased with the quarter of the garden that has been wired and dug. Many potatoes, I gather.

Brian is in London and Pat at Clouds Hill. He has cut a lot of wood for her & me: but she does not let him help her in the garden. I have got Billy Bray to give Pat jobs in my public works—water, brick-laying, cementing: and plan more for him. The fire risks this year have been really bad, and before next summer I shall have taken real pre-cautions against the danger. Pat can do most of them for us. The Knowles family is queer. They get on best apart. Pat usually lives in my cottage, but feeds with Mrs. Knowles.

{two lines omitted}

I have not yet cleared in my own mind the design of a fender for the book-room. The stainless steel top of the upstairs one is a complete success. The seat of the new one must be stainless, too.

Your cheque for £50 came early in August, and I wrote to thank you for it. It went on the cottage, of course, with my *Odyssey* money. I still have some in hand, but not quite enough, I expect. However next month more comes from the States. So please do not bother yourself to send more. It is never hard for me to make money—a rare and fortunate state that I try not to abuse!

Our marvellous summer has definitely broken. We have had two weeks of very unsettled weather. High time too, with these droughts and heath-fires all over England.

N.

{SOUTHAMPTON}

5.xi.33

Address me always at Clouds Hill, please: for though still at Birming-ham St. in Southampton, I feel it is now only for a little while more. And after this? I do not know.

Your letters take about two months and seem all to arrive: but from the little in them I read either that your life is flat, or that you are not

too well in it. It is unsatisfactory, being so far apart. There is no reality
in the exchange of only three letters in a year. All the news in them is
stale. However, to repeat the usual things. I have not been yet to
Oxford, to talk to your Bank: each time I try for it, some other duty
comes in the way. Tomorrow, for instance, I am for Cowes: next day
a conference at Hythe. The third day and fourth for Air Ministry in
London.

The *Odyssey* copy did not return from China. Lent books are very
often lost:—a truth the poor remains of my library, now all collected
at Clouds Hill, abundantly illustrates. Only the half of my harvest
survives. They fill one wall of the book-room, and one end. However
books seem to flow upon me naturally. I get some every week.

The cottage is not finished. The boiler and bath are in course of
installation, but will take quite two weeks more. I shall be so glad to
have it to myself, after they finish. The works have dragged on all
summer. Just now I am employing Pat and young Way & Cooper to
dig a great water-tank in the ground below Mrs. Knowles garden,
among the chestnut trees. This is being fitted with hydrant connections,
for fire use: and when there are no heath-fires we can bathe in it: 40 feet
by 7 by 5. I hope to roof it with glass, or leaves will choke it.

Mrs. Knowles has taken the plants from the cottage garden, and I
have made several cuttings of bushes and limbs of trees: but there is too
much growth for a week-end to cope with. I would like to spend two
nights there, some month.

I have decided to take a lease of the other side of the road, all the
tree-grown part, for £15 a year: and Godwin is preparing the lease.
My water-works made this necessary. The ram is working very well.

Mrs. Hardy and Miss Fetherstonhaugh send messages. Both are well
and at home. I see them very seldom now—but found them both on
one afternoon a month ago. Arnie is not coming to Clouds Hill this
autumn. I wrote and told him the place was too unfinished. Also he
might be disturbed by there being no bed or food-preparing place.
I must say I find the ruling-out of beds a great success. The little room
upstairs where you used to sleep is going to become a work-room, I
think, with cupboards for clothes and a food-table—Bread, cheese,
butter and jams: also fruit.

I think that is all the news. I work at boats always, and am now
getting my ideas generally accepted. Even our dear stick-in-the-mud

Admiralty wants to borrow one! When I have evening time I try to revise the *Odyssey* for publication in U.S.A. as a school-book: but I have been all the summer on this, without getting half-way. There are no free evenings.

That seems to be all worth writing you. In a week or so I will try to say it again, to give two posts the chances of getting through: but it is thin stuff to send half across the world. What's Clouds Hill to China, or China to Clouds Hill!

N.

{SOUTHAMPTON}
17 Dec. 1933

A week to Christmas, and me still in Southampton, testing boats. The *Daily Telegraph* published a note on one of them the other day, and I send you the cutting. Liddell Hart, who wrote it, has launched out a full life of me, again. I hate it. These people all exaggerate so, and make me more a mountain than a man. I read his proofs and knocked out a good deal of stuff that wouldn't do. Unhappily I had to put in something, each time, to replace what I knocked out.

It has lately been howling cold in England: the ice on the sea has been thick on all the beaches and mud flats. Clouds Hill spring froze over, for the first time in my experience. The water is now very feebly flowing, smaller than ever I have known it. It is sad, just when my bath had been put in. We dare not use it, till more rain falls. Cities like Liverpool are cutting off their water every afternoon, and hundreds of villages are carting water.

I am just back from the cottage, which is now finished, at last, and looking untidy but well. The new zipp-bedding is a great success. Pat Knowles cannot finish the water-tank (to be known as Shaw's Puddle) because of the frost, which would kill the cement. It is almost finished, however, and will come to little harm, in its present state. Such a relief to have the cottage to myself, at last, after all these months of workmen and upset. If there is ever anything more to do, I shall do it myself.

No letter from you for some weeks but no news of trouble in your part of China. I hope the "Red" party may get the upper hand quickly and settle down into something Chinese. It is the only hope I can see, as against Japanisation. No matter, though. There is a new rather good

Scotch novel out, about Ross-shire and the expulsion of the crofters.
I shall probably send it you, to keep the Barrie and Douglas company.
Your Bank I saw a few weeks ago. It says it has done just what you
want, rather against its judgement. No matter, again.

Both your cheques came. I am sorry you made them so big. The
Odyssey is paying for Clouds Hill improvements, wholly, I hope.
I shall know by the end of the month, when the last bill comes in.
Everything to date has been paid for, as it was finished: so there should
not be too much to come. You will find the little place so different.
I'm afraid it will not be so suitable for you two: but it fits me like a
glove: and if you do want to return to Dorset, and give me warning,
I will find you somewhere near. A lovely district.   N.

Arnie talks of coming to Clouds Hill for a week, after Dec. 29. I
have warned him that there are now no beds and no cooking arrangements!

WOLVERHAMPTON

2 *February* 1934

I have been here for about a fortnight, overseeing for the Air Ministry the test of a new group of motor-boat engines. As the factory is
working two shifts, I have been kept very long hours, and have had
no time at all to spare. Shortly before I left Southampton a letter came
from you. You had been away from the Hospital for a change, and
were sorry to be back in your flat land, with its muddy walks. I suppose
the winter is nearly over, and conditions will soon be fairer.

We do not seem to succeed in getting many letters through to one
another! You ask again about that *Odyssey*. Of course it never arrived.
People have little conscience about books. Do not worry about it. I
can easily get another. There are sixty or so yet unsold, and sooner or
later the publisher, the printer and myself will share them out!

Other news? Why, very little. The Air Ministry still allow me a
reasonably free hand with boats and engines, and so they get the boats
and engines that I want, and not always what they want. I have just
over a year of my time to serve, and shall then fall quietly into Clouds
Hill and stay quiet for a while, to see what it feels like. I have a queer
sense that it is all over—all the active part of my life, I mean; and that
retirement from the R.A.F. is also retirement from the stream. I shall

be 46; which is neither young nor old; too young to be happy doing nothing, but too old for a fresh start. However there is nothing that I want to do, and nothing particularly that I am glad to have done. So I am unlikely to live either in the past or in the future. Man is not an animal in which intelligence can take much pride. The cottage is finished, so far as its main lines go. The tinkering with details will be distraction for my leisure. You see, since I grew up I have never been at leisure at all. It will be a radical and not very enjoyable change.

Sometimes I think of writing a little picture of the R.A.F. and sometimes of wandering across England and Scotland by Brough and afoot. There will be time for both things, won't there? By rearranging my investments I shall bring their yield up to £2 a week, and that will easily keep me. Thanks to the R.A.F. and its twelve years of simple company, I have learnt to be very comfortable on little. I have settled on £2 a week because that leaves me free of income tax. I have not seen the cottage for a month, so cannot tell if Pat has finished the water-pool (Shaw's Puddle we are going to call it, in derision) whose brick-work was held up by the frost. We have made it nearly forty feet long and seven feet wide, to hold 7,000 gallons. It lies under the chestnut trees below the wild end of Mrs. Knowles' garden, just opposite my long upstairs window. For the moment it shows, rather; but there is a bank of rhododendrons in front of it, and in two years or so it will be quite invisible from the cottage and the road. It is only two feet lower than the ram, and so has a good fall all over the park. I have put a fire hydrant thread on the outlet pipe, so that the Tank Corps can run a hose straight out from it. And in warm weather Bill will be able to swim in it—all supposing the cement does not crack and disappoint us. The Arab doors {brought by him from Jeddah} are going to close one end of the glass house that covers the pool. Parsons, Mrs. Hardy's carpenter, is repairing them. More expense: but I hated to have them lying about, wasted.   N.

SOUTHAMPTON

21 *March* 1934

A line to you tonight. Your last letter (a fortnight ago) was written from bed. A chill, you said; and described the flat dank mud of the plains that lie round your town. I hope it was only a chill, and that no more came of it. You are not a good subject for damp.

England has been wet—at last. After a year of drought we have had a wettish fortnight . . . not solidly wet, but with heavy rains between spells of sun and cold wind. I have not been to Clouds Hill lately, but it pleases me to imagine its spring running stronger. It was down to 13 gallons an hour, and weakening daily. I was fearing its total failure in the summer; and all risk is not yet past. But things are better, far better. The ram may work again. We had to stop it off, to let the spring fill.

Pat has finished the great storage tank, and filled it from the overflow. So we have 7,000 gallons to help us through the summer. Now he is roofing it in glass. It will look ugly, from the upstairs window of the cottage, as it rises between the chestnut trees at the wild end of the Knowles' garden; but in front of it is a bank of rhododendron, already five feet high, and we have planted others to make a covering wall. In three years nobody will suspect the tank.

The Jeddah doors are to close one end of the tank, forming its north wall. They face inwards, and therefore make one side of a small glass study of mine which ends the tank-house. They will open, if their covering doors are first opened—and then they will throw the study and the tank into connection with the air and the bushes. Parsons, the carpenter, has mended the edges of the doors, and patched them with cedar, of much the same tint as the old wood. I think they will look magnificent. Pat is erecting them. The job costs money, but I am so glad to have found a use for them, after all.

Other news. You will laugh to hear that that *Odyssey* arrived, without explanation, packed as you had packed and addressed it. A day or two later Arnie came to the cottage (with his wife) and said he would like an *Odyssey*. So I gave it him.

{three lines omitted}

I think they liked the cottage and its new fittings—but they emptied the cistern (poor Ram not working) and had to carry their water. They had their Morris Minor and went out for meals.

Other news. Sir Herbert Baker had a stroke two months ago, and has a dragging right foot and helpless right hand. The foot is improving, and they say the hand may. He is well and cheerful, in his head. I have seen him at Owletts, but he will not come to the Office for some weeks yet. He does not want it talked about, for business reasons.

I have been up and down the earth—Birmingham, London, Nottingham, Brentford. Liverpool this next week. Boats of course. Liddell Hart's book on me has come out, and been very well reviewed. Not much sensation-mongering. Cape tells me that it is selling—about 6,000 already. I am not greatly interested by it. There have been interesting books (on other subjects) this year . . . new writers of promise. Yes, I got both your cheques, thank you very much. I am urging Pat to get the cottage finished, and shall then sit down and calculate how I stand, for income to live in it. I think all is well, but cannot well say till all the accounts are in. There is another £50 or so to spend.

John has had two sittings (or standings, rather) from me lately, for a new half-length. It is elongated but fine, I think, so far as it goes. He may finish it this Sunday. John very well and healthy-looking.

Mrs. Donnat sends her regards. I see her sometimes.

N. ·

{SOUTHAMPTON}
6 April 1934

There, it is a Saturday and late in the evening. I am at Southampton, in my lodging, with a little fire against the cold of the night. At Clouds Hill Mrs. Roberts is inhabiting the cottage. She arrived unexpectedly, after a holiday at Weymouth which exhausted her money and drove Roberts himself back to London to raise more. She moved to Winfrith to await it—and came to see Mrs. Knowles on the Thursday when I was at last able to reach Clouds Hill after three weeks in the North and at sea. I suggested she move to the cottage for a few days, till the money comes. It will not be long—for on the 14th Chambers (ex R.A.F.) comes to the cottage for a fortnight's camping-holiday.

Two letters of yours came, almost together. By them I learn that your two years abroad may lengthen. I had been expecting you home soon, and was beginning to wonder where you would settle to live. The cottage will be my home, then; and I have arranged it accordingly, to fit me. It will be difficult even to put up a visitor, the place is so "one-man" now. Probably when you come to see it, I shall give you the cottage, and camp myself in the little work-room by the pool.

The cottage is nearly finished. The book-room lacks only its fender-cum-log-box. Then it is complete. The bath-room lacks only its bath-mat; and the boiler its final lagging of asbestos plaster. The upstairs room is complete, but for its beam-candle-sconce. The food-room alone remains to arrange. I plan to sheath its walls with aluminium foil: to fit an old ship's-bunk across the dark end, complete with drawers: to arrange its food-shelf, its table, perhaps a chair. Then Clouds Hill cottage is finished—no, I forgot a cast-iron fireback for the book-room, and an air-vent to make the fire draw. But these are all small jobs, and could be finished in two months, if I had the time for them. As it is, I can attend to the place only by fits and starts, and so it drags on interminably.

Our last doing was to sheath the bath-room walls in sheet cork, laid on in slabs twelve inches by seven, and a sixteenth of an inch thick. These were glued to the walls and partition and doors and frames, bonded like bricks, in their vertical courses, with the horizontal courses shingled—the upper course overlapping the lower by about an eighth of an inch. The cork cost about 15/-, and has done the job excellently. Its grain and colour are beautiful. I do not know how age will change it. Today it is as good as any room I've seen. We have also hung the door-leathers to the book-room and the upstairs room, on hinged door-rods of wrought iron. They are in natural cow-hide, and very success-ful. Pat works steadily at roofing the water-pool, which has now been full for six weeks, and does not leak at all. That is 7,000 gallons of water. Your letter asks how would we make it flow up-hill, if there is a fire? Why, by the camp fire-engine, which is a powerful pump. In an hour it would pump the whole pool dry—but that hour's water would probably save our places.

The pool is not finished: it has still to be rendered over inside in fine cement; but we will not do that till the roof is finished, as rain or cold or the dust of a high wind would damage the final cementing.

So Pat is now roofing it, slowly and single-handed. He has nearly finished the wooden framing and the sash-bars. Next week the floors of my little study at its N. end, and the entrance-porch at the S. end will be laid. Then the Jeddah gates go in, to form the N. wall. They are just the right width, though unnecessarily high. However we cannot cut them down, so we have made the study too high, instead. Then the glass will arrive, and be fixed into place. Then the pool is finished. About May 15, I think. The last act will be to visit my Bank and find

out what income I shall have left, to live on, after it all. Of course, at
the worst, I can do some sort of editing or translating work, to help
me out.

Meanwhile I have the tanks running back & forward along my hill-
top boundary, to tear a bare way through the heather and heath. This
will make an efficient fire-guard, against fires sweeping in across the
plain. So between this and the water-pool I shall feel safer, this year.
The weather is still dry, and it bodes badly for the summer, from the
point of fires. Already there has been a fire near Bere Regis, besides
several in Hampshire and Kent. My spring is improving a little, thanks
to rains in March. It is up to about 450 gallons a day, as against 350.
Normal is between seven and eight hundred. I fear we shall not see
that this year; but I feel that a total failure of the supply is now unlikely. If we have a normal summer, with some wet spells, we should
get through successfully.

Easter I passed in a little R.A.F. ship, of 300 tons, which took us for
her trial trip from Liverpool to Devonport. Three of us, as passengers,
and a crew of 19. Now she has gone on, towards Singapore, her final
station. A slow little cargo-ship, to ferry R.A.F. stores from the port
there to the R.A.F. Base. I have not done anything else of note, lately.
That newspaper report of my training crews for a target boat referred,
I suppose, to a week I spent at Bridlington in 1932. At least I can think
of no other ground for the story.

I'd better repeat, in case the last batches of letters have been lost
(many obviously are, by the irregular arrival of what do come to me)
that your two cheques both came—many thanks. Also the *Odyssey*
arrived, none the worse for wear. I gave it to Arnie, who happened to
arrive at Clouds Hill almost as it did and as I did.

N.

{? SOUTHAMPTON}
17.iv.34

I sent you an account of the new Clouds Hill works in my last note,
about a week ago. Here is a sketch-map to show you how they lie.
I have marked in a line of what land, on the W. wide of the road, I
want to lease from Godwin. He agrees, and the rent of £15 per annum
is agreed to: but of course that is as far as it has got. I send him a tele-

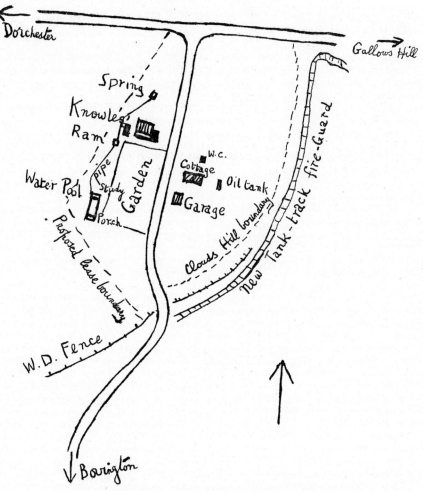

gram or two occasionally, just to keep my end up, but am not pressing
him, for so soon as he does produce the lease my rent will begin—and
his delay now is saving me money. What I have marked off is about
three acres, so I am not getting it particularly cheaply—except that the
land would fetch much more, if a row of bungalows was built on it.
No news to tell you. I put it all in my last letter, and only send this

separately in case it gets lost. I try to post the two letters by different
ships, so that they shall get to you by two different couriers. Then if
one goes, the other may not. Lady Astor, Mrs. Shaw and Mrs. Donnat
often ask after you. I saw Mrs. Donnat lately, when I went to see Sir
Herbert {Baker} who is making only slow progress. He has not come
up to London since his stroke.

N.

Your last letter asks for a copy of Liddell Hart's book on me. It is
heavy, and contains no criticism. He is a very good and keen military
writer—but unfortunately my tactics and principles happen to support
the theory of war which he urges, in and out of season.

I will send you a copy next time I get to Cape, in London—as he
will give me a 5/– trade discount on its price! It is a dear book. I gave
my copy to Sir H. Baker.

N.

{Subsequent letters failed to reach us, owing to our movements
on account of civil war in China.}

W. G. LAWRENCE

WILLIAM GEORGE LAWRENCE

BORN at Kirkcudbright on December 10th, 1889, he was just sixteen months younger than T. E. They were like twins. He was educated at the City School in Oxford and at St. John's College. Was a good runner and got a Half-Blue for the mile.

He took a great interest in all Christian work and was College secretary for the O.I.C.C.U. In the autumn of 1913, he went out to India on the staff of St. Stephen's College, Delhi. He returned in March 1915, and joined the Oxford and Bucks Light Infantry as a Second-Lieutenant, transferring to the Royal Flying Corps as an observer in August. He was shot down on October 23rd, 1915, after being less than a week in France.

Will Lawrence

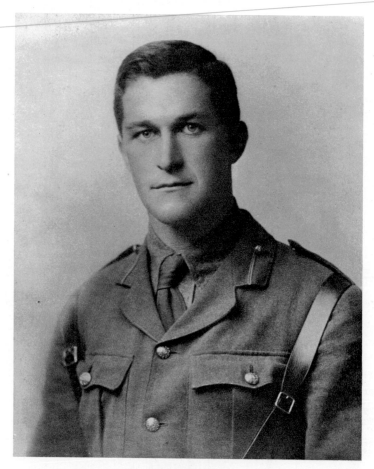

Will Lawrence

FOREWORD

By Sir Ernest Barker

It is over half a century ago that I first came to know Mr. and Mrs. Lawrence and their five sons. Three of the sons were at different times my pupils—T. E. about 1909 (but only for a brief term); W. G. from 1911 to 1913, during the whole of his course in Modern History; and A. W., the youngest, for a little time at the end of my Oxford days, about the year 1920. I am proud to be writing now, at Mrs. Lawrence's request, this introduction to the letters written to her by her son Will (W. G.).

Will was an exhibitioner and afterwards a Casberd Scholar of St. John's College, Oxford. (He was almost my exact contemporary there, for we both joined the College in 1909—he a term after me—and we both left it in the summer of 1913.) Like his brothers, he had had his schooling at the Oxford High School, under Mr. Cave; and he early became a lover of the classics. He used, if my memory does not deceive me, to go about with a copy of Pindar in his pocket (I have done the same); but his love of the classics, and especially of Greek, was greater than his technical scholarship, and after he had taken Classical Moderations in the spring of 1911, he turned to Modern History—the subject in which I lectured at the College—and became my pupil for the next two years. He belonged to a stirring generation in the College, which included some of the liveliest pupils I have ever had in the course of my life (notably Ahmed Abdel Ghaffar of Egypt, who was his friend as well as mine—and is still my friend to-day); and he was placed in the second class in the examination of 1913. He went after that, in the autumn of the year, to St. Stephen's College, Delhi, stopping on the way in Syria to meet his elder brother T. E., who was then digging in Carchemish. He spent about a year in St. Stephen's, teaching history to its students and winning golden opinions. I have treasured the letters he wrote to me; and reading them again, more than forty years after, I have been deeply moved by them. He told me in one of them about a long week-end in the hills, at the head-waters of the Ganges, where he met Mr. Ramsay MacDonald—"Imagine me," he said, "swimming the snowy river, towing the leader of the Labour party behind me, as he sat on a raft of kerosene tins." He told me, too, in another, or at least he tried to tell me, what had brought him to India. (Actually, it was almost too deep for telling.) "There's no reason I can give, beyond that I felt it was up to me somehow to come, a feeling strong enough to admit of no doubt. . . . That's faith, I think, a trust in the dark that is mainly instinctive. . . . The thing really is that there are some people—and I'm more or less in line with them—who find religion akin to human affection, not a thing to analyse but to feel. You can't explain falling in love, but you can experience it. And the danger of this position is that you get men like Tagore who seem almost to patronise God with a Platonic affection; and sentiment passing for love is blasphemy. For myself, I've said at times, and meant it, that I could never doubt love having known what beauty can be in a human being." (I know what lay behind that last sentence, but of course I keep that knowledge to myself.)

The war came: he returned to England, and was shot down in an aeroplane near St. Quentin (he had joined the Flying Corps) at the end of October 1915. He had written to me—it was his last letter—on the 18th of that month. I had answered his letter on the 22nd, and my answer was returned to me, reaching Oxford on the 29th, with the one word "Missing." How deep the memory still is! . . . He died untimely, in the flower and grace of his youth; but "In small measures life may perfect be."

He combined, above any other man that I ever knew, a great love of beauty and a deep religious sense; indeed, the two were interfused in him, as the letter I have quoted testifies. In the depth of his religious feeling, he stood near to his eldest brother, M. R., who served for years in the China mission-field (his mother with him for much of the time), as he himself served for his brief span in India. In his love of beauty and his passion for poetry he was nearer to T. E., though the quiet pervasiveness of his feeling for beauty, and the happy grace with which it inspired him, were his own peculiar gifts. I remember his zest for Provençal poetry; I remember inviting, at his request, a poet of the day—his name was Ezra Pound—to dine with me in Hall before giving an address to a College society on the troubadours. (The poet must have liked and remembered Will; for he invited him to his wedding months afterwards, not knowing that he was then far away in India.) But when

I think of Will now—and I often think of him—I do not think of Provençal poetry; I do not think even of the religious faith that carried him to India: I think just of himself. I think of the beauty of his presence, the tall straight pillar of his body, the soft voice with its winning notes, the smile that lit his face as he talked to you. I was moved, on the last day of 1915, reflecting on the year and above all on his death, to write a tribute to his memory, which I sent to *The Times*. I venture to quote some sentences from it:

"Grace was in all his doings and in all the workings of his mind. The music and gymnastic which, as Plato thought, could attune the body to harmony with the mind and harmonise all the elements of the mind in a perfect unison had done their work upon him. He seemed . . . to have the perfection of nature's endowment; beauty of mind knit to beauty of body, and all informed by a loving spirit of affection, so that his presence was a benediction and a matter for thanksgiving that God had made men after this manner. So to speak of him is perhaps to idealise him; but one can idealise only that which suggests the ideal, and at the least he had a more perfect participation in the ideal than falls to the general lot of humanity. . . . Such he was, and now he too is dead. . . . His tutor had once written in a copy of the Vulgate which he gave him: *Esto vir fortis, et pugnemus pro populo nostro et pro civitate Dei nostro.* He *was* strong—and he fought for both."

When I think of the five sons of Mrs. Lawrence, I think of a nest of young eagles—for that is what they seemed to me when I knew them in their youth. Two only are left, the eldest and the youngest; the three between them are gone, and Will was the second to go. He was the middle of the five—perhaps the gentlest, but also one of the strongest; perhaps the most winning—at any rate to me. But why should I make comparisons? If ever a mother had reason to be proud of her sons, that mother was Mrs. Lawrence. What *she* was, and what she meant to them, the letters in this volume attest.

March 1953.

DEAR MOTHER

I just want to give you some idea of the things seen by Bob and me on this last tour; now, while it is still fresh in my mind. We finished our first afternoon's walk at Bradford, a town built in tiers and terraces above the Avon, and so singularly compact to the view. There is some good old-timbered work in the alleys of the town, and the Saxon Church. Otherwise it is trying to be modern, with but little success. We cut across from there to Wells, and went into a restaurant to get some lunch. There Leonard H. Green was sitting over a plate of ham, and talked a little while with us. The Cathedral was very charming from the Bishop's palace. I tested the choir, which could not be compared to Christ Church at all. We slept our third night at Glastonbury. The abbey is very broken-down; far worse in state than Beaulieu, and covered with scaffolding for repairs. Outside the little town there is a grand hill, the Tor, with an isolated church tower on it. They say that once there was the rest of the church there, but it must have been small. Over the marshes we went to Cheddar, which lies in the low country at the foot of the Mendips. The cliffs are extraordinary, and almost weary one on account of their height. But the caves in them merit a week's stay, so glorious are the colours and shapes of the stalactites. It is a land of ferns, and almost every fifth cottage had a gorgeous japonica, and many more than one. The people balance full milk-pails, larger than buckets, on their heads, so conveying them. They make a living out of early strawberries. We walked over the Sedgmoor fens to Highbridge, near Burnham-on-Sea. In the evening I ran through the dark to the coast, which is flat and of muddy sand. Thence we made a good march over the Quantock Hills, just touching 1,000 feet, to near Minehead, which we reached by train. You have heard of our meeting with Richards. Next day it was wettish. We walked over the Myne, a great promontory, to Porlock, and up a hill into the clouds. Above 1,300 feet the mist suddenly cleared, and we saw Exmoor splendidly. Dropping down into the mouth of the long Badgworthy valley, we stopped near Oare, John Ridd's home in Lorna Doone. Next day

started very black and wet, so we did not go on to Lynton, Bob pre-
ferring to explore the valley more thoroughly. It is a wonderful rut
in the hills: very desolate and quiet save for its little burn, yet with
sweet little corners and holes off it on every side, each with its waterfall
and moss and ferns. It is famous for its trout, and also for the wild red
deer, but we saw none of them. There was a stag-hunt meet near by: of
five ladies I saw riding, four were astride. We went up the Badgworthy
Water about 3 miles, and passed the mouths of about 7 tributary
valleys, each prettier than the last. There are hardly any relics of the
Doones, whoever they really were. (Anthropologists call them a
remnant of the Cro-Magnon race.) We walked back homewards to
Bridgwater, taking the train there. Ned is going to help me with our
photos to-morrow: I do hope some of them are successful, but it was at
least a great pleasure taking them. Today has been fine here. I took
Arnie for a ride, and had a bathe, my throat being a little sore. He wanted
to join me but I thought it wiser not. Bob and Ned have been with the
Canon {A. M. W. Christopher}, helping him to send away books to
undergraduates. I wish we could have seen you just for a little, but
hope that you will enjoy the change to the full. Excuse this catalogue-
like letter. Hoping that you and Father are both very well and happy:
his arm getting better and you stronger.

your loving WILL

HÔTEL DU BŒUF COURONNE
CHARTRES
5.0 p.m. Sunday Sept. 4th 1910

MY DEAR MOTHER
    I hope this meets you after a good sea-voyage with no troubles.
It's very windy today, but the weather has time to change. I will think
of you all as you get across. For me, I had a nice enough crossing, too
rough for some but a pleasure to me. Frank will have told you I failed
to get a return ticket for him. Tell Arnie I saw a submarine submerge
itself in Cherbourg harbour. After Frank left (I hope he did not suffer
at all) Ned and I rode south over fine wooded country to Valognes,
where there is a good church and a number of old houses. Then the
land became wet and flat over the Carentan and Isigny meadows and
we made a good pace to near Bayeux. 7 miles from that town my back
tyre burst. It was not very bad happily, and while Ned very kindly

mended it I saw quite a Millet picture in the flesh. Away over the dusty road a peasant was scything a corn-plot: then a woman with a little one brought him some food and for a while husband and wife bent over the baby. Surely as sweet a sight as may be, though the man and woman were rather old. We slept the night at Bayeux. Next day we spent the morning in the Museum. While Ned tried to draw a piece of the tapestry bearing upon his pottery, I acted as decoy in another direction. He got enough notes for him to reconstruct it all right in private. At Caen we separated. He is stopping there several days: I made south to Falaise getting there after a fast ride before the wind. The castle is magnificent. Next day, Friday, I left in the afternoon for L'Aigle, on the way to Chartres. The road was terrible for the tyres, but very picturesque. For several miles it ran along a hill-ridge through fields of sainfoin and clover and with lovely upland flowers. There was a campanula there of the Bricquebec type but wild, hair-bells growing all round a thick straight stalk about 1 ft. 6 ins. high. Also I saw some queer foxglove-like flowers but yellow. Nellie would have liked to have been there. Then followed long forests with a fine lot of rabbits, etc. in them: I saw no pheasants. I got to L'Aigle about 5.30 p.m. It is a clean little town: nowhere else in France have I seen so many comely people together. On Saturday morning I rode through Argentan and Maillebois, where I believe Latham the aviator lives. There the band Ned had made the Bayeux repairers put on my tyre went to tatters, and for safety's sake I walked on the 10 miles or so here, getting in about 5.0 p.m. Don't pity me, I enjoyed the walk through the parched fields. Long before any other part of the town was visible I could see the two spires and the high back of the cathedral facing me. They grew clearer and larger as I left the kilometres behind me, but once one is in the town the cathedral is lost in a labyrinth of lanes and quite hard to find. Scaffolding is over Ned's favourite door and a hoarding prevents one seeing the Philosophus. Still there is an enormous amount of carving on the other two gates: Ned has said enough about that. The stained glass within is very lovely, and makes one long for others to be there to look at it. Also the place has a splendid organ. I got in for the tail-end of a service this morning and was pleased to be able to judge their music.

I am rather done over my tyre. I took it to a repairer's here to get another band put on. He did it, but changed the valve for a French one under the impression that it would not work! So I will have to carry

two pump-connectors and what will happen if the valve goes wrong
I don't know. Still I don't object to marching. Added to spoiling my
tyre, the man charged 3 fr. 50 for it. I wanted him to change the valves
back again at first but he said it was a three hours' job, and also I feared
he would not do it well after the way he and I had discussed the matter.
I wish Ned had been here to help me explain myself: my French breaks
down readily on such occasions though I understand almost all they
say. The town is full of soldiers. A squadron of cavalry quartered in the
hotel-yard woke me at 5.0 a.m. this morning saddling up; something
like a row! I will leave about midday tomorrow and go through
Dreux to some place in the Seine valley. Then next day down the Seine
to Les Andelys where I hope to get a note from you and perhaps to find
Ned. Thence to Gisors, Beauvais and Amiens (I hope my postcard
telling you to write to Beauvais and Amiens reached you). Next
Sunday I hope to spend at Amiens and be back on Tuesday or Wednesday. This is the farthest point south I will go. Tell Arnie I have seen
a swallowtail butterfly, black and yellow and measuring a good three
inches across. Also a dead pine-marten. If you think Miss Wright would
like anything in the way of jugs or so write to Amiens and to Dieppe.
(Though I may not come back by way of the latter). I sent a postcard
to Bob from Falaise and will send others. That's about all I have to say I
think; the row with the cycleman has made me sleepy so I must get out
again for another look at the cathedral. Ned does well to be enthusiastic.
The people wear winged lace caps here, and looked very jolly in the
service this morning. I have had no bothers. Two large hounds attacked
me the other day going down hill. I got off to throw imaginary bricks at
them and they fortunately vanished. English startles dogs I find. Hoping
that you are all four all right and that you have heard good news from
Bob and with kind regards to Miss Wright.

from your loving son,

WILL

Hôtel-Restaurant de la Gare
Boquet-Diéval
Anvin
Pas-de-Calais
Friday 4th August 1911

Dear Mother

I'm going to write a proper letter to you tonight and post it first thing tomorrow. So I'm afraid you will not get it till Monday, but the post has gone tonight.

I am in haven here at a nice little place amongst the hills. With a fast-flowing river of the Cherwell size backed by wooded chalk cliffs it's quite a pretty spot and has a nice tower by the river to set it off. So I'll feel sorry tomorrow morning to go away and leave it for St. Pol, which is a city of historical note. The Counts of St. Pol played a very clever game all through the Middle Ages, stirring up fighting between France and Burgundy to their own aggrandisement. Still I don't expect the modern town will show much signs of that.

Last night I slept at a cheap place in Fruges. (You won't know the place and I didn't till I got there.) In all it was a fairly long walk from Hardelot and very hot. Still I got the worst over, about 20 miles, before lunch. That was when I wrote my first letter to you, asking you to write to Guise (Aisne) and Cambrai (Nord). I hope you got it. From Hucqueliers, my lunching place, to Fruges, was 12 miles and they were very hot walking. When I got to Fruges I fairly swelled with soda-water which I could not get en route. It's not commonly kept at the country pubs and cafés. Then this morning I left Fruges late, not till 9.0 a.m., and first of all I walked round and round Agincourt, marking down the lie of the land. A Calvary marks the spot where the battle was fought and where Henry killed his prisoners. After I was satisfied with Agincourt I struck across the country lanes with a great deal of wandering to a place called Honcuin. I had meant to go the main road to St. Pol, but didn't after all. So there I was walking along the slopes of hills like the Cotswolds or the East Ilsley's downs with never a place where milk or soda-water or any Vichy and such like horror could be obtained. I was very glad to find an hotel here when I thought I should have to hurry to St. Pol and then arrive late for any respectable dinner. The man here fairly stared when he saw me at the eau de Seltz au citron. That's a trick Ned taught me and a very good one. The Citron makes it into a bad imitation of your lemonade and not in the least like English gaseous lemonade. Your lemonade is what one dreams about, walking.

Tomorrow I expect I will get into St. Pol by midday and stay there during the heat of the day. Then I will probably get out south to some little place amongst the hills to spend Sunday in. But the sunshine and the thirst makes one so lazy there is no knowing really what I will do. Imagine me thinking of you all in some little hill station in this hot land.

I hope Father finds the golf to his liking at Pwllheli and that you and Bob and Arnie are enjoying yourselves rarely. The name of your digs sounds very Welsh indeed, so Arnie will have a chance of learning another language. Also I hope good news has come to Frank, and perhaps after all another letter from Ned. I wrote three letters off to him before I left home, as well as to Mr. Inman. And I got Fernand Leclercq's parcel posted at Boulogne, though I could not find my letter to him till this morning at Fruges. Then I sent it.

Don't imagine I am wearing myself out with hard walking. By the map Fruges to Anvin is hardly more than 12 miles and my erring in the way can't have made it more than 20. As soon as I get a drink I fairly dance along, but it's when I can't get one and fear the water that I feel inclined for a rest. I found one little rill down from the limestone downs yesterday, with a gravel bottom and watercress by its sides, where I could not resist a long drink, but otherwise I've been very careful. Perhaps when I'm farther east among the mountains I will be able to take risks with a quiet mind. The people here are much the same as the country people of Picardy, and wheat seems the chief thing they grow. Also there are plenty of sheep on the downs. They are more polite than the Normans, though I don't like an old farmer who looks like a French Mr. Wright to cap me on the road simply because I wear a panama hat. French beliefs in Egalité are largely a lip creed.

From a queer sort of local paper I've been looking at just now, *Le Grand Echo du Nord*, I gather that England is still watching France and Germany threaten each other. France is like a cat relying on a handy tree, England, and so facing the canine Germans. If they were really going to fight I should judge they would have started by now. I wish I could go out for a swim with you to-morrow. It's thoroughly seaside weather. Or perhaps it's changed at last in England, which will make the garden rejoice.

Hoping all's well with you,

from your loving son WILL

HÔTEL DE LA COURRONNE
GUISE. AISNE

Wednesday 11.30 a.m. 9th August 1911

DEAR MOTHER

I have just arrived here and got two letters from you and Father: thank you for writing so much. I'm so glad you find your rooms comfortable. Father tells me you have bathed three times—on the 4th—so you must be fit. The mention of storms and of rain surprises me. I crossed to Boulogne in a wonderful calm and then I've been walking through days without a drop of rain or even thunder. The wind, if it has ever blown, for mostly it is only a slight breeze, is even warmer than the atmosphere so that one gets into a church to be cool. Coolness in fact is what I long for; just now I am lapped in the greatest luxury, for in this hotel where I'm going to have lunch they provide ice with their lemon and soda-water! The whole of France judging by their papers is similarly hot so your storms can only be local to England. I hope the sea will behave better soon.

It was excellent that you should get two unexpected letters from Ned, with such good accounts of him in them. I will be glad indeed to read them when I get back; you are wise not to send them to me for I can't be sure of getting all your letters. Probably you will have written again here on Monday and I will miss it, for I'm going faster than I had thought of doing. I will sleep tonight at Capelle probably or at Hirson.

I'm hoping to be back in Oxford on the 21st, Monday, just the day you speak of getting there. That will give me my 20 days, and I will have heaps of time for working at History. So I'll stick to that as a likely time for my return. It will mean my leaving France on Saturday the 19th and having a Sunday by the sea which will be well worth while. Probably I'll try and get across the Channel by the Calais–Dover route, for I could not get a return to Boulogne—they are only issued for 8 days—and I should like to see the remains of old Calais. Between then and now I hope to go to Mezières on the Meuse, where there is some fine river and rock scenery with vineyards as the chief industry. Mezières is near Charleville which I will go to see also; I will like to see Rimbaud's statue there. After Mezières I'll go west if all's well reaching Cambrai perhaps on the Tuesday. Thence it will be a march to Calais, helped probably by a ride in a train. So you have my plans so far as they exist.

I'm enjoying myself very greatly out here and walking well and
easily. This morning I've done about 12 miles to Guise, and enjoyed
every step of the way until the last 3 or 4 kilos when I was too thirsty
for words. Then one enjoys slaking that thirst and as above I'm well
off in that way here. Yesterday I had to drink Vichy Water mostly as
eau de Seltz was unknown. At the worst I am driven to black coffee,
and even that is glorious failing all else. This country is nearly waterless. Since leaving Boulogne I have crossed 3 brooks only and come to
two rivers and a canal. As a result everywhere one meets with water-
carts in the country bringing drink out to the cattle in the fields. They
allow a bucketful per cow in the afternoon which does not satisfy the
poor beast at all. There's a pest of cattle-fever which is in very many
villages. About here they grow a great deal of poppy—the large garden
poppies. Whether it's for opium or morphia or what-not I don't know.
The crops are cut with scythes and afterwards beaten out with flails.
In another day I will be in the Ardennes proper, when I hope to leave
this down country for awhile. One might be near Guildford to judge
by the look of the land in many places. So you have most of what I
want to say I think, and dejeuner is ready. I do hope you will all enjoy
your time very greatly at Pwllheli and come back much the better for
it. You're stopping a much shorter time than I had expected. Please
thank Father for his letter; I will write to him next. Wishing you all a
very happy holiday.

with love from WILL

HÔTEL DU CHEVAL NOIR
RUE DE LA LIBERTE
VERVINS
9th August 1911

DEAR FATHER
        This is being written on the same day as the letter which I sent
from Guise. Vervins is about 12 miles due east of Guise, and a place of
similar size. But it's up in the hills, whereas Guise lies along the banks
of the river Oise, the beginnings of the Seine's chief tributary. There
are some walls around the town, which I will explore tomorrow. So
far I have found absolutely nothing of a respectably ancient appearance
—except the pile of Hardelot Castle—in all my walking. As I'm not out
for antiquities that does not distress me, but it means I can take but few

photographs. The scenery is all of the long rolling down type, with the usual grey poplars marking the line of the roads. That is very delightful to look at but does not shew well to the camera. Now though I should come to more in the way of naked rock for it's only two days' walking to the Meuse and the German frontier. I want to get to Charleville on Friday night and to spend Sunday at Rocroy, the site of a battle and a place of crags and waterfalls. Or so I hope. Then I will probably use the train on my way to Cambrai. I told the post-office people to forward letters from Guise to Cambrai so if you have written any more I will get them on Tuesday or Wednesday so far as I can see. I was so glad to hear that Ned had got some other letters in, so that Mother won't have quite as long to wait without them. His liking for the Kurds is a surprise. They are a brave lot of brigands and all right in their own mountains, but they are the Mohammedan instruments for all massacres. A race of horsemen and good shots, they are pitiless hawks to the poor Armenians.

I'm stopping the night at this hotel, an expensive one. That reminds me, I will have an abundance of money for this trip, so that Mother need not think of offering me more.

I'm sorry the golf links are not good ones. Still you're lucky in having them so close and you won't have to tire yourself getting to them. The stormy sea I can hardly conceive of, nor Frank's tents blown away by the gale. I'm much luckier than you in having a continuance of the hot weather. All I need is to convoy a barrel of iced lemonade and I should be absolutely suited. As it is I must take to carrying fruit with me, since the bogey of bad water is too much for me. What would one think if one drank from a spring which tasted like Vichy? That seems dangerous enough yet one pays 4d. a bottle for it. I half think the bad-water story is an invention of the wine-loving doctors, as Savage Landor says. Still I'm not going to drink it all the same. There's a great deal of a cattle-plague called 'fièvre aphteuse' here. Many of the villages I have come to have little wooden notice boards stuck up in the fields round them with those words. Also the first day I came to them they also had the words 'circulation interdite' on them. As an amusing result I leapt to the conclusion there was some epidemic about and spent a lot of time wandering round such hamlets and losing my way. But it's really only a cattle-disease, dreadful enough for it is ruining the farmers at present. To be on the safe side I don't drink milk where such notices are.

Yesterday I came to the St. Quentin Canal, a huge affair with a mile
and a half of large barges, about 3 times as big as an Oxford barge,
moored along the bank two and three deep. It gave me a mighty idea
of the value of French waterways for that collection of barges was at
quite a little place, Hannacourt. Some of the barges were from the
Loire, some from the Rhine, but most were Seine boats. Charente is
apparently a place where many of them set out. Now I'll go to bed,
and post this tomorrow. Wishing you all a happy time.

Your loving WILL

Hôtel du Grand-Cerf
Place Nevers
Charleville
11th August 1911

Dear Father
Here I am as I intended in the great frontier-fortress of France.
Outside it lies Sedan, and it was here that the Prussians broke in in 1870.
I've had a delightful walk today, with a most refreshing bathe when the
sun was high. The country here is a great change to what I have been
coming through. It's quite as hot but the heat is a new thing to the
people. They've had quite a lot of rain during the last two months. As
a result the land is not much parched up. It's a very well-wooded
rolling country with brooks and rivulets quite common. They grow
very little corn: of course some and beans and roots, but mostly leave
the fields for pasture. The cattle are small black-and-white beasts
generally.
I slept last night at Rumigny, and there I had an adventure. I had had
a rather exhausting short walk there from Vervins—it was so hot and
the people took a pride in having no mineral waters or milk—and I
had eaten early at a small village. So I did not want dinner when I
arrived at Rumigny, a little hill-side town at 7.30 p.m. I walked quietly
through it marking down the hotels till on the outskirts I came to the
finger-post for the morrow's walk. I put my hand in my pocket for
my map and found it gone. So I sat down on the grass to think where
I had left it. I had just decided it must be at the café 5 miles away when
a man sauntered past and I wished him good evening. 'What are you
doing?' he asked, and I saw he was a gendarme. 'Thinking,' I said. 'You

must come with me,' so away we went to the gendarmerie. There he stuck me in a sort of guardroom and 4 men came to cross-question me. Of course I explained that I was English, etc., and why I was sitting there, but they would have it I was a German spy. So they examined all my baggage. The Greek Testament seemed very harmless to them and in fact they had already decided it was all right when another man turned up and persisted in talking German to me, trying to trap me into understanding him. After a while he left off and looked through Mother's letter, which satisfied him I was harmless at any rate.

So we adjourned to the hotel where they drank my health at my expense. I was in their hands about $\frac{3}{4}$ of an hour altogether and a fair crowd had collected outside. Fortunately they did not interfere with my plates. I tried a stroke of business by asking them to develop them and see they were harmless but they didn't bite. So it was only the beginning of an adventure after all. It happened just as I have said. Mother mustn't think I was lying out or anything of that sort.

Charleville–Mezières is a very large town on either side of the Meuse river. It did not exist at all till 1606 or so when it was founded by a Duke de Nevers who is honoured by a fine monument here. There is also an excellent statue of Bayard in the old town over the river. He defended it against someone or other. Also the Prussians took it the third time of trying in 1870. There is a statue of Rimbaud somewhere but I haven't found it yet.

It's nine o'clock now and I will soon go to bed. Tomorrow I will go somewhere or other to spend Sunday in, but where I don't know. Perhaps to Rocroi 15 miles off to the North, but I'm really not sure. I will have to go by train some of the way between here and Cambrai if I'm to be there before Wednesday night, so perhaps I may train westwards 30 miles or so tomorrow. I'm beginning to keep a watch on one of my boots. I got it mended by Lambert before camp but it looks suspicious. I stuck some brads in it to-day which I took the precaution of putting in my housewife. I've greatly enjoyed my little tour so far, and I'm very fit indeed. Although I've come a very long way I have not had any forced marches at all. Just a steady walk each day allowing for a midday read while it's too hot for walking, gets one along at a very fair rate. That was one of the things my gendarme friends found hard to swallow. How could I possibly have walked from Boulogne to the frontier for mere amusement? Their verdict when the

German-speaking man arrived was that I was *un drôle peut-être mais pas dangereux*. And they praised the power of my legs.

It's funny what a fuss they are making of the heat here. People go about talking of nothing else. All the shutters are up when one comes through a village making the place seem quite deserted.

I hope you are getting better weather at Pwllheli, and all enjoying yourselves greatly. It will be jolly if we both arrive home on the same day. Give my love to everyone. And tell Mother I knew about Lee, I'm sorry I didn't tell her. The school came out when I was at Swanwick. Now I will go to bed, posting this tomorrow. I will get Arnie his stamps sometime.

Your loving WILL

CAMBRAI
Tuesday morning, 15 August 1911

DEAR BOB,

I got to Cambrai about 6 o'clock yesterday evening before I had expected. On the walk over I sent a postcard to Mother from Le Cateau. But the day was cooler, for there was a breeze which even blew into something of a gale, so I was at Caudry where I had expected to sleep by 3.30. Then I pushed on and covered the distance without any fatigue whatever. I was so glad to get Father's and Mother's letters. I will write to M. Leclercq some time or other. Please tell Mother I hope she is better by now and able to bathe again. It is a pity that she should get ill just when she should be enjoying herself, and hard on you too. I was delighted to hear of your trip up Snowdon. Mother was writing while you were doing it, so I don't know how you got on. I hope the day cleared up giving you a fine view and that you thoroughly enjoyed yourself. Next time you must take Arnie with you!

Father says his cough has been very troublesome, but perhaps the return of the heat was responsible. Changes in the weather must affect it. Over here the heat-wave seems to have settled down to last. The other day the record temperature, which had stood since 1842, was beaten by one degree. I thought yesterday's wind meant a break-up but apparently it didn't. Still I like heat so don't feel inclined to complain except when there is no water.

I tried Mother's recommendation of carrying a lemon one day and it was some use, but what one wants really is just plenty of water. You perspire such a lot you get dried up and need replenishing.

Sunday I spent at a little town called Le Nouvion which lies by the side of a forest. The woods stretch for miles and are very pretty, with wild deer—I saw one roe-deer—in them and boars so they say.

I did not go to Rocroi and the Meuse valley after all. The difficulty was really that Rocroi is nothing but a fortress-town and the authorities might have objected to me sauntering about. One of the Rumigny gendarmes who arrested me was very keen to know if I intended to look at the Meuse. I was sorry of course not to see the rocks, but I don't think I could have spent Sunday better than at Le Nouvion. I went there partly by train on the Saturday, to avoid walking again over the same route. At Cambrai here there was the Fête de la Liberté when I arrived last night, which amused me rather. It's a fine town with some ruins of fortifications and a belfry. Also there is a Museum which I want to see this morning before I move on to Douai. Today's walk should be a very easy one. Please thank Father for sending Menon his £10: I expect he will explain all about it later. Congratulations to Arnie the Swimmer. Mrs. Rieder's letter must have been pleasant for Mother to read. I hope Ned will come back for the winter. If you could send just a postcard to Poste Restante, Calais, Pas-de-Calais, letting me know all's well it would make my Sunday comfortable. I would say to Dover, but perhaps as Mother suggests I may spend Sunday in France, at Dunkerque may be. At any rate I'll get home if I can the day you do. Hoping Father and Mother are feeling quite well now.

with love to all from WILL

PLACE FAIDHERBE
CYSOING
Wednesday night, 16 August 1911

DEAR ARNIE,

Try and pronounce the name Cysoing as above. It's a Flemish word and I am in Flanders now, where the country people don't talk French but a kind of Dutch. Take the names of some of the places near here. They are Wormhoudt, Houdscoote, Leffrinckhouche and Noordpeene. There are some mouthfuls for you, yet I expect I'll walk through the lot of those and a dozen others tomorrow and the next day. And yet I'm in France all right, only very close to the Belgian frontier. Just here it's about 3 miles off. The country is very pretty, flat yet well-wooded with a great many windmills. Cysoing is close to Bouvines, where the French won a great victory over us in King John's reign, and is quite small. Lille, one of the largest towns in all France, is close by though. I hope to go there tomorrow to see what the lay of the country is like round it. You see it was very important in history. Remember the *Cornet of Horse* {by G. A. Henty}. Also it has a very famous picture gallery which I would like to see. After I leave Lille, at midday perhaps, I hope to walk on about 15 miles or so and sleep at a town called Laventie. From there it is two days' walk to Calais.

You would be amused by a lot of the things they do here. Most of the carts are pulled by horses, but every now and then one meets one with a couple of oxen towing it very slowly along and looking very out of place. Then the handcarts are pulled by dogs of all kinds and sizes. One very little spaniel passed me today with a large mail-cart behind him, wagging his tail furiously as though he enjoyed it. They beat out the corn with flails and sometimes merely by knocking the sheaves of corn against the wall. And they have the same idiotic habit as the Bretons of loading their poor horses with tremendous sheepskin shoulder-capes. Yesterday I was at Douai, and at a place called Aniche outside it I saw a fête. Aniche is a coal-mining town, but the day was a holiday. First of all in a huge procession came a lot of little girls in white carrying banners with different saints' names on them. I suppose there were something like 150 girls. Then came a crowd of boys with their banners too, then the women of the town carrying a statue of the Virgin Mary, then crowds more children. Last of all came a great band and two clergymen with a swarm of little boys in uniform. They were marching about the place blessing the different coal-pits, to keep them from having accidents. At Douai the people had finished their celebrations of the Feast of Liberty, but when I came to Cambrai on Monday things were in full swing there. A great many people dressed in green coats and knickerbockers, with little red hats and feathers in them were marching about with bows and quivers. They had been shooting at something I suppose but when I saw them they were sitting in cafés mostly, drinking. There were many women in green coats and skirts with bows also. The rest of the fête was like St. Giles' fair.

They had one good game, riding at a quintain. That was an old knightly sport, galloping at full speed and trying to pass your lance through a ring, like tent-pegging. They did it on bicycles with wooden foils for lances, but it must be quite a good game. Also the miners all play a game called billons. They stick up a stump in the ground and throw clubs at it, like in bowls or skittles. Every little pub has a billon ground.

Please thank Father for telling me about my aeroplanist. M. Blériot lives at Hardelot just now and has made a kind of sand-motor for his children to rush about in along the sands, a tremendously swift machine. I didn't see it but have seen a photo of it later. There were a lot of English people at Hardelot, very nice quiet but rich people I should say. Since then I haven't heard any English at all, except from a negro at Cambrai. I've met a great many interesting people, and can talk to them more than I could last year.

I was so glad to hear of your swimming your 70 strokes. It's very good indeed. Now you can come out sailing with Bob and me next term. Give my love to Father and Mother. I do hope she is better now.

with love from WILL

CALAIS

Monday 1.0 *p.m.* 21 *August* 1911

MY DEAR MOTHER

I got to Calais on Saturday afternoon after a delightful bathe near Gravelines (another battlefield). Then I found your postcard awaiting me and a letter sent on from Cambrai. I'm so glad you are better now and that your illness was not a long one. Please tell Bob I'm sorry he did not get a good view from Snowdon, better luck next time perhaps. Arnie's swimming is quite magnificent and he can be quite proud of himself. As to golf I'm sure the heat is too much for it. Yesterday was very close and sultry here, ending in a thunderstorm in the evening. There was not a great deal of rain but it made a good show and was very nice to see. The first rain I've had this trip! Altogether I've been very fortunate indeed and have greatly enjoyed my tour. Thank you and Father for letting me loose on it.

When the rain stopped I walked down to the plage which was lit up every now and then by some of the finest lightning I've ever seen. Suddenly there would come a flash and you would see far out over the waves, and then all would be dark again. There was a great concert at the Casino and I seemed to be the only person interested in the storm. Today is a bit cooler but not much: there's more thunder to follow.

I'm going across to Dover in an hour's time and will post this there. I've seen a Saturday's *Daily Mirror* here in the Café which gives one the impression that England is an armed camp of soldiers and strikers. I hope the case is exaggerated for it sounds too absurd—and dangerous with Germany still rampant. It would give me a good excuse to stay on longer here but my walk has rounded off very well and I must do some work now. If I can't train to Oxford today I'll sleep somewhere en route and arrive tomorrow. In any case I'll wire to Frank.

My arrest was very funny and I don't wonder at your laughing. If it had been in Germany and they had thought me English it would have been the most natural thing in the world, for a solitary wanderer with a camera is obviously in a position to see things he should not. But I shouldn't have thought I would have been taken for a German. Four people on this trip have thought me a Spaniard, but that's a compliment and is due to my bronze and my panama. I was burnt very dark last week but now it's going off.

England has no monopoly of strikes. There's a big one of dockers here which makes one see sentries everywhere, and troops of soldiers patrolling the harbour. The strikers killed a blackleg and badly mauled two others in full daylight and with the gendarmes trying to protect them on Saturday. So there's a lot of trouble in the town and last night a lot of dockers were quarrelling and drunk when I came back from the plage.

Calais is a marvellously strong place, with fortifications everywhere. And so was Gravelines which was even more picturesque. The harbour is full of fishing-boats and both ports run smacks and schooners out to the Iceland cod-fisheries. I feel the usual hunger to step aboard and be off on the 'long trail, the trail that is always new'.

My trousers are decidedly on their last legs and I don't think they would stand another month's walking. As to my boots I got them mended by a cordonnier down a side-street in Lille and they are good again. My socks need mending but they are not bad. I make out that in actual marching, setting aside wandering about, I've walked 360 miles this trip, and I'm feeling extremely fit. I have £4 left, with my return fare to take out of it to Dover. So you see I've done very well for myself.

I'm very sorry that Logan did not get a second for he worked so hard and took it all so seriously. Worster is a very fine chap, one of our 1st boat two years ago. I'm glad of his first. Menzies-Jones expected nothing better than a third when I saw him after the exam. He makes a joke of everything. Thank you for telling me of the results. Of course Williams was expected to get a first. I knew nothing of Radice except that he said he got his history entire from Henty, like Mr. Atkinson. I hope you will all enjoy your last week and that the strike will be over to let you home again.

with love from WILL

TOULOUSE
Tuesday 7.0 *a.m.* 19 *March* 1912

DEAR MOTHER

As I don't know whether we won't be hurried at Les Cabanes, I'm going to write from here, and of course this may be your last news of me for some days, as this evening we should be at the foot of the pass into Andorra. I'm writing in a jolly little café where we've been having petit dejeuner.

Our train arrived here at 6.0 a.m. punctually. It's a wonderful service of trains with palatial carriages, and everything wonderfully up to time. Sleep was not difficult to get and for the most part Williams and I were alone in our compartment. All night it rained, but this morning it's quite fine down here in the South, with a warm breeze.

From Dover we had quite a good passage. The sea was rough and the wind exciting, but the boat, a turbine, went very smoothly. In the harbour we saw the wrecked barque which collided with the sunken P. & O. *Oceana*.

From Calais I could recognise many bits of road from the train. In our compartment was a Cambridge Don whom Williams had met and whom I knew about very well. He's the government nurse of the Indian Students in England. He and his wife were off to Athens to attend an Orientalist Congress. At Paris, where the rain had stopped, we walked to the Quai D'Orsay all long the Rue Lafayette and through the Tuilerie Gardens, and then along the river. Paris is certainly very fine, except in the business parts, but we attracted too much attention. 'Quelles Grandes Bêtes,' was the comment of a man we passed, which we translate What awful beasts! Now at Toulouse we have three hours to spend before our train goes to Les Cabanes. I've bought some sandals, quite decent looking affairs like cricket boots. There are none large enough for Williams! We must try again at Les Cabanes. He's very nice indeed, and I think we're going to have a most excellent time together. The plaid meets with his entire approval, as is only natural. As to Spanish, we're looking forward to having great amusement trying to make ourselves understood. As it is, down here the French they speak is very much more like English than at Paris, judging by the few people we've spoken to. I suppose it's the Provençal makes the difference; it is pronounced distinctly and without much emphasis. The Post Office isn't open yet, but in an hour's time I will retrieve the tabloids from it. It must have vexed you when you found I had left them behind. I must stop now. Tell Arnie I will see if there are any stamps of interest in Spain. Give my love to Father, Bob, Frank and him.

Your loving son

WILL

Tuesday March 19, 1912

DEAR MOTHER

I am writing this in the valley of the Upper Aston, in the twilight which will soon make me stop. It's very dark up here in the mountains, and rather cold. The valley in which we are camping is like that in 'Solitude', at the bottom of the stairs. At the far end a mountain 9,000 ft. high and covered with snow shuts out the light, an enormous cliff is opposite me like a wall, and we are lying at the foot of another precipice. Between the two runs a splendid burn.

Wednesday.   Merens near Hospitalet, road to Spain.

The dark came with one bound when I was writing the above, so I shut up and went to sleep. We were lying under an overhanging rock, in the valley of the Upper Aston, a wild solitude and very grand, 5,000 ft. above sea-level. At first the night was very fine and starlit, and we slept very soundly indeed; but at midnight I awoke to find a great wet mist everywhere. That lasted till dawn, and then it began to snow very gently. We waited an hour or two to see if it would clear up and let us into Andorra (we were already half-way there with almost all the bad part of the pass done), but the snow only became thicker so we walked very fast indeed back to the place we had started from, Les Cabanes. Getting up the valley had been as grand a walk as any in my life. The great burn running in the middle took up all the valley and along its edge lay a rough mule-path 4 feet wide, with sometimes a drop of about 100 ft. into the water below. The sides of the valley were open rock with young ash and hazel growing on it, and everywhere coated with daffodils, polyanthus, anemones, and snowdrops. There were very few birds and we did not see a single rabbit. Every stone we touched seemed to have a lizard under it; they were all over the place running along the face of the rocks. We followed the path, which was sometimes hard to find, for about 10 or 12 miles uphill all the way and at the last after a very steep climb across a hill where we touched the first bit of snow saw the upper valley and the great peaks beyond it, 9,000 ft. high. There we stopped and after eating bread and meat (such salt stuff) went to sleep in our rugs about 6.0 o'clock, when it was already dark. It had been an overpoweringly hot day, but the sun can seldom get into the Aston gorge, and it was cold there. The plaid kept me quite warm, and Williams was all right in his blanket too. But when the snow-storm came there was nothing for it but to beat a hasty retreat along the half obliterated path.

LA TOUR DE CAROL, *Thursday evening*

I've said nothing about the country from Toulouse to Les Cabanes which is a delightful plain. Olives are the chief crop I should say, and all ploughing is done, as everywhere here with oxen. On the way from Toulouse we went through Foix, where the castle is splendid. We're stopping the night here at Carol in the hotel. After getting back to Les Cabanes yesterday through the snow we walked in fine dull weather to Ax-les-Thermes, where I sent off a postcard. Thence we went up the Puymorens pass where there is a good carriage road. It is about 4,000 ft. and a magnificent gorge, bending many times and always looking as though there were no exit to it until one comes to the bend. At the end of the long gorge we came to the little village of Merens, where we slept in an old homely inn. Then this morning we went on up the pass by road, a steady uphill of about 12 miles. On the very top the road was about 4 inches deep in snow, drifted into feet in parts, but that was only about half-a-mile. Then we were about 6,000 ft. up, with mountains on either side of 8,000, looking very big and dazzling in the hot sun. From the top of the Col it was all down hill through a hot winding series of valleys here. This place La Tour de Carol is where Charlemagne won a great victory over the Moors; it is a mere village with very old houses, with carved wooden balconies and outside stairs, very pretty. The country is very different here from what it was the other side of the pass. Instead of snow mountains and rock gorges one has the rolling heather-clad type of hills, but still of great height. Spain is a quarter of a mile away and has been for a good deal of to-day since the road runs along the frontier. To-morrow we hope to cross it into a Spanish city called Puygcerda, from which we go by mule-path to Seo d'Urgel, 12 miles from Andorra. The country so far has been simply magnificent, with wonderful views, and all the peaks covered with snow (from yesterday. Before, it had melted.). The people are very kindly, and many of them very handsome types. The men generally go about wearing tartan plaids, trousers, black puttees, sandals, very red sashes and black velvet waistcoats. The women have shawl-veils (mantillas I suppose) over their heads, and shawls over shoulders. Garlic we had to-day for the first time at lunch in an omelette, and I rather like it. Fresh olives are regularly eaten and very good as hors d'œuvres.

They also have a great many vines in the fields. What we are going to do we haven't yet decided, after we have seen Andorra. But we hope to get to Carcassonne before we go to Toulouse on the way back. Probably we will stop in Spain and go East after leaving Urgel to the Mediterranean shore. At any rate I will call at the Grande Bureau des Postes at Carcassonne, in case you send a letter there to me W.G.L. since that's my name on the Passport.

I am having a most glorious time and Williams is a perfect companion. Probably I will set out home if all's well with him to arrive on the day before Easter, but of course we don't know about that. I wish I knew how you all were. Best luck to Arnie in the Sports.

Saturday morning, SEO D'URGEL

Yesterday we had a very long walk through the gorges of the Segre river here. At first we went from Carol to Puygcerda in Spain, a very picturesque walled town on the top of a high hill and overlooking all the valley called Cerdagne. From there it was a mule-path most of the way here till we came to an unfinished road, and we were both tired last night. Today we hope to reach Andorra.

The weather is magnificent. Mostly it is overpoweringly hot but whenever it clouds over down comes snow not rain; the mountains are all covered on the top. The rivers run very rapidly and are simply torrents. As to the people; this Spanish side they no longer have the same clothes as the men of Roussillon, but wear red jerseys and above them black velvet waistcoats, velveteen trousers, and sandals. They're a good-looking people, mostly, though one or two men we have seen who looked thorough scoundrels. Our landlord here speaks French, so that we have no trouble. Spanish or rather Catalan sounds very pretty. I'm going to send this off now. With best love to all of you.

from WILL

ANDORRA
Saturday, March 23rd, 1912

MY DEAR MOTHER,

Here we are in the place where we would be, and a wonderful place it is. I doubt if even Ned has come to a more primitive town in his wanderings. It is perched up on the side of a hill (7,000 ft. above sea level on the summit), in a narrow grassy valley with snow-covered mountains on the opposite side. Through the valley runs a fast clear river, which lower down cuts a wonderful gorge through the hills. The town-streets are about 8 ft. wide, and roughly paved; the tops of the houses almost meet, and are built out into balconies with old carved wood-work. In the fields in the valley are plenty of cattle and pigs, and up on the hill-side sheep are grazing in great flocks, with large herds of goats and pigs. All the carrying is done by mules and donkeys, with panniers fastened on their backs and their heads ornamented with red and yellow trappings. The men either wear red jerseys and black or brown waistcoats, or have blue smocks. All have red knitted caps.

Hens are kept in the lowest storey of the houses, where also the cooking is done, and in many places there is a proper stable by which one enters. Then there is a ladder leading to the upper rooms, which are generally bare but clean. There is a fine church here, and the Council-house.

We went over that on Sunday, after service. You go through a high gate and a door opened with a key a foot in length. Then up a stone staircase, and you come to a reading room, with maps and plans and history books. Next that is the large dining-room, like a college hall, with the kitchen opening off it. The chimney is in the middle of the roof and the hearth in the floor under it, with some pillars and chain-arrangements to hang an entire ox for the roasting. Opening opposite the school room is the Council Chamber. At one end is a small plain chapel with a fine picture presented by the French Republic; at the other is a great long table and high wooden chairs alongside. This is where the 24 Councillors of Andorra debate. There are 6 parishes in the Republic and each sends 4 representatives; besides these is the President, and two Syndics or Justices. We saw their uniforms which were much like the Mayor's hat and robes of Oxford, with plenty of gold lace.

In the lower storey of the Council-hall was a prison, always empty, and wine-cellars. The whole building is very old and beautiful, with some very fine frescoes painted on the walls inside. Our guide did not know the date of them, but said they had been there as long as Andorra had existed!

The more I saw of the valley the more I liked it and I was very sorry to leave it. There was one most charming round watch-tower, which I think is shown in Belloc's book. The snow-mountains were a perfect setting to the broiling hot valley with its clear watercourses; the costumes of the people suited them and they were all most jolly and courteous.

To-day, Monday, we have been having a new experience, a drive over the mountains in the Spanish royal mail, correo real, from Urgel to this place Puygcerda. The road at first is quite recognizable as a road but for the latter half is only a mule-track, and as we tore round corners, with only a foot of track and sometimes less to spare, and a drop of hundreds of feet below with our three horses (two leaders and one in the shafts) slipping on the loose stones, one felt what Spain was really like. The jolting was terrific, but the drive was grand through the gorges. The driver to encourage his horses makes a noise exactly like a bark, and also occasionally shouts 'Aree' at the top of his voice. There is room for eight in the cart, and for the last few miles it was full.

To-morrow we hope to recross the frontier into France. Williams is very keen to learn the news of English matters, and Spanish papers hardly mention them. Also we both want to see the Mediterranean which we will probably touch at Cape Leucate (ask Arnie to look it up). After that we may go to Carcassonne. I hope you got my letter telling you I would call for letters there. Or we may even (W's idea) go to Arles, which means a long railway trip more or less. I want to hear from you as to what I should do about coming back in view of the Strike and its developments, which we can only guess at. Also I would like to hear how Canon Christopher is, and the other news, besides getting news of you. After Carcassonne I will call at the Grand Bureau de Poste, Toulouse.

I am enjoying this trip more than I can say, and am delighted with the country and the people. Today as we drove into the open Valley of the Cerdagne the setting sun made all the tops of the snow-mountains rose-red in its light, and it was glorious. We have had the luck of meeting French-speaking Spaniards as landlords, so our Spanish has only been a joke. I couldn't get any postcards in Andorra, so I fear you won't be able to get an idea of it.

It's very queer but the people here never think of going about without a tartan blanket on their shoulders, so my plaid is quite in the fashion. We haven't slept out recently. Now it's time for dinner. With very best love to all.

from WILL

I hope Arnie did well in the Sports, which will be over I think by the time you get this. I'm extremely fit and we're walking easily mostly, and none at all today. On Sunday afternoon we walked 10 miles or perhaps 8, in order to get the Correo this morning at 6.30 a.m.; otherwise Sunday was a perfect idyllic day in Andorra. Your pronunciation of Andorra is right.

DRIVE FROM URGEL TO PUYGCERDA, *Monday 25 March* 1912

Pedro Isern called for us at five in the morning. It was already broad day, and the crowing of cocks had long given in to the donkeys braying in the plaza. As for Pedro he would have frightened a London crowd. Very tall and loosely built he was dressed in a black worked smock, velveteen trousers, and sandals and carried a huge studded whip. He had more beard than anyone I have ever seen who pretended to shave, and incessantly smoked the small black local cigars.

With this hero of the Cerdaña, we left the hotel. Across the square, down first one calle, then another, narrow cobbled streets where sunlight never reaches, he brought us to his coach, el correo real. Picture a hogshead slung between six foot high wheels, with the floor of the barrel almost on the ground, and you have the contrivance. There was straw 4 inches deep to push one's feet into, one put head between knees, and so sitting was possible. To this were attached three thin if gaudily trapped horses, one between the shafts, and two leaders side by side. There was another passenger, a swarthy bearded little Catalan with a scarred face and all the fingers but the smallest missing from his right hand. In we climbed and took our seats beside him. Then a great crack of the whip, a noise like the barking of a dog, cheering, so we left Seo d'Urgel on a spring morning.

Down the hill, over the watersplash and up again, and the valley road gave us the view. To the south and right the snow covered Sierra del Cadi, to the north, spurs of the Pyrenees, closed in the Segre to a basin half a mile across. Behind were the red sandstone crags and ruins of Castelbo, and in front the rapidly narrowing way. It was not the glistening snow peaks that held the eyes so much as the nearer slopes. Low down these were planted with vines, looking like withered cabbage-stalks, just breaking into leafage, and set thick among them were peach trees in gorgeous blossoms.

Further up where the vine-terraces ended were the olives, grey-green and shot with the light like quivering aspens. Highest of all was the broom on the very cliff top, so that to the half-closed eyes the hills were clothed in pink and green and gold. Through them we went at a canter, with much flogging of horses. The Spanish method of driving is that of the Moors. The whip is seldom used; instead a heavy stick is smashed upon the harness, and a running fire of noises, hard to make but between a cough and a bark is kept up monotonously. Only occasionally the man will crack his whip as loud as he can, shouting "Anee! Anee!" For a few miles the road ran on, and we were getting accustomed to the jolts. Then suddenly it came to an end, and our adventures began.

First we had to get down a long slope to a bridge over the river. This Pedro went straight for, with the horses sliding on their haunches and confusion of limbs rolling in the cart. The value of its shape appeared and that of the driver's crutch like a side-saddle's. Then a path narrower than the wheels climbed the opposite bank many hundreds of feet; the coach lay almost on its side and was hauled up so by the horses but this didn't matter since we helped to get it along. Then came the great drive.

The road is a rock-hewn ledge along the cliff, with hundreds of feet above and hundreds below, almost sheer. There is just room for the wheels. On this, with many 'Arees' the coach was driven at a hand-gallop, the wheels bouncing on the loose stones, throwing them into the water below, the horses trying to pull close to the safe side, Pedro standing up and shouting in excitement with us. Once we had to stop to let a mule-train clamber up the hill-side out of our way: we rushed past with one wheel off the path. More miles of this and the road opened out again, sloped down and ran into the village of Martinette, where we stopped to rest man and beast. It was a typical Catalan inn. A great meal, and almost nothing to pay, fowls and perhaps a calf in the eating-room, portraits of the king and queen, these are the things commonly found. Most characteristic are the drinking vessels; to save glasses there are decanters shaped like watering cans to pour wine into one's mouth from afar, no easy feat. These are handed round. After lunch, it is a Spanish word, Juan the Posadero came out to talk with us on the bridge. He also was a type with his blue eyes, Argivi-Greek features, dark hair and medium size, and better than Pedro too he shewed the costume of woollen vest and 8 feet long blue waistband. Interrupted by the appearance of the driver, we crouched on our seats again.

We had come 20 miles and had nearly as many to go. But now the road was mostly along the river bank, for the pass was widening out into the rich valley of the Cerdaña. So then past fields where the slow ox-teams were ploughing, under two high ruined castles, which once must have held the road to all comers, meeting mule-trains now and again and once a party of carabineros del reino, we came into Belvir, where men, women and children were dancing in the plaza. Thence the road ran through the rich wine-plain. The snow on the hills was already rose in the sunset behind us, a mist was rising from the Segre, but the horses were pushed on till we came to the white walls of Puig-cerda on its brown hill. Then the last break into a gallop up the steep winding street and the end with much cracking of whips before the old castle. Cramped and tired almost as though we had walked the journey not driven we got down. 'Gracias, Caballeros', said Pedro, then as an afterthought his one French word, 'Merci'. And that we echoed.

Wednesday Morning 27/3/1912. OLETTE

DEAR MOTHER

I posted a letter to you yesterday from Puygcerda in Spain, and at the same time left that place. We had a fine walk over the hills along the main road here, going east all the way. The highest point we touched en route was Mount Louis, 6,000 ft. The day was as hot as ever it is in England in the summer, and lizards were out all over the roads, as well as a few pretty little snakes about a foot long. The engineering of the road was wonderful from Mt. Louis down to here; huge great loops down the gorges were rather tiring however. Also there were some very fine bridges over the Tet which runs in a cañon here something like a 1,000 ft. deep, and very precipitous.

Olette is a pretty little place with sulphur baths, in no way out of the ordinary run of Pyrenean villages. It is in France however, and so there are soldiers about, and at Mount Louis, which is a frontier fortress of the 2nd. class, we came on quite an extensive field-day.

The view from Mount Louis was wonderful, both East and West. The Sierra del Cadi, which is the range of snow-mountains to the south of the Cerdagne, looked very lovely in the broiling sun, though they dazzled us considerably. Here, East, the hills are still very high, about 9,000 ft., but there is much less snow. We are coming near to the Mediterranean which accounts for this. Possibly by using the train we will reach it to-day. We talk of taking a small coasting-steamer from Port Vendres on the Franco-Spanish frontier to Cette in the Gulf of Lyons. That will be lovely.

TOULOUSE, *Thursday morning*

We didn't go to Port Vendres and Cette. Instead when we arrived on foot at Villefranche-sur-Conflans, a delightful walled fortress-town, one of the best, we bought some newspapers. Williams had been worrying about the state of things in England for some time. He lives in the north, where there are mines and docks, and the people are very rough as well as on a branch railway far from anywhere. So he feared riots and trouble at home. The papers were very gloomy of the strike's future, and painted a black picture of the present distress. He made up his mind to return at once. I thought there was no good in my coming back to make one more for you to feed, but when he was so concerned about riots thought for safety sake I would telegraph. Hence my wire. I ac-

companied him to Toulouse by rail. It was a glorious journey through
the wine-country of Roussillon. At first the train ran through lava-hills
worked into terraces with vines just coming into leaf, and bright pale
green olive-trees. Huge aloes, the Mexican cactus, were cultivated in
many places; the peach-orchards looked wonderful with rose blossom
(they had been with us all along our way) and everywhere there were
stocks and bright flowers in the fields. At Perpignan we ran into a huge
lot, quite 15, English at the station. From there the train ran through
flat country to Narbonne, touching on the Mediterranean at Cap
Leucate. Get Arnie to look it up and see the huge lagoons there are
along the coast. They were bluer than any water I have ever seen, calm
as could be and the sun was tropically hot. It was a splendid first sight
of the sea. After Narbonne we passed through Carcassonne seeing the
old town very well, and then arrived here at 8, in the evening, and I
got your wire and Blaksley's letter just in time before the office shut.
Your answer was what I expected. I'm afraid my telegram must have
been a bit of a bother, but I'm glad I sent it since it makes me more
comfortable in staying here. Williams caught a night-train at 8.45 so
we parted. We had done all we set out to do and had a most successful
trip. He is a perfect comrade. When dining here with him at the Buffet
last night we were talking with an old Light Blue of 1874 who told us
the results of the Sports. Evidently there was some wonderful running.
I'm sorry Anderson was beaten, he's such a gentleman. Evidently
Jackson ran very well. The Sports were on the day I was in Andorra!

What I will do with myself down here I have not perfectly decided.
I will take it very easy however and lounge across by foot and by train
to Carcassonne again to begin with. There should be letters for me
there. There's no use going West since there has been a great deal of
rain there, whereas in the East it's been hot as summer. Williams is an
excellent walker and faster than I am, so we travelled hard in our time
of marching. The day of just under 40 miles over high country from
La Tour de Carol to Seo d'Urgel was a caution and we were both quite
done on arrival. So lazing about in the vine-country will be a luxury.

I hope you have heard again from Ned by now. I haven't written to
him yet, but will do so in the next few days. That Canon Christopher
should take a long time to get over any illness at his age is natural; I'll
be keen to hear how he is. I wish I could see you for a while; that
Arabian Night's seeing-tube was a good invention. About coming back,

of course I would like to be home for Easter, but if the country is still
disturbed by the strike I might be in the way. That is for you to settle,
I have crowds of money and can stop on here indefinitely. What I need
is a note from you. I'll be in Carcassonne possibly for Sunday, at least
by Monday night I should think. If the letter which you have probably
sent there gives me news about this that will be all right. Otherwise you
had better write here once more to the Bureau, unless you think a letter
would have time to reach Carcassonne by Monday.

I wrote to Blaksley the other day thinking it possible he might write.
Thanks for your p.c. to him; I will write again.

With all love to all of you.
                                                     Your son WILL

                                            SAISSAC, *Friday, March 29, 1912*
DEAR MOTHER,

This is being written from a little Town with a picturesque castle
and ruined gates. It's 20 miles from Carcassonne, where I hope to sleep
to-morrow night and Sunday. After writing my last letter to you from
Toulouse I lounged about the town till lunch-time. After that I left and
walked about 15 miles through fields of vines for the most part, quite
rich country, to a town called Montguiscard. There I left the main road
and struck out over a land called the Laurageois. I slept out in a wood
near La Bastide-de-Beauvoir.

This morning when I woke the weather had changed. There was a
high wind and many storm-clouds. I set out merrily however and
walked first to a village called St. Felix-de-Caraman. It's a fine place
with a very handsome church, and a situation like that of Brill. Glorious
views from it over flat fertile wine-country.

There I lunched, and setting out again more slowly in weather which
held up though it threatened I went down and crossed the plain to
Revel, a large town. From there to my place here is about 12 miles, and
they were magnificent. First I climbed up a long river gorge past a huge
lake of St. Ferreol, coming into the Tarn department. Three miles of
gorge brought me up onto the plateau of the Montagne Noire, a great
forest which lies north of Carcassonne. The road ran through moors
yellow in the gorse which is all out. At times it was just over 2,000 ft.
high. And for three miles at half a mile from me the land dropped away
as though to meet the sea with its cliffs. And instead there was the plain
of Languedoc. It stretched for miles lit up by the sunset and shut in by

the hills. Due south of me I could count 7 separate ranges ending in the main Pyrenees the snow of which shewed up in the distance 60 miles away. I've never seen anything like it, and it was worth miles of walking.

This town Ned probably knows but it's possible he missed it so I will try and get some postcards of the ruins to-morrow. It seems very picturesque, but so far I've only seen so much of it as I passed searching for an hotel. It's very good that the rain kept off all day; at times it was quite bright especially in the distance. I could see the sunshine on the Pyrenees without having any myself.

Saturday, March 30th, 9 p.m.

Here I am in Carcassonne all right at a little Hotel, the Central, in the new town. The first thing I did on arrival was to call at the Post Office, where I got Father's letter which I hope to answer tomorrow and send with this.

To continue my journey.

I had walked about 30 miles when I came to Saissac yesterday night, so I went to bed early there and slept very sound. This morning I went out after petit dejeuner and spent about an hour on the castle. It's extremely fine, built on the point of a wedge of rock driven down a gorge, so that on either side of it are ravines. At the back of the wedge is the town with bits of old walls and bastions and towers, and all the houses very ancient-looking. For a typical old French hill-town it would be hard to beat—it even runs Domfront close—and besides it has two jolly watercourses with cascades. Everywhere grow wall-flowers and in many bits of gardens beautiful irises. Besides that the hotel is a quaint little spot with a very motherly landlady. I was quite sorry I was not spending Sunday there.

From Saissac one could see Carcassonne all right in front of the hills and the mountains.

It is really quite a landmark, for the Old Town is built on a considerable hill. But it was a walk of 20 miles, so I had just a nice distance to cover before the end of the day. The road still ran alongside the edge of the Black Mountain at first giving me very long views. Also there was still plenty of gorse. I went through a very pretty old village of Montalieu, fortified, and then through another called Mousseleus with about 5 miles between each before I came down from the hills. It was still vine-country, but also with flocks of sheep where the country was not ploughed. At Pezens, 6 miles from Carcassonne I was stopped by two gendarmes who demanded my age, business and the rest. My passport did not satisfy them till after considerable palaver, and they insisted on seeing how much money I had got. It was the return ticket to England which really convinced them of my genuineness. I had walked on, being occasionally swallowed up by clouds of dust, for these miles from Pezens were along the high road, till I was just outside Carcassonne when I overtook two more gendarmes escorting a couple of ragged fellows handcuffed together. These gendarmes also demanded my papers, but this time the Passport was at once sufficient.

A passport is legally unnecessary for a British citizen in France but after last summer and these experiences I think it will be always wise to have one with me when I'm walking. The gendarmes at Pezens were very overbearing, and it would have gone hard with me if I had not had it and the railway tickets with Cook's labels. To be sure France is in a state of terror just now. The one topic in all cafés and other places where men do congregate is about some man-slaying robbers in a motor, and to judge by a paper I took up at lunch this morning to see about the Strike, people are being arrested on suspicion of being the motorists all over the place from Beziers and Marseilles to Lille and Nantes. Still I should be sorry if I looked like a Parisian murderer even more than like a German spy.

So far I have paid one visit to the Old Town and have walked round it. It is perfectly magnificent and far above expectations. Still I don't know if my first sight of it from the train with Williams will not be my pleasantest recollection of it. Near at hand it is really too good. The excellent state of repair in which it is kept is artificial; people in the Middle Ages built their walls for defence and not for show and when the defensive purpose was no longer needed would have let them drop into disrepair. So our restorers should let the walls here be always on the way towards crumbling, and not clear-cut like the wooden walls of the Oxford Pageant. That's only my impression of the moment. I'll have all to-morrow to alter it in.

This hotel has some English people, genus bounder to judge by their language, in it, young people. Two are in the room next to me. Now it's time for bed.

Your loving WILL

HÔTEL CENTRAL, CARCASSONNE
Sunday, 31 *March*, 1912

DEAR FATHER,

It was good of you to write to me at such length. If you could have seen me enjoy it you would have felt repaid. You have given me quite a lot of news to reply to.

In the first place my heartiest congratulations to Frank. It's great his winning the cup, which I never even thought of as being likely. He has every reason to be proud of himself for a good all-round effort.

I'm very sorry for Arnie, but he mustn't mind. He's a very fine runner even if he doesn't win races on the days when he is off it. I hope he will come off as winner of the Novices race in the Swimming Sports later on. He must come bathing with me next term.

Ned does seem to have been treated scurvily by the British Museum. I saw somewhere or other that the Italians were being expelled from Syria which is just as it should be. It's good Mr. Hogarth is going out; it shews he anticipates no trouble. I was sorry to hear of Mrs. Aldridge's illness. What a beastly thing appendicitis seems, leaping on one like a wild animal at unexpected moments. I hope she's better now. About my plans. I think that unless I find a letter bidding the contrary I will try and be home for Easter. I've seen so much already that I feel as though it were months since we left, and I long to be back. And as there is nothing that I particularly want to do in France to keep me moving I may as well get back at once. Paris is not to be visited in these clothes, as our walk across it the other day shewed me. Even here it is unpleasant to be chivvied about by a horde of boys as has been my fate more than once to-day, although I am going about without bag or plaid. I have learnt since leaving Toulouse this second time to look upon every dog as a potential assailant, but boys are worse since one can't flourish a stick and shout at them.

So probably I will reach home on Saturday next. In any case I will send a wire when I reach England. (By the way I was charged nothing extra at Toulouse for receiving your telegram. Things are cheap and good here.) If by any chance I get a letter here tomorrow or at Toulouse advising me to stay longer my address for Easter should be Grand Bureau Cahors. I don't know what department it's in. But otherwise I probably will leave here to-morrow afternoon; sleep at Toulouse. Leave there Tuesday afternoon, sleep at Montauban. Wednesday

possibly walk from Montauban to Castelsarrasin and back. Then see
Cahors. Arrive at Paris if possible early in the day and see Notre-Dame
and the Venus de Milo. Then home. Thus I will avoid the rush in the
train, and will take it in pieces during the day-time instead of at one
gulp by night. The weather to-day has been very cold and grey with
some rain, so tramping for the nonce is off.

I hope by now the house is quite ship-shape and Mother not too
tired, and satisfied with her exertions. Also that Arnie enjoyed the
Circus. Mother is interested in dreams. Tell her I spent some part of
last night careering about St. Giles on a great horse and engaged in a
cavalry-duel with sabres with Mr. Winston Churchill. Madness could
go no further.

I hope the strike is settled by this. I must look in a paper to-morrow.
Also I must try and see if Oxford won the boat-race—yesterday I think.

Love to all of you.

Your loving son WILL

Hôtel Français
66 Rue Bayard
Toulouse
2nd April, 1912, 2 o'clock

DEAR MOTHER,

This is being written just after I've sent a post card to Frank, and
won't be posted immediately. I haven't much to tell you of what has
happened to me since Saturday's letter. Indeed the weather has been so
stormy I couldn't have done much even if I had been out for adventures. Sunday I spent very quietly, most of it in and about the 'old
town' of Carcassonne. Very happily the new Carcassonne which is a
great commercial city, the headquarters of the wine trade, has grown
up in the level country to the north of the river, leaving the old town
alone. The houses in the latter are chiefly antiquities dealers', and there
is only one hotel in it looking very dear. One of the best things about
the town is the view from it; built as it is on quite a steep hill above the
river with orchards on the slope and old houses at the bottom making a
little suburb it has most glorious panoramas from all over the ramparts.
It is a wonderful place and teaches one more than any number of books
would do. The only drawback to it is its very perfection; only in places
is the masonry at all old looking and mostly it looks as though it were

a mediæval 'white city' or Olympia, not genuine. I enjoyed my time there immensely, and as I only left at dusk by train for Toulouse I spent nearly all two days and another afternoon on it. Sunday was Palm Sunday and in the morning it was a great sight to watch the people buzzing about with their palms. Also I saw one queer sight I didn't understand. Outside the Church at Old Carcassonne, which is a happily built Romanesque building, the clergy and choir stood singing for quite a long time in the cold wind, with more choirpeople inside answering them. The old grandee among them—he may have been a bishop or the Archbishop for all I know—had to be held up by two men while the ritual went on. I saw the Museum at New Carcassonne which had two pictures in it which pleased me very much; one of a wood called 'Evening', and the other a vision of St. Francis of Assisi, two friars asleep in the solar chamber of an old grange and a shepherd boy coming in with his sheep. Monday at Carcassonne was as bad a day as I can remember at times, but spasmodically it became brilliantly fine though very cold always. At such times the view over the Black Mountain was very great with the sun on the snow at the top and a rainbow over the lot. I came to this Hotel where I am known when I arrived last night, and this morning have been sightseeing in Toulouse. It's a fine city but too prosperous to be pleasant for wasting time in, being of the Liverpool variety. There are tremendous quays down on the canals, and I've seen boats in them from Marseilles and Beziers and Bordeaux. France must be honeycombed with a great canal system. They have very pretty house-boats along the river where the washerwomen work, which look like the pictures of Chinese river-boats. Altogether the river pleases me most here, after the Museum. That was a place I retired to to get out of the cold, to be charmed by it. It's in an old church, with delightful cloisters in which the statues are placed. There are two or three pictures in it which I will remember. There are several good churches here, all built in brick, but the beggars about the doors are dreadful sights and make going into a church far from pleasant. In less than an hour now I will go by train to Montauban, where I hope to sleep tonight. I called at the P.O. and got your letter an hour ago, so giving the Office as much time as possible in case you might have sent a second. I'm so glad the house is nearly done, and that the strike has not affected you. The French papers talked of children dying of starvation and the like, which got on Williams' nerves, even when we made

allowance for the exaggeration of the Press. You suggest I should go to
Angers. If my ticket admitted of my breaking the journey at Orleans
that might be done, but Limoges is the nearest place where I can stop,
and that must be 150 miles at least from it. I did think of going there
till I looked it up in the map. As you say I can please myself I think I
will try and get home by Saturday night, but I may change my mind.
That will mean spending Good Friday at Amiens probably, which will
be jolly for old acquaintance sake, or else in the village of Longpri-les-
Corps Saint. It's so cold here now that for the last three days I have been
wearing my sweater all the time, and I'm quite glad to have my overcoat here. You give me the suggestion to buy a pair of trousers if I feel
remarkable. Other Frenchmen, all chauffeurs apparently and motoring-
commis-voyageurs, wear puttees down here and so there's nothing out
of the way in them. I can't imagine why people stare at me as they do,
but it's quite right here; the Carcassonne people were the great
offenders.

I've written recently to Ned and to Blaksley, and sent post cards from
Carcassonne to Florence, Nellie, Margaret and L. C. Jane. I must send
one also to Green. For some reason I feel very confident that the Canon
will get better; I'll be keen to see him when I get home.

MONTAUBAN, *Tuesday, 9 p.m.*

The journey here was through very flat fertile country. I can't
remember one tunnel between here and Perpignan on the Mediterranean, which shows you what a plain all this country is. Yet here it is
not so much a plain as a valley, and at Carcassonne the same. Then
there were the Black Mountain to the North and the foot-hills of the
Pyrenees to the South. Here Montauban itself is on the edge of the
hills, or at least looks out over very decidedly lower country. At
Toulouse the river is the Garonne, but I think the river here which is
about the width of the London Thames, is only a tributary. The
Garonne itself is a huge thing, and at Toulouse looked like the Mersey
at Liverpool.

I've made enquiries of the station authorities here about Angers. By
rail from Orleans it is 200 kilometres, with one change at Tours. And
I would have to get the Station-master at Orleans' permission to break
the journey there, since Cahors, Brive and Limoges are the only places

between here and Paris where I can stop according to my ticket. I don't think it's worth it sorry though I am to give up the idea.

So tomorrow I think, weather permitting and in spite of the wind and the cold there's been no rain today, I will go for a walk from here to Castelsarrasin, the name of which attracts me, and then catch an evening train to Paris. Only so can I get my full day in the city. Montauban is a pleasing city, very big, but not walled and on a mount as for some reason I expected. The great thing here is the Ingres Museum. Ingres, whom many think France's greatest painter, was born here something more than 100 years ago and they have a lot of his pictures. I haven't seen them yet. Those that I have seen of him so far, in the National Gallery and elsewhere, have not pleased me much. He painted in all styles, but chiefly Nudities and Sacred Pictures. I'll go to his Museum tomorrow if it's too wet for walking.

Wednesday morning, 8 a.m.

It's a fine cold day, so I guess I'll chuck Ingres and go for a walk. Then that means that I reach Paris at 9.0 a.m. tomorrow, and have the whole day there. If I feel inclined I may spend Good Friday there as well, but I feel more attracted by a quiet day at Amiens. I hope you are finding treasures in the newcomers, and are not too busy now. It will be nice being back for Easter. Please thank Arnie for the flower. I think it's one off my campanula isn't it? 'Wearing the white flower of a blameless life' is a good remark of Tennyson's. I haven't seen any campanula's this trip but then at this time they would be very tiny. In the public gardens here are all sorts of palms and semi-tropical plants, looking queer in this weather. Many roads are lined with cypresses, but it's very bright mostly with orchard blossoms and flowers. Still nothing to compare with Spain. I'll send this off now.

love to all from WILL

THE JOURNEY TO INDIA, ON P. & O. S.S. *Egypt*, 6 September, 1913

Saturday, 4.30 p.m.

DEAR MOTHER

The sea is as calm as can be with the light cooling breeze which crosses it, so I can write legibly. But I'm only going to start a letter, to be finished gradually and posted at Port Said. I had quite a nice journey to Marseilles. To Paris the train went at an enormous rate, past the places I know so well, like Hardelot Woods, and Picquigny and Amiens. It was very fine and hot, ending with a thunderstorm most of the night. The Marseilles express was crowded with people, but my reserved seat made me comfortable. In the same compartment was a very nice fellow, an accountant, who's been some years at Agra, and is going back. I've seen a good deal of him since, sitting next him at meals.

By the time the dawn broke we had left Lyons behind and were in the Rhône valley. The view of the country was magnificent: very rocky with a lot of castles. Where there was earth it was planted with olive-trees and vine-terraces. And at the background were the Alps of Savoy, some very sharp peaks and much more indented, less of a white wall, than the Pyrenees. All that Rhône country seemed just the place for a month's tramp. It was very similar though to the country A.T.P. and I went over.

Marseilles was reached about half-past eight, and for an hour before we came there we had first the Camargue, a plain flat as a billiard table, brown and hardly cultivated at all to look at, and then the sea. I saw nothing of Avignon, though we came through it. As for the coast it is very rocky, grey and brown above the deep blue. It is not so pleasing as that passed from Perpignan to Narbonne with A.T.P., but grander. Marseilles is not in the least French. Since then we have been steaming 371 miles in the day, have passed between Corsica and Sardinia in the dark, and will be at Stromboli at our present rate by 8.0 tonight. Messina will be in the dark. It's been beautifully fine and sunny without being hot.

The boat is very full, a lot of military men, of Egyptians and Indians, some missionary women (a Miss McNeile is on board I don't know where) and a large group of bounders. I chat mainly to the aforesaid accountant, a very quiet fellow of 38 who's leaving his wife and children at home, and a Captain Ivens. He's been in charge of a frontier station north of Bannu for three years, and is the usual type of army man of the best sort, a gentleman. He's just been married, a fortnight ago, so has to give up his post and go after his regiment which is in China. I've met most of the other officers with him, one of whom has done a good deal of commissioner work in the Persian gulf.

I share a cabin with a young fellow who's going out for a shop, and who's quiet and pleasant, so that's all right. It would have been nasty to have been set down with one of the whisky swillers. If only you're having something of this fine weather you must be enjoying yourself grandly in Ireland. But you'll have nothing like the stars of last night, and the blue of this sea. They are much too beautiful to leave one comfortable.

Monday, 8 September

The boat is expected to get to Port Said by tomorrow afternoon. It is now two o'clock of a perfect day with the sea hardly rippled and very little wind. The time has been passing very quietly. The only thing we have seen has been the lighted Straits of Messina. Stromboli was not glowing at all, and we did not get to the Straits till 10 o'clock. The lights were brilliant and it was very pretty indeed.

I have done very little but look at the sea, and talk with Captain Ivens. He's rather looked upon as the hero of the boat, having done some big things in frontier fighting. But he's very quiet. Also I've met Miss McNeile, who is the one at Cairo.

There is a great crowd on board, but many leave at Port Said. It's rotten just when one is getting to know people to lose them, and a lot of these fellows are pleasant. But it will be good to see Ned. There's a man on board whom I have not yet met, going presently to be introduced, who has stopped at Carchemish with them more than once. He's an engineer at Beyrout. I have seen a good deal of a Hooghli pilot, who's on board, and is the most notable India Defence official. He has done 19 years service now and is the chief regulator of the Bay of Bengal. He's very interesting. There's very little else to say now. The voyage is only a pleasant monotony in bright weather. They had two services on board yesterday, which most people were at, but they had no sermon, except a very short one in the evening.

I wonder how you are getting on in Ireland. If only you get decent weather you should have a splendid time. Now I'll stop again.

9/9/13

The land is in sight at times now, so we won't be very long. A tired nightjar settled on the boat just a few minutes ago, and we have doves flying past.

I've met the man who knows Ned, a commercial traveller named

Powell, who's going up to Beyrout. There are also an old lady and her daughter going to the same place care of Canon Parfit. And I'm told a boat leaves this evening which is very handy. If it stops at Jaffa I'll leave it there and see Jerusalem before I go on to Aleppo for the 15th.

The weather is beautiful, in no way too warm. I'll be quite sorry to leave Captain Ivens.

Now here's love to you all.

Yours

WILL

BEYROUT
10 September, 1913

DEAR MOTHER

This is the 10th, and I've come here much quicker than I expected. The *Egypt* reached Port Said a day before it was scheduled to do so, and three hours afterwards I caught an Austrian Lloyd steamer to Beirut straight. It did not stop at Jaffa for Jerusalem. Powell, the man who knew Ned, was on board, so I had company. Also there was a Medical Missionary Dr. {D. W.} Torrance of Tiberias, with whom Doughty has twice stayed. There is a great deal of cameraderie amongst these people, and I had a very jolly voyage. Now I'm at the Hotel here, where I'm intending to sleep the night, and tomorrow catch an early train to Damascus. That will give me a view of the Lebanons, which will be better than passing through them at night.

Beirut harbour is very beautiful, a splendid bay with the low hills backed by red mountains. The gunboats sunk by the Italians are still in the harbour. They put one to an odd use by fixing a Customs officer aboard her to take the number of the passengers. The disembarkation was very picturesque: we lay quiet awhile while medical officers talked and a fleet of rowboats were kept back by a man with a revolver. Then they were allowed to race full tilt for the ship and swarm up the sides shouting for passengers. As to the town it's a big place, like Marseilles only more European to look at, with the American College dominating it. Once in the streets there is a place much like Port Said.

Port Said I saw little of, going ashore with Captain Ivens (whom I spoke of before I expect). He bought me a sunhelmet while I helped him to buy some kimonos for two ladies. Port Said is very beautiful, with a caressing cool breeze, green gardens laid out in red flower-beds, and large domed harbour offices like palaces. The beach is magnificent, but bathing was out of the question. The Austrian Lloyd was quite a comfortable boat; passengers from the *Egypt* were aboard. Powell has a vast admiration and liking for Ned, and as for Cook's man here and the hotel-proprietor they'd apparently do anything to please him. Cook's man was particularly good, changing money for me after legal hours and writing a letter of introduction to the Hotel Proprietor at Baalbec.

I met Mr. Parfit, who had come to the boat to look up a friend. He's got very thin. Now for the time I'll stop.

By the time this reaches you I expect you'll be about getting back to Oxford. I hope you enjoyed the {Irish} trip, and that all is well. I had a letter from Menon, who will probably meet me. Now with love to you all.

Yours

WILL

GRAND HOTEL VICTORIA
DAMASCUS
11/9/1913

DEAR MOTHER

Here I am all right at Damascus, and immensely charmed. I've just come in from seeing moonlight and afterglow struggling for the city, and it's simply glorious. Minarets and white roofs, rose roofs and dark evergreens, all lying in a great H shaped town among miles of trees, with hills on the one Eastern horizon, hills to the north, and to the South and the West the great desert. All this I saw from an Arab cemetery perched on the hill-side, whence one could see miles and miles of beauty. I left Beirut this morning at 7.0 a.m., so I saw little of the town. The bay is beautiful, and that is about all I can say. But the country at the back which I did see was very grand. The railway winds up the hills but depends most on a cog-chain for getting up. And the fields it winds through are planted with mulberry and olive trees. There are plenty of palms, many pomegranate trees, very pretty these at present with great masses of fruit, all manner of other fruit trees especially lemons, oranges and apples, and on the ground there are dwarf creeping vines. The views from the train as it winds up are very fine. The Lebanons themselves vastly reminded me of the Pyrenees.

There was the same red colour of the hills, the same frequency of pine trees, the same terraces of the lower slopes. And the inhabitants might be Andorrans, to judge by appearances, with the same shaped houses also. I saw what may have been cedars but not the big clump.

Between Lebanon and Anti-Lebanon lay a low plain very well cultivated for the most part—all this country has been—and where it was too arid and rocky pastured over with immense flocks of black goats. I've also seen some flocks of camels, looking rather quaint and far from alive. Lying down, which seems to be their favourite attitude, they looked stuffed beasts, never moving a hair. The snow on Mount Hermon could be seen from this plain. Then the Anti-Lebanons were crossed much more cleverly than the Lebanon. They are just as high, but the railway winds along a river course all the way, a beautiful track with the river always near dressed in poplars and palms and Persian lilacs and orchard trees. All the country I came through to-day has impressed me mainly by its great prosperity. There are winnowing floors all over the place, the vines are loaded with grapes, the olives are ripe, there are heaps of cattle and horses, and thousands upon thousands of great goats, so there is no cause for complaint. All the same there has been trouble recently in the country near Beirut, some Druses having been murdered by Maronites. As to the people, they are much less different from the French than we are, and the really foreign looking people are the frequent negroes. The Hoja was a very good specimen of the average Arab countryman as I've seen him, while Mrs. Bolton would do to represent the women. The houses are just like the South of France, a strange variation between primitive balconied cottage and brick villa. If this is really the East, Provençal speaking France and Spain are altogether Eastern.

12/9/13

After writing so far I had dinner, and then walked out to the hill-side graves again. The most exciting thing was the wild dogs prowling about and fighting, but they proved friendly or indifferent.

Today I have been in the town so far, lunch-time, and have been very interested. It's quite impossible to give you any idea of the place: it stretches for miles and is full of people of all types, Bedouin, Druses, Syrians, Turks, and I think Turkomans to judge by some faces I saw. Their clothes are as varied as their features, but on the whole I think the

Bedawi dressed like and resembling the Hoja is about the most characteristic. The men are many of them quite splendid to look at, particularly the older ones: their features are mostly too rough to look well clean-shaven, though there are brilliant exceptions. The bazaars were crowded with people on foot, or on horse camel or donkey-back, and everyone seemed busy except the shopkeepers themselves who sat cross-legged and smoking. There are a lot of Turkish cavalry in the town, who ride with a loose seat on light little horses with neat heads. Then besides the Bedawi likes to ride his horse or his donkey fully armed, so it's a warlike looking place. However in a few streets there are electric trams—not in the bazaars which have no hint of machinery —and in some cafés there are gramophones.

On the whole the most interesting people I saw were the carpenters, who have a street to themselves and work at very fine mother-of-pearl inlaid work. I wish I could bring you a table. But besides these were coppersmiths hammering away, and carpet weavers and silk merchants, on all sides something of interest. The shop-fronts are woodwork curiously trellised, and one generally has a minaret or two in sight, with perhaps a lad shouting prayers from it. So last night as the sun set and I sat in the cemetery the muezzin-call went to and from men on neighbouring towers in the suburb.

Damascus is set in gardens, and has a great deal of water in it, with fruit-trees innumerable. I went walking along the outside of the wall awhile, and the air simply smelt of peaches. But though there are fruits growing splendidly there is little grass. It is very hot in the sun and very cool in the shade. I've seen curious mix-ups of the old and new manners. So there are black clothed veiled women in the streets going arm in arm with women in French clothes. The Bedawi women seem to dress in bright colours and go unveiled. Every now and then one meets an absolute negro, while there are others who in different clothes would seem English. Altogether this is much the finest place I have ever been in. The Hotel I'm at has some things for sale, carpets, tables, and other oriental wares, and the carpets I'm sure you would love to see. It's very comfortable.

Dr. McKinnon is out of Damascus at present in the hill-country, so I will not be able to see him. If he had been in the town I would have looked him up. He lives in Sir Richard Burton's old house.

Later

I've been up again on the hill-side watching the moon rise over the city. I've seen nothing more beautiful. The general effect of the city is pink, rose roofs and white innumerable minarets mingled together. And it's set among twenty or thirty miles of trees, a forest of fruit. At the back lies the desert like the sea, and with the same power of attraction about it, only flesh-tinted. I'm glad of the name Garden of Allah, but it's not adequate all the same.

The afterglow is a weird thing which comes like a flash awhile after the sunset, glows rosy in the sky for half an hour and then turns lemon-coloured. After a while it seems suddenly to go leaving the shadows of the moon. Every sunset I've seen now has been cloudless, but only at Port Said has there come the caressing evening breeze which struck me then.

I want to leave here tomorrow morning, spend Sunday at Baalbec, and reach Aleppo on the evening of the 15th, as Ned and I first of all arranged. If he meets me then I daresay we will go away at once to Carchemish. Otherwise I will stay at Baron's Hotel till he comes. It will be jolly seeing him in his native haunts, not to mention Dahoum and the Hoja.

I wonder how the Irish trip went off. It seems such an immensity of time since I went away that I can hardly realize how little you will have done in it. If only the weather has been good it will have been splendid for you. This letter may perhaps be too heavy in which case apologies. I'll be more discreet another time. Only this place is so lovely and I've had no one to talk about it with, so I've wanted to write. I wish you could have seen the beautiful things in the bazaars, or the rugs and carpets in this hotel. And the whole world would be the better if it could see the city in the sunset. Mohammed was quite right about it. The Street called Straight has tramlines down it. But otherwise the place is unspoiled. It's queer to think it is the oldest city or so in the world, but its present life is what holds me.

Over the distance my love to you all.

WILL

BAALBEC. 14/9/13

DEAR FATHER

It's Sunday evening, but as I hope to meet Ned to-morrow and so will have little time for writing I'm going to set down a few more first impressions now.

I was quite sorry to leave Damascus. It's the most beautiful town I've ever seen, with its black and white doves for ever fluttering over it and its evergreen trees round it, and the great desert beyond with towers of dust circling about like columns of smoke. And the fruit and the flowers of it. Peaches and nectarines and apples and grapes were the main fruits, with all manner of others I could not name, and sunflowers and roses the flowers. Also coming away a girl in the train gave me a little white flower like a buttonhole rose on a lilac stem, smelling sweeter than any flower I know. Altogether it's a place worth living in, which I would say of few towns. And horses are so common.

Out of it the rail ran through the Anti-Lebanon once more along the Valley of the Barada, a very rich path, into the plain between Lebanon and Anti-Lebanon. At a place called Rayak I had two hours, and after meal spent the rest of the time in the fields. They were parched up, with lizards rushing along them like the shadows of flying bees, but I came to a still stream overhung with willows, edged with willowherb, and with dragonflies just like the English ones, demoiselles and greens and emeralds, flitting over it. I walked up a few yards, and in that short time saw more than a half-dozen tortoises swimming in the water or crawling in the mud. Also the frogs were different from ours, with a brown band down the back. From Rayak the rail ran East of the Lebanons up the plain which was generally about 5 miles across. It is cultivated, but with the black tents of the Bedouins pitched on it, and great herds of camels, small kine and goats grazing on the old stubble. The Bedouin tent is a long low affair divided in two with a curtain, and is picturesque owing to the naked children and the bright-dressed women (a contrast to the grand ladies of the towns all in black and veiled). The train passed quite close to several of these camps, and again and again I saw Bedouin horsemen with guns and lances looking war-like. Horses seem very common among these tribes here, and I've seen few men riding camels. Generally there is a string of grumbling beasts moving along quietly save for grunts, and then men on horses, mules or asses (the last can gallop quite well here).

Baalbec is a market for the Bedouin so I've been seeing a lot of them here. The Hoja does as a type, though I've seen many better specimens. Their women never seem to be veiled, and are quite as good as the men in appearance old or young, though the beard helps the features of even the coarser men types.

For the rest, Baalbec has an immense spring with many streams off it, so there are even more of the poplars and willows of all this country here than elsewhere. The plain is bounded by bare red mountains tipped with snow (the big clump of cedars is a day's ride west). And the town is surrounded as it were by a water-garden of fruit-trees, and melons, and vines and maize divided into allotments and with beautiful walks through them. The ruins naturally dominate the place. For them apply to the books Arnie will be able to find you. I can only say that they are monstrously impressive as a whole, with a wealth of beautiful detail impossible to study. I sat, and watched them all this afternoon, and tried to talk to a Bedouin lad who came to chat with me. These people are very polite, and even if they beg do so jokingly. I know enough Arabic to tell them to 'ask me tomorrow', which always makes them grin and stop. This morning I spent reading in the ruins. It seems an age since I was away, and I cannot realize it is not a fortnight. And tonight being Sunday I can imagine you all at home. Now I'll stop.

Tuesday 16/9/13. 12.0 noon

I'm with Ned now, who's very well, and a great lord in this place. I had a long day's journey in the train through first of all cultivated and well-watered country, a continuation of the Baalbec plain between the hills of the Lebanon. Saw snow but no cedars. A great many Bedouin tents and villages of mud dried in beehive shapes. But after midday there were cultivated fields interspersed with sand some of it real desert. Passed one large lake at Homs several miles long. It was very hot in the train, but cooler in the carriage than facing the wind which blew dust and heat.

Ned and Dahoum met me, and brought me to the hotel. And this morning we have been spending walking about in the bazaars which are certainly far better than those of Damascus, all stone-paved and stone-roofed. Beautiful stuffs of all sorts are for sale, and there's a great variety of types of people. Also we have looked at the outside of the citadel, a wonderful castle. Ned is known by everyone, and their enthusiasm over him is quite amusing. And he is in very good form. On the day after tomorrow I will probably go to Jerablus. Have met Busrawi of the Milli Kurds, here, a marvellously-dressed and dignified person who's invited me to go over to his tribe to see some horse-racing and dancing. Means I'll have to give him a big present, but it will be amusing.

Ned sends love. He won't write just now. The plates and other things were quite right. All for the present. Love to everyone.

WILL

19/9/13

DEAR MOTHER

I've been here at Carchemish for a day and a half now, and as tomorrow will be a busy time I'm going to write now.

Aleppo was chiefly good for its bazaars, full of beautiful silk stuffs and all sorts of things in a huge stone-roofed and paved market. On the roofs are the playing-fields of the town where the goats browse on the grass and occasionally fall down through sky lights. The citadel, which in position is magnificent, up on a hill with a sloping ground front of a great height rising from the moat, has a gate-tower and bridge more picturesque than any castle approach that I've seen. The place is always closed to visitors, but by great good luck some friends of Ned's very rich Armenians of Aleppo, had got an order from the Vali to see over the place and took me with them. So I had a great view from the top.

Ned gave me a particularly interesting time in Aleppo, not only showing me over the bazaars pretty thoroughly, but also paying visits with me to various houses of friends of his, Christian and Moslem, in the town. They are very fine places, with courtyards and fountains, and wonderful lacquer roofs. Also it was jolly seeing how glad everyone was to entertain Ned. Old Busrawi of the Milli Kurds was in Aleppo seeing his son who was at the hospital there, and he has asked me out to his tents next week. We are going for two nights, which will be great fun.

So far Ned has not heard from you since he left home. That means your letter of August 16 has gone astray, and no doubt others, which is usual but very annoying. Ned was very anxious for news when I saw him.

This Carchemish comes as a surprise after the train has run over flat dried up country, very much as though the Cambridge fields were turned into thin plough-land of sand. The station shows no mound in sight and no river. There we were met by swarms of Ned's men, head of them the Hoja. And a walk of 10 minutes or so over rocky slopes brought up without really any climbing into the Kalaat of Jerablus which is thus low on one side. It is a very wide circle full of old stones and trial pits of the digs dotted about it. The house is a long low building as in the photographs. And the best part of the digs lies between the house and the high bank of the river, quite low down. The Mound is thus impressive only from the river bank. Then very much so. The river is at present extraordinarily low, but for all that it is several hundreds of yards across, shallow just now, but running very fast. Swimming against the current in most places is impossible. As to the finds, the thing that most impresses me is the company of the captains. But I will talk about them another time. Just at this moment I am being devoured by sand-flies, little white beasts, sitting alone in the big room. Ned is on the roof in bed, whither he went about 8.30 p.m. to try and sleep off a touch of fever. He's been as usual all day, but it makes him feel low. And tomorrow the Armenians who took me over the citadel are coming out to sleep one night here. They are Ernest Altounyan, Rugby and Cambridge, now at the Middlesex Hospital, Norah, very English (their mother was so) and perhaps the father, Dr. Altounyan, who maintains an infirmary at Aleppo, with a complete staff of English nurses, out of his own pocket, and is a great art connoisseur, particularly in carpets. Interesting people. Now I'm off to bed.

Saturday, 20th

Now this is in a hurry. Ned is better, but is going to take it easy. An old Kurdish gentleman has just sent him a magnificent carpet as a present, which has elated him. The weather here is perfectly fine, but not too hot. I've seen no rain since I left Oxford. The pens for Ned were all right. Also the musical box appealed to the Hoja. I wish we could hear from you. Ned is grumbling continually at the post. You have no idea how hard it is to write here, we go to bed about 8.30, and in the day-time there are too many flies for any sitting-down.

I'll write again next week after staying with Busrawi. Meanwhile love to you all. Here are a few petals of a pomegranate flower for Arnie. Salaams from Ned.

Love. WILL

27/9/13

Dear Mother

I'm on the Sea of Galilee now, at Tiberias. The time with Ned
was very good. You can get a very fair idea of the appearance of the
Kalaat from his photographs, but of course since they were not digging,
its quiet which struck me is usually absent. It is just a huge circle of
hilly land covered with stones, natural and hewn. The digs shew all
over it in trial pits, but the chief stones are all together in one corner,
and set up in a fair order. One can get an idea of the place as it was
when Nebuchadnezzar left it all smashed up. Some of the carvings are
better in stone than in photos, but generally the pictures give one a
right impression.

There are always two men on duty as site-guards to prevent visitors
taking photographs or damaging the stones. People seem to be frequently about, mostly being Germans who are very much in evidence
at Aleppo. And down on the right less than a quarter of a mile from
the main digs is the railway bridge, with swarms of workmen carrying
stones for the building material of the permanent bridge just above the
temporary one. One can walk across by the latter, more than 1,000
yards of woodwork laid down fairly loosely between the rails, with
occasional side-balconies to let one get out of the way of trolleys. They
have about a kilometre of line laid on the other side.

I didn't have much time alone with Ned. The day I wrote to you we
had quite a lot of guests, a Lieutenant Young, making his way out to
India via Baghdad, an American missionary Dr. Usher, going back to
Lake Van, and the people from Aleppo the Altounyans. These people
all stopped two days, 1 night, which were spent examining the digs and
bathing. Then they went away, all except Lieut. Young, who is still at
Jerablus. He is an interesting fellow, speaking Arabic and Persian very
well, and he went with me in Ned's place to visit Busrawi Agha, in
answer to the old Kurd's invitation. Ned had fever rather, and was glad
to escape the ride and yet leave me in the hands of someone with the
gift of tongues. We had great fun with Busrawi. He sent his son and
some retainers for us, with horses, which we got after walking across
the bridge. Then we had a ride of about 6 hours through steppes,
perfectly barren stony country rolling up and down with only a very
occasional well surrounded always by great herds of large black goats
in charge of boys with guns. Our horses were good and our escort very

wild, riding singing and shouting most of the time and continually
challenging each other to gallop. The result was the horses were dead-
beat and it was dark before we got in to the tents. On the way we
passed several camps of Kurds, guarded by large hounds (at Busrawi's
a man followed us always to keep us safe from them). On arrival
Busrawi came to greet us, ceremonially, and we were conducted to
his tent, a great open-sided sort of marquee of forty poles. He was very
proud of its size. We took off our boots, and sat down on a thick soft

mat arranged in this shape ⊔, with our places where the two

marks are. I sat on the right and Young on the left, and they served
dinner immediately. Behind us was a thick curtain right across the
middle of the tent, which shut off the private apartments, but in the
tent round us there were I suppose more than 100 men. They laid down
a long mat thirty feet or so upon the carpets in front of our mat, placed
bread all along the edges of it, and then more than 40 dishes. The old
Agha sat between us and gave the signal to start by taking a piece of
meat in his hand and putting it in my spoon. Then everyone fell to with
eagerness, saying nothing but eating at a great pace simply shovelling
the stuff into their mouths. Servants moved behind with mugs of water.
The food was very good, mostly highly seasoned hashes, some things
like mince-pies, boiled wheat, leben, tomatoes, and for fruit melons.
After we had eaten we washed our hands where we sat, in a basin like
that in Ned's house, and drank coffee. All the while we had been eating
a man had been beating a drum, and another blowing on a pipe, which
sounded at times like the real pipes, but had no bag. After dinner there
was a lot of this music, and some dancing, just of men, who capered
about waving handkerchiefs and singing, not very exciting. We slept
close to where we had eaten, touching the harem curtain, which was an
honour, and with all the rest of the men in front of us. Next day we
did very little but watch more dancing, and the playing of the 'jerred'.
This was a horse-racing game, in which men hunt each other and try
to hit with sticks. The general effect is rather like polo, and there are
all sorts of rules which we didn't understand. It was very picturesque
seeing men in dazzling robes galloping splendid horses through clouds
of sand. There was lots more feasting, and Khaleel, the successor of
Ibrahim Pasha who was dramatically murdered by the Young Turks,

came to see us. He's the greatest of all the Kurds, but very young, and rather under Busrawi's thumb.

It was very interesting listening to Busrawi's chat with Young. He's an old man, very dignified yet kindly-looking, giving the effect rather of Dr. Warren. He insisted on feeding us with his own hands, while one of his sons took off our boots. Yet this is a man responsible for some of the biggest massacres of modern times. I was very glad to have this experience.

We left Busrawi's tents in his company and with twelve horsemen next morning while it was still moonlight, and had a great ride in the half-dark getting into Ned's in time for the chief and me to catch the train to Aleppo. The galloping was grand, and we acquitted ourselves fairly well, though we had no bridles, only ropes, saddles which had to be kept on by careful balancing, and stirrups which came off if one pressed on them. Its queer that people with such good horses should have such bad gear.

Ned was quite right again when I got back. His fever was bad for two days, yet not enough to make it be obvious. I wouldn't have known anything was wrong from the sight of him. And he has Young with him still, who is going to meet Dr. Usher on Monday at Biredjik and ride with him to Van. Young struck me as a very good fellow. I left Ned very fit, Gregori had turned up, and Woolley is expected on the 31st. His house is being enlarged. It is a very comfortable place, with the mosaic floor making it cooler always than outside. And feeding arrangements are good. We always got dinner and lunches of several courses, and omelettes for breakfast. Haj Wahid is quite a character, famous throughout Aleppo for his old prowess as a fighting-man, but now quiet. Imagine a more dignified Bolton. His wife and children live in a house about 50 yards back. The house is long and flat as in the photos, with a bath-room and three good bedrooms, with English beds, wash-stands and furniture. You must not think of Ned as leading an un-civilized existence. When I saw him last as the train left the station he was wearing white flannels, socks and red slippers, with a white Magdalen blazer, and was talking to the governor of Biredjik in lordly fashion.

Altogether Jerablus is a very fine place. I got into Aleppo in the evening, and spent the evening with the Altounyans, who are the great people of the town. Dr. Altounyan is a collector of carpets and his son and daughter were both at Cambridge, Emmanuel and Girton.

Then I left Aleppo at dawn, and got to Damascus at nearly midnight, slept a few hours and caught a train at 6.30 a.m. on the Hedjaz railway.

28/9/13

The rail ran from Damascus through the old Trachonitis, Bashan and Edom, and then through the Hauran. At first the country was undulating and desert, with a surface of broken wave-like lava, perfectly horrible. The Druses call it the Fortress of God. At a place called Derat, where there is a large settlement of Tookoories, negroes from near Abyssinia, I branched off the Medina line, and thence the country was rich and cultivated, quite flat. After a good while it climbed down the Yarmuk valley through a series of gorges, very picturesque from the Hauran plateau to the Jordan valley. Suddenly we ran into a place called El-Hammi, with a jungle of palm-trees set about hot-springs and with oleanders all in flower. After that we soon got to Samach on the Sea of Galilee. On the way I saw a herd of 7 gazelles. Galilee is intensely blue, edged with white gravel and large whitish rocks, fringed with oleanders and tamarisks, and surrounded by cliffs aslope and running back into mountains of almost a flesh tint. Mt. Hermon at the north end dominates it. It is about 6 miles across, 12 long, and very deep. There are very few boats on it. I came here, to Tiberias, from Samach in a launch; its about 4 miles up the coast. Tiberias has a castle, Arab work, not very old, a large hospital run by Scotch Presbyterian Missionaries, and houses to contain a population of about 8,000, the vast majority, 7,000 or so, being Jews. They are still dependent in a measure on charity (maintained by Rothschild in the first instance) and are Polish and Spanish. But they are getting more energetic. At first they paid Arabs to do everything for them.

I put up the first night, of the 20th, at the Hotel, but am writing now from Dr. Torrance's house at the Hospital. Slept last night on his roof, and dined with another Doctor Mr. Semple, who worked once at Lahore with Mr. H. G. Grey. So Dr. Torrance, who has been here a score of years, has been telling me all about the town, which is one of the four holy cities of the Jews in Palestine. I think I told you about the Doctor, and how I met him going to Beyrout. He is very nice.

The Jews here are not quite out of their old Polish habits. On the Sabbath, yesterday, the men mostly wore fur hats and coats. They are mostly a handsome race, fair many of them. The women are even simpler clothed than the Bedouins, bare arms and legs and heads. All the inhabitants swim in the lake twice a day throughout the year, and their younger people are fine. I've seen many very good specimens. I tried yesterday to drive with Dr. Torrance to Nazareth and thence to Haifa, but failed to get a carriage. It has been better here, by the Lake. The Plain of Gennesareth, with Magdala at its mouth, has been as far north on the shore as I could get. Here is an Oleander petal for you. I have shells too, a few, but won't send them now.

I wish you could be here, to bathe and run with me, and look at the blue water in its pink lids. It's very hot, and 600 feet or so below sea level.

Love to everyone.

WILL

30 September 1913

DEAR MOTHER

Just a scrawl of a letter in the train just a minute out of Jerusalem. I sent some postcards yesterday but they may have been lost, and I think you would like to hear from the City, though this will be posted at Jaffa. I saw Jerusalem under curious conditions. I had chatted to a rich and very nice German, born and living at Bethlehem, on the steamer from Haifa to Jaffa. And his father runs an hotel here. So I went there, and found he had wired from Jaffa about my coming to make all arrangements so that I might see as much as possible in my few hours. So there was a dragoman waiting for me, and a carriage, and rather than hurt his feelings I had to see the place as though I was an American millionaire. It hurt mine, but couldn't be helped.

As a result I gained in one way, by having a drive to Bethlehem, and by seeing the usual pilgrimage sites. And after 5 hours with the drago-man I went off by myself to the Mount of Olives, which is not much spoilt, and from which Jerusalem looks beautiful. I've seen the City from there in the sunset and in the sunrise. It's very warlike looking, in no way resembling the Garden of Damascus. The Jews here, the bulk of the population, are a more mixed lot than those of Tiberias. One sees all types. As to the Christians, they each have separate chapels and monasteries at each holy site, and yell for baksheesh. My dragoman was a Protestant from beyond Jordan, an Arab.

I haven't been alone much recently. Dr. Torrance went to Haifa with

me and shewed me all the sites of the plain of Esdraelon. He's a Scotch
Presbyterian and has been about 30 years at Tiberias. And just now my
German friend came down to the station to see me off. The station is
about 20 minutes drive from the town. Also at Jerusalem I met a man
and lady I knew, the Stewart Donnithornes. At Jaffa I will lunch today
with another German. The German Colonies of Palestine breed pleasant people. It's been good to have seen Jerusalem, even in such a flying
visit (cost a good deal). But just at present I haven't yet got over the
effects of the Tiberias water. I noticed a curious taste but was assured
it was good to drink, and so it was no doubt, but a strong natural
aperient. I drank vast quantities and suffer for it.

I wanted to get you a plant of some sort from the City but couldn't.
Here's an ordinary little fern. Today I hope to get a boat in the evening
to Port Said.

With love to you all.

WILL

PORT SAID. 2/10/13

DEAR MOTHER

Such a joy it was getting your letters, everyone of them, including
the last short note. And what a good time you seem to have had in
Ireland. I'm so glad you and Bob enjoyed yourselves, and hope you feel
altogether set up in consequence. It must have been fun for you to ride
a pony over the hills. And you were lucky to get a fine crossing.
Altogether that trip seems to have been a really good success. Splendid.

I got here late last night from Jaffa. My boat, a Messagerie Maritime,
was a day late, but it did not matter, for the *Sunda* is only arriving
today. I'll get on board of her at once when she comes. This town is
full of touts, but in its sea-front is pretty in a kind of way, and at
evenings very cool. I'm stopping at the Hotel Ned recommended,
where I left my spare baggage and the sun-helmet Captain Ivens
bought me. That last has disappeared, stolen. The Hotel people will
pay for a new one. I'm not sorry that I have no time to wait. Cairo
would be interesting no doubt, but I'm a bit tired, and still bothered by
that Tiberias water I told you about in my letter from Tiberias. That
also is the cause why I'm not inclined to write at length.

I'm glad you've been hearing from Ned, and hope that by this time
he has heard from you. The post is frightful, and he was quite anxious

when I reached him. Did I tell you he approved of the pens? By now Woolley will have come—he was expected on the 31st, and the digging will be starting. His is certainly a very jolly position, and a responsible one. Although there was no work doing when I was there, I only saw him read at meal-times: all other times he was either having to arrange village land-quarrels, or discuss the question of desertion from the army, or entertain the native visitors who kept dropping in for advice or out of courtesy.

I had a long letter from Menon telling me how to get to him in case he can't meet me which is possible.

Frank will have started at College before I will be able to write again. Best luck to him. I hope Father is well and all the others.

My love to you all.

WILL

P. & O. S.S. *Sunda.* 10/10/13

DEAR MOTHER

We are now just getting out of the Gulf of Aden into the Indian Ocean. On the horizon to the south there are mountains showing up rather jagged, of the African Coast by Cape Gardafui. Nothing else is in sight, and we will only pass one more island, Socotra, between here and Colombo, I believe. My boat was some hours late at Port Said, but she didn't give me time to go inland to Cairo. A very small boat compared with the *Egypt*, and old, but quite comfortable. She is full up, but at the same time it's not a large company that she takes. And the people on board are of a very much rougher type than were on the mail-boat, jail-warders, clerks and planters for the Straits Settlements, and business men for China. But there is a large party of C.I.M. people going out, 14 ladies and a man, and two other missionaries. I've become of their party as it were, so am quite at home. Most of them are going for the first time and are young, so are less interesting than the few old ones. The leader of these is a sort of missionary,

{21 words omitted}

Altogether rather of the style of Miss Holmes. A perfectly charming lady, quite of another type, is Mrs. Hoste, grey haired and very handsome and gentle to look at, and just like her looks. It's a pity she is not in control. Bob will be very happy having her to control him at first.

Then there is another oldish lady, Miss Gregg, who came through a big experience in the Boxer trouble. I remembered the story but not the name. You will know though I expect; she was with a Mr. and Mrs. Green and two children, cut off for four months. There is another here too, Mrs. Griffith, who went through a lot at the same time, which seems to have left its mark on her face, very crooked. She is extremely nice. These are the veteran missionaries and except for Miss —— I'm all for them.   {12 words omitted}   It's very nice for me being able to be amongst them, and I'm not a little pleased to have met Mrs. Hoste.

When I came on board at Port Said I consulted the ship's Doctor, who said it was not water or a chill which had upset me, but too highly seasoned food. Busrawi's forty dishes had poisoned my inside accustomed to plainer fare. I'm quite fit now in every way except this, that the after effects are going to last awhile. I can eat everything that has no pepper or curry in it, and digest it properly, but I have to take a medicine. Nevertheless my strength is absolutely all right, and I'm not to take any precautions at all except avoiding things highly seasoned. So that's all right.

The Suez Canal is not an interesting channel, it just goes on very narrow between a desert country to the north and almost the same to the south. The only part of it with any beauty is the bitter lake, and that only gives the impression of a river estuary, with posts marking the channel. Suez is a small place and flat. And beyond that the Red Sea has only struck me by its numerous islands. One day was hot, not enough though to make me sleep on deck, and it was never so hot as the *Egypt* was just before coming to Port Said. Now for the moment I stop.

13/10/13

The biggest group of islands we passed were twelve long rocks called the Apostles, but all through the Red Sea there were islands of volcanic appearance in the distance. One or two we passed close to: bare and desert-looking with white beaches at the foot of red rocks. One had some beautiful green on it though. And stray birds kept alighting on the ship: tired swallows that died of exhaustion, and one large hawk, and a brilliant coloured woodpecker. Then after I had written the first part of this letter we came very close, within about $\frac{1}{2}$ a mile I should think, of the African mainland, of high white limestone cliffs looking quite inaccessible. It has the reputation of being the wildest coast in the world, full of perfect savages. You can't imagine how one longed to swim off and see what was beyond the cliffs. Since then there has been change only in seeing the fish of the sea. Close to the ship one day spouted and rolled a thresher whale 50 feet long, very impressive. It looked best as it went down for the last time, a long grey shining back like a sub-marine taking the water and then a last flick of an immense tail. Then we've seen flying-fish innumerable recently. They are much smaller than I expected, and look like flights of 30 or 40 little white finches. Their white colour glistens, and they go a few yards very swiftly, and disappear before one can see them go. I've seen them about 40 yards off, and I shouldn't think their whole length is more than six inches. They go so fast one sees only their colour, their fins one doesn't see. The water throughout has been ridiculously smooth though just now there is a slight ground swell. And it has never been oppressively hot, though I believe it was quite a hot passage of the Red Sea. One day only struck me as going pretty strong. I'll go on with this later.

14/10/13

We're expected at Colombo early in the morning of the day after to-morrow. That means we'll be a day late. And just now we have passed our first piece of land for days, a coral island. It is still in sight now, in the back of the sea, just a perfectly flat stretch of some miles of land, with a broad white beach, and everything behind it a mass of greenery. Some dark green bushes grow low down, and above every-thing is coconut palms; we passed close enough to distinguish the separate boughs of the trees. This is one of the Maldive Islands, apply to Arnie, is inhabited by semi-Arab and Malabar coast people, a mixed Moslem race. And they pay a tax in copra, palm produce, to the Indian Government, for which a collector goes from Mangalore to gather in every year. The island as we passed it certainly had an attraction about it.

Life on board has been very quiet and pleasant. I've spent my time almost entirely with the C.I.M. people; all of them very good and except Miss —— just as it seems to me missionaries should be. A slight groundswell we've had the last three days, never enough to move the crockery on the table, has rather upset Mrs. Hoste so I've seen less of her, and most of Miss —— and Mrs. Griffith. The latter was alone in

the Boxer trouble with a baby 8 months old, and has never I should
judge got over the experience. You can see it in her face. She has two
children on board of 8 and 6 I should guess, a boy and a girl who are
quite jolly little things. There are lots more children who are crying all
day, one or other of them, no doubt tired of the ship-life and upset by
the heat. As to that it is nothing; on deck less hot than it often is in
England, but much worse below. Still not enough to make bed-things
unnecessary.

Did I tell you I had a long letter from Menon at Port Said, and that
probably he will not be able to meet me at Colombo? His Rajah will be
tiger-shooting about this time. He gave me very full instructions as to
getting to him, and is writing again to Colombo. It's possible I will
spend two days in Ceylon. A very pleasant man, a planter from north
Travancore, is aboard, going my way as soon as the boat gets into port,
by the boat for Tuticorin (apply to Arnie) which leaves Colombo every
evening. I don't know yet what I will do, and won't make up my mind
till I've had Menon's second letter.

We still see flying-fish very commonly, but nothing else has struck
me. There are good windy sunsets, but the sea is really very calm. One
could paddle a canoe across it. I'm very comfortable and well, the
feeding is excellent, and the company so far as I'm concerned very
congenial. The Mission party is very apart from the rest of the passengers, quite as though they were officers.

16th

Tomorrow very early in the morning we get into Colombo. Then
I will post this, and also I expect will send you a wire. Nothing new has
happened to talk about, except that there were two heavy showers of
rain last night, and that this morning there was some practice in life-
saving, very badly done. They took about a quarter of an hour to lower
a boat, to pick up a dummy and a lifebelt that had been thrown over.

Once again, I will be sorry in a way to leave the ship. It is tantalizing
to make friends and lose them so quickly, and these missionaries have
treated me entirely as one of their party. But at the same time, I'm
beginning to feel a wish to do something strenuous.

The ship is going to be all day at Colombo. I don't know at all what
I will do, then, beyond getting letters from you and Menon. I'm going
to be led simply by what he says. The journey to Kandy is very beauti-

ful I believe, and of course Frazer's college is there, where Claud
Houlder is, the old O.I.C.C.U. secretary. It's possible I will go and
look him up. Howsoever, I make no definite plans.

G.O.H. HOTEL. 17/10/13

Now I'm at Colombo, which I'll leave tonight, and not go up to
Kandy. It's very hot in a moist pleasant sort of way.

I've found your letters, which have given me great pleasure. They've
all got here, including Hughes' one, and the one you feared might not,
owing to not being addressed via Brindisi. Please thank Father and Bob
very much for theirs. I'm very sorry about Mrs. McNeile, who's a fine
lady. I'm with a planter going over by the same boat, so can't write
much. This is from an hotel. I've just sent you a cable; one word only
but it will probably please you.

I'm very fit indeed.

with best love to all,

WILL

S.S. *Sunda.* 15/10/13

DEAR BOB

Just a short line to you. I guess you're in London, feeling a grain
on the sea-shore. A beastly place, and yours the most distressing view
of it. Cheer-oh though, what you can you do, and for the rest you're
not responsible. Like Joab's remark in 1 Chronicles 19/13 that Mr.
Barker copied out for me.

The ship has just passed a coral island covered with Coco-palms, a
wonderful green gem in the sea as flat as the water, with one tall white
light-house and no other sign of life. I wish you could have seen the
things I've seen, and met some of the people, C.I.M. missionaries on
board. There's a Mr. Corol who'd appeal to you greatly, and then there
is Mrs. Hoste, as good a type as I can imagine existing. I don't feel
inclined to enter into a description—I've already said something to
Mother about them and must refer you to that. Then I've seen a really
large whale, 50 feet long and heaps of flying-fish which are much tinier
than I'd expected.

I was very glad of my two days at Tiberias. No water I've ever seen
is so lovely as Galilee, even apart from its associations. And the oleanders which grow along the shore are so good to look at. There are

king-fishers and all sorts of fish, and delicate little shells of which I'll send specimens home from Delhi. Jerusalem from the Mount of Olives, as I saw it in the sunset and the sunrise, was beyond anything I'd ever dreamt of for beauty. A great pink fortress of a city set upon a hill, with walls complete about, and within close on the Olivet side a vast gilded dome. I loved the view, and the Mount of Olives is still as one can imagine it was. But inside the city I found the interest all modern. It was impossible to feel anything of the ancient spirit of the city where there were convents and monasteries everywhere. And in the Church of the Holy Sepulchre there were the murderous priests of all the different sects expecting baksheesh, and the Turkish soldiers to prevent rioting and the stink of old incense everywhere. All I wish to keep in my mind of Jerusalem is the city as one sees it from the Mount of Olives.

My stay with Busrawi made me ill, though the trouble didn't come on till I was at Jerusalem. The thing is that the highly seasoned foods set up a diseased condition of the mucous of the bowels; I can explain to you just in case Mother is worried. The result of this was diarrhœa. This has stopped: I can eat and digest everything and am quite well as far as I can feel. At the same time it's a thing which needs more than ten days in which to be removed, so I still take a medicine. The ship's doctor, who is a surgeon taking a voyage as a holiday, strikes me as knowing his business very well. So that is all right. All it means is that I must avoid curries of the stronger sort, which in any case I would do probably. With Busrawi it was different: Young and I had to eat more than we wanted to show our appreciation of what were certainly very tasty dishes.

I'll take it easy now at Menon's and go to Delhi without wasting any time or energy. Very probably I will accept a man's invitation to stop with him at Agra just before getting to Delhi. So I can see the Mission there, and at the same time rest if I am tired after the railway journey. The man I spoke of is an accountant whom I saw a lot of on board the *Egypt*, a very earnest man of about 35.

The C.I.M. clearly deals in the right sort of material, judging by this party. They are all ladies except Mr. Corol, whose wife is with him. The veterans are 5 in number: the leader to me the least attractive. The new people have no nonsense about their ideas. It's interesting to compare them with another missionary, a young man going out for the Friends Educational Mission, whose religion and his science are so far as I can see inextricably mixed up. He preached one Sunday evening on the Crucifixion and never mentioned Atonement. Modernism is thoroughly annoying at home, but out here it is appalling. This young chap suffers from conceit though: he is very clever and cares for nobody's opinion seemingly but his own. The C.I.M. people rejoiced because I made him look a fool in an argument, but that's no use.

Now cheer-oh and farewell.

WILL

Thanks hugely for your letter just received at Colombo.

WITH MENON. TRICHUR
COCHIN STATE
October 21, 1913

DEAR FATHER

The very day I got here a letter from you and Mother arrived, which was very jolly. Thank you very much for it, and also for the letter I got from you at Colombo. Though I write mostly to Mother, you know my letters are for you all.

You must have been pleased with winning the golf medal and tea-spoon. Though 4 strokes taken off will make it harder for you to do it again, still the lower your handicap the greater honour. Then too aeroplanes in such numbers and the airship were amusing no doubt. For myself mere looking at them has ceased to have much charm. It would be different to have a ride.

Then for Mother's news, it was hard lines on Jenkin. The sea-trip will put him right though: a good way of resting. And I'm glad Mrs. Monk likes the new house. My oil-skin is all right I think, but I've had no occasion to use a coat since I left England. As to Richards, Ned is writing to him. I'm sorry about Mrs. Lawrie and Mrs. McNeile.

I left Colombo the same day on which I got there, and took a boat to Tuticorin on the East Coast of South India. Tuticorin is flat and white with palm-trees on a shallow beach: very hot and moist. The sun simply shot down at one. From there I went by train to Trichinopoly: first of all through a flat country with palms and cacti, well cultivated but without water. The prevailing tint was yellow: yellow soil, yellow flowers of the cacti just like those of Palestine, where I expect I told you they form all the hedges from Jaffa inland. A more appallingly hot looking country I've seldom seen: only the desert south

of Aleppo to compare to it. Lank smooth-haired goats, bullocks
ploughing were the only animals. The people lived in straw hats, and
wore loin-cloths: a fine bronze colour theirs. The country remained
the same, with mountains on the north-west just in sight, and an
occasional high rock in the plain: like Mont St. Michel with temples
on it, till we came to Madura (see the Wonders of the World). Road-
side temples were fairly rare, and when I saw them they had carved
horses only in front of them: very few things one could call idols. At
Madura, a city of palm-trees and very pretty from the train, I saw some
way off three most glorious temples, of brown carved stone most
intricately worked. From there to Trichinopoly the country changed:
green like an English park, with trees and no palms, great sheets of
water, rocky hills near at hand and forest slopes far away. The train ran
into Trichinopoly in the dark, where I had three hours to wait. In the
Refreshment room there was a mongoose, grey and more like a squirrel than a ferret. In the grey dawn I changed again at Erode and ran
through the Palghat Gap, with mountains close in to the line and the
same green country to Shoranur, a junction where Menon met me. He
is very well: couldn't meet me in Colombo owing to a shooting-party
of his Rajah's just over, and a failure owing to heavy rain. From Shoranur the line was the Cochin State Railway. And the country was the
best I've seen yet in India. It is greener than anything we have in
England, owing to the Paddy fields (rice), it has palms where there is
water, which there is all over the low-country in lakes, it is otherwise
very heavily timbered, everywhere flowers, chiefly red, the soil is also
very red, houses pretty, thatched, like river bungalows, altogether
lovely.

I'm stopping in his house. His wife and children are very nice: the
young Menon is here too as a guest. Yesterday I went up into the
Forest on a wonderful timber tram-way several thousands of feet. I'll
talk about that another time. All this country is like a book in a foreign
tongue to me, and I find it hard to translate to you. Gradually I'll pick
it up. It is not too hot at all, and I'm very well, though with some
weight to make up. From here to Delhi is four days' journey, and I'm
going I hope via Mysore. So glad Bob had a good start. Now love to
you all and thanks for all your letters. Menon sends his kindest regards.

Your loving WILL

HOTEL METROPOLE
AGRA

DEAR MOTHER   *October 30, 1913, 7.0 p.m.*

Here I am now, within three hour's train journey of Delhi. I'm going to sleep one night here, and go on tomorrow evening, when Mr. Rudra will be expecting me owing to a wire I've sent. The train journey has been very interesting, and not at all tiring really. One or two really remarkable things happened. Of those more later.

First of all, I got your postcard just before I left Menon's. I'm glad Frank liked the look of his friend: the Prime Minister of Cochin had told me that he could not get into St. John's. It's very absurd of the President, who runs counter in this to Mr. Ball. I'll tell you about my first-rate time with Menon when I write more at leisure I hope from Delhi, so now for the train journey.

I left Trichur on Monday morning, and changed from the Cochin State Railway to the South Indian Railway at Shoranur. Then I changed again at a place called Jalarpet on to the Mysore and Southern Mahratta Railway, which ran along the edge of the Nilgherries, fine wooded hills, into the dark. The next morning I got into Bangalore, second city of Mysore, at 6.0 a.m. There was a train going to my next place of change in an hour, but I decided to wait till 11.30, and walked up a hill to look over Bangalore, a great straggling red-roofed city of many parks. I spent an hour so walking about, and then went to find a bank where I could change a £5 note. As it happened it was a public feast-day, and everything was shut but before I discovered this, in turning round a corner of a narrow lane I met Naryana! I thought he was in Germany, he thought I was in England, and in any case I never associated him with Bangalore, where however at the moment he is living. He gave me a royal time for my remaining three hours driving me about the Parks in state, and amongst other things changing my note. Also he invited me down there again for tiger-shooting next autumn. The city is very fine. Its Parks are green as can be (it stands high and has water), with great trees of which the most glorious was new to me, a South African tree, the Pathorsoria Campanulata, which is like a red-flowering azalea the size and shape of an oak-tree. Also the Bougain-vilia was flowering everywhere, a perfect purple shrub, and there were Indian deer loose in the paddocks. Immense boys' and girls' schools were the chief other feature, and an Indian-managed Eye

Hospital. I saw the ruins of the fort of Tippoo Sahib. From Bangalore
I crossed the Mahratta country to Guntakal in the Madras Presidency.
The line ran through wild grass country with bare crags of fantastic
shapes in lines as though halted on the march on either side of the line.
Lieut. Young, my companion at Busrawi's (I hope you've got my letter
from Tiberias describing that and the Sea of Galilee. Your postcard
makes me fear not, and it's my greatest impression so far), in a Marathi
poem of his which he wrote for his regiment describes the country as
"the fastnesses of the eagles", and that's exactly it. All the time we
passed through there were great eagles flapping alongside or towering
over the crags. The other wild things were very occasional deer of the
antelope sort. The grass was full of shrubs like greenhouse genistas, and
with yellow flowers. I got to Guntakal at night, and picked up the
Madras–Manmad express. Manmad is inland near Bombay. That ran
next morning through Hyderabad, the Nizam's country. We crossed
two great rivers: otherwise all the country is a flat dry cultivated plain,
with rocks rising out of it as Mont St. Michel and Tombelaine rise out
of the sea. These crags, hundreds of feet high, are often fortified. The
best I saw was one called Yalgiri, most impressive.

On the train I met a corporal of the Oxfords, who was born at
Yarnton and whose parents live in the little house on the bridge at
Wallingford. You'll remember. He had one more year to do before
leaving the service. Ran away from home, but a steady fellow, tee-
total. As he's besought me to write to him at whiles, I suppose I must.

At Manmad we caught the Punjaub mail which runs through jungle
country crossing the Narbada, and after that over dried up waterless
dust plains. There's been a failure of rain and famine is feared for next
year. At Jhansi, where Young's regiment is, I was stretching my legs
on the platform when I was hailed by one of our famous table on the
Egypt, a man I hadn't talked to much. After Jhansi the country was
desperately flat and dry. Saw wolves and many wild deer along the
line. The best place passed on all the journey was Gwalior, a town on the
top of a great flat hill, ringed round with battlements and looking
fairly impregnable. That's quite close to Agra, and here I am now in an
Hotel. Tomorrow I'll go to Delhi in the evening. I'm very fit, and the
weather is comfortable. I'll write from Delhi answering your letters, and
not as in these notes giving a diary of my doings. By the bye, if you get
my letter about Busrawi, preserve it please, so that I can refer to it later.

I'll look up a man I know here tomorrow. Meanwhile goodbye. I hope to have a letter from you waiting for me at the College. Love to all. WILL

ST. STEPHEN'S COLLEGE
DELHI
November 5, 1913

DEAR MOTHER

Here I am at my work now, and it's since Friday that I've been here. S. is all right, and all the others except M. who's run down a bit through overwork. Jenkin came last night, with Young, so I beat them by a few days.

I want now to answer a few of your letters, and not give an account of my doings. First, I'm so sorry you've been ill again. I hoped you'd got over it completely. However though I can't help you at home, at least you'll be able to rest now, with less work to do, so that will be all right. You tell me not to overwork, and I can retort similarly. Do rest more. And then from what Father said it's clear that he's all right if he can win Golf medals; so if only you go easy I'll be happy. Your letter— enclosing the flower of the choisya—came last mail: the day after I arrived. I sent a note from Agra in order to get the outgoing post. I'm sorry the Postmaster has left: they seemed nice people.

My bicycle as you say was no use in the house, neither was my gown so I'm glad they've found owners. On Saturday letters arrive. But on this Friday I'm going away with A. and Mr. Ramsay MacDonald the Labour Leader (very Scotch and very much of a gentleman whatever his opinions which I believe are fairly moderate) to the Gurukul, a school belonging to the Arya Samaj and up in the Himalayas. In this I'm amazingly fortunate, the only man from the College to have ever been there, and it's a wonderful place, a kind of monastery among the hills on the headwaters of the Ganges. We'll wear Indian dress there and live in the country way. I'll take no risks about food so don't be afraid. Besides, now I'm perfectly fit so far as I can feel, bubbling with health.

A —— was away when I arrived, and my first duty was to meet the Royal Commission on the Public Services as it steamed into the station and entertain Mr. MacDonald. Mr. H. A. L. Fisher, my Don, belongs to this and will come in a week's time, late. Everyone else has arrived.

You ask about my oilskin. It was rolled up at times in the course of my journeys, and stuck. The colour has in some parts run just a little.

But it's quite all right really, and will be very useful to me. It's hanging up now in perfect order. My racket got through all right. As to the rest I haven't unpacked everything, because I have no wardrobe or chest-of-drawers to put my things into. I've bought one which will come tomorrow or the next day. I've got two fine big rooms and a bath-room, but have to get some more chairs and things. For money, I pay 60 rupees (15 rupees to the pound) a month for feeding and household expenses. I get my salary at the end of each month. And I have money in hand at present, so that is all right. My travels cost me £41 which included some things I hadn't expected such as Doctor's Bill £1, and excess luggage. The P. and O. charged 12/- for this and the railway about £2. If ever I want money sent out, as for travelling in the summer or something of that sort, the best way will be by remittance through Cook's, which is next door to me here.

I won't give any impressions of Delhi or of the College, at present. Only you must imagine me very well and comfortable. W. W. Pearson is here. It's good to have such news of Bob. As to Arnie he's never likely to find literary work coming hard to him. Get him to look up Hardwar near Dehra Dun on the map, for that is where the Gurukul is. You mustn't worry about my getting overworked. I'm going to be as careful as I can, and if after that I get ill why it must only be accepted. Delhi is being made healthier day by day and in any case is not a bad place. And for my overdoing it, I think, there's a good saying of Isaiah that 'he that believeth shall not make haste'. I'm very lucky to be taken thus under the wing of A. : the others are quite jealous.

Getting to work means a certain disinclination to write at length. So perhaps I won't write about my southern visit tomorrow. I'll see. Meanwhile now I've just got five minutes before some men come to see me, so I'll switch off. I've got a picture of Jerusalem for you, a miserable bad print, and a photo-frame from Bethlehem, I'll send you sometime, and some shells. My visit was so short I could get you nothing beautiful. And I didn't feel well enough to spend the night on the Mt. of Olives, though I would have liked to.

Now goodbye till next week.

love WILL

Ned's carpet was a beauty. He did not say anything about when he would go home. Sorry not to write better. Not much time.

St. Stephen's College
Delhi
6/11/13

Dear Father

It's your birthday I think, or if not tomorrow is when this letter will go: many happy returns of the day. I want this to be an account of my stay with Menon, but many things will probably be forgotten and left out, since I'm writing after a lapse of days.

A great river whose name I forget separates the hills of Cochin State from the Nilgherry Mountains. When I met Menon, who was waiting for me at Shoranur Junction on the way from Madras to Mangalore, we got on to a narrow gauge State railway which took us through a country like Derbyshire, great wooded hills with steep sides, much water, and houses nestling amongst the trees. Close to the line were flat marshy fields, flooded, for rice-growing. The houses were like Thames-side boathouses, thatched open-sided cottages. In amongst them ran a numerous population of naked children, with well built graceful men and women wearing loin-cloths. Cochin is unique in these, that very little is worn in the way of clothes, that widows always can remarry, that there is no child-marriage, and there polygamy even amongst the Moslems is unknown. 30% of the people are Syrian Christians (of them more later) the rest mainly Hindus, except for some Mapilla Mohammedans chiefly of Arab blood and habits. To account for these differences between the Malabar Coast and the rest of India, Sir Richard Burton suggested that the people were Polynesian: they look like it, of an olive or a sun-burnt very light colour mostly; the women have wonderful long wavy black hair hanging down to their waists. Mostly all the people go bare-headed. Habits are much the same in all classes: thus the Rajah has only one wife, and seldom is fully dressed at home.

Trichur is like a very big village, or a collection of villages divided by garden and palm-groves. In the centre of it is a very large high-walled enclosure like a fort, with trees inside it; and this is the great temple, famous in South India. I only saw the outer wall, nothing of the architecture. Menon is excommunicated by the priests because he refused to go through the purifying rites when he returned from England. Near the temple is the bazaar, simply a road with shops on either side, mere benches where the tradesmen sit and chew betel-nut (which

stains their mouths crimson). At the end of this is a large field where
there was an elephant of Menon's undergoing treatment, a pretty
tough job for any vet., Menon's forest offices, a very large public
building, and his house, like a riverside bungalow. It's covered with
creepers, with balconies and verandahs full of flowers, and an avenue of
tall trees, mangoes, leads up to it. On these he has some forest squirrels,
large brown animals quite different to the little grey squirrels with
white stripes which are found everywhere in India, in the middle of
towns equally as in the country. I had a very nice room waiting ready
for me, looking out over a large pond or bathing-tank. All the well-
to-do have these in the country, and there are other public bathing-
lakes. Water is everywhere. At Menon's I lived a life not nearly so
strange as I expected. His wife did not feed with him and me, but sat
at the table talking, while his children tumbled about the room. That
was because he is a meat-eater, or was while I was with him, while she
lives on native food. I fancy it was merely my presence which made
this. The first afternoon I went out in a judka—a little pony-trap—with
him and his wife to tea at a large Indian house. There I met one of the
Princes of the Country, and his wife and daughter, and many other
men and women. We sat drinking tea in the garden, with lamps hanging from trees, and fire-flies, little flying beetles with drops of light as
it were in their tails, spinning about above our heads. The people are
fond of strange sweetmeats. At this tea-party, which was in no way
unusual, men and women met just as naturally as in England, but that
is Cochin custom rather than Hindu.

I went down to Cochin, the British town, and slept two nights at
Ernakulam, P. N. Menon's place. That's on the mainland with a mile
of salt water between it and Cochin. All along the coast there runs a
lagoon with coconut palms growing on it, and inside is a great series
of back-waters and more palm-islands. It's very tropical, very beautiful,
and one can travel continuously in boats for days. The people live on
coconut-farming and on fishing, with also rice-growing. I had a motor-
boat belonging to the Chief Justice, an Indian, at my disposal, and also
one of the country-craft, something like a gondola. We went over to
British Cochin, where there are two large Jewish colonies of vast
interest because one lot is as dark as Indians and the other like Europeans.
The latter came in in 500 A.D. or so historically; the others claim to have
settled at the time of the Sack of Jerusalem and their claim has been

investigated and allowed by the Rabbi Adler of London. I lunched with
a black Jew, and was shown over the Synagogue by him and a white
Rabbi. The building is of Dutch architecture (the Portuguese first
conquered Cochin in the reign of Henry VII or so and then came the
Dutch, last of all the English) and the inside of it is grand with lamps of
gold and crystal chandeliers, while on the kind of altar stand the books
of the law, in old parchment, each in a crown of pure gold. Behind are
beautiful hangings. This synagogue was visited by Lord Curzon. It is
not really simple enough for the highest beauty, but its gorgeousness
takes the breath away.

Afterwards I went back to Trichur and did little but go to a garden-
party with the Dervan, or Prime Minister, an Indian who had been in
Oxford. The Rajah was not in the country at the time. He had come
there meaning to have a shooting-party with Menon, but rains washed
it out and it ended prematurely. At this garden-party my chief gain
was a long talk with the Bishop of the country. This man was a very
interesting intelligent person from Mesopotamia: very keen on his
work and a reformer, which has got him embroiled with a conservative
section which objects to his clearing images out of the churches. The
Syrian Christian cannot be distinguished from the other Indians by any
outward sign, nor is any generalization about the relative trustworthi-
ness of Hindu, Moslem and Christian at all possible.

My best experience in Cochin State was a journey into the Forest.
I went up a wonderful forest-railway, built and used for the carriage of
teak logs down to the main railway. It's a metre-gauge, and climbs up
the hills to about 4 or 5 thousand feet. At one point when I was there,
just in a little trolley-car sort of thing, the gradient was 1 in $1\frac{1}{2}$, steep as
a flight of stairs and more so. The laden truck coming down pulls up
the empty by a wire-rope. The line runs through thick jungle, well-
watered, absolutely impassible with undergrowth. In this jungle is a
vast quantity of game, but when we came through there was such a lot
of water that the deer and wild bison and wild elephants were all back
away from the line. Also it was the day-time, so there was an absolute
quiet except for the crash of monkeys swinging through the trees,
long-tailed black animals. There were beautiful orchids, red and white,
growing in the forest, and the views were gorgeous, of great rock crags
amongst the thick trees, and of torrents pouring down through gardens
of ferns. We had lunch in a forest bungalow. From the terrace I

looked out and downwards through 2,000 feet and 35 miles to the sea, over an ocean of trees with one great arm of rocks stretched out towards the water. There was absolute stillness except for the continuous jar of the crickets, like an accompaniment to the silence. Only, high up above the forest was a great eagle climbing up in spirals to a wonderful height and passing into the sky. Weird birds of the paroquet kind hopped about quietly, and one marvellous purple swallowtail butterfly flitted below the terrace. What struck me most was the stillness.

The birds of the low-country were very beautiful: many sorts of king-fishers, some just the same as the English sort, white cranes in great flocks in the paddy-fields, green paroquets and great green parrots. As the train ran through the paddy-fields it passed man after man up to his knees in the midst of acres of water, with only white cranes about him. There were great lank goats everywhere, with short hair. The cattle are small, rather like Jerseys. Ploughing is done mainly with buffaloes, big black beasts with horns sloping back and hair bristling like that of pigs. Each night I was there nearly, there was a thunderstorm. It was hot at midday but not oppressively so. Altogether a vastly attractive country. Most of the people who are not peasants speak English. Trichur has 10,000 inhabitants. It has a High School with more than 600 boys in it—the Headmaster an Indian—and a girl's school with nearly 500 girls. Mrs. Menon—much more attractive than her pictures make her—understands English, and his sons, the two elder ones, can both talk it. Thus the country is in many ways very advanced. But it is not in any way typical India.

Now I'll stop. Tomorrow I'm going away into the mountains with A. and Mr. Ramsay MacDonald, so I'll miss the mail on Saturday. I'll be back in College on Tuesday. I like my colleagues, all of them, and my work so far has been quite pleasant. So don't worry about me.

with love,

WILL

St. Stephen's College
Delhi
13/11/13

Dear Mother

I'm not going to write a long letter this week, because I'm busy mostly. The mail goes early in the morning, and I have several letters to write, to Mrs. Hoste and Mr. L. C. Jane and others whom I owe some message to, including Ned. I'm glad some of your letters have at last got to him. As to the theory that they were being kept back maliciously, it is quite possible. Various people there probably bear him a grudge: for example one of the Effendis, who abducted a Kurdish girl just before I arrived there, and who was made to give her up by Ned at the head of an armed force. At the same time he is such a king in the district that only by such mean little tricks would they dare to touch him. You must think of him as a great power in the land for good: the Kurds apply to him continually, as arbitrator in tribal difficulties, and he has contrived to keep his village, the Hoja's people, sober, while the Germans have made drunken men a common sight in the bridge builders' cottages. The Germans (mostly Levantines who are subjects naturalised of the Kaiser) are disgusting mostly, with abominable faces and worse manners. Of course there are exceptions, and Ned's very friendly with Feldner the Director of the Baghdad company and Hoffmann, the chief engineer at the bridge. Then again for feeding he does excellently, and the Haj is quite a good servant, whose drinking is his only fault and that only very occasional, done in secret and slept off so that it does not show.

Now for my news.

I went on Friday night by train to Hardwar near Dehra Dun on the edge of the great hills, with A. and Ramsay MacDonald. We were visiting a famous monastic school belonging to the Arya Samaj, the Gurukul, which is set on Ganges' bank where the river leaves the hills and runs into the jungle. It is a wild spot, just a clearing in the forest of pampas-grass and trees where there are wild tigers and elephants still. To get to it we drifted on a raft down the Ganges about 4 miles: I'll write an account to Arnie next week. There I had a splendid time, bathing in the cold swift torrent, running about in Indian clothes, eating Indian food, and all the while having two great arms of red and green hills in sight, red sandstone and green deodars, running almost to a meeting, and where the gap came huge snow mountains as a background.

It was a very wonderful week-end. Also it was interesting not only to pick the brains of Ramsay MacDonald, who's a gentleman, but to see the actual beginning of what seems likely to be a great movement both for good and evil, this Arya Samaj monastery.

I had no letter from you last mail. Hope one will come next week, and that all is well. I'm fit, very. Just now one of my examiners, Professor Ramsay Muir, is staying in the college, and lecturing. I guess Father rejoices at the results of the Linlithgow and Reading elections. Now I'll stop. Best luck to Frank in his sports. Can you give me Bob's address?

With love to you all.

Your WILL

An oleander from Capernaum, a cactus-petal from Joppa, and an orchid petal from the jungle of Cochin.

The shoes arrived safely yesterday. Thanks very much for them and the rest.

ST. STEPHEN'S COLLEGE
DELHI
19/11/13

DEAR ARNIE

I want to tell you of a journey I had the other day to a place called Hardwar, which is in the north, near the Himalayas. It was rather interesting, and the country very beautiful.

A. and Mr. Ramsay MacDonald and I left Delhi about half past nine in the evening of Friday, and ran through the dark northwards, so that when dawn came and we looked out of the train we were already running along near the hills. They were a great wall of peaks, one after the other, but far away, so that they looked low on the horizon. By about 8 o'clock we came to Hardwar. This is the second holiest city in India in the eyes of the Hindus, Benares being the first, and our train was crowded with pilgrims, all sorts of types of people. The station was interesting for its monkeys. They were everywhere, running along the platform, on the roof, and on trees near by; great big beasts brown-haired with a little white fur about their faces, and they howl like parrots chattering. Most amusing of all was to watch them dropping one after the other from the station bridge on to the roofs of the carriages of the train while it stood still, and then running from carriage to carriage along the top. When the train starts, they have to leap all of them on to the corrugated-iron roof of the station, about 5 feet of a jump, and as many of them have little ones clinging on to them they are fairly clever to do it. We walked to the bank of the

Ganges. On the left were hills, opposite us more hills, red and green of the rocks and trees, and where the two left a gap for the Ganges there was a background of great snow mountains high in the sky like clouds. That's where the Ganges comes from. Here it is a very swift running torrent, with rapids every now and then, and about three hundred yards across in three channels of a hundred yards each. We got on to a raft of kerosene-tins bound together with ropes.

We had two bound together as a matter of fact, and five people were seated on it. Two men punted it along, or rather steered it with poles, for the current caught us at once and swept us down about 4 miles in 20 minutes. At times we got into the rapids, where the waves washed over the deck of the raft (we sat on our luggage) and the tins crashed occasionally into round boulders and nearly flung us off. The pace at such times was terrific, and in the keen cold air, with the snow behind us, and in front the extraordinary blue river (which Ramsay Mac-Donald kept saying 'might from its appearance have been in Scotland') tall pampas-grass on the bank and wild plum-trees covered with yellow fruit and thorns, monkeys trotting along in swarms (we saw about 300 all together) the sensation was splendid. So we swept down to the Gurukul, which is a school managed by the Arya Samaj (a Hindu reformed sect). There boys are taken at the age of six, and except for the visits twice a year of their parents, and occasional walking tours in the mountains, are kept till they are 25. They have a good but hard time. Well fed but plainly and all vegetarian, they have to bathe every morning in the Ganges at 4 o'clock. Then after prayers they work steadily except for breakfast and lunch till 4, after which they have to play games. The school lies in a great clearing with jungle on all sides save the river bank, so wild country that tigers and wild elephants are still seen there. I saw none. It's got a beautiful fruit garden, wide playing fields and fine college buildings, and is unique of its sort in India. This is all due not to the Arya Samaj but to the Abbot Mahatma Ji, a magnificent old man.

Their services are very strange. All sit cross-legged on mats for a quarter of an hour, thinking and praying. Then a small fire is lighted in a hole in the floor, and incense is thrown on to it, while one prays aloud, and the others join in with some prayers they have by heart, sentences from the old Hindu books, the Vedas. It is impressive, but a little weird. They wanted to know from me what our services were like, so you must imagine me singing 'Jesu, Lover of my soul' and other hymns to a large class of boys. I was in Indian clothes, a cloth wrapped about my waist like a sheet 3 feet wide and a loose shirt and cloak of embroidered crimson. On the whole the funniest thing I've done here yet was to swim across the Ganges dressed in pyjama trousers pulling Ramsay MacDonald on one of these rafts, and that was a thing I had to do. I won't write more now.

You're doing well keeping top. Also having cold baths.

Ta-ta,

Your loving,

WILL

ST. STEPHEN'S COLLEGE
DELHI
20/11/13

DEAR MOTHER

When I wrote to you last week I said that I had had no letter from you, but it was a mistake. Two letters had come, one from you, but they had got mixed up in S.'s papers, and when I came back from the hills I did not find them, nor had anyone noticed them. Bishop Taylor Smith was always excellent when I heard him. The difficulty with most clergymen, even the sincerest, seems to me that while they are 'anointed with the Holy Ghost' they are not 'with fire', and the Bishop has both.

Bob does not seem to be worked too late in the evenings at present, which is good. It was such hard luck on him that the camera was out of order. However the one photo you sent me is picturesque. Please thank Arnie for the hymn: it is the right sort indeed, such a contrast to a lot of mush we get. The test of a thing is whether it takes possession of your best memory. You talk of a lecture you went to on the South Pole. I don't think my ambition will ever lead me that way. You're seeing the C.I.M. party's photograph reminds me that I would like to see *China's Millions* sometimes, if you could send it. Mrs. Hoste was very good to me and I would like to follow her doings. As to the others, the Miss Trench you picked out was the one I was with most, a jolly person like Miss Monk, and Irish living at Killarney Abbey, Lord Ashtown's niece, I fancy. There was one man on board going out to teach in a Quaker College, whose ideas were appalling: sheer conceit making him doubt everything and weigh it in the scales of his swelled head. However I suppose he wasn't in the group so that's all right. Bob is lucky to be going to the C.I.M.

I've had a letter from Ned reporting wonderful finds, and have written to him just now. Glad his cheque got through to him. For me, I don't want any money. News of the garden always interests me. Here we have chrysanthemums in pots all about the College walls, and bushes of bougainvilia. In the gardens outside the walls are roses, crowds of them. I can't give you a picture of Delhi yet. No time or energy at the moment. I'm extremely fit, but fairly hard-worked. This week though I've done some sightseeing with Mr. Ramsay Muir, one of my examiners. It's wonderful what a lot he remembered about my papers, more by far than I did myself.

Frank's football sounds good. Best of luck to him, and in his jumping. The cheque St. John's sent sounds like being the remainder of my scholarship, but I can't say for certain. You had better not expect more and you won't be disappointed.

So glad Father is well. His golfing with Mr. Inman and beating him easily shows it. I'm as fit as I can be, well-fed and very comfortable. Also I like all the people here quite well.

I hope you're keeping well. I use the Scripture Union card you sent me, and we're very close,

from your loving son, WILL

with love to all the others.

ST. STEPHEN'S COLLEGE
DELHI
26/11/13

DEAR FATHER

I cannot write a decent letter this week, owing to lack of time. Foolishly I've left it till now, and at the moment we're in a turmoil. The South African question is just now the only thing any Indian can talk about; the only thing in fact which any newspaper mentions, with the most marvellous conflict of obvious lies in all their reports. The main point I get out of the whole business is a powerful argument against Home Rule. Assuredly we never ought to have given self-government so soon to the Boers. However this question is not so uppermost in England I expect as here. Here though they freely prophesy the wildest of doings if the trouble is not soon over.

Well, the reason why I am talking about it is that Mr. A. is going out to South Africa tonight as representative of the Indian Congress. What he will do I don't know, but most people approve of his going. I was talking to Lord Islington, the head of the Public Services Commission, this afternoon and he said it was the best thing he had heard for a long time. At the same time as A. isn't a sober politician he may do harm: to prevent this W. W. Pearson (whom Mother will remember as the best of our Camp officers) is going with him. That is at my suggestion; quaint isn't it, to think of me mixed up so soon in Imperial politics.

That however makes me frightfully busy at the moment, so that I can't write. Just now I am scribbling this between dinner and arranging some wedding arrangements for a rich Indian banker in Delhi, which latter I am doing as substitute for Pearson.

Tell Mother that I am very well indeed, and quite happy in my work. I will write a proper long letter next week, which will be Christmas mail. Congratulate Arnie on his work (I have his Greek exercise from Bob), and Frank on his very excellent football.

Now I must stop, with best love to all. I'm so glad my letter arrived for your birthday: hoping you are all well.

Your loving WILL

St. Stephen's College
Delhi
4/12/13

Dear Bob

I owe you a really long letter, because your letters have been a great pleasure to me, and they have been most inadequately answered. At the same time I'm sleepy this morning from having been up till 1 o'clock the last two nights, so the dullness of this will probably be considerable. You'll wonder what has been happening to keep me up so late, but the fact is that I have been managing a wedding entertainment for one of the Delhi grandees, and it has not only been taking up all my spare hours of the day, but has with a rehearsal and the full show last night kept me going into the small hours. Imagine an immense garden cut into small sections of green shrubs with paths of red gravel leading through them. A long avenue leading from a crowded street through high walls with houses on either side suddenly throwing you into this, where all the shrubs are hung with lanterns and smooth-boled palms are lit with electric bulbs. And in the middle, between two houses ablaze with electric light and set about with palms, a great hall of corrugated iron roof and muslin and tapestried walls, capable of seating hundreds of people. I arranged the place like a restaurant of a good hotel, thick carpets covering it all, and on them couches set about little tables piled with sweetmeats. At the far end of the room was a stage, with more beautiful curtains, and the whole was lit up by strangely twisted glass lamps and candelabra and all manner of electric shades. In this place S.S., the host and the richest man in Delhi, received his guests, the chief Europeans of the place and their wives. And then followed the entertainment on the stage, musicians playing Indian instruments, and after them a small boy of 7 years old singing— he is famous through India as an infant prodigy—and then juggling. After the juggling came some feats of Indian archery. One of the most wonderful was the blindfolding of the archer who was then turned round. Then a man held a very narrow cane and tapped it with a stick. Guided solely by the sound, and with great deliberation the archer aimed and hit the cane, at about 10 yards. Another was severing a swinging ball revolving rapidly by cutting the string. This of course was unblindfolded. He then did the same thing to a stationary ball by looking in a mirror and so aiming. And he ended by severing a string by taking careful aim, then being blindfolded, and coming up again, kneeling, finding the same aim by measuring the squareness of his position with his chin, turning it to his shoulders. He used a rather short bow, and long arrows with sharp and almost pointed tips. After the archer came some acting and then a banjo playing after which the audience dispersed. All the while refreshments were going round, and the whole place was a kind of café chantant. R., the youth who is being married, is one of the Students of the College and W. W. Pearson was his private tutor. As I was responsible for Pearson's going away to South Africa, and before he went he was helping S.S. with this show, I had to take on the duty of a.d.c., and found the work amusing, except when we drove out in an immense motor to call on generals and those sort of people, which was a bore. I mean the calling, not the motoring. Still in most cases we found people out and S.S. dropped cards on them and I did nothing.

This business of Pearson and A. going to South Africa is rather a wild-goose chase, but is mainly intended as a Christian manifesto by Anglo-Indians to the people here who are in an amazing ferment. I've seen men positively foaming at the mouth with rage and excitement in ordinary conversation. Rudra can talk of nothing else, and Mr. Gokhale, considered by all Indians of the educated sort to be their leader, and one of the Councillors of the Viceroy, does nothing but make speeches on the subject. Of course the agitators (and they are sillier out here than you could imagine) have seized on it as an opportunity and exaggerated it, but it's plain from even the South African admissions that the Indians are treated vilely, as for example in having to pay a special tax on account of their colour, and in not being considered properly married, when they are so by their own rites, sanctioned by the Indian Government.

I try to keep out of politics as far as possible, and all my instincts are against strikes, but here only a very small and unpleasant minority of Anglo-Indians seem to think anything can be said for South Africa. As to A.'s mission, he's most likely to get put into prison before he has been a fortnight in the country. We ought never to have given Home Rule to the Boers.

Talking of Home Rule Irish affairs look pretty bad, but I'm very ignorant of what is going on, since I have no time to read the papers. I trust good will come of the business, but wish neither Mr. Redmond nor Sir Edward Carson existed.

Now I must stop. I'm very well, and enjoying life vastly. At the end of this week comes a holiday, and I'm going to Jaipur in Rajputana with one of my pupils, who first of all invited me to his house there— he's a Hindu—but now we've had to make other arrangements since C., one of my colleagues, wants to come too. So it will be a case of an hotel after all. I like C. very greatly, and in fact we're all fitting together excellently.

Your work seems very much better than you expected. I'm glad you like your Doctor, and also that the Cooke family is congenial. It's hard to realize that you're having the winter in England now, but here's to a very happy Christmas and New Year, and many returns of a happy birthday.

Yours lovingly,

WILL

Frank M. gave an address to the Students the other day that you would have loved to have heard. Thanks very much for Bishop Taylor Smith's sermons. I read them last Sunday with my usual pleasure. He's a man.

Here are some tiny shells from the Sea of Galilee.

MAITLAND HOUSE
KASHMIR GATE,
DELHI
4/12/13

DEAR MOTHER

I have been writing a great many letters indeed just now for Christmas, and in a letter to Bob have described what I have been doing recently. Now to you I just want to chat quietly, without description, so get him to send you the letter if you want to hear about the wedding entertainment. I expect though that he will be with you for Christmas. How nice it will be for you having him again for awhile, and you may feel happy about the absent ones too, with Ned a royal benefactor as it were and at the same time making a great name, and me out here very well and amongst people I like. C. the Univ. man who is here and whom I had never met is an extremely jolly person. S. has been goodness itself, and we are all shaking down together excellently well.

The kind of day I lead is that at 7 I get up, after eating chota hazri, in my case a couple of bananas, in bed. Most people have quite a petit dejeuner of tea and toast and fruit before they get up. S. and I sleep on the roof of Rudra's house, and enjoy the cool air very much. The nights are quite cold; in the day there is good sunshine but never hot enough to make one wear summer clothes. Today it has been wet, in an English October style, and the roads are quagmires, but today's rain is the first except for one thunderstorm that I've had in Delhi. At a quarter to eight I work at Hindustani with an Indian teacher, what is called here a numshi. At 9 we have breakfast. At 10.20 I start taking men's essays, which continue to come till 12.20. Then there is a religious address on two days of the week. At one I have lunch, called tiffin; at 1.20 take some history men in a lecture till 2.0. From 2 till 2.40 I lecture on English Literature, and after that I am free till 6, when I take some advanced history work till 7. At present this is in Political Science and not Constitutional History, so I am quite happy. Dinner is at 8.

You see I am very busy; the disadvantage is that I have little time to myself, except in the latter part of the day when I'm tired. But I enjoy the work very much and some of the students are very good chaps, especially an M.A. Student called Bhattacharya with whom I'm spending the 6th, 7th, 8th and 9th at Jaipur in Rajputana. Also I have made friends with the son of the Principal of the Gurukul at Hardwar, who manages a newspaper here, and can walk about Delhi with him. Just of late though this wedding-entertainment has taken up my time in the afternoons. Pearson you see was private tutor to the boy who is being married (he is 17 and well grown) and was helping S.S., so when he went at my suggestion and persuasion, I had to take his place. That meant motoring about with S.S., and also arranging a stage and that sort of thing, two or three hours work every day. That's over now though. When the wedding ceremonies are quite finished S.S. wants me to come with him for a motor-tour to some ruined city near Agra, just a three days trip. We'll see. He is a strange person, very demonstrative, and in watching him I'm as it were studying the history of the Italian city-tyrants of the Renaissance period. He got all the chief Europeans in Delhi at his show last night, which went without a hitch, and was very beautiful. You see he is the richest man in all Delhi, and a tremendous grandee. What you said of Mrs. Hoste amuses me, because she asked me once if I was any relation of the Broomhall family, because I was like what Mr. Marshall Broomhall had been when he was young. She was very nice, and has a son who will be soon going up to college, besides others younger. As the accident to Arnie left him unimpaired well and good. Bicycles can easily be mended. I hope he soon got over it. How very well he is doing at school, most remarkably. I have been wondering about what I could send him for Christmas from here, but in the end I'm sending nothing but my love. It's good that he's taking cold baths still.

I lost nothing on my journey except the sun-helmet at Port Said which the hotel made good, and my knife at Agra. Altogether it was a wonderful time that I had, and except for that one affair I was very well all along. Now I'm quite fit, and finding things very good. Delhi is full of flowers, bougainvilias the best, and in the houses chrysanthemums are everywhere looking very jolly. There are hundreds of pots round the College. I'm glad you're trying to keep the Campanula alive; if it dies you will at least have done your best. Thanks for the cutting about the Gypsies, quite jolly and interesting. About our little compact, if you can't get me a card along I will spend the first weeks of January starting at the beginning of the Psalms, one a day. It's nice to think of you at the other end of the line. One of the pleasantly pathetic things about Mr. Ramsay MacDonald, who is again stopping with us, is that he keeps English time here always about 5 and half hours late, so as to know what his children are doing. He is a widower (his wife died a year or more ago) with several young ones: he is really an immensely fine fellow, with a sincerity one cannot doubt. In politics I quote Sir Walter Raleigh: "What matter how the head lies, so only the heart be right," which he said as he laid his head on the block facing west not east.

Give my love to Frank, and congratulations on his football. To Arnie also, and to you and Father all of me.

your loving WILL

A few little shells from Galilee.

ST. STEPHEN'S COLLEGE
DELHI
10/12/13

MY DEAR MOTHER

I have just got an hour so I want to use it by writing to you. It's seven o'clock, and as usual it's been a fairly busy day, getting back to work after the three days holiday of Maharram. I'm tired, because this morning an idea came to me and I spent an hour writing up an incident for the College magazine here, which has been soliciting an article some while. I'll send it perhaps to the School magazine later through you, just a short impression of a Turkish soldier. I got last week's mail today, which was jolly as it's my birthday. That was due to the visit to Jaipur, which has been the great event of recent days. Get Arnie to look it up in the Map: it's in Rajputana, and a most romantic place full of colour and clash of life.

C. and Bhattacharya (one of my pupils) and I went down together there, and as C. was with us, he and I stopped at an hotel, while Bhattacharya went to a friend. That friend incidentally was the biggest Indian I've met, about 6 ft. 6 and 17 stone, with a massive wise face. He used to be chief man in Jaipur State, and remains the Private Secretary of the Rajah, but he's not liked by Government because he's a Bengali (there's a prejudice against them due to Lord Curzon) and is suspected by the people of being a Christian, so now he's rather fallen off. The Maharajah is very fond of him, and I don't wonder.

Jaipur city is about two miles from the station, and is new, built in 1722. A wall runs all round it, and the city gates are closed every night at 9 o'clock. It lies in flat country surrounded on one side by gardens gradually merging into what is almost a flat desert, and on the other three by ridges of hills fortified all over in the most amazing way. I daresay there are photographs of these castles in *The Wonders of the World*; there ought to be at any rate. I tried for postcards but there were none shewing the hills. But just imagine a fort 8 miles long, quite uninhabited, seen by no one but military engineers (not even by the King and Queen or Lord Curzon) and crowning a narrow ridge. That's what you have at Jaipur. Within the city is laid out in great streets about 30 yards wide, the houses all built of a uniform pink colour. Up and down these streets go men in bright costumes, at full gallop, a new thing this to me in India where horses so far have been few and far between, and women in far brighter colours than I've seen elsewhere, delicate rose and pink predominating. The Rajputs are the ruling class, tall thin men, very fine-looking in every way. The people generally are more military of aspect than the short slight Delhi men.

First of all we went over the palace. I can't describe that: think though of the Tower and you get an idea of everything but the Stables, the Gardens and the Observatory. The Stables are the size of two cricket fields made into a vast oblong of cloisters where horses are kept, I should say in thousands. Wonderful horses they are too, Arabs and all others. Jaipur specializes rather in this as its form of revenue and wealth: the Maharajah gets one as a tax on every 1,000 rupees of income from his subjects, and runs a splendid body of irregular cavalry, besides a camel corps for desert work in the Thar.

Then the garden is kept for his women. He's polygamous and un-usually strict about Purdah rules. But the garden for the women which I went over with my friends (the Rajah was away at another palace with all his people) is the size of the University parks almost, with tanks the size of a cricket field in it, and Kiosks and lake-palaces and orchards all in marvellous richness and profusion. In the lake are some large crocodiles which answered to their names when fed, and were hideous brutes about 12 feet long. Altogether this palace at Jaipur is the most wonderful dwelling place I've seen. It must challenge comparison with Windsor Castle in all save the latter's fine position.

Next day C. and I drove to Amber, the old capital of Jaipur and now just a palace and a fort. The Private Secretary tried to procure us an elephant on which to ride the 16 miles there and back, but the State Elephants were all with the Maharajah. So instead we drove in country carts like Irish cars. The situation of Amber is a valley between hill ridges covered with cactus scrub, with three or four walls scores of miles in extent hedging it in. Thus we came first to a gate at the bottom of a great rise. A wall crossed from here to the ridge side and ran on the one side back the eight miles to Jaipur, on the other as far as one could see towards the Agra pass. Then the road, rock-paved, ran to the top of the hill, and went through another gate in another wall. That was the top of the pass, it then dropped down and ran level for about another mile till it came to another wall. Through that lay a great lake, by the side of which lay the palace on the slope of a hill. This palace is ruined, as is most of the small old town about it. It again is like Windsor Castle, with a dash of Carcassonne thrown in. And above it is the fort on the hill-side with a high watch tower, a fort which is the same as that at Jaipur eight miles away. From the palace one can see along the valley to the pass we crossed, and the other way more and more walls and fortresses on every slope of the hills, literally scores I should think, and then through the various gates I don't know how many a fairly wide plain bounded in the extreme distance by mountains. All the country is almost desert, but it is vastly rich, since there is the best marble of India in its quarries, and its jewels are wonderful, (Jaipur garnets and amethysts), while as I said before the horses of Jaipur are its greatest boast.

11/12/13

We also saw the Museum, which has a fine collection of Indian pictures and stuffs.

This Bhattacharya, who asked me to go with him, is a Bengali a little older than I am probably; a gentle quiet pleasant fellow, and a Brahmin. His father was Principal of the College at Jaipur, but is now dead. He is the most winning of the students I have met so far, something of an artist, and quite an authority on Rajputana history. C. is a very natural amusing sort of man, without whom we should be rather dull.

Last Friday I had a great experience, because I was invited by S.S., for whom I helped to arrange the entertainment, to take part in the Bridegroom's procession. That meant going to the centre of the town and thence walking about two miles with Indian bands and army Punjabi pipers to the Bride's house. I was amidst the most gorgeously dressed people imaginable, all the richest men of the country round, and was the only white person there except for the Chief Commissioner. The Bridegroom, who's one of the College students, a lad of 17, rode on a great black mare hung with golden trappings, and wore clothes of the magnificent golden work which they use as funeral palls. This is supposed to signify vanity of vanities, and so prevent pride. He looked very fine, since he's a tall upright man. When we came to the Bride's house people came out with lanterns to meet us; men not women carrying them, but still it reminded me of the Ten Virgins. The house which was like a mediæval palace was lit up from roof downwards, and hung with cloths. R., the Bridegroom, got down from his horse, walked up the steps, and stood for a while hidden, as two men held a sheet in front of him. It was then that the Bride was crowning him with flowers, while other girls of the household leaned out of the balcony above and rained down a shower of white rose petals on him. Then he came out again, and the special friends of the Bridegroom (me among them) went into a room and sat cross-legged on cushions while boys sang texts from the Vedas, and little girls were introduced to the new member of the household. It's something of an honour for me to have been there: in all his life Rudra has never got a chance to take part nor has any other of the professors here. The ceremony closed with the changing of the clothes of the Bridegroom, and the sprinkling of all the guests with rosewater. I did not see the Bride at all. Then I motored back with S.S., whom I haven't seen since.

On Saturday I'm going to Agra with Mr. Rudra, if our plans hold good, and I'll stop there at St. John's College, where there are several people I know. And after that I have to attend a history conference at Lahore, so you see I'm seeing a bit of India.

Two days ago I got a letter from an old soldier at some Punjab village asking me if I was any relation of Sir John Lawrence, evidently with the idea of paying his respects to me if I was. His name is one of the most honoured by both parties here.

I am sorry to hear that Mr. Wright had been ill: sent a letter to Miss

Wright for Christmas. Altogether my Christmas mail was 19 letters, to all the people I ought to have written to before, up and down the world.

I didn't sleep out in Syria: that wasn't the cause. I guess it was a combination of eating too much, drinking sulphur water, swimming in Galilee and running in the heat. I haven't heard from Ned recently: don't expect to much, while he's busy digging. You have no idea of how he's overworked. The papers the other day reported about the Rhodes Scholar rule, so I know about it.

Well now I must shut up. I do hope that you are all well. Is Father going to go away at all this winter? That will be lonely for you; I hope he'll keep fit and not have to. Love to Arnie: I'll send him some stamps of native states presently I hope. To Frank and Bob cheer-oh. And all my love to you all.

Your loving

WILL

Fit. Very.

A TURKISH SOLDIER

'Arabic, no? Feringhi speak,' he said, and his face brightened as I nodded. We were standing on the edge of the tower-head, with the hundred feet drop below to the main line of circumvallation, and we were alone together in the sunset for one moment of our lives. The hill-slopes westward were already in the shadow, only lit by the dust where the goats were being driven in, and in the East the desert was the colour of autumn leaves: I would soon have to go back to my friends. So I snatched at the chance to speak to him.

'Ever been to Bethlehem,' he went on in French. 'But no. Well, there I was born, but my old father lives now at Nazareth. It's years since I was there. Our house is at the corner of the road down the hill to Nain. Christians? Yes we are like the others of Nasirah. But now I am a soldier, and there is nothing to do here but ride behind the carriage of the Vali, and stop the fights in the cafés. Still it is a quiet life, and if we had our pay all would be well. But that we never get, and sometimes too there are wars. Those who go to the Yemen never come back.'

We stood still awhile. He was looking along the road to Djerabisse, past the barracks and the muddy river to where the great desert stretched in a silence to which all the world seems only an accompaniment, like the crickets in a jungle at noon. On a sand path a Bedawi was riding at the usual gallop, his Keffieh flying behind like a pennon and the grey tail of his mare like the wash of a ship. Two shots rang out somewhere in the direction of the bazaar, on the gardens above which the goats were grazing that sometimes fall through the skylights and cause diversion. This little moustached Syrian in his drab khaki looked out of place somehow in a land where it is not the fighting-machine which wins, but the fighting man. He was going on again.

'It is not the Yemen only which takes us. It is the worst, for the Bedawin are terrible. But now there are the Bulgary Czar's men, and the Greeks. I have lost many friends. Why should we Christians fight about Stamboul, when our women do not live there? It is different for the Tcherkessi, they love all things difficult.' Mentally I saw beside him a Circassian, a tall slender man, curbed ferocity, sinewy restraint, and I nodded. 'But we, we love our houses, and the little vineyards on the hills. In your land now, is there conscription? No, and it is England then. Ah well, and does England make redifs of all her subjects? What of the men of Hind?'

I explained that we did not force men to serve in the army against their wills. Then again came silence. The sun set with a sudden rush behind the hills that hedge Aleppo from the sea. The afterglow was left to struggle with the stars. The muezzin rose and sank. And then he turned to me again.

'So. It is more good to have the English than the Turks. My uncle is at Cairo, and I know. But to each his fate; also perhaps when the Sultan is not troubled by the Czar he will choose better Valis. Life is still good while there is love. You will go to Nasirah? That's good. Seek out my father, our house is at the corner of the road down the hill to Nain, and tell the girl who tends him that Yakoub is well, Yakoub who was born at Bethlehem. She will remember. You have been kind to speak to me, so you'll do. Thank you, Hawaja.'

So I left him bowed, a pathetic figure longing for peace among the tents of Kedar. The great eight-fold gate of Beibars clanged behind me. And in my mind remained not the murmuring of the soldier but the cry 'Allah il Allah', changed somehow to 'God is love'.

W. G. LAWRENCE

10/12/13

BOLPUR
BENGAL
24/12/13

MY DEAR MOTHER

I have little time to write to you, because I am stopping here with Mr. Rabindranath Tagore, the poet, and want to talk to him. The English mail goes this afternoon too, almost a couple of days before it does in Delhi, so I'm caught with a hurry unawares. I'm stopping today and tomorrow, Christmas, very quietly here, hardly moving from the school which is set among the palm-trees and the mangoes, on a little rise in a flat fertile plain. And the reason why I have come down South thus, is in order to fulfil Mrs. Barker's commission at Dacca. It is a long way to go, but unless I did it now I wouldn't have a chance, since in the hot weather Bengal is not the country to visit. Also as it's the Christmas season I can travel more cheaply.

My last letter was from Lahore, to Frank. Since then I've had a letter from him enclosed in yours: please thank him for it. The fire at Jesus was the chief news in your letter: a great pity this. Frank has done splendidly in his jumping. 19′ 7″ is a very good jump for College sports indeed.

I must write to John Snow, who was one of the few people I know to whom I didn't write at Christmas. As to Miss Jane, I'm glad you like her. I sent her a box of ivory inlaid with silver and ebony, rather handsome, and cheap, with two ivory mantelpiece toys. The ivory work of Delhi is what it is most noticeable for, in the way of presents.

I've had letters from M.'s sister, and also from his Mother writing through Miss Goodwin. M. and his wife are quite well now, and all the rest of us flourish exceedingly. S. and I had a great bathe in the Jumna the other day. Father will be bound to be the better for the sea-baths. I wish I had seen something of Ireland before I came away. And it will be jolly if you can get over there and join him for awhile. You don't say how you are. I hope you've had no more relapses, and that you'll get stronger and stronger. Arnie has clearly been good both about his work and his baths. Don't let him be disheartened about the Scholarship: if miracles happen like his last effort he will be lucky indeed.

I haven't time to write and explain our Maitland House system at present, but we have a very jolly time indeed, and I'm in every way comfortable. Letter-writing is rather difficult (I wrote to Mr. Grey

when I was at Lahore by the way). After this jaunt to Dacca, which is
about 250 miles from here or a bit more, I'll keep quiet. My visit to
Lahore was purely a business one and notable chiefly because I met
Bernard Wilsdon there. Frank will know him. The trip to Agra, which
I fancy I haven't described, was taken because Rudra asked me to go,
and the one to Jaipur by invitation of my pupil Bhattacharya. Rudra is
making me his walking companion in place of A. and we go and call
on all sorts of Indian grandees round Delhi.

It's very pleasant meeting Tagore in his own home. You'll remember
Ezra Pound introduced me to him. I'm sitting writing this in a house
on the hill, in the Bengal heat.

Please tell Frank if it's not too late, that he needn't copy out A.E.'s
song for me. Tagore has let me have it.

Glad Florence is with you now.

So with the best of love to all.

Your son

WILL

S.S. Vulture
27/12/13

DEAREST MOTHER

I am writing on the deck of a Padda River steamer, which plies
between Dacca and Calcutta, or rather between Naraingui and Goal-
anda Ghat. Just been up to Dacca to see the grave of Mr. Salkeld, Mrs.
Barker's brother, not that I could do anything useful there but in order
by any means to please her. I would like to do something really big for
the Barkers.

The trip means that I've travelled about 2,500 miles in 10 days, or
will have when I get back. But journeys here are very comfortable,
and my fitness is grand. And just to look around me here is to realize
that it's been a real holiday. Miles and miles of long grey water except
where the sun is getting low, where it is flashing and silvery, and everywhere in the distance lines of palm-trees marking otherwise invisible
shores. The channel for the most part must be about three to five miles
across, and it is dotted here and there by boats. Sometimes I've seen
great fleets of square-sailed craft of the junk pattern, very low and
pointed in the bows with a high cabined poop and great portholes
under the round matting roof. Let Arnie go to the Pitt-Rivers and look

for the model of a Hooghli or Sundarbans river-boat. Then there are small boats, just little cabins that follow the tide. And occasionally there come floating down great double boats of the *Swan and her Crew* pattern, carrying cattle to Calcutta. The whole thing is a new world from Delhi, and it is very good to have been here.

I had a wonderful Christmas Day at Bolpur. Tagore is an ideal person, and to be with him is great. But he went away in the evening of the 24th, to see the Viceroy and get some decoration. He's recently won a big honour in Literature. {Nobel prize for Literature, 1913.} Then the next day I got up about 6.30 and wandered out over the moor, which would be like Beaulieu Common if its palms were pines. After that, breakfast, with the teachers of the School. Then I had to give an address to the boys. 200 of them under the boughs of a grove of mangoes squatting in a dense mass, and me in a dhoti and khurta, white Indian clothes which I've worn now at the Gurukul and at Hardwar, and which are pleasantest when one has to squat and live Indianwise, standing and talking to them. That was the picture, and surely when you imagined my Christmas you didn't imagine that, the Indian clothes, the warmth of Bengal, the upturned young faces, and me making the first sermon of my life. The youngest boys didn't know English, so one of the teachers gave what he remembered of my words to them. Curiously enough, for the first time in my days I wanted to speak, and though I talked on the spur of the moment had words all the time.

Afterwards I was garlanded. That is, when I had finished tiffin, lunch, and was sitting under an awning in the balcony of Tagore's house, the place where he wrote *Gitanjali*, the headmaster came and asked me to go down to the play-ground. There all the boys were collected, and they came up and set a wreath of red and yellow flowers about my neck, and gave me two photographs, one of Tagore, and one of a memorial inscription under the great tree. That's the sort of thing which takes one's breath away. I have the photographs and the flowers which must be withered now, with me in my valise. Also I have a large pot of artificial flowers which are a terrible bother, but a small boy gave them to me and I cannot throw them away.

So you see my Christmas was a strange one. And it ended in the train, which I left in the early morning for the Dacca Steamer.

I've just sat down after seeing the sun set. While it's fresh in my mind

I must go on writing. Here the channel is about seven miles across with just a row of palms in the west, into which the sun went down after its rays across the water had gradually faded into itself. Down the stream, there is no sign of land: it might be the open sea. Up it came sailing a junk between us and the sun just as the gold was turning to a red one could look upon, and the great square-sail on the high deck and the few men tugging at the sweeps, while the vessel crept up the current was a sight to see. And then just now as the rim of the sun rested among the pines, and the water was grey or almost the colour of the white of one's eyes a catamaran came past with three men in it. I wish you could see some of these things I am seeing, or that I could paint them on paper. But it is no use: only believe that it is good for me to be here. Now I'm going to stop. The steamer will go on till about 10 at night, when we get into a train, to be set down in Calcutta at 6 o'clock. There one of the old students of Bolpur whom I met there on a visit is going to meet me.

DELHI.　30/12/13

I am back again, and have been reading my letters. One from you, newspapers, one from Captain Young of the desert-trip (he's inviting me down to Jhansi) and local ones.

The greatest news is that of Arnie and the Scholarship. It's a marvellous feat of his, and we have all reason to be proud. Don't let him work too much: with a brain such as his development rather than cramming is what is wanted. Probably his stay away from school did him more good than all his work in it, so if ever you're going away do take him with you. Presently when he is grown a bit he'll be able perhaps to go out with Ned awhile. I haven't heard from Ned and don't expect to at present. Young is full of his praise in his letter. My stop with him has given me a certainty of grasp in going about this country which I could hardly have had but for that. I'm sorry about Father's rheumatism: hope it will soon go. Your tooth seems to have been giving you a good deal of bother also.

At Calcutta I did very little. My train got in about 6 in the morning Sunday. So I had breakfast in the station, and then went to the Cathedral for service. After that I walked out to the Martinière College which took me some hours to reach (it's hard to find). Then I watched the crowd on the Howrah Bridge, the most used bridge in the world

I believe, pouring past in their thousands all the evening, and left at night. A comfortable journey put me down here.

As to Henry's son it's not a surprise to me: I remember now he hinted so much but I didn't altogether take his meaning. I'm afraid he'll find finance hard, a bit.

That's all for the moment.

1/1/14

I wear Indian clothes at Indian houses because I like them, and because A. does, whose influence in India is something terrific.

Well, now I'm going to finish this letter. Wishing you all a New Year of happiness.

with my best love,

WILL

MAITLAND HOUSE
KASHMIR GATE
1/1/14

MY DEAR BOB

Such a lot of letters I have been writing! And I always calculate that you see those I send to Father and Mother, so you must not expect a long one now. The other day I was at Agra, and met Oliphant of Exeter there. The one without the spectacles. He is a new arrival, and had the ill-fortune to break his collar-bone playing hockey almost as soon as he came. Just the day I was there he had it taken out of the splints. The St. John's College Agra people are many of them notable people whom you know, as Norman Tubbs, with whom I had breakfast and who's very well, Arthur Davies, very occupied just now in the building of the new college for which he is himself providing many thousands of pounds, he is a very rich man, and Sully. A very pleasant lot they were, and I liked them much. At the same time none of them has won the hold over India that Rudra and A. have. Then at the end of last week or rather on last Sunday I was in Calcutta, and went out to see the Martinière College. It's a long distance from the station and took me hours to find, for it stands back from the main roads and is hidden by trees. I actually walked down the road in which it is and went on without seeing it. It's a large building looking very old compared with the modern government offices everywhere else and is picturesque. It was the only thing I saw or wanted to see in Calcutta.

You'll see from my letter to Mother about my river-trip to Dacca, a wonderfully picturesque journey. Also about my Christmas day in Bolpur. I guess you did not think of me as likely to be preaching to 200 boys in a grove of mango-trees. Yet so it fell out. They asked me, and it was a clear call not to be denied. Well I'm not in the mood for writing so I'll say no more. Mother gives me news of you; occasionally unfortunate as when you are overworked but generally good. And because you have thus fallen into a pleasant place I rejoice.

                    Good-night,
                              Yours lovingly,

                                        WILL

                                   ST. STEPHEN'S COLLEGE
                                              3/1/14
DEAR MOTHER

By now I trust you are quite better, and not to be troubled again. It seemed so strange getting no letter from you last week. Please thank Frank for his, and for the Tram enclosure and Beazley's lines.

I hope it was as he said and that you were only tired. It makes me keen to see next week's mail. I had a letter from Mr. Jane, who is very grateful to you for your looking after Morwenna, but who made no mention of my present to her, which makes me keen also to get news of whether it arrived safely or not. The shop was responsible for its passage. Those were all the letters I had, and from Jane's I gathered news that Alex Wilkinson the O.U.A.C. secretary had been sent down which is bad luck on the Varsity but removes one good jumper from Frank's path. The latter needn't worry much though: let him get advice from Vassall if he has a chance but not seek him out specially to ask him for it.

As to Arnie, not having been moved up, so much the better. The emptier his brain is of new facts the better, and Mr. Hall's is a hard class to get on in with comfort. Tell Arnie to walk about a bit and get to know the hills round Oxford. That's the thing for him.

The other day, Saturday, was a holiday owing to its being a Hindu

festival, and I spent it out alone all day. I wandered down the far bank
of the river through a forest of scrub and pampas-grass, and on the way
saw a civet-cat. At least that's what I identify it as (and S.), it was like
a big heavily built animal of the cat tribe, which I would have called a
leopard only it had no spots. I had a very pleasant swim that day too
in the Jumna, which is at present low and shallow, but with swift deep
channels every now and then. Mostly I spend the small amount of spare
time I have in walking about with Mr. Rudra, who's not very strong
and goes slowly. He sends his kind regards to you. It's changed
strangely in weather recently, and last night it actually rained! S. and
I were caught in the first drops but got downstairs in time. Now to-day
there's a cold north-west wind and the ground is wet. Still they say it
is too late now: that the crops have all been killed by the drought.
Ever since I came out famine relief operations have been going
on round Agra and south into Gwalior State. I prefer the sunshine of
the past few weeks to the bluster of today: somehow it seems out of
place. So far it's never been more than pleasantly warm in the sun,
and we are still wearing our winter things. In fact just now I've got
a woollen waistcoat on, since the sun is down and my window is
open.

Next week there are exams. which will give us less to do for a
few days and then more when it comes to correcting papers. I've set
three papers, which is a new sort of experience. But it's all in the
day's work.

I heard from Pearson today who seems to have been useful. And
yesterday came news from Hughes in China, who is well, with his
wife and child, and from Tagore. The other day the boys I saw at
Dacca sent me their photographs: all this means that I have a largish
correspondence outside the home mail. Naryana sends his kindest
regards.

Somehow this paper has got stained and greasy, probably with
Boracic Ointment, but it seems extravagant not to use it. So forgive
the oily corner.

I'll put in another slip of writing tomorrow. Wish I could wait till
I heard you were about again and Father's cold gone as I hope next
mail will bring me.

No more news from Ned, which I won't expect for weeks and
weeks. Glad he's got Dahoum with him.

5/1/14

The wild winds continue, which is a great change. We are all very well here, and my work interests me quite well. Also I am getting a little more time to myself.

C. is a delightful fellow. But he and S. will be both returning in the spring, which will make things less pleasant for me.

Well that's all for this week.

Your loving

WILL

DELHI 8/1/14

DEAR MOTHER

It was hard on Arnie getting that sprained ankle. They are things which seem almost bound to come sooner or later but in his case he's started quickly and I hope it will mean has got them over for good. Let him take care of it well for a long time, and use it in walking and straight running a lot, and it will be none the worse. It's when it goes the second and third time that it gets weak.

Meanwhile I expect he's had a good rest from school-work. You must get him to work in the garden and help you there. I'm glad the Campanula is still alive. What a time it has lasted! But I should fear it won't throw up any young plant now.

I've sent a silver cup to Henry for his little son. Delhi work it is, of the Indian bazaar, and therefore rather rough but well ornamented. You must get him to show it you sometime. Indian silversmiths naturally do not use our English system of stamping, but this is guaranteed silver. As to how I feel being made a godfather I'm pleased to think of anyone in my charge even to that extent, though I fear that over this distance it will be but a nominal position in a way. It was a compliment being asked. The child is fairly sure to be a healthy one and to turn out an effective man, with parents such as it has.

It is interesting to hear of Bob's Indian Colonel. The village we go to is Kotgarh. I don't know if I'll necessarily go there, though I'll try to as Captain Young will be there, and it's the home of Stokes. The latter by the by has a child, a son, recently born to him. Let me try to give you an idea of my ordinary life while College is on. S. and I sleep in Rudra's house, but take meals on the opposite side of the road, at Maitland House, with Jenkin, C., Mukerjee and P. N. F. Young.

About 7.0 o'clock as the sun is getting up I do, from my bed on the roof of the house. Then I go over at 7.45 to Maitland House, and for an hour work at Urdu (Hindustani) with Jenkin. I've had very little time as yet for private work at this so have not done much.

At nine we have breakfast. Porridge and some second course probably a hash of stewed meat and vegetables. Then at 9.40 I take a lecture in English for an hour, explaining a book to a class of 50 3rd year students. At 10.40 I have three people for an hour and teach them history. This is three times in the week only. At 11.40 I take a class in physical drill for 20 minutes. From 12 till 1 I sit in my room and correct the essays of my English Class. Then I eat some lunch (cold pudding toast butter fruit). Then an hour's more private work with individual pupils.

At 3.30 I take a boy in English for half-an-hour. This I do because Pearson used to, and the boy is R., the lad at whose wedding I assisted.

Three times a week at 6.0 o'clock I take an M.A. class in history, and this is the work which calls for thinking in preparation. I'm teaching them Political Science and like the work.

And after 8 o'clock dinner I commonly go down to read with R.'s father, S.S. His house is about 100 yards off, set about with a garden of palms, and there I spend an hour in a great marble room covered with carpets, coaching him in English. This is important work because he is 36, yet the most prominent Delhi grandee, and likely to be a power in the future. We read poetry together or else talk, on such diverse subjects as religion, toleration, marriage-customs, teetotalism and the like.

Besides this I am going to teach English to a wild Hill-man, a Pathan soldier, in return for the privilege of picking his barbaric brains. He knows English fairly well, to speak, and write, practise only in pronunciation and reading. This only for a few weeks. You see I'm fairly busy. Exercise I take only occasionally in the form of tennis: more often it has to be in walks with Rudra who goes slowly, or with one of my pupils. At present I'm not taking any scripture.

The College stands close to the Kashmir Gate, that is, just on the outside of the town. Beyond gardens lie with roads running through them leading to the Civil Lines, like the suburb of a town. Next to the College is St. James' Church, the main church of Delhi. Kashmir Gate took a great deal of capturing in the time of the Mutiny, and the wall near it still shows the signs of the guns. And just outside it is an impressive statue of John Nicholson.

Delhi itself—that is the main Indian city—is about a mile away inside the walls though of course there are houses everywhere round here. I'll try and describe the city to you some other time.

Frank might tell Zechariah of Merton when he meets him that I met a relative of his at Ernakulam, a vakil of the court there. I would write to him myself if I had more time, but I am not likely to. I have quite a large correspondence with people up and down India already, which with letters home takes up my spare time.

The weather is very charming. The evenings are milder than a month ago. Thus I motored yesterday afternoon without a thick coat (in S.S.'s car. I was with him at a garden-party for Indians only).

The Oxford City Council is a strangely obstinate body. One would think they would accept Morris' scheme as a way out of all their difficulties. But they seem to have no sense. Mrs. M. the other day sent kind regards to you. I am very well, and find content in what I'm doing at present.

The books you sent were both very interesting. But Hardwar and the Gurukul to which I went is not that direction. Kashmir is west of this, and Hardwar East. Arnie will find Dehra Dun, or Saharanpur on the map for you, and the Gurukul is close to them, on the Ganges.

All the men here are very pleasant, and you must imagine me quite at home.

It's good to hear of you all being well.

with very best love

WILL

MAITLAND HOUSE
KASHMIR GATE
DELHI
15/1/14

DEAR MOTHER

I was very sorry to hear in your last mail's letter about the smashing of the frame. It was careless of me, but it will be a warning at any rate of what to expect. It was pretty, but badly made—by the people of Bethlehem.

With your letter came a postcard and another card from Jerusalem and from Tiberias. I am sending the card from Jerusalem because it is pretty. It was sent me by a German friend I made there, a man I must have told you about, who was very jolly to me on my trip there. Dr. Torrance is very well. If ever he returns to England I must try and get him to see you. Just the type of missionary you'd approve of.

I am sorry too about the colds. Likewise about Mrs. Abbott. I fancy her eldest son is at Lahore, but have no wish to see him. Farozpur is not far off, between here and Lahore. Thanks for the news about Ned. I haven't had more than the one letter from him, and have only written to him twice—one just a week ago.

It was very kind of the Barkers to make you a present, but indeed they're the best people. I haven't sent them anything at all, for I've seen nothing suitable. Still the expedition to Bengal would not have been made had it not been for Mrs. Barker. It has almost completed my bird's-eye view of all India.

As to Miss Wright, it is fortunate she's as great as she is, for not many things could break her down. If I have time I'll write again to her. I did send some shells to Nellie I fancy.

The only news I have to tell is of a Garden-Party I went to the other day to meet the members of the Imperial Legislative Council. Most of these are Indians, and the Chief Commissioner had got a great crowd of Delhi society together to meet them. It made a pretty show, but the English were of a fairly low-class appearance I thought, for all their titles. Hailey, the Chief Commissioner, is an excellent person. Tonight I am dining out with the Under-Secretary for Education, an Indian Christian who would have been Prince of Kapurthala if it wasn't for his religion. He was at Eton, and boxed for Oxford against Cambridge, so he's a very Englished type. I am very busy but am keeping fit as can be. The weather is charming, not so cold as a few weeks ago, and with all our work the days pass very quickly. Altogether I feel very much at my ease here, among a splendid lot of fellows.

But I'm too slack to write more just now. The stamps of native States I promised Arnie are not yet forthcoming. Sorry. As to Henry's baby, Lawrence is the best way out of the Jimmy difficulty if they want to call him after me. This week I have no time to write more than this letter, but I wrote to Mrs. Hen. last mail.

I do hope Father soon got rid of his cold, and that Arnie's ankle made a firm recovery. To Florence love if you write to her. Well now I must stop

with best love to you all

your son

WILL

Mr. Paton has sent me a photo. of his baby, a boy. I've mislaid the postcard. Will send it next week.

DELHI

22/1/14

DEAR MOTHER

Another mail-day, and half-an-hour for me to write in before my History class arrives. I don't expect I'll get the letter finished till after dinner, but meanwhile I hurry.

Such a crop of letters I had last week, one from Ned, from Bob, from Father and yours. Ned's was exciting, only a few sentences but with great romance in them. Of course you know. He had been wired for by the Palestine Exploration fund, and was off at once for Jaffa. It's very great that he has got into that job, quite the best in modern times in his line. And they too have got a useful man. He knew nothing at all when he wrote of the line of country to be explored; only that it was Arabia Petræa, which means more or less the country south-east of the Dead Sea. He'll probably take Dahoum with him, which will make him safe from any ruffians.

He said he had seen Busrawi, who had sent me in a carpet, which he was going to sell. Otherwise there was no news except the great one, which was natural. He must have been excited.

So glad ——————— turned up. I daresay I will get a letter from him next mail, which will be a great treat. As to his appearance, it could not be otherwise than changed for the worse: still I hope it may change back for the better some day. Anyhow you needn't worry about him being with Frank: he has got sense and consideration enough not to compromise anyone's reputation. I remember how he avoided a fresher he knew at St. John's, so that nobody would suspect the man of being of like sort to himself. He's my friend, so I want to hear quickly.

Sorry about Mrs. Abbott, but it sounds the sort of case where lingering on is no blessing: like Mrs. Davies of Hythe.

Thank you for all the various papers and cuttings you have sent me, and again for the books which have been a great pleasure. There's not much time for reading here, and I haven't finished the Kashmir one yet, but it's good, very. S. talks of my going with him over the Pamirs, from Shrinagar into Russian Central Asia, or rather the other way round, in two years' time. As to that, it's only a wildcat scheme at present, attractive but with several difficulties in the way. I don't look ahead at all though: his plan not mine. My work here at present is enough. My best and nicest pupil, the man with whom I went to Jaipur, will not be able to take his M.A. exam. owing to a technical flaw in his qualifications, which is an annoyance. Very. Otherwise very little has happened. The other day I squeezed in a ride on horseback into my time, and had a very good rush round the sandy paths of the new city, which is being laid down. Father's letter mentions that his arm is still full of rheumatism. I hope it's right again now. Please take this as thanks for the note, at present. I will not be able to write more just now than this one note.

I'm looking after C. B. Young's Hostel at present: that is I sleep there at night, no more. It's about a mile from the college, outside the walls. He has gone to a Baptist Conference at Calcutta. My being there is no trouble at all to me.

I'm very well. Hoping you too are all of you flourishing

your loving

WILL

MAITLAND HOUSE
28/1/14

DEAR MOTHER,

We have had a holiday today, for a sad enough reason, the death of A.'s Mother. Out of show of sympathy work has stopped. As a result I have spent the day afoot with Braja Bhattacharya, my Bengali from Jaipur, and now at six in the evening I have time to write to you at length. The last mail brought me a good deal of interest. Your letter first, with little news in it except that you hadn't been able to go to Father owing to feeling unfit (you hadn't mentioned this before). Also you spoke in it of Ned's journey telling me more than he did; he spoke only of Arabia Petræa. This is the greatest chance he has had yet, I fancy. And you commented on Marsh-Roberts' appearance.

At a change I don't wonder. He's sent me two long letters (at least one is long) and they are a catalogue of misfortunes, which I had fore-seen it's true and warned him against, some of them, but which are enough to change anyone. Poor Cyril! I have hope of him yet, but it's harder to get back than to go, and he has none to help him along hardly. Please thank Frank for his letter about him. Some of it was news to me, others not. His account of himself is nearly always made worse than truth. Well, I have written to him in answer, and hope to resume a regular exchange of letters.

Ezra Pound wrote to me too, a wonderful letter, and with it sent a lot of strange new poems. Awful rot many of them, and meant to be so, just skits and satires. When he is serious he is very good for me. I was glad to hear from him again. Perhaps he will do something for Marsh. Artie Kerry also wrote, a very comfortable letter to get. He's not going to be damaged anyway. Also I heard from Hartley, in New York, Haines, one of St. John's old people, and Yano of Japan. Quite a budget, for in addition to your's and Frank's from home there were letters from Florence (I can't answer instante so please thank her from me) and from Mr. H. G. Grey. Well, all this was very jolly, though Cyril's sent me out afoot awhile, and in the course of a night walk I saw a hyæna which Arnie would have liked. A big dog-like beast with heavy forequarters and a noise like loud chattering of teeth. It followed me along the side of the road for awhile, which was quite amusing. Don't imagine this was anything foolish: I live a highly quiet and respectable life, and walk about a great deal with Mr. Rudra, who sends his kind regards. In fact I've succeeded to A.'s position in a kind of way as Rudra's companion, and what's more, do what he tells me, which A. would not do.

Well. Today I went awalking, which will give me a chance to give you a view if possible of Delhi. Braja and I left the College soon after midday, when the sun was very fairly hot (I've still thick clothes on though. Shirt waistcoat and coat). From the College to the Kashmiri Gate is about a hundred yards. The gate is of two arches, in red brick-work like the wall of Delhi generally, but beside the arches is a narrow passage of jagged work through which Nicholson rushed the gate. That we went through, and so came outside. To the left and right the city wall stretches more or less unbroken, low and not very formidable though, toy-work compared with Norman masonry. The road split up into many avenues leading amongst fields and gardens, which are quite dusty and dried up mostly; only occasionally where there is a great expenditure of water there is green grass and flowers, with great purple clumps of Bougainvilia. On the right we passed such a garden, with a great bronze statue of John Nicholson in it, a tall strongly built bearded man with a sword, powerful work. Then a mile or so of road with trees along it (acacias mostly) and we came to the Ridge, which is a slight rise where naked rock crops out as it does in a quarry (it is largely an old quarry) and where goats browse amongst wild bushes. Altogether a barren looking spot enough, marked at the top with a monument in red stone, not unlike the Martyr's Memorial in shape. The ridge runs for miles, and gives quite a good view, but it can't be more than 100 feet above the level of the plain. I doubt if it's more or so much. Looking back from it to Delhi one sees factory chimneys, smoke, trees in great quantities, wireless telegraphy poles, and the minarets and dome of the Jama Musjid. This is probably in Arnie's book *The Wonders of the World*, but looks to me like a couple of captive balloons resting between two brick-work chimneys. We crossed the ridge and after more wild rocks crossed the end of the golf-links (a sandy course) and came into a suburb. Bhattacharya had never been there before, but I had: in fact I know Delhi better than most of the students whom I've talked with, and certainly better than the Maitland House people. That's owing to an exploring instinct which leads me among its winding alleys overhung with trellised balconies, to which quaint carved gateways give admittance over running refuse and water in the gutters. These alleys are filled by a donkey and a load: of them more later.

Well, Braja and I went along a dusty lane which was fringed on one side by a grove of pomegranates and on the other by palms in a garden. Here were old tombs of the Moghul nobles, nameless now and neglected but showing signs of old magnificence. The lane is wide as the Woodstock Road, but with ever a bend in it, and the dust lies inches deep, stirred into clouds by the passing say of a donkey with a man on it in turban shirt and pyjama trousers, or by women coming from the wells. It's the lane above all others here which has a flavour in it of the Holy Land, and I've frequented it in consequence. After a while we turned off and entered a garden, the Roshanora Gardens. This was built by Aurunzeb, the Moghul Emperor (Charles I's time) for his

sister Roshanora, and has her tomb within it. Red sandy paths run
between green bamboo clumps, under mango-trees and peepuls, ban-
yans and jack-trees, while on one part there is a large pond, unique in
Delhi, overgrown with rushes and set about with palms. Here are
waterfowl, and chattering parrots mostly green. I love to sit by its side
(which I've only done twice though. Once on a Sunday with Mr.
Rudra, and once today). As for the flowers of the garden, flowers are
dying away now, though had it rained at the usual time spring would
be coming. There are many roses in Delhi gardens though now (S.S.
my friend has 60 varieties) and there is Bougainvilia which is glorious,
almond blossom (not common) and here in Roshanora's garden violets
in pots, hundreds of them.

. After a long time we left the garden and walking out into the
Suburb took an electric tram! This ran us through a long business
street, past the Hospital for Women of the Cambridge Mission, over
a railway bridge and a canal bridge (where barges unlade wood, a
goodly sight), then through another long business street, over another
railway bridge, and through a crowded thoroughfare where there are
always camel-carts and ox-carts blocking up the way. A camel-cart is
like a cage on four wheels to which the camel is harnessed—it always
looks too big for its cart, like a donkey with a perambulator. This is
the grain-market of Delhi, and it is as though Hythe Bridge street were
a line of open shops like our blacksmiths', full of sacks of meal and
grain. Men of all the races of the East go to and fro in it. Them I must
try and describe some other time. We got down off the tram at the
entrance to the Chaori Bazaar, where iron-workers sell their goods.
At its entrance is a very fine fruit-shop, fine that is for picturesque effect,
like a coal-cellar of stone work open to the day-light, and full of
oranges. A street to the left led us up to a turn down which I took the
bewildered Bhattacharya who knew not the way, and showed him
what I think is the finest thing in Delhi. About the finest thing in the
brick and stone line I've seen in India, the Kala Musjed. Imagine a great
series of steps bringing you up thirty feet or so to where a small doorway is bounded by two towers. Great massive walls run out each side,
and over the battlements show the tops of a score or so of beehive
domes. From outside the Turkman gate, as I saw it some days ago from
the back of a horse, it has the same marvellous feel of solidity. There's
something which I call Spanish in its effect. It's all of rugged bits of

dark brown stone . . . . From the top of it one gets a splendid view
of Delhi, just a crowd of flat roofs, one or two trees, the Juma Musjid
with its captive balloons, the wall all round the city, and outside flat
country with many trees on the dusty ground (how they grow I
can't imagine) and the little low line of the ridge. Boys are often on the
houseroofs playing with kites, while the real birds soar high above the
city and many doves wheel round. Then we came back through winding streets I knew of, which are like lanes and remind me of the back
of our house at Dinard because there are open spaces every now and
then among them where goats try to graze and add to the filth that
blocks the gutter. They brought us to the Chaori Bazaar at the end of
which is the Jama Masjid. But we turned into an alley near the Bazaar
which led through an archway of old stone work, and then along a
typical old Delhi track, like one of the Rows of Great Yarmouth or the
Ditches of Southampton, or a row in St. Aldate's Street. Narrower a
good deal than Friar's Entry it ran between high walls with every now
and then a latticed window, a balcony, an old carved front to catch the
eyes upward, or a stone-work door or gateway down below. Occasionally there are open shop-fronts like the booths of St. Giles' fair, where
men sit all day working in the leisurely way of those who are their own
masters. There are always gutters in these alleys, but not always water
in them. And as to sunlight, that can hardly ever come there. I've been
exploring a good deal with Mr. Rudra, and have walked about with
S. But mainly I got my knowledge of the place in my first week here
when with no work and everyone else engaged I spent my mornings
afoot. Now I'm seldom at a loss, and will be able to act showman of
Delhi whenever anyone comes to be shown round. From these Rows
it's not far to the College. First they lead into the street of the Gold-
smith's (poor compared to those of Aleppo) then one passes the Silver-
smith's Bazaar, (cp. my silver cup for my Godson), into the main
bazaar of Delhi of which they are no end proud. That's about ten
minutes' walk from the College through a garden, across a wooden
foot-bridge over the railway-station, into the houses amongst which
St. Stephen's College stands.

Well, I've put it all down, and now it's half-past seven and I must
get ready for dinner.

I've just had a couple of photographs sent me from the boys I met
at Dacca: the elder one who had been at Bolpur is a fine specimen of

the Bengalis. And they are people whose fine specimens are very fine indeed. Well I'll write the next sentences tomorrow.

29/1/14

No news. I'm very fit indeed, and enjoying life. Also I'm making friends.

I wish I could do more than just send you a message of love over the wall of the distance.

Well, to all of you

Your loving

WILL

MAITLAND HOUSE

7/2/14

DEAR MOTHER

It's a holiday today owing to the exams., so I have the time to myself, which I want to spend in writing a letter between you and me. I've just come in from a ride on one of S.S.'s horses, a great gallop it was, terrific fun. As I spend a good deal of my time with him and take no fee for it, I have a right in my opinion to take an occasional ride of him. He is always offering me motor drives which I'm not so keen on.

Yesterday I spent most of the day driving about the town with a young couple of tourists here. They were Mr. and Mrs. Cadbury, Quakers. The man has been managing the *Daily News* for some time, and his father is proprietor of it and many other papers. So I rather welcomed the chance of influencing him. His wife was very nice in a quiet way, and was interested in girls' schools, so I showed her those we have. The Cambridge Mission has two, both Purdah schools (i.e. men can't look over them). The Baptists have another. But by far the most important is the School belonging to the Theosophists (Mrs. Annie Besant etc.). It's managed by two worn old Australian ladies—they are very much out of touch with the European community so I've seen a little of them just to cheer them up—and it has 300 girls in it of ages ranging from 6 to 23. It's not purdah; I have been all over it inspecting the girls' work, and a very jolly lot of little people they are, all Hindus. Theosophists aim at a reformed Hinduism, which is in the right direction at any rate. They may be doing good or they may not:

for my part I think these ladies are, for there's no sign of any harm in them themselves.

As to my own work here, I feel that so far as ordinary secular teaching goes I'm quite effective. In fact the students approve of my way of putting things. But of course that wasn't what I came out here for. On the other side these men are very willing to talk, and some of them want to argue. Thus I took a Scripture class the other day for M., and my impression is at any rate that many of the students read only to find avenues of attack. From that one experience I have no wish to go on in any class religious teaching. It's intellectual, and though it may do good doesn't appeal to me. Privately men who think often want to talk, and I've got to know one of my pupils, Bhattacharya, very well. He's a charming man, mostly an archæologist and artist. I feel strongly within me that in a college of this sort religion is made much too much of an intellectual thing only, cold-blooded at that. I want to be friend rather than teacher of my people.

If you asked me what I had done while I had been out I would think first of Rabindranath Tagore's school, when I was definitely given words to say, and secondly of a lot of talks I've had here with X., who's a troubled soul. He's going home to England in the spring with S.— it will be less pleasant here without them—and will probably go to Cuddesdon so I hope you will see him, some. A very charming person.

Stokes is coming to Delhi tonight, and I hope to see him tomorrow. He's a great landowner up in the hills now, a long way from his old position, and has a new-born son. A strange lack of consistency in his life, but his various impulses all seem to lead him to good results. There now as Zemindar he's making his villagers most happy. I had a long letter from Hughes in China last week, and he prospers. He has various plans for my future at which he is always hinting. But I have none. It seems to me that this position here suits me well for the present, and I'm contented in it. But an ordinary professor here, as M. is, I couldn't wish to become. Sometime no doubt I will see what I am to do. At present I don't think about it, except just now for the first time for many days. When Cadbury however asked me wherein lay the hope for India I could think of little in India at present but Tagore and Mahatma Munshi Ram of the Gurukul. I heard from Tagore last week. Men are much too fond of generalising about India. In my first-impressionist sort of journeys I've seen enough to know that any idea of a unified nation is as far off the point as is talk of a unified Europe. Undoubtedly England alone keeps the whole Indian continent together. At the same time she does it with a very unequal sort of staff (several officials I've seen are rotten. Others, as Hailey, would lead anywhere), and there's great social bitterness between European, Eurasian and Indian. A Eurasian woman for example whom I trotted round to various officials the other day (she was trying to recover her daughter who had been carried off, and came to me as head of the Baptist Mission in C. B. Young's place) spoke more bitterly of 'natives' than I've yet heard in cold blood, and she was darker than almost any of them. In anger I've heard English people abuse Indians in a way in which they couldn't possibly behave at home. And rich Indian gentlemen resent not being allowed to drive up to the door of officials' houses as English people of the meanest sort can do, and dislike being expected to salute any Englishmen they meet. It seems to me that the mental and cultural equality in every way of such men as Sir Syed Ali Imam (head of Indian Moslems and a man I've seen quite a lot of) and Maharaj Singh K   Sahib the Under-Secretary for Education (who is often playing tennis with us) with any Englishman, has made the colour-bar become more intense as the only distinguishing feature. If I was an Indian I would be bound to feel a bit bitter when a man I knew well at Oxford cut me dead out here, yet that is what happens. It's not true of the whole lot of English, but it is the general tone of society. There are heaps of exceptions, especially the Civilians and the Army men. Bankers and business people of all sorts are the real limit.

Well, you see I have been putting down some generalities, which is a dangerous thing to do. But there's a mixture of servility and suspicion towards us, even from some men in the college, which makes one bound to notice things. It must be quite easy to become an alarmist in this land.

Frank's birthday it is today I know, and I wonder what he will do to celebrate it. I guess you'll find him quite fit for life in College now: he's played up well over the Oriental in Oxford question. If he comes out to the Indian army he'll find it stand to him that he's been able to make friends with the Oxford outsiders. And I could wish him no better messmates than two or three officers in Indian regiments I've met since I left home.

SUNDAY

Your letter about Arnie's measles came soon after I had written the above. Poor little man. It seems so hard that I can't even go and talk to him for a few minutes, and cheer him up. I will wait your next week's mail with eagerness, and hope I'll get some news in it of his recovery.

I must write to Fernand: so far only a postcard has gone to him. Can you please thank Mrs. Vincent for a letter she has sent me, and a calendar: I don't know when I'll be able to answer her myself. It's good that you're better yourself, and that Father is well. As for me I flourish exceedingly; the weather here is still very charming.

Stokes came to dinner at Maitland House last night, and is coming in again this evening probably. A small neatly built man like an officer, with a moustache and no beard now, and beautiful eyes. He seemed full of commonsense and very far from the impulsive A.-like person I had rather expected.

Well I'll go on with this later.

12/2/14

I've just been writing to Ned, and have also sent a note to Fernand, and one to John Snow. I've been longing to hear how Arnie is, and will be very glad to get next week's mail the day after tomorrow. I had thought of going down to Jhansi today and stopping there over the week-end. That would have been with Captain Young. But I haven't done so, partly because of a wish to stop here and coach a particular pupil, and partly because I've ricked my shoulder slightly, and want to be quite at the best of my form when with Young, who will probably give me a sporting game.

Yesterday we had a baby four months old stopping in Maitland House, which was a bit of a change. It's father and mother have now taken it on to Peshawar.

I'm enclosing one Jaipur State stamp for Arnie as a prophecy of more to follow when my pupil Bhattacharya gets them for me.

Henry wrote to me last mail, and is clearly happy enough.

With love to you all

WILL

12/2/14

My dear Arnie

I feel that I must write to you tonight when you have been ill, though at first I thought I would go to bed. It's bad luck on you getting measles badly: what I'm looking for is a letter on Saturday which will tell me that you are all right again.

It was wonderful that you got the Scholarship, and you've made us all proud. But do remember that we want to be proud of you athletically too. Don't give up plenty of walking, which is the real thing to build on.

Out here none of the Indians of Delhi think of taking a walk for the sake of pleasure hardly. They all thought a couple of men were mad whom I persuaded to go for a tour of 150 miles to Agra. But really it's an excellent country and climate at present for trotting about in. I go wandering about in the jungle on the far side of the river quite a lot.

Mother need not be afraid of my doing anything rash in the bathing line. There are no crocodiles in the Jumna just about here at present: only plenty of fish and large tortoises the size of soup-plates which sit on the bank and slide into the water when one approaches. In the jungle I've seen one civet-cat, like a small leopard, a long low spotted beast about the size of a collie-dog. And in the night I saw or more truly heard a hyæna once. Otherwise I haven't seen much in the way of wild animals at Delhi. Down near Agra I saw vast herds of wild deer, and lower down near the Narbada river wolves. The jackals however howl in chorus in the gardens round Delhi every night, a wonderful row.

For birds, there are always kites and hawks and vultures in the sky. Most big flapping hook-beaked birds which fly heavily along the river bank are kites I believe, but they are large as turkeys and I would call them vultures. They live on carrion. Then there are parrots, hoopoes (beautiful birds—see some book), woodpeckers of gorgeous colouring, doves all over the place, and a small bird who makes a noise like the sound of metal striking metal, and who is so named the Coppersmith bird. He goes on all day long without remission. In the narrow alleys of the town as one walks about one sees mongooses appearing out of the drains, like ferrets they are, and then on all buildings, nesting in all trees, and as common as sparrows are small squirrels marked grey and white in rings like lemurs. Lizards are common too, but not very beautiful ones, and there are heaps of insects.

For trees they look mostly like English ones, except for the palms. The neem-tree is very like an acacia and the pepul is like a poplar. Mangoes have fine dark green leaves: their fruit I have not yet tasted but am told it is delicious. The trees contrive to remain green in a wonderful way considering the deep dust in the roads.

As to flowers, the bougainvilias and poinsettias are the most notable, apart from lovely roses. Mimosas are everywhere and smell beautiful, they are little yellow balls of fluff on a tree like a laburnum in shape. Poinsettias are large red leaves sprayed like the open sheath of a lily backwards on green foliage. Pomegranate flowers are pretty, fleshy red trumpets. There aren't many wild flowers just now.

I wonder if you saw the *Illustrated London News* of January 24. M. shewed it to me the other day, and it had four pages about Carchemish, pictures and an article.

Today I was helping S. who got stuck in the middle of a story he was writing for a boy-cousin of his, a most marvellous tale of pirates smugglers and boy scouts. After that I wrote a letter to the Vice-Chancellor of Calcutta University for one of my pupils. Then I wrote a literary review to give to Stokes. And before dinner I taught French grammar for an hour. In the morning I took charge of an examination.

Thus I'm very busy, in an interesting way.

Well cheer-oh and farewell and may this find you well again

your brother

WILL

DELHI 26/2/14

DEAR MOTHER

Once again I haven't much time to write to you in. Any minute I may be interrupted by some students whom I'm coaching for some acting at Speech-Day. Yet I've some news.

First of all though about your last letter. It's good to know that Arnie is getting better. He must have been very bad with it though, and for you all alone at meals as you say it was sad. It is a long way away that we all are from each other. As to the Church here I'm afraid it's a lifeless enough place, with a chaplain who talks of unimportant things in the superlative, and seldom says anything unusual. A good enough fellow all the same. There are three churches in Delhi, together with a Roman Catholic and a Baptist Chapel. Presently I really must go and see if the last is more awake than the English ones.

I haven't heard from Ned since the letter he wrote on the point of leaving Jerablus, so your news of him is interesting. This journey is a great one for him. Thanks for the *Illustrated London News*, which is good to have by one.

Yesterday I was at a Garden-Party to meet the Viceroy and the Commander-in-Chief, which has been our chief excitement in Delhi recently. There is great uneasiness in the city at present on account of some police discoveries, and they fear there's real sedition (one of the College students has been under arrest for the past week, and another man I know also). Therefore the most elaborate precautions were taken at this show, and only a very small gathering collected. I got invited, with the rest of the staff, because one of the hosts was a Maharaja who knows us. Not very regal, and quite a place where one could enjoy oneself it was, and as I know most of the Maharajas in Delhi now owing to meeting them at S.S.'s, it was all right. One of them, a renowned fighting-man of the old school, who has his own regiment of lancers and is at present stopping in Delhi with a train of about 50 camels and crowds of horses, has invited me to go out hawking with him. He hawks from camel-back, with great falcons, and is very much of a mediæval nobleman; he's famous as a supporter of the English, and an advocate of the most military measures. Also men say he is the best horseman in India.

The other day, on Tuesday it was, I took a horse and rode across the river Jumna, just fordable, and had a great gallop on the other side. And at the end of last week I saw the final of the All-India Polo Tournament, a wonderful game. So the days have been pretty full. And on Monday, which was a holiday owing to its being a Hindu Festival, I went to a place 70 miles from here and more, Muzufarnagar, to meet Sir James Meston, the Lieutenant-Governor of the United Provinces, at a Garden-Party. I had lunch with a local landowner, a friend of S.S.'s, who had an elephant in his compound on which he offered me a ride which I did not take. He is a great gardener, and I walked in a field of beans in flower, through a kitchen-garden of sweet-peas and strawberries also in flower. That was a treat, as was afterwards motoring back the 70 miles in the cool of the evening, and the early night.

Thus you'll see I'm still going about a good deal, but it's all to my advantage in learning this land. Work at the College goes on as usual; the only change is that I'm now no longer taking my Pathan soldier, but am taking a Scripture class. I have not done enough at it yet to say what I think of it. The other day one of my pupils, a Moslem M.A. Literature student, asked to come to Church with me, and accepted all the service as in agreement with Islam. Here's a saying of Mohammed's for you, 'Heaven lieth at the feet of Mothers'.

I got a letter from Morwenna the last mail from Biskra in the desert. She seems cheerful enough. And today I had a very long one from Govinda. Letter writing really takes up a great amount of my spare time, and it's a necessity here. Indians are very quickly offended if their letters are not answered, and are very swift to write in a demonstratively friendly way.

Well, that's all for this week. I wish we could see each other. But imagine me very well, cheerful, and not wasting my time.

Love to all of you. I love to think of you as all well again now, and trust I am right. Hope the breakfast was good.

Your loving WILL

{Canon Christopher's great C.M.S. Missionary Breakfast in the Town Hall, Oxford, held annually in February. This was, on account of the war, the only one held after the Canon died on 10th March 1913. There were 570 present, the largest number of all the 37 Breakfasts.}

DELHI 2/3/14
11.0 p.m.

DEAR MOTHER

I've just got back to Delhi tonight, and found your telegram about Arnie. Thank you so much for sending it: I saw it before I looked at the letters, so was able to take the appendicitis as past history. Poor little man. It must have been a terrible time for you all, but there's no need to talk of that now when joy has come that he is splendidly recovering. It was good having Bob with you; he's a tower of strength. Oh, I can imagine it all, and especially Father racing back across the narrow sea. And I'm not going to write any more but just this, and now I'm going to pray about it. One thing though first. It was on the 12th he was so ill, and it was on the 12th I think that I wrote to you enclosing two stamps for him, having first meant to write a letter to him too. But I was so tired, and busy, that I didn't. Then before I went to bed came a great feeling thrust over me that I must write to him, I could not tell why, and after all I did write, with my eyes hardly open yet the impulse forcing along my brain. I think the letter bears me witness. This is only one of several cases that have come to me, and no longer can I have any patience with talk of natural coincidences and post-imagined evidence.

I trust Ned like me will get good news as soon as bad. It would be so terrible also for him to get the letter, even though it too was so hopeful, particularly Bob's. Thank you for them all, but most for the wire.

4/3/14

It's Wednesday now, and I've a little while wherein to write, so here I go again.

It's sad to think of Arnie having been ill, all unknown though not unfelt by me, and of the few of you there to look after each other in your trouble. Such a long way off I am, and so out of reach. Yet dreams bridge the distance easily, and as you see waking dreams too; we're fairly close to each other really. By the time this comes to you, I'm hoping Arnie will be out and about, and all the better through having escaped a previous cause of trouble. But I wish I'd been at hand to help you.

The other day I went down to Jhansi, on Friday, and came back on Monday, after stopping the meanwhile with Captain Young. He gave me a great reception, and the visit was most enjoyable. On the way too I saw Gwalior, the great rock fort of the Marathas, about which I'll write to Arnie. Jhansi itself is famous for its heat, the second hottest place in India, and for its fort which is picturesque from a distance, but which I didn't see near at hand. Young was very interesting, showing me photographs which he had taken, several of Ned for example taken unawares, and of the Carchemish country, as well as a few photos of our visit to the Camp of Busrawi. They were good as reminders to me of what I had seen, but would convey no impression whatever to you. I feel all along the inadequacy of pictures and photos, except good pictures, to give an imaginative vision, which I would like best to call up by words if I could. As it is though the visit to

Busrawi was too good to be passed on second-hand in any way. Young had several writings he shewed to me, War Office reports on the Servo-Turkish war, secret correspondence with the Intelligence department almost, a sketch in words of a journey into Bashan on which he went with Canon Parfit, impressions of Egypt, and some very jolly poems. Also above everything else a theological and philosophical discussion which he read to me, amplifying it with talk for one evening and the small hours of the morning, all about his beliefs in life, and his knowledge of Christ. A strange man he is, but one I admire immensely. As to his theology he's nephew of the Bishop of Durham, and follows him I suppose to a certain extent, but mostly is original in his expression, in agreement with me, and a sheer delight.

5/3/14

Once again I'm starting, and again I want to talk about Arnie but won't. Words are no use to us when we have any real emotion to express, or hardly any use. I'll write to the pet himself. Young was very pleasant in what he said about Ned. They evidently had an excellent time together after I left, spending most of it in making carvings. Also he talked of the possibility of Frank coming to the 116th Mahrattas, about which I will write some other time.

Well, I hope you got a good letter from me the week of your anxiety. And I do trust you're getting quite strong again now. You must have a restful holiday with Arnie and Father after this trouble for you all.

My love to everyone of you. I wish I could write more but there's little time on my hands, and when I've leisure I'm not always in the mood to write.

Your loving

WILL

St. Stephen's College
5/3/14

My dear Arnie

You have had a lot to endure these last few weeks, twisted ankle, measles, and appendicitis, and then an operation. But Mother says you have behaved splendidly, so I'm proud. And now I trust you'll soon be quite strong, with your troubles over for a long time. I'm so so sorry for you, yet it is little use worrying now. And all these things are good if we let them bring the right results; as an essay I set the other day on 'The Use of Pain' was meant to make the students see.

Now let me tell you some of the things I've been doing. First of all about Gwalior. There's probably a photo. of that in your *The Wonders of the World*. It's a narrow plateau a few hundreds of yards wide and a mile or so long, with its sides sheer cliffs. On the top of them run the walls, outer and inner, with two great fortified gates. I walked up to one of them, a twisting steep way giving a great view over the plain, and then passed under the second gateway where soldiers were standing. The first gateway was at the foot of the hill. Inside it was just a clear space with barracks in places, a temple or two with Buddhist carvings, and some government buildings. I stood on the rampart and leant out, and the ground was far away at my feet, down the steep wall to where the sharp face of the rock was bearded with ivy, down, down, to at last the gardens and the road where donkeys and camels and bullock-carts passed along. There were tanks inside the walls with water lying, and one bright tree like almond-blossom but with great azalea-like flowers. I picked one, and send the petals of it to you, hoping they will give you a glimpse of the colours, just like our almond tree but brighter far. Then I went out by another gate which wound down the hill-side, past carvings on the cliffs, of Buddhas and similar figures. One figure of a man was quite 50 feet high, a wonderful sight. And after a walk of a mile or so there was Laskar, another town, with the palace of the Maharaja of Gwalior, another sight to see.

After Gwalior I went on to Jhansi, and stopped with Young. The first thing there was the sports of his regiment, tent-pegging, running races, obstacle-races, all sorts, ending with a dance of a Mahratta kind in which men leap about hitting sticks against each other quite in the style of the Morris-dances Mother and I saw at Kelmscott once. At these sports I met a man I knew, Captain Fraser of the Berkshire Regiment, which was queer.

It was a pity you couldn't see me on the Monday, mounted on a long-tailed cream-coloured horse which could gallop like the wind, inspecting the recruits of the regiment. Young asked me to go pig-sticking too with him, but my riding is not good enough for that. Then coming back there was a wonderful storm of lightning. It had been very hot at Jhansi, real Indian hot-weather as all the officers in the Mess testified, and this was the end of it for awhile. But as the train rushed along between Muttra and Delhi the lightning was almost one continuous flicker, and I saw the country, domes, tombs, trees, and fields as though in a cinematograph.

A better view of the country was in my journey by motor car with S.S. the previous Monday. I must have described that in my last letter, but it was great, that 70 mile swoop through the level country as the sun went down. And I was very delighted too with the flowers and the bean-field at Muzafarnagar. There is much to admire in this country. And now the sun-sets are getting very fine: Mother would like to see them. You will have to have a change after this illness, and so will Mother. I hope you'll find beautiful things too: it's merely a question of seeing them, for the real artist can make a fine picture out of a sky-scraper. The thing that I like best in the way of buildings in Delhi is the Kala Musjid, but the Pearl Mosque which must be shown in your 'wonders' is another thing to give one joy. Those *The Wonders of the World* are useful to help you to see where I go perhaps.

Sometime I hope to send you a lot of stamps, but they are rather hard to get hold of. And my stamp-collecting pupil, my nicest pupil in the college, has had to go away to Benares owing to a stupid blunder of the College authorities and of Lahore University. So it will be a little while perhaps before you get them in great quantities.

I wonder how the garden will get on with you not strong for awhile. By the time the spring comes well you must be about and able to help Mother. She must have found it hard to use her time when you were ill, and as to Father, it was very difficult for him indeed. Well, it's time I went to bed, old pet, so now I will shut up. Next week's mail will be good to get, but since Mother sent the telegram I'm all right. It made me quite inclined to wire back rejoicings.

I'm very fit, tell Father, and find my time spent quite usefully. There are three days holiday next week for some Hindu Festival, but I guess I'll lie quiet within Delhi in them, though the Gurukul people invite me away there.

May you be safe and happy

your loving brother   WILL

Please thank Bob and Frank for their letters, and give my love to them and to Father.

12/3/14

DEAR FATHER

It was very good getting your letter and Mother's last week, with news of Arnie, though of course it was not later than the telegram of the week before. That last was a very happy thought, more than repaying itself. You've had a lot to go through indeed, and I wish I could have been with you to share it. That's the worst of this place: it's so far off. But Bob and Frank did the work for us all no doubt. And now that it's over you must be happy. Going to France is a good idea. It's a nuisance Angers is so far off, or I'd say look up Fernand. As it is I suppose one of the Brittany places, or Les Andelys or some place of that sort is better. You won't get golf though.

The alleys of this city seem to have frightened you and Mother. They're very picturesque, a picture in fact at every step, but as you don't like it I won't go there in the future, except with good reason. There's plenty of interest in the city without them, and I wish there was some method of showing it to you but there's none. Picture-postcards and photographs I've looked at sometimes, but seen nothing that would be any use at all. The only book is Arnie's *The Wonders of the World*, and I daresay a book or two in the Union. It needs colour though to show this place, colours and smells and noises, and you don't get them conveyed in anything except a great artist's work. Down at Jhansi the other day I read Kipling's *Kim*, which gives as good a picture as anything else I remember at the moment. But like most of Kipling it's crude in places. He criticized himself rather well when he wrote to an Income-tax clerk to whom he'd pointed out some slight errors and who had retorted that he ought to be too much of a gentleman to notice such details 'I am not a gentleman, and I notice everything.' I'm the only man in India yet that I've met who doesn't adore him all the same.

Ned's letters were good reading. What a time he's having! And it will all come out of him in a book someday that will make him known. I'm keeping the letters for another week, since Captain Young is coming here to stop with me on Saturday, and I may want to show them to him. Please tell Frank that I had a letter last week, one of several, from Marsh-Roberts, and that C. will be looking him (M.-R. I mean) up in a month or so's time. Also after a while S. will see him, since they are all foregathering in the same town. I hope C. will look you up too: he'll be at Cuddesdon, so not far off, and you'll find him a very charming person. What we'll be like without him and S. I don't like to contemplate. I had hoped to have some news for Mrs. Barker this mail, but it hasn't come yet, so if Mother sees her she might say I haven't forgotten.

It's puzzling sometimes here to know what to say to people, and altogether with a staff divided very greatly intellectually, though very good friends, and students who skim over things with their brains rather than dive into them with their hearts, the water is pretty deep. But I find life very good.

Irish news seems pretty futile. '6 years limit' and that sort of thing can not surely be meant seriously. But it looks now as though one way or another there will be trouble, with no way out. The only other thing I've noticed much is the renewed campaign of the revolting women. Strange thing civilization. I'd like to write more this week, but doubt if I will. So please let this do for everyone, and give my love to Arnie in particular. Mother will soon get better I hope.

Appendicitis operations leave people stronger than ever, and the inflammation comes very often I think from some strain. That's why so many Rugger blues have had it some time or other.

I had a letter from Gaussen by the way last mail, and Frank would do no harm if he called on him.

Well, very best love to you all, and health to you

your son

WILL.   I'm very fit.

St. Stephen's College
March 19, 1914

DEAR MOTHER

I've been extra busy these past few days, with the organization of the College Sports, and also the coaching of some students in amateur theatricals. That's for next Saturday, when they will produce Act V Scene I of the *Midsummer Night's Dream*. I'm entirely responsible for the playing, so it means a good deal of work. As for the Sports, they are a three days affair, and we've had two days already, with quite satisfactory results. I wonder what about Frank and the Sports. He has had so much football that he can have had little chance to develop his jumping, which at the best of times is an uncertain sort of performance with everybody.

Last week gave me letters from you and from Father, about Arnie. It is good to know he is going on better, and that the pain was not too great. I read a book the other day in which a Father described what he felt while his little son was operated on for appendicitis, and it had a telling effect naturally. It will be some time before you settle down again to the ordinary routine. But Arnie will be able to enjoy the spring as he grows well again. About my wandering about I won't go into anywhere dangerous, and there are no wild animals round Delhi to cause harm, (except snakes in the wet season). For some time I haven't had any time for wandering at all, and have got my exercise only by an occasional game of tennis. But I'm very well. It's getting a bit warmer now, and is very dusty; in a few weeks the hot weather will be down on us. The chief event of the past few weeks for us all has been a visit from Captain Young, who came and stopped with me on last Saturday, till Monday night. He was in great form with the result that all Maitland House was charmed beyond words, though for the past few days they have been talking about him, trying to praise him. His father Sir Mackworth Young was Lieutenant-Governor here 12 years ago, and so many of the important Delhi people knew him, at a Garden-Party to which I brought him on Monday afternoon. These Garden-Parties are amusing in their way, a strange conglomeration of Europeans and Indians. But I haven't time tonight to go into them more.

Ghaffar has not written to me while I've been here. Capon, who works at the Radcliffe Observatory, is a delightful person, a friend of Marsh-Roberts' and of Logan's. Iliffe wrote to me the other day. He had been in collision with Henry (the boy in the Lodge at St. John's) a very bad accident.

Miss Tilly also sent me a letter: she has lost a brother recently.

Today week C. will go, which will be sad. Sharp stops another month.

Well I must stop now. As to Mr. Barratt I'll try to write to him when I've more time, in the hot weather. Many people there are to send word to. Please thank Father.

Love to you all, Father, Mother Bob Frank and Arnie

yrs ever lovingly   WILL

ST. STEPHEN'S COLLEGE
DELHI
24/3/14

DEAR MOTHER

It was good to get your letter last week, and to hear that Arnie was still going on well. You don't say how you were feeling yourself, and I want to know that, because the strain must have been terrible, on you, and on Father too. Let me hear always, how you are feeling too. The chief other news you gave was of the Sports. I'm sorry for Frank but he has time enough yet. Jackson seems to be in good form.

Mr. Jane wrote to me about the results, though he did not mention Frank. I had a letter from Mrs. Whitelocke, from Geneva; it was good of her to write. Last week was as busy a one as any I've had, with all sorts of things to do. The College Sports took up three days, and meant the measuring of the field and the digging of jumping places as well. They were good in results though, far better than last year, so that was all right. Then ordinary work has been tightened up because of the approach of exams. But the real thing which exercised me was some acting. Imagine me solely responsible for the production of Act V Scene I of the *Midsummer Night's Dream*. The training of students in the drama, when they are acting in a foreign tongue to them is quite hard, but they buckled to it like men, and the result was a startling success. There's been quite a lot of talk about it. In the first place I procured a great lion-skin, real and most valuable, from a German curio-dealer with whom I've struck up acquaintance. That in itself, about the biggest man in the College with a voice like a lion's would have made a triumph. But besides I noticed one youth among the students with a face not in itself remarkable, but which would make up as a woman's most uncannily, if given long glossy black hair with a wreath of white jessamine about it, a red rose behind his ear, and purple flower pendants in his ear-lobes. So I contrived it, and the effect was extraordinary. As a result of this, and of the keenness of all the actors, the audience expressed itself most heartily pleased, and it was an audience of distinguished people mostly. All the same I hardly contemplated being an actor manager when I came out here, and this is the second show I've run, counting the *Hamlet*.

Besides this I've been most busy with one of the men here who's in trouble for no fault of his own, and very low in spirits. It's meant a lot of walking about at nights. But that will soon be over, and I keep very fit. C. goes away on Saturday, which will be sad. He's a charming person, and I hope he'll look you up when he gets to Cuddesdon. S. has another month with us. When they've gone we'll be a sad company comparatively, but I'm getting so many friends among the students, more or less friends that is, that I'm not likely to be lonely ever. This acting has been a very good method of getting to know them. And in bulk, even apart from individuals, they are a nice lot, a very pleasant lot. Pearson is back in India, and ought to be here in a day or two. We had a wire from him today, from Bombay, whence he is going to come straight, only stopping en route at Hoshangabad to look up Frank Lenwood. Last Sunday Arthur Davies was in Delhi, so we continue to see people at Maitland House. Also a new lady has arrived at the Mission, who's evidently a tremendous friend of the McNeiles, and who knows Damascus and the Holy Land. I hear by the way that Mrs. McNeile is not nearly so well. She has her eldest daughter with her. Tomorrow night I will very probably go to Agra, with C., who also wants me to go to Karachi with him on his way home. But as to that he's not really serious, for I have neither the time nor the money. By the bye, it would be as well, in view of the possibility of illness, if you sent me out £5. The ways in which it could be sent are various. Either through Thomas Cook, if Father happens to be in London (or Bob could do this for you). Cook's office is only 50 yards away, so that would be quite simple, and I could use him as a banker, or withdraw it at once, as I felt inclined. Or else by way of the Post Office is I suppose quite as possible. £5 will be quite enough, and I'm without surplus funds only owing to my own travelling to and fro, which I look upon as my work just as much as sitting teaching here, and to the necessity of buying hot weather clothing.

It's not hot yet, though there's talk of the heat coming. So far there hasn't been any day in which I've wanted cooler clothes than I'm wearing now, that is a thin shirt and a thick coat; except for one day down at Jhansi with Captain Young. The climate is really delightful still, perfect days, with the temperature lower than English summer heat, but the sun at noon very strong. As to my exercise I keep in condition easily, and find life very enjoyable. I have not ridden for a fortnight owing to the fact that instead I've borrowed a car now and again from S.S. to give Mrs. M. a drive: she needs them now or something of the sort. This man S.S., who's one of the principal men of North India considering his age, is always offering me such things, so I don't think it's any harm taking them, though of course I don't enjoy it (I mean the motoring) compared with riding. But it's not for my own pleasure I arrange the drives, which incidentally are not numerous of course, only once and again.

Thursday. 26/3/14

I've just read in the paper an account of a railway riot at Jerablus, in which the German engineers seem to have had a very bad time. Ned is all right, for Fontana has wired to Constantinople that the two British subjects excavating there for the British Museum are untouched, though they had some difficulty in restraining their men from taking part. I don't wonder at there being a riot: such happenings as the carrying away of the Kurdish girl whom Ned rescued (I told you the story didn't I?) have made all Germans very unpopular. Don't fear for Ned: if the whole country was in rebellion he would still be all right, with hundreds of horsemen at his back. I daresay only his influence prevented a massacre. It will be interesting to get an account from him of the business, but probably he will make light of it.

I'm sending some stamps along for Arnie, of Nepaul and Jaipur, and a few Indian Government stamps with native state markings. If in return he has any Turkish duplicates they would please the man who sends him these.

We're rather upset this morning, because a wire has come that Mrs. M.'s father has died in Egypt. She herself is in a delicate state just now. And then another matter is a bit of a trouble to me, for some one else's sake. Pearson is arriving this evening.

Well, now I must stop. I do hope you and Father flourish and that Arnie steadily recovers. Tell Frank to cheer up and give my love to Bob.

Love to you all

from WILL

We didn't go to Agra after all.

MY DEAR ARNIE

Just a line or two to you to go with Mother's. I wish I could see you, my man, getting stronger in the spring-air, and drinking it all in.

It is good to know you are on the way towards recovery, and now that there is no more place for inflammation you ought to be a strong fellow without trying.

It's getting warmer here now, and in a fortnight or three weeks the hot weather will commence, technically speaking. Most of the Government has already left for Simla and the hills. But it is still very enjoyable, a delightful climate.

Today I had expected to go to Agra with one of our fellows, but circumstances stopped us, for which I was glad, because it was only to take him away from Delhi that we proposed going. Tonight Mr. Pearson will arrive, so all sorts of things are happening.

Here are a few stamps for you. Do you see the account in the papers of the 'battle of Jerablus'. Great excitement for Ned I should say. I must write to him about it. The other day one of my Rajah friends Malik Khan of Tirvana asked me out and showed me some hawking. Not the proper sport. That I couldn't or wouldn't go for, but the flying of his great falcons at dummy birds. Just imagine a lot of long-haired men on camels with hawks on their wrists, which shrieked like tin whistles till they were loosed, and then swooped through the air at a most tremendous speed, striking at every swoop. Fine birds, very, and you would like to watch them.

I'm just going out for a run across country with one of my pupils, Nazir Ullah, son of a Moslem convert. He's a nice fellow. That will stop me sending you a really long letter, which must wait till I have more time. This week I've been trying to rest after last week's strenuous work with the Sports and the acting. It appears though that I'm going to train another lot of actors.

Well, here's Nazir just come in, so I'll go out.

Good-morning to you and may this find you flourishing again.

your loving WILL

ST. STEPHEN'S COLLEGE
2/4/14

DEAR MOTHER

Thursday again, and a few spare minutes in the middle of the day, before an address to the students by Western, Stokes' old comrade and now one of the brotherhood! It's wonderful to see and hear the way the students listen to him owing to their respect for his old sadhuship; though indeed they are very willing to be friends with us all.

Your news last week was still favourable, so Arnie by now ought to be getting himself again, and you and Father be able once again to take breath. It's good to feel that all is well, over so many miles. Last week I had a letter from Ned too, from Jerablus. It was mostly about Aleppo art-work, and was written in a hurry, but clearly he was well. It will be interesting to get news of the battle of Carchemish. Our news here isn't particularly happy. In the first place C. has gone home (went on Monday) and has left a gap behind him. I hope he'll look you up in the summer, when he will be staying in Oxford. And then there's a sad sedition case gradually being unfolded in the courts here, concerning a group of conspirators including two old students. One of them, the ringleader, wanted to teach me and Jenkin Hindustanee, but we didn't like the look of him and so didn't take him although he was very much a persona grata with Canon Allnutt at the Mission. It appears though that he and his lieutenant (whom I've met too) were responsible for at least one bomb outrage, and probably for the Viceroy's bomb, besides various other plots. They've been caught now, and there's an end of it. But it's a miserable business that this man who most certainly has done many splendidly self-sacrificing things in his life, should have been so warped. The old St. John's man, now in California, is said to have been at the back of the whole business.

S. will be leaving at the end of the month, and it will be hard to get along merrily without him and C. But all the same we are a happy party here, and all very well.

The Government has gone up into the hills, to Simla, and Delhi is emptied of its Europeans, for the hot weather is commencing. At present it is extremely nice, like good English summer weather, with delightful nights. Last night I took Rudra out for a drive in the car, and the cool air of the evening with the grey light over the plain was most beautiful. Charm this country certainly has. It's later in the day now, and I am going on with this. Just now we are busy with work, or rather I am, because the Fourth Year are leaving for their examination, and as C. has left us, ask help from me just these days, which means the squashing in of a few extra hours into the day. But I am very fit. The other day I took a student out for a cross-country run of about 6 miles and leapt over the ground. I've heard by the way about the Sports and the Boat-race. The former is certainly disappointing. And it's a pity that Jackson did not make his record after all.

Tomorrow I am to go on an outing with the 2nd year students, to a place called Okla, about 8 miles off. S., who's their tutor, will be going too. That's about all the news. So now I will shut up, and go to bed.

Thank you so much for all your letters. They are such a pleasure. Ned said in the same way how he longed for the mail.

Well, love to you all, and hoping you are all getting on all right.

Your son

WILL

DELHI

Thursday. 9/4/14

DEAR MOTHER

Tomorrow is Good Friday, so there has been an empty College today, but all the same I've had to spend all the morning and a good part of the afternoon cataloguing and re-arranging the College Library, some of it, which will come into my charge next week at S.'s going. So I'm not in the mood to write you a long letter. Holidays last for 10 days or so, but the approaching exams mean that there won't be much leisure. Also I have to deliver three lectures at Jaipur next week, on Art and History. I'll tell you about that next mail. The chief things that have been happening here are that we've had a lecture in the College from Saunderson of the Archæological Department. His subject was Moghul Architecture (the Taj, etc.) and with lantern slides it was very interesting. Then too we've had an officer friend of S.'s stopping with us, with excellent yarns of Somaliland adventure. I hope, by the way, that Mr. Inman has recovered.

And yesterday I went to the Girls' School (the Theosophist place I've told you about) for the prize-giving, and saw some very charming sights. I was the only European invited, except the Commissioner's wife and her orderly.

10.0 p.m.

So far I had got when I was interrupted by a man who wanted me to explain some of Emerson's essays. And now it is late.

Last week's letter from Arnie was a great treat. Please thank him muchly for it, and tell him to expect a proper answer soon. As to the proposed trip, there's material for several weeks in his itinerary. I should say a journey like that Bob and I took to Ypres would do, and be less ambitious. It will be good for Arnie to get abroad. I got a letter from Florence too last week, which I would like to answer at once but can't. It's good she's well. As to A. he will be a few months of each year at St. Stephen's, which will be better than nothing. And in some respects his going may help us by removing the cloud of suspicion which hangs over this place; suspicion—that we are seditious. When there are police spies actually in the College; and men like ——get their letters examined by the police secretly, things need changing. And this suspicion is due to A. mainly, who at times has been very far from discreet. He's a Radical of the Radicals, and there's even less use for such here than in England. The College has not been suspected by the authorities much this last year, but the Conspiracy case will have renewed this attitude, particularly since the ringleader was a particular protégé of the mission. People need to be as wise as serpents, even though they are harmless as doves, {eight words omitted} Ezra Pound flourishes, from what he tells me: he would have liked you to have accosted him. By the way one queer piece of news is that Grey-Smith is at Lahore working as a journalist. I heard it last night from a pressman here. It is rather a surprise to me, but it will be amusing if we can meet. C. knew him so it's a pity we didn't hear earlier. I'm so sorry you are feeling run down. Be very careful to take it as easy as Arnie has to do for the next few months. Surely nowadays with so few of us you have less to do, and can enjoy rest.

Bob sent me two *China's Millions* last mail, which were welcome. Altogether I'm sorry I have so little time for letter-writing and so few ideas just at present.

The hot weather which had set in has broken again, with thunderstorms, and cool winds. That's unusual for this time, but pleasant. I'm very fit indeed; took the students for a long paper-chase the other day.

With love to you all, and health to you all.

Your son WILL

You don't tell me how Father is?

King Edward Serai
Jaipur
Rajputana

My darling Mother   15/4/14

I've come down here to Jaipur across the night, and am stopping with S. in the caravanserai, where 35 students will join us tonight, with Jenkin at their head. We are going to give them a series of lectures, illustrated by the exhibits in the State Museum here, and also shew them the sights of the place, the palace of the Maharaja, the stables and gardens and the famous rock fort of Amber. Those I described to you once, when I came here before with C. and Bhattacharya, so I won't go into rapture about them again. The place is indeed very wonderful, a mediæval stronghold in the Anglicized India, yet with a deal more joy in the people's faces than the Delhi people show.

Last mail I had a long letter from you, and one from Frank enclosing Ezra Pound's wedding invitation. As the letter is in Delhi now I can't answer it properly. But I remember a few of the things you mentioned.

For Ned, it was bad luck indeed on him not getting letters, yet I can hardly believe that their loss can be wilful. The Police are said to open the letters of our College professors {six words omitted} but mere malicious individual interference is unlikely. He's too popular, except among the German engineers who bear him a grudge because he prevents their vile doings. And they'd find it hard to interfere.

Talking of the Police interference with the College, now that I am away from Delhi I can talk freely without any suspicion at all of the Police reading this. It is absurd but nevertheless true that while the High Government, the Viceroy and his council, and the Chief Commissioner of Delhi, are altogether in favour of the College, and are giving it a good grant, the Criminal Investigation Department, which you'll hear whispered about as the C.I.D. every day, is very hostile to St. Stephen's. That is, because A. is a foolishly outspoken critic with a habit of appealing against wrong-doing not to the actual wrongdoer but always to his superiors and so getting him into a row. At some unreasonable performance of the police (such as the secret searching of his rooms) A. has gone straight to the Viceroy. And as to their doubt of the College methods, that is in a measure justified. St. Stephen's Students like any others in India are infested with nationalism, and A.'s Radical influence probably goes to making more of them nationalists than elsewhere. And when a case arises like the present Delhi conspiracy case, with one man, the ringleader (a man whose own handwriting shows he intended to use poisons against the English) a great friend of A., and the chief other prisoner an old student also, while one of the prisoners is in the 1st year at present, the Police can well say that criticism of their suspicions is misplaced. The land is honeycombed with spies.

I will write to Ned this week if I get time.

Margaret {Laurie} writes to me, and in her last letter mentioned how much she wanted to write to you, but how she felt that you were too busy to answer, and too conscientious not to do so. I will quote her words to you, when I get back. It's good about Kerry. And if I find time Mr. Cave will have a note. But not this week.

Mr. Rudra was very pleased to get Father's letter, please tell him, and it was a good idea writing to him. A. wrote to me saying how glad he had been to see you. He will be here, in Delhi I mean on Saturday night or Sunday morning, when we will also get back. It's not quite settled yet what he is going to do, whether he's going to remain on the College staff for 3 months of the year, which Rudra wants, or whether he'll definitely sever his connection with all missionary societies. He is an amazing genius by all verdicts, but as I say he does not work with wisdom, and many people think his action in going to Bolpur *with such a flourish of trumpets* will harm missionary work. Sen, a pupil of Tagore's and one of our professors, not a professing Christian himself, thinks this. Still most of A.'s moves have been good in result. He's looked upon almost as an incarnation of divinity by some Indians.

I'm glad you showed my letter to Miss Wright, because I really have no time to write to her myself, yet would like to do so. You don't say what sort of a time she is having? Florence has written to me and must get a letter next week, as must Mr. Jane and his sister, and a host of other people, such as the Iliffes, Henry, Mr. Barker, to name just a few. Letter-writing takes up a lot of my spare time.

I hope you had a happy Easter. I did, very; sat most of the time in the Gardens in a place where there was a breeze. Now again recently there has been thunder, and some showers, quite a phenomenon for the time of year, and it is not hot yet really. Yes I have some thin clothes. Thank you for the postal order.

It's good to think of you upon the sea's edge, and of Arnie walking about again properly. If you go to Flanders I hope you'll have a ripping time. We two ought really to have got to Ypres together once. Bob and I enjoyed that trip so. It's jolly sometimes to lie still and think of all the places where I've been, better than reading; the places one remembers though are generally only incidental, not the great views that moved the emotions, which come back more like visions.

I'm to lecture here on Art, one lecture, painting and sculpture that is of all times and peoples, on Indian Art, the second, and on a period of Indian history, the third. Jenkin will be talking too, and probably S., while one of the Moslem professors will lecture on Moslem history.

I'm glad, so glad, to hear that Father's better now at sleeping. May you all be happy

With love

your son

WILL

15/4/14

MY DEAR FATHER

I want to write to you tonight, though conditions are not very favourable. There are three of us together here, S. and Jenkin and I, in an upper room of an Indian Serai (caravanserai the books call them) in Jaipur, Rajputana. It's very like an hotel really, and we have our servant here to wait on us, but all the same it's a place where we only pay 5 pence a day, and cater. We're here, instead of in the Hotel where C. and I stayed, because we've 35 students down here for a course of lectures, of which I've to deliver 2 tomorrow and one the next day. I'm talking on art, and on Indian art, for the first two, illustrating what I say by the exhibits in the Museum, where the lectures are to be given. S. and I arrived here this morning at 5, and were only called by our servant as the train was starting out of the station again. You would have laughed to have seen us in our pyjamas, and fashionable white sunhelmets, me with red Aleppo slippers, and S. half wrapped in a skimpy Kimono, walking along the platform followed by our coolies, into a party of American ladies. What these were doing here I don't know. The plains are all deserted now. All the same the weather isn't really hot. One can walk about in the middle of the day, and I feel very energetic. The other day S. and I went with his year class to

Okla, a place about 12 miles from Delhi, where the river is tapped for a canal with the result that there's a fine lock where one can bathe. Also the engineers have boats and we took the students out rowing. It's the most changeful place I've struck near Delhi, with really good bathing in dirty water. One can get a good dive. And when we were out boating and just returning S.'s rudder somehow fell off like a stone into 20 feet of water. By our retrieving this, diving, the students were impressed.

A. comes back on Saturday or Sunday when we will be back in Delhi. We're going to have to decide then about his future: that is Rudra and he are going to do so. Rudra by the way was very pleased to get a letter from you last mail.

You are reported as sleeping better, which is good to hear. I want to get news soon of you all being as you were before the trouble.

Arnie seems to have planned an Odyssean tour in Flanders and Holland, but I suppose the reality will be more reasonable. As Mother will be in charge it had better not be too far afield. Talking in French and helping him to get stronger will be exhausting. I wish that I could see you all again for awhile.

You'll see in Mother's letter some complaints of the state of this country. If A. talked much to you he probably included some of this sort of thing, but his complaints make the position of the College weaker. It does actually stand for sedition among unknowing Anglo-Indians. Yet a more loyal man than Rudra there isn't anywhere. And A. now is fairly sensible no longer so contemptuous of the Empire. He's done marvellous things in winning the heart of India.

Well, I must stop now. The mail here goes a day earlier than it does in Delhi, which rather upsets my calculations for letters this week. I've written to Ned, though I had a jolly letter from him the other day chiefly a criticism of Indian art and a request for specimens.

Love to you all.

WILL

DELHI
22/4/14

DEAREST MOTHER
    We've been having a very busy time since I wrote last from Jaipur, but there's not much time for me to describe it in tonight.

Also I'm sleepy from going down to the station to see people come or go the last few nights. First of all for your last note. I'm glad you and Arnie got away, and had a safe journey even though a slow one. You'll be back no doubt before this reaches you—what a pity it is letters take so long—after a very pleasant time I trust. It will be interesting to hear your report of the trip. Jaipur was very amusing. You see we were in the Indian serai there which was a new experience for me, and a pleasant one too. It made our stay fairly cheap. And then one day we went out by the State Ambulance carriages to Amber, and did the last two miles by elephants. All that was new and amusing. Then Alec Fraser of Ceylon and Uganda has been stopping with us, and making the past few days very nice. He's a great man. S. has gone and A. has come back. That's the chief news. I ought to write more but it will be better for me to get to bed. Nowadays College work starts at half-past six, so one needs to sleep early.

Forgive me then for so short a note. I'm very fit.

with love to you all

WILL

DELHI
29/4/14

DEAR MOTHER

I want to start a letter to you now, though I daresay some M.A. students will soon interrupt me. The last two mails I've rather scamped so this week's should be a longer one.

Your last news was from your Belgian tour. Ypres you were bound to enjoy, and I'm so glad you got there. The ramparts with their moat and the swans in it were a great joy: when Bob and I were there the banks were gay with daffodils too. And the level country round Ostend and inland must have had the treat of novelty to Arnie. No. I didn't see any sand sailing-boats when I was there: sounds jolly. Altogether I hope you had a very delightful trip, and that the arrangement of it was not too hard on you after Frank left.

Here nothing much has been happening to me, except that I've taken charge of a Hostel. Z. has had to go to the hills for a change, and will stop there for the whole hot weather, coming back to Delhi in September, and that of course leaves his house vacant. Therefore I've taken it over. It's not that he is ill in any way to which one can give a name, but that he is generally run-down. It's due to his restlessness and feverish energy I think, and a general tendency in him to make much of trifles. I'll describe the change this makes in my own position later.

S.S. here is asking me to go as travelling tutor to his boy on a journey to various parts of India in the vac., but I'm uncertain about it. It's not altogether a position I like, for it will make me rather too much in his debt. Taking rides and drives off him is one thing, but this is different. All the same as I've been giving him for nothing just twice the work which Pearson gave him for £14 a month, I suppose my scruples are rather fine. This sort of job is easy to get out here it seems. The other day one of my Rajahs wanted me to tutor his heir at a large salary with riding and shooting, etc., thrown in, for four years at least. When you fear I'll get to wish I was rich, don't bother about me please. If life for me had been one jot different it would have been empty, it seems to me. What matters is those with us, and that is all right.

When I go on with this tomorrow I must try and describe the staff here to you.

It's hot nowadays, though still not too much for me to enjoy it.

30/4/14

I've had to go out to three meals today so after all can't write any more. It will be Arnie's birthday the day after tomorrow and I'll think of him. To all of you my very best love, and may you be happy

your loving WILL

Wednesday. 6/5/14

DEAR MOTHER

It was good to hear in your last letter that Father was over in Belgium too. I do hope you all had a very happy time together there and that it set you up well. The whole appendicitis business must be forgotten now so far as its worry went, and only the good course it took remembered.

You're surprised at Ned not mentioning the Jerablus riot. Probably it was because he has got into the habit of looking forward, not back and till the thing was quite over would not think of writing its history.

One of the great things about him is the way in which he always concentrates on the matter in hand, and puts everything else out of his mind. When he hears that the matter got into the papers, he'll be sure to tell you all about it. So far as he went, he clearly came out of it with much credit. It has not been mentioned here since, so I suppose things are quiet again. Here things have been going on much as usual. I am coaching the students in another play, and invigilating this week during an examination, otherwise work is (a) English lecture each morning from 6.40–7.40. (b) Scripture class 7.40–8.40. From then till 11 private work, then nothing till 3.30 when private work again, and at 5 till 6 three times a week M.A. History teaching. After that tennis or something of that sort. Yesterday I took three of the Hospital ladies out in the car for a drive of about 35 miles, visiting Tughlakhabad (which I probably have described to you before). They had not been in a motor any of them for years, so it was worth it, and very lovely swooping back in the moonlight. Tughlakhabad is a great ruined town, that's all, about 15 miles from Delhi, built before the Moghuls swept down as far as this, by a Pathan king Tughlakh. It is entirely uninhabited, and broken down inside so that some of the buildings look almost like volcanic rocks, quite shapeless. But great walls are all round the two miles or whatever it is of circumference, and from the tower at the southern end in the sunset it is wonderful, just a huge circle of dilapidated walls, with inside temples browsed over by goats, old walls and fallen arches, bare patches full of thorns, and the air hoarse with peacocks' crying. This is the sort of thing which really shows the passing of empires one with Nineveh and Tyre, and I could stop all night in such a place.

Thursday. 7th/5/14

Last night S.S. called for me, and took me out in the car, with Willie Pearson, who is back from Bolpur and whom you'll remember as the best of all the Camp officers, C. B. Young, whom Frank will remember, and the Baptist Minister. We ran along in the moonlight to Okhla, about 12 miles off, and eat a dinner there by the lock. Did I describe it, and how S. and I went there with some students and boated and bathed some while ago? It is where the Jumna is dammed up for a canal, so that the water is deep yet wide among sand stretches and grass, and the great lock is as big as anything on the Thames and something of the same style, overhung with sweet-smelling neem-trees and with brilliant patches of oleanders. It's really beautiful, with good bathing. Well, there we sat on a great carpet Lala Sahib brought with us in the car and ate Indian food and iced jellies and fruit, in the light of the full moon. Afterwards we ran along the road a bit further, turned back, and climbed Humayun's Tomb (for which see *The Wonders of the World*) on the great terrace of which we strolled about again for a while, rushing back to Delhi about ten thirty.

About my summer holiday I've compromised with S.S., and am going down in the middle of June to join him at Waltair on the East Coast about half-way between Madras and Calcutta. It is a well-known place for sea-bathing. From there we will go to Ootacamund, the Simla of the South, and the most like England of all places in India, which is in the Nilgherry Hills, quite close to both Naryana and Menon. Fraser wants me to go to Kandy, but we'll see. This journeying about will take up the first part of the holiday, and for the latter I am leaving plans open. Rudra will be going to Bolpur. Jenks and Young in August will go into the hills. And S.S., who's a friend of the Maharaja of Kashmir, talks of our going up there too. We will see about all that later. Looking far ahead is uncomfortable. Meanwhile it will be delightful to get some sea-bathing, and to see something of the Mass movements in the South. Of course if a hitch comes in any way such as illness, I can always move simply to the Simla hills, or join Rabindranath at Naini Tal. I wonder what you made of the latter's book. A. thinks him one of the supreme great poets of the world, one alongside of Shakespeare and Dante and Homer. But I can't subscribe to that much as I like the man himself, and enjoy reading him. It seems to me that he can give a delightful atmospheric effect, with no light in it, so far as I can see. If I hear him abused I defend him, because he is good, but if I hear A. on him all of me is annoyed, without saying anything generally. I don't think he is as big a man as Ezra Pound for the matter of that. A. habitually calls him in public 'Guruder', which means 'The Shining Master', and that is one of Sen's grievances, who says that no Christian can possibly use the term, and that every time A. uses it he puts Tagore into the place of Christ. A. refuses to believe Sen's interpretation (though Sen is a Bengali disciple of Tagore's who's lived with him) and goes on using it, while Sen keeps on coming to me fuming at the folly of it. I don't see that anyone can take a human being for 'Master', without doing himself harm: if A. used Tagore as help-mate in religion it would be different. By the way I have a group of the staff, just come, and will send it you presently when I've got some wooden sheets to protect it, and will write the names of the different men on the back, so that you'll better appreciate mention of them. They are an excellent lot, particularly Sen and Mukerjee. But it's chiefly annoying that C. has gone, whom I got to know better than S. No doubt you'll see both of them in Oxford.

Z. writes to say that he is improving. It is worry which is the matter with him, nothing else, I fancy.   {ten words omitted}
Mrs. L. has a son   {six words omitted}   and L. is up in Simla with her ill, with the result that C. B. Young and I are doing the work of these two married people.

The Hostel requires me merely for sleeping in, and nothing more. It is stocked with a very fair lot of men, one of them at least of the very best, and it is a good opportunity of getting to know the men, which I'll be able to take at the end of this week when S.S. will go with Pearson into the hills, and leave my evenings free.

Well I must stop now. It is five in the evening and fairly cool. I like this weather, and the thermometer which is about 90° indoors does not really tell the truth. And it agrees with me at present very well. I'm going to give a lecture on something or other to the College Literary Club in an hour's time, and I have not made up my mind yet about my subject. It is useful, the way in which I'm able to speak extempore: largely owing to the Essay Society and the Stafford Club.

Last week gave me a very long letter from Mr. Barker, a great joy to me at the moment. I doubt if I'll be able to answer it this week.

Your last letter was so very interesting.

Thank you so much for them all.

Love to you, all of you.

WILL

DELHI 13/5/14

DEAR MOTHER

Last mail-day was very disappointing because it brought me no letter from home at all. I daresay the cause was merely you're being abroad and so missing the post, and I hope that was it. But I'm eager for next Saturday

Miss Wright sent me a very jolly long letter, though, which was a pleasure indeed to get. She seems to be having a better time than one would expect her condition to have brought her, and that's a comfort. She enclosed a photograph, a happy thought. England won't be quite the same without Langley as our second home: it has always meant more to me than Oxford. Also there came last mail a sheaf of postcards from Fernand, at Nantes. I wonder if he and I will ever meet again.

The weather has been the chief interest of late. On Friday it was that we had a duststorm. At the time S.S. and I were walking together in a famous private garden outside the city, among a great grove of magnolias in blossom. Suddenly the sky which had been cloudy all the afternoon—it was 5 o'clock—took on a red-brick colour, and the wind blew. In ten minutes it was dark as midnight, yet not black but red, with dust whirled about in one great towering cloud and the howls of a gale. Then it began to rain mud in torrents, a weird sight while lightning started in great sheets. All this we watched from the Garden pavilion, one of the most luxurious Arabian-Nights-sort of places I've been in. After a while the strength of the rain ebbed a little and we drove home, but it started again. From the roof of the house here at 7 in the evening I could see the moon being unveiled every now and then by lightning, quite invisible at other times, one of the queerer sights surely.

Next day was cool as a result of this, with rain-clouds hanging about, what the students call a fine day. It was a holiday too, so Jenkin and I took about 70 of the men to Okhla, 10 miles off, walking. Jenks, by the way, is in every way an admirable fellow: cultivate Mrs. Jenkin: she must be good to have him as a son.

The walk to Okhla is fairly typical of the country round Delhi. First of all one goes through the town, along the Maidan, an open space between the fort on the left and the Jumna Musjid, a great mosque on the right. Then along a long street with shops on either side and a gutter in the middle, the Daryagunge Bazaar. That leads out of a gateway in the wall into the open country, quite flat except for the river a little below the road to the left. Between it and the road is the oldest of the Delhi's worth looking at, a tangle of great masonry broken quite to bits but with one tall pillar standing still, like a landmark. Two miles out comes the Puranakilla or old Fort. This is a very impressive place, another of the seven cities of Delhi, with walls fairly complete and a gateway at the end of a long causeway. Inside it is a desolation of clearance, and one big mosque with fine arches. The next thing on the march of note is Humayun's tomb (see *The Wonders of the World*) and another tomb next to it, Nizam-ud-din's. Humayun's was the model for the Taj. But all along the road there are a succession of small beehive tombs which would be remarkable any-where else, with an occasional tall pillar as a milestone. Okhla itself I've talked about already: it's the place where there is bathing—not considered safe now on account of alligators so we don't go in—and it looks like an estuary and lock combined. There are some very beautiful flowers there, and the whole spot is kept as rather a picnic place, with two heavy sea-boats in which one may go rowing. A good place to go to for a change.

Jenks and I walked back, making 20 miles in all. We're very fit, and it is still cool though fine now. This rain does a lot of harm at the moment so it is well that it has stopped.

College will close in a month's time, and then I'll go to Waltair, but you had better to continue the same address for letters. It will be jolly to get some sea-bathing, though Waltair is I fancy rather a fashionable sort of place, which is annoying. Of the rest of our men P. N. F. Young is going to Kashmir to stop with Dr. Neve (of the book you sent me which has been much read by us all) and Jenks is first of all going to do some research work in the plains and then move up into the hills somewhere with Dugdale, a C.M.S. missionary we see a lot of, who lives at Meerut. Mr. Rudra will be going to Bolpur, and to Simla. And Mukerjee is doing a trip with Shearwood (one of the teachers in the School) somewhere in the Kulu Valley probably.

Fraser was here yesterday morning on his way back to Kandy, and has taken Mr. Rudra's younger son with him. And in the evening Norman Tubbs and six other Agra men (Oliphant amongst them, Bob knows him) dropped in to dinner, rather baffling our commissariat. They are on the way to Kashmir.

Going south in my case is approved of heartily by Rudra, so that is all right. Ooty is the most English climate in India, yet close to Menon's so it suits rather well. The real idea is for me to get hold of R. a little more, who in time to come will be the most important man in this part of India probably, yet at present belongs to his old and very orthodox Hindu grandmother. The women are the real problem here.

I've heard a lot from him of his marriage, etc., and am thoroughly convinced of it. Yet very little seems to be touching them, except the work of Mrs. Besant (who personally is more than doubtful in character). Well, enough for just now.

I want very much to hear next Saturday that you are all well.

Love

WILL

DELHI. 20/5/14

DEAR FATHER

It's late in the evening, and I must go to bed, but as there's an expedition tomorrow which may keep me late I want just to start a letter now.

Two letters came last week, shewing that the first had missed the mail, so that was all right. There's always a chance, particularly there will be soon when I begin to move again, of my missing a mail too, so never think that no letter means that I'm not capable of sending one, or anything of that sort. It's hard to know which day letters for England leave a place. Thus it was only by a happy enquiry that I caught the post from Jaipur. You seem to have had a good time abroad, and it's fine to hear of Mother picking up again. I'm sorry you had trouble with your teeth though. The flying sandships were not performing in my time: glad Arnie had his ride in them. As to the whole sea-coast it's good that Arnie has been out of England: nothing like it and better than all the libraries he'll ever be in. It must have been hard on Mother having to talk and arrange business matters though. Please thank her for all her descriptions which bring so much back to me, and for the postcards.

I'm very interested in things Irish. So far as we're told in the papers they seem interesting yet much more hopeful. The Army seems to have taken a very strong stand. About that service by the way I don't know of any better men to judge by looks and the examples I've talked to than the officers in Indian regiments out here. Thoroughly good chaps. And if they need money there are all sorts of billets going, as posts in the Burmese Police, on the Frontier in charge of militia, or politically up the gulf. Having travelled gets a man an offer of a Consular post, as Captain Young who was offered the consulship at Van. Young is a supremely fine fellow, ask C. about him, and will stick to his regiment which is not one of the popular ones, and I don't think Frank can do better than join that. If he puts down his name for it he'll get in, and of course as an infantry regiment it's cheap living. Young suggested Frank as the next adjutant but one, and the adjutancy itself brings money. No doubt you'll be able to meet Young sometime when he's in England on furlough. Well I'll stop for the present now.

Now it's Friday in the early morning and I can't finish this letter. That's because I was away from Delhi all yesterday: went to a village some 25 miles off by train and footway, and stopped there in a great garden belonging to the local squire, one of the students, bathing in a swimming-tank and eating fruit. Then I and a Christian M.A. student walked back to Delhi. Impressions of the way are first a hard sea-beach of a road running through an uncultivatable country where the rocks were everywhere, then dark and the grey road, and then a sudden coming down after 10 miles without meeting anyone into a large village full of lights but heralded by ruins. After that many skeletons of Empires, just the dry bones of the old cities of Delhi.

I'm very well indeed, and hope that all of you are. Had a letter from Bob last week, and wrote to him a fortnight ago. Must write next week to Miss Wright and to Florence.

with love to all

from WILL

DELHI 27/5/14

DEAR MOTHER

I was sorry to write so short a letter to you last week but the visit to Hara and Gurgaon explained it. And then I thought that again I was not going to hear from home for my other letters came but none from you. However it arrived on Sunday so that was all right, and it was very interesting. Please thank Arnie and Father for their writings: also I enjoyed the newspaper cutting about the relay-race. You seem to have explored most of the north-sea coast, and this will be most valuable to Arnie, giving him a view of real geography, as apart from books. By the way I very heartily recommend you to buy a little book by Dr. Pennell about north India, which will make you realize the life out here more easily. It is in a series by Seeley Service and Co. Limited 38 Great Russell Street London, costing 2/–, and is called *Things Seen in Northern India* by Dr. T. L. Pennell. Its photos alone make it worth while getting. Mrs. Pennell has written a life of her husband, but it is very expensive. Try and get it out of Boots or some other library. It is so hard to make things interesting in letters that this book of Pennell's will be of use. It is a loss, his dying. It's very hot tonight, and I'm writing this in M.'s verandah in a moist condition. Temperature nowadays is about 110° in the shade, but one does not notice it much. And I'm fit as can be, and very cheery. College lasts for another three weeks, and then I will go off for a while with S.S., though very possibly to the hills after all and not to S. India, since the Delhi Conspiracy Case chains him here. Don't worry about my relations with him: I've been saving him £14 a month, and except for rides on horses, and very occasional motor drives have refused all his offers and gifts. And as to the views of Rudra, why, he paid for his passage to England once. You see he's the richest man here except possibly for one banker, and he is devoted to the College and without friends except among its tutors. A man one can be very fond of. He and I see a good deal of each other though, and he's indebted to me in several ways.

Now I must go to sleep.

28/5/14

Father tells me that Frank has turned vegetarian, and it is a phase most people go through. But here one sees vegetarianism on trial, Hindus against Moslems and Christians. The other day Jenks and I took our students on a walk to Okhla (I spoke of it at the time) and it was interesting to notice that the Christians arrived a mile ahead of all the others, and then came the Moslems. That's not altogether on account of meat-eating, because many Hindus do eat meat, but the diet in general shews a marked result. I think though vegetarianism so long as it is not on principle does no harm. It's when a man thinks it wrong to kill that he annoys me. This country is the land of cruelty to animals almost as much as it is the land of fat men, but the students all the same think they are kindness itself. For example there was a dog with a broken back lay in the sun all one day in agony, till C. shot it. And the students thought he'd committed a heinous crime! Sentiment passes for love among them to a horrible extent, and if you can gush like A. you please the Hindus very much and amuse the Christians and the Moslems. Frank will find if being peculiar agrees with him, and he's got plenty of sense.

That walk from Gurgaon is the most interesting thing I've done recently, and since then we have been fairly quiet. Work goes on the same as usual, and I quite enjoy it, and there are several of the men whom I'm getting to know well. Scripture-teaching is one of my regular duties but I don't like it. You see it's compulsory, and most of the men are not in the least keen. What would we think in England if the best College in Oxford was Moslem, and those who attended it had to listen to the Koran being taught every morning? Some men are anxious to talk about things, but not in class. And as it happens what they consult me about most is love and marriage and such matters, confidences about which they are not willing to speak to the others. More and more I feel that child-marriage is at the back of most that is wrong in this country: there is so little chance of people entering heaven by the steps of human affection. That's what makes Menon's country so much more pleasant. Individuals here are splendid, and as a whole the students are friendly. Also the professors are most of them admirable, as you'll see by the groups when they arrive. Sen is a Hindu of the Menon type, a Christian except in name, very full of fun and of experience. Mukerjee is delightful; he was at Cambridge and is a Christian by descent, very low-church. Altogether the staff is very good, and even in our differences, which in theology are very acute, we get on good terms. P. N. F. Young represents the commonly accepted S.P.G. type, and is alone, which is hard luck on him. Pearson has gone now, but C. B. Young remains as a non-Anglican on the staff.

About my clothes, they have done excellently. Collars are ruined very fast, and so I've worn soft ones mostly. But the washing people have done my shirts quite well, and all your arrangements were splendid. The light green suit I used to wear so often in Oxford is done for, and one of my warm suits, the brown one, rather dirty; otherwise I ought to start next year as I arrived very much. I've got an excellent pair of riding-breeches (3 guinea tropical corded breeches) from Pearson, who had bought them at Oxford and only worn them once, for a pound.

Things are not so dear here as one was led to expect. The most expensive thing I've bought almost was my sun helmet £1, rather a lot to give for a hat. But it will last, and one needs a good one for the shows here. Then also I bought a bicycle. But as regards money don't bother about me. If you're sending as you say another note I'll keep it, and it may be useful in case of illness. But barring such events I'll do all right at present probably.

Very fit I am, and quite enjoying the heat which sounds more than it is. It will be jolly for you having Ned back in the summer.

Father's news about his cough is most excellent, really splendid. As to Arnie, he'll be all right, and will be pack full of things to talk about to his fellows. Let him run about with Bobs.

Love to you all. It's nice to think of Oxford in the spring, and our garden looking lovely, with you in it again.

your loving son

WILL

DELHI
2/6/14

MOTHER DEAR

Last week's letter from you was quite an epic, with the account of the Suffragist disturbance at the Union. What ridiculous people they are: I wish they were agitating for something worth while talking about and taking so much pains. And you had a lot of good news in it too, of Father's cough having got so much better, which is grand, and of Ned's good fortune this season—he's going to be quite famous when the whole dig's over—and of Arnie thinking of taking up pen painting. It will be good certainly for him to learn to use his fingers, though anything but the best of art seems to me rather trivial. Why not teach him some social accomplishment like the violin? Though I doubt if he's got much more of that in him than I have: anyhow painting is jolly.

I haven't long to write to you in today, for I'm going out in a few minutes with one of the students, Hari Singh, who's a priest of the Sikhs, and wants to show me one of their sacred places. But as you say time is rather full with me, and therefore I must catch it when it's within reach. So many people write to me, and people whom I must answer because I like them, like N. W. Robertson and Miss Wright, that my time for letters is scamped. And then there are people here I have to answer.

Just now we're troubled a bit with fever. I'm all right, very fit. But Mr. Rudra has had quite a hard bout, and Roy has had what he calls dysentery, though I think it's rather a grand term for the particular trouble, and then two of the students whom I see most of have been sick too, one with tonsillitis which developed into a bad abscess. I've had to look after him a good deal, since he's in my Hostel. But term is near its end now, so that Mr. Rudra will be able to get into the hills, and be all right. It's very hot, yet thundery, and I suppose that is the reason for the trouble.

I won't be going down to the south when term stops for the Delhi Conspiracy case makes it necessary for S.S. to stop here for a while. So I'll go into the hills and loll about doing language work. Recently I've been much too busy to do any of that and in consequence I'm behind the others, and have learnt very little. In the next month I'll have much more time I hope, and so there'll be an improvement along this line. Now I must go out: sorry.

Wednesday. 3rd

The other day I sent three Photo groups to you: one of the actors some of them and the other two copies of the Professors. One is for C., the one that is without the names written underneath. Can you please send it to him. He's in the New Forest just now. That reminds me the present head of the Mission (Canon Allnutt is ill and in the hills) comes from Dibdin, but has lived at Fawley in his time. An old man he is, but it's jolly to hear him talk of those parts, which he does now that he's learnt that I'm a Hampshireman.

As for the Professors, it's not a good group particularly, though good of C.. Mukerjee and Sen in particular are not done justice. The latter is a splendid fellow, not nominally a Christian. Among the actors you'll admire Jwala Sarup, one of the men I know best, and a very handsome fellow isn't he? The big man behind the lion-skin is Shoran Singha, a Christian who used to help Norman Tubbs at Agra but who has come back for his degree. He's a jolly being, rather inflated. The man with the dog is also a Christian, and the fellow standing behind in the middle is Mrs. L.'s brother. Also the central figure with the smirk is Christian too. It's very noticeable how the Christians in spite of their small numbers are ahead in all branches of College work.

A. is away now in the hills with Rabindranath. He's talking rather wildly in public and private about the latter calling him his master, and saying that he hopes to find peace from him. It's liable to misrepresentation, and anyhow I don't see it's a healthy condition to look on any human being as one's master; certainly not a Christian position. It's unfortunate that A. is so prominent and so indiscreet.

I had an interesting ride yesterday with Hari Singh, who is a nice person, very talkative, not good at exams., but a hereditary priest of high standing among the Sikhs. Their religion you know owes most of its life nowadays to British encouragement for military purposes, and is quite a fine philosophy. He himself said 'the fault of Sikhism is that nobody puts it into practice', a pretty big admission. And now today I have been down by the river since before six with a Brahmin student looking at a Hindu festival. It's marvellous how many people there are in the country, all sorts of people, bright-eyed mostly and weak-mouthed. The women give a better general impression than the men, running less to fat, but the village men are very fine animals many of them. It was strange to see regular thousands of people bathing in the muddy river, in the most orderly manner, with the banks thronged with booths full of people. The Mohammedan is generally better to look at than these Hindus who consider, quite literally, a large stomach to be a sign of spirituality. They are very proud of such remarks as the West is material and the East spiritual, but India is par excellence the land of fat men (and of cruelty to animals). This is of the townsmen; the villagers are better, and more inclined to do their duty without talking about it. Now I must stop again.

4/6/14. 7.30 p.m.

It's raining, Mother, raining tremendously, and we have had a record dust-storm in which one could hardly see more than a yard. Mr. Rudra had never known a darker one, though it cleared quickly with this rain. It will be good, for it brings coolness which will comfort the invalids who are better by now and getting cured. Wonderful how the whole place was black with the storm, and the way in which it is pouring now with constant flickering of lightning. Certainly Nature is impressive here. Please thank Arnie for the stamps, which I haven't been able to give to the man yet. He will doubtless send the ones he has for the young'un back soon to him in exchange. No money came last week, so I suppose the Post was missed, but there's no hurry and I daresay I will be able to manage this summer fairly cheaply.

I'm becoming an examiner on the History M.A. board of Lahore University, which is absurd. And life here continues to interest me.

As I say so far as missionary work goes men talk to me about sex more than anything else, and as this is rather an unusual sort of occurrence my presence here may be useful. With regard to real religious things, they complain that while ours is a practical religion it has a bad philosophy, and they are much more interested in theology than in the love of God, most of them, so far as I can see. They want to discuss the Trinity, and the Virgin Birth and the Resurrection, and expect a scientific explanation and proof of such things. That I refuse to attempt to give.

Very nice fellows some of them are, willing to be friendly and not in the least scornful of us as meat-eaters and dirty people. Others are hostile, and suspicious: you would be if you knew that someone, for example Mr. Cave, was trying to turn Arnie or Frank into a Roman Catholic. In general it's wonderful how kind they are.

I'm sorry there is no Weller in the group. He's a splendid fellow, a man of something over thirty, at work here in the School, but taking up mission work among the Lahore Eurasians in September. He fought in the South African war. Was 9 years in America, spending most of it as a horse-breaker in Texas, and is an example of a man who has turned round completely in his attitude to life without losing his balance. Without him I would be rather solitary so far as English friends went, but he's a sermon in himself. We dined last night together with the ladies of the mission, who are rather fond of his stories and of my motor-car. They are some of them nice, one or two very, and human beings, which the men try to appear not to be.

I'm writing to Mrs. Maskew and to Florence tonight. That's all for the present. Good-night.

Love to you all

WILL

St. Stephen's College, Delhi

11/6/14

MOTHER DEAR

The money Father had sent me came last mail all right, so I'm very rich just now. It certainly should do me all right, and you needn't worry about such matters. If ever I want money I will write for it, and there'll be no hurry or need to wire because if in need I can borrow from the College in advance or elsewhere, not from individuals. That to begin with, lest I should forget it. Now for your news. I had for-

gotten that Math. Mods came on before Hon. Mods, if that is the exam.
of Frank's to which you allude. Best luck to him in it: by the time this
gets to you it will be over I suppose. It's queer nowadays to be an
examiner and not an examinee: I've been made one of the Board of
Examiners in M.A. history for the Punjab University, I believe, so I'll
know more about it even than I do now presently. May Frank do well,
and avoid a doubtful mind.

Father says Bob is being worn out by his work, so it's good he's
moving on to an easier shift. He that believeth should not make haste
is one of the true words I'm fond of, and certainly conscientiousness is
an easily abused thing. Compare Martha. So implore Bob to slack a bit
and let him get on to the river. It's not far from the slums, as we found
that queer night at Kingston, do you remember? By the way there's a
copy of *News from Nowhere* in the Library here which is a pleasure.

Your description of the garden has that same Cook's flavour. Queer
what a springtide sort of man Morris was. But it's hard to realize here
what England is like, everything is so barren. As C. says grass has to be
hand-fed and as it were taken out for walks in a perambulator! All the
same there are some fine flowering trees and shrubs if there are few
flowers here. And the fruit season is coming in, with mangoes, quite a
nice dainty.

Your news of Ned's sea-voyage with Dahoum in a biscuit-tin interested me. But don't forget that Mr. Hogarth likes to make the best of
a story. And as to Ned's caution he's got the gift of seeing the whole
campaign as well as the detailed manœuvres, so never fear for him.
So far as it is humanly possible he'll take precautions, and beyond that
he has just the faith to let him walk in the dark without tripping.

You seem to have been pulled down more by Arnie's business than
I'd thought, when you're still being tired by it. But I'm hoping the
summer will do the trick and make you well again. Anyhow it's
splendid about Father's cough. Don't worry about Mrs. Rieder. It's not
worth doing when a thing's over, and it was probably her mistake.
What about Kipling's poem 'God bless all our losses'. But certainly quiet
and Mrs. Rieder are not natural associations. You pity me for having
to look after M.'s hostel, but I fear I've misled you. It's hardly entailed
any work at all, for the Monitor or chief student does all the arrangements. And since Hindus have to arrange their own food their own
way none of the feeding troubles have touched my shoulders. No!

I've only had to nurse a fellow a bit, whom I made ill myself by taking him for too long a walk, to pay the servants, and to see that people were in at night, as well as a certain amount of coaching work with the students and of course conversation. It's given me a nice roof to sleep on outside the city and the surrounding gardens, and a little walk to keep me fit. That last I still am, happily. Though the weather since the storms began has not been so bracing as the dry extreme heat.

The storms are indeed very wonderful things. At present it's all serene again, with the thermometer high, but still it's cooler and a bit damper. Also the grass is green where it exists. But indeed round the city there is no grass growing naturally: only dust and stones and rocks and ruins, with a lot of thorn-trees like acacias and clouds of dust. Here and there the goat-flocks go, but how they live is a bit of a mystery. It's fascinating, absolutely, to be in a skeleton of a country like this, but it makes the change of the seasons little noticeable.

You think I should have a business arrangement with S.S. So I would have done, but our relations grew naturally, from my spending a few minutes every now and then with him to my giving him 2 hours a day. And we kept off money matters. In the future perhaps we will make a deal. But as to hiring horses I've tried and failed. No one rides in Delhi hardly of the Indians, and the English all own their own horses. There is no way of riding but my way at present, and there is no feeling in my mind of a favour. There is a bit in regard to his motor, which I only borrow for the ladies' sake at times, but he's continually offering me drives. The other day I had quite an exciting time driving it myself in the dark along a rough track over a hill some dozen miles off. But I don't often go out in it. Most of my exercise is tennis just now. It's too hot to walk much, and Mr. Rudra has been ill. In the small hours of Monday morning I hope to take him away to a hill-station near by, Kasauli, for about 10 days, to let him recuperate. That will be a jolly change. After that I will go with S.S. for a while. He wants me to teach his wife English, so I'll be fairly busy. Letters will be forwarded. Well, that's about all for the present. As you say L. has gone through a hard time: he's more sociable now that his wife is out of the way, so I may get to know him a bit. M. and Mrs. M. are all right at Dalhousie, and should come back in October probably. We will be getting news of Mrs. M. some day soon now: I hope it will be all right.

Farewell then with love to you all.   WILL

Postal address is still THE COLLEGE   KASAULI. 18/6/14

DEAR FATHER

There is plenty of time for the writing of letters now, so here's one for you. I only wish you could see me, under a vine and near to an apricot-tree dripping with ripe fruit the stones of which I can throw many feet down a pine-grown gully at the bottom of which a farm shows like a toy house. We look East, but at present can't see far, because the monsoon has broken and there has been rain. This is S.S.'s house at Kasauli which he has put at my disposal for a while, and which I've brought Mr. Rudra up to. It's a fine big bungalow, gloriously situated.

About S.S., my relations with him are rather queer I suppose. As a matter of fact I simply took Pearson's place when the latter went to S. Africa, but took no money. He had been paying Pearson £160 a year with board and lodging, and has profited by the arrangement therefore with me, particularly as I've actually given more time to him and his son. I thought it important not to take money, since the real thing is to get hold of the lad R., who will be immensely influential when he comes of age (he's twice as rich as his father and much more independent and strong-willed) and one could only do that by being in the position of a friend, not a tutor. The boy despised Pearson and treated him at times like a servant, but he couldn't do and hasn't done that with me. As to the rides I've taken, some of those have been in R.'s company, others with S.S. himself and the rest alone. And I've refused many offers of the motor. You can see easily that R. who has been filled with a hatred for everything English, and who is bitterly orthodox refusing to have anything to do socially with non-Hindus, will be a very adverse force in the land unless his prejudices are removed, and that is my work at present. With S.S. himself I'm a sort of political adviser (he's a man of some standing politically you see) and for the rest I read English poetry with him and try to improve his English.

If R. has got through his examination and S.S. wants me to go on with tutoring him I may make some nominal business arrangement, but in any case I'm certain to go on being on familiar terms with the father. He wants me to teach his wife English (she's a purdah woman of course and it's a revolutionary proposal) but there his Mother (a stern old orthodox lady hating everything European) will probably put her foot down. S.S. himself is an interesting study, a contradictory mix-up of tendencies some good some bad, but may be summed up as a man of excellent impulses ruined by slackness. R. is the stronger man, but less amiable.

Well I wonder if you approve my attitude in this matter? Mr. Rudra does at any rate, and I feel fairly confident that it's right. As to people misunderstanding me it's possible that might happen if I were a more conspicuous person, like A., but as it is I don't suppose anyone who matters has noticed that I visit him, except the police who are everywhere and about whom people here are afraid to speak. Considering the facts brought to light by the Delhi trial I think the police suspicion of all Indians quite justified. After all Amir was guaranteed as loyal and virtuous by the Cambridge Mission officially to the police, at a time when he was circulating documents advocating the use of poisons for political purposes.

Enough of such things for the present. It's a quaint land, and sometimes its politics seem like a volcano, other times like a squib. The most curious thing is the venom with which even loyal people talk of the officials. They don't object to the government, but they hate the governors. For my part when I've been in big gatherings of English I've felt that the I.C.S., probably owing to the competitive system which sends young clever upstarts to this country, is bad. The swagger of men who find themselves socially important here from being nobodies at home, would be amusing if it wasn't dangerous. But on the other hand when I've been among officers I've felt that the best of the English were here after all. It's good Frank is going into that service; the clean appearance of the average officer is a joy to look on. It's amusing by the way how both officers and missionaries are classes apart. Coming out to Port Said I was in a set of the former, and hardly spoke to anyone else, and it was really quaint to see how no one dared to accost them. That is due to two things I fancy, in the first place because they stand for the old hereditary Anglo-Indians and do despise the modern examinees who run the country, and secondly because the civilians are afraid of their daughters getting to know them and so marrying poorly. Of course even a Major's pay is small compared with the Civilian's, and as to the subaltern, he hardly gets more than we do and has a certain standard of living to conform to. But I'm glad Frank is doing that job.

As to the unpopularity of missionaries, that's natural. If you get into any set here not military you will find conversation turn chiefly on 'pay'. Most of all does that seem to be true in the educational service which is full of second-class men who at home would be school-mastering (I'm about their standard!). To such people it's an offence that there should be educationalists around doing it for so little, and since the Mission Colleges have at times criticized too freely it's not to be wondered at. Still educational missionaries are fairly popular: the Agra men for example, and with us S. and C. The real trouble is that there are a lot of missionaries in the country whose ideals really seem doubtful: young ordained men getting prestige by serving awhile abroad, and worst still —— —— making money by ex-ploiting their converts. I know one such who is not only a minister in charge of a large district, but is also a farmer who sweats his congrega-tion by making them work on his land. He's conscientious enough no doubt and it doesn't occur to him that when he sends off consignments of grain and rubs his hands at the price it fetches him he's puzzling critics a bit, but so it is. There is enough evidence about for people to say with a grain of justice that Mission-work is a method by which poor men at home may become important abroad.

{14 words omitted}

Then there are men like A. who represent the British officials as monsters, and seem to claim (this is quite true) that they alone are sympathetic. They make the labour of ordering the country so much harder that if I was an I.C.S. man I'd hate them most certainly. These are the men (A. for example) who are by nature at home and abroad out and out Socialists and Radicals, who think Home Rule a religious obligation and the Empire a fraud. You should hear A. on Ireland or on the South African War. Then you see how it is that a country where all the English are Conservatives except the highest officials who are appointed by the Liberal Government writhe under one-sided criti-cism. They've got a lot to put up with, criticism and no appreciation from Indian barristers (this is the country par excellence of the Bar) occasional visits from Keir Hardies and Ramsay MacDonalds (honest men except in so far as they are politicians) and anti-Indian feeling in the colonies which they have to attempt to explain away.

By the way though Kipling does seem to me to be the best authority for this country, I mean the writer who is most vivid, take his view of

Anglo-Indian society with a very large grain of salt, particularly representation of the mem-sahib. As a journalist he was only just tolerated at Lahore, and wrote about things from the outside, not from within. There are matrimonial mixes-up here as elsewhere, but one need only use one's eyes and knowledge of faces to realize that to take Kipling's picture as a landscape is wrong. I haven't mixed among the English, or only a very little, but men have talked to me, and I've seen people and their dresses, and met some officers' wives, and I'm sure of this. It's true though that I haven't been to Simla yet which is the place with the bad reputation. The real trouble with the English here is their preoccupation with their pay and consequent social rivalry.

Being on the College Staff means one quaint thing, and that is that I have to try to get jobs for old students. The other day I wrote to the Chancellor of Calcutta University, and got one of my M.A.'s on to that body. And just now I'm trying strenuously to get another of my men, a Christian, into the Police, and another fellow into the same job. Fortunately De Montmorency the Commissioner's Assistant is a thoroughly good fellow and there is no bother in approaching him.

I've been made one of the Examiners in the M.A. degree for the Punjab University, so next year I'll see something of the working of that body. Quaint isn't it, to think of me examining, and travelling about on the Board of a University! On the whole the Educational system here strikes me as a beastly mistake: degrees lead to blind-alley employments or else to the Bar, and a great proportion of students, puffed up with John Stuart Mill, etc., become political agitators and malcontents. Relations between English and Hindu professors are bad, and there is a distinct colour bar except in the Mission colleges. On the whole an American Mission (Presbyterian) College at Lahore, the Forman Christian College seems the best in this district. I'm inclined to credit to some extent the very wide rumours which go about of unfair dealing by one of the {one word omitted} College professors, a man I've had lunch with, who's pressed me to stop with him and his wife, who's very interesting, but hard to trust, and who boasts of his mercenary attitude to what he calls 'this pestilential country'. These Government people are highly paid, yet want more. One good man at Lahore is —— whom I knew well at Oxford and who is very efficient as a chemist, and from him I've heard a lot about his colleagues. But I'll know more presently.

It's very jolly up here. Mr. Rudra had been ill, so I wanted to get him away, and it was only a night's run in the train through a very hot night. From Kalka the junction from Simla it's a winding road of 9 miles. Mr. Rudra went by rickshaw, I walked, and very interesting it was to go from zone to zone of vegetation, starting with bamboos, then cacti, then trees like ash, and ending with the pine forest here, and chestnut-trees in flower and cherries ripe beside the roads. The cuckoo is a familiar sound. We're about 6,000 feet up, which isn't high for a hill station, and it's chiefly military here, with a Pasteur institute, and sanatoria and that sort of thing. There's an English Church, and a Presbyterian one, and a Baptist Chapel. There's a Highland regiment and other bodies of troops. This house is far away from the main part along a cliff-edge where a road runs among pines, rather a Bourne-mouthy effect, and the valley below in the mist and at night with its lights from native villages looks like the sea. Simla is a day's walk away over the hills and from there the road runs into the interior to Kotgarh. I don't know at all what I'll do in the vac. For some time I'm booked with S.S., who's an uncertain individual, and then C. B. Young is trying to persuade me to walk up the Chini valley with him. S. will be able to describe that journey to you. It's the way into Thibet. He took it with C. Unless S.S. goes to Ceylon I probably won't look up Menon and Naryana after all this summer, although they both pro-mised me tiger shooting which is attractive. Menon has written to me today to say that he's been laid up with a strain, but is now better. As to my health, at present I'm in great form, and I enjoyed the heat. All the same I'm going to be taking it easy for awhile, except that I'll probably spend a few days in the beginning of July riding about on horseback in the Delhi village district with one of my students whose father is a big country magistrate.

It's great news about your cough, and I'm so glad. By the time this reaches you Ned ought to have arrived, so you'll all be very happy together. I hope Frank's exam. will go all right, and that Arnie will find it easy to get to work again. That seems to be about enough for the present. So with love to you all

from WILL

KASAULI. 24/6/14

DEAR MOTHER

Last mail brought me your letter and Arnie's, with all the photographs of the tour. They are really excellent, and, as I know the places mostly, gave me a lot of pleasure. Photos are little use except as reminders of people and places. All the same Mrs. S. seems to have been of use with her Delhi pictures, which is good. I can't describe life out here at all, and only someone who has seen the queer mix-up of modern and mediæval things can realise it. A type of India was an altar I saw at Jaipur to the goddess of slaughter Kali. They kill a goat there each morning. And hanging by the altar was on one side the great bloody sacrificial sword, on the other a Waterbury watch. That is India: one side of it at any rate. It's an amazing country. Sometimes one feels it's like a volcano. Other times it seems more like a great stagnant pond with gas-bubbles and smell and a certain amount of iridescence due to decay. Really it's not like either but the educated minority attract the attention and prevent one realizing easily the changelessness of the villages and their stability, which is a foundation for anything good or bad. And then there's all the difference in the world between the rationalistic conceited Hindu, who has a philosophy but hardly seems to know what a personal religion is, and the faithful Moslem who hates civilization and is a man. The thing that makes one happy is the character of the Christian students in the College, and the way in which Hindu and Moslem alike absorb the teaching and seem really to be in touch with the personality of our Lord without confessing it. Even the Christians have their difficulties which are going to cause trouble, between the Modernist with his higher criticism and his persistent questioning of miracles, etc. (the Hindu spirit rejects miracles. Moslems accept them without difficulty) and the simple faith. The bishops and others at home seem to be threshing these questions out, and yet talking does no good. It's a matter of temperament. But meanwhile tolerance on either side is hard, and signs of a conflict are fairly plain. In our college the difference in the scripture teaching between say the two Youngs must strike the students, and it's a pity indeed that there's no general agreement. Then again one gets division in regard to Sunday observance, teetotalism and the like. 'Life is a queer mix-up, and I suppose we're not meant to understand it but just go on unseeing.'

I heard from Marsh-Roberts last mail, from Amiens. He's walking about in France, and seems all right. Also a letter came from Green, who's had scarlet fever very badly but is mending now. And I had a receipt for 2/- from the British and Foreign Bible Society for literature. What this means I don't know, unless you've ordered them to send me papers. At any rate there's no hurry about finding out, so I merely mention it now. You'll have Ned with you now, which will be A.1. It's good to hear too that Bob is having more time on his hands, and altogether you ought to have a very happy summer together at home. I wish it were possible for me to look you up.

The chief news here is that the Z.s have a daughter, born on the 20th. It's a comfort to have that over. All the same I look upon it as in a way the beginning of troubles. Mrs. Z. too young to shift for herself and a family in this country,   {eight words omitted}. And Z. himself is incorrigibly conscientious.   {seven words omitted}.   Some day I'll feel tempted to write a book on marriage and that sort of thing. But though our absurd boy and girl marriages and the worse custom of grown men marrying infants— bolstered up by the lie that a woman of 20 is 7 years older than a man of the same age whereas they are both children—are bad enough in all conscience, they are sunlight compared with the pitiable state of affairs here. There's a youth in the 1st year at college whom Arnie could knock down yet he has two children who'll be like him when they grow up I suppose. I've talked to a man who told me how he'd lain in wait for days in a temple just in order to get one glimpse of the girl he was to have for second wife. Never a word to her. And this sight of her veiled struck him as enterprise. What wonder that this Delhi is famous for its vices. And then when people do marry, custom decrees that husband and wife only see each other for years, for an hour in the early morning, and an hour at night, no more. What can they know of each other? Our system substitutes ignorant reverence for matehood and may bring disillusionment, but here there is nothing at all. When these fellows talk to me about their position, and ask me for advice I'm driven desperate, because they don't even know what they're aiming at, and I don't understand at all what they feel, which blocks out sympathy. I've understood when Englishmen have asked me my opinion of their going off with other men's wives. Here I see no light so long as there are mothers and grandmothers living. In two generations when the old people have gone there'll be a change. The women

govern this country by the wildest of ways, and our Suffragettes aren't
in it with them. What do you think of a mother's threatening, with
every serious intention, to commit suicide by burning herself with
kerosene, a common trick, if her son carried out what to my mind was
a magnificent plan for the education of his young boy. She beat him
there, and naturally, and she's a type of the old ladies of this country
with their hatred of change, their bigotry of religion, their wish to
rule with the rod. And they have the whip hand owing to the joint-
family system which makes grandmother, mother, and sons' wives live
all together, only as I say seen for two hours in the 24 by their menfolk.
Oh, the wrong of unshapely things is a wrong too great to be borne.
I'm sorry to write to you in this way, but I'm muddled a bit personally
at present. And when I look out over this valley 2,000 feet deep
with palms and bamboos and cacti at the bottom, and pines at the top,
when I see the hills in ridge upon ridge on the other side with only
today's fine-weather haze hiding the great snows, the contrast between
this nature and the Delhi town hits hard. Not that the villages in these
hills are perfect by any means, but at least the people in them are fairly
free to follow their instincts, and not killed by custom. They're still
Hindus in custom here, not as one gets them further back Tibetan with
many men marrying one wife and that sort of thing. Very fair in
complexion they are mostly, and the women wear great ugly nose-
rings far worse than those of the women of the plains, and are in
trousers like Punjabis. The hill-slopes are all worked into narrow little
terraces sometimes not more than 4 feet broad, and planted with
maize. Men and women work together, and the children are all penned
together in one cottage in each village, built over a stream so that the
little babies may have water dripping on their heads to cool them.
Round Kasauli there are 100's of such villages, but further off, as far
as I've been in my wanderings, one comes to great wild hill-sides not
safe to move about in without a gun, on account of bears and leopards.
One such I wanted to go to, to inspect a great Gurkha fort with round
turrets at the four corners, but it's too far, and hardly safe, so I'll give
it up. There are occasional English flowers on the hills, and some birds
which sing, and the cuckoo. Also down in the valley where water is
(not much, but I've found one stream where I can bathe as though I
was in the tropical house of the botanical gardens) there are ferns of
many sorts. If I find any of unusual beauty—so far maidenhair is most

prominent—I'll try to get some to you. And the views here are very distant, very fine. One can sit on a hill and look north-west and south-west over the great plain with the Sutlej 30 or 40 miles off like a great estuary winding away for hundreds of miles. The clearness of the air at times has been marvellous and I must literally have been in control of 200 miles of distance. There's wild thyme up here but no heather or gorse. As to the climate it's hot in the sun still, but the air is delicious, a perfect drink.

Well I'll stop for the present now

Love

from

WILL

SHANTI KUNJ
KASAULI
30/6/14

MOTHER DEAR

It's raining now, so I can't go out, and there's a good chance of writing to you. The whole valley is full of wet, rain and mist, and one can only at whiles see the dim outline of the other side where there is a village and church Sonarvar, with a school for soldiers' sons founded by Sir Henry Lawrence. I went there for a service on Sunday, and will be lunching with the headmaster tomorrow, a pleasant person and an old Blue. The rain is very pleasant, but the changeableness of the weather is queer. This morning it was very hot and sultry, sleepy in the extreme, and now comes the storm. But I'm very fit, though not so energetic as in Delhi.

I suppose that's a sign that the work was tiring me. All the time I was very fresh and not in the least bored, but as soon as it was over it seemed nice to do nothing but look at the hills. Occasionally these days I have been very strenuous doing long marches, but mostly have spent them dreamily. There's so much to look back over which I haven't had time to get into clear outline, and when I've nothing to do—I'm without books altogether just now—it's pleasant to remember, as talks with Young in the desert (one could make a book, several books out of him) or Captain Ivens on board ship or Miss Trench in view of Minicoy the coral island. Very wonderful all this time has been. And when I read the Bible it's queer to have pictures in my mind of Simon the Tanner's house or of the Bethlehem road to Jerusalem. Then again people I met, like the Mrs. Donnithorne (did I mention how I went with her from Charing Cross to Beirut and then met her in Jerusalem? I was sorry not to be able to accept her invitation to dinner that night) or Theodor Fast, who sent me a postcard the other day. He was a rich German born in Bethlehem, and living in Jerusalem, a fine fellow. People more than places for me. Your last letter said again that you were weak, less strong this summer. Why not really get someone to help you? Do take it easy though, when you find moving about tires you. I daresay it's mainly a matter of the mind still unsettled after Arnie's illness, which is natural enough. Ned's homecoming will do you good.

The best news is always of Father's cough. It's going is supremely good. Very jolly it was of Arnie sending the little photo of him at Ostend, and likewise the one of you by the sea.

For last week's news the biggest item was that of Bob as an Ulster army doctor. Out here it is hard to see what is happening in Ireland and in English politics. Every Indian practically is madly pro-Redmond without understanding anything of the matter—Mr. Rudra for instance—but the Anglo-Indian press is almost all Conservative. However as there's been no fighting yet, perhaps there won't be. If there is, will Frank join?

Frank I hope satisfied himself in his Mods. Exams are all very fluky, and the motto in regard to them is to make game of that which makes the same of you, as Omar Khayyam says. Still of course I'm an examiner myself now, on the Board of History of the Punjab University for the M.A. degree, which incidentally is amusing considering my age in actual years. Jenkin is too, for Chemistry in the B.A., but then his qualifications are terrific and his subject more of a speciality. Tell Father that as to the way in which Government think of our College, some of them think it is a hotbed of sedition and distrust. A few who know it better approve, and the Chief Commissioner of Delhi—although he's rude to A. has given us a splendid grant. I don't in the least blame officials for distrusting us: the mixture of radicalism, etc., which it has given its students is quite bad, though well-meaning. But Education here under the circumstances of government is almost of necessity seditious. Very little sense people have: they talk and talk and talk. Someday I'll give you my views of the government perhaps. The best thing in India to my mind is the Army.

Last mail brought me a postcard from little Fernand at Rennes. I do hope I'll see that child someday: his faithfulness is awe-inspiring. Also there arrived, a great pleasure, the *Bible in the World* from January to this month. Now and again I've seen a copy in Maitland House, but it's nice to have them for myself. There's no paper I know which gives you such a feeling of the world's breadth—it's like reading Walt Whitman—owing to its photos. And it's much easier to forget that there are other parts of the earth here than in England, because of course when one thinks one goes homewards. Thanks many. It's stopped raining now, but the climate is still short sighted. On clear days from this verandah one can get most glorious views, ridge upon ridge of fir-clothed red hills with the lower slopes in terraces for the Indian corn of the hill-villagers, and then far away, about 50 miles, the Snows. In the evenings one can see Simla with its lights, and the general effect of the valley is that one is looking down into a bay of the sea. That is better still westwards the other side of the hill. I go each day to a promontory about 7,000 ft. high to see the sunset, and look out over the great plain of North India for 100's of miles. There's nothing but my eyesight's humanity to prevent me seeing to the sea. And the only thing that marks the great flat panorama is the Sutlej, a great snake of a river 40 or 50 miles to the westwards, looking like an estuary with its flooded pools from the first rains and winding away southwards till it's out of sight. When one gets a really good sunset it will be splendid. So far there have been no sunsets in India to compare either with storm-sunsets I've seen in England and in France or with the afterglow of Damascus and Port Said, though there have been a few afterglows in Delhi. Sunrises have been better, yellow, gold, then rose, but not recently. I hope Edgar Vincent did better than he expected. Will you kindly let him know that I'm simply stuffed up with Indian corres-pondents and have little time for writing. So he must wait a long time before I write to him. I still owe Mrs. Vincent a letter.

Ned will be with you now, and I'll enclose if I have time a letter for him in this.

At the end of the week I'm going back to Delhi for a day or two, to see various officials for Mr. Rudra, but since it's hotter than ever there, they say a record, I won't go for my tour on horseback through

the villages, but come back here as soon as possible. After a bit I'll go
to Simla probably, since Sir Syed Ali Imam wants me to stop with
him. He's the only Indian on the Indian Government, the Viceroy's
Council I mean, officially; a Moslem nominally and rather like Dr.
Whitelocke in his manners.

The Z.s have called their baby —— and Z. writes about its admira-
bility. He's an extraordinary man, more centred in work, more
conscientious, than one would think possible {four words omitted}
It's a vice with him, and he's ill again in consequence. Yet a good
colleague, very.

Lee Abbott, whom Father writes about, is stationed not far from
Lahore. If you like I can look him up sometime. Where is Harold
Inman? Do you know? He's one of the people I haven't known whom
I've most wanted to know of men I've met. I'll leave this now.

Thursday. 2/7/14

The £10 will doubtless come by the next mail. Barring accidents
there'll be no need to use it.

I'm very well, Mother, and only anxious that you and Father should
be the same. Don't worry about me whatever you do; there's no point
in having a doubtful mind and it's much better to live in the moment.

Love to you all, all of you.

your son WILL

The money came all right in the middle of last week so I'm very rich.

DELHI CLUB

DEAR MOTHER

Last mail brought me, besides my usual letters one from C., who
reported that he'd seen you—he writes every other week—and another
from Cyril who's walking about in the Morbihan or was when he
wrote, from Vannes. He was going south-east into Touraine, and then
going to Russia again, and had been ill. Then too Mr. Cave answered
my letter, and Nellie wrote, so I was fairly rich.

All the same your letter was distressing. Why this feeling miserable?
Possibly it's just the heat which takes some people that way though
it's bracing to me. But do, do, take care of yourself, and above all
don't work unless you've nothing to do. In Z. we have a continual
warning here of what it is to 'be busied about many things'. The week-

days as well as the Sabbaths were made for man, not man for the weekdays.

Captain Noel is a Palestine Exploration engineer. Although it would be good for Ned to have seen the Gulf still as you say a rest is important. I notice a Capt. Shakespeare has just done a ride from Kuweit to Suez of 1,800 miles in 3 months, good going.

KASAULI. 9/7/14

I was down in Delhi for a few days of business, seeing all sorts of officials about the new College, the Conspiracy case, the mission's constitution and the like. It amuses me to be in touch with these lofty fellows, who are mostly very nice. The Anglo-Indian difficulty is chiefly the young civilian new to society who swaggers in a nouveau riche way, and his wife. In Delhi I stopped with Mrs. Hibbert Ware, the largest woman I know, Irish and nice. Irish affairs engross conversation nowadays too—de Montmorency who's Irish from the south was very gloomy about things, Captain Evans-Gordon another good official (young) much more hopeful. A queer mix-up the world is. Can you please ask Frank to go down to Ned's house, find a book in *Everyman's Library* called *Mediæval Stories and Romances* or some such name, look at the end of it for a story called 'Sir Guy de Tabarie', and copy out for me what Sir Guy says to Saladin about the Rule of Chivalry. Just a short piece, of the style of Tennyson's 'Sir Gareth' 'live pure, right wrong, etc.' I want it for a popular exposition of chivalry. There's a lot of talk in the book, but just one speech is unmistakably the thing I want. If he's in doubt Ned will help him. Delhi was mighty hot: I played tennis there yesterday and it was like having a bath. As to sunstrokes, of course one can only take precautions: I'm quite a sober person really and you needn't be anxious about me. Very well I've been, happily, with nothing worse than a sore throat since October, and that I got up here the other week due no doubt to the change. What did you think of C.?

{27 words omitted}

He's not coming out here again—marriage and that sort of thing will stop him.

For Scripture teaching my own work doesn't seem to me valuable along that line, except so far as I hand on Christ's teaching in regard to moral conduct. I mean it's not so much a showing of Our Lord that

I'm given to make, as of His teaching. But that's not my business to worry with. 'The thing done without God is better kept stillborn' as Pindar has it. There's no use trying to be intellectual. So in place of arguing with them about the hen and the egg, I praise its eating and show how best it can be cooked. I'm sleepy today, by cause of a night-journey {10 words omitted} This land never ceases to be interesting. And up here it's far more relaxing than in the plains. Probably I'll be moving further north presently with S.S., who had arranged that I should teach his wife (a purdah lady: if things weren't told me in confidence I'd love to write about this side of Hinduism) to speak English. But his mother has put her foot down and it's off. That old lady is a kind of Dowager Empress of China in her methods. At Delhi I went out to dinner with a Hindu of the College, in his house, and he introduced me to his daughter, a girl of 16. Rudra is amazed beyond measure, for the man is quite strict. So I progress still: non-smoking, etc. helps me with Hindus: it would be better still from that point of view if I gave up meat-eating. (All right. I have no intention of doing so!) But there are many things in their attitude which are hard to grasp, and no one can learn the East easily, the East as it is shown in this little part of Delhi.

It's a dingy looking day now though beautifully sunny as I walked up the 6,000 feet and 9 miles here from Kalka. The plain is spread out in front of one like the wash of a ship getting wider and dimmer the further one looks. How I wish you could see what I've seen. But also of course I'd like, say, to be at the Varsity Match on a warm day, and see some English grass, with you.

The children up here are a pleasure. One sees babies in Delhi, but seldom any boys or girls between 12 and 20. Here there are plenty. There's a large school for soldiers' sons, and another for girls. The Principal is a Mr. Barnes, late of Summerfields School, Oxford, an Oriel man. He gave me lunch the other day, and I met there an old St. John's man, rough but strong. Oh yes, without doubt I lead quite a good time. It is not good to see only Indians.

Also I'm getting a little to know L., or was before I came away.

{19 words omitted}

Well, that's all for this week, and I'm sorry it isn't more interesting. Glad you're getting Pennell's book. There was a good photo of him in one of the *Bible in the World*'s. Thanks for Children's S.S. report. I do hope your next letter will shew you healthier. To all of you best love.

WILL

College address always

15/7/14. (SHANTI KUNJ KASAULI)

MY DEAR MOTHER

Your letter last week with the news of Ned's return was good to get. By the time this gets to you he'll be nearly off again I suppose: can you tell him therefore that if he's in Stamboul again he should go to the shop of Sébah et Joaillier, 439 Grande Rue de Pera and buy a photo or two of an Ephèbe drapé newly arrived in the Museum. Captain Young got one on the 26th June 1913 for 10 piastres, and it seems to me a masterpiece.

With your letter came the books on China, for which many thanks. I haven't been able to read them yet of course, but in the next weeks will have time enough. As a matter of fact I read very little: Tolstoy's *Anna Karenina* is all my bag of recent weeks and that only cursorily. Only I read a little with S.S., who's down in Delhi again (Morris. *News from Nowhere* is our text with Isaiah and some poetry.) I've seen such a lot that I need to digest it more than to hear the opinions of other people. It's nice to know that you enjoyed the photograph. The Staff are really excellent fellows, though Sen is the cream of the cup. You don't say by the way what you thought of C., who interested me more than most men I've met, and also pleased me very well. I've found life very different since he left, with little outside interests to keep one human, and if it wasn't for the ladies of the hospital I might at times have got tired. As it was though there was no flagging at all, so this country agrees with me. Up here it's much more relaxing than in Delhi, as was easy to find out from my visit there the other week. But it's delightful to watch the changing lights on the hill-sides, and to clamber about on the rocks. At times when the wind moves about the pines there's a sound as of the sea, and the lights in the valley ride like ships at anchor, so that I am out again in the wide spaces of God. It's the restlessness of horizon-seeking coming on me again I suppose. If only I could go and see Hughes in South China! Though of course mostly it's queer but restlessness takes the form of wanting to be home.

I'll be very busy tomorrow probably so I'm writing this to you late at night, and won't do much. It's been a tiring day with a long walk in the rain to the Simla railway line, to meet a student, and to look up another in a sanatorium. Mr. Rudra and S.S. are both in Delhi as witnesses in the Conspiracy Trial, but Shudhir Rudra is with me. When he goes to Cambridge in the autumn I'll write more about him. He's possibly the best modern product of the college, a brick.

Don't be afraid of my getting sunstroke or anything of that sort. So far as is possible I take precautions, and beyond that it's not our business to be anxious. I wish you were as well as me: what you said in your letter of two weeks ago has worried me a bit. How is Mr. O'Connor by the way? Remember me to him, if you have a chance.

Frank knows his own business best I suppose, but scratching is a risky sort of gamble. He knows what happened to Pavière in that business.

Lady Hardinge's death is the main topic now: she is very popular in India. But Irish affairs also take up attention. In Delhi I had a little talk about them with some I.C.S. men, who took a very gloomy view. But surely something can be done to keep the peace. Well, I'll go to sleep sitting here if I keep writing much longer, so enough for the present. The Mail goes from here tomorrow Thursday, and comes in on a Sunday, so we're further away from each other as a result of being in the hills. I'll finish this tomorrow.

16/7/14

There's really nothing more in my head today, so it will be only a short letter you'll be getting this week. Do tell me how you are when you write next. It's annoying that letters take such a time moving across.

Love to all of you

Your son WILL

DEAR MOTHER KASAULI 22/7/14

The mail-steamer broke down last week somewhere between Port Said and Bombay, with the result that we haven't any letters yet. So I am writing without knowledge of how you were a fortnight ago, and can only talk of my own doings. The jolliest of them is that I've seen Captain Young again; he wrote to me saying he wanted to stop with me for a few days in Delhi, but as I wasn't there he went straight through to Simla and saw me *en route*, giving me breakfast. An admirable fellow, as Ned will tell you; he said by the way that he was sending two walking-sticks to Busrawi Agha. Also he was full of stories of Captain Noel, with whom he used to wander about in disguise through the bazaars of Bombay. I have an invitation from him to his brother's in Simla, but probably won't go. The death of Lady Hardinge has of course thrown Simla out of gear; also if I do go up there I can hardly avoid stopping with Sir Ali Imam. Simla however is a place where one has to be in grand garments, and just at present most of my clothes are in Delhi.

It's raining here, raining tremendously. But there are days of brilliance, and on one such the other day Sudhir Rudra and I, with two students who had come up by train to see me, had a gorgeous bathe under a waterfall in a mountain-burn. There was a high bank near by absolutely overgrown with large wild roses, and down below there were bananas in a grove, with bamboos. There are good things here too, most certainly. And on the morning of the next day I went to a Gurkha hill-fort and examined it. There are four near Kasauli, that is about 10 miles off each of them, on different peaks. The best is infested with leopards and bears and much too dangerous to approach even in the day-time, without a rifle. The second best also has a cheetah living in it, which has lately been robbed of a cub for the Puijore Zoological Gardens. So we could only see the third, not so big. But still they are alike in planning and construction. The Gurkhas were dominant here in the 18th century, which is therefore the probable date, and the scheme of the forts is clearly just to command the passes. They are built of stone, rather roughly mortared for the building had cracked badly in one place, and being on the summits are so far as I could judge waterless. In size they are very small, the walls about 20 feet high only, and they are of oblong shape with four round turrets at the corners. These are very curiously adjuncts, and not parts of the oblong. The walls are all well pierced with slit-windows of the ordinary English pattern. The turrets have newel-staircases, and there were clearly two storeys once or three, throughout. The interior was very dirty and full of refuse, so I couldn't judge that easily. As to the purpose of a short double wall on one side I suppose there must have been a gate once, but the wall had been taken away by the neighbouring villages on the slope below. The wall at the gateway had also been broken down. There was a small ditch, round, and signs of an outer wall, but on the right hand side the cliff was precipice. The ditch must always have been dry. The sides of the bastions sloped out queerly, and a moulding ran round at the height of the ordinary walls, but otherwise the fort was a very plain building. The Gateway is on the left of the picture hidden by the bastion, and there was no path whatever except one approaching from the Himalayan oak on the left, which was on slightly higher ground than the fort. This fort is on a slope, rather than a peak and in the wet season has water below it not very far off. The cliff is very stiff climbing. So much for Ned's benefit. There's been rain in the plains now, and at the end of this week I will probably go down to meet one of my students, whose father is a great land-owner in the country, and who wants me to go for a tour on horseback with him among the villages. That will be interesting, and useful. However we'll see: to-day with its steady rain makes me feel lazy.

An annoying piece of news is that Z. has had fever again, rather badly, for four days.

{46 words omitted}

If he goes though it will be a real calamity: his name carries influence among the English, he's a splendid teacher, and most valuable of all he's married. However he's bound to stick it a year or two longer—he's wild always at the suggestion that he should go home—and then S. will be back again, and we'll have a new man too. This next year the College is to be run most absurdly short-handed; they are getting no-one in place of S. and C. The latter by the way has determined—he may have told you—to settle in England, owing to many reasons, and he will try to get a job at an Oxford college.

{23 words omitted}

But I'm sorry we're losing him.

Well, I'll stop now, and go on with this later.

23/7/14

The mail came last evening, letters from Father, Mother Ned and Frank. It's hard lines on the latter that he's been given a pass, but so long as Jesus College doesn't mind it won't matter. As to his reading history, he'll enjoy it though he'll have to do it in a different way from mine, learning more history and less human nature. If I were him I'd keep off occultism which often is a path to insanity. Will his history do all right for the army, I wonder? He mustn't give that up.

I'm having a remarkable time here just now, for S.S. has given his wife to me to teach English ways to her. Mr. Rudra has had to get out of the way therefore: it was good that I was able to bring him up here. As to him, he's a man I like very much, and respect. But never in my life have I met anyone more fond of being wise after the event. For the lady, I'm the only man besides her husband and male relations that she's ever spoken to or gone with without a veil, so it's the most interesting thing I've done yet. She knows a little English, taught her by an Indian Christian woman (her husband will have nothing to do with the Mission ladies) and has got over her shyness. We laugh now. She's very fair, and would be handsome as well as pretty if her mouth were firmer. Smiles very nicely. She wears just the tiniest silver stud in the left nostril, great ruby ear-pendants, and her arms are loaded with gold. Of course she wears Indian clothes, very magnificent. Yesterday, when the rain stopped, I took her out for a walk! I'll tell you more about her later. From the point of view of learning India this job is very important, and I won't care even if it makes my holiday rather a sedentary one.

As a matter of fact though I'm going to Delhi next week, there to meet a wild Punjabi Squireen who's coming into the city with horses, and we're going for a ride of a couple of hundred miles perhaps, just for the fun of it. There's been rain now in the plains, and they're growing green visibly, so it will do me good. And the Maharaja of Cassim-Bazar, the man who wanted me to tutor his children, has some wish for Kashmir. But I don't think there will be time to go there with him.

It's good to know you're feeling better a bit. Ease of mind is the great thing. This letter will reach you two days late. Please thank Frank for his information. The man is notorious as a discontented political I believe. Also the Photograph was jolly to have. John Kettlewell figures in it as well as your group. I had a very jolly letter from S. who's been sailing on the Shannon. Well that's enough for this week I think: I'm very fit and enjoying myself vastly. Mrs. M. and the infant both flourish. It's a nuisance about him.

May you all be very happy

Your loving WILL

I hope you won't be nervous at the late arrival of this. Nowadays I'm a complete vegetarian, keeping off eggs even. But it's not principle only politeness. You see I've been eating Indian food mostly for 5 weeks. But with Captain Young I had fish and beefsteak and devilled kidneys and bacon! Much better food.

KASAULI
30/7/14

Three splendid days I've had, Father, three days of the old India in which Englishmen were perfect, capable as men thought of no wrong. To start from the beginning. In the early hours of Monday, I walked through the black night down the 9 miles to Kalka, groping along the way, having to be very wide awake, but safe as a house so long as I was. Then to Delhi by train, and to Mr. Rudra's house where I changed into my riding-kit, which fortunately looks well. By the time I'd finished breakfast at C. B. Young's, Jai Narain Singh, one of my class, a Jat Hindu clumsily and heavily built and a good fellow, came driving up and I went to the station with him and sixteen miles or so north-west of Delhi to a place Bahadurgarh. Coming out I saw a glorious half-Arab mare from Jacobabad, with another horse, and on these we rode 10 miles or so on field paths to a village Mitraon. The country was very wet, very green; quite flat with a sandy soil and acacia trees growing. I was on the grey mare, which was said afterwards (and I believe it) to be the fastest horse in the south Punjab. So we rode till about 1 o'clock we came to the fortified house of my student's father, Rai Bahadar Raghunnath Singh. The family has ruled the district for twelve generations, and the father of Raghunnath won the battle of Najaf Garh for England, the last battle of the Mutiny, in which the rebels of Delhi were exterminated. They had the title Maharaja but it's lapsed under British rule though we've kept them lords of the land.

Raghunnath Singh was waiting as I rode up, a tall man 6 foot high looking taller for his wild turban, and weighing 190 pounds; and with him were some 20 men, retainers of the house. As I leant from the horse to shake hands with him he bowed with 'This is a happy day, your Honour,' and kissed my hand. And then after I was on my feet the servants came up man after man and touched my knees with their hands to shew respect. Comic it was, but explanatory of Anglo-Indian pride. We went through the great archway of the building and I had a bath and changed into Punjabi dress, having no luggage with me. And then we sat on the roof of the house for a while in the cool of the rain-clouds, and talked of Indian affairs.

Things were very different here to the continual dropping of contentious critics wearing out the patience to which I've got accustomed. Here was an old man, 62 he is, with a military point of view, who said 'We train our young men to talk of duties, not of rights.' A man whose father had served General George Lawrence—they treasure some letters of the latter's still, and possibly my name was the main cause of my royal treatment. A man who every morning as I was to see, after his prayers, did Indian club and sword exercise despite his years. He called servant after servant up to me to exhibit them, old men with wounds from the Kabul War under Lord Roberts, whose father and grandfather had served the family in battle. He complained of the leniency of the government in dealing with sedition, and said 'If Lord Kitchener is the next viceroy India will be heaven.' And then he talked of horses and guns till up came a Sanskrit-speaking poet with verses about me, the ruler from over-seas, and after that we went to the village sports-ground. The Jats are all agriculturists, worshippers of Krishna, very simple people most of whom serve a while in the army. And their spare time they spend in all sorts of sports, wrestling one of the most spectacular (catch-as-catch-can with a square shoulder fall). All the men of the village now performed, long-jump, high-jump. sprinting, wrestling. At Jai Narain's suggestion I competed in the Sprint and fortunately for the prestige of the British raj left them behind. Then the village school-boys were brought up and drilled before me, and we did a 'grand tour' about the place, my right arm going up and down all the time saluting. The sunset from the roof was glorious, a colour I've never seen before in the sky, something like what we mean by 'golden' applied to hair. And four peacocks stalked up and down before us all the while.

Another student from the neighbouring town of Najaf Garh dropped in in the course of the evening, a Brahmin too, but we all ate together of food one could stick one's teeth in, thick Zamindari bread. Then Jai Narain and Rup Narain Sharma the other student grumbled to me about their Hindu marriage system, and the old man prayed never moving a muscle but breathing in through one nostril and out through the other very slowly in the Yoga fashion. And after that we went to bed in the courtyard till the screaming of the peacocks at the sunrise woke us up.

Then prayers and exercise, the latter with Indian clubs and in all sorts of gymnastic ways, walking on the hands, etc., after which came in huge bowls of hot milk. That over Jai Narain and I rode off again to see the site of his grandfather's battle (Buldeo Singh his name was, and he was Regent of Bhurtpure) and beyond that to a tower in a village 11 miles away. We walked, cantered and galloped, no trotting, and my mare could give his horse 50 yards in 200 I should think. It was very hot by the time we got back from the village to Najaf Garh, where I was given a public reception. First they had me to the Courthouse, there to look learned and say nothing while a case was compromised. Raghunnath Singh is the magistrate for the district, of course. Then a meal with Rup Narain Sharma, and after that an expedition to the School. Here they'd got up a notice 'welcome', after which all the 450 boys were paraded before me, drilled, and shouted 'Huzoor Lawrence' (or rather Lalun). (Huzoor = Captain or very respectful sir.) A select squad did a very excellent performance on the bars, a deal harder things than I've ever done, some of them. And then came the horses again and we rode through lines of townsfolk saluting, out through the fortified gates and over the two miles of sandy firm path to Mitraon.

The evening passed as before, except that the old lord talked more and more reactionarily, till I marvelled how Mr. Rudra and he could be in the same land. And next morning there was another performance.

By dint of a reckless gallop over rough ground from which the mare and I had emerged unscathed—a horse like that makes one mad with joy—I'd got a wholly fictitious reputation as a horseman, and had to mount a wild buckjumping beast. He was fortunately rather blind in the right eye, so it was a case of throwing oneself into the saddle from the off and sticking on for a plunge or two, when he quietened down, not so bad as I expected. And Jai Narain's wife (who's a daughter of a famous Jat fighting man Hon. Captain Hanwant Singh V.C.— he got that for saving Kitchener's life) then presented me—through him of course—with some work which I'm sending to Mother. It's not very beautiful but is the sort of cloth which brides bring as dowries. She also gave some bead-work, and Raghunnath Singh presented me with a rosary such as the Hindus use. Can you please get some

photos printed of me at Gillman's and send me five for future use, by
the way? I'll send the young children of this Mitraon household some
presents sometime, but it would please the old lord if I gave him a
signed photo. I felt more at home in that house than anywhere else in
India so far; Raghunnath Singh is such a gentleman and his relations
with his villagers are so jolly that the place was a glorious contrast to
the luxurious, mysterious Delhi. He came in with me on horse-back to
Bahadurgarh yesterday, and I've promised to go back there.

These Jats are less hair-splitting than the other Hindus, more
inclined to faith than to philosophy. Raghunnath Singh struck me as
very genuinely religious. And he wasn't in the least unwilling to listen
to my religious views, though of course as an old man of such standing
he was inclined to lay down the law.

When I got back to Delhi it was very hot, and I went to C.B.'s to
get my mail. Then I looked up R., my pupil, who has done very well
in his exam. He's stopping in Delhi, because his father is keener now
on my teaching the lady. I dined with Canon Allnutt and this morning
climbed up the 9 miles again getting tremendously hot.

Mrs. Barker has written to me about her brother. Please thank her:
I've no mind to write today. Likewise Frank: he's been very good to
carry out researches for me, but he's told me quite enough I think.

That's enough for this week.

Love to you all

WILL

If Ned is still with you, give him birthday greetings.

KASAULI. 5/8/14

Yesterday evening I learnt through a private wire to the C.O. here
that England had declared war. It's an awful prospect of a world-
struggle, though our own position appears better than any other belli-
gerent's. Just at the moment though the personal aspect is what I feel
most. What will Ned have to do, stop at home or go East again and
steer his country into safe waters? And how far will there be a need for
the British army in addition to the Navy: how far will volunteers be
wanted? These are the sort of questions troubling me. I wish I were at
home, and yet if supplies fail it will be good that you have one less to
feed. Today I must write and compare notes with Jenkin, and find how
the business takes him. He's got a brother in the Navy. Austria seems

altogether to blame for the struggle, and no doubt Germany instigated her. Italy's abstention, on the ground that they are the aggressors, at least shows that history will absolve the Triple Entente, all of whom seem bound by honour to stand or fall together. And humanly speaking there doesn't seem to be much likelihood of the latter. The C.O. here thinks it will be all over with Germany in six weeks, and we can only pray it will be so. A long protracted death-struggle would be the most terrible war of Europe. I'm trusting that the English fleet will begin by an overwhelming victory, and then our part will be over, and you'll be assured of food coming into England safely. News, news, news, we long for, and we don't get. Too far away. Yet at any rate it's good that I'm not merely enjoying myself touring in Kashmir. All leave has been stopped here for officers and men, none of them are allowed to go home, and altogether the country is mightily affected, especially commercially. Lady Hardinge's death was providential; it's stirred up loyal feelings to the Viceroy so that I don't expect any disturbance here. Our isolation is what strikes me most; I haven't any idea for example whether you'll ever get this letter.

There's no paper published today. It's the Sabbath of the pressmen. Tomorrow we'll know more. It's a strain to feel so useless and so out of the way, so very far from you.

6/8/14

The newspapers haven't yet got the news of England's declaration, so I'm still in the dark. This does make me feel far away from you all.

Your birthday is coming along. And yet with this trouble in the world it seems mockery to hope you will be happy. A merry day it can't be, yet a happy one, in faith, it may be. I wonder if this letter will get to you in time. It hardly seems safe to send you the cloth I have for you, and in any case since it can't go overland it will come late. I'll ask the post-office people, when there's a chance of getting there. The rain has been too overwhelming for two or three days to get out almost. Please thank Bob for his letter. And I'm glad about Arthur Barker's success. Yet all this sort of thing is swallowed up in the War.

Out here we're so isolated that we don't seem likely to be of any use except by praying. And as I hope it will be a naval affair I suppose one would be equally useless so far as action goes at home. That for you will save one trouble, of the individual finding it his duty to volunteer.

When I said the other day that a European war alone would give peace to Ireland, how little I realized what I was saying.

There's no use in more talk. Love to you all, love.

WILL

KASAULI. 12/8/14

DEAR FATHER

We're still moving about miserably, longing for war-news, of which we get nothing certain, but the wildest of rumours. As I spent Monday and Tuesday, and for the matter of that Saturday too, over the valley at Sonawar with some friends of mine, English people, I felt it particularly there. Here as I'm alone in my anxiety more or less, it's only an individual case, and not an epidemic.

On Saturday I represented Sonawar in a Rifle-Shooting Competition and did very fairly. So I'll be of use when the row comes here, if it does. There's considerable fear of trouble amongst the Sikhs, which will be due, if it comes, rather largely to H. D., our St. Stephen's and St. John's Oxford man. But if the war's over soon all will be well. Meanwhile everyone volunteers, and there's a censorship over the papers which is beastly, for we can only surmise that the news is bad when there is none.

I was stopping with Sanderson, head of the Sonawar College. He's an old St. John's man, who had become a kind of myth in my time for wild behaviour, and is nicely married with one little boy a year old. It was jolly to be English again; Indian food and ways are very scrappy. Also it was wholesome for me to get alongside of a keen young mind of the Imperialist sort. There's a tremendous temptation here to become a machine with a clerical pose, but so far with the help of my riding and my lady-friend in the Hospital I've avoided it. By the way, to counteract what Mr. Rudra appears to have told you about me here's a scrap from the *Delhi Mission News*: "Lawrence gets through a great deal of work, while preserving the air of a 'man about town'. He is said to be a great favourite with the ladies, owing to his mysterious powers of borrowing motor-cars and using them for the public benefit." A libel.

Yes. I'm getting a useful knowledge of people, though how am I to use it? This latest experience of the purdah lady is very possibly unique in the world. At least it amazes Rudra, who again was astounded at my going to R.'s Hindu Wedding ceremony. If only I could suddenly learn the language I'd be pleased. But in Delhi there was much too much to do, and here I find it hard to settle down to such work. Still even if I can't use my knowledge it's interesting and amusing. And someday perhaps I'll be inspired to write: I almost was the other day about a Jewess friend of mine. The trouble is most of the things I know were told me in confidence. It's very hard to chatter in a letter now, when this trouble is heavy on the world. If only we could get news of a crushing naval victory by England we'd be happier. But nothing comes. Only it appears as though the Belgians and the French were both doing well, and the German manifestoes appear very hypocritical. I'm anxious about individuals, as to how it is hitting all of you, whether Bob and Ned and Frank are training Terriers, and what Cyril is doing out in Russia. I do feel far away.

Well that's enough for just the now. Please thank Bob for the *China's Millions* (I enjoyed Dr. Apricot's book vastly one Sunday) and Frank for his painstaking about Riza; he need bother no further at all. Indian students are asses to hate Cromwell Road; they hate to look facts in the face. Riza sounds rather a shady customer methinks. Education is the curse of this country, or one of its many curses, but since it's come to stay the adding of a Christian influence such as we're trying to give is vitally important; our men really do run better morally I believe than the rest. But it's typical of their thought that we are really suspected of immorality because we're unmarried. Delhi is like the decaying carcase of an Empire with the bones sticking through and the whole foul thing swarming with maggots. Sorry if Mother doesn't like the metaphor! I'll write something more tomorrow, though I haven't an idea when this will get through to you. Hope your cough's reappearance was only fleeting.

13/8/14

Still there's no news whatever of the doings of our fleet: the press censor here is keeping a tight hold on things, but we can't help fearing ill, since there'd be no harm in letting the masses know if we'd won a victory. Ugh! It's beastly. S.S. came back the day before yesterday, with his wife after all. The poor lady had been very sad leaving here— I think she's enjoying the experience as much as I am—and after all she over persuaded him. So here she is again. In ten days time we should get a move on, but we won't go far for there's need for readiness to meet all emergencies. If the war is soon over there should be no trouble: in the other alternative, why we fear our Sikh regiments, the very men who saved us in the Mutiny!

Rudra and I are upset just now about A. Another precipitate move on his part! You'll hear about it in time, when it becomes public property, meanwhile Mr. Rudra is almost broken-down. There's need that a man should be wise out here if he's going to take his own line, and above all need that he shouldn't take himself too seriously and get conceited. Compare Stokes. Though *he* isn't proud. Tell Frank that Rabindranath used to be registered a member of the Brahmo Samaj, that is of the old sort, not Keshub Chunder Sen's New Dispensation. But I believe that he has little to do with the Society now, and I doubt if he'd call himself a member. They're a very small body numerically, the Brahmos, though it's no doubt fairly true to say that there are more Brahmos outside the society than in it! That is, their influence is very wide. If Rabindranath were more of a man it would be a jolly good thing for India.

If this war is not fairly decisive and productive of a large indemnity I doubt whether the New Delhi will be built after all. It will give the Government their exuse to retire from a hare-brained undertaking. So the course of the war will affect the College. I'm glad Frank liked Keswick, but his Free Kirk Camp must have been finished by the war, wasn't it? Now no doubt he's training. I see Kitchener's forming a second line. It's good he was in England, not in Egypt. A great fellow— certainly great.

You'll observe that my letter-writing faculty is failing me. You don't need to read descriptive passages about the hills at this time. In fact all you need is the word that I'm well, which is set here. The only news for you really is about my stay at Sonawar which was a pleasure; it's jolly to be English again, to take a lady into dinner and help her to her horse. Also I admit meat tastes well after long subsistence on rice and lentils fried in butter. You can't imagine all the different roles I've filled since you saw me last, teacher, preacher, lady's companion, chauffeur, Inspector of His Majesty's Schools, of his Army (when at Jhansi), Actor-manager, throat-doctor (lancing an abscess), consumptive nurse (not much), physical culture instructor, financial agent (I negotiated concerning a loan of £7,000 the other day), art critic, night-watchman (spent one night crouching by a wall, in running-costume, with a mashie ready to smite, to no use), cookery teacher to a Kahar cook, and I forget the rest. It's interesting even when it's not amusing or useful.

And next I suppose I'll be soldier. But when I talk of trouble here don't let Mother worry. There's no fear of it whatsoever for months, and if the Sikh Regiments are mostly sent to Europe there'll be no fear at all. And surely the war should be over quickly. To judge by German proclamations they've lost their heads which is a good sign. Presently I'll have to write to my German friend in Jerusalem, I should think, to show there's no personal feeling.

Well, may you all be well, and as happy as is possible.

Love. WILL

31/8/14
BAJAURA
KULU

MOTHER DEAR,

It's been your birthday, and every now and then I have wondered what you were doing, and how you were feeling. This war is beyond the beyonds. And it's so long since I heard anything: we've sent a runner off this evening to the Post-Office, and hope to get our letters and newspapers by the end of the night, and then we'll know if England has fared well. But I won't know how you are bearing it, nor in what ways it is hitting you hard. Forgive me if grumbling in this manner makes things harder for you, but I want to write quite naturally and it's grumbling that comes swiftest to me. I am writing this in a place about as far from war in its aspect as you'd find anywhere. On the left there's the valley we came down just now, the Dulchi pass, and a river in it which is a pace or two off in front, just a mountain torrent. Opposite there is a great fruit-garden—apples, pears, plums, peaches, apricots, everything—going up a hill-slope and belonging to an English settler Col. Rennick, who's married a Kulu woman. Behind it is a pine-crested hill. To the right the river runs into another bigger one the Biasse and there the skyline is cut by a high ridge caught up in the mists of the gathering night. There is the gurgling of the water mixed with the cricket's jar, and altogether it's Arcadia.

This Kulu valley runs up between two ridges of hills for 60 miles, and it's fruit-orchards all the way, most like England. The people in it are of a delightful complexion, red on brown, and dress like Japanese somewhat, the men in woollen shirt-coats, the women in very short coarse woollen clothes shaped like kimonos. The valley is hard to get at, but is famous for its fruit. And I'll ride along it tomorrow.

Coming here was difficult, for the rain had washed away the road in places, and several bridges were broken. That meant that we had to ride across streams like the Dee at Llangollen, and had to spend a lot of time in repairing the track by the simple process of throwing down more of the cliffs to make a possible descent for the mules. This is my business: I'm leader of the expedition when it comes to difficulties. Still we're here with no casualties, and some people who joined on to us for a while killed a mule and saw the baggage of two ponies smashed at the foot of a precipice. So we've done well. The responsibility amuses me: my chief regret is that we've seen no bears which are said to be plentiful. By the way, believe me that I'm sober as a judge nowadays: never fear for me so far as my own caution goes. Accidents are happily not in our hands. One of our muleteers has fever: otherwise we're very fit.

There's been a lot of rain and I wish you could have seen me having lunch today, in a cottage where my eyes ran with wood-smoke, with 7 wild men sitting around dressed in their woollen sacks, with a pony dripping moisture standing with lolling ears outside, as I swallowed various indigestibilities with the greatest gusto. Here again believe me I'm very careful, e.g. milk is boiled!

The Dulchi Pass isn't particularly high, about 10,000 feet I fancy, and is wooded to the crest chiefly with pines but also with Himalayan oaks (not in the least like ours) and Rhododendron *trees*. There is a great profusion of ferns, but I'm not in the mood just now for gathering such trifles, and don't suppose you are for receiving them. I'd meant of course to send you something for today. I've got some embroidery (a present to me) and have more or less ordered a spinning-wheel if you'd like the latter. But all parcels must bide a wee

{The second sheet is missing.}

DEAR FATHER

DELHI. 23/9/14

Here I am back again in Maitland House. Except for visits to the Chief Commissioner I've been pinned down to the College steadily since Saturday, examining and correcting papers and getting things started again. As to the Chief Commissioner, I was arranging with him about the College's relations in the future with A., which are to be nil. It was hard to break that news to Rudra.

Mr. Hailey (the C.C.) is a very good man indeed at his job, clever as anybody can be, though he always thinks before he speaks. Hailey says there's no chance of English Volunteers being sent from India to help in the war, so all our volunteering is no use at all. Things here are quite quiet. Hailey approved of an idea of mine of going home in the spring, but as a matter of fact my real inclination is to sprint at once and get in with Frank. I wonder what you and Mother would think if I left here for a year next May? Whether you think the country or the education of India on Christian lines the more important. Because I'm sorry that I'm here at the moment. I've been writing to Frank by this mail about the war, a foolish letter I daresay of advice about water and washing etc. Mother was wise to get him inoculated, though as a matter of fact the English must have learnt to imitate the Japs' methods of sanitation.

The *Gazette* the other day had a list of quite a lot of men I knew who'd become Lieuts., and people seem to have been waking up well. The other day I was talking to the Resident of Sikkim who was regretting that the Germans had not succeeded in getting into England just to raise the moral tone of the lower classes! That doesn't seem necessary. There was a lot of rain here, a record fall, at the end of last week, 4 inches an hour for several hours. The result of that is a flood of the Jumna for many miles across the country through village after village. It's a wonderful sight from Rudra's roof. There have been washes out in many parts of the town which looks as though it had been bombarded. This rain at the moment is good for the health of the city.

We are all here now, for P. N. F. Young and Jenkin broke their trip on account of the rain and came here this week. M. isn't very well; the rest of us fit.

Your news of Edgar Vincent was very bad. I do hope he's better now; miserable it must be for him. When a few more mails have come I'll write direct.

Ned's returning to Carchemish surprises me a bit. Turkey has mobilized through Syria and digging will be absurd. Perhaps though there's the political motive. We ought to get to some arrangement about the Bagdad Railway.

Latest news seems to me rather disquieting. That East bank of the Aisne is mighty bad terrain for attacking in, and we must be fighting with tired troops against reinforcements. Still the Indian contingent is arriving now. There seems little chance to my mind of peace before the winter of 1915, by which time the misery of the continent will be intense. Russia and Germany have got a lot to answer for, or, at any rate the latter. Leather's brother, an officer on the *Pathfinder*, has been lost: otherwise we haven't been touched any of us in the way of personal losses.

24/9/14

Tonight we have the news of three cruisers being lost, a bad business. I have just come in from dinner with Mrs. Ware a couple of miles away, and haven't much time before sleep. These days I've been examining, a dull but necessary job. Work will be very hard for no-one has come in place of S. and C., therefore you mustn't expect long messages from me for the next few weeks. I was sorry to hear of your cold picked up on the meadow. This winter you'll hardly feel inclined to go away for a golfing hotel-life, so you must get rid of it soon. Eating meat is the way to do it. If Frank is sent to the front there'll be one of the five of us doing something, which is as it should be, but you and Mother will be glad that Arnie is still too small. No doubt Bob is going to do medical work too in England or abroad.

Well that's all I'm up to tonight. It's very hot here and muggy but we're all well. Best love to you and Mother and the others

Your son

WILL

1/10/14.   DELHI

DEAR MOTHER

Tonight I'm in no mood for writing; the days and nights have been busy ones recently and I've cause to be tired. So you must forgive me for a very little news. As a matter of fact I ought to be able to write quite a lot, for Delhi has been very excited recently with Hindu processions loathsome enough but interesting. You should have seen me the other midnight, with the Chief Commissioner, being garlanded with gold-worked embroidery (I have the wreath hung on the wall in front of me now and someday I'll send it along) in a strange room in a long gleaming bazaar where the crowd was massed like the drops of a sea except for one place where four women pirouetted in a dance. When I'm fresher I'll describe. Meanwhile as I say it's better for me to rest. Work is very hard owing to the removal of A. which I had to arrange for political purposes.

Last night I dined with Hailey, the Chief C., who approves of my going home in March.

The news of the Russians surprised us much, but it was in all our letters; also in Hailey's and most other people's whom I've talked to. About Mr. O'Connor of course it's natural to think of it as one thinks of the man who at last, after many knocks down and painful rallies, takes the full count. But it's very sad too, and Mrs. O'Connor fought a good fight and now has still to go on. Women suffer most though in in England and everywhere just now, and in a great calamity one can see things in proportion.

We had a riot the other day here, no one killed. And down at Calcutta a man I knew, police officer, has been shot with about a score of others, in a shooting affray. It's lucky we sent the disloyal Sikh regiments out of the country.

I hope Ned will get his job. But Turkey ought to have the sense to remain neutral.

Marsh was in Russia probably when the war started. It's his great chance and I hope he's taken it.

As to the Tilly's, it's bad luck on them but so it is on everyone. Well, good-night. I write that I'm tired, but I'm fit as usual. But work is a bit of a rush owing to the loss of two of the staff.

Love to you all

WILL

8/10/14. DELHI

DEAR FAMILY

I'm going out to a wedding-show this evening, so before that happens must snatch a half-hour for a letter.

It seems so absurd that life goes on here just the same. In fact the funniest thing about the war is that we're at peace. All my time is taken up with work, from 7 in the morning to 8.30, and then from 9.30 to 2, and then from 6.30 to 7.30 and then from 9 to 10, with an hour or so of preparation in the afternoon, so you mustn't expect much in the way of letters. My recreation is shooting and driving or riding or motoring to the place. Yet for all this rush of work I'm very fit, and only troubled because the war takes one's heart out of it. There's not much news to chronicle. The Delhi Conspiracy Case has come to an end, and three men have the death sentence, two of those I knew. It's what we expected and they deserved, I think, so one can't make a fuss in one's emotions. Then another man I knew has been shot with a lot of others in a riot in Calcutta; about 30 killed altogether, by Sikhs. And we're on tenter-hooks here about Turkey, with all sorts of wild bazaar-talk. Talk in the papers about India's loyalty makes one grin; though the masses are loyal, there's a bitter feeling even among Indian Christians which opens one's eyes. Still there are no leaders in the country, and the trouble won't be yet awhile.

Well, it's no use talking of the war for letters are so late. And there's nothing else worth talking of at the moment. So I'd better shut up.

With love to you all, best love

Your WILL

3.15 p.m.   14/10/14

Dear Father

This is the only hour I have to myself each day, since I ride from 6.30 to 7.30 and shoot vultures from 4 to 5. So you mustn't expect much in the way of letters from me this term.

Things here are much the same. War news is scanty and disappointing. Delhi is empty. Flying rumours reach us of likely riots but nothing happens. The Conspiracy trial is over and three of them (two College men) are to be hanged. Quite right and just that is. The Government has annexed all rifle ammunition and no range-firing even for regular recruits is allowed. I've a Greener .310 bore: hitting vultures on the wing with a rifle is hard but I bring them down. For the rest work, work; it's good to bear the yoke in one's youth. And the College makes the most of us. The C.M.S. have announced that they expect their laymen to go to the war, but the S.P.G. seems to ignore it. Anyhow if I move from Delhi before March I'll throw things very much out of gear. All the same it's beastly to poke about here, and it's a good thing

I have so much to do. Also I've known a good many casualties, like Manners and Henderson, so that it's sickening to feel so far away.

The other day I was amused by a deputation of Jats (from that old landowner whom I visited) who came to offer 40 troopers fully equipped for the front if I would lead them. Jimmy's Light Horse! The poor beggars will be disappointed, but if Turkey joins in they may have their knock out here after all.

Your last remark in your second letter last mail gave me such a strange picture of you doing household work for Bertha was still away. By now I hope the tonsillitis has gone quite. I lanced a man's throat for an abscess in a tonsil one day out here with great effect!

What a business it has made of the world, and as to missionary effort it's an obstacle. Once again I wish I was home.

Well I'll finish this tomorrow.

15/10/14

We hear today, unofficially, that Turkey has gone in. That will give Ned employment. There's nothing else for me to say just now, except to hope you're all right

with love

yrs.

WILL

Birthday greetings by the way.

15/10/14

DEAR MOTHER

It was very sickening to get news last week that you were ill. As a matter of fact I was very anxious about you on the 1st for some reason, and will be glad to get a letter next week and this one. As I've told Father the College is making the most of me at present and there's no time for writing, so you must imagine my letters rather than read them. After such a lot of brain-work one is best resting, and so it is that mostly I'll just send a line.

News here is slight: many rumours but nothing real. The Mussulmans are a bit above themselves, that's all, and of course nobody trusts the Sikhs. The bulk of the people are splendid, and if I were willing I could raise quite a hundred horsemen for the army so I can't help noticing it. For some reason the military-minded among the students, and many of them are village squireens, have made up their minds that I'm an officer in embryo and they come along and then go away disappointed. As a matter of fact none of them can be so disappointed as I am myself. Altogether things are not very far from triste. We hear of indecisive fighting, and I see the names of men I used to know who have gone under. We've had one bit of barbarity from first-hand information. M. isn't well. My friend Amy Storrs is going into Bengal. Then you're ill. Howsoever it's no use railing at the circumstances in which one is entangled, and there's nothing to be done but one's immediate work.

The heat has broken in rain—last night it was. And as I write there's a rumble and belching of thunder, so the winter is coming. Thanks to the stores you gave me I've heaps of clothes for that, and also I'm well supplied with money. Therefore you need not give me a thought these months on business lines. And I'm fit, very; also very cheerful in spite of my position.

Bob wrote to me last week but there's no time to write to him. Please thank him very much and tell him how busy I am. The only disadvantage of having so much to do is the way in which it blocks one's own private time, but still a lot of it's mechanical, merely lecturing, when one can think of two things at once. Well there's a lecture to give now, so I must stop. I do want to get a letter from you on Saturday.

Now I've my free time and so again I'm writing. It's no good my talking more about the tonsillitis because of course it'll be over now. But I do want you to feel me loving you though there's no energy or speed in my mind to say it just at present.

The other day I had to go to a great show here in the evening, the wedding of a Mussulman grandee's son. These eastern festivities are quaint rather than beautiful but I'd like you to come to them with me sometime, to see the great candelabra and the starred roofs, to see the chairs all around with English people in evening things and nawabs in all their splendour, and then in the middle some fat oily horror singing and clapping its hands. The Indian singing is quite a different thing from English, a throaty business altogether, yet strangely musical in conjunction with the pipes. But if you were here it would break you down, to realize the world can be so cold-bloodily beastly as it is.

I must stop now because really I have nothing to say beyond the obvious.

So with love to you, best love

Your Son WILL

NAKODAR
20/10/14

DEAR FATHER

This is a castle I'm writing in, in the North Punjab, about 250 miles from Delhi. There's a four days holiday and by travelling two nights in the train I get 3 days here, with a country-bred stallion for me to ride, and fields and jungle to tramp in, all the change of the country. A Rajput chief's my host.

I'm in an upper room and it's the afternoon. Through the tunnel-like windows one can see the sun in the courtyard and hear the horses stamping. Up above there's a pair of doves cooing and there's the regular Indian feeling that earth's holding her breath. Also I'm tired, so forgive me if I'm uninteresting. It was good to get news that Mother was better, but how hard it seems to have hit her. Now she must rest indeed. There's no good talking, but I want very much to get the mail next week, and hear how she prospered. In this war nobody in England can be cheerful, and getting well will be hard. But at least she's the satisfaction that Frank's in it. I'd a letter from Ivens the other day. Do you remember the officer I talked to en route for Port Said? He's at Hong-kong and has a daughter. But his regiment and he are maddened by being there. And that's the normal state of mind of most men out here. Grumbles at being left, and guesses at the war's length, are the stock subjects in Delhi, together with rumours of alarms and riots. However everybody is getting so sick that presently there'll be no talking at all. I've spent today after buck, but unfortunately didn't bring my rifle. So the result was that after much walking I was fool enough to shoot at the leader of a herd about 90 yards off with small shot, wounding him. He went with a limp; may he soon recover. Coming back there was an experience. It was hot very, along dry sand and pampas grass in a flat plain. But suddenly looking northward I saw the line of the great snows high in the sky a hundred miles beyond the horizon of the plain. That sort of thing does one good.

For the rest I've done nothing today except ride a few miles bareback for fun on a pony that had never been ridden. It went well but erratically.

Yesterday—I left Delhi at 11.0 p.m. on Sunday and got here on Monday about 9—yesterday I spent on the big bay, which goes a treat. I'm lucky in my horses. And it's an experience to use the native saddles which are not good though. They're without knee flaps and one is meant to curl the legs under the beast's belly with one's heels against it. Also one has to sit a little forward if anything at the canter, and not well back, because there's a peak behind. Live and learn is a good motto though, and riding does me good.

Tomorrow we're to go off on riding-camels, Sawari-unt (isn't oont a good name for a camel) and hunt for jungle-fowl. Then back to Delhi, working and watching and waiting again.

That's all just now. I'll finish this later.

22/10/14

I wonder what you think of my intention of volunteering. Western the second-in-command at the School is taking a commission out here probably, but I feel it's my duty to stop till March. Sorry not to be back sooner: it's a shame on you that I'm out of it. All the same it's not irresponsible out here in the College, and when the war is over or rather when I can talk instead of write there'll be a lot to tell you about.

A. is back in Delhi but I've got him segregated in the Hospital. He came into my room this evening just when I was taking a class and behaved characteristically: that is he went straight to my wardrobe looked in, said 'Have you any sheets?' I said 'Yes', he said 'Well I'll take this one' and decamped. He's got a pillow of mine too. He goes about in a dressing-gown and pyjamas nowadays: even called for tea on the M.'s in that garb. What a fellow it is!

Well that's all for the nonce. It's after 11 at night and time I turned in.

By the way have you ever read *Kim*? Not a nice book but wonderfully true to the general atmosphere of life out here. Kipling's it is.

Please thank Bob for a very jolly letter last week.

Good-night.

Best love to you all

Your son

WILL

Dear Mother

I've a few minutes to spare, precious few, and want to use them well
—Yet as you must easily understand, letter-writing is difficult now-a-
days with so much to do, so that it's best for me to do nothing generally
when I have the chance.

But this tonsillitis of yours has been so bad that it makes me long to
write all sorts of things to you which can't be said. How you must be
glad to be well again. And what a bother it and the war and me and
everything else have been. Well anyhow I'm hoping you're well again
now and that I'll be having the old sort of letters from you in the
future soon. When we have faith that all these things are for our good
we ought to laugh longer than most people.

Yet it's hard to rub along here as though the world were at peace
when regiment after regiment is sent out and news comes in of slow
progress in the lands I know. I'd a letter from S. last week who's in the
South Wales Borderers at Seaford. And Western is thinking of taking
a commission out here, so that you'll easily guess that the dutiful path
is not the easy one. However in the end I ought to be able to play the
game for you. News here is slight. I can't tell you all that I'm doing or
what's happening because of course letters are not the place for it. But
at any rate I'm not wasting my time altogether. And it's interesting
here at times. Thus we've had Rabindranath Tagore stopping with us
a few days. Frank will get out of taking him as his 'guru' now that
he's meeting the bigger things; he's a poet no doubt but only half a
man. And A. has come back to Delhi and is stopping with Mrs.
Hibbert Ware who's trying to convince him of the error of his ways.
I like A. but can't help feeling India would be a better country
if he wasn't in it: he has ideas but no balance, no power of sitting still.
The result is that when he's exhausted an idea he goes on without one.
Also he has little power of seeing another point of view than his own:
he is always dreadfully cock-sure though he ought to remember how
he has changed his ideas often before this.

I'm annoyed because my friend among the ladies is leaving us for
Bengal, has left us in fact. She came round to say goodbye the day
before yesterday. And Mrs. M. has been down with fever again.
Happily M. is all right and as Friday and Saturday are Moslem festivals

and holidays I'm taking him out into the country on horseback. We have a 20 mile ride for Thursday afternoon and more afterwards. It'll do him good, and with him I can always think quietly, though he irritates every one else with his worrying. We start tomorrow then, so I'll have to finish this letter before then.

About my own health of course I'm very fit. It's easy enough to cultivate a receptive sort of mind. The students call me the 'must-molla', the man who takes everything with a laugh. And as to the vegetarianism, it agreed with me very well though of course I've chucked it now. Meat is bad for the liver out here. There's nothing wrong with my balance, mother dear, and as long as the mind is all right through faith the body will be likely to run smoothly. Only this is a responsible position.

The other night I was having dinner with the Tibetan Resident, one Gould, and had no end of an interesting talk with him about Lhasa and the north. And now after that Lamasery at Rampur Bashahr I have seen enough to catch hold of the country from hearing the tune of it with him. Very wonderful all this world is, and though India some-times seems like a sick man full of eruptive sores and sometimes like a volcano-giant it's always interesting. I wish it were possible to tell you more than it is. But when we meet again there'll be lots to talk about. Here's Abdul Khalig one of my men.

That's over and there's more time. I had a long letter from C. the other day and one too from Bob who's been writing very often. If I can I'll get a note done to him tonight and send it with this, tho' indeed it's hard to manage. Beyond that I haven't heard from anyone west-wards for some time. And there's no time for reading anything but what is necessary. The worst of this rush is that it limits one's reading of the Bible but at any rate one reads nothing else.

Here's another interruption so I'll stop for the nonce.

Thursday. 29th

I'm just waiting for M. to come but the horses are outside being walked up and down and in a few minutes we'll start on our score of miles of riding. Very nice it'll be. And then back again on Saturday night and a letter from you on Sunday.

I'm anxious to hear what you think of my coming home, and sur-prised you haven't suggested it yourself yet. For it's only doubtfully right in my own mind to wait so long as this. However all things will be clear in the end.

Well, goodbye for another week. Oh I wish we were together again awhile. But you ought to be well again now

with love to you both

from WILL

I'm escaping a tea with a grand Lady by this ride. Jolly that.

19/11/14

DEAR MOTHER

Last mail came father's letter saying that the scarlet fever was better. But what a time you've had and how tired you must be. Poor Arnie will remember this time of war as his bad year I should think. And you must be careful of yourselves more and more.

The College has closed for an hour because of a state memorial service to Lord Roberts. And as I have no mourning I can't go, so I've time to write awhile. Only for this service I'd be giving an address to the College now.

Incidentally our cook was cook's boy to Lord Roberts in the Kabul War. It's a fine thing that the old soldier was able to see the troops before he died though one would have liked him to have seen the beginnings of victory. And that looks a long way off still. Father says he isn't surprised at my wish to come home, so that's all right. Nevertheless it's easier now to be content here for I've work to do: training with the 9th Gurkhas 2 or 3 times a week and other jobs still more to my taste. Delhi keeps fairly quiet and more troops have come in, Wiltshires (Territorials). It's strange to see raw recruits about in the city, men from the works at Swindon; they'll have a lot to learn, both manners and manœuvring, before they'll be fit for the war. And their inefficiency is a demoralising sight out here.

Later

Then I was interrupted again and now I'm too tired to write. So it will be a small letter again.

The best thing I've done recently is the hearing of some skylarks singing, the first I've heard in India, out yesterday on the plain north of the city with the 9th Gurkhas. And for the rest there's been some interest for me in a Moslem wedding. One of my students asked me, and others of us, and we went down to the Moslem quarter of the town one afternoon and through lanes such as I've described before—not of the extremely narrow high sort though but more like those of Aleppo—and through an archway into a big courtyard. Through that a passage led into another where there was a little courtyard full of plants and with a fountain playing: beyond at the far end was an arched covered space like a very wide cloister. There when we came in were hundreds of people sitting in their finest clothes, with Turkish caps (The 'Enver Bey' fez is the one patronised by the young Delhiman, which is symptomatic of their feelings) just talking in the Indian fashion: war-news probably of the lurid sort; they are fond of describing the latest Turkish and German victories with gusto. By the way the other week a report that George V had been carried off in a Zeppelin won very wide belief in the bazaars.

After we'd sat down opposite to the bridegroom we were able to look about. He sat on a fine carpet and cushion, in a long black coat and a fez, with a garland of flowers round his neck and a veil of gold tissue on his head. Before him crouched two mullahs, one his agent and the other the bride's, who began after a while to chant the wedding-service which is mostly an old formula not Koranic but still attributed to Mohammed. It lasted for a few minutes, and occasionally ran into a chorus which all the assembly took up together. The bridegroom had nothing to say, and there were no women present. Nevertheless the service did strike me as reverent and suitable, only I knew of how the bridegroom had wanted to marry another girl but could not, being a Shiah, and how he'd never met his bride, and I felt sorry for him somewhat. As a matter of fact this ceremony is only part of the wedding, which will be finished next year.

I wish Bob would send me a copy of *Field Service Training* which he probably has. Not the Infantry training pocket book. And please thank him for his letter again last week. He has been writing to me very regularly of late, and I would answer him if only I'd the time.

The other day Ned's Carchemish book was mentioned in a book catalogue, so that's out all right. Not a good time for publishing though.

News from the front is depressing: Dixmude captured and Ypres the centre of the fighting, Russians slowed up again and desultory fighting in bits of country round Arabia. Also the naval fight off Chile was not much credit to us. However I suppose one can't expect much at present. Opinions as to the war's duration are hugely varied.

That's all for tonight. I hope Arnie is better really, and through with his troubles. And may Bob Ned and Frank flourish exceedingly. Ned's gone east I daresay.

Love to you both, best love

Your son

WILL

MAITLAND HOUSE

21.1.15

DEAR FATHER

It's rather late and I'm not much in the mood for writing: also there was no letter from you last week so there's nothing to answer. That was due to the disorganization of the Christmas mail no doubt, for I got one letter, from Bob, posted on the 23rd. Well, today I've taken an important step which had to come sooner or later, in writing to apply for a commission, to the Adjutant of the O.T.C. The letter will reach him the day after you get this, and in it are recommendations from the Earl of Radnor and Colonel Porteous, with a Medical Certificate also. I merely state my qualifications and ask for a post in any regiment, in Special Reserve or K's Army. And that it's the thing I ought to do I'm satisfied, though it's annoying having to put myself in the hands of the authorities, and I'm sorry for Mother's sake. Still it's obvious enough that if it's anyone's duty to fight it is mine. Probably I'll start for home on the 16th March: Rudra is quite willing and the College won't be hit by my absence till October, when perhaps the war will be over though that's optimistic very.

The Chief Commissioner here has written to the head of the War Office General Bingley recommending me so there's not much doubt I'll get a Commission. It'll be an expense returning, but I hope that it won't fall on you. However we'll see. The real trouble of this position of our being so far apart is that I can't ask you for advice but I think you'll approve. Every available man will be wanted, and in the summer here I'd be wasting time. And since it's inevitable that I come home, the quicker I get gazetted the better. It would be worse than useless for me to go to Ned as Bob recommends for I don't know Arabic nor the position in Egypt, and if I couldn't go to France my duty would be to stop in Delhi I think, where I'm of some value politically. As it is though, France is the place I must go to, willy nilly.

Well you won't be in the mood for gossip after this news so I won't give it you, though it's been a very interesting week. By the way I've referred the Adjutant to Mr. Barker as sponsor for my character, and to you for birth certificate: you can see him of course too if you like though I think my letter contained enough. Jenkin is writing to Cambridge too, and I've got the C.C. to include his name too in his letter.

As I said before, I'm sorry to have had to act without taking your advice. Yet what else could I do? And as it seems to be the only course before me you won't be opposed really though I daresay you'll feel sorry that I'm committed now to a definite course of action. But it had to come sooner or later, and sooner was better than later.

By the time this reaches you I hope Arnie will be feeling fit and well again, and that you'll all be as well as the circumstances permit. It will be strange to see you by the middle of April won't it, though the conditions will be different to those I had dreamt of.

I'm well very: galloped round the racecourse here the day before yesterday at a marvellous pace, and yesterday motor-cycled over the Aravalli hills 50 miles and rode a borrowed horse afterwards to an orange garden where the fruit hung ripe. Don't worry about my health: you'll see me looking fit I hope, fit as ever I was.

Now I'll wind up. On Saturday there should be news of you three and of Frank: also Bob is writing very regularly now.

With best love to you all

your loving

WILL

DELHI. *Jan. 27th,* '15

DEAR MOTHER AND FATHER

Last week came three letters, your Christmas one, and one each from you on the next mail day. Also the scripture card, for which, thanks. It pleased me very much, Father telling me I could do what I pleased about coming back: it annoyed me to have to arrange that sort of thing without asking advice. This letter had better be answered to Port Said, care of Cook's, since I'll probably leave Delhi on the 17th of March before your letter can come back.

The biggest thing you speak of is the project of boarding school life for Arnie. As to that it's difficult of course to say anything at once, and we'll be able to talk about it, but personally I think it might be very good for him in two years time, or one year and a half, not before. The matter is mainly one of the question of moral influence, and so far as that goes I don't know Arnie enough to say properly so this is all the answer I'll give you. Personally I'm glad I was at the High School but I fancy being there has made it harder for me to treat such ideas as *esprit de corps* seriously, also has made me dislike the whole idea of discipline and of organization. Let's leave it at that now. Florence was coming to see you, and that was very good indeed. Thanks for the Langley news.

Last mail brought me a long letter from C., very pleasing, and also one from Mr. Barker. I'm going to write to him probably tomorrow, or if not then next week.

For our news there's been rather a lot on my hands just at present; in particular I've been involved in rather a big domestic quarrel about the engaging of a lady doctor in the confinement of an Indian lady I know: not Mrs. S.S. However all is over now, and I'm satisfied that the course I advised was right. Then also there have been some political matters, not very important though, and as Captain Young is rejoining his regiment leaving tomorrow I've been seeing a lot of him. It's a strange life here, stranger than ever I expected: for example yesterday you might have seen me sitting in a dim room where old carved walls showed Mogul remains, being served with food by a Gond woman of the savages of South Indian hills and talking to one of the men who turned King's Evidence in the Bomb case. Then I came out through dingy lanes and noisy bazaars and dined with a man just arrived from Burma and going up the Persian Gulf. On Saturday again for example we talked camels steadily and Somalis and the Upper Nile with two military men who were my guests at dinner, and on Friday I'd been at an Indian wedding feast in which the bridegroom was 12 years old. Certainly there's no monotony, yet one general thread runs through it all, and the various things are all part of the one job.

It was on Friday that I'd a most delightful bicycle ride to Okla where everything is green, where it isn't yellow with the mustard flowers, or white with tumbling water in the weirs. I was with R. my pupil, and we watched the fish leaping up a run, a regular fish-ladder, and we could hear the roar of the whole place with everything unlike Delhi yet only 11 miles away. It's unsafe to bathe there though because of alligators which hereabouts we call 'muggers'. And then on Saturday I'd a ride on horseback for a change, and earlier in the week had gone round the racecourse like greased lightning on a great waler belonging to the Master of the Delhi Hunt. Every day too there's the military work till 12 involving a 9 mile bike-ride: today we'd a very interesting attack. One of our fellows, Mukerji, has just got engaged to be married, which is about the only house-news. It's to some Indian Christian girl in Lahore whom I haven't seen, but he seems very pleased with everything except with the cost of an engagement ring. Oh, by the way, on Sunday I met the first unpleasant Anglo-Indian lady I've seen yet, a very vulgar half-grown middle-aged creature. One such is enough to discredit a society: mostly people here have faced big things and are big themselves however, and you can see that in their faces. And as to our race-pride which causes so much disagreeableness—it's bound to be so as long as the principles of the two races are so much apart. {45 words omitted} It's not that we're better than Indians but that their religions are definitely diabolical at times and a curse to them. And our real difficulty is to avoid shrinking from the sores of the morality here as one feels inclined to shrink from the sores of the lepers who gibber at the alley-corners.

Well, there's enough. I'm afraid that you find me too direct when I talk, but I don't often do it to you and I've wanted to tonight. It's a pity we can't have someone like Isaiah to walk naked for three years and show what a man is—I don't mean as he did, literally—these people don't realize what they are or what they ought to be, and we're a little better in that clearness of sight thanks to Christianity. That's the difference between us.

Good-night and may you be very happy. Don't worry about me: and take my love

Your son

WILL

DELHI CLUB. 16.2.15

DEAR NED

There was a letter from you on Sunday which must have crossed mine, but there was nothing to answer in it. Why I am writing is that the *India* on which I should have sailed has been requisitioned by Government, so it'll be some other boat about the same date which you'll have to look out for. I'll send particulars later. Of course you're busy so I won't expect you; at the same time Port Said isn't far from Cairo so I'll hope for you. You gave good news of Ghaffar. Of course he'd told me he was married and settling down, but at the same time now's his opportunity so it was a surprise to me he'd done nothing. By rights I should ask him too to meet me, but I don't do it in case of awkwardness with the three of us possibly together. It's strange to think of you at Cairo doing office-work, but no doubt things will quicken up later. As to Young he's at Bannu now having rejoined his regiment, another case of a man being wasted.

Do you remember Powell, a commercial traveller who used to travel eastwards? He was here the other day, and Young and he and I dined together, having an Aleppo night. There's nothing much to talk about here. A bomb exploded at the Club the other night, no damage done and due apparently to an enterprising Police candidate trying to make a case for himself. An ex-St. Stephen's man too, the ass. The Viceroy is back safe from the Gulf, and is starting some social events. And the scarcity of corn in the city is getting very serious. That's about all. I understand that the Indian Army is very little use, so we'll be having it back again presently probably, and that will mean trouble. When the war is over there'll be the deluge without doubt, and it'll be interesting for me back out here. Meanwhile the sooner I get to Europe the better pleased I'll be, and as to entering the Indian Special Reserve that would be simply throwing the chance of doing anything useful right away. And being attached to the Wiltshires is only for training purposes.

Mother tells me you've taken out your motor-cycle or at least got it sent after you. What sort of a bicycle is it I wonder: nowadays I ride furiously at times on a Premier, bumping over Indian roads. 40 miles an hour is the most I've reached, and about the most that's possible hereabouts. That's one of my recreations, and the biggest other at present is shooting in the Aravalli Hills which lie out on a red ridge full of rocks about 10 miles from the city and give one a really decent change. As to books recently I've been overworked and so have read little, and that consists of novels. Ever read the *Virginian* by Owen Wister? I recommend it. By the way *The Lovers of Gudrun* has caught hold of my literary pupil no end. And no wonder. It's getting warm already but there have been very heavy rains, and hail-storms too, so a good harvest is assured which will help things at home a lot. But what an absolute fool Mr. Asquith is, giving away things as he does. There'd be much less chance of a row here if he were out of the way and some-one with knowledge in his place.

Well, this is nonsense so I'll stop

Yours ever

W.

18.2.15

They haven't been able to give me a berth yet, the P. & O. people, but I'm hoping to get off by the *Egypt* and *Salsette* combination arriving at Port Said on March 22nd. I'll try to let you know later.

No news more except that yesterday I re-wrote the first part of the *Taming of the Shrew*, changing Shakespeare into Anglo-Indian bur-lesque for our Speech-Day Play. And today I motored Jenkin over to the Aravalli hills in the side-car and shot partridges: it was a holiday.

Well, so long. Good luck

Yrs.

WILL

4.3.15. DELHI

DEAR MOTHER

Here's the last letter between us, and then we'll meet. And this won't be a long one because I'm so sleepy: it's only 3 in the afternoon but there's a hot-weather feel in the air and the coppersmith bird call-ing, and the last three have been strenuous days. So this will be empty. Monday, Tuesday and Wednesday were packed with good things, for you see I went with Jinks into camp at a State Bungalow made over to me by Hailey the Chief Commissioner at Badar Pur, a place 12 miles south of here and on the edge of the Aravalli Hills. There we went out field-firing with a company of the Wiltshires, and went out shooting on our own too, partridges and hare and duck, filling the pot with the spoils of our shikar. Yesterday we walked something over 30 miles. And what made the time such a treat was that we found a lake in the hills which was as good to be at as any place I've seen in India, a lake hidden away among a wilderness of rocks in a country where nobody would expect it, a country dry as a skeleton and just as bony, not at all nice. There we came suddenly on a stream, with huge surprise, and went up it to see how it came to exist, and after following its windings suddenly came to a bank, an old water-bank of some past dynasty and topping it saw a lake about 600 yards long, deep water and clear with red rocks overhanging it our end and palms here and there beyond and two or three ranges of hills flowing back. We bathed with any amount of delight, and saw evening close in afterwards while we waited for duck to come over.

And yesterday we were up there again and explored the far end of it, where it runs into a narrow stream between grass lawns with kingfishers on the banks and goldfish in the water. There's a grove of palms there, tall narrow ones, and peacocks walk up and down the grass or screech from the palm branches while the white paddy-birds dip to and fro among the reeds. At the far end is a great masonry wall ending the valley, and a little ruined temple beyond which 20 feet or so above the valley-level stretch some rice fields which might be in South India. And all around are set the barren hills, rocks on which nothing grows but thorns.

Who built it, how it came to exist, this green valley in the wilderness, I don't know. It must mostly be artificial but anyhow it's a Paradise.

The contrast in the afternoon when we walked up the river-jungle was immense.

You ask me about getting inoculated. I think it will have to be left till I get back because a ship's doctor won't be likely to have the things or to be a good one, and here I'm going to be too busy in the remaining 7 days to risk having to rest for an afternoon. Also the long railway journey might be irksome if the arm swelled. There's no need really to get it done: it'll last another six months, but I suppose the precaution is best.

Well as I say there's a drowsiness on me that's huge, and I'd like to try a siesta. But as a matter of fact I'll be interrupted in a few minutes and will have to go out for awhile. The voyage is going to be a treat, with rest, deep baths, and nothing to do but eat and sleep. And I've told Ned when I'm touching at Port Said so there's a chance of seeing him there.

Don't think for an instant of going to London to meet me, Mother. I'll keep, and Docks are always the limit. It seems funny that we'll meet about a week after you get this. May you all be looking and feeling well then.

Love to you all

from WILL

27.3.15

DEAR MOTHER

This boat is touching at Marseilles after all (it seems a pity not to go overland but not worth the uncertainty and the cost), so I'm sending you a line. We went through the strait of Bonifacio a few hours ago.

There was a letter from you at Port Said for which many thanks. But of course I'm quite without news that's up to date and it's useless to speculate therefore I'll chat about my own doings. Ned came to see me at Port Said but there was fighting in the Canal, a mere empty parade of Turks, which delayed the ship and he had to go back to Cairo. He left a letter for me, and other things. As we had time to go ashore I called him up on the telephone and had a chat about things political chiefly.

He's a Staff Captain nowadays and Dr. Mackinnon of Damascus who's on board (Mrs. Mackinnon is sitting next me at the moment) has been seeing a certain amount of him. He's very fit they say and having a great time. As to Egypt it's as quiet as a mouse and the Egyptian Army has been used against the Turks. You needn't have any anxiety on that score. And Abd El Ghaffar is settled, married and quiet in his home out of Cairo.

This voyage has been a pleasant one with only two days of heavy weather so far, and pleasant companions. We had rain in the Red Sea, and it was cool at Aden where I went ashore with a young couple who are the nicest people on the ship, a Cambridge Botany Don and his wife. He's been for the past year on New Caledonia, and is only just married to a charming Australian.

Since Port Said I've been spending most time in the First Saloon with a strange person, Lady Evelyn Cobbold and owing to her had amusement at Malta. We were there yesterday and at breakfast her maid asked me to see her. To be short I escorted her ashore where we looked up the Governor Lord Methuen in the palace. That resulted in a very interesting talk about the war, and as I knew a lot of his friends in India it was most jolly. Afterwards we drove round the island in his car.

It's a picturesque place Malta; gray on a gray sea it looked as we came in in the dawning, with walls round it and walls everywhere on the fields, a perfect olive country one would think but without olives.

Chief occupants of the roads goats, goats everywhere.

I heard various things from Lord Methuen which I'll tell you about in a few days.

There's little news of the war comes aboard. No casualty lists. And the plans of the ship are impossible to discover: some people say she is not going to London at all but some other port. So that's all.

Your news at Port Said was mainly about Frank's doings. Best love to you and cheer-oh

Your loving son

WILL

Tomorrow morning early we get into Marseilles where I'll post this ashore. I'm lunching with Lady Evelyn at some villa she has a few miles out of the city: if we're allowed off the boat.

This Lady by the way met Ned at Petra.

F. H. LAWRENCE

BORN February 7th, 1893, at St. Helier, Jersey, Channel Islands. Educated at the Oxford High School for Boys, and gained a King Charles I Exhibition at Jesus College, Oxford, for mathematics.

A very good athlete, he was first in the School gymnastic competition in 1911–12–13; Captain of the Football Eleven for two years and Vice-Captain of the Cricket Eleven. He also won the School's Challenge Cup for Athletics. He played regularly in Jesus College First Eleven Association Football Team, 1913–14.

From an early age he was a keen miniature rifle shot, winning several prizes, and was Captain of the City of Oxford Twenty Club, 1912 and 1913.

He became a member of the Officers Training Corps on entering Jesus College in 1913, and was given his commission as Second-Lieutenant in the 3rd Gloucesters on the outbreak of war in August 1914, and joined the 1st battalion at the front on February 9th, 1915. Killed on May 9th, 1915, at Richebourg l'Avoué leading his men forward preparatory to the assault.

Frank Lawrence

Frank Lawrence

FOREWORD

By the Rev. E. W. Cox, M.A.(Oxon)

*Vicar of Holy Trinity, Oxford, 1910–19; Vicar of Steyning, 1919–45;
Assistant Master at Oxford High School, 1899–1903*

It was in 1899 that my long friendship with the Lawrence family began. We might have known each other earlier as neighbours, for we lived not far apart; but it was the boys who brought us together. At that time there were only four of them, though in the following year their number was increased to five. I saw much of these four both in and out of school, and I cannot remember any band of brothers more united or more helpful to each other than they were. They were attractive boys, all four of them, and it was a pleasure to teach them. There was the same sturdy uprightness of character in them all, but each one had some quality which was peculiarly his own.

I think I can best describe Frank simply by saying that he was a *dear* boy; a very real boy—lovable, affectionate, happy and gentle, and with a most attractive smile. One could not help loving him. He was still at school when I returned to Oxford in 1910, but three years later he entered the University, as his three older brothers had done.

Then came the war, in which all the four brothers served. Frank and I wrote to each other when he went to France, and I remember one letter in particular in which he described how one night he went forward alone to the place where there had been fought one of the early battles in which our losses were very heavy. In a few graphic words he told how he stood there in the silence, and in the light of the full moon; the stillness being broken only by the hooting of the owls. Not long afterwards, on May 9th, 1915, Frank was killed in action at Richebourg l'Avoué; and about five months later his next older brother, Will, was also killed in action near St. Quentin, on October 23rd, 1915.

After only three or four days' illness, Mr. Lawrence died in the great influenza scourge in March 1918. Ned was still away in Paris at the Peace Conference, and Will and Frank had each a soldier's grave in France, but when we laid their Father in his burial-place in the cemetery at Wolvercote, I felt that they, too, were with us then.

28/8/09

DEAR BOB

Thank you very much for your letter, which I got today (Saturday). The address about God wanting us when we have fallen was given by the Sub-adjutant {of a Free Church Camp for Schoolboys}. He drew it from Peter's fall and Jesus seeking him out afterwards. One of the officers, I don't know which now, likened a Camper to a person walking along a somewhat dark road; and then he comes to a hill on the top of which the sun is shining, and then beyond there is a dark valley again. He said that Camp was on this hill, and that during Camp one comes closer and nearer to God than at any other time of the year. This seemed to me just to describe Camp. But you can form no idea of what Camp is until you have been there. Could you not manage to come to Camp next year as an Officer or visitor? I am afraid the Camp people will only take fully fledged Doctors as Medical Officers. The principal cases to be treated are sun-burn and often straining of the knee and sometimes broken arms. But you would enjoy Camp. It would appeal to you. The Bathing at Camp is also splendid. Beautiful sands. But the inner side of Camp is what you would like indeed. The officers are all men of the right sort. The Chaplain (Rev. G. E. Darlaston, Sydenham) I liked very much. At this Camp, somehow, I formed no friendship at all close with any of the boys, and on the last night after prayers in the Chapel tent all the campers were in little knots scattered everywhere about the field. It was quite dark, just about 10.0. I was standing near the tents feeling rather lonely, as I had no-one to talk to, when the Chaplain came along with a boy, and invited me to walk with him. The other boy left us after a little, and then I told the Chaplain. So you see that His hand was in it all, leading me up to tell the Chaplain, without which it might even have passed off. Very likely this was in answer to your prayers. I was moved all through Camp by the addresses, but was especially moved on that last night. I was longing to speak to someone about what I felt, and God sent to me just the person I needed. If I had missed that opportunity I should not have had another. But just

597

lately I have been feeling the relapse after Camp, and have not been doing what I should have done. But I must get over this laziness of mine. I am going to write to the Chaplain soon.

Phillips has sent a P.C. to you here to say he has changed his address. I took charge of it meaning to send it on to you, and write to him. The P.C. only says he

{The second sheet is missing.}

GISORS. *Friday, Aug.* 19
{1910}

DEAR BOB

We have now got to Beauvais on our return journey. I have enjoyed the riding very much, though I dont like pavé and the roads might be better. The country we have passed through has been mostly very pretty, especially the forest of Compiègne, which we went through yesterday, finding some splendid large blackberries. We went to Reims, but there was not a single aviator left. When we got there there was a bank holiday and a fair, and the whole town was crowded. We had to search 1½ hrs. before finding an hotel, owing to the curious lack of hotels Reims has. We were afraid we would not be able to sleep there. Now I may as well tell you about Camp, in case you have not heard. Shylock & I got there all right early on the afternoon of the first day, before the other boys came. Several of the officers there I knew, which made it very nice. Our baggage was brought all right by Patterson. I found there were 6 boys (counting myself) and the officer in my tent, so we were rather tightly packed. One of the boys I had already seen at two preceding camps, the others & the officers were unknown to me, but they were all very nice. The officer was a man named Micklem of New Coll. Oxford. I liked him very much. He was at the last of the Baslow Camps. The Subby was orderly officer at all three Baslow Camps, so he must have seen Will, although he does not know him. His name is Beale. He is a Cambridge man, but he is coming up to Mansfield for 3 years next term. He is also a very nice man. I am sure you will like him. I have promised to go to Mansfield Chapel on the first Sunday of next term to meet him and the other officers. This time I did not get sunburnt, but to make up for it I sprained a muscle in my back, just badly enough to prevent my running a single step without a good deal of pain. I did it playing football. We got up games between teams of association-playing boys and rugby boys, so you may imagine that the games were rough. I played for the association side, and in one game I charged into Shylock, he put out his elbow quite unintentionally, caught me in the back with it, and sprained a muscle. After a couple of days I thought it was all right, but in the relay race in the sports I sprained it far more badly. The doctor rubbed it a good many times with embrocation and it was almost all right by the end of Camp. At any rate it has not interfered with riding. Our tent was quite a successful one. We won the tug of war in the sports without losing a single pull. I was able to pull although it was just after the relay race. Then we also won the puddocks {a team game for scoring runs by hitting a ball with a short broom-stick}. I scored fairly well in our matches, my scores being 21, 69, 47, 36, 8, 11. The last two scores were made when my back was hurting me, and I could only make a pretence of running. The subscription to the sports this year was $2^{d.}$, and the prizes were baby's toys. I sent mine by Shylock to his little baby sister Mary. For the puddocks we got $6\frac{1}{2}^{d.}$ knives. Do you remember my telling you last year that one of the Camp officers was going out to India as a missionary? A letter from him was read at Camp this year, and we sent back another letter signed by all the boys who knew him last year. But as he would know half the officers and boys of this year's camp, I thought it would be a nice thing to send him a photo of the Camp. So I have ordered one for him and will send it as soon as it comes. Shylock and Ballard and Patterson all liked the Camp very much and really enjoyed themselves. On the excursion we went by boat to Arundel. At midday it began to rain, and it kept on till the evening, so everybody got fairly wet, I especially, as I had not taken a waterproof with me. But all our clothes were dried in the ruined coastguard station just next camp, and as I had a dry sweater and a pair of football trousers, I did not mind. Some people whose shirts were wet wore pyjamas. There was more ragging at this Camp than at any other I have been to, mainly because one of the officers was extremely fond of it. A day or two before the end of camp he and the chaplain tried to let down a tent on some boys. The attempt failed, but the boys retaliated and let down their tent (the chaplain and this officer were in the same tent together). Then as the ragging continued, three officers were carried off by the boys and ducked (clothes and all) in a large horse trough in the camp field. The chaplain was as nice and helpful as ever, and the commandant (whom I had not seen since Matlock) was also very nice. The adjutant was the same as last year, and I liked him very much. One of the boys in my tent while bathing one day towards the end of camp almost took the nail of his big toe off by hitting it against a break-water. It was still painful and bandaged at the end of Camp, so I lent him my sandals to go home in, as he could not bear a shoe even if he could have got one on. We had a fair amount of rain, but my tent held out well against it and we did not get any rain inside, but one of the tents was quite flooded out. They had left a piece of the tarpaulin out-side the brailing of the tent and there were puddles covering the tar-paulin and soaking their bedding when they wanted to go to bed.

When Camp stopped I rode over to Littlehampton, joined Ned at the Church, and rode on with him to Rye, making my longest ride, 72 miles. We passed through Hastings and Winchelsea and it was pleasant to see them again. Winchelsea seemed just the same, except that they have completed the building of the house which we saw beyond the church. Next day we rode on another 26 miles to Folke-stone and caught the 12.0 boat. I had taken Dr. Inman's tablets, but I really did not want them, as the sea was beautifully calm. At Boulogne we passed the customs without having to open our bundles, and went on another 20 miles or so, before stopping for the night. Even now I cannot make out what they say, except a few scattered words or unless they talk very slowly. The nights were all alike, so I shall not attempt to describe them, as you probably know them better than I do. At Noyon we came to a very fine Cathedral, as also at Amiens. At Coucy we came to the finest castle in France according to Ned. It is most massively built and almost impregnable. The keep is now 180 feet high, and was originally 200 feet. The other towers and walls are on a similar gigantic scale. Cardinal Mazarin wished to blow up the keep, so he put barrels of gunpowder on the floor of it and set fire to them. The explosion clean took out the whole of the inside and the roof, but did no harm to the walls beyond cracking them from top to bottom, which crack has now been repaired. This will shew you the strength of it. The internal diameter at the bottom is 63 feet, and as the walls are 24 feet thick there, the total diameter at the bottom is 111 feet. The rooms in which the seigneur lived are 46 feet high, and the windows 10 feet high, and the window seats 2 feet high. Everything is huge. The steps in the stairs are much bigger than ordinary ones. The gallery which runs round the floor above the seigneur's is 13 feet above it, and 20 feet wide. Ned and I spent a whole afternoon in the keep measuring and looking. Ned has a 50 foot measure with him, so the distances I give are quite accurate. Looking from the top to the bottom it seems a vast way. In the hour we had in the morning we went over the other towers and parts of the castle, exploring the vaults under the old hall, of which there is now hardly anything left. In the bottom of the keep there is a well now 150 feet deep, with another 50 feet filled up by rubbish, etc. There were 3 drawbridges at the entrance, and the whole castle stood on rising ground. Its walls were about 60 or 70 feet high, and very thick. The town of Coucy is still surrounded by its walls. Another town we came to, Montreuil, is also very well walled, and is a favourite resort of painters. At a place not far from Picquingy there were in the hotel 26 English lady painters. We have been very fortunate in our weather as to-day is the only day at all wet that we have had, and it has not been too bad. I started this letter at Beauvais, but being unable to finish it that night have brought it on to Gisors, where we are now. Beauvais Cathedral is, I think, the highest in the world. You could put inside it any Oxford church with its spire. Each part of it has tumbled down at least once, and it was found quite impossible to complete the building. I have had three splendid hot baths just lately, one to-day. The baths are very nice and I like them very much. I expect you have had them yourself, so I won't attempt to describe them. One night at dinner I asked for bread, and was rather astonished when the waitress gave me one of those long 3 foot loaves whole. Ned had to hold one end while I cut some off. I have not yet had a single puncture, although Ned has had some trouble with his tyres. I have written to Shylock reminding him about the magazines. I hope you are having a nice time without any troubles. I wish you could have come to Camp with me. It was just as good as any other camp. Ned is rejoicing over some books he has discovered at the price of a franc. Each time I have a bath he goes and buys a book instead. This place has also a strong castle, but it has no striking features and is not nearly as good as Coucy.

To-morrow we go to Château-Gaillard, where we will get letters and I hope to hear about the Locals. In a few days more we shall go to Louviers, where a boy from Camp is staying, whom I hope to see. I have greatly enjoyed the trip, although I have got saddle-sore now and am not very comfortable. Are you not coming back till September?

It seems a long time. I hope you are feeling quite well. I have seen one of your P.C.'s the first, I think, but nothing else. I am afraid I cannot give you any address to write to.

FRANK

Le Petit-Andely (Eure)
HOTEL BELLE-VUE
Sunday, August (21) {1910}

DEAR MOTHER AND FATHER

We got here yesterday and got your letter and a P.C. from Bob. I am indeed delighted about the Locals. I never thought of getting off Additionals, though I was hoping for Responsions. Can you tell me when you know what Shylock has done. It makes the ride all the pleasanter now I know what I have done. Our ride from Gisors yesterday was chiefly noticeable for 4 punctures and a head wind. When we got here I was very surprised to meet a boy from Camp, who is staying here with his father and mother and sister. I thought he was at Louviers, and was going to try to see him. They are very nice people, and I am enjoying myself with them. I had a splendid bathe in the Seine yesterday just opposite the hotel in the picture. The Seine is several hundred yards wide here and has a very swift current. It was quite hard work trying to swim against it, and 20 yards up stream was as much as I could manage. This hotel is full of artists. Every person in the hotel except the servants, etc. speaks English. It is very nice to be among English-speaking people again. It is a very comfortable place, with a nice terrace looking out on to the river and plenty of rowing boats for hire. To-day I have been over Château Gaillard with Ned. It seems a very poor place after Coucy. The interior of the keep is only two feet more than the walls of the Coucy keep. There is a marvellous view from it. The Seine is very pretty, and the surrounding country exquisite. There are continually passing up and down before the hotel four or five or more barges pulled by a tug. They go about $2\frac{1}{2}$ miles an hour up stream and $4\frac{1}{2}$ down stream. My sandals I do not expect for a little time, as I asked the boy not to send them too soon after Camp. The 3/– was lent to Shylock so that is quite safe. When the Camp photo's come you will find there are two of the same photo. It seems extravagant, but I can explain it. Do you remember my telling you that one of the officers of last year's Camp was going out to India as a missionary? At Camp this year a letter from him to us was read. We have sent back another letter signed by all the boys who knew him last Camp, but as he would know quite half the officers & boys this year, I thought he would like a photo of the Camp. It is only 1/6, so it will not ruin us. His name is J. Gordon Bennett, and I believe you said last year you liked his face the best of all those at Camp. You ought to come & stay at this place, the river is so pretty, and the country so exquisite. There is here a great big dog belonging to one of the artists. He is a huge strong animal but not fierce, as French dogs are. I don't much like French dogs. They usually try to bite if you ride past at all fast, and are most of them half-wild. Ned went up to Château Gaillard this morning at 11.0, and has just come back now at 6.30. I have not been with him all the time. I hope you will get better very soon. I am having a very nice time, but will be quite glad to get back. I hope Henry has come by now. Mr. Cave's letter was very nice. I have written to Bob, and will do so to Florence {his faithful nurse} in a day or two. We will be at Cherbourg on the 30th, and I will cross on the 31st. I have Dr. Inman's tablets all right.

FRANK

Do you notice that this paper is at least 10 years old?

HOTEL DE NORMANDIE
CAEN
Aug. 25, Thursday Night {1910}

DEAR FLORENCE

Doubtless you have heard from Mother the results of the Locals as far as they are yet known. I am wildly delighted at getting excused the Additional Subject as well as Responsions. It is far beyond what I had hoped. Now I do not mind much where I come. The full result will be out on Monday, according to Father, so I hope to hear on Tuesday at Cherbourg. Will is coming over on Tuesday afternoon from Guernsey to Cherbourg, & I think he will have a little tour himself in France. Ned and I will meet him, & I go over to Guernsey by the boat the next morning about 8.0 or 9.0 a.m. I shall be quite glad to get to Guernsey & the others, although I have enjoyed the tour very much. We have had splendid weather, only one at all wet day. Today we have spent at Caen, getting here quite unexpectedly yesterday, by riding 50 miles. There is a good deal to see in the town, several churches. William the Conqueror & his wife Matilda each built a large church

here to pacify the Pope, who was angry with them. There are also here
4 desecrated churches. They were desecrated at the Revolution & are
now used as warehouses. They have been gradually falling into ruin &
are a very sad sight. Such a state of affairs would not be tolerated in
England. My French is still ludicrous, & I cannot yet understand what
they say, unless they speak very slowly. One night at dinner I asked for
bread, & was rather astonished when they gave me one of those great
long 3 ft. loaves (you may remember them) quite whole. Ned had to
hold one end while I cut some off. On our tour we have come to
several very interesting churches & castles. The cathedrals at Amiens
& Beauvais are rivals in height. You could put inside either of them
any Oxford church & tower, & the top of the spire of the Oxford
church would not touch either of the roofs. It is very hard to get an
idea of the height of them. The cathedral at Beauvais is so high that
every part of it has tumbled down at least once. The tower & spire
came down soon after being built, & smashed up the roof & most of
the sides of the part that had been built. The spire has not been built
again, & another part of the cathedral has not even been started to be
built. The people of Beauvais built their cathedral so high just to beat
the Amiens cathedral. At Coucy we came to the most interesting castle
in France, so Ned says. It is still very complete, although partly ruined.
The keep dominates the whole. It is a huge building 180 ft. high. At the
bottom the walls are 24 feet thick. It is almost impossible to get a good
idea of its size. Its internal diameter at the bottom is 63 ft. Just think of
it. You could put the ordinary large town house, ours for example, in
it, & there would be plenty of room. It would touch no part of the
walls, & would not even reach to the ceiling of the first flight, since
each storey is 46 ft. high. Ned has a 50 ft. measure with him, so these
distances are quite correct. Cardinal Mazarin wanted to destroy the
keep some hundreds of years ago, so he put barrels of gunpowder inside it and set fire to them. The explosion completely cleared out the
inside of the tower (ceilings & floors of the different storeys, & the
roof), but did no harm to the walls beyond cracking them, which has
now been repaired. This will give you an idea of the strength of it.
When you have got up to the top of it (it is quite an effort as may be
imagined) people at the bottom seem quite insignificant little creatures.
The view from it is splendid. Ned & I, evading the 'gardien', went
over the rest of the castle by ourselves, & by dint of forcing locks &

climbing over doors & up walls succeeded in getting into every part of it. There are some very fine cellars under parts of the castle (the place where the banqueting hall was), & these we explored. When we had got to one end Ned felt himself slipping down into a pit, & got rather a shock, as we could not see in the least how deep it was. However he saved himself, and, coming back later with a few matches, we found it was only about 6 ft. deep. We went quite a long way in the cellars, getting into the bottom of towers on the walls & other places. It was very interesting, though until you got used to the light (it was almost pitch dark) it was very hard to see where you were going. Several times I walked straight into pillars, & was brought up with a bump. We went round the bottom of the moat (which is nearly 30 ft. deep, now quite dry), wading waist deep through a fertile crop of nettles. I only got stung once however. We entered a passage which originally went all round the keep below the moat to prevent & detect mining. It is now mostly filled up, but some of it is still free, and Ned, who was walking first, only just saved himself from walking into a pool of water. We stayed in the keep the whole of an afternoon, from two to six, so much did we like the place. When we at last came out we had to climb over the entrance gate to get out, as it was locked. The whole castle is on a most massive scale. Each of the towers round the walls would be a keep in a smaller castle. The steps of the staircase going up the keep (they are still intact) are larger than ordinary ones. It is very hard to go up two at a time. The gallery that runs round one of the floors is 13 ft. above it. It took four seconds & a little more for a stone dropped from the top to reach the bottom. There is a well in the bottom now 150 ft. deep. It was originally another 50 ft. deeper. It has to be deep, as the castle stands on a hill. It does not look nearly as large as it is. The ordinary tourist I am sure does not get any idea of its size. It was never captured, and I think is quite impregnable, as it could keep enough provisions in its cellars for years. The town of Coucy is still surrounded by walls, very high ones too. After leaving Coucy we went on to Reims, where all the flying has been. There is not a single aeroplane there now, so we were disappointed. We got to Reims on a bank holiday and there was a fair being held. The whole town & a lot more people were in the streets. Reims has a great lack of suitable hotels & we were riding about for 1½ hours before we got one. Fortunately we got there early, so we had plenty of time. The fair I was very disappointed with. It consisted of 1 miniature rifle range and about 20 drinking booths. That was all. The trams were very active that night. There were three sets of rails outside our hotel, and in five minutes nine trams (electric) passed.

Friday

I wrote this much at Caen, but being unable to finish have brought it on with me to Bayeux, where we are now staying for the night. The ride to-day has been quite a nice one with no mishaps. At a little village half-way where we stopped to look at the church I bought some flint & steel. It is not a curiosity, it is meant for work, and they use it in the village instead of matches. Ned has been practising a great lot with it for his next Syrian trip. He lit a person's cigarette with it this evening, but failed to get the candle to light. The tapestry is very interesting, and must have taken years to make. It is wonderful it does not seem to have faded at all. The roads in France we have not found very good, some of the high roads being unrideable. After going 20 yards along one of them we stopped and turned off to a by-road, the main one was so bad. There is no speed limit for motors in the country, and as the high roads are absolutely straight for 5 or 6 miles or more at a time without any obstruction they generally go as fast as they can. One motor passed us going quite 60 miles an hour. On one ten mile stretch of road 13 motors passed us. The stones with which the town streets are paved I do not like at all for riding, and they seem to throw any spare piece of glass they may have on to them. I do not much mind now where I come in the Locals. Getting excused these two exams. is delightful. If I had not, I would have had to go in for Responsions in September, and the Additional Subject in December. I should almost certainly have failed for Responsions owing to the short time for preparation, so that would have meant another try. Besides the worry of any exam. is great. One of us of course will write as soon as the results come out. I do not think the results of these exams will be in any paper, as they are hardly public as yet, though quite official. I am looking forward to next term, as I will almost certainly be in the 1st eleven in football, and have a chance of being captain of it. It would be very nice if I did become captain, but I am not at all seriously expecting it. I think I may also say that I will be moved up into the upper Vth next term, which is in all but name identical with the VIth. A miniature rifle club will be started in the school next term mainly owing to me. I expect it will be a great success. Can't you manage to come to Oxford again soon? It seems such an age since you were here last. I hope you are quite well and are having good weather.

FRANK

DEAR MOTHER

Please excuse this paper & pencil, but it was all I could get hold of. I expect you would like an account of things from the beginning. We were delayed 2 hours in Oxford before we started owing to punctures & other things. When we did start all went well till we were past Littlemore some way. Then Ballard's chain broke. We walked & towed each other for some way & then we came to a smithy where they advertised mending bicycles. The only person there was a boy of about 15, but he was fairly clever with tools & after an hour's job managed (with our help) to mend it after a fashion. It broke after another mile. Then one riding & towing the other we managed to get to Dorchester by 1.50 p.m. where we had dinner. We called at two cycle shops on the way only to find the man had gone out for the day in each case. From Dorchester I towed to Benson, whose repairer had also gone on the spree. Then I towed on to Wallingford which we reached about 4.0 p.m., thus doing 15 miles in 7 hours. Here a new chain was put on, and we got to Reading without mishap about 5.30. Having tea there with relatives of Ballard's (an uncle, aunt, & two cousins) we left at 7.0 p.m. & got to Basingstoke at 9.0 p.m., just missing lighting up time. Here we stayed at an hotel for commercials, very cheap & quite good enough for us (3/3 each supper bed & breakfast). Next morning we started to cross the downs (North & South). The North downs were not too bad, except that the road in many places was absolutely unrideable, being 3 inches deep in loose gravel & flints. It was not a main road. As we wanted to get to Chichester by 1.30 if possible we pushed on to tackle the South Downs. As we were pressed for time we decided to go straight over them instead of riding another 8 miles round them. We got something then. We had to go over a hill 600 ft. high at least, & proportionately long under a broiling hot sun on the usual sort of country road, white to the eye & a loose surface. After that one we had a couple more of about 200 ft. each, and we got to Chichester at 3.30 p.m. It was the hills that did it. After tea there with Ballard's relatives (grandfather & aunt this time) we went on to Camp getting here just after 6.0 p.m. just before the rain, which came down heavily all the evening. You can judge what kind of wind there was when the big marquee used as a chapel tent was blown over, nearly killing one fellow who happened to be underneath it. Another man who was trying to hold it up by one of the poles turned a few somersaults quite against his will. Just after 7.0 p.m. the day before yesterday evening Valentine flew a few miles away from Camp over the hills towards Shoreham, going a great pace, and this morning about 6.0 a.m. Cody flew right over the Camp about 200 ft. high also towards Shoreham. We had a very fine view of him the whole Camp turning out. Yesterday we had our excursion. We walked to Littlehampton, trained to Arundel, & were towed by motor boats about 3 miles up-river to a very pretty place, where we had dinner. After dinner we were towed another mile or two up stream to bathe, afterwards coming back to the same place for tea. Then we motored down to Littlehampton & walked to Camp. This time there was not a drop of rain, a striking contrast to last year. The Camp this year is a very good one. We have got an exceptional number of very good officers, and everything has gone with a hum. In tent competitions we have been knocked out of the puddocks & won 1st match in Soccer. In the Camp cricket match with Feltham we were beaten. Scores 108—47. But they had playing for them a county player who a few days before had made 30 & 16 against Notts. He made 33 not out, which on a good ground would have been 70 or 80. He was a very pretty player to watch with beautiful strokes. Also quite young, about 23. I am sending a couple of postcards with this. I have made a dot with a blunt pencil under my tent in the view of the Camp. I have not yet settled my course after Camp, but will tell you as soon as I do. Got your letter today. Glad to hear about the shooting and that you are all well. By this time I expect you have got my other P.C. of Camp. I am all right, no sunburn to speak of.

FRANK

Glad to hear about Ned. We leave here Wednesday morning. I have paid Will's 1/–.

309 COWLEY ROAD
OXFORD
July 28, 13

MY DEAR JIMMY

We fellows in 1st XI thought that you couldn't finish your 13 years at the School without having some tangible memento of them. We know the good work you have put in all along for the School, and much of it very thankless work, and we ask you to accept these to show that we aren't ungrateful for it. Hoping you will find them useful.

Yours,

1st XI

{A pair of cricket pads were sent with this letter.}

FREE CHURCH CAMP
WHATSTANDWELL
DERBYSHIRE
Tuesday {1913}

DEAR MOTHER

It is now all settled about Arnie, Bobs and the two Phillips. They can come up on Monday (Aug. 11) with Edgar, although the Camp proper does not start till Tuesday. Mr. Phillips is writing to the two Phillips to tell them this, but Bobs Hutchins I undertook to do. I do not think he is at home now, but if you arranged it with Mrs. Hutchins she could tell him. Douglas Phillips will not be going from Oxford. He will meet the others at Birmingham. I will fix up a definite meeting place and tell you later. Tickets from Oxford can be taken to Matlock (Bath), or if preferred to Birmingham and then rebook to Whatstandwell. Luggage it is best to label for Birmingham and then relabel to Whatstandwell. Although it is only six or seven minutes walk between the stations at Birmingham, yet it is through a busy part of the town, and it would be best for them to take a cab. At Derby they must particularly remember to get into the Whatstandwell train and not the Matlock express. I have just written to Edgar telling him practically the same as above. Please either you or Edgar write back as soon as you can saying which day Arnie, Bobs, and he will come. It would be best for Arnie to bring either one or two rugs with him, in addition to the valise I have, as the nights are cold. I can get all the blankets I want from Ballard. I should be very glad also if he would bring me a clean collar, and two or three handkerchiefs. I am going to have a bigger office in the Junior Camp than I ever expected. At the request of H. E. W. Phillips & Standing (an officer of this camp who is going to be Adjutant of the Junior) I have taken on the post of Subby. They were very hard put to it to get one. Griff had tried hard before Camp began, and when it was seen that one of the tent officers would have to be Subby they pitched on me. The Camp will be a small one, almost certainly less than 50. I have been following the present Subby about for a few days now and know practically all the routine work. Standing is an exceedingly nice fellow, & altogether I am beginning my office under very pleasant circumstances.

The weather in Camp so far has been very good, and it has been a very nice time. The night before last the officers and a few of the boys were fetched up from 2 to 3.0 a.m. to stop the mess tent from being blown down, but otherwise there have been no very remarkable incidents. I wish I could be at home to see Florence. I am very glad she had a view of the Arabs, and hope she is having a pleasant time with you. I expect you are glad that the Arabs have gone.

I am glad Arnie is not at this Camp. It is an exceedingly good one, but I am sure he will be more happy at the Junior one. I shall be very glad to have him with me, and as Subby will be able to do things for him I should not be able to do otherwise. Shaggy Phillips is remaining on for the Junior Camp.

I have now missed the evening post from Camp, so have to take this letter down to Whatstandwell myself. I hope Ned will get back safely.

FRANK

{An address given by Frank to the Free Church Camp at
Whatstandwell in 1913.}

I wish to give you an idea of what I think Camp should mean to each of us.

To do this I would like to take an illustration from an outgoing Atlantic liner. Let us suppose the ship is steaming along the Cornish coast by night. The Captain of the liner, alert to his responsibilities, is keenly on the watch for the various lighthouses he passes. From each one he takes his bearings, and marks out his course on the chart. Each lighthouse he passes tells him his position more certainly, till when he has left Land's End behind he can steer his vessel out into the ocean with confidence. Every lighthouse on the voyage of that steamer symbolises a Camp which we have the privilege to attend. Just as the Captain of the liner takes his bearings from the lighthouses he sees, so we should take our bearings from every Camp we go to. Each Camp should give us more and more of the grace of God to enable us to lead the life which Christ would have us lead. But the Captain of the liner, if he had to navigate his ship across the Atlantic by the aid of lighthouses alone, would fare badly, if indeed he ever reached the port he was bound to. So we must not rely on Camp alone to reach our goal. To steer a straight course the Captain has to refer constantly and carefully to his chart. If we would steer a straight course in our lives we must likewise be in constant touch with our chart, Jesus Christ. Camp is for us a unique opportunity of getting to know Christ, but it is not enough by itself. Very few are able to go to many Camps, and to everybody there must come sometime an end of Camp, just in the same way as an end of lighthouses comes to the Captain of the liner. What would happen to a liner if her Captain sailed her in dangerous seas without care either of the lighthouses or his chart? It would beyond a doubt be wrecked. In such a case it is not the Captain's life only that is endangered. The lives of the passengers and crew are also risked. In like manner if we attempt to live our lives without reference to God we shall not only destroy ourselves but also adversely affect the lives of others, whom we know not, but it is certain that if any of us falls, his fall will be reflected in the lives of others. As the Captain is responsible for the lives of his passengers, so are we responsible for the lives of those around us. So if we, like a wise and careful Captain who brings his ship safely to harbour, lead the life Christ would have us lead, our life will without our knowledge influence for good the lives of others. We cannot go through life without influencing for good or for bad, there is no medium, the lives of others.

Let us therefore use this Camp as one of the lighthouses of our lives, as a place at which we may obtain strength to sail forth into the future in the power of God, doing everything that Christ would have us do, that we may finally meet again in the life that has no ending.

Extract from *Camp Chronicle*, Volume IV, June 1915.

F. H. LAWRENCE

Matlock, 1906, 1911, 1913.
Elmer, 1907, 1909, 1910.
Redmire (Subby), 1914.

When we stood at our tent doors in the chill of early morning on the fifth day of Camp, and cheered our Subby as he struggled up the slope of the Camp field with his luggage, on his way to Redmire Station, we did not know these would be his last sounds of Camp. Now news has come that he was killed in action, on Sunday, May 9th.

If ever a man deserved cheers he did, always quietly looking about to see what he could do to give other people a good time; who never shirked any job, however dirty or difficult or even desperate it might be, if he felt it was his duty. We can imagine how he must be missed in the home and our sympathy goes out to his relatives, and especially to his mother in her loss.

{His report to the "Twenty Club" of best Oxford Miniature rifle shots.}

Before we start our business to-night, I should like to make a few remarks about the Meeting. I think it may rightly be described as an entire success, and we may all congratulate ourselves upon it. We have, on the whole, given satisfaction to everybody, which is saying a great deal, and should we, at any future time, decide to run another open Meeting, I think we may confidently look for more support than we had last week. We have all gained valuable experience, but I should like to mention a few things which particularly appeal to myself. I hope no-one will think that I do so with the intention of putting any blame upon anybody; it is simply to try to ensure their not being forgotten at any future meeting we hold. First as regards the 50 yards range. Luck being on our side, and making the entries small, we managed to complete the shooting, but to enable us to do so we had to have an extra three hours shooting on Friday. I think it must be plain to all who took part in the management of our meeting that it would be very unwise to again attempt to run both 25 & 50 yards shooting under the same conditions. The inconvenience of moving from one range to the other was great, and the total stoppage of 25 yards shooting while 50 yards was going on was most annoying. If we had had many more entries we could not have got through the meeting, and as it was we had not a second to spare. If the three hours shooting on last Friday had been left till Saturday, we should not have finished our shooting till after 8.0 p.m. (and that by cutting off all unlimiteds) and would have had to have sent for candles so as to distribute the prizes about half-past nine.

The only dissatisfaction I heard expressed that was not of a temporary kind was allowing men to shoot two or more targets successively when others were waiting to fire. There was general grumbling about this, and to remove it at our next meeting the range warden must always be collecting the next set of targets while one squad is firing, so that a competitor will never have to wait more than about 10 minutes, after he is fully prepared, before being able to go down. Of course if there are not enough competitors waiting to form a squad some of the squad shooting at the time will be able to go down for a second target, but not necessarily at the same place on the firing point. The remark of one competitor which I overheard may well be pondered over. "Yes, this is a very nice range, but it's miles from anywhere." If we ever hold another meeting, we must try our best to obtain a temporary range for the occasion as close to the station as possible. This year, of course, we have been hampered by lack of time & lack of knowledge of the work entailed by such a meeting as we have just run, and we had to use the material ready to hand. Now that we have some knowledge of the work, for our next meeting we must start preparing four or five months beforehand, instead of only $2\frac{1}{2}$. We must also manage, if we possibly can, at our next meeting to have refreshments sold on the range. The lack of such an arrangement last week made itself keenly felt, judging by some other remarks I heard.

To wind up our meeting properly we ought to have a balance sheet distributed to those who gave donations towards it. If we rely on the local papers only for this purpose many of the donors will not notice it, while others will not trouble to read it. They are all of them people accustomed to balance sheets, and if they each receive one properly drawn up they will be much better disposed to support us if at any future time we ask them again for donations. I do not consider it would be of any use inserting such a balance-sheet in the local papers, both for the reasons I have just stated, and because it would be no compliment to the donors to read an account that 50,000 other people, who have no connection with our Meeting, have the opportunity of reading; also I do not like the idea of displaying our financial matters so openly. It would, however, be a very good thing if the names of the donors could be put in the papers, but this, together with the matter of the balance sheet, can be discussed later.

I should also like to see letters of thanks sent to the men who did hard work for us although they were not members of the Twenty.

I have now nearly finished but I have an announcement to make concerning myself. It is with very great regret that I have to tell you that I must resign the captaincy of this club. I have had a very pleasant time in that office, and I only hope I have given half as much profit to others as I have obtained myself. It is an honour on which I shall look back with pride all my life that at the age of 19 I should have been elected captain of the picked shots of Oxford, and should have been re-elected the following year. The reason why I have to resign my office is that I am, as most of you know, going to the University next October. This means practically entering a new life, and as my time will be more fully taken up than that of the average undergraduate I know I shall not be able to continue to help to run this club. My reason for wishing to resign so early is that my successor may have as much of the year as possible to work in. I will, however, keep on the office till another captain is elected, so long as I may leave it in July when I leave Oxford for some time. I feel I owe you a most humble apology for leaving my office like this, but I am afraid I have no other alternative. At the time of my election I did not know for certain I was going to go to the University, or I would not have taken office. I should like the reasons for my retirement to be clearly understood. It is not on account of the Meeting that has just passed, or because I am tired of rifle shooting, but because I know that I shall be too fully occupied next October to attend to the business of the club. I wish to retire now and not wait till October so that my successor shall have time in the remaining part of this year to accomplish good results, and that he should not come into a new position just when the indoor shooting season is beginning, and the claims of his own club are calling him.

{August 1914}

DEAR MOTHER

I have filled up the form for the Special Reserve not lightly nor without thought. Please get it taken at once to 9 Alfred Street. If there is anything you want to say about it please wire. There is only one post a day here. If you give the form in, and any order comes for me (please open all the O.T.C. correspondence) you must wire. I will always give you my address. This is enough for this place: Camp, Redmire, Yorkshire.

Should the Broads still hold, I will most likely stay here as long as possible and then go there. I will write about clothes shortly. Bobs will be disappointed that Ladram {Bay Camp} has been scratched.

FRANK

{September 1914}

DEAR MOTHER

I expect to be orderly officer next Saturday or Sunday, so I don't think it likely that I shall be able to come home. It is a pity, but if I do not manage this week I will try the week after. I hope in any case to get off very soon, but I am afraid it will not include any part of Monday. I wish I could have got up to London on Saturday. I was stopped most unexpectedly just at the last minute. I think I shall be regularly on route marches now, three times a week. It will be a change, and a much-needed training. I shall also be with the company a good deal. I am perfectly fit physically.

I have had another day's shooting duty at Gravesend, and again it was very pleasant. The train was crowded coming back, and as no carriages had been reserved for our lot there was a good deal of squashing in places. The men got in through the windows where the doors were locked. In the butts I got a shower of sand down my neck because some bullet hit a sand-bag just above me.

Washing I meant to have mentioned before. It is now being done in Abbey Wood, quite well, and not too expensive. I have had no mending to do yet.

My tent has just bought a stove between us. It costs 12/9, burns paraffin, & gives a good light & heat. It will be very useful I expect.

I will continue this tomorrow if I can.

FRANK

I hope very much you & Arnie are going on well.

DEAR MOTHER   *Wed.* {*September* 1914}

Thanks very much for your long letter & Will's enclosed. If I do not write for a few days at any time you can be absolutely certain that it is not because I am going or gone out. When I do get away you will know almost as soon as I shall. I have been very much occupied the last few days. I got up to London last Friday, but have not yet got the clothes. On Saturday we expected a draft to go, several officers having been warned. On Sunday I went on guard again at the Sewer and had a mildly exciting time. I had been back from that about an hour on Monday when I was sent to Bristol to bring back some men on Tuesday, which was a very nice change. The guard was noticeable as my corporal told me there was a wireless installation in a house in the sewage works which was kept secret. So in the evening I went to the house with the corporal and a private and demanded to be shown a shed where the wireless was. There was no trouble about that, and I found the installation there all right. It was a very small one, not in working order, but it could have been put into working order in a very few minutes. The people said it had not been tried for two years and was of no use at any time. My corporal however knew it had received messages from ships (or rather intercepted them) about six months ago. Two poles for aerials were standing about 20 feet apart next the shed. There were no wires up, but they could have been put up in a few minutes, there being pulleys on the top of each of them and the best & thickest blindcord I have seen in position all ready. Only two men in the works knew of this wireless. It was not very important both because the information that could have been sent by it was scarcely likely to be valuable, and it could not very well be used now as it is in full view of a sentry, who would of course see the flashes. Still, it was quite amusing going to the house. I reported it next day, and the result is that it has been pronounced harmless by the police and also by Colonel Bryant, who is in charge of the defences of the Arsenal. I have not heard details of his visit, but I know the whole house was searched.

Bob has interrupted me here. He came for about an hour & a half. He brought me a compass from Ned which is most excellent for its own purpose. I will get a marching one as well.

I gave Bob Will's letter.

I have no more time, now, I'm sorry. Will try & write tomorrow.

FRANK

Very glad you & Arnie are going on so well.

I may unfortunately not be able to come home next Saturday, but don't know yet.

{*Sunday September* 1914}

DEAR FATHER

I am very glad to hear that Mother is really getting better now. I hope it will not be long before she is downstairs again. I think after this she ought to have a change of air, if possible. What is Arnie going to do for the next few weeks? I suppose he won't go to school.

I hope in about a fortnight to be able to send you £22, which will I think nearly cover what you have paid for me. I will be very glad if you will tell me the exact amount.

I have had a great time with the Colt. It took me some time to find out how to dismount it, and a longer time to put it together again. Then this afternoon I took the greater part of it to pieces, & couldn't get it back for a long time. The Colonel happened to pass when I was trying to put it together, and was very interested, watching me putting the sear in wrong way round. After that difficulty had been disposed with I went on all right, except that it took a long time. When next I am free I shall take a little more to pieces, most likely the whole thing. Please ask Ned why the following happens. After replacing slide & barrel on the receiver, holding them upside down & having the link forward, why does the slide not come back freely when pulling it backwards to put the safety catch in place? It sticks when pulled back slowly, & requires a jerk to overcome the resistance, whatever it is. The hammer is at full cock. Except for this I have no other question at present. Bob came down yesterday & we had a nice time together. I expect I shall be able to see him next Thursday in London. I hope that before long I will be able to get off for a weekend, so will be able to get home. I may be able to manage it this week, but scarcely expect to do so, as the Adjutant is not fond of letting men go away for long. It will be very nice if I can do so. My sword came yesterday, from Wilkinson. I had to have it while I am here, though I fancy there are not many being carried at the front. Most of our men will send them home as soon as they go out.

Huts are going to be built for us. I expect we shall be in them in a fortnight.

FRANK

Dear Ned   {*September* 1914}

I think you were quite right about that projecting pin, which is the end of the disconnector. I had it out some days ago, but don't know yet how it works. It really will be quite hard for me to get a range to shoot on. There is no range attached to the Camp, as we are within Woolwich Arsenal, and no shooting is allowed there because of the large number of magazines dotted about and also because there is a fairly large amount of picric acid out in the fields. If a bullet hit that it would go off. I have tried at the King's Norton Ammunition works here but their range is too much occupied. The only other one is a 30 yards one a mile & a half away. That is a Government one, and is being fairly constantly used. This is, I think, my only chance locally.

I have got 200 rounds of ammunition & can get plenty more, at 12/6 per 100. The address of the Colt place is the London Armoury Co. (not Ammunition as I said before), 31 Bury Street, St. James, S.W. Spare parts can be had there, and in a few days I shall try for a spare magazine. They were out of them when I got the ammunition.

The Colt is a lovely pistol. The more I examine it the more I like it. There is a vast gulf between it and the ordinary revolver.

If you want anything in connection with it which you don't want to write for I could get it for you. They keep two weights of bullet, I think 200 & 230 grains. The lighter weight has considerably higher velocity and greater penetrating power, though I suppose less shock.

Frank

3RD BATTALION THE GLOUCESTERSHIRE REGIMENT

Dear Father   *Friday* 25 {*September* 1914}

I hope Mother is going on all right. I have not heard today as yet. I got the handkerchiefs all right. Thanks very much. If it is not too much bother, could you send me my footer things. Football is being started here. Just my shirt, shorts, & two pairs of stockings. I have not got any proper football boots, & do not want any, as the black boots I have at home will do. Please send them also.

Tonight the fish factory is on the go, with a mist rising also. Fogs are rather frequent here. I have heard today that huts are going to be built for us, so we shall stop here. I expect we shall be in them in a fortnight, which will be an improvement.

Four officers left camp yesterday to go to the North Lancashires, who are rather short. I fully expected one of them, who was in my tent, to want to take my Colt & glasses, as he had not got any. He offered me £5 for the Colt in the morning, before he knew he was going. As I had to be on parade till shortly before he went I was very relieved to find he had not tried to pack them up when I came back. As it is he has only taken a handkerchief of mine.

I was talking to the Colonel today & find he was at Maclarens school, & later at Merton, where I think he was rather wild. Another officer, the second in command of the company I'm in, travels greatly & has been to Carchemish. His name is Captain Salmon. He is a short, thick-set, middle aged man, not particularly nice. I was not talking to him myself, but Vere was, & he told me. I will get talking to him when I can.

I expect Bob down here tomorrow.

I have not yet been able properly to examine the Colt.

I hope I hear good news of Mother tomorrow.

FRANK

I should also very much like to know how you are.

Tuesday 29 {September 1914}

DEAR MOTHER

I was delighted to get your letter today. I am very glad you are feeling better. I hope you will soon be out of pain. It is a very good thing you are going to Boar's Hill. It ought to be very nice up there just now. I wish I was going with you. I will try to get off for the weekend after this one. I am afraid weekend is rather a misleading term, as it will be a very short one. I shall have to get back here on Sunday night. I could not possibly get leave for any part of Monday, except under very exceptionable circumstances. Of course I need not get back till late on Sunday, but it would be easier to be here before 8.0 p.m. On Saturdays I can get to London at the latest, barring accidents, by 2.15. This will be Charing Cross, and I think it takes between 15 & 20 minutes to get from there to Paddington. Please tell me what trains I can get then. I can't properly get it out of Bradshaw. If I make a dreadful rush I could get to Charing X by 1.40. I can have about 24 hours at home by this, so I think it will be worth it, though it does mean travelling back on Sunday. It will be very seldom that I will be able to get off for Sunday.

I can get plenty ammunition for the Colt in London. Their depot is not as printed on the box & the booklet that came with the pistol. It is now the London Ammunition Co., 31 Bury Street, about 6 or 7 minutes walk from 15A Pall Mall. I hope to do some shooting to-morrow at the King's Norton ammunition works here. The more I look at the Colt the more I like it. It is beautifully made. The pull is a lovely one, both for sweetness and straightness. Vere is one man who greatly covets it. He has got a ·320 Webley Scott, but badly wants mine also. My glasses attract him too. He appreciates automatics & high-power glasses, which more than one here do not. I am very glad he is here. He is such a thoroughly nice man. Unfortunately it is quite likely he will be sent off soon, while I have not got that to look forward to. He will be very glad to get away.

I have just got your parcel, but have not yet opened it. The Colonel has just asked for the two stamps off it, for his little boy. Thanks very much for the parcel.

Yesterday morning all the recruits were taken in Company drill, the junior officers having charge of platoons. There were some queer results obtained. Most of us knew a fair amount of the drill, but the N.C.O.'s were absolutely new to it. It has not been tried today. All the men are well provided with new thick blankets, a very large number of them Witneys. I have asked each lot of men I have had if they were cold at night and they have all said they were not. The blankets are really very good ones, white. They are much better ones than the brown kind.

More officers are being inoculated, and I think there will be a few more later.

I tried Major Menzies with one of the only two sentences of Gaelic I know. It meant something like "Good morning" or "How do you do." You know it all right, but I won't try to write it. He said he didn't know any more Gaelic than I did. This was a few days ago, I think. I will write more tomorrow if I can, but hope to see you soon quite well.

FRANK

Wednesday {October 1914}

DEAR MOTHER

I am very sorry you have been so ill, & that it will take you so long to recover. You have had a very hard time. I hope Arnie does not have to have another operation. Dr. Gibson has given you a long time to recover, but I hope you will get strong again before the month is up. I don't think I shall get the £10 back, as I have had a receipt for it. If I get the £6 from the Stores paid to me it will do nearly as well.

I'm always asking you to send me things, but I would be very glad if you sent me a small strip of old carpet or a small rug. The boards of the tent are very cold to stand on when going to bed or getting up. A bit two feet long would be heaps. If you send a rug don't send a good one. It will be spoilt in no time with the clayey mud here.

I'll write again tomorrow, & answer your letter more fully. Now I'm just going in to mess.

FRANK

Practically every man in the camp is going to be inoculated for typhoid.

I shall be orderly officer on Sunday next, I think, so will not be able to get home this week.

Monday {October 1914}

DEAR FATHER

I'm very sorry to hear about Arnie. It is of course a good thing to know definitely what's the matter with him, but I hope he will not get anything else after this. I'm glad he is not in much pain. Ned's version is commonsense and lively. Bradley must be mystified. I will write to him. Mother must take care and not do too much when she is not strong. It will be now quite a long time before I get home.

The Adjutant said an interesting thing the other day. Speaking about drink, he said that if he had the power he would make it a penal offence to bring drink into England, and would hang anybody trying to do so. He is not an abstainer, and is very fond of port. He was speaking from his experience of men. The lot here, he said, work three days a week so as to be drunk the other three. Yesterday I was orderly officer, and had a little extra excitement, for a man broke his leg and also a tent went on fire. I had to telephone to the Argyll's camp for a doctor for the broken leg, but the fire was very amusing. One of the men in the tent, a bell one, must have been smoking, I think, and thrown a cigarette end or a match against the side of the tent. Only part was burnt, but some blankets and equipment and two rifles were damaged. It was beaten out in a few minutes.

One unfortunate thing is that we shall most likely after all not be moved from here. Well built wash houses & cooking huts have been built already, and the authorities don't want to waste them.

I saw Bob on Saturday & hope to see him again on Thursday. I very much hope Ned gets that post. It must be a good one.

I will get the money as soon as I can. In the matter of the belt I will send it to Walters tomorrow to try and get an allowance for it. I don't expect I shall however. I have tried to sell it myself, but can't manage that. The belt is a very badly made one. An important part broke just after I got it. So please do not pay the bill till you hear further. I have had a letter from Will. He is feeling wild at not being able to take part in this business. I am quite sure I do get £40. I will write to Cox and try through him.

FRANK

{October 1914}

DEAR MOTHER

I was very glad to get your letter this morning. Could not you stay at Boar's Hill longer, till you were more recovered at least? It seems such a pity to come away so soon. I hope in any case it will not be long before you are all right again. I don't think Bob means to come home next Saturday, as we have arranged to meet in the afternoon in London & in the evening to go to Mr. Webster's meeting. I think I can almost promise to get off for Saturday week, which will be very nice. If I wait till Monday to come back I should not get to Camp till after 11.0, which means missing three parades & orderly room. It is very unfortunate there is no midnight train from Oxford.

There is just a chance I shall get back that £10. It is not caution money, but a donation to the mess. As I joined in war time I may escape it. If I do get it back I will return it to you.

There is another man come into my tent. He is a good cricketer & footballer. He plays for Gloucestershire, and in football for the Casuals. He knows Kerry and B. O. & A. L. Corbett. He seems a very decent man. In all large camps (Public School & University included) men must have their meals in the open except when it is cold or wet. That is usually a standing order. The reason is to keep the tents as clean as possible. Refuse would get between the floor boards & underneath them and the rats would soon appear in camp. When in the open all refuse can be picked up, but it could not be done to the same extent in a few hundred tents. The rats here come from the sewer, and all huge animals. I am very glad Father's cough is good.

I have not yet had any football. The ground at present is very hard, and full of ridges & ruts. I have twisted my ankle once about a week ago, happening to jump on an uneven place, & am rather frightened to play at present. It would be all right if the ground was level, but it is not at all. It would be a very great nuisance to damage myself now. As I would lose vastly more than I would gain by playing, I don't think I will till the ground gets soft. I think my tent will (between us) buy a small oil stove. From other things I have heard the huts may not turn up till Christmas, and even perhaps not then. At times it is a little cold now. I have not yet got my £40 nor 2/6 a day field allowance, but have got enough money to go on with. It will be very nice to see you again soon.

FRANK

Tuesday {End of October 1914}

DEAR MOTHER

I got to Camp on Sunday just before twelve. Something, I suppose it was the pears, had upset me, so I had an uncomfortable night, but I had a long sleep last night and am all right now. I have been reckoning up different things I want to get and I'm afraid I will have to ask you for money after all. I am going to get a kind of knapsack, which with other things will get up to £2. I will be very glad if you send me that much. That will be quite enough. I will try & get another visit home in. I shall not, I expect, be leaving very soon. A fairly large draft is going off tomorrow or the next day, but I am not for it. I will write a longer letter tomorrow if I can. I shall be on guard again at Mugly.

FRANK

Oct. 22

Dear Father

I return the cheque endorsed. I had not expected it now. I hope Arnie is going on all right. We had another easy march this morning of about 8 miles. I expect we shall soon do longer distances. Three mornings a week are given to marches. They are sometimes quite amusing. Our men won't make much noise on them however. We usually go up on the high ground about a mile from the camp, to where we were once going to move. It is very nice country, and it is really very enjoyable. We are all in full marching order.

There have been several changes here lately. Most unfortunately (for me alone) Vere has been sent off to the front. He was very lucky to get the chance, as there were several men who ought to have gone before he did. But as they all happened to be out of Camp he went instead. He was told late one evening and went nearly mad with excitement. He went away the next day and I went up to London with him. He was smiling all day. Another subaltern and two senior officers went at the same time. The day after three more captains went. So we are very short of captains now. I think we shall be getting more in soon.

The lecture on inoculation that was to have taken place last Thursday is on again today, so I shall not be able to get up to see Bob. I hope I shall be able to manage Saturday.

I have now stopped doing orderly work, & am instead put on to keeping guard. This will mean occasionally having charge for a day of a small number of men guarding part of the Arsenal. Yesterday I fired 8 shots from the Colt. I foolishly started too far away, and out of the 8 shots I missed the target (6 × 6 ins.) twice. The bull was the same size as the one Ned shot on when trying the pistol. One shot was in the bull, two very close to it. The other three were all high. The distance was 30 yards. Another man with me firing with a revolver hit the target once in 10. I think I shall be able to go to this range fairly frequently. It is a government one, much like the Cherwell in a disused clay pit, only rather better kept. The pistol shot beautifully. The light was not good, as it was a quarter to five.

I will write again tomorrow. Just now I have to go on parade shortly. I hope Mother is not getting too tired.

Frank

Tuesday 27th {October 1914}

DEAR MOTHER

It is very good of you to write such a long letter. I had not expected one from you for some time. You must be very busy with Arnie. I hope you will not do too much. It is very hard indeed on Arnie having all this trouble. I will write to him tonight if I can or else tomorrow and tell him about my going on guard, for I have come off it a few hours ago. Father must be kept busy with ordering everything. I wrote to Menon a day or so ago. Vere is at present at Winchester. He will be going out with the 8th Division in a few days. The notice he had was not really short. Some men have been sent off from here at 8.0 a.m. when they were told at three or five o'clock that morning. Men going out on drafts usually have two or three days notice. Vere was such a truly nice man that it is a great pity for me that he has gone. There is no-one like him here now. Don't get despondent about the war. We are doing very well, and at present cannot expect to win smashing victories. We are winning more & more every day. Our forces are being constantly increased and reinforced.

It will be very nice indeed if I can get home soon. But I would rather not go anywhere else. I cannot be long at home in any case so it would be a great pity to waste any of the time at another person's house. I hope Dr. Gibson will allow it. But I am now more uncertain when I shall be able to get away, owing to going on guard. I cannot change guard either. I hope to see Bob tomorrow afternoon down here. I have had a letter from Janet wanting me to go to lunch with Mrs. Laurie some Sunday. I will do so if I can.

I have been using my O.T.C. uniform lately, which is very warm. I shall get something in the line you suggest soon.

I don't really think we can be kept here much longer. The field is in a terrible state of mud after only a few hours rain. It is regularly flooded most of the winter. Skating is frequent on it. Rheumatism and pneumonia will be rampant soon.

I will write to Will as soon as I can. I wrote to Florence lately. I have not heard from Ned. It's too late now to write to Arnie, so I will have to leave that till tomorrow.

I hope very much I will be able to see you soon.

FRANK

Wed. 28 {*October* 1914}

Dear Arnie

You must be having a very nasty time, I am afraid. But cheer up, it won't last much longer, and by it you are doing good because you are giving Mother a complete rest from her ordinary work. So you have a cheering thought to console you.

I'm not sure if I shall be able to finish this letter now, as Bob may be coming down here. He had arranged to come, but as it is now nearly 5.0 p.m. I think he must have been prevented. When going on guard officers have to be in marching order, which means a Burberry rolled up on your back, haversack, sword, glasses, & water bottle. The only thing I did not have was my pistol, which is not necessary for the guard I was on. The water bottle was taken for show only. I have not used it yet, and do not expect I shall want it for a long time. There were nearly 80 men on guard altogether, my company officer being in command. We had to go about 1½ miles to the place where we were to stop, half a dozen tents for the men and one for Capt. Scott and myself. Twenty men went off to a hut on the river bank as a picquet.

Later.

Bob came when I had got as far as this. He was here a little over an hour only. It was very nice seeing him. He said he would write to Mother tonight or tomorrow.

To continue as before:

These twenty men had a fine time according to their own ideas. There was a fireplace & chimney in the hut which looked as if they had been put up for working in metal of some kind. The fireplace was like a square box without a lid, the sides & bottom being gratings. It was about 14 ins. deep & the same across. There was coal near used for cranes, so the men helped themselves to it and had a huge fire going all night. They filled the box thing as full as possible, and whenever I went there it was too hot for me to stop inside the hut. During the afternoon it was once too hot for the men themselves. They seemed to enjoy it though. The place might have been the stoke hold of a steamer. There were ten sentries on in all, each for two hours. We got to the place about 3.0 p.m. on Monday, and were relieved the same time the next day. The Argyll's took it on then, for they have it on alternate days with us. The sentries were posted by Scott and myself as soon as we got there. Four patrolled the river bank, and the other six were distributed on magazines and a searchlight. The searchlight was put up just after we got there. It is touching the tents, but is not very much use. It is not powerful enough, and cannot be elevated sufficiently. Also it cannot twist round like a top. It has a starting point which it cannot pass. It starts from there and goes round till it comes to this point again, then it has to come back. It cannot go completely round. The gross stupidity of the body of workmen who put it up has managed to get this stopping place when the thing is pointing to the only part of the sky in which it is required. The glass is arranged as a motor searchlight, a number of different vertical strips of varying power. The thing is about 2 feet in diameter, but is really only a toy compared to what is wanted here. My food for the 24 hours had all been sent out by the mess, and when I came to look at it I found there was no knife nor fork, nor even a cup, though they sent a tea pot and nearly $\frac{1}{4}$ lb. of tea. Scott had no knife etc. either. I had plenty to eat though. I went round the sentries about 7.0 that night. It took just about an hour to do them. The idea in visiting them is to see that they are on their beats and are keeping awake. Going to one man I had to walk along a rickety old jetty the planks of which had gaps in them occasionally and there was no railing of any sort on it. Underneath was a drop of 20 feet on to stones, at low tide. At high tide the water was about 10 feet below. The sentries enjoyed that beat. When I got back we did nothing till 11.15, when the two of us went round, taking half each. I had the longer round and the more awkward. I kept on stepping into ruts & holes anything up to a foot deep, or on bricks or bits of wood on the ground. Scott was in bed when I had finished, & I went to bed as soon as I had arranged to be called soon after four. Neither of us took our clothes off. I took my boots off, but was not really supposed to. I had been walking through such mud that I didn't like keeping them on. I was called as arranged, and started off round at half past four. It took an hour and a half this time, as I had to hunt for some sentries. They happened to be at the furthest limit of their beat, or going round a large magazine and I had to guess which way to go. All of them were very wide awake. I took good care always to make a noise before coming to where I thought a sentry was, for some men get very nervous and will fire at anything. Our men are not bad in this way, but the Territorials who were on the job before us were so dangerous, firing at anything they saw, that the police refused to go round. I badly wanted a flash lamp, but mine unfortunately had just run out and I was not able to get a refill before I went on guard. I will take care to have one next time. The Arsenal is all patrolled by police as well as our men. The night was quite warm, and it was not at all unpleasant going round. I had a lovely view of the comet. This is quite a bright light, and has been mistaken by some of our men for an airship's light. I got back at six, and did not wake up again till nine. We got up then, but couldn't get any water to wash with. So we had a dry clean instead. I went round the sentries again soon after 10.0, which was the last time. The Argyll's reached us sometime near 3.0, and we got back to camp about half past, when I went off and had a bath. Scott had his meals in a Major's house close by, so I was alone for them. I expect I shall be on guard again about next Sunday, but not at the same place most likely. It will be at the Sewage Works then. There was really very little to do on guard, and there will be less still at the Sewage Works. They have been keeping quiet lately, and have not treated us to their peculiar smell. The fish factory has been active fairly often though.

I must stop now, but hope to have good news of you soon.

FRANK

3RD GLOUCESTERS
ABBEY WOOD
LONDON, S.E.
Oct. 30

DEAR WILL

This is not an essay, though the paper must remind you of one. It is only the nearest approach to foreign paper I can get just now. Thanks very much for your letter. I am indeed very lucky, and you are unfortunately most unlucky. It must be maddening to be out there while all this is going on. If you do come back I don't think you will have difficulty in getting a commission. There are still a very large number of people wanting commissions, but many of them have no knowledge at all of this kind of work. Ned would be able, most likely, to get you in anywhere. The casualties among officers are very great. Nearly 80 per cent. are killed, wounded, or missing, and in the case of officers 'missing' generally means wounded. It will be very few men, if any, who will go through much of this war without being hit. One man who went out from here three weeks ago has been dangerously wounded, and over half of the officers sent out from here since the

start have been, or are, badly hit. My battalion, the 3rd, will not, I
think, go out as a battalion. It acts as a feeding ground for the 1st
battalion which is out there, and a number of drafts have been sent.
Another draft ought to go any day, as the Gloucesters got badly cut up
lately attacking somewhere around Ypres. They were in Ypres a week
ago. The 2nd battalion, also of the line, is on the way from India, and
will go straight out when it comes. Then we shall have two battalions
to feed. Some Territorials have been sent out to India to take the
Gloucesters' place. That is what has been done with most of the
foreign service volunteers of the Territorials. They are sent out to allow
perfectly trained men to come back to fight, and they must be sick now
when they have realised that there is very little chance of any fighting
for them. We are, as you know, stationed in Woolwich Arsenal, at
present the most important place in England. Work never stops for a
single instant in the Arsenal from one month to another. There are
25,000 men employed by day, and about the same by night. There are
enough magazines within three hundred yards of our camp to wipe all
our lot right out, should one of them only go off. An airship would not
have any difficulty in finding this place, for they must know every
inch of this place. For years a German had a farm just outside, with
grazing rights for his cattle inside the boundary. He was also very good
friends with the police here. He disappeared a week or so before the
war, and has not been heard of since. There are many more cases rather
like that. A Zeppelin would be able to blow up any of these magazines
quite easily, provided it did not try to get away itself. If it did it would
be more difficult. One has been over Southend not long ago, and one
may come any night. Still that danger is problematical. What is certain
is that we are going to have terrible illness unless the camp is moved.
We are in tents on marshes, which are flooded some months of each
winter. We ought to be under water now, but owing to the exception-
ally dry weather the rain has only been on for a few hours and we are
only in a terribly muddy mess. It is raining now, and if it keeps on all
night the water will be over the floor boards of some tents by the
morning. The Thames once flowed over these fields, but they have
been reclaimed. They are still several feet below high water level. The
subsoil is peat to a depth of about 15 feet. There is a contract out for
building huts for us on some high ground near, which is a very nice
place, but it will be 10 weeks at least before they are completed. Also

I hope I shall not still be here in 10 weeks time. I can't say of course when, if ever, I shall get out, but I hope it will be before Christmas. I expect I will just come in for the latter half of the winter. Our business here is training ourselves and the men. It is very nice work, and I very much enjoy it. We are not very hard worked. We start at 7.0 a.m., and finish usually at 3.0 p.m. I am also on guard nearly twice a week, for 24 hours each time. That means being in command of a small body of men at some point in the Arsenal.

I really cannot describe the language, sentiments and thoughts freely expressed here by the officers. It is beyond words abominable. I never thought such a state of things could exist anywhere. There has been one really decent man here, from B.N.C. He has now gone to the other side, and there is no-one left here like people I have been accustomed to. I see Bob usually twice a week, which is very nice, and hope next Saturday or the Saturday after to get home for a night. I would have been home before but for Arnie's illness. He is going on all right now. It is hard on him getting scarlet fever after all his other troubles. I hope also to see something of the Lauries soon.

I will write again to you very soon. I wish you were here with me.

FRANK

{On the envelope:}
W. G. Lawrence Esq.
  Maitland House
    Kashmir Gate
      Delhi
        India.

Better put this address on letters in future. 'Kent' is all right, but Abbey Wood, London S.E. may be better for some obtuse postal official who scribbled on the envelope of Father's letter.

3RD GLOUCESTERS
ABBEY WOOD
LONDON, S.E.

Sunday, Nov. 1

DEAR MOTHER & FATHER
    I have only just got your letters today, as I was on guard again yesterday & they were not brought out to me. Thanks very much for the £1. I will use it as you suggest. I have got back the £10, but am

holding on to it as I want it to pay my mess bill. I paid Vere's bill when he went, and I have not yet got it back again. He told me to write to his home for it if he did not send it me in a few days. I have written to Vere so will have it in a little. I went on guard yesterday morning at 10.0 a.m. & am now feeling rather tired. I was on the sewer, but it was very nice. I was in charge of one picquet, and Captain Scott had charge of the larger picquet. He did not come to me at all during the 24 hrs., so I was quite on my own. My men were split up into two bodies, each of which were 6 men and a corporal. I was with one lot, and the others were about ⅓ of a mile away on the other side of the sewage works. I had a little hut to myself with electric light and a stove. The men with me had a tram to sleep in, also with electric light. The other lot had a hut with stove & electric light and were quite comfortable. Bob came down in the afternoon which was very nice, and as I expect he is writing I will not describe these arrangements more fully now.

I have just moved to the other writing place so as to be quiet, and there is only red ink obtainable here. I went round the sentries once or twice only during the day as there is no danger of them going to sleep then. They were armed with Martini carbines, firing buckshot. Rifles are very dangerous there, as there is a very high explosive, picric acid, in barrels out in some fields a few hundred yards off, and a bullet would send it off if it hit the stuff. Picric acid is very slightly changed by some process and then called lyddite. I went round the sentries at night at 10.0 or a little after, 1.0 & 4.0, the corporal waking me up the last two times. Other men do not go round nearly so often, once being about enough for them between 11.0 & 12.0. There is no rule that I know of laid down for this business, but of course in war the officer goes round every two hours or more. It is, I think, very much safer to visit each man during the night. They are on for two hours each, and might go to sleep. Also they, purposely or otherwise, muddle up their beats, and go wandering off where they are not wanted. One of them did that last night, and gave me an extra mile to walk the second time I went round. I couldn't find him at all, and thought he had gone to sleep somewhere. When I did get him in the end it turned out he had gone twice as far as he ought to have done. Should anything happen during the night it would be far better for me to be able to say I had visited each sentry on duty, rather than having left them to themselves for 7 or 8 hours. We are guarding one of the most important places in

England just now, and there are continually men trying to get information of some kind or other. They pose as officers, police inspectors, workmen, or anything just to get past the sentries, and naturally we don't know when they may come. Also a few weeks ago there was signalling from some house on the hills to a boat on the river, and we have to be on the look-out to see if there is any more of it. About 4 or 5 nights ago one of the sentries on the sewage works reported to the corporal that there was signalling going on from a house in the works built for the men. When the corporal got there he saw a light in the window, but it was quite steady. The sentry, who was young but perfectly in earnest, then brought the corporal to the place from which he had first noticed it. The corporal found he had got a small tree without knowing it between himself and the light, and as he looked first from one side of the tree and then from the other of course the light went in and out like signalling. I bought the men an egg each for breakfast, very fine large ones at $1\frac{3}{4}d$. each. They were splendid eggs. I got back to camp at 11.0 this morning, just in time to take the Wesleyans to their service, which is held out in the field. There were about 30 of them, and a Wesleyan clergyman came & took the service. It was quite nice, though I thought it was rather long. I expect it was just because I was tired, as it only lasted half an hour. I had not been detailed to do it, but took it for another man who lives in London and wanted to go home for the day. He is the Gloucestershire cricketer, and the nicest man here now, so I did not mind doing it for him. I am now feeling rather tired and very sleepy, though I have had a sleep this afternoon. I shall get to bed early tonight, and have a proper sleep, as last night I could not undress.

Captain Scott has gone away this morning till tomorrow night, and as the other man senior to me in the company is on guard I shall be in charge of it tomorrow. This will mean interviewing the men brought up at orderly room tomorrow, and either settling the case myself or sending it to the Colonel. The limit of my powers is giving a man up to three days C.B. When a man is C.B. he has to report himself to the guard in camp every half-hour, and is also put on various fatigue duties. It is very difficult to get in contact with the men at all. I do not see them really except on parade, and it is only when on guard that I can speak to them quietly. Then it is difficult, as although of course I speak to all the sentries yet I have to talk about their business to make sure they

know it, and switching off on to religious matters with very many of
these men would do no good at all. They would have to listen as I am
an officer, and that would not be the best way to go about things.

I should very much like to know what Ned is going to do. The man
with the broken leg was removed to hospital the next morning, and I
have not heard anything about him since. He trod on a tent peg when
drunk. I will not go to the Laurie's on Sundays.

We are, I am glad to say, definitely going to be moved to the top of
the hills. The positions of the huts are being planned out, but it will be
a number of weeks (8 or 9) before they are all built. I expect that before
then we shall transfer all the tents up there. We have only had a very
little rain, but the condition of the lines is terrible in mud now.

I very greatly hope the King does not come & inspect us. Many of
the men are slovenly and careless, others so old as to be incapable of
doing anything well. A fair number of them have certainly been dismissed from the Army years ago as undesirables, and they come up
here, being taken on because they pose as old soldiers and do not have
to show a certificate (of character), just for the money and the food.
Many of the N.C.O.'s also are not nearly as good as they might be.

I did not intend to write as much as this when I started, but there
being nothing I had to do I thought I would go on. I wrote to Florence
some days ago, but could you send on to her any letters you think fit.
I will write as often as I can to her, but there are so many people I
ought to write to that my time is rather taken up, and I cannot always
be writing.

I am very glad Arnie is going on well. I have got no fear about
Mother. This rest ought to be a very good thing for her.

I have written to Will and will do so again before next Friday.

Please tell me whether a book of 'Everyman's' series has come from
a shop in London. I should like to know, as they may not have sent it.
It should have come some days ago.

FRANK

I am in no want of money, as I am fitted out now in everything
except a compass, which I must get soon unless Ned has one to spare.
I don't think he has, but you might find out from him if you can. I
have £7 owing to me in field allowance, which I hope to get sometime.

Please don't bother to make any more socks. Those I have are quite thick enough, and I have plenty of them. It would be no use having more. Thanks very much.

Friday {End of November 1914}

DEAR MOTHER

I have just come off guard today & as I shall not be on duty next Sunday I have asked for and obtained leave for Saturday night. So I hope to reach Oxford at 5.52 on Saturday. I don't expect I shall be able to get there at 5.15. It is an opportunity not to be missed. I might not have another for a long time like this. Also there is talk of large drafts going next week or very shortly, and although it is not nearly yet my turn to go of course there is always a chance that I might be taken. It will be lovely to see you all again. We'll risk infection. The danger of that can be very slight now, I should think, and I am in perfect health. Arrange for sleeping how you please, Ned's house for preference. I had a very nice time again on guard, at the same place. The men with me were nearly all good class old soldiers, and gave no trouble. We were all very much on the alert, as the day before two men in plain clothes had come down in a motor and had, very stupidly, been given information as to the sentries and allowed to go away by the officer in charge. He should never have done such a thing, but ought to have sent them under escort to the camp. The Colonel & Adjutant were very much annoyed about it, as it is impossible to tell who they were. They may have been our men come on a surprise visit, or spies. In any case they effected their purpose, and left with complete knowledge of the positions of the sentries. There are only the bare minimum of sentries on the sewage works, and it is almost impossible to prevent a person who knows the beats from coming in any time he likes. In addition to this visit a sentry soon after 11.0 that night saw a man hiding just outside the works, and challenged three times, which gave him time to run off before the sentry could shoot. My men weren't going to be bothered with scruples as to challenging the regulation number of times, but would have shot rather quickly. Nobody would try to get into the works at night over the palings unless they had an illegal purpose, and the men who had a purpose in getting in would be well armed and desperate. Everything was quiet for me all night, and there was a very bright moon. I was up most of the time, but got in three hours sleep in two detachments. Bob came down to my great surprise. We had arranged I was to go to London that afternoon (Thursday) to see him, but I sent him a telegram in the morning to say what I was doing. He was not free till 5.30, but got to me at 7.30. It was very nice his coming. He stayed an hour very nearly. I went a little way back with him when he was going off, and we met the cook of my guard coming back from the main camp with a stone jar. We found out it was beer he was bringing to my men, a thing I had never heard of before. He said at first it was two pints, but later it turned to four. It is quite against regulations as far as I know. In the end we paid him the price of the stuff and poured it out onto the ground. There were four men to share the beer, so they would not have got drunk, but they would have been made queer. The man had gone to camp without my permission, so when I got back to the post I told the corporal a little about things. The cook asked me next time he wanted to leave. I am now going to have a bath. I'm feeling a little tired today.

I will be able to tell you more when I see you, as I hope tomorrow. It will be very nice to get home.

FRANK

DEAR MOTHER *Friday* {? *November* 1914}

I can't get home this week end. I have just asked the Adjutant, and he has told me I shall be going on guard on Sunday. We will hope for better luck next week, if I am still here. I also asked him if he had any idea when I might be going out, and he said he had not the very least, as the War Office was sending down the names. The order might come at any minute, or it might not be for weeks.

I was expecting to hear from you today, but I suppose you have not written as you may have been hoping I should turn up myself. I am afraid that it is unlikely I shall get off during the week even under these circumstances.

Today I went with the company to Plumstead Wash Houses, and later on paid the men their weekly money. This job lasts an hour usually. The company quartermaster sergeant makes out the pay books, and all I've got to do is just to give out the money. Today we had £15 in notes & about £45 in silver. No coppers are paid out. The money for all the companies is fetched every Friday morning from the Bank, and is paid out as soon as we get it. Sometimes a profit is made, others a loss. I was exactly right today. The profit comes from the bank putting in an extra shilling or so, as the money is weighed, not counted. They cannot count out £400 in silver. Loss comes from giving a man more than he ought to have. This has to be made up by the officer paying. At the end this morning there was £4 in notes and 5/– in sixpences left over. The usual pay a married man gets is 1/– a week. The rest goes to his wife. An unmarried man 6 or 7 shillings. N.C.O.'s up to 25/–. Hope all is going on all right at home.

FRANK

DEAR MOTHER   *Thursday {End of November* 1914}

 Have just got your letter, and you must have had mine by now. I have again had no time for writing much today. We have just had a very good lecture on shooting from a staff officer. I'm very sorry I shall be on guard on Saturday for certain, and as I shall not be off it till Sunday I will not be able to get home. It is a great pity, but it cannot be helped. There has been some rain today, and the mud in the field I do not remember ever having seen excelled, even on paperchases. The whole field is mud & puddles. It is impossible to walk properly. Men slip over everywhere. The Adjutant has written a furious letter to the War Office, and we are going (definitely I think) to be billeted in a day or so. The huts have been started on the top of the hill.

 I'm not sure if I told you yesterday that Vere has not gone after all. I met him at Bristol and I expect him back here soon. It will be very nice to be with him again. At the last minute there were promotions from the ranks, so he was not wanted. I will tell you about going to Bristol tomorrow I hope. It's washing day, & I think I will be more free.

 Everything is all right with me. I am perfectly warm at night. I don't think I will be able to see Ned before he goes. Bob has told me all he knows about him. Ned ought to have a good position there. If he lets his services get known (as he will have to most likely) he may be 'D.S.O.' soon.

 Glad Arnie liked the books. I am going to collect some in camp & send them.

 What is Ned gazetted in? (I mean regulars or reserve).

More later,

FRANK

Saturday {End of November 1914}

DEAR MOTHER

I am on guard again today, at the sewer, so have time to myself. I hope Bob will come down this afternoon. Vere came back to camp last night, which is lovely for me. He may not stop long though. Three subalterns & a major left this morning, also 80 men. Our 1st battalion is now having a rest at the base, while our 2nd is at Winchester.

I came off guard last Monday, and had only been about an hour in camp when the Adjutant asked me if I would like to go to Bristol to bring back a draft. Of course I said I would, so I put all I wanted in my haversack and just managed to get the 3.0 train from Paddington. I badly wanted to go to Oxford instead, but could not do it. I got to Bristol about 6.20, and went straight to our depot there, Horfield Barracks. They are very nicely situated on high ground about 4 miles from the station. After I had seen the Adjutant there (he told me I was to start at 3.0 p.m. the next day) I went for the night to the home of one of the officers here. I did not know his family in the least, but he gave me a letter for them. His father is rector of a fairly large parish, and they are both very nice people. The others of the family were away. I had a very nice time there, and it was quite the next best thing to being at home. Next morning I had a look at their church, which is modern and not striking. It & the parish make up their world. Their other son, a scholar of Trinity, is in Kitchener's Army. The draft I had charge of was just 100 men, including N.C.O.s. We left the barracks, which were very fine buildings, at 1.30, and got to the station at 2.30. On the way we were photographed by a pressman. It had not been arranged. He just happened to pass us. Two carriages were put on to the train for us, and we stopped in them all the way. At Reading we were changed to the S.E. Railway, and had to wait an unnecessary hour owing to a guard's fault. From Reading we went to Aldershot, Guildford, Redhill & Cannon Street. We got to Abbey Wood at 11.0 p.m. It would have been far quicker to go by London, but the War Office had arranged it as above. There was a meal waiting for the men when they got to camp. Seven N.C.O.'s were in the party. They & 20 other men had all come back from the front, some wounded.

Later: Now its Monday morning. Bob & Vere both came down on Saturday afternoon, and stopped some time. The night was quite quiet as usual. I was up most of it, and was so sleepy yesterday that I slept all the afternoon & evening. That's why I did not send this off last night. This morning we were to have a battalion parade at 10.0, and a company one at 11.0. But as our company this morning consisted of three officers, the sergeant major, and three corporals, the parades have not come off. Another company had two corporals representing them. The men were all on guard, except a few sick.

I am going to London this afternoon, to get the clothes. I am perfectly warm however. Next week-end I hope I may be able to get off. I ought to be on guard on Friday, but can't tell properly, as another guard of 100 men has been taken over by us.

FRANK

I suppose Ned is leaving London today. I don't expect to see him though.

I hope Arnie is going on all right.

Tuesday {November 1914}

DEAR MOTHER

I was very glad to get your letter yesterday. Your note on scarlet fever including Arnie's views are scarcely what I would like myself. I'm afraid we differ on that subject. Arnie ought to enjoy a change of room. It will be a pity if the disinfection does take the paint off.

I'm very sorry but I don't think it's possible for me to get back this week. I will tell you later. It must be a great puzzle to you where to go now. I think you had better accompany Ned to Egypt. The country round here would scarcely do for you. It will be rather cold soon. I'm not sure if I have ever really described the land on the hills. It is one huge market garden. There are fields here three or more times the size of the raised portion of the meadow which are very neatly planted with strawberries. Greenhouses abound growing tomatoes or flowers, mostly chrysanthemums. Large fields in the open even now are a fine show of colour. Raspberries, currants, cabbages, etc. are everywhere. The soil would suit Father, being a mixture of gravel & sand to a depth of nearly 100 feet. Houses are frequent, nearly all comfortably sized good ones standing in their own grounds. Villages or small towns are scattered about at intervals. The roads are largely tarred & good. Where they are not tarred they are like those in the New Forest. I think I have mentioned the lovely white dogs one house has here. They are really beautiful. What spoils this place is the awful railway service. Also at certain hours of the day there is scarcely standing room in the trains, all classes alike. The new equipment Bob told you about is, I think, a very good thing. It will do away with conspicuous leather belts, and from a distance it will be impossible to tell it from a private's equipment. This may be useful, as of course the officers on both sides are specially looked out for, and the casualties among them have been very heavy. It will be better than a private's equipment as it is only about half the weight. A large percentage of officers now are leaving their own belts in England and going out in the men's equipment. The holster for my Colt will be, I think, just covered over with the new stuff, which is webbing. It will also not be expensive. A private firm is producing it, and they are being inundated with enquiries & orders already, though it is not yet on the market.

This morning we had a march of about 13 miles, not very much. I was expecting a longer one. Tomorrow morning my company will go to the top of the hill & dig some trenches, if fine. Also if we have any men on parade.

I saw Bob yesterday for an hour in London. The cough he told you about lasted for a short time when he happened to be with me. I am perfectly well.

I am hoping to get into the same tent as Vere. I think I told you he has been put into my company. I don't know if you noticed a tiny paragraph in the papers a few days ago about an airship flying over the country one night. We fully expected it down here, all lights having been turned out. It did not materialise.

I will try & see you as soon as possible, but cannot mention any date.

I hope you are feeling stronger yourself now, and that Father is keeping well.

FRANK

Wednesday {25 November 1914}

DEAR MOTHER

Unexpectedly I have been put on guard today, taking the place of an officer who has gone off. Four subalterns left this morning, which leaves me second on the list. Vere is the one in front of me, & it is just possible he may not go for a little. So I may be the next. Of course it is quite impossible to give any date, but I might go any minute, and am quite likely to go in the next fortnight or three weeks. I do not know in the very least, and have not heard a whisper to guide me. I will do all I can to get home, but cannot promise that. I have not got the clothes yet, & don't think I will. Vere told me he bought a large stock of clothes when he went to Winchester meaning to take them out with him, but has sent them all to his home, as good clothing can be obtained from stores out there. This also saves weight.

I am hoping Bob may come this afternoon. I sent him a telegram this morning, but he may find it hard to get to me, as this is a fresh guard I am on. It is at one of the entrances to the Arsenal, and we are in tents in a fairly dry field. There are 100 men but only 4 sentry groups wanted. So most of the men have nothing at all to do. I am the only officer here. A large number of men are sent so as to be effective in case of aircraft. A few rifles would not have much effect on a Zeppelin.

I have had your letter card. I am very glad to hear about Arnie. It is a good thing its over now. He must not get anything else. Ned must be a little annoyed with the W.O.

I'm afraid this letter is not exactly a comforting one for you. Still it has to be. If I had got to camp the second time I came here on Saturday instead of Tuesday I should now be at Southampton. It is only those three days that have stopped me this morning.

I hope I will be able to come home.

FRANK

ABBEY WOOD
LONDON, S.E.
Mon. Dec. 7

DEAR MOTHER

Thank you very much for the little book you sent by Bob. It is extremely interesting, though also very humiliating. Bob, to my great joy, came down this afternoon for an hour, as I was on guard. If I can, I will see him in London tomorrow, I hope. I ought rather to say today, as the time is now 2.0 a.m., and I am just waiting for a little before I go round the sentries. This is certainly a queer existence for me. There are only 40 men on guard here today, with four sentries as before. The positions of the sentries have been changed, and now it is practically an hour's walk to go round. The night is beautifully fine, with a good moon. When going round sentries I have almost my only chance of talking to the men individually, as they are all willing enough to talk then. It is very difficult to turn the talk to serious subjects however. Tonight I came across an old man from Stow-on-the-Wold who has two sons in the Gloucesters and one in the Navy. He is keen enough to get out. I am going, if I can, to try to get some plate-armour shields with Bob. They are meant to fit in the two top pockets of the tunic, covering the heart & lungs to some extent. They are not meant to stop a bullet, but to turn one. Bullets are capable of such curious twistings in their course. One hit the stud in the front of the shirt of a private of the Gloucesters, travelled round his neck tearing his coat collar on the top, and came out at the back of his neck just opposite to where it first hit him. It is possible that the shields I have been told about are not made now, but I will try & get some. Vere has gone out with thick steel ones. Such things may not be wanted at all, but one officer of our 1st battalion had his life saved by a bullet striking a whistle he carried in one of those pockets and then glancing off sideways. So I will try for them.

I am going round now, so I will stop this scrap of a letter. Bob tells me that a letter from you is waiting for me at camp, which is something to look forward to. If I do get up to London when I get back to camp I don't expect I shall be able to answer it till Wednesday.

Will's thoughts must have been particularly with us today.

I hope you will all have the nicest possible time at Torquay, and that the air will quite set you & Arnie up again.   FRANK

Don't think of meeting me if you are at dinner.

Friday {December 1914}

DEAR MOTHER

I've got leave for Saturday night, so you may expect me at Paignton at 7.46. I think I will be able to get that train all right. If I do not manage to get it I will send a wire, but not otherwise. I will have to come back on Sunday night. The 8.45 train will do me very well, as then I will be able to get the 4.30 a.m. train from Charing Cross, the only one that suits in the early morning.

It will be most delightful to be with you again. I am glad Arnie is going on well.   FRANK

17. 12. 14

Dear Mother

You must have been wondering why I did not write sooner. I had a fairly busy time on guard, the Adjutant coming down to see what could be done to improve matters. The field had a little water in it and was muddy. In the end he told me to make paths of bricks everywhere. Then one of the Majors, the Indian Army man, came along, and found that none of the men had the slightest idea who he was, nor did any of those he asked know who I was. Bob turned up soon after, and stayed quite a long time. The next day I got up to London, and met Bob. We went to the Stores together, where we ordered the two steel pocket plates. Also we chose a watch for me, quite a good one, with illuminated figures & hands.

Yesterday I went to Woolwich, or rather some place past it the name of which I don't know, and had a photo taken. I don't expect much from it, though.

It's very good about Scarborough, isn't it? It will give a shock to some people.

My captain has gone to Winchester today, to do some work for the 2nd battalion. He may be away a few days. I shall be in charge, I think, till he comes back. I hope you are all going on all right.

Frank

29. 12. 14

Dear Mother

I am quite all right, though it was rather windy on guard. The tents were not very comfortable, so the men & I all slept in a barn, on some hay. I had to walk about when the storm was fairly heavy, so I got coated with ice & the lower part of me could not have been more wet if I had been wading. Most of our big main camp was blown down, my tent included, and all my stuff in it got soaking wet. It's all right now though. We are going into billets tomorrow, or at least part of us, so we will not have any more of these incidents.

I will go to Cox's tomorrow if I can.

Frank

3RD GLOUCESTERS
ABBEY WOOD
LONDON, S.E.

2. I. 15

DEAR WILL

Thanks very much for your long letter. You really should not have troubled to write it, as every minute of your time must be occupied. It's all very well to say you give long lectures to the College, but you never mention the hours of preparation you must have for them. It is a wonderfully busy life you are leading. The training must be a very welcome interlude. I should like to know more of what it is. I don't suppose you are always in sole command of a company, but you must have one a good deal. By this time I expect you know the drill, and must now be doing attacks, trench digging etc. If you have not heard this order before you might, if you want to, try it on your company. It is a perfectly legitimate one, but unusual. Get them marching in column of route, and then give 'Facing right, advance in column'. The leading platoon commander will give on his own, 'right turn', and the other three will give two 'right inclines'. I expect you know it, but if you do not, & they do not, you will certainly muddle them up with it.

Four hours a day three times a week is not too little time to put in, I think. To do a great deal regularly seems here to take the spirit out of men & officers. You will always be fresh & eager for your work at your rate of going.

I should be very sorry to see you enlist. I really think it would be an entire waste of time for you, besides being very unpleasant. You would be under officers who might (and the majority have not) not have reached twenty, and who behave like babies. You would be immeasurably superior mentally & physically to every subaltern in this regiment supposing you were a private here now, and we have got a better lot here than the men who are getting commissions in Kitchener's Army. For some time we had in our camp the officers & men of the 11th battalion of the regiment, one of Kitcheners, and there were junior officers in that who would not have been taken under any circumstances in any Regular regiment. One of them fell out once, without leave, when passing a railway station on a route march, and went up to London for the day. He is still in the battalion. It's that type of man who is now getting commissioned, and it will be still worse in

another few months' time. Elementary school teachers, ex-C.L.B. boys,
and others like them are all getting in. You will not meet, except
rarely, should you enlist when you come back, the Army Officer you
have been accustomed to. I have said all this to try & show you a little
of what you would have to go through in the ranks. The ages of the
junior officers in Kitchener's Army, and in fact everywhere will become
younger & younger as time goes on. The wastage in officers is very
large. I do not think you should have any difficulty in getting a commission. If you have to leave the Gurkhas (it would be scarcely fair to
the regular officers to have you taking their place on service) their
Colonel ought to give you a recommendation to the War Office at any
rate, and you would almost certainly get a captaincy in Kitchener's for
the asking. The New Army will not be sent out entirely. The later-
formed divisions will be kept as feeding regiments to others doing the
fighting, and if you went into the New Army it would most likely be
one of them you would be attached to first. I don't think it would take
you long to get out. If you go for the Special Reserve I cannot give a
guess as to what rank you would get. Everything would depend on
what your Colonel said about you and if a Colonel here got interested
in you. I don't think for a minute you would be kept for months of
further training in England. You might be here for months waiting for
your turn to go out, however. I don't think I can say anything more
about enlisting, except to assure you that doing your present work you
are putting far more in the scale of 'services rendered' than by coming
back here and going out as a private. You would undoubtably get a
commission from the ranks if you lived, but it would be very much
better that you should get the commission immediately.

I can't say now when I shall be going out. It ought to be soon, as we
have lost rather heavily lately in officers, that is our 1st battalion. Our
2nd battalion is now out, but has not yet done any fighting. There were
10 officers on the square when I joined in September, and four of them
are now dead, four wounded and one missing. If I had come to camp
three days earlier I should have gone out in place of another man some
weeks ago, and as he has been killed I expect I should have been. The
proportion of killed in officers is very nearly one in two. Sam Browne
belts are of course entirely out of the question. Web equipment, rifles
& bayonets are almost compulsory. I shall not, I think, take a British
Warm with me, but instead have my Burberry lined with oil-silk and

fleece. I will also have my tunic lined with oil-silk in the same way. Should you want a sword when you come back you will find mine at home. If glasses are carried the case is now being covered with khaki cloth. I will not go without mine, but will try & get some way of carrying them without the case. That gives you away. I am now using riding bags, as they are very strong and most comfortable. I have got a large dark coloured handkerchief to use round my neck, as collars are one of the first things to be chucked away. Wool scarves are too hot for me. I am going tomorrow to get a waistcoat with sleeves made of oil silk lined with thin fleece. I have got these various ideas from officers who have been out & from what has been taken out from this camp. I have been lucky enough to find a shop that has just brought out a set of webbing equipment which with pouch, holster, & a pack about the same size as a Tommy's one weighs about $\frac{1}{4}$ or less of the ordinary kind. It is waterproof as well. I will write & tell Mother or you how it wears. Bob knows the shop & all about the equipment and will order one for you should you wish it when your time comes.

The feet is the great unsolved problem at present. Trying to sleep with cold feet is not easy.

The men have now been moved into three large schools here, and are quite comfortable. About half the officers are in them also. I am stopping in the camp here, as I could not have a room to myself in the schools, so it would be very stuffy with a fire, gas-stove & gas light in a small room with two or three others. Last Monday evening nearly the whole camp was blown down (the second time it has happened). My tent went too, and the men who put it up abstracted my razor & spare blades. My canvas bath & bucket also disappeared. I was on guard that night, & managed to find a barn to sleep in with the men, 40 of them. This barn had one side open, so as the men got to the barn first, while I was wandering round beating up strayed ones, I found I had to sleep near the open side, and had the rain falling like dew on me all night. I had my valise, so I was all right, but it gave me a fearful cold. The officers here now are quite a decent lot. The old ones have all cleared off, so the mess is a very different place. What you say about dirty talk is very true I can see now, but I am glad to say that has stopped now. I imagined the Regulars were different. One of the captains here said to me some weeks ago that he would not recommend the Army to anyone who wanted to do more than walk pleasantly through life. There was always someone on top of you, to prevent you making the fullest use of your mind & opportunities. One of the majors here, an Indian Army man, also said much the same. He added that you could not reach a position which adequately rewarded you for your life till long after it was possible to obtain it in civilian life. Naturally I have been thinking about this question a lot. I can see that the Army is a pleasant life, decidedly not a soft one, nor a slack one unless one wishes. I very much like the life I am leading now, out of doors all day long. The Army is attracting me more than ever now I have had a glimpse of a small part of it, but the other side of the question is 'Would it be better to do some job like Mathew's in Nigeria, or that sort of place?' There is much to attract in that business. I would be very glad if you would tell me what your idea roughly about this is. I know you like the Army, and I know also Ned does not. But Ned is so very different from me that I am not putting too much weight on his opinions in this matter. I have not decided myself, and am very much puzzled. I have been wondering about it since the war started. I must stop now, but it would be very kind of you to tell me what you think about the above.

FRANK

{January 1915}

DEAR MOTHER

The carpet came today and will be excellent. Thank you very much for it. I think I will be able to come up on Tuesday & Wednesday & if I can will also stop till fairly late on Tuesday night, somewhere about 10.0 or so. It will be delightful to see you & Florence. I suppose you mean the Clifton Hotel. It does not sound as if you were stopping for Wednesday night.

The wind that night nearly blew me over once or twice. Walking against it was very slow work.

If you can send me that letter of Ned's in which he asks us to find out about the £50 Cox will tell me. Not otherwise. It was silly of Ned not to give directions as to his department. As I thought, Cox has no miscellaneous dept., & I had no end of a hunt before I managed to find his account in the miscellaneous ledger of one of the many divisions of the bank. They must have authority from him before they will say anything.

All the men are now in three schools about 20 mins. walk from the camp. Half the officers are also. I am not for the present. The amount of money wasted on schools is enormous. Each of these schools is larger than the High School, though more compact, having three stories. Captain Scott is going out tomorrow, to the 28th. I expect. They have lost a number of officers lately. Nearly all went out from this camp. I think I told you that if I had come to camp three days earlier I should have gone out instead of another man. That man is the last one to have been killed.

I hope Florence will enjoy her time with you very much.

I am glad Father is feeling more chirpy.

It will be lovely to meet next Tuesday, though of course I will come back on Saturday if I can.

FRANK

3RD BATTALION THE GLOUCESTERSHIRE REGT.
ABBEY WOOD
S.E.

Tuesday {January 1915}

Am dreadfully tired, as I was on guard last night & did not get any sleep at all. I was just going to bed at 4.0 a.m. when one of the sentries told me a policeman had appeared twice on the sewer bank. The silly sentry had let him go without even approaching him. As no policeman had any right to be anywhere near the bank, I turned out two N.C.O.'s & some men & searched the place. It was futile, as the sentry (whose brain powers seem nil) had not told me till much too long after it had happened. The matter has been cleared up fortunately, a bobby having owned to doing part of the things that were done, but there has been no end of reporting about it. I had to go to Mugly this morning after I had come off guard, and was not finally able to rest till nearly 5.0 p.m. And I started to go round the sentries (during which round I was told) at 3.0 a.m. Practically the whole time I was going somewhere. The report the Police have in hand is to go to the Chief Commissioner, then the War Office, and then Colonel Bryant. I was put on guard quite unexpectedly too, out of my turn.

I shall not go in to mess tonight, but am going to bed now instead.

I can't write decently, but I hope you are going on all right, and will get much better soon. I suppose this will come before Florence goes.

I wish I could have seen her more. I hope she has enjoyed her time. Vere is going on well, though slowly.

FRANK

22. I. 15

DEAR MOTHER

Just got your letter. I enclose paper. I will send the socks. It started to snow last night & is still going on. The woods look awfully pretty. It is really very nice. The tents have got an accumulation of snow round each, about 2 ft. deep now. I don't think they'll come down with that lot round them. The snow woke me up this morning, falling on me. I was sleeping in the doorway as usual. It has given the country quite a new aspect, and a wonderfully fine one. When it thaws it will be slushy, but at present it is lovely. I have to go down to the schools about 10.0 tonight. It will take me some time to get back. I am very sorry you say you have got a cold. I hope it will not be a bad one. I expect Arnie did just have a cold. He must not get anything else.

In haste,

FRANK

{Telegram}
Abbey Wood   9.10 p.m.   8 February 1915.
Lawrence   2 Polstead Road   Oxford

Leave with Draft 7.15 tomorrow morning. Cross from Southampton probably almost at once.

{On a postcard}

DEAR MOTHER

This departure is rather sudden & unexpected. Two men were unfit, so it came to me. I was told yesterday morning that my name had been sent in for it, but it was not till ten minutes before I sent the wire that I heard the W.O. had confirmed it. I was expecting it all day, but as it was quite possible that they might have refused me I did not like alarming you. I was with Bob some hours, which was very nice.

A lieutenant is in charge of the draft (200). I know him very well and like him very much. We are going to our 1st Bn., which is not fighting just now I fancy. I am writing this in the train, just after passing Redhill. We have picked up more men, & now have a huge long train. Bob knows about my clothes. I have plenty of handkerchiefs for some time, but when the dirty ones are washed you might perhaps send them out. I will give you my address as soon as I can.

I can't say much on this card, so will get off a letter before I reach France if I possibly can.

F.

SOUTHAMPTON DOCKS
9. 2. 1915

DEAR MOTHER

We have lost no time in getting on board. We got here about 2.0 p.m. (coming straight to the docks). We stopped in the customs sheds, and the men were issued there with field service dressings, knives, gloves, & body-belts. Then we came on board, where I now am. I think we are starting about four, another hour's time from now. It is certainly a strange transformation from the day before yesterday. The post card I wrote in the train will most likely reach you at the same time as this. We are going to Havre I think. The steamer is a fairly large one, and there are a lot of men from different regiments on board.

I never expected to be parted from you so soon, after the quiet Sunday. But for those other two officers being unfit I should not have gone for some time.

I will write as frequently as possible, but after this letter my other ones may be censored.

I have not to my knowledge left anything behind, but if I have will tell you.

I must stop now, as I have to meet the officer with me, Churchill-Longman, in a few minutes.

Goodbye for the present,

FRANK

Thursday Feb 11

DEAR MOTHER

At last I have time to write to you. I have been most fearfully busy up to now. We left camp as I told you at 7.15 on Tuesday morning,

getting a special train about 8.0. This train went a very long way round
to get to Redhill, where we picked up more men. We went almost to
Chatham, before we started to come back. At Redhill we found
another train waiting for us rather longer than we were, so together
we made quite a good show. From Redhill we went to Southampton
getting there about 2.0. We formed up in the custom's sheds, and were
issued with knives, field service dressings & body-belts (I have not got
one of these). We then went straight on board, the boat being a troop-
ship the name of which I have forgotten. We did not finally get away
till 6.0, there being five other boats going that night. When we got to
Portsmouth we were in the middle of about a dozen searchlights,
eight being visible at one time when I counted. There were also others
in S. Water. Outside Spithead all lights on deck were turned out and
the portholes covered over. Our escort joined us here, two torpedo-
boat destroyers. You will have found this out I think from one of the
postcards. The boat rolled a bit going over, but I was all right. There
were 15 officers on board of 12 different regiments, having 800 men
in all. We were easily first in numbers. We got to Havre about 6.0
a.m., and after a hurried breakfast issued out ammunition (100 rounds
per man) and rations for the day. Then the business of disembarking
began, and that did not run so smoothly as the quay space was very
limited. After a lot of bother everybody finally got on shore, and then
when the men moved off I was left behind with 30 men to do a little
more unloading. That took only about 20 minutes, and then we too
got off. We had a guide to shew us the way, as it is about 5 miles.
There is a line of hills 3 or 4 miles north of Havre, and the camps are
situated on the further side of these hills. There are not less than 20 of
them, ours being No. 9. There are about 1200 men in it. The men are
in tents, the officers in canvas huts with a wooden framework, two to
a hut. I am in with a very nice man, of the K.R.R. The ground is clay,
so although there are pathways of boards everywhere still it is very
slippery (being on the side of a hill) and also very muddy. The officers'
mess is in a tin hut, with French cooking but meals in the English style,
at French hours. We get French bread also. There is plenty to eat for
everybody. The mess closes altogether at 9.30, and most men are in
bed by then. Last night I was by 9.0. Yesterday I went to Harfleur,
which is about $\frac{1}{4}$ mile away, to get some candles. They charged 1d.
each for them, so I was rather done in. I had to have them however.

By the way there is one thing I would be glad if you would send me, and that is some compressed milk tablets. I've seen some out here in a fairly large glass flask by Horlicks, and they are very useful things. Get any you come across. Today we have been fitting out our men with all they want, and it has been a job. First there had to be an inspection of kit, which I did, and that took some time. Longman was doing other work then. After the inspection we had to send in a list of what was wanted, and when we had done that a pile of letters came along for us to read and sign. All the men's letters have to be signed by an officer, for we are all censors here. There were just about 500 letters & post-cards, which rather appalled us. Especially as one of us had to go to see to the drawing out of store of the articles we had applied for. Longman went off for that job, while I took on the letters. They had to be done by a certain time to catch the post, nor could the drawing of kit be postponed a minute. So we were both fully occupied. I read a lot of the letters & postcards, but as they were all announcing their safe arrival (the men did not have a chance to write yesterday when they got to Havre), and hoping those at home were well, describing the voyage etc. I signed away as fast as I could only reading, after the first 50 or so, a casual letter here and there. Just now the men could not write anything that wants censoring, and there is no need to read every one. In a few days and for the future it will be different, but then there will be fewer letters. I got the letters done at last, and then it was lunch time. Immediately after that we had to collect all the men's pay books (each man has one to record casual payments), and write a certificate in each that they were in possession of a full kit. At the same time there was more kit to be drawn & then issued to the men. Longman did that job again, while I got a few men together to write the certificates (which were only a couple of lines) in the pay books, which I then signed. This meant 211 signatures, so I am having plenty of practice in writing my name. When that was done I went off and had a wash, and then had to go and get some kit which had been overlooked. Then I came in to the mess and started this letter, only to have to go off to get kit for two men who have come back from the front, but certified fit again by the doctor. So they will go back with us. Since then I have not been interrupted, but it is now almost 7.0 p.m., mess time.

The address of this camp is: Inf. Base No. 1, Havre, France. Letters here will be forwarded. Better not put 1st Gloucesters on any address till you hear further. Just 'Gloucesters' alone. I may be sent to the 2nd battalion.

I'm very well, and very happy, so do not worry at all about me. I have heard that the 1st battalion is having 3 weeks rest, but it may not be a fact. I don't know of course when I shall go up to the front, but it may be in the next two days, or it may not be for 6 weeks. We will not have any notice, only orders to go. No one is allowed out of camp after 6.0 p.m.

I seem very far away from you here, and as a matter of fact I am farther from the firing line than I was at Abbey Wood. I fancy it takes about 2 days in the train to get to the front, as we go slowly in a very roundabout route.

This letter will not go till midday tomorrow, and I think it is a rather slow post home, so it may not reach you for some days. I will write tomorrow, but I don't expect it will be before the afternoon. One very nice thing is that I censor my own letters, at present at any rate.

FRANK

{On a post card stamped 18 February.}

1ST GLOUCESTER REGT.
BRITISH EXPED. FORCE
c/o G.P.O.

DEAR MOTHER

I have got to the regiment all right, but cannot describe the journey just now. It was quite a good one, though long. I will get off a letter today or tomorrow if I can. I am perfectly fit, and quite ready for anything. I don't expect I shall get any of your letters for some days, as it may be a slow post up to here. I have got a room in a very nice clean house, so I shall be very comfortable. We will probably remain here resting for some days, perhaps ten. But no-one knows exactly. Don't worry about what may happen to me. I shall be all right whatever does. It's a lovely day here, with bright sun.

FRANK

Address exactly as above for everything.

1ST GLOUCESTERS
BRITISH EXPEDITIONARY FORCE
Tues. Feb. 16

DEAR MOTHER

Now begins the time when I cannot mention names, and you must just be content to think of me as 'somewhere on the other side of the Channel'. I still censor my own letters though, so that is very nice. We left the base camp at Havre just after 1.0 last Sunday afternoon, and marched about 3 miles in mud to a small station. Here we gave out 2 days rations to each man and then got in the train. The whole operation of distributing rations with the delays that always occur took nearly two hours, during most of which time it was raining. About 900 men in all went off when I did. Most people were rather wet when they got to the train, but that did not matter. I was very lucky and got in the luggage van where all the valises were, so I was able to change at once all my wet things. There was a sergeant only with me, so we had plenty of room and could not have been more comfortable. We could walk about as we liked, and had the door open (it slid back like most van doors) all the daytime and some part of the night, getting a most perfect view of the country. The train was crowded, most of the men being in luggage vans like ourselves. There can be nothing like a troop train in the world. Our van was the last of the lot, and looking along there were literally hundreds of men to be seen, clambering along the footboards, running by the side of the train, and generally doing everything but obey the order not to leave their carriages. The train went very slowly (a good pace for it being 14 miles an hour), stopping frequently. There was a breakdown on Monday near some place very well known to English people (I have passed through it) and that helped to delay us. We started just after 4.0 on our journey, and detrained about midnight the night after, about 32 hours in all. Much of this time was, one may say, wasted doing nothing through stops. During Sunday night I found out from the guard we were nearing a town I wanted to see again, so opening the door I tried to see what was passing. I found there was, as I thought, a thick fog, so shut the door again for a few minutes, then opening it again there was the same fog. I gave it up then, but the guard came in after about 5 minutes and then shewed me we were going through a tunnel, and the wall was not more than 18 inches away. It seemed so absurd to mistake it for a fog. We stopped once during the night at a place where some R.A.M.C. Territorials had boiling water ready for us, for tea. Hot water was the great need on the train. It could only be obtained from the engine, and our train was such a very long one that men half way down and lower could not go right up to the engine. Another train was following us though, and occasionally caught us up, w (a little dog smudged this) when the men took full advantage of it. At every stop, in spite of orders to the contrary, the men used to swarm out on to the line, and as the train often stopped only a few minutes there were some wild races to get it again. One of my men had to run nearly a mile and a half, and two men were left behind early on Sunday night, but caught us up the next morning, coming on by the train following us. These stoppages were all, except a few, unplanned, but it usually happened, unfortunately rather, that they took place where there were cottages near. The consequence was that the inhabitants came flocking down to sell the men bread, chocolate, beer, and spirits. It was impossible when once there were some hundreds of men on the line to see what each were doing, when they were often determined to get spirits, so several, at a terrible cost later, got them. The cost was a man's life, who tumbled off on Monday night in a very busy part of the line, and I am afraid there is no doubt he was killed. He was one of the Northamptons. What made it so impossible to control the men was that they had, most of them, very little idea of discipline, and the N.C.O.'s were often as bad. Our men were fairly good, but some regiments were very bad. Some Black Watch were not too good. The men used to go off to the cottages, perhaps 200 yards away, when they knew the train might go off any minute, and there get bread and hot water and perhaps other stuff. Often the train's pace was not more than three miles an hour, and forty or fifty men might be seen walking and running alongside. All the way the French children and those who lived alongside the railway kept shouting out for biscuits etc. Being at the rear of the train, I could see a great deal of what the men gave away. Every few miles or less there would be a knot of a dozen or twenty small boys & girls and old women. I could see them counting their spoils and it was rare to see one who had less than 6 biscuits. These biscuits are about $3\frac{1}{2}$ ins. square, and very good satisfying things. They are meant to take the place of bread when that is unobtainable. Each man was issued with two days ration of biscuits, as I said, when we started, but I don't suppose more

than 1 per cent. of those biscuits were eaten by us. The men also gave
away tins of corned beef. The population on the railway need not buy
any food as long as our trains are passing. As you may imagine from
the time we took, we went a tremendous long way out of the direct
road. I can't imagine why we did, but we almost toured the north of
France. Of course I was quite comfortable all the time, and have never
more enjoyed a railway journey. I had a good sleep on Sunday night,
having my valise and plenty of room. The springs of the carriage
transmitted rather more bumps than I had expected, but that I did not
mind. I cannot, of course, tell you where we went, but I will do so
when I come back, as I hope to do all right. When we finally got to
our detraining point on Monday night it was fortunately quite fine.
We got out all right, and found all the men were present, which was
a good thing. Then we set off to the village the regiment is billeted in.
We started off in the wrong direction, so altogether we had about 5
miles to march. Of course it was quite dark, it being about 12.30 a.m.
when we started. We got in soon after two, and quite 60 men fell out
on that march. It was a rotten time for me. I was at the rear, and after
we had gone a mile or so I used to come across two or three or more
men sitting by the side of the road saying they were too tired to go on,
or were ill. If they had stopped behind we should have had to have sent
out a patrol to bring them in, as of course they did not know the way,
so I had to bring them along. It was a dreadful job to make them come,
but I managed it, as we left none behind. We passed two pumps, and
when I got up to them I found about 20 men fighting round each just
to get some water, which they should not have wanted at all, as they
could have got plenty on the train. I got more than I wanted on it. If
I had waited to let them all get a drink we should have lost the main
body altogether, and there being only one guide I could not do this.
The main body all this time were marching faster than the stragglers
in the rear, and the party must have been almost a quarter of a mile long
when we reached the second pump. As matters stood like that I had
regularly to drive the men away from the pumps, as we could not stop.
We all got in all right in the end, but I don't want another march like
that. Last night I was in a house here, and had a most comfortable bed.
But it was not a very nice house, so I have changed today to a splendid
one, spotlessly clean. The men, husband and brother, of the woman
who is in charge are both fighting. She is very nice, and will do

anything for me. I am going to have a hot bath tonight. There is one sergeant with me here, but I know him well and like him so it is very pleasant. I have got a very sunny room, also clean, so I could not be in a better place. I have been posted to a company with a very good captain in charge. He seems a nice man, so I will be all right that way too. Altogether I am very lucky. Many of the officers here I know, as they have been at Abbey Wood. We are billeted in a typical village, about 10 miles behind the fighting line. As I said in the postcard, we will almost certainly not be going up for some days. I will tell you more about the village later.

The dog I mentioned earlier belongs to the house, and is a very nice, playful animal, a year old. It is lovely having him here. I am having meals with the other officers of my company, and as I am not quite sure when the evening meal is I must go to the house to find out, as it is about 6.0 p.m. I have had nothing to do this afternoon. I will write again as soon as I can.

I hope you and everybody else are all right.

FRANK

Wed. Feb. 17

DEAR MOTHER

I could not send off the letter I wrote yesterday, so I will add some more before despatching it today. I got the soles from Lambert today. They will do very well. I think I had better have a second pair of them made for me. Please tell him to make them slightly wider and also of thinner softer leather (if he can). The soles as before.

Today it has drizzled most of the time, so we have done nothing again this afternoon. In the morning I had a look at all the men of my platoon (50 men roughly). They seem quite a good lot, with only about two regular grousers. There are no weaklings among them as far as I could see. They are all distributed in the different houses, usually two to a house. They can't speak French, and have no text books, but they all said they got on all right and were as comfortable as could be. Practically all have proper beds to sleep in. I have not got a bed, but it is really nicer without it, as I can get right underneath the window, which is the usual French type and very nice. I am getting on perfectly with the woman in the house. Occasionally we have complete deadlocks in speaking to each other, but generally we get round them all right. The sergeant with me is not much good in that way. I had a very decent bath last night, though the 'bath' might have been larger. As to meals each company feeds by itself, officers and men. I go to the captain's house for our mess. There are four of us, and the food is very good. Some tinned goods have been brought out for our mess, if I can call it so. There will at no time be any difficulty about that. The village we are in is really a small town. There are a number of regiments represented in it, as it is Divisional Headqrs. as well as Brigade Headqrs. The Gloucesters are now at full strength. I know rather more than half the officers, and a good number of the N.C.O.'s. I was very glad to meet today a man I knew very well as a corporal at Abbey Wood. He is now a sergeant. He was looking out for me, as he had heard I had come. Bob will remember him, as he was the corporal of the guard at the Sewage Works once when Bob came down, and we gave him a gospel then. He is a very nice man. I wish he was in my company.

I am perfectly happy here, and there are no discomforts at all. It is really altogether too luxurious for active service. I have still got your last letter, and see I have not answered your question re shirts. 16 in. is the size I should like, but at present I do not want any. Please send the boots when they are made. Don't keep them, but there is no hurry for them.

I am very glad Father has got someone to play in the morning. I hope that the next letter I get will announce the rout of the Rev. Vincent. It is a very good thing he is a decent player.

I will if I can send Arnie one of our biscuits. They are splendid things, but I may not be able to get one for a little. The woman of this house gets paid something for keeping us, but in addition I should like to give her something for the trouble she has taken. Could you send anything? I don't know what to suggest. She is very intelligent & sensible, about 35 as far as I can guess, of a very good country type. There is also a young girl of about 14, and a small baby. I cannot get anything here for them. If you send anything, be sure and wrap it up securely, so that there is no chance of its coming undone.

Will write again tomorrow.

FRANK

1ST GLOUCESTERS
BRIT. EXPED. FORCE
Sat. Feb. 20 (or 21)

DEAR MOTHER

Your letters have still not yet reached me, though I expect they will soon. I want to know how you all are. It is just a fortnight ago today that I was with you.

The trench digging last night did not come off, as there was bother about spades etc. so it was an easy day. This morning we went out some miles and then attacked some gorse on the top of a hill. The ground was undulating, so we did not have long rushes in the open. My platoon was the 1st line of supports, so I had an easy time personally. The whole thing was really very enjoyable. The ground was mostly plough, so it was heavy and muddy to lie on, but it all went off very well. This afternoon we have done nothing, as is usually the way on Saturday afternoons. Tomorrow there is a Church parade, but I don't know anything about it yet. Of the company officers the captain, Blunt, is a most capable calm man. He seems to be much calmer under fire than at ordinary times. I think he is by far the best of the captains here, judging by what I have heard here & at other times of the other captains. He has been out a long time. The second in command, a Lieutenant, I knew at Abbey Wood, and he is also very capable, though naturally he does not know so much as Blunt. One of the 2nd Lts. is an ex-President of the Union, and was at Balliol. He is a very nice man. The other 2nd Lt. is a newly promoted corporal from the 61st, our 2nd battalion. I think he will be all right. The acting sergeant major of the company I also knew at Abbey Wood. He is a really fine man, with no flaws in his character. He has got the D.C.M., and also threw up a good position to come out here. My platoon sergeant has been out all through, one of the very few men to do so. He naturally has great knowledge, which will be most useful. The other N.C.O.'s in the platoon are a mixture of capacity & mediocrity. One of them is a Jew, and a very nice, decent fellow. He showed me today a Prayer-book the Government have issued to all Jews serving, and it is very beautifully drawn up. The men are all as happy as can be. They have all got feather beds to sleep in (I think I mentioned this before but I'm not sure), and are living well. The inhabitants bring some of them coffee in bed in the morning. I am perfectly comfortable myself.

I will write again tomorrow, as I am sure to get time to myself then. I will be thinking of you as 11.0 a.m. comes round.

Please tell Lambert to put a tin of brown Dubbing in with the boots when they are sent.

FRANK

1ST GLOUCESTERS
BRIT. EXPED. FORCE
Feb. 21

DEAR MOTHER

I cannot quite make out how the postal arrangements work here. I fancy most of my letters have not gone till the day after I wrote them. I can never write till the afternoon. I have not had any of yours yet, except that one at Havre. They ought to find me soon. I have had a letter from Isaac, my captain at Abbey Wood, and one from Doreen and one from Vere written before he knew I had gone, and that is all. Those letters were all addressed to the regiment, so evidently the Havre people are slow in sending on. Please tell me if you can when you are sending the boots. Parcels sometimes don't get through, if they are useful things like that. I have written once only, I think, to Florence. I will write very soon to her, but I expect she sees all the letters you get. I do not manage to get off many letters either. If we do anything in the afternoon we are not usually back till nearly five, and the evening meal at the captain's house is about 7.0 or 7.30, & it's no real use trying to write after it. The five officers of the company (which includes myself) are very comfortable. We have a sitting-room in the house the captain lives in, and we use that for all meals. It is about 8 minutes walk for me. Blunt is a very quiet man. His voice is low, and sometimes he does not say anything for hours, except when spoken to. The meals are quite well cooked, with a few peculiarities. The woman always cooks hen's heads & necks and sends them up, also the heads of rabbits. We are living very well. The men are also living well, though today I came across one letter which was grumbling at everything. The man thought he was having awful hardships. He came out with me, and is going to get a shock when we do get to the real thing. Letters that would give a false impression to the people at home are not sent. This particular one might have been written by a German to try to stop recruiting.

I am sending a field service post card at the same time as this letter, just so that you will have had one. So many people have got them by now that it would be a shame if you had not. I am also sending one to Florence.

1st Gloucester Regt.
Brit. Exped. Force,
Tuesday, Feb. 22

Dear Mother

Thank you very much for sending those extra things. They are all very useful. The coffee I don't think I want, so I gave one to my servant and the other to the sergeant living here with me. The milk tablets are very good things. I am glad they have reached me, as there is talk of leaving here on Thursday for the reserve trenches, but I rather fancy we shall not go on that day. I expect we shall go soon however. A move may mean further delay in the delivery of letters & parcels. By the same post I also got letters from Bob & Florence, and two large boxes of chocolates and some peppermints from Mrs. Mitchell of Abbey Wood, the lady who kept my things for Bob to take away. It is very good of her to send them. I had no idea of anything of the sort. They were expensive boxes too.

This morning the regiment was inspected by General Munro, under whose command I believe we are. It meant a lot of fuss and bother and great attention to kit, seeing that all was complete, but it all went off all right. The battalion formed up in mass (Bob can explain that formation) and the general & his staff just walked round the various lines. Then we formed into a square and he talked for a few minutes. After that we went back to our various parade grounds & dismissed. Each company has its own parade ground. One of the two dogs who came out with my draft from England was on parade with us, where he had no business to be, but fortunately he was not noticed. The dog in my house is a lovely little animal, very lively and sweet-tempered, also very nicely built. He is small, but not by any means a toy. When I am sitting downstairs he often comes and jumps up on me. He is also perfectly at home with the sergeant. We shall, I think, almost certainly be going into the reserve trenches when we go up, so we shall not really be fighting at all. Things most likely will be fairly quiet out here till about the end of March, as it is then that the weather may be expected to become decent. A general advance on both sides seems probable. A great many men have come out in the last fortnight.

If you send out anything for the woman of the house, and I have left before it comes, I will send it on to her. I wish I could give you her address, but that would give the show away. I will write again to-morrow if I can. My address will not vary.

FRANK

I'm very sorry but I can't send Arnie those biscuits.

1ST GLOUCESTERS
BRIT. EXPED. FORCE
Thursday Feb. 25

DEAR MOTHER

I got your letter of Feb. 16 late last night, so the post as you can see is very uncertain, and if any of my letters take a long time in coming you must not get anxious or think anything has happened to me. It is so easy for a letter to be lost here. I know letters that have been sent by men here which have never reached England. Mrs. Mitchell, a letter from whom I got at the same time, said she sent 1,000 cigarettes to me for the men at the same time as she sent the chocolates, but they have not come yet. If letters go wrong when going to England they are much more likely to go wrong coming out, and there must be several sent to me at Havre which have not yet reached me.

I am very glad you & Arnie had that long walk. I hope it did you both good. I can quite follow your description of it. Mrs. Mitchell has been very good indeed. It would otherwise have been a job for Bob to have got to the station with my things. I would like the towel sent out again, though it is not much use saying this now, as you most likely will have sent it by the time this reaches you. I sent one of my photo's to her with the bag, so you will not have to send one. I find we have some tins of Café au lait out here.

You say you expect I wrote in the train, but I could not do so. My letter describing the journey will I think have shown you there was a great deal to do on it, and also when the train was going it was far too uneven & bumpy to write. It was not quite like a well-sprung English carriage.

There is one thing I would be very glad if you would ask Bob to do for me, and that is a refill for my torch. The last day in London I bought a torch not much larger than the small ones, and lighter than the two together, which burns for 8 hours. He ought to go to the shop I bought it at, a small one on the left-hand side of the Haymarket walking down from Piccadilly. It is just above, as far as I can remember, the Theatre Royal, near the bottom. I think half the shop is iron goods, but one window has some electric torches in it. The number to be asked for is 1626B.S. The fill I have will easily last me a long time, as I am scarcely using it, not having yet wanted it.

I also had a letter from Florence.

The other pair of soles you sent have reached me all right. Please do not send any more, as I have plenty now.

The day before yesterday I was orderly officer. The only difference it made was not getting back to my house till midnight, and then I had to climb up to one of the windows to get in. I don't think this will go till tomorrow, but I'm not quite sure. I will write again tomorrow, though I may only be able to manage a card.

I am always looking forward to your letters.

FRANK

1ST GLOUCESTER REGT.
BRIT. EXPED. FORCE
Monday night {1 March 1915}

DEAR MOTHER

We left our town last Wednesday afternoon, and marched about 7 miles to another larger & better town. We stopped there that night sleeping in a huge boarding school for girls. It had been a hospital, but the Germans shelled it & so they took the wounded out. We were very comfortable in it, having our valises. We have not seen them since, and I don't think we shall till we go back for a rest. There were good shops in this town, and I changed a cheque at the Banque de France. This bank will cash officers' cheques up to £5. It is the only one that will do so. It is of course most convenient, as English paper money cannot be cashed anywhere over here, and is perfectly useless. I bought a few quite useful articles there, including the small writing paper book I have written two scraps of letters in. I can carry it in my pocket, and it is convenient as it is self-contained. Most of the officers had their meals at an hotel, but Newman (the latest joined officer in the company) and myself had our meals in the school, buying extra stuff outside. We left the town at 4.0 p.m. the next day (Thursday) and went about $4\frac{1}{2}$ miles to our position. Two companies of the battalion stopped in reserve behind, the other two companies each sent up two of their four platoons to the firing line by day, and increased the strength by an extra platoon each by night. The remaining platoon of the two companies stopped behind as reserve. My platoon, as I said, went up on Thursday night, and stopped till about 8.0 p.m. on Saturday night. It was most queer there, entirely different to what I had imagined. There were no trenches, but breastworks of sand-bags. These of course were above ground, and there was no water in them though plenty of mud. The breastworks were in heavy ground, open and flat, about 350–400 yds. from the German lines. We (our company) had a small portion of the line as our share, about $\frac{1}{4}$ mile or a little more in all. This was split up into two approximately equal parts, each platoon having one of them. The breastwork was not continuous, but had gaps at intervals. These gaps were covered by hurdles, and naturally the Germans used to snipe at anybody crossing them, as they were then in full view down to the waist. It was really not safe to cross in daylight. I only had to do so once. At night the Germans sent out a few snipers who came quite close up to our line, and then potted at anybody they saw. They did not succeed in hitting any of our men, though they had some good attempts. They very nearly got Captain Blunt, and had one or two tries at me. The odds are vastly against anybody being hit at night, except by a purely chance shot, as it is so impossible to aim. Please don't imagine I go wandering about aimlessly everywhere. I am strictly preserving myself as far as I can, and only go down the line when I ought to. On Thursday night we did not hit any Germans so far as we know, but on Friday five were wounded by absolutely fluke shots. My quarters were beautifully cosy. A small hut had been made, the sides of sandbags the roof of corrugated iron covered with earth: one side was the breastwork itself. It was of course entirely waterproof. There was a layer of straw on the floor, two chairs and a small table. There was a fire just in the entrance, of wood & coke. On Thursday night the Captain stopped in the work till about 11.0 p.m., and then left it to go down to the reserve platoons for the night. We always, the whole regiment, stand to arms at dusk, and again about 5.0 a.m., or 5.30 in the morning. So when the Captain left us on Thursday night there were six hours before we stood to. These six hrs. the other officer & I divided between us, three each. One officer must be awake at any time during the night. This gave us three hours sleep each, but that was interrupted as it was a little cold. We made it up during the day. Very fortunately it did not rain at all in our time there. The ground is very muddy, and of course has been made worse by many people walking on it. It is planted with mangel wurzels (I hope I have not spelt this too absurdly), and these project 3 or 4 inches above the ground. On Thursday night I could not very well see them, and as I only came across them in the gaps I could not use my lamp. The consequence was I slipped about all over the place, but escaped going down flat. I often went in in muddy places half way up my leg and more. I got in a most fearful state by the time I got relieved. I shall use those waterproof things Father sent as leggings, so they will take the thick of the mud I hope, in future. Friday was a brilliantly fine day, and many aeroplanes (of ours) flew over the German lines. They were all fired at, mostly with shrapnel & machine guns. Watching them we saw little white clouds of smoke appear all around them, each of which was a bursting shell. No aeroplane was hit. I have found out what the German shrapnel is like now. The shells they fired at the aeroplanes of course had to come down somewhere, and many of the little pellets came down round us. I have got one that fell about 10 feet away. Others were closer. One man was hit a glancing blow on the head, but beyond raising a very tiny bump it did no damage. The pellets are of steel about the size of a small marble, and when the shell bursts have great velocity.

Our lines were not shelled at all by the Germans. On Friday night the captain stayed with us. The German lines opposite have a great deal of barbed wire in front of them. We have got a good deal also. They have a trench as well as a breastwork. Very few of their men show during the daytime, not more than one or two. The others may be there, or behind somewhere. They are working each night improving their position, and our people are doing the same, directed by R.E.'s & Sappers. That was the job I was on last night, with 100 men. Rather more shots are fired by night than by day, but there are very few altogether. On Saturday night we came back about a mile & a bit, and were spread over various houses close together. These houses have all had shells near them some time, and I don't think there is one window intact in the whole village. Roofs also. They are quite empty of course now, that is of population. We occupied only the bottom floor in each, but were quite comfortable with a fairly thick layer of straw. The officers all had their meals together, and so we fed very well. The feeding has been excellent, and I think will continue so. Just as we got into the houses I was handed a bundle of letters, about six, and two parcels. I did not see who they were for, but imagined the mail had come in for the five of us, for all the officers were in the room at the time. So I told the captain and gave him the letters. The first one was for me, & he handed it over. The second was also mine, and he handed that over. The third was the same. Then he began to get suspicious and quickly looked at the rest. When he found they were all mine he fairly banged them at me. None of the others got any letters that night. The letters had accumulated during the three days. That was why I got so many. Most of them were yours, & one Father's. I was delighted to get them, for I cannot get too many to satisfy me. It is so lovely to hear from you & Father. The scarf will do beautifully, thanks very much for it. The waterproof things will be most useful in keeping some mud off, as I have mentioned I think. One pair is all I want. The hat cover came all right. I wish I had told Bob of one shop, for he could have got it there and would have been saved much trouble. The shop is Dunhill in Conduit Street, near the Piccadilly end of Regent Street. It was very good of him to take all the trouble he did. I have managed to get a hat cover issued to me here also, so I am well off. I did this before Bob's came.

Will's position is very interesting. I will write to Port Said if I can. Have you heard from Ned lately? I got Father's letter tonight, with yours also. Very many thanks. The periscope I have seen, but could not carry it about with me. It is far too awkward an article. I have got a pocket one which is just about as efficient and is very handy, as it weighs nothing and measures only about $3\frac{1}{2} \times 1\frac{1}{2} \times \frac{1}{4}$ ins. So I do not want the big one. It was very good of Mrs. Mitchell to write so warmly. She has been most kind certainly. Her parcel of cigarettes has not yet come. I hope someone has not kept it. The Miss Holmes you sent one of my photos to was de Vere's nurse in London. She was exceedingly good to him. Letters come here in three days, or less sometimes. So we are not far away from each other. I shall not get them, however, if I am in the firing line till I come out. I may as well tell you that we are in France here.

I have written rather fully about the position here so that you can see for yourself that I am not to be pitied at all. It is for me war wrapped in cotton wool. The feeding is splendid, I have got plenty of clothes with me, and the works we are defending are the best men who have been out here all the time have ever seen.

In the matter of papers I would like one sometimes. Florence wants to send me things so I will ask her to send *The Times Weekly Edition*. It is quite a useful thing to see.

A most surprising thing happened the other day. One of our men caught a well grown chicken in the village. This place has been occupied more than once each by Germans, French, Indians & English, all of whom were on the look out for chickens. How it can have escaped for so many months is a wonder. I am as fit as possible, and enjoying things. My platoon is in reserve tonight, which means a quiet night and an easy day tomorrow. Tomorrow night we will go into the firing line just to strengthen it, which will be another quiet night.

I hope Basil does get a commission. He must be having a most uncomfortable time at Northampton. I'm afraid he will find it not easy however to change from Territorial to anything else.

As I said above, I cannot get too many letters from home. It is very nice for me I get so many. I hope Mr. Cave is all right again now. The school will be considerably altered when the building is completed.

By your next letter I hope you will be better than 'all well enough'. That is not quite so good as I should like.

I have not yet a third got through the milk tablets, though they are very good. If you send some more, could you try to get them in a flat, flask-shaped bottle (they are sold in it) as it would be so much handier for carrying. Otherwise I really do not know anything I want, except perhaps occasionally chocolate. The English milk or nut milk variety is so much nicer than the French I think. Now I am going to sleep, as it is after 10.0. Going to bed does not entail much preparation here.

I will always censor my own letters, but sometimes letters are opened before they reach England. This is very seldom however. The censor's stamp on my letters is that belonging to the regiment. You need not put 'on active service' on your letters to me. It is only on mine to you that it should be put.

FRANK

I will write to Bob when I can. I was very pleased to get his letter.

3. 3. 15

DEAR MOTHER

I am perfectly all right, though I had my closest shave this morning of being hit. Close shaves are unavoidable. Some bullet is bound to come close to you in 12 or 48 hrs. under fire. The term 'under fire' is really not correct, for the tiny number of bullets that come over cannot be called fire. The breastwork has now been completed, all the gaps having been filled up. So we do not have to walk across the open now when going down the line. The arrangements about relieving the regiment have been altered, so I shall be in the embankment again in about three days time. Don't worry about me. You know you will see me again.

FRANK

1ST GLOUCESTER REGT.

4. 3. 15

DEAR MOTHER

I got your most welcome letter of Sunday 28th last night. I am glad the boots are coming, though I don't know how to carry them just now. I shall have to tie them on outside somewhere. Of course I don't mind Henry seeing the letter. I will write to them today if I can. I hope you did not get anxious when no letter came the next day, as I don't think one could have got to you till Tuesday or Wednesday. When in the firing line letters are neither delivered nor sent. I notice you say you have the little map from *The Times*. You might keep it, as my own position is in it, I am almost sure. I really should not tell you, I suppose, but it is not giving away any military secret letting you know that a map of a few square miles of country, I think, covers my position. I cannot quite remember the places in the map.

Mrs. Mitchell's cigarettes have come all right. The little dog you mention did not require any teaching to eat chocolate. I wish I could have brought him along with me, he was such a lovely animal, and beautifully built.

I am glad Menon had one of my photos. It is a very good idea of yours to give one to Shylock's Mother. It seems much more than three weeks since I left. I am certainly in very different scenes now. There are batteries of ours about $\frac{3}{4}$ mile on each side of the house we are in, and they are constantly firing, nearly over the house sometimes. The Germans don't know exactly where they are, but try to silence them by shooting as near as they can in the right direction. So we hear their shells shrieking through the air as well. It is perfectly safe, as at the nearest they burst $\frac{1}{2}$ mile away. The day before yesterday I was in another house in the village and then shells dropped 200 yds. away, but came no closer. The Germans do not know our exact positions. Their aeroplane service cannot find out, as it is dominated by ours.

I have just had a letter of yours dated Feb. 25, and also the one from Doreen you sent on. The oil you are sending with the boots is excellent stuff. I have got a tin of it in my valise, but that might as well be at home as I don't know when I shall see it next. The oil is called Mars oil.

Mrs. Laurie has had bad luck with Selina's insurance. I have written to her, and will write again soon. The shave of being hit I mentioned in my last note was quite a close one. My platoon had been in the firing line for one night (Tuesday), and came out in the morning. An attack was going on a few miles off so we could not leave the position before it was really light, as we had intended to. The road down which we went to get back to the village was quite open and fairly frequently sniped. Of course the Germans could see the men walking along, so they sent a few bullets after us. The men went down in twos & threes with intervals between each man. I came last with my platoon sergeant. We were walking along side by side, as if we were on any ordinary road, and of course made rather a good mark. One of the Germans, who was rather on the flank, fired a very well aimed shot, which passed between our heads. After that I walked a few paces behind the sergeant. The bullet went quite close to us, as it was travelling obliquely. I am very glad to hear your cough has so far improved, and also about Arnie. I hope you all keep well. The cutting you sent about the clergyman ranker is very interesting. Our brigade padre is a splendid man, liked by everybody. He is not the old man I mentioned before. Last Sunday morning there was a small service followed by Communion. I don't think there is anything in the way of papers you can send, except perhaps the *Oxford Times*, or anything specially interesting. As I said, I have asked Florence to send me *The Times Weekly Edition*. Books I do not want here.

FRANK

1st GLOUCESTER REGT.
BRIT. EXPED. FORCE
4. 3. 15

DEAR MISS WRIGHT

If I surprised you with my letter you have done more for me with yours. I am exceedingly grateful to you for writing it. It is words such as yours that mean a great deal to people in my position, when injury or death is so possible. Just a few minutes ago a shell came closely past the house I am in, which must have been fired at random as it is now dark. I have just had 60 hrs. altogether in the firing line, and for some days have been in reserve in this village, which is less than a mile behind the firing line, and is fairly often shelled, though none have fallen closer to me than 200 yards. The firing line we have (that is our regiment) is a breastwork, not trenches. This of course is far more comfortable in every way. I will try and give you some idea of what a modern battle-field is like. In the first attacks are mostly purely local. The breastwork of which we hold a part stretches for many miles in both directions, and then becomes trenches. Various amounts of it are handed over to different regiments. We have about $\frac{1}{2}$ mile or a little more. Each regiment makes its own arrangements for relieving those in the firing line. Usually it sends up half its strength at a time, for 24 or 48 hrs., keeping the other half behind in reserve during that time. Then the two halves change places. After a certain number of days the whole regiment leaves its position and goes a few miles back for a rest, while another regiment takes its place and carries on. Thus we expect to be relieved next Monday night. Our breastwork is about 400 yds. from the German works, and this is a fair average. It varies up to 50 yds. in places. When I said that attacks were local I mean that only a very small portion of the line is affected by them. We have twice heard attacks going on about 2 miles away from us, but it made no difference to us at all. It is seldom that more than two, or at the most three regiments take part together in an attack. The objective is most likely some definite trench or part of a trench or work, with a front of perhaps 300 or 400 yds. The trenches on either side do not participate. When several regiments are employed they are usually arranged in depth, not in breadth. So you see that there are no 'battlefields' strictly speaking. The whole line of 200 miles or more (I don't know the length of it) is the battlefield, and men in one part of the line do not know what another part is doing.

We did not know who was engaged in the two attacks we heard and have not yet heard for certain except that it was either the French or the Germans who captured some trenches. If one part of the whole line was really routed it would affect every man fighting on both sides. The trenches or breastworks are not continuous. There are frequent gaps in them. We have our part divided into two by about 200 yards and one part lies rather behind the other. Then there are usually gaps between regiments. Regiments are self-contained units, and fight by themselves, though giving help if required to other regiments near them. The men of one regiment are not mixed with those of another if it can possibly be helped. At present things are very quiet. The ground is too heavy owing to the weather to make attacking easy. All we have done is to improve our position and keep a watch. We have only had one man wounded after five days and nights, as of course nights are rather more active than days owing to snipers coming up close to our line. We have all had narrow escapes. Yesterday morning I was coming away from the breastwork walking side by side with a sergeant, when a bullet came between our heads. A few inches lower or to one side or other would have hit one of us. I have also had several shots go just behind me as I was walking along exposed portions of the line, which was because the men who fired them fortunately did not know enough about shooting to allow enough for my travelling at right angles to the bullet. The way the fighting is done is by men behind loop-holes firing at any mark they see in the enemy's position, or just aimlessly to let them know we are in readiness.

You are not by any means alone in praying that peace may be restored. I am sure there is not one man in the English army who does not echo that wish, though all are determined to go through with things, and hope that peace will not come till a definite result has been obtained. No result at all has come about yet. I am truly pleased at your sending so many thoughts to me, and Mr. Wright also. It is not the physical danger I wish to be preserved from, but the spiritual. It is a very great help to me to know that so many people are interceding for me. That moonlight night you mention I was in charge of a party of men improving our embankment, and had 5 hours of that job. During that time I went and inspected some dead bodies lying in front of us. Most of them were Indians. They have now nearly all been buried. They had been there some time. I will remember 3.0 p.m. on Fridays.

Drink is a terrible curse. His price is life itself here, as elsewhere, but here the payment is often exacted very soon. Men get a small amount of alcohol served out to them, but many when writing home say how they would like some beer or spirits. It is much more sad, I think, than all the deaths in this war.

I do not quite remember Ida, but I think she has done quite right.

I am very glad to hear Mr. Wright keeps well. I hope he will continue to do so. I wish I could have a comfortable morning or so in bed. It is a wise thing not to let him know the full extent of the war. Mother I am very sorry for. She is the one who feels most the danger I am in.

I will write again later.

Very many thanks for your letter.

FRANK

I am glad Nellie is well.

Sunday {7 March 1915}

DEAR MOTHER

I have now almost completed another 48 hrs. in the firing line, which will be the last for some days, as we are being relieved tonight by another regiment. It has been a fairly quiet time, except last night. We had some shells over us yesterday but they did not do any damage, though they were quite close. In the night we did get startled. About 11.0 I was just free to go to sleep, as I did not go on duty till 2.0 a.m. I was along near the far end of my platoon, when suddenly the French guns behind us (about 1 mile back) opened rapid fire on the German lines, and the regiment on our left did the same. Of course this set our men off, so the pandemonium was terrific. We only had the sentries on duty when the guns started. I thought the Germans were attacking us, so I passed the word along for all my men to stand to, as we call it. Then as it was very dark I told one of my N.C.O.'s to fire two cartridges from a special pistol we have. These cartridges give a brilliant light, and shew up the ground in a circle of about 100 yds. radius. The flare goes about 60 yards usually, and burns about 15 seconds. Last night there was a high wind blowing from us to the Germans, which carried the flares along right down to their lines shewing up the whole ground in between. The first flare was fired straight towards the Germans, and shewed that there was not a single man between the two lines. The next one I had fired towards the left, in front of the next

regiment, and that again showed there was no one about. All this time
the guns were going behind us, the shells whistling over our heads, and
rapid fire was being kept up on our left and also on our right. I could
not imagine what it was all about, but as there was nobody attacking
us I began to make the men stop firing, as I did not want them to waste
their ammunition. I had stopped about half of them when the captain
came along, and then he told me that it was only being done to distract
the German guns from some work the French were going to do on our
right. The show had started before the time advertised, and the captain
was just prevented from warning us by that. He did not want the men
to fire, and told me to stop them all. He also said that it was going to be
repeated at 1.0 a.m., and then we were to open rapid fire. The Germans
put 9 or 10 shells over my part of the line during this time, but although
some burst only 30 yards behind no damage at all was done. When all
the men were quiet I found many of the older men who had been out
some time had not fired a shot, as they had seen when the flares went
up that there was no one to shoot at. It was the young men who lost
their heads completely and nearly went mad. Several cowered down
behind the breastwork and fired straight up into the air. The Germans
had an awful fright, I should think. They continued firing back for
some time after our men had stopped. The French gunners fired very
well, putting shot after shot right into the German line. The Germans
in return were poor, not hitting our line at all.

At the second go our men were all standing ready, and as soon as our
guns started they began as well. It was a very fine experience to me
watching. The noise was tremendous. There were huge flashes from
the guns behind us, lighting up the whole place. It was impossible to
hear the return rifle fire of the Germans, but their shells came quite
close. One just grazed the top of the parapet, but I was not in that
particular section at the time. Again their shells burst 30 yards behind,
some of them, but no one was hit or even had a narrow escape. The
younger, newly arrived, men were again in an awful funk. It was surprising to see how many rifles jammed during the firing. I went along
once or twice, and it was nearly always the younger men who got their
rifles jammed. Half of them did it on purpose so that they could avoid
firing. The rest of the night was quite quiet. We have not heard if the
French succeeded in their attempt. I did not use a rifle myself, and was
more use than if I had made one more to shoot. I can always get a rifle

when I want one, but I don't think I will carry one. If I do I will have to carry ammunition as well, which is heavy stuff.

The boots came safely, just before I started for the firing line. Many thanks for the contents. If you send another parcel, you might include a couple or so of decent sized candles. They burn quickly in the shelters we have.

I was lucky enough to get your letter of the 3rd when in the breast-work. It was very welcome. I hope you did not have to wait long for news, though there must have been a gap somewhere about there, I mean in my letters.

This part of my letter is being written about 16 hrs. after the first part, that written in ink. The regiment is now about $2\frac{3}{4}$ miles behind the firing line, and the officers are in a most comfortable house. Also we have our valises, so could not be better off. We expect to stop here some days, perhaps up to 10.

The flask-shaped bottles of milk tablets are just what I wanted. Please don't send any more just yet, as I have heaps. I will answer your letter later.

FRANK

Monday {8th March}

DEAR MOTHER & FATHER,

I have just had your two letters dated March 4th & 5th. I was hoping for one or two today, as there was only one of yours brought to me when in our embankment. That was quite unexpected, but all the more welcome. Could you sometimes enclose a couple of sheets of writing paper and an envelope in your letters, as I shall soon get a little short. I have plenty to go on with for two or three weeks, and may be able to get some more in the place we are now stopping. It is a very small place, but all the same I am most comfortable. Also we do not have to stand to arms at 5.30 each morning. In the firing line all men stand at their posts at dusk and again before dawn, just now at 5.0. When we were in reserve in that village about a mile back we stood to at 5.30, so as to be ready if we were wanted.

The artillery business on Saturday night was really very amusing in its unlooked for suddenness. The captain got a telephone message at 10.45 by his watch that the guns were going to start firing at 11.0. He was walking along the line to tell us when the whole show began, and then he started raving at the men to stop rapid shooting at nothing. There were about 20 to 30 guns more or less behind us firing rapid, with many more farther away each side. The South Wales Borderers on our left made an awful row, the whole lot shooting as hard as they could. I suppose for fear of the news getting to the Germans they had not told the reserve companies, so they all turned out in the village. It only kept on a very short time.

I will try and describe the position we have just left, as we may not have the luck to get back to it.

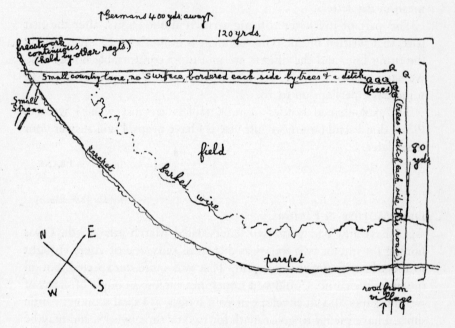

A small road leads up to the middle of the part held by our company, running almost straight from the village (eastwards). It is just a little more than $\frac{1}{2}$ mile. The rough drawing is of half our position only. When there were gaps in it my platoon held it all, but the last time I only held half of it, the left-hand half. The road from the village comes on at the bottom right-hand corner. The rest of the embankment held by our company stretches on in just about the same direction as the last bit of it shown. The compass points are approximately correct. The German line, 400 yards away, runs very roughly as ours does. The country between is quite flat, intersected by another stream and some wire of ours. The Germans have a lot of wire in front of them, which they have placed a few yards from their line. The captain took a photo of myself and Newman, the ex-ranker officer in the company, yesterday with a V.P.K. I will send it to you if it comes out at all, though it may take some time. Newman is a very nice man, I am glad to say.

You say you are sending two more tins of Café au lait. I would rather have Cocoa rations, which are mixed with milk & sugar, but are in small packets six in a tin box which I can carry fairly easily. They are very light, and have the great advantage of being able to be used one at a time. The coffee tins are heavier than they should be for their size, and once opened cannot be carried from one place to another. I would be glad of not more than two boxes of the cocoa tablets. They would only be a reserve, as cocoa is usually carried in a basket which travels with us and is the company officers' mess. Please don't send any more boot soles.

When you told me Ned was getting 15/- a day I knew at once he was a captain. I will write to him in the next few days.

It is very unlikely we see again the towns where I joined the regiment.

A dirty towel ought to have come back with my things from the camp. It does not mind much if it did not. I can get the one I have washed here, and I cannot carry more than one with me. I have heaps of socks now, thanks very much. The boots travelled perfectly, and were splendidly packed. They went up to the firing line as they were (the whole parcel). I had no place to leave it behind me. My servant carried it, and said a bullet nearly hit it on the way.

Captain Blunt is a very fine man and a very nice one. He is more lively when under fire, though he never takes the slightest notice of it however fierce it is.

My mention of the Banque de France could not have told you much about where I was. You ought to know fairly well now though from my last letter. I will tell you if I ever would like some money from you. I hope Arnie will not have an unpleasant time with the dentist.

Mr. Jenkinson's business is amusing certainly.

I will write to Mr. Cave & Mr. Jolliffe (please note the spelling) if we stay here more than a few days, as I hope. Father's ending of his letter is delightful, but I don't consider it an empty one at all.

I shall get a most lovely sleep each night now, which is a thing to enjoy. Also I am able partially to undress. The house is a very fine large one. There are ten officers in it, but as we can use the upper floor there is heaps of room for many more.

I did not mean to send this off today, but as the letters have not yet gone I will do so. So you will get two from me today. I will write something tomorrow. I am very glad you are writing so often, but please don't do so if you feel tired or not fit. It would not be a pleasure to me to get letters if I knew they were written when you ought to have been resting. But I cannot have too many from you.

I am perfectly fit myself.

FRANK

Friday Mar. 12

DEAR MOTHER

I had another of your ever-welcome letters last night. It was dated Mar. 8, and enclosed Mrs. Whitelock's to you. It is certainly very nice the post being so quick. In the matter of clothing I am completely equipped. I have got a warm woollen waistcoat, which is much more convenient than a sweater, and quite as good. Also I have got with me in my pack the oil silk waistcoat which I use as a kind of overcoat, and the fleece lining of my Burberry. I have never been cold yet, except when sleeping, and it is impossible to carry enough in the way of clothes to keep you warm then. I am using drawers, so you might send out the pair you have. I've got two here though, so I am all right in that way. The spare pairs stop in the valise. I will be glad to get the refill, bulb etc. Could you try and find out (through Bob if he has time) whether *wet* batteries can be obtained for my size of lamp. They are far more useful than dry ones (the ordinary kind), as to recharge them you only have to fill them up with water. It may be difficult to get them, as shops won't like keeping them because of the difference they will make in their sales. I shall want a fairly constant supply of the dry batteries.

The country is still very wet, but it is drying fast. It will be a very good thing when it has dried up.

I should like to tell you exactly where I am, but that information would be most useful to the Germans, so I had better not mention it.

You say you were thinking about me at 2.0 a.m. I hope you were not worrying at all. 2.0 a.m. at this time of year is a particularly safe time. In our position we have on an average only about a dozen blind shots in the hour between 2.0 & 3.0. No attack would be made at 2.0 a.m. just now.

You describe the two places very neatly. The first place you mention is most important. It is held by the Germans. There has been fierce fighting there, and probably will be more. The French will most likely take that in hand. The forward movement that is being made now, if well pushed on, is calculated to turn that place without further fighting in it itself. Our position is a few miles north slightly east of it. The second place is, as you say, a large town. It is the place we stopped one night at when on our way up to the firing line. We are now 5 miles from it, but are going much closer tomorrow, as the brigade is going into reserve, which means no fighting for us for some more days. I don't know how long we are going down for. Yesterday there was very little doing. The results of the day before were quite good, the fighting taking place a few miles on our left. The Indians did particularly well, which is the first time they have really shown up. Trench work did not suit them. Sitting still in trenches is now practically over. We shall not be just looking at each other much in future. The general advance has not started by any means; only preliminary movements are taking place now. We must expect a determined forward movement on the part of the Germans. They will try to break through our line. Once that has failed, always supposing that they try it, an advance will be steady and will achieve great results at odd times. The cost to ourselves will be very small compared to that of the Germans, and the war will probably not last very much longer. The end can be foreseen, but the time cannot, as the Kaiser will be sure to try and get peace before his army is too badly beaten. If peace was proclaimed now there would be another world war in a few years. The Germans I think are saving their big gun ammunition. They have plenty when they want it, but do not shoot much here in answer to our guns. For one thing they can't find them. They have put over about 300 shells today and the last two days, but all have fallen about a place 300 yards from where I am which had had a battery in it but the battery has been taken away several days ago. We are in the thick of our batteries here. French & English are in a line about $\frac{1}{4}$ mile to our rear. There is an immense number of guns, the line stretching for miles in each direction. Before the various attacks came off on Wednesday a bombardment took place, lasting about 1½ hours. About 6,000 shells were fired, and they did immense damage. The noise here cannot be imagined. I cannot describe it at all. The batteries are firing a good deal just now, as there will be more forward movements today. The purpose in firing so many shells is to cut the wire in front of the German lines, otherwise the infantry would be held up. That did happen once to the Indians. If this advance is published in the papers you will be able to see from the map how it is threatening the first place you mentioned. Our line is now east of Neuve-Chapelle. Our late position, for it is by no means certain we shall go back to the same place again, is about midway between Neuve-Chapelle and the other place, to the west of the direct line between them. My equipment is very good indeed. I would not change it for the ordinary kind for anything. The oil-silk lining to the Burberry makes it a perfect coat. Nothing could be better. It is quite waterproof.

Photography is going strong out here. The V.P.K. is the most popular camera. I wish I could have Arnie's here. Some most interesting photographs could be taken. The usual difficulty is in the way, carrying it when it is here. I should like to know what Gilbert has done. Whether he gets the R.H. medal or not he has given himself a great help up in his career, though I don't think he can get promotion simply on account of it.

I am glad Mr. Cox is able to get about now. He has had a very nasty time.

If you see Major Rowden please thank him very much for doing that. I will write if I can, but there are such heaps of letters to write, and you always come first. Mrs. Cave is very kind, but I hope she will not put herself to any trouble about me. I will try and get off a letter today to Mr. Cave. Parsons has done well, even if competition is slightly less keen than usual. I don't know if it is, but it may be.

I am glad the pony (a delightful word) is coming over safely. The Captain certainly seems a very exalted person to do it.

The food in the firing line is always exceedingly good. The rations are brought up each night, and given out to the various sections. They are cooked on fires of wood or coke, in buckets pierced with holes all round. Cold food is the exception. By the way, I have heard that some clergyman is preaching that the rum given out to men in the trenches is the curse of the Army, sending more to hospital than anything else.

This is absolutely wrong. There is no degree of truth in it. The quantity each man gets is very small. There is no compulsion about taking it. It sometimes happens that the N.C.O. sent to fetch it for any detached post drinks it all himself before he gets back, and in that way it does do harm. As you can imagine those cases are scarce. I have never had it myself, and one cannot rely on the testimony of any person who drinks alcohol in judging it, but Vere (otherwise an abstainer) told me he found it valuable when he was in the trenches. When men are soaked through from the knees downwards and it is freezing they cannot possibly go to sleep. A thimbleful (which is about the allowance) of rum drunk just before lying down warms you enough to let you get to sleep. Of course the effect does not last long, but you do get an hour or an hour & a half of sleep which it would be impossible to get otherwise. I must stop now for this time.

FRANK

Tuesday Mar. 16

DEAR MOTHER & FATHER

Very many thanks for all your most interesting letters. I have been able to write very little the last few days, not more than letter-cards or F.S. Postcards. The day I sent you the card the letters were collected before I expected. I was in the middle of one to Mr. Cave, and was going to write a short one to you afterwards. As it was I could only get off the card. They are marvellously useful things. As I said in the letter-card that went off today, we were on very short notice to leave for those three days. The difficulty in moving a body of men quickly is not in getting them out of their billets with their equipment, but in starting the march. The second morning on which we stood-to at 5.30 (when we were in first line reserve) my platoon was not called till long after 5.0. It was 5.20 by my watch when I was called. I was sleeping with everything on including equipment, so it did not take a second for me to get out of the room I was in. My platoon was in the same house, all asleep. Also many had taken off their boots and puttees, which they should not have done. Still they all got out fully dressed and marched 150 yards inside 10 minutes, which was distinctly good I think. I hope we don't have to go back to the same quarters again. I had a room without a door or a window (the holes were there, but nothing in them except a little glass left in the window) but that did

not mind. There was also the accumulated dust of ages, except where
it had been disturbed by the many men who had inhabited the room
before me, or by the straw on the floor which was the favourite bed of
two cats. The cats everywhere here are more faithful to the places than
to their owners. There were two large beds in it, and also a large
cupboard like a wardrobe. There was just room for me in one corner.
To enter I had to go through another room in which a dozen men slept.
I had fresh straw put down for myself, and with two blankets was
perfectly warm. I would not have slept on the beds for anything. The
smell was musty and all pervading. My servant did hang his waterproof sheet over the doorway, but that merely blocked the view,
nothing else. I slept three nights there altogether, but was lucky enough
to get off with a few fleas only. I expected a good deal more, and
thought I had got it till I investigated. I always keep my own blankets
separate from the men's, which is a great help in saving me.

You mentioned in your last letter, I think, Dr. Soutar's writing on
the deeds of the Germans. I have not come across anything like that
yet. What have suffered here are the houses more than anything. The
inhabited ones are full of refugees. There is one woman in the house
I am now in who lives near Lille. Her husband is fighting. Her two
sons being at school in Boulogne. She will be lucky if she finds the
walls of her house standing, when she gets back to it again. The houses
are stripped bare unless their owners stop on living in them. Then they
are not disturbed by us. It is wonderful too how the people do hang on
in their houses, although shells burst near and bullets (stray ones) sometimes go near. There has been much wanton destruction of houses by
the Germans, and those that remain have been utilized by everybody.
We must have wood for our purposes now, to make roads and paths
through the mud. The only wood we can get is from the various
buildings, so everything we do not want has to go. There are not many
doors left in houses near the firing line, and most of the huge wooden
bedsteads are broken up also. The various men who have stayed in the
village I am thinking of have all taken their toll. Today one man
wanted to send home about 100 postcards which he had collected from
various houses, and probably the same man would say in his letters what
great pity it was that the houses should be so destroyed. Instead of the
ordinary room with small ornaments pictures & chairs there would be
four bare walls and perhaps one chair. Every other single thing in the

place gone. There might be two spring mattresses left in what was once a bedroom, and perhaps another one lying in the yard at the back. But absolutely nothing else. That is the condition of the houses I have seen. It will be rather worse the farther we go. That is a tiny part of what England is spared from by its position. The towns some miles back from the firing line are even now fairly well frequented by tourists (American mostly needless to say). The battlefields will be practically for all time visited by swarms of ignorant Americans, souvenir-hunting. They will be the showplace of Europe.

We are now in another large village, and quite comfortable. I and two other officers of the company sleep in the same room. It is a large one, with tiled floor, and perfectly clean. We have our valises, so are all right. I have got a place right under a window which is always wide open. I should like to take a photograph of the house.

In the mornings we have a company parade, which takes the form of drilling and musketry practice. The drill is peculiar, as the captain combines the old and new styles (the old should have been entirely given up) and also gives orders which do not belong to either. I am not accustomed to him, and so find it awkward. His voice is not a particularly loud one, and as he does not use a horse when on these parades it is quite impossible to hear him if some way off. The older men of my platoon are used to it, and they have put me right once or twice. I will soon get into it. In the afternoon there is either a march of about an hour or football. There are also fairly constant small things connected with the platoon to be looked after. In most of these houses there is the usual French cess-pool in the court-yard. One of my men tumbled into one the other night, owing to forgetfulness. He won't forget again, for he went up to his neck in foul-smelling liquid, and it was lucky for him he could swim.

We have had a package from Queen Alexandra. They are being sent in her name to the officers of all the different companies. There is not very much in them, and they are interesting more for the sake of the name on them than for their own. I have got a tiny pillow, in a white linen case marked with a crown and the words 'a gift from Queen Alexandra'. I will keep it in the valise, as it does fulfill its purpose, and is softer than a tightly crammed pack with a book nearest the surface of the only part of it your head can rest on. It is valuable, as I am never likely to get another gift from her.

The electric lamp I have sent for is a most useful one. Refills are no more expensive than the ordinary type, as they cost 5/–. The lamp itself is, and that is why I have sent a cheque myself instead of asking you to buy it for me. But to get one burning for 50 hours is very useful. It has a shutter on it so that the light can be switched on and yet only a tiny gleam appears shining directly downwards, a considerable advantage if having to use it when not in cover. In size it is very little larger than the one I have now, which I will send back. I have ordered a refill for the new one. It is possible that if there is much fighting for us the postal service will never reach us for days at a time, and the ordinary battery lasting 8 hours could easily be used up in three nights. I have written to Bob asking him not to get any more batteries for the lamp I have.

We are today under notice to move in one hour's time, but tomorrow and most other days we shall have two hour's notice given us. That is much more convenient. I have told you about being under 10 minutes' notice till Friday. On Saturday we were put under an hour's notice, so seized the occasion to have a bath in a canvas one which Newman has with him.

When shooting is going on, especially artillery as well, it is perfectly impossible to make oneself heard. You have to go along the line and shout at every few men, or else pass the message along from man to man. I don't know if I was cool that night, but I know I was in a horrible funk when the shells came just overhead and hit only 30 yards away. Shells, in the little I have seen of them, frighten me badly. Bullets really don't mind much. I was in bed one night when in the village just behind the firing line, and suddenly heard a shell coming. I could tell it was a big one, and also that it was coming close. I seemed to see it surrounded by rejoicing evil spirits. The thing burst 200 yards away, and did no damage to anything. Many shells came that night, all more or less in the same locality. When shooting at night to repel an attack it is absolutely necessary to have an unobstructed field of *view*. So men must have their heads & shoulders above the parapet when firing. This is what those young boys (for they were nothing else) did not like.

Who is Mr. Meyrick of the school?

The lovely cat must be amusing and also very nice.

Kitchener's Army have very many good ex-regular officers, and ex-ranker officers who are out here now are being sent to them also. So the battalions which will come into action as units will not be composed of entirely untried officers, though they will be very largely. The Parkin will be very acceptable. We do not get much of that here, and there are five of us in the same mess to share what there is.

The battalion of the S.W.B. near us is one of their regular ones, and no New Army officer would be in it. Colin Sharp must be in the New Army if he has been given a captaincy.

I should like to hear the results of the Sports.

The matches in the tin box would be very useful, though a dozen is rather more than I want. Half that would be plenty. I cannot start supplying the men with matches. There are too many of them. I don't think I have answered the question of cigarettes yet. Woodbines are always acceptable, as most men like them best and the mistake is often made of sending dearer brands which are not so much appreciated. They cost 1d. per packet, and 4½ dozen packets are wanted to go round the platoon. Large numbers of cigarettes are sent for the men, but very few Woodbines.

My servant is a very good man. I got him after I joined the regiment.

I will write something, if only a F.S. card, each day if I can.

FRANK

Mar. 18

DEAR MOTHER

I got two letters from you this morning, of last Saturday night & Sunday. I did not have any from you yesterday or the day before, so there was some hitch this side. I should like to see that cat. As to food I am far better off than you seem to imagine. We run a most efficient mess, and feed as well as we do at home. Milk we have very few days been without. We are living really expensively, getting things sent out from Fortnum & Mason as we want them. The total expense is getting on to 2/- per day. I am perfectedly all right in all necessities.

It does seem a very long time to me since I left.

The country is drying rapidly, and we may expect things to move on both sides. Our losses at Neuve-Chapelle were heavy.

I have misled you I think, about the news we get. When actually in the firing line I do not hear much, but the captain has fairly frequent messages sent him if anything is going on likely to affect him. When we are in reserve he gets perhaps six a day. In addition every odd day or so we have what is called a summary sent round giving the most detailed information of what is happening everywhere. This summary is never published in any paper. It is the official newspaper of the Allied Armies.

I am glad Bob got home for the week-end, and that he is quite well.

FRANK

Washing sent off today. Have plenty to go on with.
(Letters just being taken.)

Sat. 20

DEAR MOTHER

Received parcel safely. Many thinks for contents. The leggings are just what I wanted. I had a letter from you & Father today, and another one this morning. I have not got them with me just now, & won't bother to answer anything tonight. I had a 4 hour walk this afternoon hunting up places where guards were posted, and in addition the usual before breakfast run & morning parade. I have to take fresh guards round starting tomorrow morning at 8.0 a.m., but will have a horse to save me another 4 hr. walk. I hope the beast does not chuck me off anywhere.

Am going to bed now.

FRANK

Tues. 23rd {*March*}

DEAR MOTHER

We moved about 8 miles yesterday, and are now several miles away from our old breastwork. There is more breastwork here though, so we will be all right. I think things are being worked on a different system here, and I don't know how we shall manage with letters. Don't be surprised if you do not hear anything for some days, or a week or more. I will not miss an opportunity for writing. This position is no worse than the last, so don't get nervous about me. I could not be more fit. The horse I had on Sunday was a lively beast. He has run away with his groom, and a few days ago with Captain Blunt. He was a good deal too lively for me. I had to show my party of men the way, and wanted the animal to go at a walk. He refused to do so, and seemed to me to be gradually working up for something really exciting. It took exactly two hours to post the last group of sentries, and if I had made him walk all that time when he did not want to he might have done anything when I did start to ride him, along a canal bank. I thought it was safer to walk. We started to move earlier than was expected yesterday. So when I was packing up about 9.20 a message came along I was to go off at once to collect these guards, and bring them on after the battalion. They were going to be relieved at 10.0, so although I had another horse I could not reach them all before they were relieved. I went off in a hurry, and left my torch behind. I have sent for it, but don't expect I will get it. The new one I am hoping for today though, so it will not matter much. The horse belonged to the Colonel, but was quite quiet, so I got on all right with him. All the guards were due to come back over a certain bridge, so I went down to that bridge and waited for them. The nearest were not very long in turning up, and about half were in at 10.45. Then I heard that 4 men had been sent off at 9.0 to collect all the blankets of the guards. This was an absurd thing to do, as of course they should have started an hour sooner. These men were the most awful nuisance possible to me. I had to bring them along as well, but they could not get back till 1.0 at the earliest. Then they had left their equipment in their billets, as they had been told the battalion was not starting till the afternoon. It did really start at 11.0 a.m. It was half an hour's walk from the bridge I was at to the village in which we had been billeted. I reached that bridge as I said before 10.0 a.m. and left it to follow up the battalion at 2.15 p.m. I had got 30 men by then, several of them tired and weary. We had about 7 miles to go, in a hot sun, and none of us had had any food since break-fast. Half the men got their rations just as we moved off, but the others were without theirs. I had not got anything myself. We went by a canal bank, and had no opportunity to buy anything till we had gone nearly 5 miles. Then I got some loaves of bread, some butter and some chocolate. I walked the 7 miles, as the horse would have made me too stiff. I am only a very little stiff this morning. We have got comfortable quarters once more, in a farm.

We may be up here for three weeks, and will not have quite so easy a time when in support as in the other place. It is no more dangerous. I don't know how long we shall be here for certain though.

I would be glad if you would send me a Stylo pen. I don't want a very good one. The pen I have with me is the one the Vincents' gave me, and I'm afraid of it's smashing. Then I should be left without one, which would be awkward. Please get a strong, fairly short Stylo. I have smashed the top of my pen already. Could you try and get me a tin top such as one sees on pencils. The size of the pen is approximately the same as an ordinary Swan. No thicker.

I am not going, under any circumstances, to touch the rum. I don't think there is anything else I want just now. I understand your feelings about getting me things, so will not hesitate to mention anything. I wrote for that lamp myself both because I would get it quicker, and also I thought I should pay for it myself.

I have seen a fairly large number of Indians the last few days. All those I have seen were fine built men nearly all in the prime of life. No young boys such as swarm with us, in some regiments more than others. It is very good of Miss Hales to think so of me. Please thank her very much.

I had forgotten to mention the St. Andrew's matter. I suppose it is better my name should go down, but I wish they would not read it out. Still it could not possibly be avoided as it happened, so we can just leave it. I hope the posts will not be too irregular, as it is always such a pleasure to me to get your letters. I am very glad you both write so often. I am afraid I can't answer your last few letters in detail today, but will try and do so tomorrow if I can. Tonight my platoon will be in support a short distance behind the firing line, and tomorrow we expect to move back to about 500 yards (perhaps $\frac{1}{2}$ mile) behind the breastwork. After that we may go up to the breastwork, but I don't know. It is really very easy warfare, almost lazy.

An order has come out forbidding cameras, so that settles the question of Arnie's for me.

I expect Vere got the photos all right. I will write to him when I can.

FRANK

Mar. 24 Wed.

DEAR MOTHER

I have got some time to spare now so I will start a letter, though I don't know if I will be able to send it off today. I and my platoon have been sent away from the Company, and now are in houses rather more than a mile behind them. The reason for this is that there was no room for my platoon to get anywhere near the part of the embankment

allotted to us. The regt. we took over from is only about half our
strength, but they declared they had a number of men in the firing line
far greater than could possibly be crammed in, using every inch of
space. They could not have had nearly as many as they said. In consequence of what they said three platoons of the company were to go
into the firing line last night, my platoon being in the reserve line
behind. That was the arrangement made. What happened was that my
platoon got into the reserve line all right, but when the others tried to
get into the firing line they found it quite impossible to get more than
two platoons in. So the Captain had to wander round trying to find
some place to put the third platoon. He found some odd trenches in a
corner out of the way, so the third platoon went in there, and had a
comfortable night, there being a very large dry dug-out. The rest of us
had the reverse of comfort. The weather has been most beautifully fine,
just lately, and any shelters that had been built in the firing line
embankment and the support line had been taken away. The parapet
was of just the same type as at Festubert, the other place I was at,
except that there was a trench to stand in behind it about a foot deep.
There must have been shelters built, but there was no sign to be seen
of them last night, except two or three in the firing line. It started to
rain about an hour and a half before we paraded to go up to our
position. The ground was dry the day before, but by the time we got
there it was a quagmire of clay. We had a walk of about $1\frac{1}{2}$ miles
across country in a very roundabout way, on paths through ploughed
fields for some distance. More of the path was supposed to be a road
made with bricks, but the bricks had been just loosely put down and
were lying about all over the place, which did not give a good surface
for walking. Just at the end we had 200 yards of wading through water
up to 6 ins. deep. We were in position about 7.30, and between then
and 12.0 all the men were at work getting up rations and collecting
any sort of wood to make shelters with. It was drizzling most of the
night, with occasional showers. Of course only the roughest shelters
could be rigged up. My shelter was a framework of sticks tied together
about 5 feet square and 3 feet from the ground in the highest part, with
three waterproof sheets as roof and one side. There were earth banks
about 2 feet high along two sides. The fourth side was open. There was
a good space between the top of the earth banks and the roof, and the
waterproof sheets forming the roof did not meet exactly as they ought

to. There were two boards to sit on with the earth banks to lean against. My servant & I stayed there, and for some time also the platoon sergeant. It was not quite the same as being in a house. The rain would come and drip on my face. When the sergeant was in it I was half lying on & off one of the boards with my feet in a muddy puddle outside. I was rather glad when a quarter to four came as then we started getting ready to come back to our present position.

We started just before half-past four, so as to pass a certain point before it was really light. Our job now is to bring up the rations to the battalion each night, and nothing else, for as long as the battalion is in the firing line. This will not be very hard work, except that it will take most of each night. But we can sleep in the day as we are on our own. I had a sleep this morning. I will not be on duty in the firing line at all this time I think. I don't know how long we shall be at it. There will be nothing doing on our part in the next few weeks in the matter of attacks. I have been talking to officers who were in the Neuve-Chapelle business, and the affair was really a terrible failure. It was a marvellous chance completely thrown away for good. One division failed to make good its attack, and to accomplish now the results that the attempt should have brought about will cost hundreds of thousands of lives, besides adding greatly to the duration of the war. I had not realised its full possibilities before.

The waterproof leggings were wonderfully useful. They kept all the mud off from the ankle upwards. I should have been in a terrible mess otherwise. They also kept me dry to some extent, and I am glad to say I did not get water in my boots at all. I was wearing the new ones, and they are very good. Mud of course was all over my Burberry and equipment. It still is, by the way.

Mar. 25 Thurs.

I am having a luxurious time on this job. The rations last night only took 4 hours, everything working without a hitch. It should be shorter still tonight. I was in my house soon after 10.0, and as we did not have to stand to arms at 4.0 I had a really good sleep, never waking up till 7.0, and not getting up then. I shall have another sleep some time today also. Now there is nothing to do all day, except inspect rifles and do a few minutes drill. I am in a very comfortable house, my platoon

sergeant and servant being with me. We have found several tins of
Maconochie Rations & also Jam in the house, left behind by men who
have been here before, so we are well off. Maconochie Rations are very
good things. They are complete dinners in tins, ready cooked, only
wanting a few minutes warming up. Meat, vegetables and everything
is in them, and they are very good. The Camerons (I don't know what
battalion) are occupying the houses round us.

This morning the Germans have not been shelling this locality much.
They usually shell it fairly often during the day, as there is one of our
artillery observation posts about 150 yards away and they don't like it.
No shells have fallen near this house for weeks, so we are all right.
They do not shell the various houses, only the roads and cross roads.

Two officers of ours were wounded yesterday in the firing line, one
in the arm, the other in the shoulder. Neither serious. They were both
in the same company, not mine.

Wandering about round here yesterday I picked up the brass nose
cap of a small shell which had pitched in a field. It is quite thin & weighs
almost nothing. I will use it as a drinking cup.

The regiment's letters have disappeared somewhere. We did not
get any yesterday or the day before, and I don't suppose we shall get
them today. The brigade post office knows where they are, but we
can't find the b.p.o. They will turn up soon, and there ought to be a
fair number for me. I will try and get this sent off today if I can, but
don't quite know how to work it. If I can get to a French Post Office
I will send it that way.

I have had a letter from Menon, and will answer it soon. He was
ploughed.

My bicycle was not in a particularly good state, I know. It was a
surprise to me to hear it had gone. I think it is better to give it than
lend it.

I want to see that cat. It must be a lovely animal. I have not met any
A.S. Readers.

The newspaper cutting was only giving the order of seniority. It has
not been done before. I have done more than my six months probation
now, so such a list is wanted.

The war will not be over quickly. The country is far too wet to
allow of any advance yet. It is absolutely necessary to dig trenches
whenever any advance is made, and it will be quite another month

before we shall be able to do that. At present water is met with just about a foot down, and the country well back of the German lines is far worse than that here. The Dardanelles job must be a slow one too.

I think myself there are about $2\frac{1}{2}$ of Kitchener's armies out now. Men have been coming out in large numbers during the last two months.

I do not think it is at all necessary to declare parcels. The last letter of yours I have had is dated Mar. 18th. Can you tell me what Gilbert did? I have not heard the full account.

The letters the men write are sometimes marvellous affairs. Some men think that stirring deeds are expected of them, and as they have not done any they invent them. The bombardment I spoke about some time ago was described by one man as a fierce attack on us, the Germans coming on in swarms and being mowed down like sheep, piles of them lying dead out in front. The bombardment I mean was the burst of fire by the artillery, when we were occupying the breastwork at Festubert. I don't know how the man could write such stuff. There is no reliance at all to be placed on the accounts of the ordinary soldier, and letters in the paper describing any great hardships or anything very out of the way should not always be taken too literally.

I will write again at the next opportunity.

FRANK

Mar. 26

DEAR BOB

I got your letter of 21st last night, with a big bunch of others. I am very glad you say it is a pleasure to you to write to me. It is a very great pleasure to me to get them. There is so much here to try me, and I have fallen so far short already. Your letters make a great difference to me. I do not get any others quite the same as them.

Pavière is at Abbey Wood, and not enjoying the men there very much.

I wrote to Mother yesterday, & have nothing more to add today. When I go up at night with the rations there is a horrible smell of decomposing bodies buried under a pile of debris, the remains of some houses. The thousands of unburied dead will, practically certainly, bring about some epidemic when the warm weather starts.

FRANK

Mar. 27

DEAR MOTHER

Last night I had two letters from you, dated Mar. 20th & 23rd. Also the card of the Sports. I will write to Mr. Gillespie, as he wrote it out. I wrote yesterday to Mrs. Cave, a short letter with not much in it. I will write again to her soon. There is no word yet of our leaving this place. Today is Sunday, and I woke up this morning to hear a service going on in the next room. Our brigade chaplain was taking it. He is an exceedingly fine man, liked by everybody. I was on a working party last night, and did not get to bed till 2.0 this morning, so I was having a good sleep to make up. I saw the chaplain after it was over.

I had an interesting job last night, fortifying a house which looked straight down a road. About 400 yds. along the road were the German lines, but as they were busy working themselves they did not fire at us. There were half-a-dozen men with me, and we did some quite good work. We had to pull down part of the house, which was a rickety concern as a shell had taken the inside out already. I should scarcely think our 2nd Bn. would be sent to the Dardanelles. I have not heard anything about it.

Will's mile is the School record all right.

It most likely was Bridson you saw. He would not be in uniform.

I will try and write a letter tomorrow if I can.

Because it is Sunday the Germans have put some shells over here, and caught several men. None have come near me.

FRANK

Mar. 29 Monday

DEAR MOTHER

I have just seen Captain Isaac, who was passed for service after a struggle and has joined the regiment. It is delightful seeing him.

I have had a time today reading my platoon's letters. I told them yesterday they could send them, having previously asked the Captain's permission. I thought I should only have 60 or 70 but the number that turned up was more than double. I don't know how they did it. There was another big dose today. Some of the letters are sickly sentimental, some mad, some talking a lot of rot about leading better lives when they get back, a thing these particular men are absolutely certain not to do. Occasionally they write in answer to a clergyman. Then they are in the last degree hypocritical. Many are very good letters, also sensible, and written fully meaning every word in them. The men who write these are among the best in the platoon. A very few invent all sorts of bloodcurdling stories, and talk of shells bursting a few yards away from them. These are the men who will run like hares if they get a chance when shells really do start falling within 150 yards of them. Yesterday night I had two parcels from Mrs. Mitchell & Miss M. They contained a cake, chocolate, raisins, and two brown silk hand-- kerchiefs on which Miss M. had embroidered my initials.

No change here.

FRANK

Mar. 30

DEAR MOTHER

My men have been very good today, and only about 30 letters have come in. So they are quickly done. This gives me more time to write myself. I had a letter from Vere last night. He is having treatment at Bath twice a week but hopes to be all right soon. He is not going back to Abbey Wood till April 8. He said he had received the photos all right, and that it was very kind of you to have sent them. He asked me to go to his home for a visit after the war was over, all things being right, of course. One of my lance-corporals lives in St. Aldate's. He is the only Oxford man I have come across yet in the regiment. There are quite a number from Oxfordshire nearing the border of Gloucestershire. Please always send an envelope to each piece of paper. I have no proper writing paper at all left of what I brought with me. These letter-cards are my substitute.

The rations are an easy job. The whole lot for the battalion are brought up to a house about 200 yards away, where the four company quartermaster sergeants sort them out for the different companies. There is a light railway running up to about 300 yards from the firing line, on which trolleys can run. The end of the railway is behind some buildings and quite safe. There is a trolley for each company. At about 6.30 I bring my platoon along to the house where the rations are by this time divided up into companies. The men carry the rations from here to the trolleys, about 200 yards. Each man when he is given a load is told what company it belongs to, and some N.C.O. goes with each party to see the rations are put on the proper trolley. When all the rations are on we start off. Four men shove each trolley, others walking alongside and helping in difficult places. When going round curves the trolleys are very liable to come off the line. The rails are made of wood, so that no noise at all is made. Two of the companies at present are in trenches through which the railway runs. Each company sends about 24 men to unload its trolley & carry the rations to their separate platoons.

The country is absolutely flat, or the railway would be impossible. My own platoon carry the rations up to our company, when the trolley has gone as far as it can go. The job is very simple, and really quite well managed. It would be possible to make an awful mess up of affairs. There is no credit due to me for the way it is worked. As soon as I have seen all the rations off the trolleys I have nothing more to do with them except my own company's. When the men have carried the company's rations to the proper place they go back again, while I go on to Capt. Blunt to see him & ask if he has anything to tell me. Last night I made a wooden platform along a communication trench which had got water in the bottom of it, or rather a dozen men did the work. That did not take very long, and I was going to sleep about 11.45. I am sleeping luxuriously now. I have got a feather mattress (it is perfectly free from all animals) and a blanket. Yesterday I got letters from you & Father, written on the 26th. If that horse would have jogged I should have been able to control him. The beast would not do less than trot, breaking into a canter occasionally. That was what fed me up with him. The stylo in the dining room is not what I want. A long pen like that is very easy to smash. A short one has far more chance of lasting. I've forgotten when I sent the parcel. It will be nice for Bob to get home.

It will certainly be very hard for Will if he has to wait a long time. Things will be moving here too. I would far sooner be on duty all night if it was very cold rather than attempt to sleep in it. The night you mention though I was in bed about 10.30, and quite warm. It freezes every night. My valise I won't see till we go away from here.

Harold Inman must be very close to me. I have forgotten his regiment if you told me. Could you tell me again? He has got most dangerous work. What is it Father did not like in the sentry business, kit, equipage & fatigued men? I don't quite see.

The cat must be a wonderful creature.

Our chaplain has been in to see me, and has stopped about half-an-hour. He is a really nice man. I have not heard anybody say a single word not to his favour.

I have just had your letter of Mar. 27, also one from Mrs. Maskew. I am very glad you have bought the short stylo. That is the sort of thing I want. Barnes must have been excited over the baby. I will send a letter to Miss Wright when I can. We do not make such use of snipers as the Germans do. They are merely annoying, not dangerous. They very rarely hit anybody.

Our 2nd battalion is within about 40 miles of us, but that is all I know. I don't know how they got their casualties.

If peace was declared now it would be as great a calamity as the whole war is. There would be another world war within 10 years. The Germans are defeated already, but it must be carried into effect. It is an awful pity the Neuve-Chapelle fight failed so badly. If it had succeeded another month's fighting might have seen the end. It was a most marvellous opportunity for striking a blow which would have been felt along the whole length of the Western front. Now it is impossible to estimate how many thousands of lives and how many more weeks of fighting will be required to repair that defeat. The fighting that will occur now will be the fiercest possible. The chaplain tonight said what a near thing it was that the N.C. fight failed by. Also that the next affair like that must not fail. The hospital accommodation was all ready before Neuve-Chapelle started, and they had prepared specially for the fighting expected from it 150,000 beds. That shows something.

It's getting near the time for parading now, for the rations, so must stop.

FRANK

Sun. Apr. 4

DEAR MOTHER

Am quite all right, but very much occupied. I rejoined the Company after all the day we moved (when I last wrote) and since then have been in trenches, with no opportunity for writing. I don't know when this will be posted. We are really in trenches now, but they are very good ones and dry. We come out on Tuesday or Wednesday evening, and expect to go for about a week's rest. I have not felt inclined to write at all these few days as I have not had much sleep. So any descriptive letter I will leave till I get at rest. We have not been in any attack, nor do we expect to be.

Parcel came safely. Very many thanks for contents.

FRANK

Tuesday Apr. 6

DEAR MOTHER

As I have an hour free now and don't feel inclined for sleep I will at any rate start a letter to you. I hope you have not been too worried at not receiving anything for a week at least, but I could not manage otherwise. I expect you guessed I was in the firing line. I did not have word that I was going into it last Wednesday till late in the afternoon, when I had no time to write. I have had rather a tiring time in them, as there was a lot of work to be done. The regiments before us had left the parapet very low in places, and it was hard work getting it up higher. It was my part of the line that required this. I have had some working party or other each night. When raising the parapet, which took two nights, there was a great deal of work to be done on top of it and on the further side. No one was hit, but we all had to flop down whenever the Germans put up a flare, and there were very many of these during the night. The country is perfectly flat and open, so flares from all round lit us up when in any exposed position. One light every two minutes was about the average.

Our line runs very roughly like this

the dotted line being the Germans. The vertical line is where my own position is in it. We had bullets coming into the line from behind, at each side, as shown by the arrows. Flares on either side of us were nearly as good as flares in front. The diagram is not to scale. The German lines are 400 yrs. away in the narrowest part, which is where I happen to be. Lights going up were a very great nuisance. They interrupted the work, as one had to throw oneself down when they appeared, which was a dirty business. My dug-out opens on a traverse which is at right angles to the German lines. The parapet when we took over was very low just here, and the Germans had fixed a rifle so that the bullets just skimmed the top of the parapet and used to pass my door, which is about 4 feet high, just roughly 6 or 7 inches above the lintel. The other people were too lazy to raise it. We altered that at the first opportunity, and have had no more trouble. The position here is half trench, half breastwork. The trench part is where the ground permits it, and is about half the total length. The ground is clay, very nice when dry, but not quite so nice when wet. Yesterday it was wet. My dug-out is a little over four feet deep, a bare yard wide, and not more than 6 feet long, about 6 inches of which are taken up by a shelf which serves as a pillow. The first night I slept on some sacks only, and it was very cold. For the next night I had a couple of boards put down and I have been perfectly warm since. The boards are like a spring mattress, as they are thin and bend nicely. I have got an old sack hanging down to form the door, and am really perfectly comfortable. It might be better fitted up, as it is an awkward place to write in. I am writing in it now. The night before last I had got some iron loopholes to fix in the parapet. These are thick bullet-proof plates about 18 inches square, with a small loophole in them. I was not able to supervise the placing of them myself, but went along to examine them after they were up. The absolute necessity for them is cover from view. One of my sergeants, a silly fellow, put his so that it projected several inches above the parapet and there was also a hole a foot square on the further side. Such a one would have been shot at all day and all night. It was very lucky I looked at it. I covered the whole thing up and have told a competent man to do it again. I was the farther side of the parapet looking at another one when I got a fright. I was crouching down seeing how it had been concealed when about 10 or 12 feet away there was a flash and a bang. I thought it was one of the men in the trench firing, and shouted out to my sergeant, who was in the trench, to find out who it was and take the man's rifle away from him. The sergeant came back and called out that nobody had fired at all. This really frightened me, as my next thought was that someone on my side of the parapet had fired at me. Just in front of the place where the flash had come from was, I knew, a large hole 8 or 9 feet deep made by a shell. I pulled my Colt out pretty quick, and then slowly crawled towards this hole, ready for action. I was relieved when I found it was empty, as I fully expected a German in it. What had really happened was that a German bullet had hit another loop-hole plate close by, which had produced the bang and the flash.

Last night I was on another working party, which was making a trench about half way to the German line. There is an old trench there which we used to hold, but it got flooded so we moved back to our present position, leaving isolated posts here and there. One of these posts is manned by our company, and I have to visit it at night when I am on duty. It is about 200 yrds. from the German lines, and the first time of walking out is not very nice, as there is no cover at all. The authorities have now decided to make another trench next the old one and to move our line forward to it. So we send out forty to fifty men a night to work on it. This work of course is almost entirely exposed for the men, and altogether for the officer. Flares are constantly going up, as I mentioned before, and when they do we all flop down. The ground is very muddy there, and the mess everyone gets into is appalling. In addition to the intentional lying down there is a good deal of unintentional work as well. There is a fine large shell hole near with about 2 feet of water and mud at the bottom of it. One very dark night the Captain thought this was a turnip heap, so stepped boldly over the edge. He knows what it is now. The sergeant-major followed his example the night after. The Germans know of course that we are working, but I don't believe they see us. They do not fire very many shots, and no one has been touched yet. I was at one time standing in part of the trench we had completed when a bullet hit the parapet near and scattered a little earth over me. I think the bullet passed in front of me. That job kept me up till 12.0, so I had four hours sleep. One officer has to be walking about the trench always, so the hours of the day and night are split up between us. In the day we do 3 hrs. each, at night two. The reason is that the day lasts from 5.0 a.m. to 7.0 p.m., and the night from 8.0 p.m. to 4.0 a.m. I was on this morning from 5.0 a.m. to 8.0 a.m. Between 4.0 & 5.0 a.m. & 7.0 to 8.0 p.m. we are standing to, and so all are on duty. When on a fatigue lasting to about 11.0 p.m. that counts as your night duty, and you don't do any watching in the trench. After the rain yesterday in places the water was up to 5 ins. deep in the trench, but today we have got it quite dry again. The water drained off between the bricks with which we had paved the bottom, and the remaining mud was removed by shovels. It is very nice again once more. We shall only have one more night in it, as we are being relieved tomorrow. Unfortunately we do not expect the relieving regiment to arrive before 11.0 p.m., so if that is the case it will be 1.0 a.m. before we start for our billets, which we think are 6 miles off.

Our mess here is in a very fine large dug-out, with a table composed of a door covered by a waterproof sheet. There is a chair for each of us. We took the place over from the S.W.B.'s, who preceded us. I wish you could see us as we are. We are not at all depressed or uneasy, but quite a happy party. You wrote in one of your letters when referring to the man who tumbled into the cess-pool as if you thought we were very anxious and worried and overcome. This is quite a mistake. I very much enjoy the open air life, and am in the best of health. Bullets do not worry me in the least, though I do not take any risk that I can avoid. To get hit for no reason at all is not an honest or right thing to do, it seems to me.

My new lamp is most useful. It is larger and heavier than I expected, but it is worth it. There is a shutter on it which regulates the amount of light showing. Several of the last few nights have been pitch dark, and I must have used the lamp for hours. Walking along a trench on a dark night is a dreadful job, and much of it tires one out completely. There are so many things to tumble over. Having a light robs it of all its difficulties. The name of the lamp is 'The Courier', and the address of the firm is:

The Essex Accumulator Co.
497–9 Grove Green Rd.
Leytonstone
London N.E.

The refill costs 5/–. If you ever send for one be sure to ask for it in an airtight tin.

This letter is being written in odd scraps, but I will finish off the account before I talk of other things. I was on duty on the night we were relieved up to 10.0 p.m., and then I went in to the mess to have dinner. The Captain made room for me to pass, and I sat down on a chair next him. It was an uncomfortable one, and I said so. When I got up some time later I found I had been sitting on the Captain's hat, which was very nearly flat then.

The relieving regiment turned up just before 12 midnight. We started to clear off soon after 2.0, it being a very slow relief. We had some distance to go along a muddy communication trench, which of course took some time. We got to our billets soon after 6.0 a.m. They are about 2 miles from the last place we were resting at. The valises were ready for us, so after breakfast we had a most lovely sleep till dinner time. I was looking forward to that sleep all the march. I had another long sleep last night, not getting up till 9.30 this morning. Now I am perfectly fit again, and not a bit tired. I have had various letters from you when in the trenches. They come up with the rations at night. Sending off letters is a different thing. It is most delightful Will has got back safely. It is a wonder you went to bed at all when he did not arrive till late. Of course he can use my sword. Also my belt, but that pattern of the two straps meeting in a ring at the back is only used, I think, in the Oxfords besides ourselves. Will could get on without them if he bought a canvas sling for his overcoat. I have got with me the two small straps used for carrying the coat.

Please ask Arnie to fix the photo of Father and the cat and then send it to me again. I should like to keep it. The parcel came safely. I opened it in my dug-out. Don't try too hard to send the candles whole. They are lovely ones, but I have to break them in two to carry them in my pack. I am very glad they came. The shirt I am using now. I had a bath yesterday in a canvas bath like the one I had. Some of my men found it in the trench and gave it me. Could you try and get me a canvas or rubber (canvas better) washing basin. It must stand by itself without supports, be very small and as light as possible. If I could take such a thing into the trench with me it would be a great comfort. It will also be most useful at all other times. It would be better, I think, to get it from London, but you might try Oxford first. I have got a whole pack of raisins now, with those Mrs. Mitchell sent me. Could you instead of them send some other dried fruit, figs, apples or dates. Anything in that line.

The stylo is a very good size, just right. Bob sent a Fountain Pen top which I made to fit mine, but that has got cracked already. The tin one will be all right.

I have got a small pocket writing book, one of many sent out by Vickers Ltd. It will be very useful, as I may be able to keep it dry. The writing paper I had in the trenches got damp and then the envelopes stick themselves up. Could you either send yourselves or ask Bob to get for me two refills (of paper & envelopes) for the writing case made by Letts for Vickers Ltd. I enclose a bit of cardboard from the case in which the thing was sent. There can be no mistake made I think.

I left some books in the top drawers of Will's chest of drawers.

I am going out very soon to make two of my men do some work. One of them is the laziest slackest old beggar going. I don't think he cleaned his rifle once in the 8 days we were in the trench. The other man came on parade with his butt covered in mud. I have been hoping for a chance to wake the first one up a bit. The Captain has too, so I shall give them about an hour's rifle exercises and marching round. I am in very comfortable billets here, and as I have got the valise I don't want anything else. We expect to be here for 8 days, and then go into the firing line again for another 8. This last time we had a number of Territorial officers and men sent to us to be instructed a little in trench work before their battalion was put in the firing line. Ballard's regiment sent a good many. The officers we saw of it were an exceedingly decent lot.

Colonel Lovett has been in charge of the regiment from the start. For the last few weeks he has been on leave and I don't think will come back. He does not seem to be exactly pined after. Major Gardiner is the 2nd in command. At present he is commanding. He is a very nice man. My company is B.

Our chaplain has been along this morning and has arranged to hold Easter services next Sunday for us. The photo Blunt took of me at Festubert has not turned up here yet.

I will write to Will very soon.

Bob's suggestion of searching the debris of that house in Neuve-Chapelle I cannot, of course, do now. I did one job of burying a dead German in the trenches and I don't want another like it. The smell was far, far worse than anything I have ever yet come across. He had been in a ditch for many months.

I am very sorry I have not been able to get off letters for so long, but I hope you did not get too anxious. That may happen always when in the trenches.

FRANK

There was a big row over the artillery business you mentioned lately.

Saturday 10 *April*

DEAR MOTHER

I got your very welcome letter of last Tuesday about 11.0 p.m. yesterday evening. I am very glad Arnie sent the two photos. I think they are both good, though it is a pity your face is so entirely hidden. I would very much like other ones if you have any.

I have found a way of sending letters when in the firing line, by means of the company quartermaster sergeant. So I hope to get notes off to you almost as usual. I hope the spring cleaning will not tire you too much. It must be most irksome. I am glad you are going to London with Arnie for a day or two.

I had a letter from Mrs. Mitchell last night, and am sending it to you as you may like to see it. It will give you more of an idea of her.

Last Saturday I quite forgot to write. All the morning was taken up with company training, and then in the afternoon I played footer for the company against another coy. The thought of writing never came into my head till after the post had gone, as I was fully occupied. The scheme I was on was a very skeleton one. It would have taken days to work if we had had all the men out, so the regiments were represented instead by five officers. One officer was C.O., and the other four company commanders, the companies being ourselves. About six regiments took part. The scheme was divided roughly into two parts. The first was an attack on the enemy's position, the second was arrangements for holding the ground gained. The whole idea was to practice the various signalling officers in maintaining communication with the regiments on either side and with brigade headquarters. In the first part we were in reserve, and had nothing to do. In the second we took up a position, put out imaginary outposts, and got connection with the people on either side of us. Our signalling officer is the ex-N.C.O. who was in the company, Newman. He has done 9 years of it, and is one of the most expert signallers out here. So as some regiment had to be in reserve we were, for the whole scheme, as I said, was just for the signallers. I started out at 8.45 a.m., and got back at 8.30 p.m., as we had to walk some miles and some regiments were slow in putting out wires etc. We moved up here on Thursday, and B Coy., as I said, went into the reserve trenches. We have been very comfortable. The dugout I am in is a huge one, holding eight easily. It is about 5 feet wide, and very long. A small sort of trench, 1 ft. deep and 18 ins. wide, is dug along the centre, leaving ledges each side for sleeping. I have got some straw and am all right, though it gets rather cold. The Captain is in here as well, and two or three telephone men live at the further end. Last night we had working parties out improving (remaking in places)

a communication trench with the front line, which is about 300 yards
in front. The German line is a short distance in front. My platoon were
put on widening part of the trench, and also in building an embankment of sandbags over a ditch. First I had to remove a few planks
which had served as a bridge across it. It was a simple business, as two
doors on two thick beams sufficed for the new bridge. What made
things difficult was that it was pitch dark, so dark that literally I could
not see where my next step was going to be, and the men digging had
to feel to find out if they had got the right width or depth. It was
perfectly impossible to see. About half way between our present line
and our front line is a ditch, with a number of bridges across it. I had
to find them out and mark them, so that if we had to reinforce the
firing line we should know how to go. My platoon sergeant went
with me, and we had a funny time. We found one bridge, went across
it, and then started to walk about 150 yards to the reserve line. We ran
into what seemed like miles of our barbed wire, and started to cut our
way through it. The stuff was no good there, as its purpose had been
fulfilled. When we got somewhere about half way we had lost ourselves and might have had trouble in getting out if a flare had not
shown up the ruins of a house we knew. It was hopeless to try and find
the way. I was treading very gingerly as I expected to run into wire,
but even so I could not stop myself tumbling into a shell hole. It was
not a very large one, only about 9 feet across. But I could not see it.
My sergeant and I went out again at 3.30 this morning to see the
bridges, and then did things all right, as it was light enough to see. We
found a small road running straight up towards the front line, stopping
at the ditch, which for night work will be most convenient. We shall
of course only use it in case of emergency. There were a few bits of
wire across the road, which I cut, but we avoided nearly all the mess of
entanglements. We found the bridges, marked them with biscuit tins,
and then went straight up to the front line to see what part of it was in
front. This was a most necessary thing to do, in case we ever had to
reinforce a particular part of it at night. We were not doing it to see
the view or anything silly. When we reached the front line we suddenly
found we were entirely exposed, as the ground where we had struck
the trench was rather high. Of course the Germans could not see us,
but I don't think they were more than about 100 yards away. As they
were putting some bullets over we only stayed long enough to learn

what we wanted and then retired. It was quite a surprise to both of us finding ourselves above the level of the front parapet. We expected to be sheltered by it.

This afternoon I want to get to sleep, although I am not feeling very sleepy now. I had three hours sleep in the night, and also slept from 5.0 a.m. to 8.0 a.m. So I am doing all right.

Tonight we go up into the front line, for 48 hours. After that we will go into reserve again, probably in more trenches farther back. We will have another 48 hrs. in our present position sometime I expect. The position is a fairly quiet one. Yesterday they fired a lot at some houses just behind us (about 150 yards), but did not try to hit the trench, and their heavy shells do not come within $\frac{1}{4}$ mile of us. It will be quieter still in the way of shells in the front line, as there the two lines are too close together for the artillery to fire at either just for nothing. Please send me another tin of Mars oil (for boots).

Also I would be very glad if you would send me a periscope. I have written for one, but it is better to have two. The best type is called 'Trenchoscope', and is to be obtained from Adams and Co., 16 (?) Charing Cross Road, London, S.W. I'm not sure of the number. Price somewhere about 11/6. They will pack it up well for you. Periscopes are useful things, but the clumsy box type is no use at all at short distances. It is smashed in no time.

If Bob can get the refills of the little writing book I am using now which Vickers sent out I think I will do all my writing with it. It is nice paper to write on, and the case can be easily carried about. It is more handy to use when one is practically in the open air than sheets of note paper. So if refills can be got easily could you send me them in future and not the sheets of writing paper? I wish I could have that cat out here. I should love it. If I have to stop out this side when the war has finished I will certainly come back with a dog, always supposing I am all right. I would not like to have one now as I could not take it to the firing line, and would have to be constantly leaving it uncertain whether I should see it again. The two dogs that came out with my draft are still in the regiment, but as their owners are in other companies I very seldom catch a glimpse of them. They are not intelligent animals. At our last billets there was a lovely dog, large enough to pull a dog cart, but very sweet tempered and friendly. I badly wanted to bring him along with me.

It is almost 1.0 a.m. now, and I must stop.
I will write again tomorrow.

FRANK

Sunday {April 18}

DEAR FATHER

All's well, and a lovely day. It has been quite quiet. The company
is in the firing line. Last night I put 5 loophole plates in new positions,
and they have been quite a success. We shall annoy the Germans considerably by them. Am making another one tonight which will en-
filade part of their trench, firing across our front. We have got a rifle
now with telescopic sights. Received your letter last night, at 1.0 a.m.
Was about to go to sleep for an hour. Please don't send 1,000 cigarettes
all at once, if that is your intention. I can't deal with so many. A box
of 250 would do nicely. At present the men are not getting much
tobacco. Am very glad to hear you are going to the links again. My
electric lamp is called the 'Courier', the firm being:

The Essex Accumulator Co.,
497–9 Grove Green Rd.,
Leytonstone,
London, N.E.

Price 30/–. Refills 5/–. The reason I got it was that I do not know of
any other lamp which burns more than 8 hours. This means frequent
refills, and as the post is not to be relied on for parcels it is quite possible
one might run out of batteries at an awkward time. As I have said
before, the post will be the first thing to be disorganised if there is any
activity, and parcels will be left behind before letters are interfered with.

A very great defect of the ordinary flash lamp is that it gives too
much light. Its rays go in all directions. Mine has got a shutter on it
which allows one to regulate the amount of light. When I am walking

along the trench the ground is lit up like this:

The black dot represents myself, the shaded sector the amount of
ground lit up. I have the shutter so that about 18 ins. only is shown.
This is as much as is wanted, and it absolutely prevents any bit or
reflection of the light from showing above the parapet, a most important thing when the parapet is low, as they mostly will be in future.
I have used my lamp in perfect safety when in front of the lines at

times when an ordinary flash lamp would have been seen at once by
the Germans. The small lamp in leather case very much used by
officers has the same attachment on a worse scale, but it only burns for
8 hours and costs 50% more to refill than mine. The drawback to mine
is its weight and size. The measurements are roughly $6 \times 3\frac{1}{2} \times 2$ ins.
Weight somewhere about 2 lbs. It can be carried either on the belt or
slung like binoculars. Its advantages I think far outweigh its disadvantages, and I would not change it for any other lamp. Walking along a
trench is the most tiring kind of procedure I know. Always turning
corners, stepping over men sleeping, the floor never being level for
more than a few yards at a time, and if wet more slippery than ice, at
night a light is a wonderful help. One is certain to be feeling tired, and
one's feet are usually tender. Some wet nights I have stood still, almost
in despair of taking another step, just wanting to lie down & rest. A
light would have saved all that, and I have not seen any lamp so good
as mine for any purpose out here for which a light is wanted. It is not a
very bright light, nor is a bright light a good thing. It is made to last,
not wear out. Will, of course, must decide for himself. The above is
only my own ideas. The total weight I carry on the march is about 75
lbs., but as almost all of it is on the back I have never felt the weight
of the lamp. Another officer in the company has a lamp like mine, and
he is completely satisfied with it.

Must stop now as I have to walk about the trench for a couple of
hours to see everything is all right, and after that want to get to sleep.

FRANK

Monday Apr. 19

DEAR MOTHER

I'm all right, and tonight we go back into reserve about $\frac{3}{4}$ mile
behind. I'm writing lying down in my dug-out. I'm too lazy to sit up.
I shall be glad to be out of these trenches, as it has been fairly hard work
here. The Captain gave me the first turn of day watch this morning,
so I finished my duty till 7.0 p.m. at 7.0 a.m., and have done nothing
but sleep since except for half an hour when some bombs came over
near by. It has been a lovely day. The dug-out I've got now is not a very
good one, merely box shape with a top on it and one side open, which
wants two waterproof sheets to cover it. At night it is cold, but I have
not been in long enough at night to get cold.

I received your letter yesterday, written on the 15th from the Montague Hotel. I hope you did not tire yourself too much. It is good Morwenna & her baby are all right.

A shirt will be welcome. I bought a dark green one from Walters but both the collars for it have been lost. Could you try & get a collar for it from him. I expect he will know more or less the colour. It is much darker than the last one you sent. It is not always possible to get things washed. Has that parcel ever turned up yet? Will write tomorrow if I can.

FRANK

The mud splashes on this were shaken down from the roof of the dug-out by the explosion near of a German bomb.

Wed. Apr. 21

DEAR MOTHER

I have had two lovely days rest, and am going back to the firing line again tonight. My periscope has come, I am glad to say, as such things are most extraordinarily useful. I have seen many types of periscope in use, but none to come within miles of this one. I enclose a paper about it. Will should not come out without one. Do not hesitate to recommend this type if you ever get enquiries about them.

I cannot write more than a few lines now, just to tell you what I am doing. I got your letter yesterday enclosing Thornton's. If the refills cannot be obtained I would be glad of some other paper. Will tell you later when I hear. I am glad you have got the washing basin.

The waders came from Vere, for me to try. They are not wanted now.

I am glad Will has got a watch, and a good one also. I would not be without mine for anything.

No more at present.

FRANK

By the way, my Lance-corporal from St. Aldate's is a married man of about 29 who does not know either Bob or Ned.

Monday 26 [April]

DEAR MOTHER

It is good of you to take so much trouble over making socks. Clean socks & shirts are very nice to have. I can get washing done here, so will not risk sending other parcels home, except that I may send a pair of boots to be repaired. I am very comfortable here. We have the same room as before to use as a mess, but I have got another bedroom. This one is in a very nice house, beautifully clean. It is a small room with a window which opens wide, and looks on to a fruit garden. The plot is about 150 yards square, and well cared for. If anything I should say it was too thickly planted. There are rows & rows of currant bushes, with other rows of apple & pear trees among them. It looks very nice now, and as I practically cannot see beyond it except to some fields in the distance I am very pleased with the place.

I hope Will likes the 3rd Oxfords when he reaches them. They are far safer than any kilted regiment if one is taken prisoner. Hatred is not the word for the feeling that exists between the Germans & Highlanders. Brutal ferocity has been the rule on both sides in very many cases up to now.

I have just had your letter of Apr. 23, also *The Times Weekly* and a periscope. Very many thanks for sending it. Periscopes are a wonderful help and save many lives.

The pocket looking glass may be useful, but I have the periscope glasses.

The Colt automatic bullets are covered with nickel and keep their shape. It is the Government revolver ammunition which has a lead bullet, and this expands as soon as it hits anything hard. They have a dum-dum action. The Germans have mostly stopped shooting men because of revolver dum-dum bullets, but I know several officers who intend, if they can, to throw their revolver bullets (Government pattern) away if they are going to be captured. Officers (and N.C.O.'s) may have exactly what kind of revolver or pistol they like. There is no necessity at all to have one taking Gov. ammunition. If Will wants to sell his Colt write to Ballard (Cromwell's House, Woodstock). I have about 90 rounds with me. I have not used any yet over here. In trenches it is not necessary to. If we have an attack I shall use it entirely. By the way in the matter of losses you must be prepared for very large ones soon, though I don't know if we shall have many in the regiment or not. The losses in fights up to now will be far excelled by what is coming.

I hope Will will ask any question he wants to know. I cannot think of all I want to at the time of writing. This afternoon there is a lecture being given to the officers & N.C.O.'s of the brigade, which cuts up the time I have now. One or two small things about taking over a trench I will write tomorrow if I can. I am glad you are sending more than 50 pkts. of Woodbines. Only 50 pkts. would not quite go round once.

If the 3rd Oxfords are at Portsmouth it will be a good thing, as that is quite a good place to go I should think. I can understand Will would prefer the Seaforths though. My B.W. Coat may be useful to him if it is long enough. The ordinary great coats are, I think, abominations.

In the matter of overcoats I suppose Will has a Burberry. The oil silk coats are so easily torn that they are not much use here. I have not seen anybody with one. My Burberry, of course, is lined with oil silk, and I am very pleased with it. The Burberry proofing alone does not keep out much rain. I have still got my fleece lining also with me. I have not worn it for weeks, but it is useful when sleeping in dug-outs. As far as I can see now the oil silk poncho will be the solution of the rain coat question.

I am very glad also I have got my lamp. There have been several wonderfully dark nights lately. I now have two refills for it, as I have not yet used up the first one, although I have not spared it at all. The refills for the writing book have not turned up. If they do not come in a few days I will tell you.

Certainly if Pearson wants my rifle sell it him. The aperture back sight wants to be screwed down tight, a job which would take 10 minutes for Venables or any man accustomed to those sights. It cost 10/6 I think, as far as I can remember, and is quite the best type of aperture sight.

Turrill's rifle is worn out in the barrel. Everything is so uncertain that it is far the best thing to get rid of my rifle if Pearson offers to take it.

I must close up now as we are starting very soon to walk three miles to this lecture.

FRANK

Captain Isaac has just been given the job of taking charge of a convalescent company, stationed in the place I am now at. He cannot march, but will be doing quite useful work there.

DEAR MOTHER & FATHER

I got your combined letter of Apr. 24 today. I am glad the refills
are coming. I got hold of this writing pad which I am now using today,
but it is not a very big one. The collar will do very well. Stiff collars of
a different colour to the shirt might be found in Kitchener's Army. In
regular battalions one would be very severely sat on for trying to use
them. In peace time almost every regiment has its own shade of khaki,
from which there is no departing.

500 cigarettes came from Mrs. Mitchell today. The men will greatly
enjoy them, as they have had very few lately. The story Jenkin got
hold of about the Colt bullets is really very funny. The bullets for an
automatic pistol must be hard, or it would not work. The Tommy was
most likely talking of Colt revolvers, which of course have lead bullets,
and Jenkin must have thought the automatic had the same bullets. I
think the Germans have stopped objecting to revolver ammunition
now. I have not heard of any case since I have been with the regiment.
The regiment's number is 28, as you must know, and Henty's book
'*One of the 28th*' is about it.

I am glad Father's cold is going off, and I hope Florence will not have
hers long. It is not what she ought to get when she comes to Oxford.

The lecture yesterday afternoon was a very good one, but not
particularly comforting, to us. The German latest gas can be circum-
vented. One of our doctors was experimenting with asphyxiating gas
yesterday and put himself unconscious for 4 hours. I have just seen
yesterday's *Standard*. Evidently they have not got the least idea of the
effect of the German gas used in their attack at Ypres. Owing solely
to the use of the gas the Germans got right through our lines (or rather
the French ones) but have been driven back on almost the whole front
of their attack and part of their own front line trench has been taken.
There was fierce fighting nearly all last night. The gas renders unconscious all those who come under its influence, if their breathing is
undefended, and its effect was felt for a mile. It can only be used when
the wind is favourable. For this reason their attack was postponed for
two days. It will probably not succeed to the same extent again. It was
not fired from bombs or shells.

The canvas basin you sent will do very well, though I don't think I
will be able to carry it. The figs etc. I was very glad to get. They (the

figs) must have been expensive in that shape. Could you sometime or other send me more of them, but the ordinary type will do perfectly well.

It is a most lovely day, and I am feeling rather wild because I can't leave our billeting area. Blunt is in England on special leave, while the second captain & the senior subaltern have gone to Béthune for the afternoon. So I am left in charge, the other officer, the ex-Union & Balliol man, being junior to me. I don't feel able to write this afternoon.

Phonetical spelling is abominable. Our men use it largely. One gets 'roat' for 'wrote' and 'year' for 'bear' and 'porsble' for 'possible'. Many other things like that. Sickening stuff, if it was not so pitiful. I should like the Reformed Spelling cranks to see some of it.

I am afraid Florence will have gone before this letter reaches you. You must wish she could stop longer. I hope she had a really nice time.

FRANK

The candles are excellent. Just right.

It was the bombs mostly that shook my dug-out, not shells. Only one of those dropped anywhere near. I saw it in the air just before it reached the trench. It dropped about 20 yards behind and sent a shower of mud over us. I got a lot of that, as I was not in the dug-out at the time.

Thurs. 29

DEAR MOTHER

I am glad to say I have received your letter of last Monday, also the parcel in perfect condition. You did pack it up carefully. Very many thanks for all you have sent. The potash I will certainly use, as it is more wanted now than in the cold weather. I had brought out with me a small pot of Boracic ointment, but the tube will be useful also. The cigarettes will be greatly appreciated. I am delighted you included the figs. *Punch* I can see out here, as it is always sent to two officers in the company. I will give any you send to the men.

It is a good thing Father & Florence are both getting rid of their colds. I hope Arnie will soon also. It is a pity Florence could not be longer with you. I can imagine you today thinking & hoping that Bob will come to morrow. I am afraid I shall not get any leave for some time. There are eight before me on the list, and no leave is being given this rest, so far as we know. I have an idea the Germans are threatening an attack. I hope they do, it will make it so much easier for us when we attack. It is a pity, as I should love to get home, even for three days.

Marsh has turned up to scratch well. I will write to him if I can.

Can't you make arrangements for keeping the cat? It must be one in a thousand, and between you all you have completely won its heart. I should love to see it.

I must stop now as the post is nearly going. Yesterday's practice only took till soon after 4.0 p.m., but that meant over 5 hrs. walking & running in the heat of the day, and the days are very hot just lately.

Today the company have had a bath, and I have had 100 letters to read. I am feeling rather washed out now. More tomorrow.

I hope you are all right yourself. Now that Arnie is quite strong & Bob is at home also you should engage a punt on the Cher. They will be cheap this summer.

FRANK

Fri. Apr. 30

DEAR MOTHER

Got a letter from you (undated) including some photos of Arnie's. These are very good, & I would much like to see others, as I know there is plenty of printing paper in Ned's house. I cannot really answer your letter, as I am rather occupied today. From 9.30 a.m. to 2.0 p.m. we were on a route march, which finished by doing the attack twice. It was done on purpose as a test to see if we could stand heat. Only one man of the battalion as far as I know fell out. Packs were not carried, as it was what is called 'fighting order dress'. Very much nicer. I have just come back from taking some of my men to have a swim in the canal near by. I went in too, as it looked so inviting, although the water was not quite as clear as crystal. It was very nice though. In about $\frac{3}{4}$ hr's time I am turning out for the company at footer, against the R.A.M.C. here. So I am having quite a busy day.

Please don't send the shirt just yet. I have got three clean ones, & 5 pr. socks. I would be very glad of the shirt after we have moved from here, but that will not be for a number of days if things are all right. I will tell you that later.

FRANK

Sat. May 1

DEAR MOTHER

We are really having a rest today. The men are cleaning up generally, so there is nothing much for us to do. Tomorrow I expect we
shall do the attack again, or something like it. In your letter which I
got yesterday you mention some casualties of ours. Both our last time
and the time before my company was lucky in that way. The other
companies got shelled & bombed rather badly. Our total casualties for
those two times were about 100. The nearness of the two lines was
mainly responsible for this. The Germans made excellent use of their
fixed rifles, and things were much more lively than at the first lot of
breastworks I was at. There the Germans kept only a few men in the
line by day, and it was perfectly safe to look over the top as much as
one liked. Rather a funny thing happened soon after we left there.
Some Irish Regiment took over that bit of the line, and there were
handed over to one of their subalterns two red rockets and a number
of flare lights, with a pistol for the latter. The red rockets were to be
fired if our artillery was required to open fire. They were only to be
used when the telephone was broken. The fellow, I suppose, wanted
to see what the rockets were like, so he fired off both of them and sent
up a number of flares at the same time. Of course the artillery started
then, and all the neighbouring regiments, who knew what the red
rockets were for, stood to arms and opened fire. There was a huge
commotion. I don't know what happened to the fellow who did it,
but for that sort of thing a man is marked 'permanent base'.

A photograph was taken of the company officers this morning. I
don't know if I shall be able to get one. The Adjutant of each regiment
is allowed to have a camera.

The hymn you sent lately is a very nice one.

When Shylock has been sent to Salisbury Plain it means he is leaving
England very shortly. The whole army out here has heard at one time
or other that it is going to the Dardanelles. It is quite possible though
that he may go there.

{Four lines omitted}

I am sorry I did not remember Arnie's birthday when I wrote yesterday. This will come too late for it. I have made the enclosed cheque

payable to Father, as I don't know what the law is about cheques made payable to minors, but it is for him. I hope he will get what he likes with it.

It is a most glorious day, with lovely sunshine. There have been some very fine sunsets lately.

Has Ned sent any explanation of those photos of the dead men? I cannot imagine what he did it for. I could get plenty here if I had a camera and wanted to. The human body after death is a most vile & loathsome thing. The one I helped to pull out of the ditch at the last trench but one absolutely defies description. I dislike wood fires because the smoke makes my eyes run, but I went to the nearest one and put my head right over it to get out of the smell for a little.

The potash is very good stuff, I think. I am glad you sent it.

Could you send me some tooth stuff? Powder is awkward to use when out of doors, and is not so convenient to carry as paste. I have been using paste up to now, but am just running out of it. I would prefer paste, if you can send me some. I don't know how parcels go when sent to The Forwarding Officer, Southampton, but if you do this you have only to pay postage as far as Southampton, not France. You might try it if you like, as it would be cheaper. Put my name, regiment, B.E.F. on it above

c/o Forwarding Officer,
Southampton

I have just got Father's letter of 28th.

I am sorry you had all that great bother about the Vermijelli. I expected you would have had the address somewhere.

Vermijelli (1 lb. tin 1/–)
W. H. Strickland & Co.,
23 Cromwell Place,
South Kensington.

It was very good of Will to take all that trouble. $8 \times$ glasses are those the War Office issues (when it ever does issue any), but there is no order or law, even unwritten, as to what power an officer should have. He can get exactly what he likes. One officer in the regiment has a pair almost the same as Mother's small ones. The usual $8 \times$ glass is a most cumbersome, heavy affair. Their sole supposed advantage over higher powers is that in fog or a dull light they can be used easily. I think there is very little in it. So far, in nine cases out of ten, I could have very well done with a higher power glass than my own (12 ×).

I will answer Father's letter if I can today or tomorrow.

FRANK

Monday, May 3

DEAR MOTHER

Got your letter of Friday night, the parcel & the refill. Please don't send any ordinary writing paper now. I have enough now to last me a long time. The parcel I have not opened, as we are shifting billets this afternoon. I have had a job given me of looking at aeroplanes today. No connection with the R.F.C. I have had a sentry outside to tell me when an aeroplane was in sight, and I have been going in & out fairly often since daybreak. It got me off a general's inspection this morning, which was a good thing. I hope Arnie gets all right very soon.

Mr. Chapman has been anticipated by many days out here. Blunt had 5 days leave only.

I'm feeling rather tired and not up to writing now, so will not go on.

FRANK

Photos good. Will keep that of Father & Bob.

Wed. 11.0 a.m.

DEAR MOTHER

I am writing early today, as I shall have no chance later. We are practising an attack on some specially prepared ground, and start in about an hour for that. I do not expect to get back till about 5.0 p.m. or so. I must go off now to get my things ready; this note is only to tell you what I am doing.

I have just come in from a parade, and have no time to spare now. Sorry.

FRANK

Wednesday May 5

DEAR MOTHER

Yesterday I started two letters to you. One I left unfinished at 2.30, when I went off to pay out the company. When I got back the letters had gone. The other I started in the evening, but did not go far with it. As I knew Monday's letter did not go till Tuesday I did not bother to try & get a late letter off, as can sometimes be done.

The aeroplane job on Monday was quite amusing. The whole company was intensely interested, though of course they did not know what I was looking for. A good part of the morning I was sitting in a chair in an orchard adjoining the road, while the company was lined up in the road waiting for the general to turn up. They had to wait two hours for him. I am taking the business in turns with Griffith, the Balliol & Union man. He had it yesterday. I have got it again today. I have not seen any aeroplanes yet of the type I want, though it is now after 10.0 a.m. It was misty this morning till soon after 5.0 a.m., and there were no aeroplanes up. B.E. & Maurice Farman biplanes are fairly common.

The company is going to a wood this afternoon to practise sham fights in it. I get out of that.

Nothing came from you yesterday. It is good Bob is back with you once more. You ought to take a boat now for the summer, as I said a few letters back. Vere is not all right, but has gone to Abbey Wood again. I don't suppose he will be sent out yet.

I have had another change of platoon sergeants, and now have a man who used to have charge of it before he was wounded. He was hit in the leg and is not really fit yet, but was keen to come out again. He is a very good man, with a tremendous voice. It is queer how very much like a dog's bark commands sound from a distance, if properly given.

Yesterday was again very hot, and we felt it as we had a route march up to nearly 1.0 p.m. There was a thunderstorm in the evening, preceded by a violent wind. One of the windows of the room we feed in has only got hinges to one half of it; the other half just stood more or less in place. The squall coming without any warning at all caught this half and there's only the frame left now. It made an awful noise on the tile floor. There are people living in this house, and they will be sure to want to charge us for it. Prices of everything the French country people sell to us are regulated by what they are able to get out of the men, not the market price. I suppose it is only natural, but they might be Jews in the way they behave. Nearly all the farms & houses near the firing line are inhabited by refugees from other places, who have settled down in the first empty building they came to, often neither knowing nor caring who the real owners were. There will be plenty of squabbling after the war, these people being a tight-fisted lot. There are very few men left. It is very seldom one sees a man of military age.

The stylo you sent has been very useful. I have done all my writing with it, except for one or two letters. I carry it in my writing book, & am not afraid of smashing it. The top Bob sent for my fountain pen is still doing service, but not much more splitting is wanted to make it useless.

There is a girl of about 16 in the village our last billets were in. Her home is in German hands. She lived in it for 16 days before she could get away, and during that time had to sleep on the floor. A German private turned her out of her bed. I wish some of the old hags I have come across could have a taste of German manners.

I will tell you in a few days about boots.

Today's mail has not come in yet, which is a nuisance. It is always nice getting the mail, and when it is late everybody gets in a bad temper.

4.30 p.m.

I hope you are all right yourself. The hot weather is trying. I have not been able to answer Father's letter yet.

FRANK

Thursday 6

DEAR MOTHER

Am all right, but no time to spare. We had a fairly long route march this morning, & now am going to get a proper bath, I hope, at a place $1\frac{1}{2}$ miles off. It will be the second good one I have had, if I get it.

FRANK

{On a Field Service Post Card.}

I am quite well.   *Friday*
            F.

{"The last letter my darling wrote"—his Mother.}

Saturday {May 8}

DEAR MOTHER

Quite unexpectedly I have got the chance of writing today. I am at present in the headquarters of the London Scottish. Yesterday morning I started off at 6.30 a.m. with 20 men to do a fatigue near our last position in the firing line. I found it was to fortify a room in a house, the top part of which is used for artillery observation. The job took till 6.30 p.m. It was hard work, as we filled and placed rather more than 1,400 sandbags. My sergeant & I worked together and did more bags than any other pair I think. We were twice interrupted by small shells coming too near, that is within 50 yards. One pitched 10 yards away but as it was inside a wall it only sent bits of brick flying about. Two men were slightly grazed by them. I expected the battalion would come up during the evening to where I was, and I was to join them when they came. Instead of that they were, after they had started, given orders not to come and were sent to a village for the night. I heard about 7.0 p.m. that they might not be coming, but nothing definite. I went to the Scottish Headquarters and got them to telephone to the 3rd brigade for me. As the regiment was on the march the brigade could only reach them by cyclist orderly. This I could only guess; after two hours & a bit I was told where the battalion was for the night, but nothing else. The men had got rations for yesterday, but not for today. The Scottish came to the rescue & said they could manage that. So as the men had got a place to sleep in I decided to stay where I was, sending a message to the brigade for them to forward to the regiment saying so. The Scottish most kindly have put me up in their Headquarters, and are feeding me today. I got orders this morning to stay here and that rations would come up. The battalion will come tonight I expect. The Scottish are a very nice lot, that is the few officers there are here. The Colonel, Adjutant, a Captain, Padre & a Subaltern are all there are. The men I have met are all of the City man class. Every day one or more applies for a commission.

I am sending this letter through them.

The battalion is about an hour & a half's march at least from here. What stopped me from going to find it early last night was thinking that it might have moved, in which case I should have been completely stranded.

Of course I have not got yesterday's mail.

FRANK

Going to have a sleep.

{On the envelope:}

Not to be delivered till after my death.

F. H. LAWRENCE

ABBEY WOOD
Nov. 26, 1914

DEAR MOTHER & FATHER

This letter is a solemn one for me, as I do not mean it to be delivered to you till after my death. I am writing it because it is quite likely
I shall be killed very shortly. I only know of one officer who has been
out at the front since August who has not been hit yet. I do not think
I shall escape being wounded at any rate, though I hope to come home
again all right.

If I do die, I hope I die with colours flying.

Do not grieve for me. God's purposes are too vast for us to see, but
I know He is always with me, and whatever happens will be with His
foreknowledge and by His orders in accordance with His plan. It will
be very hard for you both, but you must think that however I die will
be best for me. Also the parting will not be for long. Merely for an
infinitesimal space of time out of eternity.

I can never be sufficiently grateful for having been given such parents
as you, and also for all you have done for me. I am afraid I have ill
repaid you on earth, and must have caused you great trouble. Arnie
must now be your solace, as he will be I expect.

In these last three months I have gone through indescribable depths
of infamy, living in the midst of it, and if I had been accustomed to
going to theatres, music halls etc. in the seemingly harmless way other
boys go I should have found it trebly hard to have kept myself clean.
I do not think Arnie will ever live as I mention above, but should he
ever feel inclined to I hope he will remember the words of one who has
experienced a little.

Please give the enclosed letter to Pavière, together with a number of
books, about a dozen, which are in the two locked drawers (the small
top ones) of Will's chest of drawers in the Brass Room. You will find
the keys in my room. One is in the painted wooden box with a picture
of Ventnor on it in the top drawer of my chest of drawers. The other
I think is in a black pocket book in a cardboard box on top of the
wardrobe in my room. There are 8 books by Ramacharaka, one large

one by Alan Leo, one on the Rosicrucians, and a few others on various subjects, included some printed like large exercise books on Hypnotism etc.

Do what you like with anything else of mine.

Well, I will be watching over you all, and will know what you are doing.

Goodbye, till we meet again not on this earth.

Your son still,

FRANK

Sat. May 1

DEAR MOTHER & FATHER

I am leaving directions so that should I be killed this letter will be sent to you. We know fairly well that the attack has been fixed for about May 12, if all goes well in the meantime. If the Gloucesters are in it there will most likely be very few of the regiment left, as it will be a huge affair and no means must be left untried to help it to succeed. It is quite possible I shall be killed, though I have no premonition about it. I am glad I have not. It is a queer thing to be out here in this beautiful weather & to think that perhaps I have only another fortnight to live. I am writing this letter on the hypothesis that I have been killed, so will treat it in that way. I am glad I have died, not so much for my country, as for all the many wrongs by which the war was mainly commenced and also which it inspired. The purpose for it all I do not think can be seen by us in this life but there is a purpose all the same. Now I come to a harder part. I know you will grieve for me, and it is no use asking you not to; remember me as one who has gone before, not as one parted for ever. This present earthly life is after all a very limited space of time. Although I have been parted from you on this earth for 8 months, yet all the time I have felt in closer communion with you than when I was at home. This more especially applies to my time in France. I think you have also felt much the same. I do not think this communion will be broken now. It will still exist, though there will be no letters travelling between us. If you cannot see me, yet I hope I shall be able to see you. I have many times felt how much I owe to Him who put me in my family. It has been a very, very great help to me all these last months, though I have fallen very short in many things.

This letter will be written in bits, as I do not mean to close it till the attack is near, unless of course death overtakes me first. We have been told we leave here (Hinges) on May 10, as at present arranged, which means we shall practically go straight into the attack. The bombardment on the German line where some division, which will most likely be ours, will attack is going to be fierce. I hope it will make the gaps in the wire as has been arranged. The ground on which we have in the last few days been practising the attack has been made as much like the real place as possible. The bayonets are all being sharpened, and the photo this morning I expect was taken by order.

Thursday May 6

Have learnt tonight when & where the attack will be made (by us). I shall be on a fatigue all day tomorrow, starting from here at 6.30. It is now after 12.0 m.n. & as I don't suppose there will be any rest now till the job is over I want to get a few hrs. sleep.

Goodbye,

Still your son,

FRANK

Friday evening.

Have finished the fatigue (6.30 p.m.). It was hard work. Am expecting the battalion to come up any time now. The fight tomorrow will be a big one. Cannot say all I want to, but I will not say 'goodbye' again. Rather, by His grace,

AU REVOIR,

FRANK

Saturday evening.

As I said this morning, only not in quite so many words, the attack was postponed 24 hrs. It will come off tomorrow morning I expect. I am not looking forward to it.

No time for more just now.

{On the envelope:}

In the event of my death, please close up this letter & send it with my effects to

Mrs. Lawrence,
2 Polstead Road,
Oxford.

May 11th

DEAR MRS. LAWRENCE,

Will you please accept my sincerest sympathy in your sad bereavement.

Your son was in my company and at the time of his death was leading his men forward preparatory to the assault. The assault I regret to say was unsuccessful.

Your son was a very promising officer—very keen on his work and most painstaking. The Regiment has lost a good officer in him and I cannot say how much I regret his death.

I have collected all his effects and they are being despatched today.

The enclosed letter was found in his pocket book also the 120 francs in notes.

I have packed up his watch separately and sent it by post today.

With my deepest sympathy.

Yours sincerely,
[Signed] A. ST. J. BLUNT, Captain,
B Company,
1st Gloucestershire Regt.

May 18th

DEAR MR. LAWRENCE,

I received your letter of 15th inst. today. I am glad to say your son suffered no pain, being killed outright. He was hit by 3 shrapnel bullets.

Yours sincerely,
[Signed] A. ST. J. BLUNT

3/GLOSTERSHIRE REGT.
MILLER BARRACKS
GRAVESEND

29 May. 15

DEAR MR. LAWRENCE,

I am sending you herewith the Commission of your late son, which we received today—will you kindly acknowledge receipt of it. Will you please at the same time accept my deep sympathy & allow me to express to you how very sorry I was to see your son had been killed. Though he has lost his life in a great cause, the loss can be none the less sad to you. I only heard the day before yesterday from our late adjutant, who is now at the front, that your boy was doing very well, and I mention it, as being all I know about what happened, & in case you have not heard more directly, that he was coming up with some reinforcements to the help of the front line, when he was killed by the base of a shell which burst and blew back. I understand he was killed at once.

Believe me,
Yours very truly,
[Signed] GEORGE H. BURGES, Lt.-Col.

INDEX

Letters of T. E. Lawrence, later T. E. Shaw

INDEX

Letters of W. G. Lawrence

INDEX

Letters of F. H. Lawrence